COMPETING GLOBALLY THROUGH CUSTOMER VALUE

COMPETING GLOBALLY THROUGH CUSTOMER VALUE

The Management of Strategic Suprasystems

Edited by MICHAEL J. STAHL
and GREGORY M. BOUNDS   *1991*

Q

QUORUM BOOKS
New York • Westport, Connecticut • London

"Institutes for Productivity Through Quality"ᴹ is a federally registered
service mark of The University of Tennessee.

Library of Congress Cataloging-in-Publication Data

Competing globally through customer value : the management of
    strategic suprasystems / edited by Michael J. Stahl and Gregory M.
    Bounds.
        p. cm.
    Includes index.
    ISBN 0-89930-600-4 (alk. paper)
        1. Strategic planning. 2. Organizational effectiveness.
    3. Customer satisfaction. 4. Competition, International.
    I. Stahl, Michael J. II. Bounds, Gregory M.
    PN761.P38 1991
    809—dc20   90-26410

British Library Cataloguing in Publication Data is available.

Library of Congress Catalog Card Number: 90-26410
ISBN: 0-89930-600-4

First published in 1991

Quorum Books, 88 Post Road West, Westport, CT 06881
An imprint of Greenwood Publishing Group, Inc.

Printed in the United States of America

The paper used in this book complies with the
Permanent Paper Standard issued by the National
Information Standards Organization (Z39.48-1984).

10 9 8 7 6 5 4 3 2 1

CONTENTS

F. Conclusions

FOREWORD

DAVID T. KEARNS
Chairman, Xerox Corporation

Editors Michael Stahl and Greg Bounds have produced a valuable and much needed book. The contributing authors argue persuasively that

- The overriding priority of management is the delivery of value to the customer.
- Management must continuously improve organizational systems to focus on the customer.

That certainly has been our experience at Xerox.

In the late 1970s, we realized that we had lost our customer focus and that to be a worldclass competitor in the eighties and nineties, we had to challenge everything we had done in the past. We had to change dramatically – from the way we develop and manufacture our products to the way we market and service them.

For us, that amounted to a major cultural change. We had to change the way we managed and worked. We had to train people in new processes. We had to change the way we rewarded people and the criteria we used to promote people. We had to communicate more with people and share information with them. We had to bring more discipline and teamwork to our corporate culture. And we had to make decisions that were based not on intuition and feel but on hard data and statistical analysis.

We've been at that process of changing the corporation for about six years now, and, although we still have a long way to go, the results are gratifying. Let me give you just a few examples:

- We have reduced our average manufacturing costs by over 20 percent despite inflation.
- We have reduced the time it takes to bring a new product to market by up to 60 percent.

- We have decreased our billing errors from 8.3 percent to under 3 percent.
- Dataquest has reported that customers rate Xerox #1 in our industry in terms of product reliability and service.
- We have decreased our defective parts from 8 percent to less than three-hundredths of 1 percent.

Perhaps our greatest achievement is that we are the first American company in an industry targeted by the Japanese to regain market shares without the aid of tariffs or protection of any kind.

We're also proud that we did it without closing our factories or moving our manufacturing offshore. The point is that there is nothing inherently wrong with American business. We lost our way in the 1970s, but we have found it once again.

People sometimes ask how we are doing it at Xerox – how we have reversed our slide and begun the long tough road back. Believe me, there is no magic formula. We are doing it by involving all of our people – union and nonunion alike – in problem solving and quality improvement.

We've all heard a good deal about quality recently. We define it as "conforming to customer requirements" – pure and simple. It's an axiom of business that's as old as business itself, yet many of us lost sight of it. And when we speak of quality, we mean more than just product quality. We take the view that every person in the company has a customer for the work they do. For many people, the customer is someone inside the company – the person we type reports for or the person to whom we deliver parts.

It follows from this view of quality that it must work its way into the entire organization – into manufacturing, sales, service, billing, training, finance, and so on. Our quality policy sums it up well. It says simply: "Xerox is a quality company. Quality is the basic business principle for Xerox. Quality means providing our external and internal customers with innovative products and services that fully satisfy their requirements. Quality improvement is the job of every Xerox employee."

Xerox is hardly alone in this approach. Scores of corporations – some of them represented in this book – are finding that quality improvement is a powerful way to improve business results. This heightened interest in quality is not surprising. The Japanese have realized for years that you don't have to sacrifice quality for cost. In fact, quite the reverse is true. A focus on quality – on satisfying the customer and meeting customer needs – actually drives cost down. That clearly has been our experience at Xerox!

Today, more than 85 percent of our workforce is involved in some five thousand Quality Improvement Teams around the world. These teams are creating a sense of excitement and fun at Xerox. More importantly, they are improving customer satisfaction and impacting our bottom line.

But our journey is far from over.

That's because as we improve, two highly dynamic forces are at work. First, as we get better, so does our competition. Second, as we meet the requirements of our customers, their expectations of Xerox also increase. What we see is an upward and never-ending spiral of increased competition and heightened customer expectations.

If you had told us that six years ago, we would probably have been discouraged by the thought of running a marathon race with no finish line. Today, we find that prospect invigorating. The pursuit of quality has taught us that as good as we are today, we must be better tomorrow.

In *Kaizen*, Masaaki Imai says that in the Western world we have an expression: "If it ain't broken, don't fix it." In Eastern culture, the philosophy is: "If it isn't perfect, make it better." That's a powerful concept for all of us. Our success as a world power may depend on it.

And that's the message in this book. The contributing authors are arguing in no uncertain terms that American management had better get back to the basics: Focus on the customer and continuously improve.

FOREWORD

JOHN PEPPER
President, The Procter & Gamble Company

When Greg Bounds and Mike Stahl asked me to write the foreword of this book, I readily agreed because I believe their work makes a significant contribution to understanding what we call Total Quality at Procter & Gamble.

Doctors Bounds and Stahl have done an excellent job of selecting, organizing, and editing chapters covering virtually every key aspect of Total Quality. They have obtained contributions from many industry leaders in their fields and have themselves contributed a great deal to the content of the book.

The Procter and Gamble Company made a formal commitment to the concept of Total Quality in 1986, when we first began to realize how much its principles could help us achieve our corporate goals. We have always been a company that has focused on serving the consumer. This focus is embodied in the first sentence of our corporate statement of purpose. "We will provide products of superior quality and value that best fill the needs of the world's consumers." We have found Total Quality to be a means of achieving this objective better than ever before.

It is helping us reach our objective by aligning everyone in the company to a far greater degree against meeting and exceeding the expectations of our consumers. Total Quality is also teaching us how we can serve consumers better by improving our systems and work processes. We are learning that "measurement systems" are essential to achieving improved quality and competitive advantage on a global basis. At Procter and Gamble, we have instituted tracking systems that are telling us how well we are satisfying the needs of our consumers and customers and how well our manufacturing plants support these needs in terms of their process reliability and outputs.

Our experience at Procter and Gamble demonstrates that Total Quality leads to improved consumer satisfaction and better financial results. Procter and Gamble's improved financial performance over the past several years can be attributed to many factors, including stronger technical innovations and more rapid global expansion; but no factor has been more significant than the application of Total Quality principles to more and more of what we do. These principles are communicated very clearly in this book, written and edited by Doctors Bounds and Stahl.

The book begins with the need for organizational strategies focused on delivering customer value and then moves to a very practical discussion of the role of management in leading, developing and deploying Total Quality. It also includes practical discussions of how to apply Total Quality to improve specific business activities and it provides several Company case histories of how Total Quality has led to improved results.

In recent years, more and more top U.S. corporations have been adopting Total Quality as a means to compete more effectively in building their businesses.

That trend will continue. Indeed, I am certain the use of Total Quality principles, no matter how they are described, will become an essential element of any truly successful business in the years ahead.

This book should make an important contribution to helping business and other leaders understand how to use Total Quality principles to dramatically improve their results.

PREFACE AND EXECUTIVE SUMMARY

MICHAEL J. STAHL
Associate Dean, College of Business Administration
University of Tennessee

GREGORY M. BOUNDS
Research Associate, Management Development Center
University of Tennessee

To survive and prosper in the white hot international competitive business environment of the 1990s, organizations must shift to a new role model for organizations and the practice of management. The contributing authors argue, first, that the ultimate managerial priority is the delivery of the best net value to the customer, and, second, that management must continuously improve strategic suprasystems which provide that value. The following paragraphs summarize each of the chapters contributed by the various authors.

GLOBAL COMPETITION: THE NEED FOR EDUCATIONAL AND BUSINESS RESPONSES

As global competition intensifies, business schools and business must develop and implement new ways of managing and competing. In documenting a new model of management and organization, the authors of this book develop two themes. The first and the *central* focus of management should be the determination, creation, enhancement, and delivery of the best net value to the customer. Net customer value consists of that which is realized minus that which is sacrificed by the customer. Best refers to excelling all competitors. Three critical dimensions of net customer value are quality, cost, and response/delivery time of products and services. Second, management must design and continuously improve strategic suprasystems that focus on discovering, creating, improving, and delivering value to the user/customer. Such strategic suprasystems cut horizontally across vertical organizational structures and integrate functional silos. The results of such a strategic suprasystems management approach focused on competing with customer value include consistently higher quality, lower cost, and quicker response time.

COMPETITIVE ECONOMIES AND THE ECONOMICS OF COMPETITION

The concept of evolution is stressed in showing that world leadership passed from the United States to Japan and Germany. Simple models are developed to show major features of the latter economies. The crucial differences are found in managerial methods, with the Japanese approach appearing to be given broad "lip service" as the new paradigm for success. The competitive model of economics is described with highlights of its failure to explain the evolution set forth above. The principal reason for the failure is the fact that the competitive model takes both technology and managerial methods as given. The model assumes that technology and managerial methods are "on the shelf," available for purchase by any firm, and that firms will purchase the combinations of technology and managerial methods that will maximize profits, both in the short run and the long run. A crucial fallacy is the implicit assumption that new techniques are easily adaptable, that they are "on the shelf" in the sense that money can buy them and make them operational. Changes in the firms' cultures and in the broader society are required for them to be adaptable.

COMPETITIVE ADVANTAGE THROUGH CUSTOMER VALUE: THE ROLE OF VALUE-BASED STRATEGIES

Managers using current strategic management models, process, and content have focused on, but not achieved, competitive advantage for many U.S. firms. The new global context requires that managerial leaders alter their current predisposition toward stockholders and financial performance and focus instead on continuously improving value for customers as a means to organizational success. This change suggests new processes and new content in competitive strategy paralleling those in current models.

BUILDING RESPONSIVE UNIVERSITIES: SOME CHALLENGES TO ACADEMIC LEADERSHIP

Universities face a difficult task in responding to societal problems. Information growth coupled with the rising tide of professionalism gives the individual professor a personal identity while precluding any cross-discipline understanding of problems. Such a narrow functional approach is reflected in curricula and teaching. Hence, graduates tend to be function specific in their approach to issues. If business needs to emphasize cross-functional systems approaches, then universities need to educate future managerial leaders to think in cross-functional terms.

MANAGERIAL LEADERSHIP

To compete domestically and internationally, managerial leaders must more competitively create value for the users of their products and services. Managerial leaders at various organizational levels must personally engage in two sets of strategic activities: (1) to determine what customers and users value in products and services, and (2) to improve strategic suprasystems that create value. This chapter presents an implementation strategy to ensure that these two sets of activities are integrated to achieve and sustain organizational competitiveness.

CUSTOMER VALUE DETERMINATION AND SYSTEM IMPROVEMENT CYCLES

In this chapter the authors elaborate the managerial leadership model in order to give managerial leaders and system owners a better understanding of their required tasks. This model consists of two interrelated cycles of activities: value determination and systems improvement. The Strategic Value Determination cycle is an exercise in seeking and confirming knowledge of customer value. It consists of four sequential steps, suggested by the quadrant labels: PROJECT, INVALIDATE, DISCOVER, CONFIRM. The results of customer Value Determination must guide the work of the Organizational Systems Improvement. The Systems Improvement cycle of managerial activities consists of four quadrants labeled DESCRIBE, ASSESS, STANDARDIZE, and CHANGE. Organizational systems management must be viewed as perpetual, improvement activities.

THE MANAGER'S JOB: A PARADIGM SHIFT TO A NEW AGENDA

Continued reliance on the classical functions of management will not be adequate to ensure organizational viability over the long term. The practice of the classical functions has deteriorated into activities that are more similar to the administration and maintenance of the status quo.

Continued reliance on such a classical functional approach to management ensures the status quo and does not encourage managers to proactively set an agenda focused on continuous improvement of organizational systems that will increasingly create value for their customers. This chapter reviews models of the classical approach to management, points out shortcomings pertaining to this work, and offers an alternative for the manager's job. This alternative emphasizes an agenda that drives managerial interest and activity toward customer value creation. Two themes of this agenda are knowledge development and continuous improvement.

THE ROLE OF MIDDLE MANAGEMENT IN IMPROVING COMPETITIVENESS

This chapter builds the bridge between the role of managerial leaders and the role of operators. The bridge rests on the shoulders of those who fill the traditional hierarchical levels between managerial leaders and operators, the "linking pins" called middle managers. After a brief review of the evolution of middle managers, the authors propose a new set of role activities for middle managers which integrates and links the managerial activities of leaders and operators.

THE ROLE OF THE EMPLOYEE IN IMPROVING COMPETITIVENESS

Many managers have responded to competitive crises by establishing employee-focused programs to improve productivity and quality. These programs have varied in their scope and objectives. Implementation vehicles have included Quality of Work Life programs, Quality Circles, Team Building, Statistical Process Control, and Work Group strategies. Employee-focused programs have generally fallen far short of correcting the fundamental shortcomings of the organization to improve long-term competitiveness, often even failing to sustain themselves over time. This chapter describes the appropriate role of employees in improving organizational competitiveness within the context of managerial leadership.

MANAGING STRATEGIC SUPRASYSTEMS: THE NOBLESSE OBLIGE OF LEADERSHIP

Critical strategic (transfunctional) suprasystems are inherent in the selection of organizational strategy. A new strategic orientation and a new methodology for discovering strategic suprasystems are offered, and examples of this new thought process are included. Organizational implications that may result from such a reorientation and their operational considerations are discussed.

ORGANIZATIONAL CHANGE: THE SYSTEMS APPROACH

This chapter suggests that managers must adopt a systems view of the organization in better understanding how to invoke long-term change. They must recognize that the organization represents a transformation system that consists of a multitude of layers of subsystems that are interdependent and are put in place to provide what customers value. Managers are responsible for utilizing human, capital, technological, and raw material input resources effectively. They must initialize the improvement effort by ensuring that an organizational system is in place to determine what customers most highly value. The current and future instability of the market in which those customers reside suggests that this accumulation of knowledge will not be a single event. The system must allow management to be aware of what is currently of value and what will be of value in order to proactively respond to changing needs. Managers must recognize that work actually gets done in an organization through systems that cut horizontally across the entire organization.

MANAGING IN THE PRESENCE OF VARIATION

This chapter describes management behavior and practice in the use and response to process system information, primarily of a numerical nature. The meaning of variation in numerical information, and how that variation affects and is affected by management practice and purpose, is explained. The descriptions and experiences of managing variation need to be understood in the larger context of the management of critical systems.

UNDERSTANDING CAUSE AND EFFECT RELATIONSHIPS FOR SUPRASYSTEM IMPROVEMENT: DESIGN OF EXPERIMENTS AND BEYOND

Owners of strategic organizational suprasystems need tools to work causal issues that arise in system description, assessment, standardization, and change. This chapter briefly discusses use of the design of experiments as a tool for robust product and process design and as a tool for organizational suprasystems management.

ASSESSING PROGRESS IN MANAGING FOR CUSTOMER VALUE

To compete, an organization must increasingly create value for customers. Quick fixes and partial approaches to competitiveness doom an organization to mediocrity, at best. Competing globally requires comprehensive managerial attention to many factors in the organization. These factors include individual, cultural, and management system considerations. To maximize their competitive impact, leaders must make sure that these relevant factors are complementary and congruent. Doing so requires a lot of managerial thought, attention, and hard work. Managerial leaders must identify these factors and track progress for improvement within their organization. This chapter provides a framework and method for doing this work to improve organizational competitiveness through managing for customer value.

MANAGERIAL LEADERSHIP AND CULTURAL TRANSFORMATION

Organizational culture is important because it can defeat organizational change or serve to reinforce and sustain it. Therefore, culture is an important consideration in assessing the degree of difficulty an organization will have in digesting a given set of changes and can help inform the change strategy. This chapter addresses the issue of cultural change in relation to managerial leadership and organizational competitiveness in creating value for the users of the organization's products and services.

MANAGERIAL PERFORMANCE MEASUREMENT

Performance measurements are critically important managerial tools. These tools may be poorly designed and misused to the detriment of organizational competitiveness in value creation. Alternatively, performance measurements may be used to encourage continuous improvement and the consistent creation of value for customers. The shortcomings of traditional systems include the assumption that optimization of local objectives results in optimization of systems objectives, ignorance of variation, measurement of what's easily available, and internal orientation. The proposed alternatives emphasize broader system measures, external orientation, and a cascading set of measures for continuous improvement. Guidelines for making changes to these proposed alternatives emphasize managerial behavior change.

ACTIVITY-BASED COST SYSTEMS FOR FUNCTIONAL INTEGRATION AND CUSTOMER VALUE

Organizations are asked questions such as: are all products profitable, should we accept this order, should we continue to do business with a customer, and what is the cost impact of process waste and improvement? These questions imply that organizations need to know the cost of the product, process, and serving customers. Without such information, firms are unable to establish direction with regard to product and customer strategies. These questions cannot be answered under traditional costing frameworks. Activity-based costing provides a methodological break through that can help provide operational and strategic knowledge.

IMPROVING THE PRODUCT DEVELOPMENT PROCESS

This chapter outlines some "essential elements" for improving the product development process. The "essential elements" presented in four articles in this chapter are part of a comprehensive effort to build an integrated product-development methodology that product development teams can practice successfully.

The first article, entitled "Some Essential Elements for Superior Product Development," provides an overview of the entire product development process. The second article, "Some Essential Elements for Product Technology Selection and Development," focuses on the critical technology selection and development phase of the product development process. "Qualification of Critical Product Characteristics for Superior Product Development," the third article, discusses the identification and effective use of product performance and quality measures throughout the product development process. Finally, the fourth, "Some Essential Elements for Superior Product Manufacture," examines the development of superior manufacturing processes.

A NEW ROLE FOR ENGINEERING PROCESS CONTROL FOCUSED ON IMPROVING QUALITY

The new role of engineering process control will focus on managing variation beyond designing and implementing control systems. This chapter discusses a broader role of engineering process control that includes studying variation and how it affects quality. Several cross-functional liaisons are suggested that could provide important new perspectives on both understanding and managing variation. The technical and organizational issues presented in this chapter are particularly salient to the continuous process industries; yet, they apply to any industry that operates continuous or semi-continuous process equipment.

CLOSING THE GAPS IN SERVICES MARKETING: DESIGNING TO SATISFY CUSTOMER EXPECTATIONS

Many companies are beginning to recognize the importance of providing high-level quality in the services that support the products they make. These firms are striving to give better total value to their customers. They are failing in spite of their efforts. This chapter describes a model to improve customer value creation in services by identifying the gaps in services marketing.

THE PRODUCTION AND INVENTORY CONTROL SYSTEM

Improvements in production and inventory control translate directly into customer value through better product quality, cost, and delivery. This impact dictates that the production and inventory control system must be a focal point in a manufacturing firm's strategy to compete through customer value. The inability of many firms to achieve good production and inventory control stems from fundamental deficiencies in certain organizational systems. The role of management is to identify and improve those systems. Unless management accepts this role, implementation of any faddish technique for coordinating production will, at best, result in marginal improvements.

ACHIEVING CUSTOMER VALUE THROUGH LOGISTICS MANAGEMENT

The logistics area encompasses unique opportunities to create value for the customer. Defined as "the management of product and information flows from original source to final customer in a manner which adds value to the external customer," logistics represents a key bundle of resources that can be applied successfully to the task of providing best net value for the customer.

MARKETING IN A VALUE-ORIENTED ORGANIZATION

Marketing has a tremendous opportunity to increase its contribution to organizations because of its customer-oriented dimension, but only if it reconsiders its role. This chapter presents a framework for understanding marketing's changing role responsibilities in organizations in the decade ahead.

FINANCE AND THE CREATION OF VALUE

The traditional functions encompassed by corporate finance include (1) the selection of viable projects, (2) the acquisition of capital from the financial markets, and (3) the management of short-term assets and liabilities. Although the role of finance in an organization committed to delivering customer value spans these same activities, the continuous creation of value in today's complex environment may require new approaches and different tools. This chapter summarizes the new approaches that are currently known and directs attention to areas that require more insights. In particular, attention is devoted to concepts and techniques required for effective capital budgeting. This chapter also addresses changes that may be required in the management of financial institutions if they are to adapt to a competitive global market.

MANAGEMENT ACTIVITY FOR COMPETITIVE CAPABILITY

The types of activities critical to competing in global markets include creation, innovation, incremental improvement, standardization, routinization, maintenance, and execution. The domains of these activities also vary greatly, ranging from strategy to operation. These objects include value strategy, design strategy, strategic systems, corporate policies, management systems, strategic subsystems, process technology, operating methods, operational tasks, and operational motions. This chapter offers a framework, the Management Activity Topograph, which can be used to articulate the roles of all employees regarding these activities and objects. Human resource needs can also be inferred from this framework.

HUMAN RESOURCE MANAGEMENT FOR COMPETITIVE CAPABILITY

Human resources represent a key to organizational competitiveness. Although productive organizations increasingly rely on automated and advanced technologies to transform, transact, and transport information and material, people provide the brainpower, ingenuity, and creativity required for orchestrating the creation of value for customers. Traditional approaches to human resource management have been too individualistic. This chapter presents a model that emphasizes systems and team performance, as well as jobs and individual performance.

APPLICATION CHAPTERS

These chapters contain case examples from some well-known organizations of how some of these new concepts have actually been used. No one organization has applied all the concepts. These applications are not perfect. They are reports of the experiences of some organizations grappling with customer value and strategic suprasystems issues. However, in the spirit of continuous systems improvement, the managerial leaders of several of these organizations have launched their organizations on the path of linking customer value and strategic suprasystems.

ACKNOWLEDGMENTS

The contributions of several individuals to this book must be recognized. Indeed, this book would not have been possible without their collective contributions.

The authors and coauthors of the thirty-four chapters and two forewords must be recognized as providing the essence of the book. Within this group, two people need special recognition.

Dr. Richard Sanders was one of the cofounders of the University of Tennessee's Institutes for Productivity Through Quality. The Institutes have provided a living laboratory for many of the coauthors in this book to develop, test, and validate their ideas. Richard's tireless efforts in developing the Institutes over the past decade must be acknowledged.

Dr. Harlan Carothers is another individual who deserves special recognition. He was instrumental in developing the major themes central to the book. Harlan also helped to generate the concept of writing the book.

Deans Warren Neel and William Snyder of the Colleges of Business Administration and Engineering, respectively, encouraged their faculty to rethink the paradigms of their disciplines and to publish their knowledge concerning this new managerial and organizational model.

Tami Touchstone assisted administratively with the book's development and production. Jeanne McDonald, Joan Snoderly, Patricia Hunley, Lynn Landry, Julia Elkins, and Patricia Flynn helped prepare the document for publication.

Our wives, Barbara Stahl and Tuck Bounds, understood our marriage to this book and endured our editorial activities on many long evenings and weekends.

We deeply appreciate the multiple contributions of this team.

Michael J. Stahl
Gregory M. Bounds

A. INTRODUCTION:

THE COMPETITIVE CHALLENGE

CHAPTER 1

GLOBAL COMPETITION: THE NEED
FOR EDUCATIONAL AND BUSINESS RESPONSES

MICHAEL J. STAHL
Associate Dean, College of Business Administration
University of Tennessee

GREGORY M. BOUNDS
Research Associate, Management Development Center
University of Tennessee

SUMMARY

After a decade of unbridled growth in competition, global competition promised to be white hot in the 1990s. As more countries experience growing political freedoms and gravitate toward market-based economies, as Europe becomes further integrated, and as Japan targets new industries, the worldwide competition should become even stronger. As international competition intensifies, business schools and business must develop and implement new ways of managing and competing.

In documenting a new model of management and organization, the authors of this book develop two themes. First, the *central* focus of management should be the determination, creation, enhancement, and delivery of best net value to the customer. Net customer value consists of that which is realized minus that which is sacrificed by the customer. Best refers to excelling all competitors. Three critical dimensions of customer value are quality, cost, and response/delivery time of products and services. Second, management must design and continuously improve strategic suprasystems that focus on discovering, creating, improving, and delivering value to the user/customer. Such strategic suprasystems cut horizontally across vertical organizational structures and integrate functional silos. The results of such a strategic suprasystems management approach focused on competing with customer value include consistently higher quality, lower cost, and quicker response times.

GLOBAL COMPETITION

This chapter uses many examples concerning the decreased global competitiveness of industry in the United States, partly because so much has been written on the subject. However, these North American examples can be used in a much broader global context concerning the fate of any country's business which ignores customer value when competing globally.

As the 1990s opened, many recognized the United States' diminished global economic competitive position. For example, a nationwide poll of over 1,500 registered voters conducted in early January 1990 indicated widespread awareness of the weakened global economic competitive position in the United States versus that in Japan. The poll contained the following question. "When it comes to economic power, which country is currently in a stronger position – the U.S. or Japan?" A strong majority of the respondents (73 percent) answered Japan. Only 20 percent picked the United States. The other 7 percent answered "About equal" or "Not sure" (*The Wall Street Journal*, January 19, 1990: 1). It is informative to see if those perceptions are supported in reality.

Market Share

Market share data are important to the customer value theme of this book since changes in market share indicate relative changes in value realized by customers. The worldwide market share held by U.S. firms has fallen precipitously in a number of industries. Most readers are familiar with the declines in market share in autos, textiles, steel, shoes, and consumer electronics.

The trend of declining U.S. market share has also included high technology industries. The challenge in these industries is especially troubling to those who view high technology industries as the seed industries of the future. Although not exhaustive, Figure 1 shows the U.S. market share of six important products reviewed by *Fortune* over a ten-year period. *Fortune* viewed the six products as important because they are integral to several high technology industries.

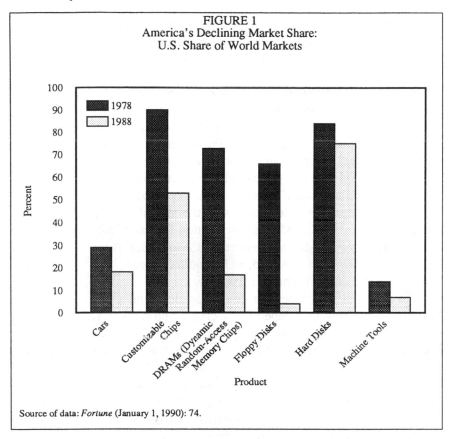

FIGURE 1
America's Declining Market Share:
U.S. Share of World Markets

Source of data: *Fortune* (January 1, 1990): 74.

In addition to the specific products with their indicated market shares in Figure 1, *Fortune* also lists twenty-two technologies considered vital to U.S. security by the Pentagon. The United States leads the world in just ten of them and is holding its own in four technologies according to the *Fortune* article. The United States lags in eight technologies, including biotechnology, gallium arsenide semiconductors, high-power microwaves, integrated optics, machine intelligence and robotics, microchips, pulsed power, and superconductors. The U.S. failure to maintain preeminence in products for which there is a critical defense need has frightening economic and national security implications.

A good example of the U.S. firms' loss of significant market share is the automobile industry. General Motors' (GM) domestic market share declined from about 46 percent in 1979 to about 35 percent in 1989 (*The Wall Street Journal,* December 14, 1989: 1). After a decade of declining sales, GM President Robert Stempel articulated his insight into the problem. He remarked: "Our market share was in the 40s, and now we're in the 30s. Those are the facts. We've made those facts, and we've got to own up

Some have also pointed out the formidable economic power associated with the European Community after most economic boundaries fall by 1992. Given a history that has been spotted with protectionism, there is concern about some European ambitions to create a superstate (*Forbes*, January 22, 1990: 85). A good example of potentially greater global economic competition is contained in the reunification of East and West Germany.

We should not forget the growing economic power of Japan. Not only do the Japanese dominate a number of manufacturing-based industries, but also the presence of the Japanese is growing in banking and world finance (*Business Week*, February 12, 1990: 24). Other Pacific Rim countries, which are poised to emulate the Japanese story, should not be dismissed.

Should governments solve global competitiveness issues, or should firms? Some argue that the governments should, but recent examples of U.S. and Japanese trade issues suggest the firms should. As the Japanese continue to post a substantial trade surplus with the United States, pressures are mounting in this country for a U.S. response. Some want a U.S. industrial competitiveness policy (*Business Week*, February 5, 1990: 54), while others are clamoring for a U.S. protectionist response (*Business Week*, January 22, 1990: 50). However, given the Reagan and Bush administrations' market-based philosophies, it is unrealistic to count on either U.S. protectionism or a U.S. industrial policy to solve the competitiveness issue. It appears that business in the U.S. must implement its own competitiveness solutions.

BUSINESS SCHOOLS: HELP OR HINDRANCE?

How can business schools help in this quest? Are they part of the solution, or are they part of the problem?

Recently, a raft of criticism has been leveled at business schools because it appeared that the schools were not a part of the solution. A recent article documented a number of the criticisms, including the following four (*Business Week*, November 28, 1988: 84-86). Lester Thurow of MIT's Sloan School, remarked: "If our B-Schools are doing so well, why are American companies doing so badly?" Paul Allaire of the Xerox Corporation noted: "The academicians are too busy writing about what other academics are interested in." Robert Hayes of Harvard commented: "There is no evidence the money spent on business schools has served this country well." Curtis Tarr of Cornell stated: "For a long time most schools abandoned manufacturing. They got swept up in this financial thing." Some critics claim that business schools churn out MBAs who lack leadership skills and operations knowledge. According to the *Business Week* article, partly because of the above problems, a number of companies have stopped recruiting MBAs.

What do the business schools teach in their curricula? Many of these schools still teach the primary functions of management as planning, organizing, directing, and controlling. Functional specialization is also frequently taught in terms of production, marketing, finance, personnel and accounting. How many schools teach that a central function of management is to discover, create, enhance and deliver best net value to the customer? How many teach that management needs to create strategic suprasystems that integrate across the functional silos?

The preceding indicates that many business schools were a part of the problem, rather than a part of the solution, in helping U.S. industry regain its global competitiveness. The authors of this book argue that business schools can be, and need to be, a part of the solution. This issue is described in more detail in the fourth chapter in this part of the book.

A MANAGEMENT RESPONSE

As already indicated, there are two major themes in this book. The first concerns the role of management in determining, creating, enhancing and delivering best net customer value. The second theme argues that management must design and continuously improve strategic suprasystems to insure the focus on best net customer value.

Customer Value

Three major dimensions of customer value are quality, cost, and response/delivery time.

Quality. Several other chapters in this book in Parts B, D, and E establish the conceptual importance of quality as a major dimension of customer value. In introducing the topic, there are numerous examples in the business press of the overriding importance of quality as a critical component in customer value and as a competitive factor.

The most important rules America's successful high technology companies were following at the dawn of 1990 to improve their world competitiveness were recently listed. One of the rules focused on "QUALITY, QUALITY, QUALITY." Even high technology won't get far in the marketplace if it isn't produced with high quality. "The Malcolm Baldrige National Quality Award administered by the U.S. Commerce Department signals government recognition that American companies need a push to match the competition. In November, President Bush handed out awards to the 1989 winners, Xerox and Milliken" (*Fortune*, January 1, 1990: 76).

Motorola was recently recognized for regaining market share from its Japanese rivals. One of Motorola's secrets was described as "Built-In Quality. CEO George Fisher's mission has been distilled into a handful of key goals, capped by attaining Six Sigma quality. That's statistical jargon for near-perfect manufacturing – a rate of just 3.4 defects per million products. Only relatively simple products, such as calculators, have reached this level, but Motorola expects to do so across the board by 1992" (*Business Week*, November 13, 1989: 108-110).

Michelin was recently recognized for its successes, including its unrelenting pursuit of quality. "One of Michelin's secrets is a business style remarkably similar to that of a Japanese company. It consistently sacrifices all short-term concerns for the pursuit of just two objectives: quality and market share" (*The Wall Street Journal*, January, 5, 1990: 1).

However, all is not well on the quality front. Many companies continue to define it relative to the company – rather than to the customer. Such an approach misses the entire point of this book concerning customer value – not company value. "Though managers increasingly acknowledge the importance of quality, many continue to define and measure it from the company's perspective. Closing the gap between objective and perceived quality requires that the company view quality the way the consumer does" (Zeithaml, 1988: 17).

It may be some time yet before American consumers associate high quality with many American products. The poll described in the first part of this chapter also dealt with quality perceptions. "Yet the poll found that most Americans don't pin the blame for the country's competitive woes on foreigners but on the U.S. itself. Fifty-four percent say the problems are mostly the result of U.S. management and labor falling behind in productivity and in the quality of goods" (*The Wall Street Journal*, January 19, 1990: 1).

Unlike the above examples of firms that have integrated quality into their corporate fabric, a number of firms still view quality as just another program. "More than 80 percent of the Fortune 500 companies have made some type of in-house quality and productivity improvement effort. Unfortunately, in many instances, these improvement efforts have not been tightly interwoven with the organization's strategic management practices. When quality improvement is not linked to the organization's key strategies, employees will perceive it as just another faddish program" (Bremer, 1988-1989: 11).

Cost. Cost/price has always been a major dimension of customer value. Indeed, cost leadership has been recognized as a major generic competitive strategy (Porter, 1980). However, many who view cost leadership as a competitive strategy do not seem to recognize that in today's international competitive setting, the vast majority of customers will not trade off quality for the sake of low cost. Quality has become an absolutely necessary condition in most markets. For example, although GM offered all kinds of rebates to increase sales, its market share continued to tumble in the late 1980s partly because of its earlier quality problems. "Consumers remain angry about poor cars in the past though quality improves" (*The Wall Street Journal*, December, 14, 1989: 1).

Low cost must be maintained but not at the expense of quality. Indeed, high quality keeps costs low owing to fewer reworks, less scrap, lower warranty costs, and larger market share (Deming, 1986). High quality and low cost are compatible, not contradictory.

Response/Delivery Time. Recently, some companies have realized that many customers place a high value on the speed with which a product can be delivered. "Today, time is on the cutting edge. The ways leading companies manage time – in production, in new product development and introduction, in sales and distribution – represent the most powerful new sources of competitive advantage" (Stalk, 1988). The number of firms that recognize time as a competitive advantage seems to be growing. "A majority of chief executives surveyed say their firms have begun programs to shorten product-development cycles" (*The Wall Street Journal*, February, 1, 1990: 1).

Nonetheless, it appears that some firms are still unable to compress the time to deliver a product. As of 1988, it took Detroit five years to develop a new car, while it took Toyota three years (Bower and Hout, 1988: 112).

Strategic Suprasystems Management

In order to deliver value to the customer, it appears that a new way of conceptualizing the managerial role is required. The old way which focused on the traditional functions of planning, organizing, directing, and controlling ignores the importance of providing customer value. The old way of conceptualizing organizations consisting of production, marketing, and finance hampers the ability to discover, create, enhance, and deliver the customer value. The old emphasis on functional silos almost precludes focusing on the customer because the functional specialists tend to concentrate on functionally specific criteria – not customer criteria. Competing internationally in the creation of value for customers requires the cross-functional management of suprasystems to integrate diverse organizational resources.

OVERVIEW OF THE BOOK

Now that the dual themes of customer value discernment, creation, enhancement, and delivery, and of a strategic suprasystems management approach have been introduced, it is appropriate to describe the parts of this book.

The first chapter in Part A introduces the competitive challenge. Following this chapter are three chapters on competitive economies, global competitive strategy, and the challenge facing our universities.

Part B defines and describes the new managerial role in great detail. The dual role requirements concerning customer value and strategic systems management are described in the first chapter and contrasted with the traditional managerial role requirements. Subsequent chapters in this part describe the implications for managerial and nonmanagerial behavior. Statistical concepts used in quality programs, especially as they affect managerial behavior, are described in the last few chapters of Part B.

Part C describes the role of the organization, including assessment and systems. The transformation of the organizational culture to serve the new role of customer value management and strategic suprasystems management is also described.

The new role of traditional functions in focusing on customer value creation and delivery, and in terms of managing strategic systems, is described in Part D.

Part E contains industrial and governmental applications from several organizations.

Part F concludes with implications and a call for the future.

REFERENCES

"Americans Have Uses for 'Peace Dividend' That Aren't Selfish: Japan's Perceived Supremacy." *The Wall Street Journal* (January 19, 1990): 1.

Bower, J., and T. Hout. "Fast-Cycle Capability for Competitive Power." *Harvard Business Review* (November-December 1988): 112-113.

Bremer, M. S. "Linking Strategic Management and Ongoing Quality Improvement." *National Productivity Review* 8, no. 1 (Winter 1988-1989): 11-22.

"Carla Hills, Trade Warrior: She Must Battle Japan and Europe – and Keep U.S. Protectionists at Bay." *Business Week* (January 22, 1990): 50-55.

"The Dark Side of 1992." *Forbes* (January 22, 1990): 85.

Deming, W. E. *Out of the Crisis.* Cambridge: Massachusetts Institute of Technology, Center for Advanced Engineering Study, 1986.

"The Future of Silicon Valley: Does the U.S. Need a High-Tech Industrial Policy to Battle Japan Inc.?" *Business Week* (February 5, 1990): 54-60.

"Getting High Tech Back on Track." *Fortune* (January 1, 1990): 74.

Ishikawa, K. and David Lu. *What Is Total Quality Control? The Japanese Way.* Englewood Cliffs, N.J.: Prentice-Hall, 1985.

"Long-Term Thinking and Paternalistic Ways Carry Michelin to Top." *The Wall Street Journal* (January 5, 1990): 1.

"Many Americans Fear U.S. Living Standards Have Stopped Rising: Nagging Lag in Productivity." *The Wall Street Journal* (May 1, 1989): 1.

Mitroff, I., and S. Mohrman. "The Slack Is Gone: How the United States Lost Its Competitive Edge in the World Economy." *Academy of Management Executive* 1 (February 1987): 69.

Porter, M. E. *Competitive Strategy.* New York, N.Y.: The Free Press, 1980.

"The Rival Japan Respects." *Business Week* (November 13, 1989): 108-118.

"Shorter Product Cycles Become a Top Corporate Objective." *The Wall Street Journal* (February 1, 1990): 1.

Stalk, G., Jr. "Time – The Next Source of Competitive Advantage." *Harvard Business Review* (July-August 1988): 41-51.

"The Tokyo Stock Market." *Business Week* (February 12, 1990): 74-84.

WEFA Group. *U.S. Long-Term Economic Outlook* (Third Quarter 1989).

"Where the Schools Aren't Doing Their Homework." *Business Week* (November 28, 1988): 84-86.

"Who Gains from the New Europe?" *Fortune* (December 18, 1989): 84.

"With Its Market Share Sliding, GM Scrambles to Avoid a Calamity." *The Wall Street Journal* (December 14, 1989): 1.

Zeithaml. V. A. "Consumer Perceptions of Price, Quality, and Value." *Journal of Marketing* (July 1988): 2-22.

CHAPTER 2

COMPETITIVE ECONOMIES AND
THE ECONOMICS OF COMPETITION

WILLIAM E. COLE
Professor of Economics
University of Tennessee

SUMMARY

Quality products and quality processes are said to be key factors differentiating market leaders from market followers. It is therefore interesting that the discipline of economics has had almost nothing to say on the subject of quality. A perusal of the latest comprehensive textbooks devoted to economics shows that quality is taken up in only the most cursory fashion and never accorded an important competitive role. The advanced texts ignore the subject entirely, focusing on price formation. This omission is all the more relevant when we consider that the applied business fields such as marketing, finance, and logistics, for example, consider economics to be the "mother discipline." Indeed, because economic theory is at the core of all business curricula, graduate and undergraduate, its failure to consider quality may have important consequences. Specifically, decision makers in business and government may have failed to give importance to the topic of quality partly because they had been unwittingly trained to view the world through the lenses of deficient theoretical models. At this point it may be useful to recall the words of John Maynard Keynes (1936, 383): "The ideas of economists . . . , both when they are right and when they are wrong, are more powerful than is commonly understood. Practical men, who believe themselves to be quite exempt from any intellectual influences, are usually the slaves of some defunct economist."

The pages that follow trace some important facets of the economic evolution since World War II. Emphasis is on the emergence of quality as a central competitive feature and on the difficulties in understanding those events when they are refracted through the prism of standard economics. It is then proposed that the economics of the firm should be developed from a new point of view, that of net customer value. As defined and elaborated throughout this volume, the concept of net customer value subsumes price, product performance, serviceability, aesthetics, and timeliness. In explaining the key differences between leading firms and follower firms, a broad definition of technology emerges that includes organizational characteristics and strategies. The logic of the argument then moves to the role of top management of follower firms in finding a way out of their competitive dilemma. In concluding, it is argued that both business decision making and government policy making will be better served by economic models that are fashioned within the framework of the net customer value perspective.

THE TRANSITORY TRIUMPH OF YANKEE INDUSTRIAL GENIUS

The brilliance of its officer corps, the valor of its troops, and the willingness of its general population to endure sacrifice are duly credited for their contributions to a nation's performance in war. Of equal, if not greater, importance, however, is the ability of the economy to gear up for the production of war goods while still providing essential goods for the sustenance of the nation. There can be no doubt that the triumph of America and her allies in World War II was due in great measure to the abilities of America's several economic sectors. Moreover, the victory on the battlefields encompassed another important aspect, the destruction of the major industrial and infrastructural components of the principal economies of Europe and Asia. Indeed, by the end of the war, the economy of the United States, because of its productivity and because it was now largely uncontested, reigned as the world's foremost productive entity. The rise to the leadership pinnacle had been long in the making. Some would say that it had been reached before World War II, having been based on the development of the assembly-line factory system. The extent to which this leadership phenomenon resulted from the intrinsic merit of its productive systems and the extent to which it was an artifact of the war cannot be pursued here.

The fact that the U.S. economy was momentarily uncontested meant that the manufactured goods entering international trade flows immediately after the war were for the most part American. It also meant that the private investments that flowed to the less developed countries of the world were associated with American firms. Moreover, the official flows of aid that helped restore the economies of Europe and Japan came from the economic largesse of the victor. In terms of natural resources, the American cornucopia seemed boundless. Moreover, the domestic market for which the industrial system produced was made up, on average, of the richest consumers and in enough numbers to provide economies of scale for large numbers of firms in a broad range of possible industries. The American industrial system was also blessed with a highly skilled workforce that was the product of what was called the first and foremost system of public education in the world. In other words, from every viewpoint, the American economy was the uncontested industrial champion of the world. That all of this would create a sense of pride is understandable, and that the pride would promote the development of myth might also be conceded as a natural course of events. Emerging from those events, therefore, was the mythical American manager who was considered to be the keystone of American "know how."

An academic response to the postwar economic developments was the rapid emergence of colleges of business administration at major universities. American industrial know-how was studied by a new breed of scholars and its essence analyzed, modeled, and diffused by new scholarly disciplines. Management techniques were studied, systematized, analyzed, refined, and transmitted to the cadres of MBAs who moved into the managerial ranks, slowly but steadily replacing the self-made businessman. The academic analogue to American management gave new impetus to the theme of scientific management that had been around, albeit furtively, for decades. Indeed, some observers unabashedly referred to the cumulative product of this synergistic interaction of industry and academia as a "managerial revolution." That coupled with the fact that the technological revolution was considered to be largely an American phenomenon gave promise that it was truly an American century.

AN ASIAN AND A EUROPEAN PHOENIX RISE FROM THE ASHES

As the European and Asian economies began to rebuild, they did so not by simply restoring that which had been destroyed but by utilizing the most modern of the feasible technologies then on the drawing boards. That was especially the case with Germany and Japan because their industrial sectors had suffered the most damage. Steel was one of the first sectors where that trend became noticeably important. After focusing on domestic rebuilding needs, both the Japanese and European steel firms turned opportunistically toward global markets. The new technologies and modern facilities caused some stir in America, but many observers initially dismissed the foreign competitive position in steel as being based on allegedly low wages and poor working conditions. Only slowly did the realization dawn that the mighty steel industry that had served as the backbone of America's war effort was both technologically and managerially obsolete. The scenario would be repeated again and again in other industries.

The nature of Germany's postwar development was brought home to the United States in the form of imported German goods. Precision instruments and tools, cameras, and automobiles had been the prewar forte of German industry, and it came as no surprise that she returned to those lines. In terms of Japanese development, however, much of the growing industrial acumen remained hidden for a time from the United States because what we saw as imported goods did not reflect the growing strength of Japan's basic industries. It was during the early postwar years that the label "Made in Japan" was synonymous with low price and shoddy quality. All the while, Japanese heavy industry, with its new look, was busy rebuilding the Japanese economic infrastructure. Slowly, but surely, the mix of Japanese exports underwent transformation, and just as surely, the image of Japanese quality changed. In less than two decades, the change was marked: "Made in Japan" had become a synonym for the highest in quality.

The era of transcendent American know-how had been short indeed. In only three decades, it had been superseded by the mysteries of the alien management methods. However, neither the American managers nor their academic counterparts gave up the myth gracefully. "Cheap labor," government subsidies, and "dumping" were all held up as factors that might account for ostensibly inferior methods having triumphed in the marketplace. Then, and reluctantly, the argument shifted to technology. Next, the foreign achievement of high quality with lower prices came to be seen as the result of their having adopted more modern technology. Modernization through investment became the new American watchword, another flag behind which to rally the effort to put our industry back in the race.

The new panacea did not take. Slowly and inevitably, American industry came to the realization that differences in quality were not readily explained by differences in technology. In the next phase, the current period, it is suggested that the source probably lies in the way firms are organized to utilize the technology and in the methods used to manage and motivate the labor force. American managers and American thinkers have begun a long odyssey in which the search for the keys to quality involves peeling back layer after layer of the institutional structure of the Japanese firm. That search has come to focus largely on alleged aspects of the Japanese approach to quality, and it is realized that many more layers are yet to be peeled. As will be clear from the several contributions in this volume, it is also important to peel back the layers of institutional matter that envelop the American firm if we are to learn how to close the competitive gap.

THE COST OF QUALITY PARADIGM

Formal economic theory has nothing to say about the problem of quality, except inferentially. The ability to produce quality products, in the narrow sense of meeting standards, is held to be implicit in the nature of technology. The technology is seen as imbedded in forms of capital, human and machine. In that view, better quality requires the technological forms that produce it, and the technology, in turn, requires investment. In other words, quality costs. All of this is implicit. It is not spelled out in economics texts because technology itself is almost always taken as an exogenous factor in economic analysis. The theory of the firm *assumes* that if a new technology is available, managers (decision makers) will acquire that technology when and if doing so will result in maximizing profits on investment.

Whereas standard economics takes quality to be so simple and straightforward an aspect of cost analysis that it need not be modeled, the fields of industrial engineering and quality engineering have developed a formal analysis of the cost of quality. Assuming that the market has determined a given standard, failure to produce that standard is said to involve costs in the forms of scrap, rework, and repair under warranty. By holding total output constant and starting with a given level of quality conformance, greater conformance can be obtained by more inspection, better machines, better materials, and/or more effective maintenance, all of which contribute to improved quality. In this analysis each of these aspects is perceived to involve costs and benefits.[1] The analysis is usually graphed as shown in Figure 1.

Curve B represents outlays for improved machinery, increased inspection, more maintenance and other methods for obtaining closer conformance to standards. Conversely, curve A represents the cost of scrap, rework, and repair under warranty. Following the internal logic of the model, expenditures on quality improvements should be made as long as the present value of added benefits outweighs the present value of added costs. With reference to Figure 1, the profit-maximizing firm would choose to provide additional quality by making improvements out to the point where the rising cost of quality curve intersects the curve representing

---

1. This accords with the bedrock foundation of standard economics: the concept of opportunity costs.

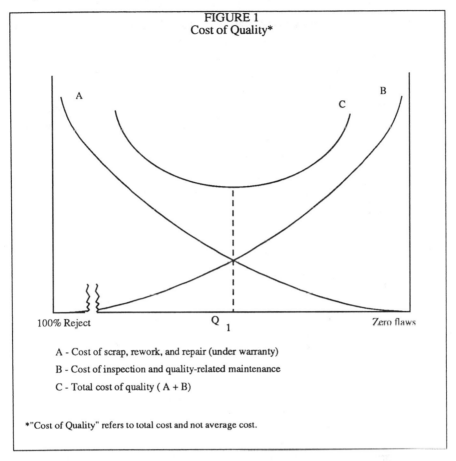

FIGURE 1
Cost of Quality*

100% Reject Q_1 Zero flaws

A - Cost of scrap, rework, and repair (under warranty)

B - Cost of inspection and quality-related maintenance

C - Total cost of quality (A + B)

*"Cost of Quality" refers to total cost and not average cost.

declining cost of nonconformance. Any additional expenditure on quality would increase the total cost of production and therefore lower profit. The profit-maximizing firm would therefore operate at the level of quality represented by Q_1. If economists had shown interest in this analysis, they would have added that this argument applies in competitive markets in which the products of the several producers are perceived to be very similar to each other.[2] However, in the real world, some firms may choose to differentiate their product from those of other firms by moving further up the cost of quality curve. Such firms would then endeavor to promote a "high-quality" image for their product, which would necessarily cost more. This might be thought to represent the behavior of some German automobile firms.

2. In the formal presentation of the economics of perfect competition, the assumption would be that the product would be identical across the several competitors.

We can visualize successful manufacturing plants that use the cost of quality model as consisting of numerous inspection stations, intermediate rework points, and inventories of parts and work-in-progress queues. Moreover, inspection implies rejects and scrap. The costs of quality therefore show up in many ways, and some of those are highly visible: the additional workstations and inventory locations that imply floor space and more working capital tied up in inventories. Those direct and visible costs of quality can be illustrated by the simplified three-stage production system shown in Figure 2 where stations representing inspection, intermediate rework, scrap, inventories, and so on, have presumably been added up to the point where the cost of investment in quality equals the benefits obtained from such investment. Figure 2 will be referred to as the "G" model.

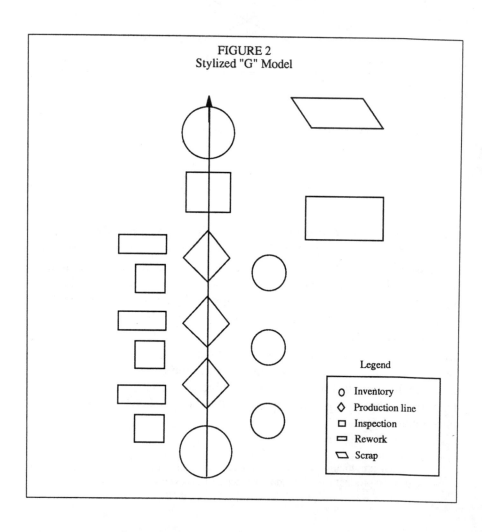

FIGURE 2
Stylized "G" Model

Legend

o Inventory
◇ Production line
□ Inspection
▭ Rework
▱ Scrap

Although the discipline of economics has found the cost of quality model to be of no apparent interest, the approach is nevertheless in accord with standard economics. In the world of economic theory, it is assumed that any profit-maximizing manager automatically chooses to operate at point Q1 in Figure 1. Production engineers and accountants will have provided management with analyses and data to support that decision. Economics *takes it for granted* that engineers will design processes correctly and that accountants will count accurately, at least for the most part and over the long run. Given profit-maximizing behavior by management and full availability of pertinent information, the proper decisions will automatically take place in the long run. If better ways of doing things emerge anywhere in the world, those ways will come to be adopted here if they are appropriate to the resource base. Moreover, if new methods are not appropriate to the U.S. resource base, those same economists might suggest that perhaps the United States should no longer engage in those activities. In the final analysis, economic theory teaches an optimism whose "flip side" is fatalism: Free all relevant markets from artificial fetters and "que sera, sera!" But whatever is will be assumed to be for the best.

GETTING BEYOND THE COST OF QUALITY PARADIGM

This cost of quality approach is in accord with the foundation stone of the supply side of standard economics, the principle of opportunity cost. Improved product quality requires investment outlay, and improvements beyond some point imply higher costs of production with consequently higher prices. From the point of view of the demand side, the higher prices associated with improved quality require greater sacrifice on the part of the consumer. We will see, however, that what might be termed the Japanese approach or "J" model has turned the cost of quality paradigm on its head, by yielding higher quality products at lower cost.

In contrast to its "G" model counterpart, the "J" model is sleek and trim, as illustrated in stylized form in Figure 3. No inventories and no inspection imply fewer workstations, less work space, and less capital tied up in inventories. If we approached this illustration solely from the perspective of the cost of quality paradigm, viewing it side by side with Figure 2, it might be thought to represent a firm that had made no investment in quality, a firm that is producing junk and letting the rework be done in external repair centers and allowing the scrap to show up in consumers' households. Moreover, it might be speculated that total downtime would be great here because there are no inventories of work-in-progress to tide the process over when glitches develop at particular workstations. The starting point

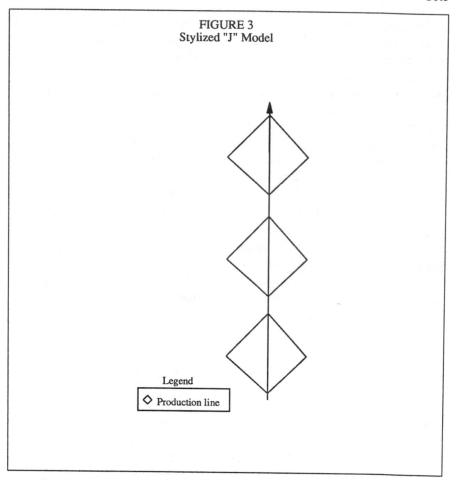

FIGURE 3
Stylized "J" Model

Legend

◇ Production line

with this figure, however, is the assumption that the quality emerging from this process is just as good or better than the quality emerging from the "G" model. With high quality assured, we quickly see that the absence of inventories, inspection, rework, scrap, and the like, represents cost savings.

This system that produces higher quality at lower costs can be reached only when variation within the manufacturing systems has been reduced to predictable and very low levels. In "G" type systems, inspections are made because of the nature of the variation, inventories are kept to meet seemingly inevitable emergencies, and scrap and rework result from unacceptable variation in terms of defined standards. Moreover, Figure 3 cannot show the relatively thin profile that lies in the unseen third dimension. That thinness derives from the "J" model's paucity of middle management which, in turn, results not only in lower costs, but also in the ability to respond quickly to external and internal stimuli. Nor can it reflect the necessarily amorphous nature of knowledge flows and decisionmaking that move both vertically and horizontally through the organization.

The reasons for reductions in variation in the "J" model may be found in a host of sources, some of which are widely recognized. These include statistical process control, close alliances with selected suppliers, internal organization that utilizes a cross-functional systems approach, and active participation of all levels of the workforce in process and systems improvement. There is also the recognition that the overall volume of improvements is undoubtedly more than the sum of gains from these several sources. That is to say that we have not identified all the important factors contributing to the ongoing improvement process. And we may never find all of them. Just as in collegiate football, it is some mysterious "x" factor that distinguishes the number one organization from the also-ran organizations.

At this point we will highlight another major shortcoming of the cost of quality paradigm: an exclusive focus on the manufacturing processes. This volume makes clear that the quality and cost achievements reflected by firms that are market leaders derive from systems improvement activities that span all parts of the organization. Marketing, design, purchasing, accounting, finance, logistics, and manufacturing all contribute in simultaneous and interacting fashion to an unending string of improvements in net customer value. The important lesson for the economist is that those improvements in processes and systems that promote higher quality, for the most part, have not entailed opportunity costs. Quite the contrary, they are the wellspring of persistent cost reductions.

If we were to undertake a historical study of a "J" model type of firm that features continual self-improvement, it might be possible to identify some past investments that were made as a conscious effort to build continuous improvement systems. In such cases, it would be correct to say that those specific improvements entailed an opportunity cost at the time they were made. For the most part, however, the stream of improvements that now come as a normal consequence of the routine activity of the "J" firm cannot be said to entail an opportunity cost to the firm. That is the case because the organizational design that produces a never-ending stream of improvements is itself largely the product of evolution. It was not a matter of purchasing technologies of quality "off the shelf." Nor was it a case of the improvements resulting from expenditures on research and development. Rather, it was largely a matter of the management and the workforce in the process of day-to-day operations finding new ways of improving processes that would yield increases in customer value. In such cases, the standard cost of quality approach that is reflected in Figure 1 is of relatively little use.

STANDARD ECONOMICS AND NET CUSTOMER VALUE

In economics, technology is said to be embodied in capital goods and in knowledge that is called human capital. Improved technology is pictured entering the firm through new investment, which acquires one or both of the forms of capital in which the improvement is imbedded. The investment in technology may take the form of off the shelf purchase or R and D expenditures. In either case, the technological improvement should result in increased output per unit of input for one or more inputs. If there is competition among firms, the productivity gain should result in a reduction in unit costs, which would be passed along to consumers in the form of lower prices. If it is assumed that information about this technology is available, the standard economist would say that competition is all that is needed to force firms to adopt the most appropriate technology.

To the extent that markets are imperfect, there will be some information costs in acquiring the technology. In any case, however, the profit-maximizing firms of the economists' models would supposedly adopt the technology that yields the best returns given the relative factor costs facing them. Otherwise, they would not be maximizing profits. If the matter were as simple and straightforward as assumed, the optimum national policy would be the promotion of competition through such policy devices as free trade internationally and antitrust domestically. The matter, however, is neither simple nor straightforward. We have seen that firms like those represented by the "J" model have organizational characteristics that promote continuous improvement of quality and productivity. Accordingly, those characteristics should be seen as playing the same type of conceptual role that academic analysts have reserved for technology, as narrowly defined. It is therefore necessary that those analysts now expand their conception of technology to include organizational characteristics.[3]

In the standard approach to the economics of the firm, new technology requires an investment and therefore has an opportunity cost. This would be the case, for example, for a firm that did not currently feature continuous improvement but wished to adopt some of the features that have evolved in a "J " model setting, such as Just-in-time (JIT). In fact, hundreds or possibly thousands of firms have made expenditures to learn how to utilize such features as quality circles, Statistical Process Control (SPC), and JIT. The point to keep in mind is that the firms that have developed systems that internalize continuous improvement are often able to make advances

---

3. Although there have been some mavericks, most economists have not used the term *technology* to refer to aspects of organizational design, managerial style, or organizational dynamics. (For exceptions, see Cole and Sanders, 1983, and Cole and Mogab, 1987).

in productivity and quality without having to make specific investment outlays. For them, the improvement is a normal outcome of the day-to-day method of operation. It is the follower firm, on the other hand, that *always* faces an investment cost in its efforts to internalize a system advance that was produced in evolutionary fashion by leader firms. This dilemma facing the follower firm might properly be termed a competitive lag.

An illustration of the dilemma which the follower firm must deal with is found in current developments in the automotive industry. As American and European firms struggle to improve product quality through such investments as the introduction and implementation of SPC and the development of close relationships with suppliers, very large financial outlays are required. Meanwhile, the competitive leaders move up to new plateaus of net customer value. Custom design for almost immediate delivery is one of the latest benefits of the continuous improvement systems. The reduction of variation to a bare and manageable predictability allows JIT to be refined to the point that, for example, each car coming through the process can differ from all the others produced the same day. This breakthrough, which might properly be termed *economies of scope*, is not associated with higher costs. It is simply the latest advance in the evolution of organizations that feature systems for continuous improvement. In fact, it is not inconceivable that this latest competitive leap would mean reductions in cost, just as did earlier stages in the evolution of those systems.

INSTITUTIONAL RIGIDITIES AND THE ECONOMIES OF NET CUSTOMER VALUE

What should be clear is that firms will have difficulty remaining in business over the long run if they persist in being followers because of the costs associated with trying to stay in the race. The process of catching up on the quality and service sides of net customer value continually adds to cost, which through higher prices reduces net customer value. "Catching up" adds cost because the follower is always in the position of trying to adopt through a formal educational process the new organizational innovations that have evolved within the institutional structure of the market leader. Meanwhile, for the market leader, the evolutionary process is continually providing new ways of enhancing all aspects of net customer value simultaneously. In this scenario, the competitive gap can do nothing but widen. The only possibility for a current follower firm to stay in the race over the long haul is to develop itself into an organization that features continuous improvement in all aspects of creating and providing the best net customer value as a normal aspect of its operations. To accomplish the implied restructuring would obviously require a tremendous effort on the part of top management.

Unfortunately, the matter is not exclusively in the hands of the managers of firms. Institutional rigidities to radical change are found in the broader attitudes and institutions of the society. As one small example, Just-in-Time as a concept may be on the shelf in the sense that the information is available. And there may be gurus to explain how it works on paper. However, the ability to move a firm to Just-in-Time requires that variation be driven to a bare bones minimum which, in turn, requires a host of fundamental systemic changes across the organization. Moreover, to be able to make those changes without it involving excessive costs to the firm will require broader societal changes such as in the system of public education, for example. The investment in human capital, both by firms and individuals will require that both managers and workers come to be viewed and to view themselves as assets rather than agents. This latter point will be pursued shortly.

It is important to remember that the techniques that "follower" firms are attempting to take "off the shelf" are systemic elements that were developed within the institutional framework of the "leader" firms and are therefore specific to that framework. The question would seem to assert itself as to whether soft technologies such as organizational systems can be transferred easily from one firm to another if the originator and borrower belong to different societies.[4] In other words, to what extent are the soft technologies contextual to the institutional framework within which they were developed? One analyst who approaches technology from the point of view of social systems suggests that technologies cannot easily be disassociated from the institutional aspects of the broader society within which they are developed. Using the assembly-line system of the early U.S. auto industry as his example, Goonatalake (1984) argues that the assembly-line system was produced by and in the context of the norms of a society that, for example, saw a sharp division between those who were decision makers, that is, managers, and those who were sweat hogs. The structure of organizations, the nature of labor relations, even the philosophy of the public school systems, as well as the hard technologies and the way they are implemented, must, by this approach, be seen as fitting together in a mutually supporting whole.

Even the hard technology bears the scars of the social system within which it emerges. Take, for example, the plumber's wrench. Is there surprise in the fact that its weight and torque are appropriate to a society

---

4. The concept of soft technologies in reference to administrative and managerial systems is developed in Cole and Sanders (1983) and Cole and Mogab (1987).

in which the role of plumber is tacitly reserved for males. The sexual division of labor has become part and parcel of the wrench – it is designed in. If such a simple example of hard technology as the wrench and such straightforward a matter as the organization of production technologies into an assembly-line system have been greatly affected in their design and functioning by the nature of the societies in which they were developed, how much more important these societal factors must be in the development of and functioning of soft technologies such as managerial systems and organizational strategies. Just as the transfer of assembly-line technology to a society that treats workers as assets might produce inefficient results, the use of soft technologies developed in societies where managers and workers are mutually viewed as assets might entail difficulties if the host society treats those persons as agents.[5]

If managers and workers are considered assets in the same vein as capital, then it makes economic sense for those individuals to invest time and effort to acquire firm-specific information. This concept of self-investment is especially relevant to the cross-functional activities of the firm. Aoki (1990: 18) notes that "skills effective for the creation of information value in the context of horizontal coordination may not be classifiable along well-defined job categories, for which market contracts transferable between firms can be unambiguously written." It follows that if employees expect to remain with a firm and prosper or falter with it, they are more likely to expend time and effort to master activities related to functions other than those corresponding to their job titles. Moreover, shallow programs that largely consist of announcements that "workers are important and will be listened to" are not sufficient for changing job behaviors of managers or workers. "Saying it doesn't make it so." The institutional changes that are needed to effect and support the necessary revolution in attitudes are fundamental and would ideally be diffused throughout the society as well as the firm.

---

5. The view of managers and workers as agents is an integral part of the standard approach to the economics of the business firm. With ascendancy of the corporate form, the venerable artifact of profit maximization was salvaged by assuming that stockholders hire management as their agents to maximize returns on their investments (Aoki, 1990). Management, in turn, hires workers as their agents. Agency implies a tenuous tie to the firm, based on the perceived needs of the absentee owners. Some say that this aspect helps explain the focus on short-term profits for which some U.S. firms are notorious. In this cited work, Aoki argues that leading Japanese firms treat all employees as assets, and he develops the economic implications of that viewpoint.

THE POVERTY OF ECONOMIC POLICY

The answer of standard economics to the competitive dilemma has been to recommend dropping protection and other barriers to perfectly free functioning of markets. That advice assumes that as a matter of course competition will force follower firms to utilize the most efficient technologies. A major problem with that approach to the problems facing national economies is that it gives the appearance that the relevant information is available and unambiguous and that the required changes can occur quickly. This, however, is an oversimplification that borders on deception. Economists, when pressed, will acknowledge that over the period that they call the long run many firms may go out of business in declining industries and many new ones will come into operation in rising industries.[6] The deceptive impression that the models make on political debates may be something else, however. In the naive model, the removal of protection and deregulation gives the appearance of yielding relatively swift and certain results, and the appearances may be tempting. However, if information is not fully available, if it is not unambiguous, and, most important of all, if it is specific to its original cultural and institutional settings, change efforts based on emulation will always be deficient. This follows from the argument that there are persistent cost and quality gaps between leader and follower firms.

When economists thirty years ago were telling policy-makers that international competition would force American steel to adopt competitive techniques, it was genuinely believed that all that could keep our steel industry from matching that of Germany or Japan would be some form of misguided protection that would shield it from the discipline of the market. A decade later, that same sentiment was expressed relative to the American automobile industry. By now, however, the argument of the economist has changed. Facing a reality of industrial decline over what must surely be considered a period of sufficient length to qualify as the long run, a standard economic answer now says that perhaps the U.S. economy was not destined to remain in those lines of production. Our comparative advantage is now said to lie elsewhere: maybe in services, maybe in agriculture, or possibly a combination of the two. According to that reasoning, if our comparative advantage is in services and/or agriculture, our standard of living will be better in the long run if we concentrate on those areas and import steel, automobiles, and so forth. From the point of view of pure and simple comparative advantage theory, it might be a perfectly natural journey for

---

6. An industry may decline because its output is no longer in demand, as in the case of buggy whips. Or, as in the case of the auto industry in the United States, the reason may be impaired ability to compete.

the U.S. economy to have traveled from being a nation of hewers of wood and tillers of the soil to the industrial pinnacle and then back again to its agrarian roots. It is doubtful, however, that the American people or their leaders would have bought that round trip ticket, if such an eventuality had been foreseen as having a reasonable probability of occurring.

The present analysis would suggest that a government policy largely limited to dropping protection was doomed from the outset. In order to devise policies that effectively meet the competitive challenge, the analysis must be based on theory that recognizes the role of endogenized and costless technological change on the part of leader firms in the global economy. This will lead to the conclusion that there should be well-planned mutual support between government and business. For example, tariff reductions should probably be selective, conditional, and implemented in stages that allow time for the necessary structural changes in the ways firms are organized and managed. Furthermore, a plan for promoting competitiveness should provide for important institutional changes in such areas as education, antitrust, and other aspects of the legal framework. The deterioration of schools, the extreme limits on interfirm cooperation, and a legal atmosphere that encourages speculators to burden otherwise competitive firms with heavy debts have all contributed to the competitive decline. Since the days of Adam Smith, it has been said that the role of government should be limited to that of a watchdog over competition. In the modern age, it may be necessary to replace this view with a vision that recognizes the complexity of the problems of global competition. In that regard, it is instructive that firms rated as competitive leaders appear to consider themselves to be partners with their governments rather than adversaries.

CONCLUSION

First, let it be suggested that economists should expand their view of the economic world. Where interest heretofore has been almost exclusively placed on price formation in stylized markets, a more worthwhile approach might suggest the study of the other components of customer value, quality, and product service. It is also suggested that a broader view of technology be taken so as to include aspects of organizational systemics. Furthermore, the dynamics of technology formation and technology transfer should be studied by economists rather than assumed away. If, as argued throughout this volume, systems design and systems management are key factors in the development of an industrial unit that features continuous improvement, then those factors are themselves technological. Furthermore, if the ability of U.S. firms to compete depends on the ability to develop continuous process systems that are uniquely appropriate to the institutions and attitudes of this society, it would seem imperative that we open the "black box" of technology and study its contents.[7] If economics is to remain as a foundation stone for the functional business disciplines, it cannot continue to neglect robust variables that explain the competitive gap. Moreover, shortsighted economic models help to shape and reinforce the continuance of the shortsighted behavior that characterizes the lagging firms' and government policies.

In terms of policy, what is needed for the follower firm is a leap forward into evolutionary forms that feature continuous improvement. However, these new forms must necessarily be peculiar to and compatible with the broader institutional framework of the firm's internal and external environment. Simply trying to copy systems that were born abroad will not do the trick. The imported models will function but imperfectly, and imperfect functioning will insure continued relegation to a follower role. In such a context, where catch-up efforts entail attempted emulation, improvements in customer value will always cost the follower firm while being a natural byproduct of everyday functioning for the leader firm.

The ideas reported throughout this volume all lead inevitably to the argument that the managers of firms must become personally engaged in a massive overhaul of the goals of their firms and must undertake massive organizational restructuring. The goals will entail a focus on all aspects of customer value, and the reorganization will focus on how to maximize it. A particular thrust of the present writer is to urge that the broader society must also undertake to make important institutional changes to support and enhance the efforts of managers if the economy is to enjoy broad-based success. In promoting the necessary societal and institutional changes, government will have to assume the role of partner rather than limiting itself to being a regulator.

REFERENCES

Aoki, M. "Toward an Economic Model of the Japanese Firm." *Journal of Economic Literature* (March 1990): 1-27.
Cole, W. E., and J. W. Mogab. "The Transfer of Soft Technologies to LDC's: Some Implications of the Technology/Ceremony Dichotomy." *Journal of Economic Issues* (March 1987).

7. Rosenberg (1982) referred to the economists' concept of technology as a "black box." This refers to the almost universal tendency to take technology as exogenous to the analysis.

Cole, W. E., and R. D. Sanders. "The Transfer of Soft Technologies from the Tennessee Valley Authority to Mexico." *Papers and Proceedings of the North American Economics and Finance Association* (Mexico City, 1983).

Goonatalake, S. *The Aborted Discovery: Science and Creativity in the Third World.* London: Zed Books, Ltd., 1984.

Keynes, J. M. *The General Theory of Employment, Interest and Money.* New York: Harcourt, Brace and Company, 1936.

Rosenberg, Nathan. *Inside the Black Box: Technology and Economics.* New York: Cambridge University Press, 1982.

CHAPTER 3

COMPETITIVE ADVANTAGE THROUGH CUSTOMER VALUE: THE ROLE OF VALUE-BASED STRATEGIES

G. HARLAN CAROTHERS, JR.
Senior Lecturer, Institutes for Productivity
University of Tennessee

MEL ADAMS
Assistant Professor of Management
University of Alabama in Huntsville

SUMMARY

Despite the use of strategic management process and content models, many managers fail to maintain or improve their firm's competitive position. The new globally competitive context requires that top management alter its current predispositions toward certain stakeholders and financial performance measures and refocus on continuously improving net customer value. These changes suggest new strategic management processes and new strategy content paralleling those in current models.

INTRODUCTION

The driving force behind world economic growth has changed from manufacturing volume to improving customer value. As a result, the key success factor for many firms is maximizing customer value. Rather than price, quality has become the dominant influence on customers' perceptions of value. Thus, quality is now a necessary but insufficient factor in gaining and retaining customers. A strategy of providing the best net value provides the most sustainable long-term competitive advantage.

Thus, value is much more important to customers and managers than previously imagined. With rising consumer expectations and legal requirements for better quality, customers are loyal only as long as the firm provides the best value. For managers, statistically-based value management processes provide the only systematic way to continuously improve relative value (and cost) positions and thus recapture market share. This fundamental shift in the basis of long-term competitive advantage suggests that the strategic management process itself needs to be reexamined.

Purpose

Complementing the macroeconomic view of the preceding chapter, this chapter takes a microeconomic view and focuses on the firm or strategic business unit, viewed from top management's perspective. After defining terms, widely accepted concepts and processes of strategic management are briefly reviewed. Then an alternative set of concepts and processes based on customer value are suggested. Finally, a typology of value strategies is developed.

Fundamentally, we argue that the firm's single most important strategic obligation is to provide best net value to customers; it is so important that it constitutes every firm's superordinate goal. All other goals represent distracting self-interest. Managerial leaders must design strategic organizational suprasystems that continuously improve the firm's and its members' abilities to provide and improve value for customers.

Accordingly, the paramount managerial leadership activities, formulating and implementing strategies to provide net value to customers, are indigenously linked. Since later chapters detail implementation issues at the operating and supervisory levels, this chapter focuses primarily on formulation issues at the business unit level.

Definitions

Customers' perceptions of realizable net value are the single most important determinant of long-term performance. Broadly defined, *customers* include purchasers, end users, intermediate customers, distributors, internal customers and users, and others who derive value from or make sacrifices because of a firm's product or service. Thus, employees who use the output of a previous stage of production or a staff function are also customers. The value provided to each type of customer is a direct result of the firm's strategy.

Objective measures of value by managers are less important than value through the customers' eyes. *Perceived value* has been defined as "the consumer's overall assessment of the utility of a product based on perceptions of what is received and what is given" (Zeithaml, 1988). Customers' sacrifices cannot be measured in dollars alone; the price paid includes both monetary and nonmonetary components.

We use the term *net comparative customer value* to emphasize recognition of customers' total sacrifice (including opportunity costs) and the existence of competitive or substitute products/services. We use the term *comparative* to suggest that customers choose a firm's product/service from a set of competing alternatives that go beyond immediate alternative suppliers and substitutes to include all personal choices in their unique context. Nevertheless, for brevity, this and other chapters will use the term *net value* to mean *net comparative customer value*.

Net Value is defined as that value realized by a customer which justifies the sacrifice made to acquire, use, and dispose of a product/service, in comparison to available alternatives. *Best net value* is defined as that product/service set which customers perceive as superior to all others in providing what is expected, after considering alternatives and the required sacrifice. This combination of the customer's perceived value and his or her potential to realize that value minus all sacrifices determines how much value the firm can create.

Strategy has been defined as "the pattern of organizational moves and managerial approaches used to achieve organizational objectives and to pursue the organization's mission" (Thompson and Strickland, 1990). Thus, strategy refers to the *means* a firm uses to reach its ends. Fundamental to every firm's mission and competitive strategy is its value strategy. Generically, a *value strategy* is the pattern of decisions and actions that constitute the firm's overall approach toward providing realizable net value to customers. A value strategy inherently involves all parts of a firm's functional and organizational strategies that provide value realized by customers or require sacrifices by customers.

All firms have a value strategy, but few have completely conceptualized and clearly articulated value as the basis for competing. In fact, many firms are more competitor-oriented than customer-oriented. As a result, many managers are more familiar with their firm's competitive strategy than its strategy for improving customer value. Some inadvertently compromise net customer value either by producing products/services perceived to be of low quality or by requiring excessively high sacrifices of customers. Ironically, the most competitive firms are the customer-oriented, not the competitor-oriented firms. Customer-oriented firms are nearly driven by value-based strategies.

Given a defined set of value expectations, a *value-based strategy* is that pattern of decisions and actions in which managers take responsibility for: (1) delivering products/services that provide best net value, and (2) creating strategic suprasystems to improve that value and satisfy the obligations of the enterprise. Most fundamentally, value-based strategies are customer-oriented, business-level strategies aimed at providing **best** net value.

Value-based strategy should not be confused with generic strategy. The one-dimensional generic strategies of low cost, differentiation, and focus (Porter, 1980) are the three most extreme examples of producer-based, value-added strategies (Porter, 1985), but they are not customer value-based strategies. Each of the three is more competitor-oriented than customer-oriented. Each strategy can be pursued with no assurance of providing best net value.

While low cost and differentiation are usually seen as mutually exclusive (Porter, 1985), a value-based strategy may require and achieve both. Since many customers now count time rather than dollar cost as their most precious asset, a high-quality strategy provides little competitive advantage unless it is paired with low cost (i.e., low price and/or sacrifice reduction). Similarly, low-cost/price strategies may also fail if they are not complemented with quality perceived to be of sufficient value. The synergistic combination of low cost and differentiation that may come with a value-based strategy is a direct result of managing critical systems that contribute to value. To analyze the systemic nature of value-based strategies, we turn to the processes and content of strategic management.

STRATEGIC MANAGEMENT PROCESSES

Current models of strategic management can be traced to the way in which strategy itself was defined and applied to business (Chandler, 1962): "the determination of the basic long-term goals and objectives of an enterprise, and the adoption of courses of action and the allocation of resources necessary for carrying out these goals." Chandler identified two parts of the strategic *process*, formulation and implementation, which, by the early 1980s, came to be known as strategic management. Current process models expand formulation and implementation to at least five components (e.g., Thompson and Strickland, 1990):

1. *Mission*: Developing a concept of the business and forming a vision of where the organization needs to be headed – in effect,

infusing the organization with a sense of purpose, providing long-term direction, and establishing a mission.

2. *Setting Objectives*: Translating the mission into specific long-term and short-range performance objectives.

3. *Strategy Formulation*: Crafting a strategy to achieve the target performance.

4. *Strategy Implementation*: Implementing and executing the chosen strategy efficiently and effectively.

5. *Strategy Evaluation and Control*: Evaluating performance, reviewing the situation, and initiating corrective adjustments in mission, objectives, strategy, or implementation in light of actual experience, changing conditions, new ideas, and new opportunities.

Clearly, each of these five components involves subprocesses that develop specific strategy content (see Table 1). As a process, strategic management is usually assumed to be objective to the extent that the strategist takes an open systems view and addresses the concerns of all stakeholders. But this theoretical objectivity is frequently limited by any personal dispositions the firm's strategist(s) may have toward certain stakeholders; many firms' goals appear to represent only selected internal stakeholders. Although strategists' personal predispositions are rarely considered in these models, they often determine the strategy formulation process, the strategy formulated, and the resulting path of strategy implementation.

According to Webster (1980), *predisposition* is an inclination or tendency; here we use the word to mean the inclination of a firm's management to serve a particular stakeholder group. Managers frequently recognize customers as the principal external group, while shareholders or top managers themselves usually top the list of internal stakeholders since these groups drive the firm's expectations. However, two dramatically different predispositions arise from managerial leaders' emphasis on external (customers) versus internal stakeholders (top management or stockholders). These different predispositions lead to two relationship models: one contract-based, the other reciprocity-based. A predisposition toward serving the other party (reciprocity-based) is best characterized as one of "providing," whereas a predisposition toward gaining from the other (contract-based) is one of "expecting."

Figures 1a and 1b present alternative models of these fundamental predispositions of both parties in every exchange process. In each figure, both the internal groups and the customers hold predispositions of expecting and providing. The difference is in the order of priority and therein the dominance of one predisposition over the other. In each model the top half

TABLE 1		
Strategic Management Subprocesses and Content		
Process Component	**Subprocesses**	**Content**
Mission	Business definition	Product, Market, Technology
	Value clarification	Philosophy
	Stakeholder analysis	Broad goal statements
Setting objectives	Environmental scanning	Opportunities and threats
	Industry analysis	Strengths and weaknesses
	Strategic group mapping	Long-term objectives
	Competitive analysis	
	Competitor analysis	
	Key strategic issues	
	Internal analysis	
	Activity-cost chain	
Strategy formulation	Long range planning	Generic and grand strategy
	Strategic choice and fit	Resource allocations
	Portfolio analysis	Pro forma financials
	Sensitivity analysis	
Implementation	Short-term planning	Annual objectives
	Organizational design	Functional strategies
	Institutionalization	Structure and staffing
		Culture, policies,
		Leadership/role of CEO
		Budgets
		Reward systems
Evaluation and control	Monitor performance	Key success factors
	Evaluate deviations	Gap analysis
	Feedback	Corrective actions

dominates the relationship. In both models, customers' predisposition toward the firm is very stable; they expect to realize best net value with minimal sacrifice.

Predisposition of Classical Strategists: The CONTRACTUAL Model

Classical strategic process models clearly focus on organizational performance: "long-term and short-range performance objectives", "target performance"; and "evaluating performance," in components 2, 3, and 5, respectively, in Table 1.

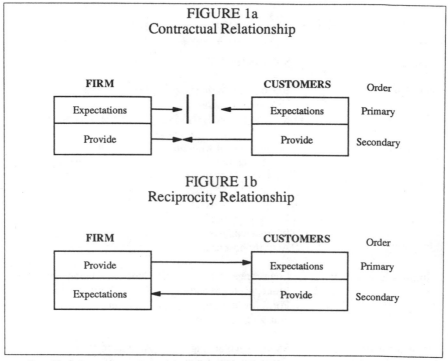

FIGURE 1a
Contractual Relationship

FIGURE 1b
Reciprocity Relationship

Implicit in component 4 is the notion that strategy implementation and execution are best judged by the efficiency and effectiveness in achieving "target performance." Thus, four components of the existing strategic management process are predisposed toward firm performance.

For publicly and privately held firms, economic measures of performance dominate both business practice and research. Managers, as employees of the shareholders (or owners themselves), expect a return on their investment; they influence the predisposition of the organization in the process of setting objectives for the firm for their own personal gain. Many managers center almost exclusively on financial performance as measured by sales volume, sales per share, cash flow per share, earnings per share (EPS), book value per share, net income, rate earned on capital (ROI), rate earned on net worth (ROE), and operating margin (Karger and Malik, 1975). The fact that researchers have adopted most of these measures as dependent variables (Rhyne, 1986) is further evidence of this predisposition.

Shareholders are interested in these financial measures per se only to the extent that they influence the growth of (or risk to) positive cash flow. Yet top and middle managers' personal rewards (e.g., bonuses, raises, promotions, etc.) are often tied directly to such measures. Thus, the current paradigm appears to emphasize internal stakeholders (shareholders, managers, or employees). This sets in place a predisposition toward "expecting" financial gain by stockholders and managers in which internal stakeholders' goals are considered a higher priority for the organization than those of the external customers. Any inclination toward "providing" is lost in management's predisposition toward the dominant internal expectations.

Figure 1a models the predisposition of a firm focusing on internal performance as a contractual relationship. Even though the mission may headline the customers' need, management's emphasis on established product line(s), earnings, growth, and profitability suggests it is really driven by the internally focused self-interests of stockholders and/or top management. When driven internally rather than externally, such firms usually provide a "satisficing" (i.e., providing of a necessary minimum) of customer needs, offering only that which is sufficient to gain what is desired in return. With such a stance, the prevalent producer attitude becomes "give as little as possible while gaining as much as possible – caveat emptor! (let the buyer beware)." With this view of the exchange relationship, the selling concept becomes the (unstated) driver in the firm's relationship with its customers. As management attempts to maximize shareholder and personal gain, it adopts an insidious, internally focused predisposition of "Expecting."

Needless to say, this shortsighted view does not enhance a continuing association with most customers. Since customers were expecting the firm to take responsibility for satisfying their needs, the selling concept provokes them to adopt an attitude of "getting all you can while giving up as little as necessary." Thus, each party is expecting from the other, a condition of conflicting predispositions of protective self-interest. The exchange process often becomes a bargaining contest, a relationship that is at best "Contractual."

Implications of the Contractual Model

This internally focused predisposition of the organization does more than bias the exchange process between internal and external stakeholders. Most important, a predisposition toward internal, financial indicators often also proves internally dysfunctional. Determining how to manage the organization to meet internal stakeholders' expectations (dominated by stockholders, owners, and managers) usually becomes the agenda of short- and long-term strategic planning processes (Ansoff, 1965). Given the best of intentions (as advertised in mission statements) but rigorously bounded by emphatic financial expectations, managers usually formulate strategy from this predisposition. Internal quantitative objectives, coupled with organizational control and reward systems, define appropriate behavior for subordinate functions, processes, and tasks throughout the organization. Long-term organizational purpose and direction give way to short-term (i.e., annual, quarterly, monthly, weekly, even daily) functional-level financial goals and objectives. Individuals' perceived roles and personal performance are focused by reward and incentive programs that reinforce this dominant predisposition.

Ultimately, this leads to goal conflict and a behavioral paradox for managers and employees who are torn between providing for the customer and expecting personal gain. Organizational members, like most humans, seldom serve two masters well, and most seek ways to resolve this struggle. There are three common outcomes in organizations: (1) the reward system motivates behavior contrary to the mission, (2) individual behaviors fulfill the mission with no relationship to rewards, or (3) the reward system is directly tied to realization of the mission.

This first of these three situations is most typical. In keeping with the predisposition to satisfy internal stakeholders, managers attempt to protect financial results at all cost. Carried to extremes, some managers even manipulate operations and accounting results to accomplish short-term goals; strategic budgets are "adjusted" to preserve operating margins. Line managers and employees may cut product/service corners to reduce short-run expenses, thereby compromising customer value realization, increasing customer sacrifice, and risking customer loyalty.

Why then the emphasis on financial performance? What is the relationship between mission and performance? What is the significance of performance indicators? Performance measurement is generally thought to be the most important indication of how well the mission has been accomplished. The problem is that, while the mission is appropriately defined in terms of the task to be performed in satisfying customer needs (not firm needs), the typical financial performance indicators directly contradict the mission by measuring how well the firm satisfied its own needs (not customer needs). Thus, while the ideal strategic management process aims to satisfy both customers and organizational objectives, the organization's financial performance is at best a surrogate for how well customer needs were met and mission accomplished.

This need not be a chicken and egg problem, nor is it a matter of choosing between serving either customers or the organization. The way out of this dilemma is to change the predisposition of the firm. Resolution lies in the simultaneous consideration of the expectations of both internal and external stakeholders.

An Alternative Predisposition: The RECIPROCITY Model

An alternative predisposition may be more appropriate, particularly in the developing intense, international competition. Although many firms and researchers have studied consumer behavior for decades, the predisposition of a firm studying consumer behavior is *not* the same as that of a firm predisposed toward its customers as the primary stakeholder group. Echoing early advocates of the "marketing concept" (McKitterick, 1957), many have suggested that organizations should be customer-oriented, that "organizations need to stay close to their customer" (Peters and Waterman, 1982). Unfortunately, those who have suggested such reorientations have treated the managerial and organizational behavioral implications with such extraordinary superficiality that very few organizations have completely adopted the marketing concept.

Only recently have many firms seriously considered moving customers to the top of the list of stakeholders. Figure 1b models such an alignment in which management commits itself to satisfying user expectations. Such an alignment requires a top management predisposition to "provide" what the consumer needs or wants within the framework of what the customer is willing to "provide" in return. Given customers' corresponding predisposition of "expecting," the model depicts a complementary match between the two groups' predispositions. Unlike the contractual model, however, the firm is, first and foremost, committed to "providing" what the consumer expects and the firm expects only what the consumer is willing to provide. The consumer, though still predisposed to "expecting" first, is now also willing to provide the firm a fair market price and a continuance of association in return for the firm's demonstrated commitment to meet his or her expectations. Rather than a relationship based on contracting to protect self-interest, this alternative is based on mutual self-interest and the rule of interdependent reciprocity. Essentially, in the classical model, management has said, "You scratch my back and I'll scratch yours." However, the new model says, "I'll scratch your back in anticipation that you'll scratch mine."

When predisposed to providing for a particular set of customer needs, understanding customers' expectations for realizable net value becomes imperative. While marketing studies of customer satisfaction are interesting, organizations must refocus on finding the determinants of satisfaction and dissatisfaction. Predisposed to provide, managerial leaders will attend to managing these determinants, a process that results in customers increasingly valuing the firm and viewing the firm as more responsive. As the firm increases customers' realization of value, customers will reinforce the firm's predisposition to "provide" and encourage its behavior by way of product/service selection and financial sustenance (profit). This builds sustainable competitive advantage for the firm. In short, this alternative predisposition, coupled with appropriate organizational actions, leads to managed reciprocity between producer and purchaser rather than conflict or bargained compromise.

Implications of the Reciprocity Model

This alternative model has distinct implications for the mission statement, the goal-setting process, for what is provided to customers, and for management's internal focus on certain activities.

Currently, based on the contractual model, managers first ask, "What do we want?" and then "How are we going to get it?" But this existing, seemingly preferred logic of means following ends may be backward. If a firm is predisposed to providing best value, then defining *how* the firm provides that value (the means) supersedes the firm's specific financial objectives (the ends). Thus, in the reciprocity model, management reorders these questions: first, "What will we willingly provide?" and then "Will what we are provided be sufficient to support our commitment to provide in the future?" Only when these types of questions come to the forefront of the organization's attention and are answered first can management possibly be assured of having predisposed the firm to serve customers' expectations. When this has occurred and been institutionalized, a firm should experience reciprocating relationships. Thus, reciprocity is the natural outcome of being predisposed to "provide" best net value for customers and is therefore in the firm's own "self-interest" (Smith, 1937).

Changing the firm's predisposition from expecting to providing also changes *what* the firm provides. The providing of a minimum is replaced by the intent to provide best net value. This requires all internal stakeholders of the firm, including shareholders, to take the initiative in developing the organization's capacity and capability (discussed later) to improve the net value provided to customers.

What if customers do not return the favor, that is, provide for the firm's expectations? This, too, may be more common than thought as firms abandon their responsibilities to customers. In an increasingly competitive environment in which customer power is also growing, more firms are retreating from markets by rationalizing "niche" strategies, divesting product lines, abandoning markets, or liquidating. Many managers, feeling the effects of deteriorating market share and profitability, turn to financial and accounting wizardry to improve shareholder value, rather than refocusing on providing enhanced net value to customers as the source of shareholder gains. Before they can expect to see customer reciprocity restored, however, managers must reverse this trend. What one gives is most often what one receives, and vice versa (Narver and Slater, 1990). Still, current strategic management process models provide little direction on how to refocus on customers. Obviously, without new value-based strategic processes and content, a new predisposition for the firm will prove to be insufficient.

ALTERNATIVE STRATEGIC MANAGEMENT PROCESSES

Figure 2 shows five major steps in an alternative strategic management process which roughly parallel those of current models. The fundamental difference arises from the predisposition toward fulfilling customer expectations. Each step of this new model presents different subprocesses and strategy content consistent with a predisposition to "provide." To reiterate, value-based strategy is the pattern of decisions and actions that form a firm's overall approach toward providing net value for customers.

In Figure 2, the five major components are: responsibility determination, environmental factor analyses, strategic suprasystems determination, strategic suprasystems management, and confirmation and correction. Although some of the labels in this figure might seem familiar, none of

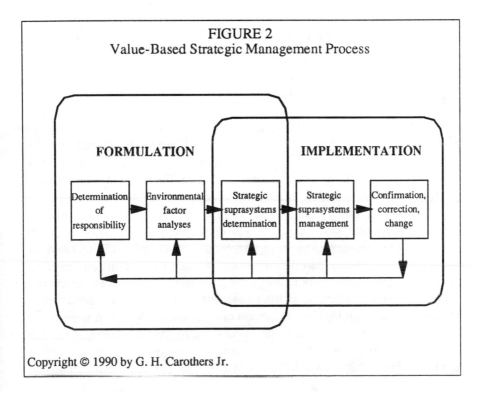

FIGURE 2
Value-Based Strategic Management Process

FORMULATION   IMPLEMENTATION

| Determination of responsibility | Environmental factor analyses | Strategic suprasystems determination | Strategic suprasystems management | Confirmation, correction, change |

them describes the traditional subprocesses or content. These new sub-processes are defined as:

Determination of responsibility: Specifying a set of fundamental cus-tomer needs and wants for which the organization takes responsibility, defining a complementary set of products and services that satisfy those needs, and committing the organization to continuously providing the best net value in satisfying those needs.

Environmental analyses: Analyzing external factors that affect the value criteria of customers and those internal factors that influence the capacity and capability of the organization to provide the best net value.

Strategic suprasystems determination: Discerning and describing the required strategic suprasystems to meet the responsibility to customers and designating managerial ownership for these systems.

Strategic suprasystems management: Operationalizing a process for continually knowing what is valued and coincidentally providing and improving strategic systems to ensure that products of best net value are provided.

Confirmation, correction, and change: Evaluating net value perfor-mance and financial performance and initiating adjustments to defined responsibilities, capacity, and capability, in light of changes in environ-mental factors, competitive offerings, and new value contribution alterna-tives.

Each of these processes and subprocesses is described in the following sections.

Determination of Responsibility

The alternative process in Figure 2 begins with determining the respon-sibilities of the firm. Although current stakeholder models should provide a systematic way of defining the hierarchy of goals for the firm, they actually provide little guidance (Ansoff, 1965). The new paradigm is also grounded in a stakeholder model but a very prescriptive one based on providing best net value. Specifically, such a mission requires a predisposition that ranks customers over employees, management, and stockholders. Rather than being internally focused, employees and management must (1) identify customers' value expectations and percep-tions and (2) take the responsibility for providing the best net value now and in the future. Much more than a semantic distinction, this predisposi-tion places the ongoing determination of what the customer values above the self-interests of internal stakeholders. Thus, instead of searching for financial rewards for the firm, management looks for opportunities to create and provide value for present and prospective customers. The internal stakeholders' values will be realized by virtue of customer preference and purchase of products and services provided by the firm.

In addition to moving customers to the top of the stakeholder list, this new model is also dramatically different in content. Typically, mission statements focus on the firm's products or services, but many firms fall captive to their own technology and fail to adapt to changing customer needs. Whereas mission statements specifying products/services *assume* customer need, a statement of responsibility focuses emphatically on the customer need and value, and then commits the firm to designing and producing products/services to meet that need.

Determining responsibility means that top management willingly chooses to perpetually act so as to satisfy a well-defined set of needs and values of clearly defined groups of customers. Only then can managers specify the products/services that meet the defined needs. Such a firm's statement of responsibility would focus on "the creation and continuous improvement of best net value products/services," and the firm would thereby intend "to become increasingly preferred by customers when compared to alternatives." Artificial value offerings achieved by overselling product value or short-term price reductions on the product/service would be a violation of the mission.

This describes a covenant view of the relationship between firms and customers based on bona fide provisioning, not bargained exchange. Instead of a mercenary role in conforming to internally defined job requirements, the firm's employees, management, owners, and suppliers hold a self-imposed intent to provide for the value needs of customers now and to improve the firm's capability to do so in the future.

The firm's predisposition to providing for customers and its commitment to continuous improvement of value will serve as the keystone of every element of its mission statement. To remove the temptation to substitute the bottom line as the chief end, the mission statement should also specify appropriate predispositions and behaviors for each and every element of the organization in fulfilling the firm's obligation to customers. Taking ultimate responsibility for satisfying a specified set of customer needs and for finding ways to improve the value provided to customers can maximize long-run returns to internal stakeholders (Miller and Dess, 1988; Narver and Slater, 1990).

Since every firm requires a clear sense of purpose, the new mission statement of selected obligations becomes the outcome of a new subprocess for value contribution analysis. Defining potential customers and users, analyzing current value contribution deficiencies, and evaluating new value-creation opportunities are imperative. Value opportunity analysis (VOA) methodologies move to the forefront of strategic subprocesses by providing a way to discover and validate value contribution opportunities. Woodruff (1990) has provided one methodology based on a behavioral system view of market opportunity. In Figure 3, macroenvironmental forces such as economic cycles, social and cultural trends, demographic changes, and technological advances affect end users, channel customers and competitors.

In the subprocess shown in Figure 4, managers first make a rough definition of end-user markets with promising value contribution options. After initially describing products/services and markets, managers must build detailed profiles of end users, channel customers, and competitors. These profiles should focus on customers' needs and usage behaviors that determine potential net value. Based on the definition of net value, Figure 5 shows three generic value opportunities: (1) improving realization potential (customer-valued benefits or consequences of a product/service); (2) reducing sacrifice required of the customer (e.g., money, time, aggravation, inconvenience, energy); or (3) offering some combination of better realization and reduced sacrifice.

Value contribution opportunities must then be evaluated against both external and internal considerations. Externally, two factors are critical: vitality (likely growth in demand) and viability (potential market share gains), taking into account competitive profiles and likely competitor

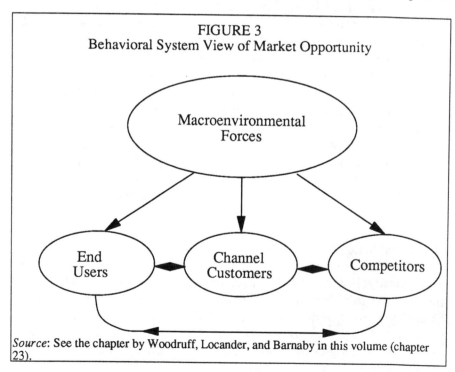

FIGURE 3
Behavioral System View of Market Opportunity

Source: See the chapter by Woodruff, Locander, and Barnaby in this volume (chapter 23).

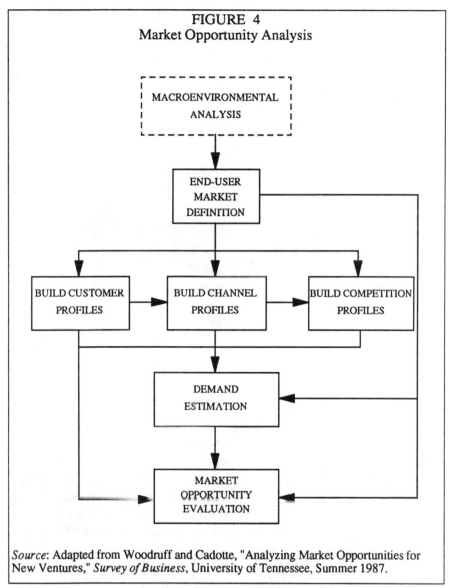

FIGURE 4
Market Opportunity Analysis

MACROENVIRONMENTAL
ANALYSIS

END-USER
MARKET
DEFINITION

BUILD CUSTOMER
PROFILES

BUILD CHANNEL
PROFILES

BUILD COMPETITION
PROFILES

DEMAND
ESTIMATION

MARKET
OPPORTUNITY
EVALUATION

Source: Adapted from Woodruff and Cadotte, "Analyzing Market Opportunities for New Ventures," *Survey of Business*, University of Tennessee, Summer 1987.

responses. At first glance these may appear to return the firm to internal expectations. Quite the contrary, they are significant to the firm's long-term ability to provide and continuously improve net value. Without a fair assessment of likely reciprocity from customers and market barriers to potential reciprocity, a firm naively enters into fulfilling its responsibilities only to discover it is doing its internal stakeholders a major disservice.

FIGURE 5
Components of Customer Net Value

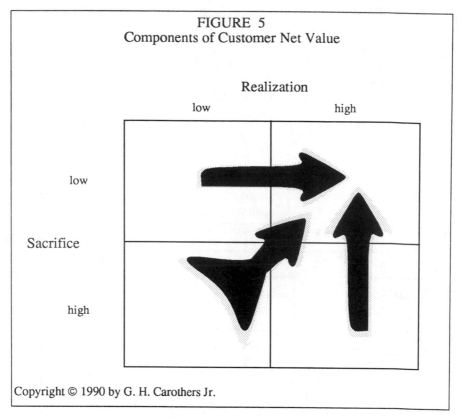

Predicting reciprocity, in the forms of anticipated sales and profits, is the responsibility of the managerial leadership. Naturally, these yields should justify the responsibility assumed.

The primary criteria for their sufficiency must be the degree to which reciprocity ensures the organization's ability to sustain its commitment to providing best net value in the future. This might well include other considerations – for example, in the case of a publicly held firm, the ability of the organization to retain investor confidence.

Value contribution matrices suggest a typology of value-based strategy content that can help managers evaluate opportunities. Since these may vary over time, Figure 6 suggests that an organization may choose to contribute different types of net value to different markets, including (1) bringing new value to any or all markets (e.g., the ability to fly brought about by the creative genius of the Wright Brothers); (2) bringing enhanced value to existing markets (e.g., teleconferencing, replacing the need to travel); and (3) bringing the old value of certain markets to completely new markets (fast foods to the Russians). Since the firm may choose to enhance realization of value, to reduce sacrifice, or some combination of these and

FIGURE 6
Value-based Strategic Content

NEW VALUE OFFERINGS

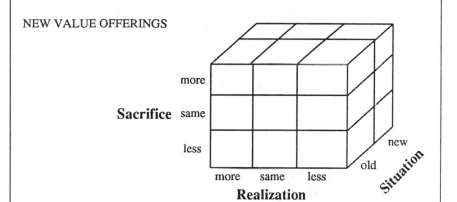

EXTENDING EXISTING VALUE OFFERINGS

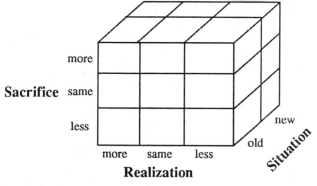

OLD VALUE OFFERINGS

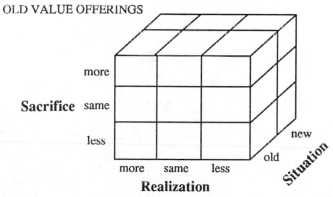

since this choice depends on the customer's situation, managers should assume that each of these value opportunities is totally different until proven otherwise. Value contribution decisions must be well understood and clearly articulated to provide organizations clear direction.

The *vitality* of market opportunities (Figure 7a) is determined by (1) the potential to increase value realized by customers or to reduce their required

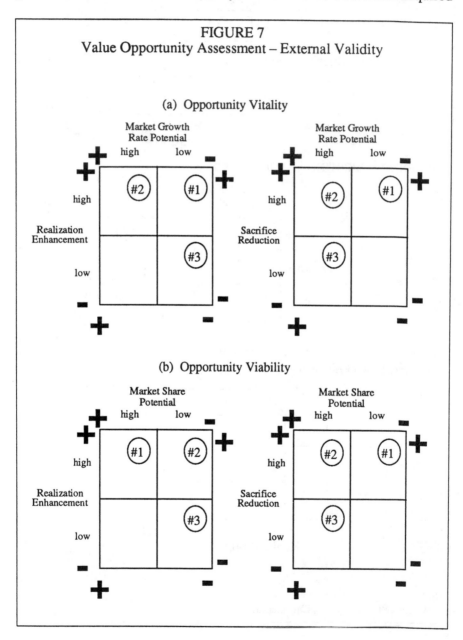

FIGURE 7
Value Opportunity Assessment – External Validity

sacrifice, and (2) the potential for market growth. For example, in Figure 7a, a firm may have identified three value opportunities, #1, #2, and #3. Each of these value opportunities is evaluated as to potential for improving customer value realization and reducing customer sacrifice. In addition, since vitality is necessary but insufficient, each is examined for potential market growth in the short term and long term.

The *viability* of market opportunities (Figure 7b) is a function of the potential to capture market share by improving value realization and reducing sacrifice. The viability of each opportunity is analyzed in a manner similar to that described for vitality. These evaluations will ultimately be used in the final selection of actionable value opportunities.

Ideal opportunities have high potential for customer realization of improved value and reduced sacrifice in markets where both the growth rate and market share gains may be high. For example, opportunities like #2 in +/+ cells of the vitality and viability matrices are attractive, while those such as #3 in - / - cells must be justified on some other basis. Note, however, that #2 in the left-hand matrix of Figure 7b indicates that, even with enhanced realized value, this opportunity has low market share potential. BMW finds itself in this position; it stands a far better chance of gaining market share by reducing the required sacrifice than from increasing value realization. These least desirable opportunities show little potential to improve realized value or to reduce sacrifice in markets and offer only low growth and low potential for share gains. Since they are truly customer value driven, these initial evaluations establish the *external* validity of market opportunities.

Market opportunities must also be evaluated for *internal* validity. As mentioned earlier, the firm's predisposition to "provide" carries the requirement of internal stakeholders (including stockholders) to exercise initiative in the exchange relationship toward providing best net value. Management must focus on developing capacity and capability to improve the firm's ability to provide net value. A firm that can demonstrate continuous improvement of both capacity and capability has taken the initiative in the exchange process.

Capacity is defined as the degree to which the firm intends to provide the best net value with its products/services. Capacity reflects a firm's drive and motivation to fulfill its commitments to customers. Capacity assessment involves a review of the intensity and tenacity that currently exist or that might be required of the organization for each opportunity. *Capability* refers to the resourcefulness of an organization, the degree to which the firm successfully acquires and manages the inputs required to make an offering that is valued by customers. Capability assessment involves

FIGURE 8
Organizational Capacity and Capability Assessment

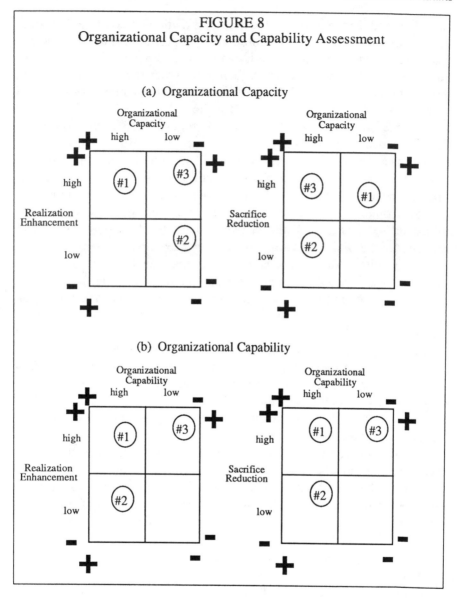

(a) Organizational Capacity

(b) Organizational Capability

comparing existing resources to the resourcefulness required to improve value or reduce sacrifice for customers.

In this stage of the process of evaluating market opportunities, each internal factor, capacity and capability, is paired with the potentials to increase customers' realized value and lower sacrifice. Figures 8a and 8b show four matrices used to evaluate opportunities for increased customer realization of value and sacrifice reduction against organizational capacity and capability. Just as with vitality and viability, ideal value options combine high existing capacity and high current capability with opportunities that maximize customers' value realization and significantly reduce sacrifice. The least desirable opportunities are those where the firm has little commitment and few resources to bring to bear on opportunities that hold little potential to improve customer realization or reduce required customer sacrifice.

Each value opportunity should be summarily reviewed as to its relative external attractiveness and the internal strength available for pursuing that opportunity. For example, from Figures 7a, 7b, 8a, and 8b, the individual evaluations of value opportunities #1 and #2 have been aggregated in Figure 9 in an opportunity profile of external attractiveness and internal business strength. Opportunity #2, as summarized in opportunity profile #2, is externally attractive but internally lacking. Such summary comparisons help managers determine if they can marshall the intent and resources required to pursue attractive opportunities.

Although tradeoffs on the various dimensions are inevitable, final selection should be based on the anticipated reciprocity from customers. Short- and long-term gains to customers should be reviewed carefully. The form, timing, and volume of reciprocity must be conceptualized, operational descriptions decided and documented, measurement systems developed and validated. Methods for testing critical assumptions must be developed and thresholds established to justify the organization's continued pursuit of each value opportunity. Without methods, financial projections lack credibility and market opportunity estimates are hollow.

Responsibility statements (missions) are the natural outcomes of this first subprocess. To remove the temptation to substitute the bottom line as the chief end, missions should explicitly describe the value obligations that managerial leaders willingly choose and then clarify what these obligations mean for the behavior of all internal stakeholders. Top management needs to articulate clearly for employees acceptable and unacceptable behaviors that contribute to realized net value and reduced sacrifice for customers. These appreciations become the foundation for behavioral choices required of all the members in carrying out their daily responsibilities for helping provide best net value.

Strategic Factor Analyses

As a result of the increasing complexity, dynamism, and turbulence in business environments during the 1970s and 1980s, many managers now analyze the largely uncontrollable economic, political, social, and technological environments along with the industry forces and competitors that

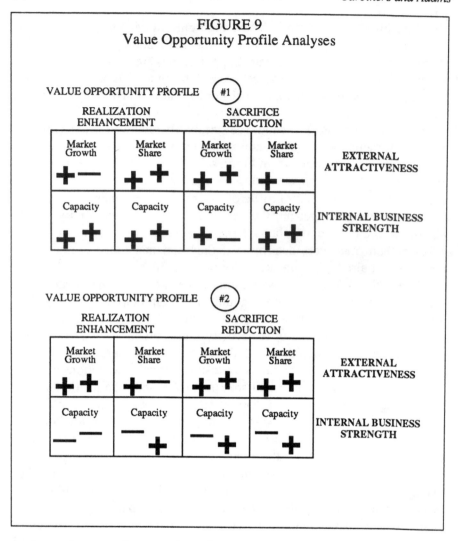

FIGURE 9
Value Opportunity Profile Analyses

make up the operating or task environment. But these approaches often fail for several reasons.

First, environmental scanning came and went as another management fad when managers found it difficult to incorporate broader, longer term trends into operating strategies. Second, the overly simplistic SWOT analysis (Strengths, Weaknesses, Opportunities, and Threats) is fundamentally grounded in warfare theory. Industrial organization economics suggests that a firm's performance is directly related to the degree to which it can achieve and sustain competitive advantage, a view based on rivalry between competitors rather than providing for the needs of customers. Finally, Dill (1958), in coining the phrase "task environment," suggested it refers to those parts of a firm's external environment that are potentially relevant to goal setting or goal attainment. But researchers seldom suggested what those goals should be. Organizations predisposed toward providing and improving customer value will consider different factors than those firms predisposed toward expecting financial performance. Both the subprocess and the content of this second component will differ significantly from current practice.

A value-based organization continuously studies the factors that influence net value perceived by the customer as well as the factors that influence the organization's capacity and capability necessary to provide that value. Figure 10 suggests that macroenvironmental forces remain a key consideration. But in addition to assessing political, economic, social, and technical changes for impacts on the firm, managers should determine the effect of any such trends on *customers'* perceptions of realization and sacrifice.

Figure 11 further develops this focus by showing that a customer's situation and circumstances may determine his or her propensity to realize value or make the required sacrifice. Too many firms do not anticipate the impact of the customer's situation on the net value of their products/services. Managers must understand the context in which the customer views the value offered and the potential sacrifice. The firm must offer value in the customer's context. Customers' sources of assets, personal values regarding needs versus luxuries, situational priorities, shopping options

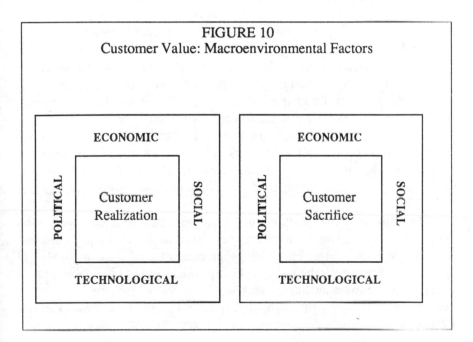

FIGURE 10
Customer Value: Macroenvironmental Factors

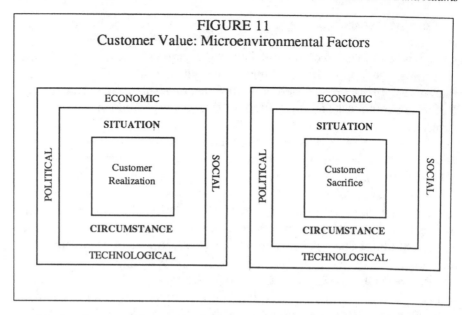

FIGURE 11
Customer Value: Microenvironmental Factors

and behaviors, purchase criteria, and usage factors are the basis of perceived value and sacrifice made.

Only after customer analysis is complete can the firm assess the macro- and microenvironmental impacts on its internal capacity and capability. Figure 12 shows macro- and microenvironmental forces affecting the organization's capability and capacity. Again, the importance of these forces on the firm lies in the potential impact on the intent of the firm to satisfy customers by providing best value and on the resourcefulness of the firm to do so.

Fundamentally, managers can offer relatively high or low sacrifice and high or low value realization to customers, based on the customer's contextual situation. Referring back to Figure 5, we see that the arrows suggest that managers must work toward continuously reducing sacrifice and improving realized value. In turn, this implies that organizations predisposed to continuous improvement of best net value must also be thought of as being in continuous transition. Thus, both content and process issues arise when determining the factors that influence customers' expectations.

The content of the situation analysis should be customer rather than only competitor driven. Since best net value to the customer includes comparison with competitor offerings, customer-based situation analysis subsumes competitive alternatives. Using competitors as the standard for comparison removes the direct focus on relative value from the customer's perspective. Thus, a firm might "improve" its products relative to competitors and actually reduce value to customers. American auto producers

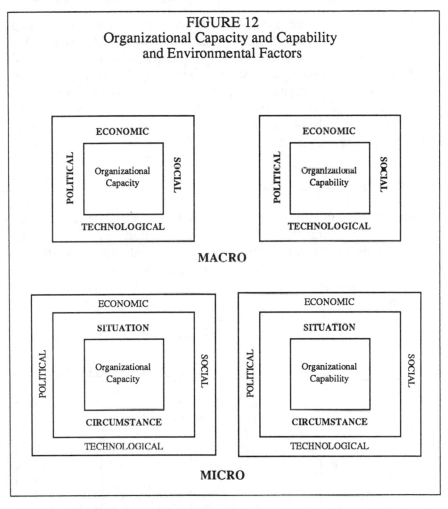

FIGURE 12
Organizational Capacity and Capability
and Environmental Factors

have almost always relied on adding less valued features while foreign producers improved highly valued reliability. This comprehensive customer-based perspective drives the analytical process.

This framework (Figure 5) provides the basis for two methods of evaluating an organization's success in continuously improving net value. Current net value can be evaluated relative to both the past and to competitors. First, it is the customers' perceptions of net value over time that matters. Analysis of longitudinal data provides a basis for assessing whether customers actually perceive any absolute improvements made by the firm. Second, although a firm may have made major improvements in value which were perceived by customers, it may have actually lost ground in the customers' views if competitors improved even more. Thus, managers must understand the *relative* value they offer.

Figures 13 and 14 extend this mapping process into tools for assessing relative success in creating best net value. These two figures extend this mapping process into tools for assessing relative success in creating best net value. Systematic investigation of customers' perceptions of an organization's value contribution and sacrifice reduction compared to that of each of its competitors can be conducted. These comparisons are critical to any evaluation of the organization's current position. In later processes, they also assist appraisals of managerial effectiveness.

Strategic Suprasystems Determination

Traditionally, managers formulate business-level strategy based on either logical incrementalism or a somewhat ambiguous matching of strengths with opportunities while minimizing weaknesses and threats. Although both approaches stress environmental fit, neither explicitly focuses on the customer and providing best net value. A better approach

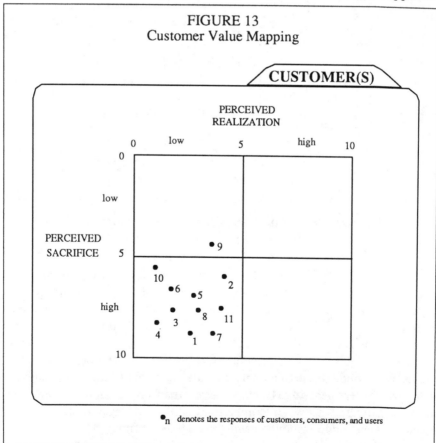

FIGURE 13
Customer Value Mapping

$\bullet_n$ denotes the responses of customers, consumers, and users

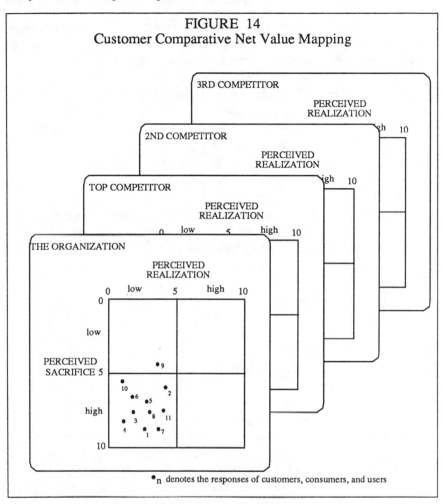

FIGURE 14
Customer Comparative Net Value Mapping

•n denotes the responses of customers, consumers, and users

defines a business-level strategy based on providing net value and the strategic suprasystems required to implement that strategy and thereby improve net value.

The third component of the new process is labeled Strategic Suprasystems Determination. The critical outcomes of this component include (1) identification of the strategic, transfunctional suprasystems inherent in the chosen strategy, (2) general descriptions of these suprasystems with an appreciation of their scope, (3) complete understanding and operationalization of net value, value realization, and sacrifices expected by customers, and, (4) most important, designation of managers as responsible owners of specific transfunctional systems. A written form should be used to record these agreements. The key benefit of these agreements is establishing ownership of each system. Such agreements also build an

accountability bridge between strategy formulation and implementation by
delineating the architecture of the systems, confirming their scope, and
validating the congruence of interactions and interdependence.

Strategic suprasystems are those transfunctional systems derived from
management's commitment to provide certain customer-valued
products/services. These systems always fulfill personal roles and responsibilities otherwise required of the customer. In taking responsibility for
providing the products/services that meet the customers' need, the firm has
explicitly chosen to accept full accountability for setting up systems that
provide net value equal to or better than that which the customers provided
by themselves. These accountabilities dictate transfunctional systems,
processes, and tasks that must be designed, operationalized, and managed
by system owners. The integration required of transfunctional systems
demands the subordination and support of all other functional unit subsystems, activities, processes, and tasks.

To the degree to which systems theory addresses input, process, and
output and that tasks are specialized and organized in these categories,
systems often connote structure. However, systems theory is first and
foremost based on the content of transactions between elements within the
system, not the structure of the system (Katz and Kahn, 1966). A *system*
is defined as a "regularly interacting or interdependent group of items
forming a unified whole" (Webster's, 1980). *Structure*, however, is "something arranged in a definite pattern of organization" (Webster's, 1980).
Thus, structure is only one dimension of every system. Traditional organizational structure is inherently vertical; transfunctional suprasystems
are inherently horizontal. While systems are frequently modeled by flowcharts, these do not show the "hidden factors" that usually moderate the
relationships between the steps in the process. The focus on suprasystems
providing customer value attempts to overcome the barriers to integration
in vertical structures.

Thus, suprasystems are not the same as formal organizational structure.
As in the traditional model, implementation of a value-based strategy
through suprasystems involves much more than structural changes. Unlike
the traditional model in which systems are usually perceived within functions, suprasystems bridge and integrate those responsibilities to the customer which are common across departments and functions. For example,
delivery of a product goes beyond the shipping department to the degree
that accounting is involved in billing, and to the degree that marketing
establishes customers' expectations for delivery. Since suprasystems
delineate the organizations' responsibilities but do not dictate the structural
arrangements, suprasystem management establishes an informal

mechanism to overcome the limits of authority inherent in the formal structure. Suprasystems form the synthesis of formal structure.

We cannot overstate the importance of this component as the bridge between strategy formulation and strategy implementation. This has been the weakest link in previous strategic management models and is a key reason why managers find that their emergent strategy is often not the same one they had intended (Mintzberg and Waters, 1985). The key to defining a value-based strategy for the entire organization is specifying which tasks in each function are relevant to each responsibility to customers; these aggregated tasks form the associated suprasystem. It is critical to the success of the enterprise in fulfilling its obligations to the customer that this part of the process be well managed.

Strategic Suprasystems Management

Much of the frustration with strategic management in general and popular quality management programs in particular stems from ambiguity concerning strategy implementation. Other than translating long-term, top management objectives and strategies into functional-level counterparts, current models provide little direction as to how implementation should be accomplished. Emphasis varies widely on such factors as structure, corporate culture, leadership, motivation and reward systems, and control systems. The last two stages of the proposed alternative strategic management process are only briefly introduced here since they are detailed in later chapters. The first four chapters in the next part of the book explain the role requirements of this component in detail.

Successful implementation of these roles, by those appointed as suprasystems owners, completes the long-sought linkage between strategy formulation and strategy implementation. Determining responsibilities, understanding environmental factors affecting customer net value, organizational capacity, and capability, and establishing managerial ownership of suprasystems eliminates the disjointedness that has characterized the formulation and implementation process. But this link will be made only if those managing the suprasystems of the organization specifically attend to the obligations of the firm. Continuous contact with customers by suprasystem managers is necessary to keep emergent strategy as closely tied to intended strategy as possible, especially if the customer's environmental context is volatile.

Confirmation, Correction, and Change

Classic strategic management process models generally conclude with a feedback loop following the last component (evaluation and control). Similarly, value-based strategic management includes confirmation of the effectiveness of strategic suprasystems management, correction of these suprasystems, and/or adaptation of suprasystems to maintain or regain the focus on net customer value. Suprasystem confirmation and correction must be analyzed and evaluated using both external market performance data and internal firm financial performance data.

Externally, the validity of assumptions, decisions, and actions must be continuously reexamined. Initial planning assumptions about vitality, viability, capacity, capability, and reciprocity should be tested for current and future validity. The original value attributes accepted as obligations and the resulting transfunctional system responsibilities must be reassessed. Therefore, there is much to confirm, correct and change.

First and foremost, managers must confirm that customers' perception of realized value and sacrifice match their expectations. The questions, "What did we say we would do and have we done it," can be answered only by asking those who assisted in defining what was expected, the customers. Using the perceived net value maps (developed in the strategic factor analyses) in a longitudinal study, managers can measure the value realized and sacrifice made by customers. In Figure 15, the circles suggest the possibility of measuring statistically customers' repositioning on net value. Changes in the centroid and dispersion will provide evidence of improvement in customers' perceptions of net value.

Finally, since the commitment of the organization was to provide best net value, a firm must routinely measure the organization's position relative to its customers' view of delivered best net value. Figure 16 compares plots of perceived net value, taken at different times, which may be used to assess its customers' perceptions of progress and or problems in managing the providing of value in comparison to the firm's competitors.

With acceptance of determined responsibilities, the organization is also committed to providing for the customer's net value for some time to come, not just for the moment. Managerial leaders must confirm the appropriateness of choices they made on net value to be offered. Customers' selection behavior, as measured by validly obtained market share, provides key confirmation that they perceived best net value. However, managers must discount illegitimate selection behavior brought about by the constrained availability of alternatives or by offers of artificial value.

Confirmation of organizational performance becomes much more comprehensive with the necessity to examine (1) the organization's current

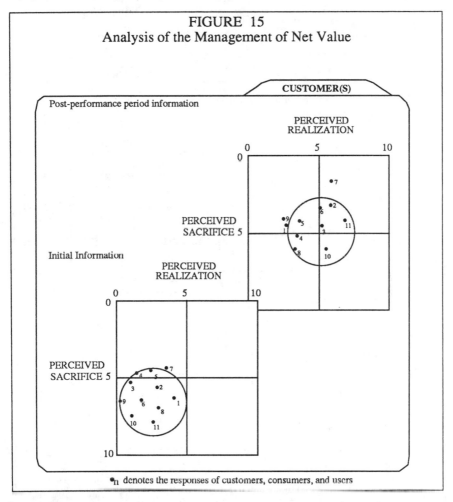

FIGURE 15
Analysis of the Management of Net Value

●ₙ denotes the responses of customers, consumers, and users

proficiency at providing what is now valued by customers, along with (2) its ability to improve at providing what will be valued in the future. To the extent that the organization cannot simultaneously generate *margins* from which to gather profits, retained earnings, and dividends (if necessary), it is deficient in its capability to fulfill its long-term commitment to provide best net value.

Similarly, to the extent a firm cannot demonstrate its ability to provide liquidity or leverage, it has limited its ability to quickly arm itself with its resources or to convert to alternative resources. However, if an organization can manipulate its activity (as measured by turnover ratios) without manipulating value provided to the customer via false promotion, compromise of margins, and so on, the firm may actually enhance net value. Obviously correction of formulation or implementation deficiencies may

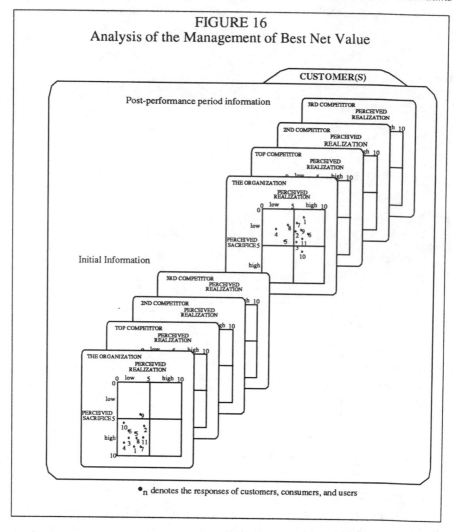

FIGURE 16
Analysis of the Management of Best Net Value

•n denotes the responses of customers, consumers, and users

be indicated in this comprehensive evaluation. Such correction should be understood in terms of what currently exists and what should be expected upon correction.

Change is the last subcomponent of this step, and it activates the feedback mechanism. Strategic environmental factors may have been over- or underestimated. New environmental factors may affect customer net value expectations or organizational capacity and capability. Competitive actions or responses may have been different than anticipated and impacted comparative net value. Customer expectations may change, requiring further sacrifice reductions or value improvements.

Implications for Managers

The ideas presented in this chapter have direct application to most managers in both the formulation and implementation of strategy. First, managers need to adopt a predisposition toward providing what customers value. Strategies based on providing best net value will succeed only with top management's personal participation.

Second, the strategy formulation process itself must begin by focusing on customer net value dimensions. Value opportunity analyses should be used to continuously determine the net value perspectives driving customers' behaviors. These data direct the firm in fulfilling its accepted responsibilities and systemic management obligations.

Third, business-level value-based strategies must center on the concept of continuous improvement of provided net value. They are therefore much more comprehensive and customer oriented than the generic competitive strategies of differentiation, cost reduction, or focus.

Fourth, since implementation is much more difficult than imagined, top managers must take personal ownership of suprasystems. Management is first and foremost concerned with creating, providing, and improving the suprasystems, not administering existing functional systems. Managerial leaders must be given ownership and held responsible for each suprasystem impacting customer net value. These managers will be recognized as imposing transfunctionality on all organizational structural elements.

REFERENCES

Ansoff, I. *Corporate Strategy.* New York: McGraw-Hill, 1965.

Chandler, Alfred D. *Strategy and Structure: Chapters in the History of the American Industrial Enterprise.* Cambridge, Mass.: MIT Press, 1962.

Dill, W. R. "Environment as an Influence on Managerial Autonomy." *Administrative Science Quarterly* 2 (1958): 410.

Karger, D. W., and Z. A. Malik. "Long-range Planning and Organizational Performance." *Long Range Planning* (December 1975), 60-64.

Katz, D., and R. L. Kahn. *The Social Psychology of Organizations.* 2nd ed. New York: Wiley, 1966.

McKitterick, J. B. "What is the Marketing Management Concept?" In *The Frontiers of Marketing Thought and Science*, Frank M. Bass, ed. (Chicago: American Marketing Association), 1957.

McKitterick, Proceedings of the American Marketing Association, 1957.

Miller A., and Dess, G. "The Appropriateness of the Porter (1980) Model of Generic Strategies as a Research Paradigm: An Empirical Examination of Its Generalizability, Accuracy, and Simplicity." Working Paper Series, University of Tennessee, 1988.

Mintzberg, H., and J. A. Waters. "Of Strategies, Deliberate and Emergent." *Strategic Management Journal* 6 (1985): 257-272.

Narver, John C., and Stanley F. Slater. "The Effect of a Marketing Orientation on Business Profitability." *Journal of Marketing* (October 1990).

Peters, T. J. and R. H. Waterman, Jr. *In Search of Excellence.* New York: Harper and Row, 1982.

Porter, M. *Competitive Advantage: Creating and Sustaining Superior Performance.* New York: Free Press, 1985.

Porter, M. *Competitive Strategy: Techniques for Analyzing Industries and Competitors.* New York: Free Press,1980.

Rhyne, L. C. "The Relationship of Strategic Planning to Financial Performance." *Strategic Management Journal* 7 (1986): 423-436.

Smith, Adam. *Wealth of Nations.* New York: Modern Library ed., 1937.

Thompson, Arthur A., Jr., and A. J. Strickland, III. *Strategic Management: Cases and Concepts.* Homewood, Ill.: Richard D. Irwin, 1990.

Webster's New World Dictionary. New York: Simon and Schuster, 1980.

Woodruff, R. B. "Market Opportunity Analysis: A State of the Art Evaluation." Unpublished Working Paper, University of Tennessee, 1990.

Zeithaml, V. "Consumer Perceptions of Price, Quality, and Value: A Means-End Model and Synthesis of Evidence." *Journal of Marketing* 52 (1988): 2-22.

CHAPTER 4

BUILDING RESPONSIVE UNIVERSITIES: SOME CHALLENGES TO ACADEMIC LEADERSHIP

C. WARREN NEEL
Dean, College of Business Administration
University of Tennessee

WILLIAM T. SNYDER
Dean, College of Engineering
University of Tennessee

SUMMARY

Universities face a difficult task in responding to societal problems. Information growth coupled with the rising tide of professionalism gives the individual professor personal identity while precluding any cross-discipline understanding of the broad problems of society. We have become an academy of researchers, not scholars, a faculty of highly trained specialists without concern for how the depth of our understanding applies between and among other disciplines. The challenge of university leaders is to foster an organizational climate that values breadth, not just depth.

BUILDING RESPONSIVE UNIVERSITIES: SOME CHALLENGES TO ACADEMIC LEADERSHIP

Imagine this scenario: The guests at a cocktail party are community leaders and scholars from a nearby university. The conversation swirls around topics of local interest as well as those concerning the global village. One small group over in a corner of the room is involved in a discussion of careers, and as you approach you hear a townsperson asking a distin-

guished professor about his career. Since he is new to the campus, the
professor begins his response by speaking of his involvement in cutting-
edge research of his field. He tries to give meaning to his studies by noting
that his particular endeavor focuses on the spring offense of a particular
Napoleonic battle. Since few people in the circle are familiar with that
subject, he adds that he is a professor of Western European history with a
specialty in the Napoleonic era. That, too, needs some explanation, or so
it seems from the continuing discussion, so later he suggests that he is a
member of the distinguished faculty of the History Department and there-
upon elaborates on the quality of the faculty within the department. Still
later, he suggests that he is part of a larger unit on campus referred to as
the College of Liberal Arts. Finally, he announces himself as being a faculty
member of the university. As the conversation continues, someone asks
how he became an historian, to which he replies that he has always loved
history and teaching.

This scene is symptomatic of a major set of problems facing universities
today. In some measure these problems parallel the greater society
problems, particularly those that face American business in a global
economy.

The professor at the cocktail party is a specialist, a professional, and a
nationally recognized researcher in his field of endeavor. In the course of
that particular evening he defined himself in very narrow, vertical terms,
never once suggesting to his audience that he was an educator first. In the
practice of his chosen field, he selected the field of history. Most complex
businesses today have their own set of "professors" who profess a particular
discipline for a particular function. They see the problems facing a particular company in highly structured vertical terms. Like the university, the
manager of today is a well-trained specialist whose chief contribution has
been largely determined by continual specialization of labor in highly
fragmented hierarchical structures. Universities mirror that same dilemma.
As a matter of fact, they may magnify the problem.

How did we get to this position? Wasn't it absolutely essential that we
design this kind of structure in a modern university given the information
explosion? Isn't it in keeping with the traditional land-grant mission of
comprehensive universities in this country to have scholars pursuing the
cutting edge of their field? The answers to all these questions is an obvious
yes. But something has gone astray. The land-grant university concept is
over one hundred years old, founded in a period of time when the dominant
employment pattern was agriculture. It rose to a position of prominence by
being responsive to the societal needs of an educated labor pool during the
blossoming of the Industrial Revolution. Its growth paralleled the burst of
energy that resulted in an exponential increase in new information. Now,

over a hundred years later, its mission still intact, the public is asking the cadre of scholars who inherited the academic mantle, "Are we being responsive to societal needs at the turn of the twenty-first century?" Thoughtful leaders are suggesting that the answer is *no*.

When we look at the university as it is organized today, we find that its structure mirrors the information explosion. Naisbitt and Aburdene say in *Megatrends 2000*, "we are drowning in information and starved for knowledge." Each department is set up so as to accommodate a body of information and give identity to that body by way of a professorate and a degree. The department is comprised of a group of faculty members with specialties and subspecialties. Generally, all members of the field can get an independent evaluation of their scholarly output through journals or other publication media whose editorial boards are from similar departments and specialties. Getting published becomes the sign of success and the currency that is "spendable" in the job market. Furthermore, more often than not, the editorial boards focus the area of interest, and thus the research agenda, by soliciting the articles for publication that address those areas of specialty already accepted as "interesting." The market plan for academic positions, particularly in comprehensive universities, places a high value on publications. They are countable, a sign of research capability if the research is funded, and there is independent judgment of quality.

All these elements are important to an academic community. But can that community value other equally important activities of the faculty, namely, teaching and service? Perhaps those leaders who are questioning the responsiveness of comprehensive universities and higher education in general are asking how institutions lost sight of who the customers are, of who the professorate really serves, and how. Thus, a university, if we dared draw an analogy, is a large community made up of small households: each often having a separate language, a separate set of goals and aspirations, and a separate sense of identity. Each house may be painted a different color, have a different roof pitch, and a different size family, but it is part of a larger community. Or is it? What makes a community is a common set of shared values, not a disparate group of houses lined along the street. So the question to the modern university is, how can we develop a common set of shared values, bridge the gap between our specialties, and develop breadth as well as depth in our body of information so that we do indeed have a community of scholarship rather than small independent households of narrow research?

Some would suggest that this analogy is counter to the information explosion era in which we need the specialist whose entire energies are devoted to a particular aspect of a field. That argument is certainly appropriate. However, not everyone pursuing those small glitches in the armor of a particular discipline will build a great university that is responsive to the larger needs of society. Thus, the challenge is to build breadth as well as depth, to get a common, shared set of values that build a community rather than a disparate group of houses.

That analogy is not totally unlike the problems that face American business. The huge American corporation, with its line and staff positions, each fragmented into highly specialized units, has been the hallmark of American economic dominance since World War II. Today most executives are finding that those same specialists no longer talk to one another, yet the problems are multidisciplinary, requiring individuals from different points of view to work together, debate together, and come to a common solution. That need, as well as the pressure to be responsive to that need, is driving American corporations to experiment with different models and different staffing needs for those models.

There is no greater challenge to university leaders today or to those captains of industry than addressing the narrowness and the professionalism that have isolated and insulated both professor and manager from the major threats facing the country today.

It is often said that American business (or for that matter any business operating in a competitive environment) has as its force of change the need to make a profit in order to remain in business. That pressure of competition in the marketplace is supposed to exert sufficient influence on the structure of the corporation. But universities don't have the same set of market pressures. As a matter of fact, universities have generally been isolated from such pressures. Certainly, there is the public outcry to hold tuition costs down while admitting additional students to the academic programs. Generally, however, universities have been able to pass along the tuition costs. Tuition has actually risen far faster than the inflation rate in the last dozen years or so without any material change in the delivery system of education. Now, however, the pressures are mounting for public accountability, for the wise and frugal use of public funds. Those pressures suggest that large comprehensive universities must respond differently than they have anytime in their history.

The public's increasing insistence on accountability by the American educational system was initially felt by the K-12 segment of education. The public perception of the quality of American education, what is right and what is wrong with education, is influenced primarily by the perception of the condition of this level of education. This is understandable given the larger K-12 student population relative to higher education and the greater involvement of the public with K-12 rather than higher education.

It was natural, therefore, that the initial wave of dissatisfaction and insistence on accountability would be focused on K-12. The skill deficiencies of students certified by K-12 are initially more readily discernible in K-12 graduates than in higher education graduates. In looking for scapegoats for our educational problems, the public has centered on the school boards and on the preparation of teachers by colleges of education. While there is great need for improvement in the preparation of teachers, the public criticism has at times become unfair and oversimplified.

Criticism of colleges of education is the cutting edge of public insistence for more accountability by higher education, yet other professional disciplines are also experiencing increasing criticism and insistence on accountability. The law profession and law schools are being criticized for contributing to a more litigious society. Business schools are being criticized for producing graduates more interested in optimizing corporate quarterly profits than in issues of quality, customer satisfaction, value added, and international competitiveness. The engineering professions are being criticized for being insensitive to environmental issues and the social implications of technology.

The common thread of criticism centers on the inward focus that has come with excessive specialization and inadequate emphasis on cross-functional, interdisciplinary education. Universities, like American business, are being challenged to give greater attention to value added to the students they matriculate, to have more concern for customer satisfaction. This emphasis on accountability can be expected to increase in a future of finite financial resources as education competes with other societal needs for funding.

Interestingly, the proliferation of professionalism within the narrow distance of a modern university is detrimental not only to the quality of education, particularly at the undergraduate level, but also to achieving any economies. As disciplines are further fragmented, specialists are hired, teaching loads are reduced to enhance the image through research, and class sizes fall. The result is lack of responsiveness by comprehensive universities to their various constituencies (publics).

Several other elements suggest that the university is insulated from change. One is that in many instances the most important "currency" for enhancing the reputation of the individual faculty member and/or the department or college is that of research funding and publications. While indeed that is important to the continuing process of inquiry, the faculty member of a narrow specialty often picks an esoteric research agenda so as to appeal to a particular editorial board of a particular journal – not because the agenda item chosen is of national concern, not because the students in the faculty member's charge have a need to understand both breadth and depth of a discipline. Imagine if you will a large comprehensive faculty of a major land-grant institution, say, one thousand or more professors, each seeking an outlet for their critical research in a narrow discipline as the major driving force behind their behavior. In such an environment, it becomes extremely difficult, if not impossible, for the leadership of a campus to materially affect, or for that matter address, multidisciplinary problems, the kind of problems that are generally those of society and the world marketplace. In such an environment it is left to the student to follow the path of the curriculum to gain breadth by being exposed to a host of highly vertical narrow disciplines. Ironically, most major universities today leave that responsibility for gaining any disciplinary understanding and knowledge primarily to the student.

In many instances, especially in professional schools, faculty members as in the cocktail party previously noted view themselves as members of an academic household, that is, a very narrow specialty, and do not see themselves as educators or as members of a larger community. This of necessity means that the leadership of comprehensive universities today has the challenge of rebuilding a community of scholars, rather than producing narrow researchers.

The agriculture-dominated campus of the old A&M model of a hundred years ago was epitomized by large surrounding fields with handsome silos standing watch over the various research projects whose findings would ultimately benefit the farms of the citizens of that state. Today we don't see concrete silos; rather, they are functional silos representing every discipline on campus. There is no concrete or brick, but they are made even more durable. Today they have the same hardness and insularity that they have always had, but the concrete is being replaced by a unique language, and the bricks by a set of understood acronyms. They are the professional silos. Clustered together, they stand watch over curricular and budget turf. The research outcome of these silos is often returned to the silo and recycled over and over and over. It may never get to the domain of public debate and use. The challenge to the leadership of the universities is, therefore, to break down the silos, to find the richness of inquiry (research and scholarship) matched by quality classroom teaching (professing) that collectively builds a mosaic of breadth and depth so as not to leave students responsible for breadth. Tomorrow's leaders who come from that cauldron of intellectual fervor will be capable of handling those problems that require the competence of depth with understanding of breadth. But first American higher education must value those traits and organize itself to engender them in the next graduating class.

REFERENCE

Naissbitt, John, and Patricia Aberdeen. *Megatrends 2000*. New York: Morrow Publishing Co., 1990.

B. THE REDEFINED MANAGERIAL ROLE

CHAPTER 5

MANAGERIAL LEADERSHIP*

G. HARLAN CAROTHERS, JR.
Senior Lecturer, Institutes for Productivity
University of Tennessee

GREGORY M. BOUNDS
Research Associate, Management Development Center
University of Tennessee

MICHAEL J. STAHL
Associate Dean, College of Business Administration
University of Tennessee

SUMMARY

To compete domestically and globally, managerial leaders must more competitively create value for the customers of their products and/or services. Managerial leaders at various organizational levels must personally engage in two sets of strategic activities: (1) the determination of what customers value of products and services, and (2) the improvement of organizational suprasystems that provide value. This chapter presents an implementation strategy for integrating these two sets of activities to achieve and sustain organizational success.

*These authors are greatly indebted to Richard Sanders for his contributions to the development of this chapter.

COMPETITION AND CUSTOMER VALUE

The industrial-organizational microeconomic shift from producer power to consumer power in the emerging international markets points to the need for managerial leadership centered on creating and providing customer value. Over three-quarters of U.S. output in 1980 was produced under true competitive conditions, up from one-half in 1939 and 1958 (Case, 1989). Significant increases in the number of worldwide competitors have intensified this dramatic change in microeconomics. Following a timeless strategy, many of these new entrants offer better products/services while requiring less from the customer, thus creating a customer perception of increased net value. Successful competitors recognize that organizational success depends on the customer's perception and/or realization of the increased value of their products or services. Less successful competitors define and manage value from their company's perspective, not the customer's, much to their detriment.

Customers make choices based on relative comparisons of the net value of competing alternatives (Hardy, 1987; Karger, 1987; Zeithaml, 1988). Managerial leaders must recognize that net value is that which is realized by the customer of a product/service which justifies the sacrifice required (Carothers, 1989). The net value, therefore, results from combining that which is realized and sacrificed. Managerial leaders must attend to each of these dimensions of customer value. The level of attention devoted to each of these complex components may involve comprehensive strategic decisions based on analyses of the tradeoffs and potential interdependencies among the components.

A good example of increasing value for the customer is found upon examining IBM's value-enhancing approach to customer service. Even if it meant helping to install some competitor's products, IBM attempted to integrate whatever hardware and software the customer needed, independent of the manufacturer (Jeffrey, 1987). Thus, IBM increased perceived and real net value by reducing the customer sacrifices, and by eliminating frustration, mental energy, and work time that might otherwise have been required of those who choose their products. IBM recognized that the customer's sacrifice entails more than just funds required in purchase.

The following example illustrates how Tandy Corporation ignored the customer's need for timeliness, much to its chagrin. Tandy planned its first Christmas promotion of Radio Shack stores in Holland in anticipation of December 25, as is customary in the United States. After experiencing disappointing sales, a dismayed Tandy discovered that the Dutch exchanged gifts on December 6, St. Nicholas Day (*Business Week*, 1977).

Timeliness is becoming important in industrial as well as consumer products and services. With the advent of Just-in-Time (JIT) manufacturing, timely delivery and availability is becoming an important element of net value for customers of industrial products. In addition, undesirable variation in important quality parameters insidiously contributes to the sacrifices required of the sequential customers linked in the classical industrial value chain. A JIT manufacturer may be willing to pay more money for a component that consistently arrives on time, in the right quantity, and has very little variation around targets in important quality dimensions, thereby eliminating headaches for the customers of that component. This manufacturer understood that the industrial customer's potential sacrifices entail more than just purchase prices. Reducing each of these sacrifices potentially enhances best net value for the customer.

Toyota offers another example of value enhancement. Toyota found that customers want new automobiles with new technology, and they want them now. Toyota shortened the time to develop new cars to three years in 1988. At that time, it still took Detroit five years (Bower and Hout, 1988). The shortened development time created value for customers by providing availability of the latest in designs and product technology and coincidentally reducing the costs associated with longer development cycles.

Marriott also discovered the importance of value to the customer. "For years, Marriott's room service business didn't live up to its potential. But after initiating a 15 minute delivery guarantee for breakfast in 1985, Marriott's breakfast business – the biggest portion of its room service revenue – jumped 25%. Marriott got employees to devise better ways to deliver the meals on time, including having deliverers carry walkie-talkies so they can receive instructions more quickly" (*Business Week*, 1990). Marriott increased value to the customer by reducing customer sacrifices in sleep, worry, delay, and frustration and by increasing consistency of delivery, convenience, and availability of breakfast.

A good example of initially ignoring the customer's perception of value was the experience of Campbell's Soup in Great Britain. "Campbell's Soup tried to sell condensed soup in Great Britain but the British were convinced that they were receiving half as much soup as before. Campbell's Soup was obliged to modify the product by adding water to conform to the accepted mode of purchase" (Hardy, 1987). The customer may have actually realized the same taste and palatability in the condensed soup, with comparable sacrifice in terms of price. But the perceptions actually determined the customer behavior. These perceptual processes make it even more important to confidently determine what the customers of products and services specifically value.

Figure 1 summarizes the concept of net customer value as consisting of that which is realized and sacrificed. The figure also lists some potential elements of each.

The preceding examples suggest how success in the competitive creation of net value for customers contributes to organizational survival, prosperity, and longevity. A company's products and services must be continually chosen from among competing alternatives for that company to remain viable. Creation of best net value for the customer becomes the most critical strategic imperative and, therefore, is mandated. Barring monopoly, only organizations that compare more favorably to their com-

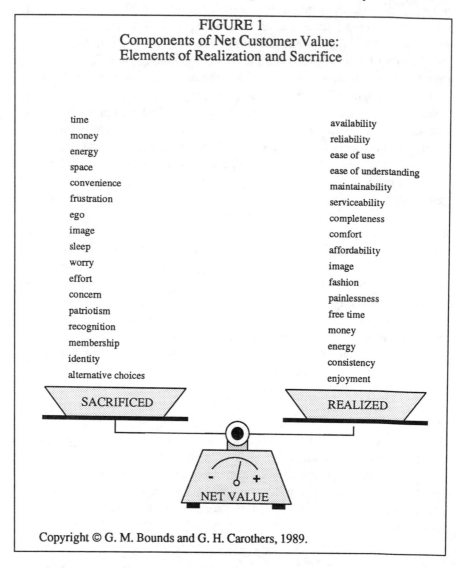

FIGURE 1
Components of Net Customer Value:
Elements of Realization and Sacrifice

SACRIFICED	REALIZED
time	availability
money	reliability
energy	ease of use
space	ease of understanding
convenience	maintainability
frustration	serviceability
ego	completeness
image	comfort
sleep	affordability
worry	image
effort	fashion
concern	painlessness
patriotism	free time
recognition	money
membership	energy
identity	consistency
alternative choices	enjoyment

NET VALUE

Copyright © G. M. Bounds and G. H. Carothers, 1989.

petition in value creation will remain viable, especially in the intensely competitive global market of the late twentieth century.

This dramatic microeconomic shift of power provides for the framing and defining of managerial leadership. Managerial leaders must respond to this new, compelling requirement. Even organizations currently enjoying the last vestiges of producer power and little competitive pressure should engage in managerial leadership proactively in order to maintain and extend their competitive advantage and avoid future crisis.

DIFFERENTIATION OF MANAGEMENT AND MANAGERIAL LEADERSHIP

In the past, microeconomics caused the evolution of the new subspecies of economic man: the salaried middle manager. Current microeconomic changes have created a new need for managerial leadership within organizations intent on long-term success and competitiveness. In the following discussion, a distinction is made between managerial leadership and management. Managerial leadership involves setting and directing the transcending organizational purpose. That purpose should be to create and provide value for the customers of products and services. Management involves the execution of that purpose. Management is subsumed within and is subordinate to managerial leadership. In this chapter we make the case that managers must adopt and enact the following definition:

Management consists of creating, providing and continuously improving strategic organizational suprasystems which, when used by organizational members, ensure the creation of value for the customers of its products/services (Carothers, 1989).

This definition of management takes on meaning within the framework of managerial leadership and organizational strategic purpose, and is deficient without such a framework. The above definition of management requires that managers know what the customers of their products and services value. This knowledge should never be presumed to exist within the organization. Managerial leaders must recognize that "The selection of a strategy for a particular product or market segment depends on its *customers'* definition of value. Strategies based on *customer* value standards and perceptions will channel resources more effectively and will meet customer expectations better than those based only on *company* standards" (Zeithaml, 1988). [Emphasis added.]

The concern for value creation as an integral part of managing has only recently been recognized and must now be operationalized. For the most part, such roles have been assigned to "the organization" and only implicitly to "top management." The following two quotes are representative of the role that the impersonal firm or company should play. "For outstanding performance, *a company* has to beat the competition" (Ghemawat, 1986). "To compete in the new global environment, *companies* must constantly map the terrain in which they operate, alert for significant change" (Rothschild, 1984). [Emphasis added.] The role of creating and providing value must be specifically defined in terms of a set of prescriptive managerial tasks. These tasks must be specifically assigned to managers within organizations.

Given the organization's dependency on its environment, knowledge of customer value must not be taken for granted (Hambrick, 1982; Thomas, 1980). Such knowledge represents the cornerstone of organizational sustenance. Managers must be led to work on strategic suprasystems that advance the organizational agenda. The development of knowledge about customer value, which is taken for granted in the above definition of management, is a prescribed agenda for managerial leaders and a prerequisite for suprasystem improvement. Managerial leaders are responsible for developing and confirming knowledge of what customers value, as well as creating systemic ability to deliver it. Continuous improvement of net customer value becomes the preeminent integrating force, and therein the strategic and tactical imperative for viable organizations.

The expanded responsibilities of managerial leadership, beyond "getting things done through others," can be identified in the following definition:

> Managerial leadership consists of continuously knowing what is currently of value to customers, discovering what will be of increased value to the customers of its products/services, and creating, providing and continuously improving strategic organizational suprasystems which, when used by the organizational members, ensure the creation of value for the customers of its products/services (Carothers, 1989).

Managerial leaders are responsible for establishing the substantive and purposeful focus of the organization, that is, for establishing continuous creation of customer value as the strategic thrust. They are responsible for determining value elements, tracking discovered elements, and anticipating customer value changes. They must also provide the means of creating that value, that is, creating, providing, and continuously improving strategic organizational suprasystems. Strategic (transfunctional) suprasystems are those systems derived from the strategic decision of an organization to willingly accept responsibility for providing certain customer-valued products and/or services.

Managerial leaders are no longer expected simply to write mission statements, state broad goals and objectives, and then review financial or other performance indicators to ensure control of fiscal variances. Managerial leaders must not be driven solely by the short-term objectives of the next quarter or the stock market.

Managerial leadership consists of managers leading purposeful, value-contributing organizations and providing the means of achieving the purpose by improving strategic suprasystems. The word "leadership" is appended to the word "management" to emphasize that managerial leaders must lead the organization to the appropriate strategic focus of customer value. This organizational leadership differs from the classical interpersonal processes emphasized in traditional leadership models.

The interpersonal and social leadership processes of influence, inspiration, guidance, and direction are clearly important to managerial leaders and managers of all levels of the organization. Interpersonal and social leadership will be necessary for managerial leaders and managers to sustain their efforts to manage suprasystems that create value for customers. Managerial leadership focuses the manager's efforts on the task of managing the effectiveness and efficiency of strategic suprasystems, and thereby creating customer-valued outcomes. Providing strategic focus and equipping organizational suprasystems to enable organizational members to succeed in creating value for customers constitute the backbone of managerial leadership.

Managerial leaders must recognize that value creation has to be sustained over time if the firm is to maintain a competitive advantage (Coyne, 1986). The importance of constantly improving value creation is being more broadly recognized. Note the recent attention devoted to the strategy of value creation in manufacturing and the strategic choices associated with emphasizing a customer service-oriented strategy in manufacturing contexts (Bowen, Siehl, and Schneider, 1989).

In summary, managerial leadership entails leading the organization to (1) the appropriate purpose, that is, best net customer value, (2) knowledge of what customers value and (3) creating, providing and improving the means of achieving that purpose. Within this context, the tasks of managers are subordinate to and necessarily congruent with the tasks of managerial leaders. Managerial leaders determine what customers value, identify the strategic suprasystems that create that value, and in conjunction with managers, assess, standardize and improve these suprasystems. The superordinate goal of an aligned team of managerial leaders and managers is to ensure the competitive future of the organization by creating value for the customer of its products and services.

Managerial leadership provides the bridge for integrating strategy formulation and strategy implementation in theory and practice. Managerial leaders bear the responsibility for developing the organization's strategic capability, that is, to align the organization's abilities to meet current and future demands and to pursue future value-contributing opportunities. The following model of managerial leadership suggests the behavior required of leaders to ensure strategic alignment.

AN OPERATIONAL MODEL OF MANAGERIAL LEADERSHIP

The model describes the appropriate tasks and activities of managerial leaders. Based on the above definition, the two critical tasks within the model are (1) determining what customers currently value and deciding what they would value even more in the future, and (2) creating, providing, and continuously improving organizational strategic suprasystems. These two tasks may be regarded as interdependent cycles of managerial activities (see Figure 2). Since these task cycles recur throughout the life of organizations, we may think of them as interlinked spirals of activities continuing through time.

Most people are familiar with the concept of a cycle, that is, a complete set of events or activities that recur sequentially. Many have seen the concept of cycles applied to the management of organizations. For example, Shewhart is credited with the PLAN-DO-CHECK-ACT (PDCA) cycle (Shewhart, 1939). The uniqueness of the cycles in Figure 2 is that they behaviorally specify and prescribe managerial leadership and management. These cycles are not a rearticulation of the PDCA cycle. Unlike Shewhart's cycle, these highly interdependent cycles are not problem-driven heuristics, which are optional, situational, or temporal managerial activities. Instead, these cycles constitute the organization's life process, and they must be perpetually engaged to ensure survival and ultimate organizational success. Since these cycles of activities are so important to organizational viability, the components and interdependencies of the model are discussed further.

The Strategic Value Determination cycle consists of four sequential task activities, suggested by the quadrant labels PROJECT, INVALIDATE, DISCOVER, CONFIRM. The first set of activities, PROJECT, consists of making an educated guess of what the customers value. INVALIDATE means to continually seek to disprove the correctness of one's guess. DISCOVER includes the affirmation of the guess or the articulation and operationalization of what was found to be erroneous about the guess, and further specification of that which is imperative from the customer's perspective. CONFIRM involves examining customer

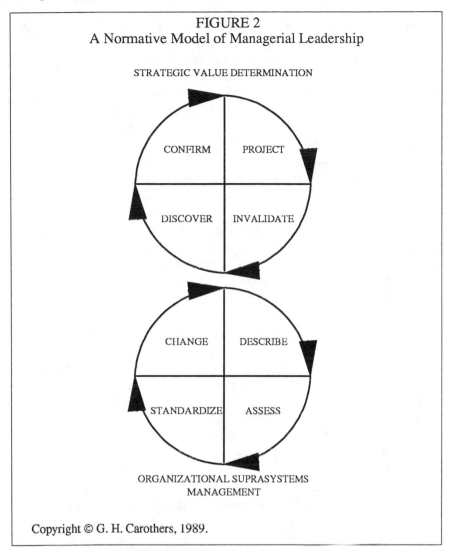

FIGURE 2
A Normative Model of Managerial Leadership

STRATEGIC VALUE DETERMINATION

CONFIRM   PROJECT

DISCOVER   INVALIDATE

CHANGE   DESCRIBE

STANDARDIZE   ASSESS

ORGANIZATIONAL SUPRASYSTEMS
MANAGEMENT

source selection behavior to determine any discrepancy with prior discovery of what customers value. These exhibited customer behaviors serve as a basis for inferring whether best net value has truly been created and provided for the customer.

Given that managerial leaders know what customers value, the managers of organization suprasystems are either responsive or nonresponsive. Obviously, there may be varying degrees of responsiveness to customers. Customer source selection behaviors CONFIRM managerial success in determining what is valued and in responding to create suprasystems that provide value. Confirmation gives managerial leaders the knowledge they need to assess the performance of organizational suprasystems and to realign strategic focus. Strategic organizational suprasystems management must be intensely directed toward the resulting specifications of the value determination activities. Suprasystems improvement is pointless if devoid of this intent. This conclusion implies that some organizational suprasystems are critically linked to organizational strategy and that these are the strategic suprasystems on which managerial leaders and managers must focus.

These strategic suprasystems are derived from the strategic decision of an organization to willingly accept responsibility for providing certain customer-valued products and services. Managerial leaders determine what customers value and prioritize them in accord with the imperative strategic focus. Managerial leaders thus elect and specify the responsibilities for which all organization members willingly choose full accountability. These responsibilities dictate the strategic suprasystems to be conceived, designed, operationalized, managed, and improved. The following example provides insight into the necessary linkage between strategic value determination and suprasystems management.

Consider the case of Federal Express. Ask an individual with a volume of paper (too large to fax) how he intends to get it to a specific person in another city quickly. The strategic question Federal Express must ask itself is: "What service would the customer have to do for himself/herself if Federal Express had not accepted the responsibility for doing it?" Federal Express answers with the following services: (1) Upon demand (e.g., a phone call), Federal Express will respond by scheduling, and then, picking up the material, (2) Federal Express will provide careful, secure, informed and timely movement of the material, (3) Federal Express will find and place the material in the hands of the intended recipient, and (4) if Federal Express cannot complete the obligation of delivering the material to the intended recipient or complete another agreed upon arrangement, then Federal Express will similarly find and return the material to the sender. These chosen responsibilities reveal the obligatory suprasystems that Federal Express must manage in order to satisfy the commitment of the enterprise. Customers have come to expect Federal Express to have suprasystems for (1) responding upon demand, that is, pick up, (2) careful, secure, informed, and timely movement, and (3) confident placement of the material in the hands of designated recipients. Failure to accept or execute the above responsibilities may be met with customer rejection, particularly if alternatives prove more responsive to that which is valued.

Strategic value determination may be viewed as a set of ongoing, investigatory, or seeking set of activities. The execution of each successive set of activities in the cycle produces more sophisticated and refined understanding of what customers value than exists at the preceding set of activities. Rather than treating these successive activities as independent and mutually distinct, they should be viewed as complementary, with investigatory activities flowing sequentially from one set of activities to another. Findings in earlier stages of investigation serve as foundations for later investigatory activity.

The continuation of these activities yields an increasingly refined and detailed knowledge base and understanding of what customers value. The failure to engage in customer value determination may reap costly organizational and personal outcomes for negligent managers. Many organizations fail to move beyond the naive and superficial PROJECT activities in value determination. Subsequently, managers base strategic and tactical decisions on untested assumptions and guesses. Stubborn and inept reliance on the activities of this first quadrant poses a risk to organizational success. Blind faith based on unconfirmed guesses often results in ineffective trial and error product introduction. Major consumer products firms indicate that market failure rates exceeding 50 percent and even 90 percent for new products based on this trial and error approach are not uncommon.

Managerial leaders may use the initial guess concerning what is valued to begin the Organizational Suprasystems Management cycle. This complementary companion cycle of managerial activities also consists of four sets of activities, with quadrants labeled DESCRIBE, ASSESS, STANDARDIZE, and CHANGE. These four sets of activities are applied to organizational suprasystems. Managers need to DESCRIBE the specific organizational suprasystems, ASSESS the ability of these suprasystems to create customer value, STANDARDIZE the implementation of the suprasystem with the members of the organization to ensure its maintenance and stability, and accelerate constructive CHANGE of the organizational suprasystems that demonstrate enhancement of the value realized by the customers. Thus, the results of value determination must guide managerial leaders and managers in creating, providing, and improving strategic organizational suprasystems.

Strategic suprasystems management must be viewed as ongoing improvement activities. The initial activities of suprasystem management require knowledge development aimed at increased understanding of existing strategic suprasystems. Suprasystem managers are required to

---

1. Deming, Ishikawa, and Juran stress the need for new management behavior directed at continuous improvement (Deming, 1986; Ishikawa and Lu, 1985; Juran, 1964). Only a small fraction of managers in the Western world show evidence of having understood and responded to their entreaties.

learn about what currently exists through description and assessment of suprasystem architecture, operations, and outcomes.[1]

Managerial leaders must identify those organizational suprasystem elements, that is, activities, processes, tasks, or inputs, which contribute to or detract from that which the customer values. Designation of an organizational suprasystem owner from the managerial group is imperative, and not optional. The manager who exclusively owns the suprasystem and leads other managers in improving the suprasystem must understand how his or her suprasystem contributes to or detracts from what is valued.

The suprasystem manager must diagram and justify the elements of the suprasystem. He or she must also operationally define the desired intermediate and ultimate outcomes of the suprasystems and the activities of the suprasystem, design measurement methodologies, and ensure that confidence can be placed in these methodologies. The work done on definitions and measurement methodologies forms the basis of subsequent suprasystems assessment and standardization. Standardization is defined as the process through which the suprasystem owners validate the operability of suprasystem architecture when used by the organizational members to provide customer value.

The improvement of suprasystems requires that the suprasystem manager master operational definitions, procedures, inputs, outputs, measurement methodology, causal relationships, current capability, and contribution to and detraction from customer value. Suprasystem managers must standardize and ensure the maintenance of existing suprasystems performance through education, communication, policy enforcement, and quantitative confirmation to ensure statistical predictability, statistical capability, and performance capability. All organizational members must be led by suprasystem owners to challenge and change existing suprasystems to meet changing customer demands. Suprasystem standardization and maintenance must be viewed as providing not permanency but operable stability and a confident basis for directed, orderly, continuous, proactive suprasystem changes.

Stability provides the launching pad for the acceleration of further improvement through change of existing suprasystems architecture or the introduction of novel or innovative suprasystems architecture. Organization members must be led to constructively flow from standardization to change, introducing and maintaining improved levels of suprasystem performance without regression. Change of suprasystems must provide improved creation of value for the customer. Changing existing suprasystems will require strategically directed experimentation, identification of value-enhancement leverage points, statistical analyses of relationships, and breakthrough analyses. Managerial leaders must narrow any gap between what the suprasystems currently provide as value and what customers will value in the future via suprasystems improvement realized through alternative suprasystems architecture. Managerial leaders must work to eliminate the potential for any gap to occur. Successful integration of customer value determination and suprasystems management activities improves the creation of value for the customer relative to competing alternatives and thereby increases organizational sustenance and success, and thereby stakeholder returns.

The PROJECT: INVALIDATE: DISCOVER: CONFIRM cycle for value determination and the DESCRIBE: ASSESS: STANDARDIZE: CHANGE cycle for the management of organizational suprasystems are highly interdependent cycles of managerial activity. These cycles operationalize managerial leadership within the framework of organizational strategy and are intended to provide managerial leaders an appropriate response to evolving microeconomic demands.

THE IMPLEMENTATION STRATEGY

Models are nice but of little value if managerial leaders and managers cannot understand how to use them and succeed through their use. The challenge of succeeding with this new model of managerial leadership is increased by the complexity created by the ongoing nature of most organizations. The model must be engaged "on the fly" without jeopardizing current operations within an organization. Although space limitation precludes a full discussion of implementation, key elements, which increase the likelihood of success, are embodied in the following suggestions for the implementation: (1) Emphasize the responsibility of managerial leaders for strategic suprasystems, (2) strategically focus on continuous creation of customer value, (3) integrate the improvement efforts of managers, (4) ensure the interdependence of the value determination and suprasystem management, and (5) provide educational resources and assistance for managerial behavior change.

These suggestions are based on experience gained from a decade of regularly teaching and assisting managers from 80 percent of the top 30 *Fortune* 500 companies through the Management Development Center at the University of Tennessee. In the 1980s, this Center has moved into the top four in executive education program market share among American and Canadian universities (*The Bricker Bulletin on Executive Education*, 1989).

Emphasize Responsibility for Strategic Suprasystems

Organizations that produce products/services must be led by managerial leaders who attend to strategic suprasystems that are intended to create value for customers. These suprasystems are composed of interdependent patterns of activities that organizations use to assure desired outcomes, and include processes, functions, activities, tasks, and various material inputs. Managerial leaders must go beyond the focus on the subordinate activities and processes within functions or within departments or subsystems. They must concentrate on the critical superordinate suprasystems of organizations which are tied to the organization's fundamental strategy. These critical suprasystems are by their nature interdepartmental or transfunctional, that is, transcending functional units.

Subordinate managers, supervisors, and operators will undoubtedly focus on functional activities or processes or tasks in their work to improve suprasystems. However, the work of managerial leaders resides at a higher level and transcends the many boundaries that subdivide an organization. Unfortunately, existing strategic suprasystems of organizations have typically evolved in a piecemeal fashion, inherited from previous generations of managers. Although current managers may have never traced the origin of existing suprasystems, the mandate for managerial leaders is to become masters of these strategic suprasystems, steering them toward organizational competitiveness in the creation of best net customer value. These suprasystems must not be taken for granted. Quite the contrary, they demand continuous attention, care, concern, and enhancement.

Strategically Focus on Continuous Creation of Customer Value

Successful implementation requires that the managerial leader's fundamental and long-term responsibility be to identify the critical customer values to which managers must attend. These critical customer values offer clues in identifying the superordinate strategic suprasystems. Since organizational resources are often limited, not all elements of value can be maximized. Determined customer value cannot be pursued outside the framework of organizational strategy. Priorities must be set to focus managerial efforts on achieving advantageous value creation. The chosen focus must integrate both organizational performance outcomes and customer value in formulating long-term strategy. Managerial leaders must also attend to the constraints and opportunities extended by various other organizational constituents, in the creation of value for the customers of their products and services. These constituents include broader society, employees, unions, governmental agencies, governing bodies, and other private and public institutions.

Managerial leaders bear the primary responsibility to engage in the activities of the Strategic Value Determination cycle. Although they may seek assistance with the task of value determination, *under no circumstances are these activities to be delegated* to subordinates or staff assistants. Value determination must be conducted and led by those who have authority commensurate with the responsibility for determining the purposeful focus of the organization. Managerial leadership may be present throughout the organization. Managers at various levels may assist in value determination and strategic suprasystem improvement. Determining what customers value may be complex, however. Customers may be varied and have conflicting values. Therefore, active involvement in value determination at the highest managerial levels is important to ensure proper prioritization, and the integration of strategy and customer value. Otherwise, customer value may be neglected. Personal involvement of managerial leaders creates awareness of and commitment to whatever is discovered about customer value.

Managerial leaders must identify the critical value creating suprasystems of the organization which are peculiar to its strategy. They must also personally engage in the activities of the Organizational Suprasystems Management cycle. The goal of these activities is to develop organizational suprasystems that continuously create value for the customer. Managers will likely discover components of their suprasystems that actually detract from value by increasing the sacrifice required of the customer, for example, high product cost due to high overhead or high inventory costs. Therefore, managers should create viable suprasystems by putting in place value-enhancing components and, ideally, eliminating value-detracting components. The objective of this work is to improve the capacity of organizational suprasystems to create the best net value for the customer, which clearly exceeds that of competing alternatives.

Integrate the Improvement Efforts of Managers

Engaging in value determination will likely reveal more work than managerial leaders can possibly do by themselves. This means that they will have to engage other managers, perhaps subordinate managers, in the task of suprasystems management. Managerial leaders determine the focus of subordinate managers' organizational suprasystems and subsystem work, and assign subordinated personal ownership to managers for the responsibility to improve these subsystems which are components and microcosms of suprasystems. Managerial leaders must convey to managers

that their ownership of these subsystems and the engagement in suprasystems management is not a fad, or "the flavor of the month," or a temporary
assignment to be terminated once the report is filed. Suprasystem and
subsystems management must be *the job* of managers. They must be
rewarded and appreciated for it.

Managerial leaders will hold subordinate managers responsible for
ensuring that these subsystems are improved with regard to creating value
for the customer of the products/services. Managerial leaders will review
the progress of subordinate managers in subsystems improvement. Thus,
managerial leaders are responsible not only for value determination, but
also for creating, providing, and continuously improving the critical organizational suprasystems, while overseeing the subsystem management
activities of their subordinates. They must fulfill all these responsibilities
to ensure the integration, congruence, and consistency of strategy formulation and strategy implementation throughout the organization. Integration
of diverse managerial activities is explained further in the framework
presented in Chapter 25 by Bounds and Pace.

The work of managerial leaders and managers will be integrated by
ensuring that the results of value determination are used to direct attention
to the appropriate organizational suprasystems and subsystems. The goal
of long-term organizational competitiveness through the continuous creation of best net value should guide these activities. Therefore, the work of
managers on subsystems must necessarily be subservient to and integrated
with the work of managerial leaders.

The fragmentation and self-serving actions of specialists, departments,
functional areas, or fiefdoms, which typify organizations, can be averted
by making managers responsible for work on suprasystems that cut across
these functional or arbitrary boundaries. Organizational culture and structures must be constructed to support and demand managerial leadership
and suprasystems management. The managerial leaders must ensure congruence of rewards, appreciation systems, promotional criteria, information systems, performance evaluation, and reporting systems with the
definition of the managerial jobs.

Ensure the Interdependency of Value Determination and Suprasystems Management

Managerial leaders have two tasks: they engage in both strategic value
determination and organizational suprasystems management. As part of
managing these suprasystems, managerial leaders may assign whole systems or subsystems to other managers. This delegation is permissible only
after managerial leaders have determined their own personal and non-

delegatable systems. They must personally retain responsibility for managing at least one suprasystem, as well as overseeing the management of the other systems. This suprasystem responsibility extends to the highest level of the organization.

Personal participation and leadership by top managers are needed for success. In addition, managerial leaders and managers will, by necessity, employ groups of managers or other employees to assist with the thinking and work of suprasystems management. Such collaboration is useful and typically necessary, given the transfunctional nature of organizational suprasystems. Managerial leaders must set the focus for the suprasystem improvement work, and the focus must be consistent with the organization's strategic purpose. Without strategic focus, efforts are fragmented and tend toward disorder or entropy.

Managerial leaders may begin application of the two cycles with obvious, PROJECTed customer values, while working to determine actual customer values. Thus, the sequential starting points are PROJECT and DESCRIBE in the two respective cycles of activities. Managerial leaders must continue to engage in Value Determination and Suprasystems Management cycles. Managerial leaders must integrate the work of the two cycles to ensure organizational viability within dynamic environments. These activities must continually be reiterated, with the focus of the suprasystems work contingent on the discoveries of value determination. Through inspection and assessment of managerial behavior, managerial leaders must continually ensure that managers are working on suprasystems that are related to what customers value. They live by the credo, "One gets what is inspected, not what is expected."

The interdependence of the two cycles of activity must be remembered. The cycles are most aptly described as spirals of activity that continue through time. The basic activities are to be repeated over and over, through time, since organizations and their external environmental situations change.

The activities of value determination and suprasystem improvement never end, unlike the resolution of a problem in problem solving. These cycles do not represent problem solving. The activities are not driven by reaction to "today's crisis" or some salient, recurrent problem. Rather, these managerial activities are proactive and, most appropriately, anticipatory, driven by the imperative of continuous improvement of suprasystems to increasingly create competitive value for the customer. Thus, the work of suprasystems improvement should be contingent on what is determined to be valued by the customer. This interdependence and intertwining of the two spirals of activities are necessary to ensure the organization's competitiveness and viability.

FIGURE 3
Managerial Leadership as an Ongoing and Integrated Set of Activities

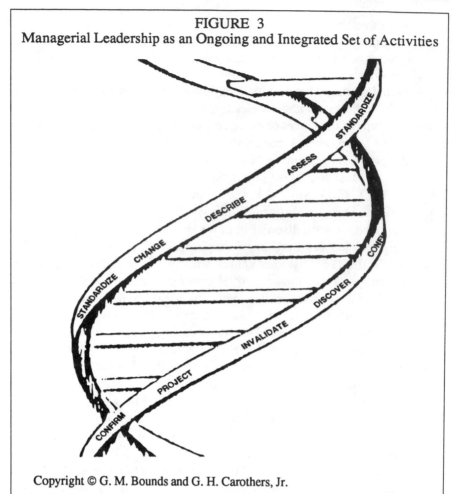

Copyright © G. M. Bounds and G. H. Carothers, Jr.

A robust metaphor for this interdependency is the structure of DNA (deoxyribose nucleic acid), the double helix (see Figure 3). The double helix is composed of two intertwined helical polynucleotide chains that are held together by hydrogen bonds. The picture of the double helix in Figure 3 is certainly a simplistic representation of reality. The DNA molecule is infinitely more complex in its real and life-giving form.

As the analogy suggests, the two spirals of managerial activity, value determination and suprasystems management, are to be intricately interwoven. They exist simultaneously, and they are symbiotic. One set of managerial activities alone will not ensure a viable organization. The spirals are necessarily interconnected with the bonds of mutual interaction and aligned congruence. The work of suprasystems improvement must continuously be focused and refocused on the appropriate creation of value for customers. The spirals of managerial activity are intended to continue into time as a never-ending process, with continuous improvement in value created for the customer of the products or services.

Provide Educational Resources and Assistance for Managerial Behavior Change

Managers are typically ill equipped and inexperienced in the methodologies implied by the model's cycles. The equipping and development of the manager's personal competence and confidence must be established in the real setting of ongoing organization, demonstrating significant contributions to organizational success. Changing to the new managerial-leadership model consists of a paradigm shift within the organization. This paradigm shift requires a radical reorientation of managerial thinking, role perception, behavior, methods, systems, and strategic focus. Organizational structural modifications may be required, but they are not to be treated as the panacea.

Although this transformation process requires more than just education, it should begin with education. The purpose and nature of managerial leadership must be understood. Whether the educators are internal or external to the organization, they must familiarize themselves with the organizational architecture. The specific study of the organization's situation, mission, vision, strategy, organization, managerial practices, and work content should precede formal classroom training. Informal contacts, site visits, and interviews of participant managers serve the purposes of gauging the commitment of the critical members of the hierarchy. This exposure to the organization is also important in building rapport, gaining permission to influence, getting to know the organizational and managerial people issues, and behaviorally and operationally baselining the organization with formal methodologies developed specifically for the assessment of managerial leadership.

Organizationally specific examples should be prepared, and the most appropriate applied techniques and methodology for the needs of the organization should be determined. The tailoring of the content to the needs and interests of the organization makes the educational experience more meaningful, eliminates the excuse of individual managers that the education is not pertinent to their specific context, and assists in transferring the educational experience to the specific job setting.

The educational course should be composed of activities aimed at imparting skills to the individual managers and managerial leaders which are pertinent to determining customer value and the management of organizational suprasystems. The course should also motivate these individuals to engage in these activities. The rationale for continuous improvement of suprasystems should be discussed, as well as new approaches to managing organizations. The message to be conveyed is that organizational suprasystems are the means through which value is created for the customer, and the corresponding implications for their jobs should be cited. Managers must be led to the understanding that purposeful suprasystems improvement represents their key to organizational success.

The content of the new managerial leadership role and the processes of value determination and suprasystems improvement should be discussed in several contexts. Various applied concepts and improvement tools should be presented, including the cycles of managerial leadership activities, decision processes, cause/effect diagram, Pareto, flow diagram, time-ordered charts, correlational techniques, and designed experiments that are strategically directed. The participants should have an opportunity to apply their newly acquired skills each day in group exercises aimed at

1. Identifying what customers value and what the organization must do to become increasingly competitive.
2. Identifying and describing the critical organizational suprasystems that create these outcomes.
3. Designating ownership for the management of these suprasystems.
4. Developing a means of measuring customer value creation and current suprasystem performance.
5. Outlining a plan for organizing and continuing the work of value determination and improving organizational suprasystems.

Extensive education and assistance will be required. However, implementation requires more than just sitting through a course. Implementing managerial leadership does not end with the wrapup of the initial educational course. Maintaining the work to improve organizational suprasystems initiated during the evening activities requires continued attention and effort. Review sessions and followup contacts should be scheduled as needed to sustain, encourage, and convey the importance of the work through appreciation, coaching, continued education, and personal attention. Those who accepted the responsibility for facilitating implementation should continue these followup efforts. Shifting an organization to the managerial leadership model will require managerial leaders to rethink all aspects of their organization, including strategic planning, human resource systems, engineering processes, information systems, manufacturing processes, logistical and transportation systems, marketing, accounting, and financial functions.

Implementing the managerial leadership model will often require a resocialization or rescripting of managers, in terms of new role perceptions and new behaviors. The behavior of managers represents the key to competitive improvement. All employees must ultimately be involved in improving and maintaining organizational suprasystems. Managerial leaders must regard all employees as human resources with great potential for contribution. Without the appropriate managerial behaviors, however, programs focused on the lowest levels of the organization will fail to reach their full potential, and people will not be given the opportunity to grow and contribute. Managerial leaders and managers must purposefully pull worker participation into their personal improvement efforts.   Any "employee involvement" should have strategic focus and exist within the context of appropriate managerial behaviors and organizational culture.

When the managerial leaders have created the right culture for their organization, stories and symbols will arise among the ranks to reinforce the theme of customer value. For example, Procter and Gamble circulates stories about how its line workers get close to the customer. "At the Duncan Hines angel food cake factory in Jackson, Tennessee, the line workers are given letters from customers who have problems with the product. One factory hand called up a customer whose angel food cake didn't rise, and helped figure out why by asking such questions as 'How long did you beat the mix?' and 'At what temperature did you bake it?'" (*Fortune*, 1989). A good example of how corporate culture can help reinforce the customer value concept among employees exists at Delta Airlines. "At Delta Airlines, Inc., a focus on customer service produces a high degree of teamwork. Employees will substitute in other jobs to keep planes flying and baggage moving" (*Business Week*, 1980). In a culture driven by managerial leadership, stories like this should permeate every level of management, not just the bottom, and especially the very top of a hierarchy.

In implementing the managerial leadership model, leaders must assess progress by focusing on behavioral criteria in the early stages of transition or resocialization. Results criteria should be met over time but will not likely be observed immediately. Discussion of impediments and facilitators may assist the cultural transformation to ensure that customer value determination and suprasystem management continues.

MANAGERIAL LEADERSHIP TO COMPETE

Implementation of managerial leadership represents a strong alternative for organizations seeking a more competitive future. Managerial leaders must lead organizational managers to the appropriate strategic focus and correspondingly manage the organization for improved suprasystems to ensure themselves a competitive and viable future. Managerial leadership consists of continuously knowing what is currently of value to customers, discovering what will be of increased value to the customers of its products/services, and creating, providing, and continuously improving organizational suprasystems which, when used by the organizational members, provide value to the customers of the resulting products and/or services.

Although adherence to the preceding suggestions for implementation will be helpful, managers will not readily abandon old habits. Organizational inertia will be apparent. Those who dare to walk this way must recognize they have chosen "the straight and narrow"; it will not be easy. It is hard work. It is time consuming. It demands discipline. Implementing managerial leadership may appear deceptively easy. Managers who mistakenly walk this way, without the resolve for personal toil and struggle, may have chosen the primrose path.

The challenges of growing global and domestic competition will make it difficult for managerial leaders to remain dormant. Managerial leaders must assume that their competitors, both global and domestic, are improving strategic suprasystems and creating improved net value for customers. The competitive challenges will not go away but only grow. Those who do ignore the challenges of international competition and fail to respond appropriately may find themselves fading as competitors. Those who meet and surpass the competitive challenges with managerial leadership may earn the right to remain in the race. The race is one among the management groups of organizations, and managerial leaders must accept their personal responsibility for remaining and competing in this race. The model presented in this chapter should help equip managerial leaders for this competition.

REFERENCES

Bowen, D. E., C. Siehl, and B. Schneider. "A Framework for Analyzing Customer Service Orientations in Manufacturing." *Academy of Management Review* 14 (1989): 75-95.

Bower, J., and T. Hout, "Fast-Cycle Capability for Competitive Power." *Harvard Business Review* (1988): 112-113.

Carothers, G. H., Jr. "Managing the Managers of Competitive Strategic Change: An Exploratory Study of Variables of Organizational Context and Individual Managerial Personnel in Four American Manufacturing Business Units" Ph.D. diss. College of Business Administration, University of Tennessee, 1989.

Case, J. "Competitive Advantage." *Inc.* (April 1989): 33-34.

Coyne, K. P. "Sustainable Competitive Advantage – What It Is. What It Isn't." *Business Horizons* (January-February 1986): 54-61.

Deming, W. E. *Out of the Crisis*. Cambridge, Mass.: Massachusetts Institute of Technology, Center for Advanced Engineering Study, 1986.

"Procter & Gamble Rewrites the Marketing Rules." *Fortune* (November 6, 1989): 91.

Ghemawat, P. "Sustainable Advantage." *Harvard Business Review* (September-October 1986): 53-58.

Hambrick, D. C. "Environmental Scanning and Organizational Strategy." *Strategic Management Journal* 3 (1982): 159-174.

Hardy, K. G. "Add Value, Boost Margins." *Business Quarterly* (Summer 1987): 63-64.

Ishikawa, K. and D. J. Lu. *What Is Total Quality Control?*, Englewood Cliffs, N. J.: Prentice-Hall, 1985.

Jeffrey, B. "The Great Value-Added Push Revolutionizes IBM." *Business Marketing* (November 1987): 68-72.

Juran, J. M. *Managerial Breakthrough*. New York: McGraw-Hill, 1964.

Karger, T. "Listening to Consumers Can Yield Value-Added Distinctions for Brands." *Marketing News* (July 31, 1987): 3.

"King Customer." *Business Week* (March 12, 1990): 91.

"Radio Shack's Rough Trip." *Business Week* (May 30, 1977): 55.

Rothschild, W. E. "Surprise and the Competitive Advantage." *Journal of Business Strategy* (Winter 1984): 10-18.

Shewhart, W. A. *Statistical Method from the Viewpoint of Quality Control*. Graduate School, Department of Agriculture, Washington, D.C., 1939.

The Bricker Bulletin on Executive Education, Princeton, N. J., 8, no. 1 (1989).

Thomas, P. S. "Environmental Scanning, the State of the Art." *Long Range Planning* 13, no. 1 (1980): 20-28.

"What Corporate Culture Is and How Shared Values Contribute to the Success or Failure of Strategy." *Business Week* (October 27, 1980): 43.

Zeithaml, V. A. "Consumer Perceptions of Price, Quality, and Value: A Means-End Model and Synthesis of Evidence." *Journal of Marketing* 52 (1988): 2-22.

CHAPTER 6

CUSTOMER VALUE DETERMINATION
AND SYSTEM IMPROVEMENT CYCLES*

G. HARLAN CAROTHERS, JR.
Senior Lecturer, Institutes for Productivity
University of Tennessee

GREGORY M. BOUNDS
Research Associate, Management Development Center
University of Tennessee

SUMMARY

The managerial leadership model was introduced in the preceding chapter. The purpose of this chapter is to elaborate this model to give managerial leaders a better understanding of their required tasks. Because of the brevity of this chapter, some of the particular analytical techniques associated with each task are only suggested and not fully discussed.

INTRODUCTION

This chapter rests on three basic assumptions. First, you have formulated a strategy to create and deliver value to the users of your products and services and have identified the strategic systems that create and deliver value. Second, you have been assigned the ownership responsibility for

---

*The authors would like to acknowledge the unmeasurable contributions of Richard Sanders, Bill Parr, Ken Kirby, and Jerry Toomey, for their help in developing the managerial leadership model discussed in this chapter.

managing a strategic suprasystem (or subsystem). Third, you accept this responsibility and seek to learn more about how to fulfill this responsibility. Note that the material in this chapter specifies the content of the managerial job proposed in the chapter on managerial leadership by Carothers, Bounds, and Stahl.

Recall the definition of managerial leadership:
Managerial leadership consists of continuously knowing what is currently of value to customers, discovering what will be of in creased value to the customers of its products/services, and creating, providing and continuously improving organizational suprasystems which, when used by the organizational members, ensure the creation of value for the customers of its products/services.

Also recall that there are two critical cycles in the managerial leadership model: (1) determining what users value and deciding what they would value even more, and (2) creating, providing, and continuously improving the organizational systems that provide that value. The four quadrants of each of these two cycles were briefly described in the preceding chapter. In Figure 1, the many activities of managerial leadership are sequentially listed for each quadrant. In this chapter each of these activities is explained to operationalize the managerial leadership model. The Strategic Value Determination cycle is discussed first.

The interrelationship of Value Determination and Systems Management cycles is especially critical for managers to understand. One set of activities has little impact on an organization's competitiveness without the other. These authors place value determination as the lead set of activities, which makes a lot of sense if you consider a single iteration of the cycles. In practice, over time, however, it may be more difficult to establish which comes first under the mandate of continuous improvement. The activities of the two cycles may appear simultaneous and intermingled, as the two strands of the DNA model presented in the preceding chapter. Managerial leaders and managers should be prepared to flow from one set of activities to the other to ensure their integration. For example, value determination may be used to seek opportunities where existing/modified systems can be more competitive, and experimentation for continuous improvement may reveal understanding about user value.

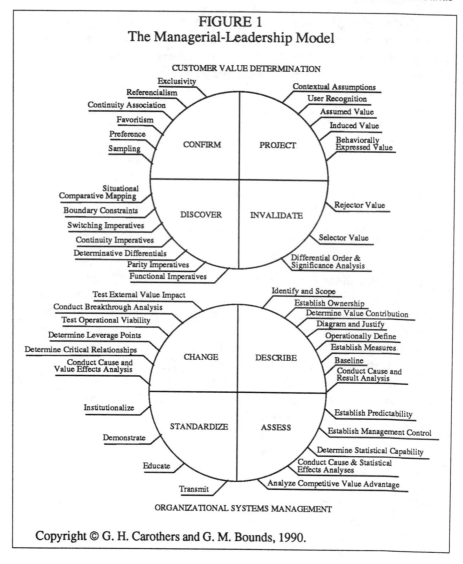

FIGURE 1
The Managerial-Leadership Model

Copyright © G. H. Carothers and G. M. Bounds, 1990.

STRATEGIC VALUE DETERMINATION

The purpose of strategic value determination is to establish a base of knowledge and understanding about what users value. As discussed in foregoing chapters, the strategy of the organization is to create and deliver the best net value for the user. Best net value is that which is realized by the customer of a product/service which justifies the sacrifice required while acquiring and using the product/service. The net value, therefore, results from combining that which is realized and sacrificed. Managerial leaders must attend to each of these dimensions of customer value.

A value-based strategy inherently involves all systems and activities of the organization which contribute to the realizations provided and sacrifices required of the user. Some firms effectively maximize net value by producing products/services with high customer realizations and low customer sacrifice. Others inadvertently compromise net value either by producing products/services perceived to be of low realization and/or by requiring excessively high sacrifices of customers, or both. Managerial leaders must ensure that user value determination provides guidance to the management and continuous improvement of organizational systems for best net user value.

Throughout this chapter the broad term *user* is employed to simplify the writing. "User" encompasses intermediate customers, end-use customers, and consumers, and others who might derive value or be required to make sacrifices because of the product or service. For example, in a subsequent chapter (23), on the role of marketing in creating value for customers, Woodruff makes a distinction between the end-user market and channel customers. As system owner, you must recognize that products and services may have many users sequentially and/or simultaneously. These diverse users must be explicitly recognized and considered separately in determining what they value in your products and services.[1] Their perspectives will vary.

Relative to the following discussion, consider that the Strategic Value Determination cycle is an exercise in seeking and confirming knowledge. It consists of four sequential steps, suggested by the quadrant labels PROJECT, INVALIDATE, DISCOVER, CONFIRM. The first step, PROJECT, consists of making an educated guess of what the users value. INVALIDATE consists of attempting to disprove the correctness of the guess. DISCOVER includes affirming the guess or restating what was found to be erroneous about the guess, and further articulating that which is imperative for creating and delivering user value. CONFIRM involves examining user behavior to determine any discrepancy between what is valued by users and what is provided for users. These exhibited user

---

1. The Watervliet Arsenal in Watervliet, New York, and Greg Conway distinguish three sets of users: consumers, deciders, and beneficiaries. The consumer is the actual person/organization who actually uses the product/service. The decider is the person/organization that selects, chooses, specifies, and authorizes payment for the product/service. The beneficiary is the person/organization that benefits or makes sacrifice due to the use of the product/service. In some cases, such as a person who buys a hot dog from a street vendor, one user embodies all three sets, as the consumer, decider, and beneficiary. Other cases are more complex. The producer of a cannon faces many diverse users. The soldier may be viewed as a consumer, the acquisition agency (Department of Defense) as a decider, and the American public as a beneficiary.

behaviors serve as a basis for inferring whether the best net value has been created for the user.

Keep in mind that strategic value determination is a perpetual, investigatory or seeking exercise. You must examine user value from a number of perspectives, with various purposes in mind, and you must intend to continually test your understanding of user value.

Rather than treating these successive activities as independent and mutually distinct, they should be viewed as complementary and cumulative, with the investigatory activities flowing sequentially from one step to another. These activities are intended to be partially redundant. Execution of each successive cycle produces more sophisticated and refined understanding of what users value than exists at the preceding cycle. These activities are interrelated. Findings in earlier stages of investigation serve as foundations for later investigatory and analytical activities.

The continuation of these activities yields an increasingly refined and detailed knowledge base and prescriptive understanding of what users value. This knowledge and understanding then becomes the focus of your efforts to create, provide, and continuously improve organizational systems. The activities of each PROJECT, INVALIDATE, DISCOVER, and CONFIRM are discussed below, and the relationship of these value determination activities is briefly related to market opportunity analysis (MOA) to suggest value opportunity analysis (VOA) as a strategic opportunity and necessity for managerial leaders.

Project

To PROJECT requires that you make an educated guess of what the users of your products and services value. If you accept the guess as truth and fail to proceed to subsequent activities of value determination, you risk grave error. The guess simply represents current knowledge about user value and should be skeptically regarded as only a starting point in value determination. The activities that compose the PROJECT quadrant in the Value Determination cycle involve contextual assumptions, user recognition, assumed value, induced value, and behaviorally expressed value. Each of these components is discussed below.

Contextual Assumptions. In order to more accurately project what the user values, you must take into account the underlying assumptions made regarding the user's context. Assumptions such as the following must be stated: "Their basic needs will not change in the foreseeable future." "They will not choose to perform the service you offer or make the product you offer themselves." "Their strategic plans for the foreseeable future will not change their needs, for example, through divestiture, merger, or acquisition." "New market offerings will not offer viable alternatives." Stating these types of assumptions provides a basis for understanding the projected user values.

User Recognition. Typically, organizations have many users of their products and services. Some of these users are frequently overlooked. For example, while focusing on the end consumer, managers may fail to consider those who handle or "use" the product in the distribution channels. Various users will value different aspects of the product or service. Prior to guessing what users value, you must explicitly recognize users and perhaps logically group them into groups that completely represent the users. To effectively execute the activities of value determination you must know who your users are. Thus, user and market definitions are critical precursors to value determination. Market opportunity analysis (MOA) can be helpful in this regard. These issues are more thoroughly discussed in Chapter 23.

Assumed Value. Once users are identified, managers should have some current assumptions about what each of these users values. These assumptions may have a number of bases: past experience, current information, or logic. Put yourself in the user's place. Assume the role of the user, and from that position indicate what the user values. In putting yourself in the user's place you should adopt the user's perspective. When guessing what the user values you must consider two factors: what it is that he or she receives and, coincidentally, what sacrifice is required to obtain that which is received.

Induced Value. The users of most products and services have been led by your actions to expect certain value out of products and services. You may have suggested what the users of your products/services can expect via advertising, proposals, discussion, promises, promotions, and past performance of products/services. Guessing what users value requires you to identify these induced values for specific users or user groups. These induced values should reflect the inherent or explicit obligations included in your chosen organizational strategy. For example, as a bread manufacturer you obligated yourself to make bread available at specific times, places, and in quantities and quality expected.

Behaviorally Expressed Value. Users of your products and services express what they value by their behavior. You can infer what users value from their choices of products and services and how they use these products and services. Both those who currently use your products/services (choosers) and those who could, but chose not to (rejectors), provide a basis for making guesses about value. What do their behaviors express in terms of user value, that is, that which is realized or sacrificed, in choosing and using your products/services? Consider the following behavioral examples: (1) a person will not go across town to purchase your product because it isn't worth the trip, pain, or the like; (2) you won't stop at a fast food place if the line is over four cars long because there is a value difference between fast and slow service. What does each of these behaviors express about value?

Invalidate

To INVALIDATE requires that you attempt to disprove the correctness of previous guesses. You must adopt and perpetuate a set of activities intended to disprove your guess of what users value. It is imperative that you genuinely intend to disprove your guess. Maintaining this disposition helps you avoid manipulation or self-deceit, which might erroneously confirm your guess. Do not selectively sample users to confirm your guesses. Unfortunately, if you do, you may discover your error later, when the result of such manipulation shows up as user dissatisfaction, disapproval, or, worse yet, total rejection. The activities of INVALIDATE involve identification of rejector values and selector values, and differential significance analysis of these two sets of values.

Rejector Value and Selector Value. Rejectors are those who could, but currently do not, use your products/services.[2] Selectors are those who do currently use your products/services. Establish a plan to contact those who would be most instrumental to your strategic improvement, and who would influence your organization's short-term and long-term market and financial performance. Clarify the following: what is valued, what is realized, what are the required sacrifices to realize value, the difference between you and your competitor, and an expression of the order and significance placed on each value and sacrifice? The objective is not to determine customer satisfaction or dissatisfaction. Rather, you should seek information pertaining to the factors and rationale used in the derivation of user satisfaction and dissatisfaction. This is not a selling or telling mission but a purposefully managed reconnaissance. The purpose is to learn how to more competitively create best net value for the user. Competitors' current success in value creation must be studied through the user's perceptions. Initially, you should use the value found common to both selectors and rejectors to check

---

2. In reviewing this chapter, Bob Woodruff suggests that the idea of "rejector" can be expanded to fit more than the existing product and existing market situation, which seems to be implied. A broader set of situations should be defined by a two-by-two figure yielding four combinations of existing market versus new market on one side of the two-by-two, and existing product versus new product on the other side. In each of the four cells of this two-by-two, "rejector" has a different meaning.

the appropriateness of the measures being used to assess system performance.

Differential Order and Significance Analysis. You should conduct further analysis after gathering data from the selector and rejector groups. Next, you should analyze the differences in perceptions and the relative importance attached to these perceptions by the members of the two groups. The commonalities and differences across the selector and rejector groups should be identified, in terms of what is valued, what is realized, the required sacrifices to realize value, the difference between you and your competitor, and an expression of the order and significance placed on such values.

Discover

The competitive success of an organization may well be determined by the quality of its effort in the value determination DISCOVER activities. To DISCOVER involves the affirmation of previous guesses or the restatement of what was found to be erroneous about the guesses, and further articulation, differentiation (in terms of order and significance), and description of that which is imperative for creating user value. It is here that you either succeed or fail to learn the basis on which you are judged by the user. To the degree that you know, understand, and successfully operationalize these expectations, you will be considered for choice by users and ultimately earn the privilege of user choice over the long run. The activities of DISCOVER involve finding the following: functional value imperatives, parity imperatives, determinative differentials, continuity imperatives, switching imperatives, boundary constraints, and situational comparative mapping.

Functional Imperatives. Given any product/service, it is likely that there exists a set of user value expectations, which, if not met, represent a fundamental breach of promise to the user. An organizational system that does not ensure these functional imperatives risks the survival of the business. Examples of functional value imperatives include: a printer must print, an automobile must transport, and an insurer must insure. You should identify these functional imperatives.

Parity Imperatives. Parity imperatives represent the value that you must provide to the user in order to be equivalent to that of competing alternatives. The discovery of competitive parity imperatives is second only to functional value imperatives in strategic criticality. Both are necessary to compete and be perceived by the user as best in comparative net value.

Determinative Differentials. Obviously, in any competitive contest, your success is dependent on your ability to create a difference between you and your competitors. In a net value contest, knowledge is needed to guide the creation of value to overcome any negative gap between you and your competitors, or to further any positive gap. The most important knowledge in a net value contest is a clear understanding of what value differences determine user choice. Why do users choose one organization's products/services over another? What are the users' criteria which determine their selection of organizational products/services? You must understand the order and significance of the components of value to the user, that is, that which is realized and sacrificed. This understanding provides direction to strategic improvement in old value offerings and/or selection of new value offerings.

Continuity Imperatives. Continued and repeated use of products and services by users sustains the organization. You must seek continuity with users, and therefore you must determine what set of value expectations determine continuity of use. Why do users continue to use your products and services? Why do users continue to use the products and services of your competitors?

Switching Imperatives. Because users make choices when they switch, there must exist some set of values on which they are discriminating among alternatives. This set of values is useful in evaluating strategic improvements of current value offerings as well as additional value offerings. These become most important in a mature market with limited competitors and/or limited users. What value would justify a user switching? You must answer this question regarding existing users of competitive alternatives. Why do users switch to or from your products and services and those of your competitors?

Boundary Constraints. User value may be affected by considerations other than competitive offering. These considerations might include broad (macro) factors such as cultural norms, and economic, social, and political factors that may constrain the selector choice. You should identify any and all factors that the user might consider in selecting among value alternatives. Insight into potential influential variables must be gleaned from discussions with users and verified interpretation of their behaviors.

Situational Comparative Mapping. Refinement of your knowledge of user value will lead to the realization that what the user values varies with situations. Often, what the user values is moderated or completely changed as personal or organizational situations change. Factors closer to the person (micro) include personal values, patriotism, and personal and family economics. You must understand the situational factors that impact user values. Coincidentally, it is necessary to identify the situational factors that could significantly and negatively affect user value. Situational risk analysis, in the form of probability of occurrence of both supporting and rejecting factors, needs to be conducted on a regular basis.

Confirm

The ultimate proof of user value is to be found in the behavior of the user. User behaviors CONFIRM managerial success in creating best net value for users. Selection or choice behavior manifests the extent of perceived value. For example, continuous reselection may affirm that the user finds a product/service to be of competitive value. CONFIRMing behaviors give you the knowledge to assess the performance of organizational systems and to realign strategic focus. The results of all value determination activities, especially the CONFIRM quadrant of activities, must serve as the basis for system improvement.

User behavior can provide an understanding of current levels of user-perceived value of system outcomes. These behaviors provide insight regarding implied comparative deficiencies. However, these deficiencies may result from mistakes in value determination and system management. These mistakes include: (1) misguessing, (2) misordering (3) misinterpreting significance, (4) miscategorizing, (5) misjudging competitive strategic value responses, (6) inappropriate systems implementation, or (7) misexecution.

Comparative deficiencies may result in switching behavior by the user. Switching usually results from either a breach of producer/supplier responsibility or an extraordinary value improvement made by a competitor, or from both. Since switching can result from both events, care must be taken in interpreting this behavior. It is best to conduct a thorough investigation of the reasons for a user switching before drawing any conclusions. Once the switching behavior has occurred, subsequent user behavior reveals more information about perceived user value.

There exist many levels of perceived value. The following behaviors represent increasing levels of perceived value by users. These behaviors should CONFIRM user value and should be studied to determine the causes of and rationale for such choice behaviors. The behavior provides a means of uncovering the truly important information. Users can be grouped according to their behaviors to study their rationale and the reasons for using your products/services. What components of value, that is, that which is realized and sacrificed, lead to these behaviors? What components of value are important in getting increased levels of perceived user value and behavior? User rationale for choice must be mapped and understood. These behaviors represent the ultimate yardstick of system performance in the creation of value for users. These behaviors include sampling, preference, favoritism, continuity association, referencialism, and exclusivity.

Sampling. Sampling behavior may convey that the user perceives some potential value in your product/service but has not yet experienced it. The user may sample because of price, curiosity, or desire for a change. Upon sampling the product/service, he or she realizes some value that may be confirmed in subsequent choice behaviors.

Preference. The lowest level of value is that of being preferred. However, preference is a loose binding between the user and creator of value. Given reasonable alternatives, the users' first choice is their preference. But other products/services are, and will be, considered and selected at times. Preference smacks of objectivity and practicality.

Favoritism. Favor is given for favor received, contractually. This simple relationship may be the first level of social obligation. Implicit in this relationship between user and provider is a social contract. Objectivity and practicality become subordinate to personal reciprocity.

Continuity Association. A state is reached where the user will continue to seek out the product/service. The relationship between the producer/supplier and the user has gone beyond transaction and contract. There exists a bona fide commitment based on confidence that satisfaction will result.

Referencialism. The users hold little or no reservation about referring another potential user to your product/service. User confidence has reached a sufficient level that they consider it no risk to their reputation as competent to refer others. If asked, they willingly volunteer your organization as the most likely to deliver what is valued.[3]

Exclusivity. When exclusivity is reached, other competitors find it difficult, if not impossible, to gain the consideration of users. Exclusive use is the ultimate strategic barrier to be created for the purpose of eliminating any competitive threat. This privilege is reserved for those most responsive in creating user value.

Conclusion: There is no conclusion with these managerial activities. With the evaluation of confirming behavior, the next cycle of strategic value determination begins. Beginning with PROJECT activities, you must

---

3. The hierarchical arrangement of this classification bears further empirical testing. "Referencialism" may vary in its location in this hierarchy depending on the rigor in definition and measurement of the behavior. Past studies of word-of-mouth referrals suggest that far less commitment to product/supplier is necessary to stimulate referrals.
4. On subsequent cycles of value determination activities, management might PROJECT about each of the types of value listed in the DISCOVER quadrant. If managers had the kind of value typology listed in the DISCOVER quadrant, their "educated guesses" might be better.

continue to cycle and recycle through the activities of value determination, with increased understanding and intimacy of knowledge resulting over time.[4] This knowledge should guide the system improvement activities.

Value Opportunity Analysis

The activities of the Value Determination cycle overlap and complement those of market opportunity analysis (MOA). An MOA specifies the three following dimensions: (1) the types of information needed, (2) the sources of each type, and (3) the analysis of the information to draw conclusions about market opportunity.

Although the MOA complements the activities of value determination, this chapter does not fully present the most challenging and strategically important aspects of an MOA. Determining who the users are and should be is not as thoroughly discussed as it would be if MOA were being elaborated. The interrelationships between various components of the MOA are suggested, but not sufficiently developed from a systems perspective, that is, the market arena as a system. It would be unwise and misleading to isolate value determination from the MOA process. The MOA and marketing's role in value determination are also discussed in Chapter 23. The integration of MOA and value determination activities represents a strategic opportunity and necessity for managerial leaders, who must be willing to invest in these activities. The resulting combination of these two domains of market and value investigation may be labeled "value opportunity analysis."[5]

ORGANIZATIONAL STRATEGIC SYSTEMS MANAGEMENT

As system owner, you may use the initial guess concerning what is valued to engage in the Organizational Systems Management cycle of activities. Organizational systems management must be viewed as per-

---

5. Parallels between an MOA and value determination might be drawn. 1. The PROJECT stage addresses the second of the three MOA dimensions, that is, the sources of information, by demanding an educated guess from management (a source). 2. INVALIDATE is an imposed safeguard for overrelying on management's educated guess. Too often, managers mistakenly think they know what users value. Since starting with their own educated guesses may bias the process, managers should be prepared to consider alternatives to revise and update their knowledge. 3. DISCOVER addresses the first MOA dimension, that is, the types of information, and offers a typology of value information. However, it does not address the second MOA dimension, that is, the sources of each type. 4. CONFIRM also addresses the first MOA dimension, that is, the types of information, but offers a behavioral typology.

petual improvement activities. The initial activities of strategic systems management require the development of knowledge intended to increase understanding of existing strategic systems. Strategic system managers are required to learn about what currently exists through description and assessment of system architecture, operations, and outcomes. You should identify those organizational system elements that contribute to or detract from that which is valued, realized, and sacrificed by the users. You must ultimately control and change those elements to create increasing value for users.

This companion cycle of managerial activities also consists of four quadrants, labeled DESCRIBE, ASSESS, STANDARDIZE, and CHANGE. These four sets of activities are applied to organizational strategic systems. See Figure 1 for identification of the managerial activities composing this cycle. Managers need to DESCRIBE the specific systems, ASSESS the ability of these systems to create user value, STANDARDIZE the implementation of each system with the members of the organization to ensure its maintenance and stability, and accelerate constructive CHANGE of the strategic systems to enhance value for users. Thus, the results of user value determination must guide this work in creating, providing, and improving organizational systems.

Describe

In order to improve organizational systems, managers must first DESCRIBE strategic systems to provide understanding and familiarity with those systems. Ultimately, this understanding must be validated against reality. The following activities require you to DESCRIBE those systems: identify and scope, establish ownership, determine value contribution, diagram and justify, operationally define, establish measures/metrics, baseline, and conduct cause/result analysis.

Identify and Scope. A terse statement should identify the system, suggest the user's underlying expectation, and reflect the organization's strategy. For example, a commodity food product supplier may be required to have a "system to insure product replication." A short statement describes the objective of this system: "The user can expect to find the food purchased today to be very similiar to, if not identical to, that which they last purchased." The scope of the identified system must be determined. Of what does this system consist? With what other systems might this system interact? What is the potential interdependency of this system with other organizational systems identified as critical to the strategy of the organization? What boundaries, interfaces, relationships, interactions, and potential interdependencies exist with the other systems? An understanding of system scope helps you decide who may assist you in describing the current system, assessing the current system, standardizing the system, and changing the system.

Establish Ownership. Establishing ownership requires more than just assigning an individual's name to a system. You must clarify what you (as owner) think ownership means. What will be required of the owner? What will be required of others throughout the internal organization? What may be required of others outside the organization, for example, suppliers and government agencies.

Determine Value Contribution. Using the best guess(es) about user value made in the last three activities of the PROJECT quadrant of the Value Determination cycle (i.e., Assumed Responses, Induced Values, Behaviorally Expressed Values), you can tentatively decide about what users value. Common sense will guide this initial selection. This information can be used to determine a preliminary set of user value expectations that are required from your systems. Your systems must be managed to contribute to these value expectations.

Diagram and Justify. In diagraming the system you should convey the way it really is, not the way you would like it to be. Record your initial understanding of the parts of the system: What do they do? How do they do what they do? What result can you expect from each? Ultimately, you should confirm the validity of the diagram through observation, inquiry, and investigation. To gain knowledge, you should hold discussions with those who are part of the system or use the system and/or subsystem. As you develop a valid diagram, which is tested against reality, you can document the justification for each part of the diagram. Why is each part required? What necessitates the existence for each?

Operationally Define. An operational definition requires (1) a written statement that communicates what it takes for a product to conform to user requirements, (2) a decision criterion by which you can judge whether or not an item or group conforms to requirements, including specified sampling and test methods, measurement, and method, and (3) the ability to make a consistently correct decision on the basis of the decision criterion. You should operationally define quantitative measures to assess the ability of the currently existing system and its principal subsystems to make the value contributions represented by your best guess.

Establish Measures/Metrics. As the strategic system owner, you must establish and confirm a methodology that can be used in repeatedly assessing the system's performance. Confirming a methodology will entail examining the validity of the test methods, test instrumentation, and testers. Confirmed measures/metrics should produce data that are representative of the system parameters chosen for study. Planning data gathering is critical. You should carefully develop a competent data-gathering methodology; otherwise you run the risk of wrong decisions, suspect results, and invalid assumptions. You should test the credibility of your plan in light of its ability to reliably report the knowledge needed about your system and/or subsystem outcomes. Does the plan provide for the capture of the system's statistical variability? Will it represent the system performance?

Baseline. Using the confirmed methodology and your data-gathering plan, you can begin gathering and recording data to document (baseline) current system performance. Statistical charts are valuable in the analyses of system performance. Baselining provides information on current system performance, as well as a basis for comparison over time.

Conduct Cause/Result Analysis. As you begin to study the performance of your strategic system, you will likely observe results that the user would not value. Fishbone diagrams are useful in examining what might cause such results. While it may be premature to begin changing any system parts, since the system is not yet fully characterized, it is very appropriate to map the potentially interactive/interdependent parts of the system through cause/result analyses. You should avoid the impulse to react and tinker with the system before you understand the system causes.

Assess

The time will come to characterize the system you own fully and quantitatively. You must ASSESS the ability of these systems to create user value. Although you may not have a finally confirmed user value set, you know that some values are obvious and will prove themselves obvious in further discussion with users. To ASSESS involves the following activities: establish predictability, conduct cause and statistical effects analyses, establish management control, determine capability, and analyze comparative/competitive advantage.

Establish Predictability. Analytical methods of statistical control charts are useful in determining the current performance predictability of the valued system outcomes. You should determine whether the system outcomes are predictable using statistical control charts. In the event that the outcomes prove unpredictable, the use of cause/result analyses and Pareto analyses may prove useful in correcting such deficiencies.

Establish Management Control. Predictability doesn't necessarily confirm that the user-desired outcomes are realized. A system may produce predictable but inappropriate outcomes. You should investigate how well your now predictable system does what is desired (expected) of it. The analysis consists of comparing the anticipated predictable distribution of system outcomes to the target and limits desired (expected).

At this time, you should focus on managing the system parts so that they collectively produce predictable, desired, valued system outcomes. This may require the revision or even the elimination of some parts of the system. Such changes must be documented by the system owner. In all first-level experiments on system change, you can avoid confounding system performance information by trying many things at once.

Determine Statistical Capability. The management system owner must decide the degree of capability that will exist in his or her system. Statistical capability can be determined only when the outcomes are predictable. In addition, to the extent that the system is incapable, net value is compromised. You should calculate the statistical capability of each element of value, that which is realized and sacrificed.

Conduct Cause and Statistical Effects Analyses. At this point "capability" becomes more important. If a system-valued outcome is not capable and a decision is made to improve its capability, it will become necessary to construct cause/statistical effect diagrams. These differ from cause/result diagrams in that their contents provide insight into what might cause either (1) the average variability or (2) the extremes of variability of a given system. These diagrams provide guidance for the system owner in directing changes aimed at moving (repositioning) the average and/or reducing variability.

Analyze Competitive Value Advantage. The system owner must make every effort to glean from the value determination DISCOVERY activities any actual and/or perceived competitive value advantage held by a competitor. You should review and analyze the outcomes of DISCOVERY activities and summarize the comparative advantages and disadvantages. Although there will always be a variety of ways to create net value, the system owner must never jeopardize his or her organization by neglecting reported deficiencies.

Standardize

The results of the DESCRIBE AND ASSESS activities should be a system that is described, operationally defined, metrically manageable, and capable of ensuring best net value. Yet, this work remains incomplete if not successfully institutionalized by all contributing organizational members. Therefore, you should STANDARDIZE the implementation of the system with the members of the organization to ensure its maintainability and stability. STANDARDIZE does not mean routinize. Standardization of system architectures means managers fulfilling their obligation of verifying the operability of systems prior to releasing them for use by organizational members. It consists of providing and enabling organizational members to predictably create value for customers. Standardization is a prelude to empowerment. You should STANDARDIZE the system to ensure statistical predictability and stable system performance, which, in turn, provides a confident basis for directed, orderly, constructive, proactive system changes.

Rather than maintaining the status quo, managers must alter existing systems to meet changing demands. System standardization provides the launching pad for further improvement through change of existing systems or introduction of novel or innovative alternative systems. Organizations must be prepared continuously and constructively to flow from standardization to change, introducing and maintaining improved levels of system performance. To STANDARDIZE requires the following activities: transmit, educate, demonstrate, and institutionalize.

Transmit. A methodology must be developed through which you can transmit or impart to all supporting organizational units the system-specific needs and permissible latitudes. If you as system owner do not transmit such detailed description of system-specific needs, then you cannot justifiably hold subordinates accountable.

Educate. You should educate those who make a contribution to your system. This responsibility must not be interpreted simply as training those who make a contribution. To educate means much more. Education means a seeking of new knowledge. As system owner you should lead all others in seeking and developing new knowledge about the system, in light of its critical contribution to organization success and survival. You should learn the limitations to and/or opportunities for improving customer/user net value. This learning can be turned into constructive, purposeful, ongoing system improvements to meet and exceed value expectations.

Demonstrate. As system owner, you must demonstrate your knowledge by being capable of teaching others (who make subordinate contributions). As the architect of the system you must have a working familiarity with all parts of the system, their intricacies, and their interdependencies. You and your subordinates must be able to answer all the who, what, where, when, how, and why types of questions. Furthermore, the ultimate demonstration of education comes in the successful quantitative demonstration of a system to predictably and capably produce what is required when it is required.

Institutionalize. This demonstrated knowledge must ultimately be institutionalized or installed as part of ongoing systems. The mark of an institutionalized system is that the system should remain as part of the organization, until it is purposefully modified or replaced. It should be able to stand up, even if the developers of the system leave the organization.

Change

An organization's security and future success is related to the rate of managed change that enhances value for the users. Demonstrated system change should be the norm. You may accelerate the constructive CHANGE of the organizational systems which demonstrates enhancement of the value for users. Change of systems must provide improved creation of value for the user. You must narrow any negative gap between what the systems currently create and what customers will value in the future via systems improvement. In addition, you should eliminate the potential for any negative gap to occur.

Successful integration of value determination and systems management activities improves the creation of value for the user relative to competing alternatives, and thereby increases organizational competitiveness. All rewards, appreciation systems, and policies should promote systematic and orderly system change to increase user value. The quality of such changes must be directed toward higher and higher user behaviors that CONFIRM user value. Ideally, changes would be led by user articulation of next levels of expectations, but organizations should not be tied to this constraint. Organization initiatives may be required to anticipate new value expectations.

Proactive pursuit of system knowledge is required to CHANGE systems for improved value creation. This learning for CHANGE involves the following activities: conduct cause and value effects analyses, determine critical relationships, determine leverage points, test operational viability, conduct breakthrough analysis, and test external value impact.

Conduct Cause and Value Effects Analyses. This is the third time that causal analysis has been mentioned. (First was cause and result analysis, and second, cause and statistical effect analysis, i.e., what causes the average and/or the extremes of variability to change.) In cause and value effects analysis, another type of cause is sought. What causes user value effects to change? What causes significant improvement in value effects? What might be changed and in what way is it possible to create enhanced value? What determines the limitation of value which can be produced or supplied with the existing system?

Determine Critical Relationships. System studies must be directed in order to discover relationships between system input variables and the dependent system value outcomes. The first level of such investigations may take the form of gathering scatter diagram data, studying correlational associations, and identifying associations between system input variables (potential leverage points) and system value outcomes. This work may provide clues to system leverage points.

Determine Leverage Points. Since scatter diagrams and correlation imply association but not necessarily causation, it will be necessary to conduct studies to establish causation and to establish the effects of causal changes on dependent value outcomes. Controlled, designed experiments provide a methodology for such detective inquiries.

Test Operational Viability. Potential change options identified through systems leverage point studies may or may not prove viable to an organization. Organizational resource availability, and/or net value after investment, may not justify change. An organizational analysis must be conducted to determine viability, by identifying the factors that inhibit and facilitate the use of these system leverage points. Viability might also be tested with trend-setting user(s).

Conduct Breakthrough Analysis. While value breakthrough can result from current system studies, alternate system designs will likely be necessary. Innovation and creativity must be managed in conceptualizing, evaluating, and confidently introducing alternate systems. The credibility of new alternative systems can be judged in comparison with existing system performance. Statistical control charts and other statistical methods, for example, analysis of variance, can be used to evaluate the significance of alternative systems breakthrough. Furthermore, you should test the objective significance of statistical results against the confirmed subjective appreciation of users.

Test External Value Impact. The value impact of decisions to change current systems and/or introduce alternative systems needs to be tested. Since the users are the final judge of value, a representative group of users should be maintained with whom new value contributions can be evaluated, in terms of order and significance of value components. Practical and valid survey research instruments must be developed by which you can assess the potential effectiveness of new offerings of value.

Conclusion: There is no conclusion with regard to these managerial activities. The new potential offerings should be viewed as projected (guessed) new value of user(s) prior to testing. This begins a new cycle of value determination and strategic systems management. You should continue to manage your systems for improved user value creation.

CHAPTER 7

THE MANAGER'S JOB: A PARADIGM SHIFT TO A NEW AGENDA*

GREGORY M. BOUNDS
Research Associate, Management Development Center
University of Tennessee

GREGORY H. DOBBINS
Associate Professor of Management
University of Tennessee

SUMMARY

The classical activities of management include planning, organizing, commanding, coordinating, and controlling. Despite widespread confidence in these classical activities, continued reliance on them does not ensure organizational viability over the long term. In many organizations, reliance on the classical management activities has deteriorated into administration and maintenance of the status quo. This chapter offers alternative activities for the manager's job based on a shift to a new competitive agenda. This alternative challenges basic assumptions and requires different methods and practices. The new agenda refocuses managerial activity on improvement of strategic suprasystems and subsystems to produce and deliver valued goods and services for customers. The two themes that underlie this managerial agenda, knowledge development and continuous improvement, are discussed. For educational institutions, including business schools and executive development firms, to remain relevant, this new approach to management must be incorporated into educational curricula.

*These authors thank Mel Adams, Harlan Carothers, Angela Evans, and Earl Conway for their helpful comments on this chapter.

CHANGE TO COMPETE

There are those who dare for change and those who do not. The creativity and aspiration of those who dare prompt change in organizations. Those who do not dare stifle the initiatives of those who do. Some stifle change out of conservatism and regard for stability, continuity, and order; others do so out of complacency, habit, or dogmatism. Managerial leaders will always face these ever-present tensions between change and stability. They have to delicately balance change and stability because both are necessary for an organization to compete. The competitive conditions described elsewhere in this book dictate that many organizations make a change in management approach.[1]

What kind of change? On what information and activities should managers expend their finite mental, physical, and temporal resources? What should managers know? How should managers develop this knowledge? How have managers changed in the past few years? How should future managers be trained and educated?

The literature on classical management activities does not provide adequate answers to these questions. In the past, researchers and educators in management have focused on the classical management activities of planning, organizing, commanding, coordinating, and controlling, as introduced by Fayol (1949). Although some researchers have questioned their usefulness (e.g., Mintzberg, 1975), the classical activities are still commonly used to train managers. Continued reliance on these classical activities will not ensure organizational viability and prosperity; such reliance ensures only the status quo. In practice, the administration of existing systems through these activities distracts managers from a more important agenda.

The traditional approach to management, embodied within the classical activities, is becoming obsolescent.[2] The time has come for a paradigm shift to an improved agenda. Rather than assume the classical framework

---

1. For simplicity the terms *manager* and *managerial* are used throughout this chapter. Comments suggesting managerial responsibilities do not refer only to middle managers, and should not be taken to exclude managerial leaders, strategic leaders, or lower level supervisors. The concepts contained in this chapter generally apply to diverse managerial positions. On occasion, more specific terms are used to indicate particular relevance to managerial leaders or strategic leaders.

2. The notion of the technological life cycle suggests that a new technology enjoys a period of time wherein effort put in for this technology yields increasing benefits. Continuous incremental improvements might be made. However, at some point in time the returns start to diminish, and improvement plateaus. Further gains can be made only through a shift to a new technology, to yield discontinuous improvement or a jump to a new level.

of management as a base for refinement or elaboration, we offer an alternative framework. This new agenda can be summarized as *managing cross-functional (or transfunctional) systems for the competitive production and delivery of value for customers*. In this approach, system owners lead teams of diverse contributors in improvement for increasingly valued system outcomes.

What does cross-functional management have to do with competing? A clear example of the disastrous consequences of failure to appropriately manage a team of individual contributors comes from the 1988 Olympic Games. The 1988 Olympic 400 meter relay team was composed of the fastest athletes the world had ever seen. The world expected the U.S. team to win. With virtually any combination of four runners, the U.S. team was the "fastest" group of four individual runners. Each of the best four runners could run his or her leg of the race in unbeatable time. However, the relay race is not run and won by aggregating individual performances. The relay requires a modicum of teamwork. The baton must be passed from one runner to the next, and be done so within a prescribed stretch of the track. Winning requires timing and coordination of efforts. The U.S. team failed in this teamwork; the baton was not passed in accordance with the rules. The team failed before ever reaching the finals.

Rather than take a few star individuals and practice to master the teamwork required, the coach decided to vary team composition throughout the qualifying trials.[3] The teamwork was taken for granted. It was assumed to be adequate, but it was not. This example illustrates that even with the best available talent, while pursuing individual objectives, the "team" fails.

Even in an event that requires minimal interaction at the interfaces between individual stars, teamwork spells the difference between winning and losing. However, most organizations resemble football and basketball in their requirements for cooperation, collaboration, and integration, and teamwork is much more important. To make their organizations competitive, managerial leaders are charged with the formidable task of integrating diverse human, material, mechanical, and technological resources. This organizational task is much more challenging than the relatively simple

---

3. As reported by Carl Lewis (on "Larry King Live," July 4, 1990), the team was not managed properly. Lewis reported that the manager had used his position as Olympic coach for apparently selfish purposes. The coach reportedly induced runners to sign with him as their trainer, with the promise that they would get to run in the qualifying trials of the relay and earn a gold medal. Lewis reports that one of these runners would later contribute to the demise of the team.

task of the track coach who coordinates the handoff of a baton among four talented and highly motivated sprinters.

Integrating these diverse resources is a difficult task, but it is now required to compete. This chapter briefly addresses some of the inadequacies of past approaches and prescribes an alternative agenda. It prescribes, rather than describes, a knowledge base and some specific behaviors for managers. The approach offered in this chapter defines the manager's job in terms of this competitive agenda, that is, learning about and continuously improving organizational systems for customer value. Prior to elaborating this new competitive agenda, we briefly review the classical management approach and agenda process.

THE MANAGER'S JOB AS CURRENTLY CONCEIVED

Recently, we reviewed ten of the leading Introduction to Management textbooks published in 1989 or 1990. We found that all ten of them were organized around Fayol's classical activities. The only exception was that Fayol's term *commanding* was replaced by more contemporary terms like *directing* or *leading*. Fayol's five major activities are described below.

Planning, in both the short and long term, is the process of determining in advance what should be accomplished and how it should be accomplished. Planning requires managers to set goals and strategies. *Organizing* is the process of prescribing relationships between people and resources in order to accomplish goals. It involves grouping activities and resources in a logical fashion. *Commanding* is the process of influencing or affecting the behavior of others. It involves getting members of the organization to work effectively to accomplish the organization's goals. *Coordinating* is the process of adjusting the activities of independent groups to ensure harmonious action. Coordination is essential if the independent work of groups is to blend together to accomplish the organization's overall goals and objectives. Finally, *controlling* is the process of comparing actual performance with standards and taking any necessary corrective action.

Research on the Classical Activities

Over the past thirty years, researchers have used a variety of descriptive approaches to study the behavior of managers.[4] The major conclusion of

4. Examples of descriptive methods include direct observation of managers, asking managers to keep diaries of their daily activities, and conducting interviews with managers focusing on their typical activities.

this research is that, although examples of the classical activities may be observed, much of the work of managers is not easily classified according to the classical activities. The work of managers tends to be episodic and punctuated by disjointed verbal communications with a variety of people. There are numerous interruptions, and much of a manager's behavior is reactive, driven by crisis and salient problems, rather than proactive. Managers are constantly interrupted by subordinates, peers, and superiors, and have to respond immediately to problems with production, personnel, customers, and suppliers. In addition, managers' activities tend to be strikingly brief and fragmented, wherein managers respond to the needs of the moment. Planning may appear disjointed since it is often difficult to find the long periods of uninterrupted time that are necessary for this activity. In addition, most information is most often gathered informally, through brief, often unplanned, verbal encounters (Mintzberg, 1975).

The above description of managerial work verges on chaos. It also suggests confusion about what managers actually do. Observation of managers reveals that their activities are not easily categorized into the classical activities. However, such disjointed behaviors are consistent with observations (discussed below) that managers operate under a self-developed "managerial agenda".

Managerial Agenda

Although managers' highly interpersonal and informal activities appear fragmented, purposeless, and wasteful, there may be method to their madness. Several writers agree that managers work from an individually developed framework. This framework has been called an agenda (Kotter, 1982), foci of attention (Stewart, 1982), programs locked deep inside a manager's head (Mintzberg, 1975), lists of concerns (Elliot, 1959), and thrusts (Peters, 1979). All these orientations indicate that managers have desired objectives they are trying to move toward. The fragmented and reactive managerial activities described above may serve as a means of developing this agenda and the network of relationships needed to implement the agenda. This agenda process may be seen as a mutation of the classical planning function.

Guided by their developed agenda, managers episodically pursue selected activities and purposes. Based on performance, their current knowledge base, and key management skills or competencies, managers revise their agenda. Further agenda revision, continued cycles of activity, performance, and subsequent agenda revision ensue. The classical management activities may be regarded as the means used by the manager to fulfill his or her agenda. Figure 1 presents the agenda revision and fulfillment process.

THE FAILURE OF CLASSICAL ACTIVITIES AND MANAGERIAL AGENDA

A recent review of management textbooks and curricula reveals the widespread belief that "the classical functions [activities] still represent the most useful way of conceptualizing the manager's job, especially for

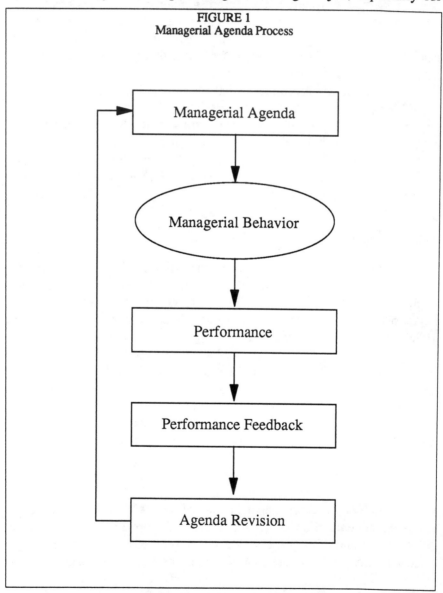

FIGURE 1
Managerial Agenda Process

management education" (Carrol and Gillen, 1987: 48). This belief may seem plausible for the manager's job as currently practiced. However, the classical activities are not currently the most useful way of guiding organizations toward a more competitive future. The classical approach is inadequate because it is maintenance oriented, prescribes the future to be the same as the past, allows arbitrary agenda setting, and treats customer value as incidental. These issues are discussed below.

Maintenance Oriented

The classical activities and typical agendas of managers are maintenance oriented. A maintenance-oriented organization is one wherein the managers, along with the rest of the organization, administer existing procedure, policies, and tactics. Managers accept the structures and broader systems of the organization as givens, as unchangeable constraints within which to optimize performance. The adaptability of the organization to its environment gets ignored. "Managers" often engage in firefighting or problem solving to ensure system maintenance, but these activities do not constitute improvement. The managerial agenda of a competitive organization must reflect the quest for competitive improvement. Competitive improvement has to be a central thread in a manager's agenda. Managers should be proactive, not simply reactive. The term *manager* does not mean "administrator" or "problem solver." Controlling and problem solving to maintain stability in current systems does not suffice for competitiveness because of the need for change and improvement.

Prescribes the Future the Same as the Past

Mintzberg (1975, p. 54) made a damning observation about upper echelon managers:

> Executives . . . are fundamentally indistinguishable from their counterparts of a hundred years ago (or a thousand years ago, for that matter). The information they need differs, but they seek it in the same way – by word of mouth. Their decisions concern modern technology, but the procedures they use to make them are the same as the procedures of the nineteenth-century manager.

Regardless of whether management practices have changed in the last century, circumstances can and do change. Current circumstances are characterized by greater demand for higher quality, reduced costs, and better service and delivery, in an environment of short product life cycles and high technology turnover, with growing pools of international competitors. Customers increasingly demand that producers of goods and services do more with less. In such a dynamic environment, organizations may not survive, and will certainly prosper less, by adhering to the status quo.

The classical conceptualizations of managerial activities, as derived from Fayol, merely describe managerial practices as they have been observed in the past. It seems as though researchers observed and described managerial actions and then, over time, concluded that their descriptions (what is done) represented prescriptions (what should be done). Developing prescriptions from a normative description of that which currently exists represents a circular activity that preserves the status quo. Such conceptualizations will not be adequate in the future. Researchers can no longer afford contentedly to describe current practices, but must invent and discover new approaches to management that meet today's competitive challenges. Correspondingly, managers must engage in practices to achieve improvement.

Allows Arbitrary Agenda Setting

Establishing and maintaining a focused, relevant managerial agenda can be a critical component for enhancing organizational competitiveness. An organization can no longer afford to rely on its managers' uncertain and often arbitrary agenda development process as the cornerstone of its future viability. Managers should have a specifically prescribed agenda pertinent to organizational competitiveness.

The setting of a managerial agenda should be guided neither by individual predispositions nor by the situations, episodes, and problems of today. Managers may work diligently and successfully on the problems of today and still have their organization go out of business tomorrow.

Numerous social scientists (e.g., Katz and Kahn, 1978) have pointed out the danger of assuming that an individual's goals will be synonymous with those of the organization. Human beings are typically most concerned for their own good and that of their own social group. Individual and social needs are powerful motivators of behavior which may induce managers to adopt goals and courses of action that undermine the good of the larger organization. Agenda setting will be influenced by these individual concerns and, therefore, must not be left to chance or be left unchecked. An arbitrary agenda may be gravely inconsistent with the organization's competitiveness goals. A competitive organization does not result from the summation of many arbitrary and idiosyncratic agendas of individual managers which may be uncommon or unintegrated.

Treats Customer Value as Incidental

Classical approaches to management treat the job of continuous improvement for customer value as incidental. Competitive organizations will enhance the priority and intensity of this work beyond that implied by traditional descriptions of managerial work. Producing and delivering value for customers must be more than incidental; it must be intentional, purposefully pursued, and consistent.

Managing an organization for customer value requires attention to many causes that determine system outcomes. This task can be overwhelming for any individual who assumes responsibility for the performance of the overall organization, or even for a single system. How does a manager or leader handle this problem? Managers often adopt proven methods and approaches from other sciences for application in their organizations. One such approach adopted by management, often with unfortunate consequences, is reductionism.

Reductionism. As the term implies, a reductionist approach to management involves breaking a complex whole into discrete and manageable elements. Ideally, mastery of the elements allows mastery of the whole. Many scientific breakthroughs have resulted from this approach, for example, in atomic theory and biochemistry. However, there are limits to reductionism in science and management.

In a reductionistic approach to management, the organization is broken down into "manageable" pieces, with explicit task descriptions, individual objectives, and narrowly defined measures of performance for each piece. The pieces are then passed off or delegated to subordinates who report to a manager. This "divide and control" approach to management assumes that the manageable pieces should be run by specialists, who master their respective piece. The specialists are accountable to do the best they can to operate their piece of the organization as measured by specifically focused goals, objectives, and quotas.

Meanwhile, the overseers of this divided organization "manage" by watching production numbers, with centralized vertical information flows and feedback through the hierarchy in the form of written and verbal reports, and oversee the results of subordinate operations through various control systems. They control the organization through budgetary allocation and various outcome reporting systems that keep tabs on operations, and they reveal deviations from budgeted standards. Management hierarchically coordinates and controls the work activities of various specialist groups to meet internally driven goals and objectives. They assume that performance on all the pieces will add up to overall organization performance, for example, financial performance as shown by increased profit, return on investment, or return on assets. Periodic planning sessions are conducted, employing forecasting models and planning strategies, to craft a "plan" to ensure forecasted performance, which is measured in financial terms. The results are heavy on "goals and objectives" and light on the means of how to achieve them through the systems, processes, and business operations. Individual agendas are freely self-determined, whereas each manager independently pursues the goals and objectives in any way he or she sees fit. Managers do not collaborate with those in other processes, or with customers, but strive to produce the numbers that are attended to by their superior, the "real" customer. As long as subordinates adhere to standards and make reasonable progress toward goals, they do not expect to be bothered with inquiries from superiors.

Hampers Integrated Efforts for Customer Value. In the traditional reductionist approach described above, customer value is considered, at worst, a necessary evil delivered to meet financial goals. At best, customer value is genuinely important to managers, but it is assumed to result automatically when individual units accomplish their individual objectives. Too often, no manager orchestrates the organizational activities of various individuals, departments and functions to ensure integrated and competitive provision of value for customer. Rather, the activities of various functions are coordinated through the hierarchy. An overseeing manager relies on conflict resolution to handle problems that are brought to his or her attention by disgruntled or quarreling subordinates. This approach to management assumes that the best outcomes for the whole organization are achieved by balancing the diverse initiatives and needs of the various functions. At best, functional interfaces, across functional boundaries, are managed by the involved parties themselves for mutual accommodation and compromise to allow peaceful coexistence. Typically, no one "owns" and manages the entire system for customer value.

The above description, though an oversimplification, is not far removed from reality. In fact, this results-oriented approach to management has proliferated with the rise of functional specialists to organizational power in the 1950s through the 1980s. The unfortunate consequences of this "divide and control" management mentality often include factionalism, internal competitions, subversions, passivity, myopia, negative stereotyping, and functional prejudice among various functions, departments, and individuals. These consequences are usually created by poorly designed systems put in place by well-intentioned managers.

These organizational circumstances are all the more damaging when the organization is required to institute radical changes in order to remain competitive. The use of a reductionist approach can delay or preclude the implementation of new ways of operating that could improve its competitive position. In essence, the organization becomes bound up in its own knickers, strapped to outmoded policies and deficient systems that remain unimproved, and manned by a band of lone rangers, each with his or her own agenda. Consider the difficulties such an organization might have in implementing changes that are inherently multifunctional and inter-departmental, for example, a Just-in-Time (JIT) manufacturing strategy.

JIT places extreme demands on an organization, in terms of lead times, inventory reduction, equipment reliability, and balanced flows. Simply pressuring the traditional functions to "do better" does not suffice, espe-cially when traditional control systems are still in place. Purchasing may have a mandate to grant low-bid supplier contracts, without consideration of quality and delivery capabilities. Infrequent and large order quantities of incoming material with inconsistent quality preclude or nullify JIT from a manufacturing perspective. To maintain high efficiencies and utilization rates and still meet delivery schedules, production managers may be encouraged to anticipate uncertainty regarding incoming materials and the incapability of machines and processes and respond by building inventories as a buffer. With scrap and rework built into standards, errors and waste are tolerated. Setup costs remain high and unimproved, so high inventories and long production runs are commonly used to reduce unit costs. All these parochial actions are incompatible with JIT.

These circumstances preclude any action by individuals to move toward JIT. None of the departmental or functional managers will be inclined to risk their own necks. Unilateral action by either purchasing or production to move toward JIT can be punished with poor evaluations on their traditional performance measures and control systems. The critical agenda for top managers is to work on overall systems, to pull in participa-tion and contribution from all functional and departmental managers. Only then can leaders expect integration of diverse functional activities and processes.

Avoiding Reductionism

Managers cannot simply manage through reductionism. Competitive approaches require that managerial jobs expand to encompass more of the value-providing system as a whole. This value-providing system includes the diverse activities from all the individuals, departments, functions, processes, or subsystems that contribute to or detract from customer value.

A core set of demands should be placed on the manager, and these demands should be synonymous with the long-term needs of the organiza-tion, as well as be acceptable to the individual manager. A manager should have a prescribed work agenda. We recommend prescription but caution against dogma and rigidity. Managers should have some flexibility to pursue other agenda items as afforded by the constraints and choices of the situation. In addition, the manner in which the manager pursues this agenda should be flexible enough to allow use of his or her individual strengths and idiosyncratic style.

What should this prescribed agenda be? The thrust of the managerial agenda centers on identifying what the customer values and in creating, developing, and continuously improving organizational systems that provide that value to the customer. Some managers are already shifting to this new agenda. Consider how Buick demonstrated that the promise of improved value can affect a customer's purchase decisions, which ultimately determine organizational prosperity. "Sales of Buick LeSabre rose 4% last year – vs. a decline of 6.6% for the division as a whole – after Buick began promoting the car's No. 2 position in J. D. Power's 1989 ranking of manufacturing quality" (*Fortune*, February 26, 1990).

Continuous improvement also yields benefits that directly contribute to operating margins or profit and improves the marketability of products. For example, Giddings and Lewis assembled a "cross-functional team" to simplify and revamp its Masterline lathe, an industrial metal-cutting tool. "The team designed a tool that performs as well as the old one but costs $171,000, or 35%, less" (*Fortune*, May 21, 1990: 56). Anecdotal evidence also comes from leaders such as John Pepper, president of Procter and Gamble: "We started, as most companies have, focusing on processes and systems in manufacturing – improving reliability. The improvements in quality and savings that have come from that have literally been worth hundreds of millions of dollars" (Pepper, 1990).

Unfortunately, traditional reward and control systems encourage reductionist management which takes system performance for granted. Linking rewards and punishments to individual and other narrowly focused evaluations impedes the teamwork, collaboration, integration, and coordination needed for accomplishing organizational objectives. These reward and control systems worsen the effects of the "divide and control" approach to management.

Narrow goal definitions and individualized performance appraisals encourage the individual to pursue self-interests rather than group interests. The organization may resemble a constellation of fragmented and warring tribes rather than collaborative and united members of the same body. When the goals of different groups are in conflict, or are mutually exclusive, competition and hostilities tend to rise between the groups (Aronson, 1980). The addition of performance appraisal and contingent rewards and punishments increases the tensions and frustrations. These tensions may be relieved by aggression, subversion, or passive resistance.

Unfortunately, once this dynamic is set in motion, the mere removal of the competitive conditions may not eliminate the hostilities, which may endure for years. Simply forcing the groups to interact may not diffuse hostilities and distrust. Forced interaction does not ensure cooperation and integrated effort. As an example, consider the racial violence and turmoil associated with public school integration in the 1960s. One effective means of insuring integration and cooperation is to impose circumstances that require mutual interdependence for the accomplishment of superordinate goals. Team sports served as an arena to bring the races together. A similar requirement for teamwork, collaboration, and integration of efforts for mutually valued outcomes can have a similar effect within organizations.

Such an arrangement has a higher chance of success if it is seen as nonreversible; that is, uproar, subversion, and resistance will not result in the reinstallation of former circumstances. People either convince themselves that they can live with the new circumstances, or they leave (owing to the psychology of inevitability). Over time, through mutual exposure, understanding, and interdependency, old prejudices can be revised and new behaviors emerge.

In organizations, the organization leaders must create the new circumstances requiring integrated effort toward system outcomes. Leaders must change the behavioral requirements and managerial culture, as well as the management systems that demand and support the behavior, for example, appraisal, reward, and information systems. Furthermore, leaders must lead by assuming personal responsibility for the strategic systems of producing and delivering goods and services. Simply mandating behavioral changes without changing other aspects of the organization will not suffice. Managerial leaders are accountable for changing the organization. No one else can do it.

In response to competition, many managerial leaders have responded with "programs" or "processes" that are often regarded as "extracurricular," sideline activities, or remedial treatments that promise to hasten recovery faster than the world's greatest snake oil. Leaders "apply the antidote liberally," prompt others to the task, and sit back to await the results. Unfortunately, the alphabet soup of methodologies and techniques has enhanced confusion and has proved disappointing for many companies. Managers are often left with no idea of which or how many acronyms it takes to spell success from the rapidly multiplying list, for example, SPC, TQM, QFD, ABC, MBO, MRP, JIT, CAD, CAM, MOA, QWL. Some of these methods and techniques are quite useful but still represent only partial answers.

Jumping from program to program yields, at best, partial solutions and fatigued jumpers. Even worse, the implementation of many programs simultaneously can be especially disappointing, since such an approach typically suffers the effects of reductionist management. Many managers falsely assume that each program incrementally and proportionately improves the organization's competitiveness, as if each contributes independently. But these programs often become competing efforts, vying for resources and managerial attention, detracting from an organization's competitive capabilities. Only the comprehensive management of strategic systems will ensure that all parts fit into the whole. Any special programs, methods, or techniques must be integrated, mutually compatible, complementary, and orchestrated by managerial leaders to contribute to the customer value. Managers may choose either to persist in the quest for the modern-day miracle salve or to roll up their sleeves and pursue a challenging, less glamorous agenda. The new managerial agenda, alluded to earlier, is more fully described below.

MANAGERIAL AGENDA FOR CUSTOMER VALUE AND ORGANIZATIONAL COMPETITIVENESS

Although specific assignments may vary, every managerial agenda should be directed toward competitively providing value for customers.[5] This proposed agenda outlines the demands on the managers and leaders of a competitive organization. This agenda may also serve as a guide for the curriculum in managerial education for business schools and executive development firms. The items for this customer-driven managerial agenda include the following:

- A customer value-driven strategic management process
- Selection of strategic systems for customer value
- Determination of the value customers derive from the systems
- Improvement of the systems for customer value

To properly execute this agenda of managerial behaviors, managers need knowledge, understanding, skills, and abilities for

- Strategy formulation and implementation
- Concepts and methods of value determination
- Concepts and methods of system improvement
- Managing the effects of variation within systems
- Experimentation to learn about systems

---

5. Other chapters in this book address the managerial agenda for managers of various positions of the organization.

- Interpersonal and organizational leadership

To install and sustain this managerial agenda, managers craft the following social mechanisms of organization:

- Role definitions, perceptions, and relationships
- Managerial structures and systems
- Organizational culture

Organizational Chemistry

The dynamic relationship among all the above agenda items is modeled in Figure 2. The model employs the analogy of a chemical reaction. In this "chemical reaction," the managerial behavior is the basic phenomenon of interest. Managerial behavior improves the systems that competitively produce and deliver value for customers. The organizational chemist wants to generate this behavior from available, controllable elements. The essential elements are the knowledge, understanding, skills, and abilities of the individual managers. These elements represent potential that may or may not be translated into observable changes in behavior. These essential elements remain inert and nonvolatile, producing no behavior changes until the catalysts are introduced.

The catalysts include the social mechanisms of organization, for example, role perceptions, reporting systems, rewards, and various other aspects of culture. The primary catalyst is role perception. The manager

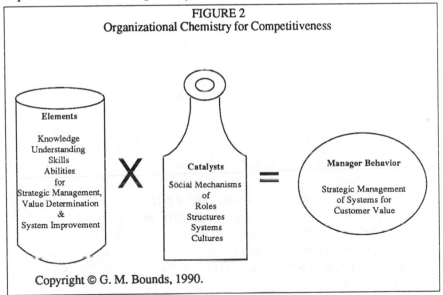

FIGURE 2
Organizational Chemistry for Competitiveness

Elements

Knowledge
Understanding
Skills
Abilities
for
Strategic Management,
Value Determination
&
System Improvement

X

Catalysts

Social Mechanisms
of
Roles
Structures
Systems
Cultures

=

Manager Behavior

Strategic Management
of Systems for
Customer Value

Copyright © G. M. Bounds, 1990.

must be convinced that "system improvement" and "value determination" define his or her job. Otherwise, the desired behaviors never result, and potential remains unrealized. In a chemical reaction a catalyst acts as a stimulus to make a result possible or hasten a result. Just as the addition of a catalyst enables or hastens the rate of chemical reaction, the addition of catalytic social mechanisms enhances the behavior in organizational chemistry. The addition of one catalytic social mechanism, such as redefining managerial jobs and roles, yields some increase in the desired behavior. The addition of other catalysts, such as reporting, rewards, information systems, and resources, yields and sustains higher rates of change in the desired behavior.

Although quite simplistic and limited, this analogy illustrates some basic principles of organizational change. For example, the multiplication sign implies an interaction between the elements and the catalysts in the organizational chemistry equation, rather than simple addition. If one of the variables, for example, knowledge, skills, and abilities, is zero, then the multiplication yields zero. (Addition would imply something greater than zero.) This multiplicative relationship implies leaders can train all they want, but if they do not demand and reward new behavior, they do not get it.

Models provide guidance. However, the complexities of organizational chemistry require thought and action to produce the desired behavior. Continuous learning, thinking, and action are required to pursue the two general themes that underlie the above list of agenda items: (1) knowledge development and (2) continuous improvement. These themes are discussed below.

Knowledge Development Agenda

Since their organizations depend on the environment, managerial leaders must lead the learning process to know their various constituents and their organizational systems. The specific knowledge requirements about (1) the environment and (2) organizational systems are discussed below.

Organizations Depend on the Environment. The relationship between the organization and its environment is very important in setting the managerial agenda. Organizations are open systems, receiving inputs and delivering outputs to others in the environment. They are in a constant state of flux with the environment and are dependent on the environment for the energy that sustains them. Organizations may be conceived as an energetic input-output system in which the return from the output to the environment reactivates the system. As long as the organization transforms inputs into an outcome that is demanded or valued by an outside group or system, then the organization remains viable, and even prospers. However, if the organization is unable to create outcomes that are valued by external constituents, then the organization will not receive needed inputs and will be unable to continue operation. Managerial leaders identify and understand the strategic suprasystems that ensure the production and delivery of valued goods and services. (Carothers and Adams discussed these strategy formulation and implementation processes earlier in Chapter 3.)

In organizations that manage for customer value, the managers engage in activities seldom emphasized by researchers and theorists of the managerial job, for example, knowing the environment. As was noted by one CEO, "a major determinant of success for a manager is knowledge of the customer, knowledge of the organization's culture and technology, and general knowledge of economic and political conditions" (Carroll and Gillen, 1987, p. 48). Such knowledge is important, and it should not be taken for granted. Managerial leaders are responsible for systematically collecting data that provide information about environmental conditions.

Leaders Lead Learning. Managers today operate in increasingly competitive organizational environments. They sift through potentially relevant information and study the information most pertinent to organizational competitiveness. Word-of-mouth data gathering and informal, "intuitive" analysis do not suffice. The knowledge development must be systematic and purposeful.

Managerial leaders assume ownership and responsibility for identifying customers and developing knowledge of what these customers value. These leaders determine the desired features and the sacrifices associated with the acquisition and use of their products and services (Zeithaml, 1988). Developing such an agenda requires more than the occasional venture from the office, casual stroll through the plant, or watching performance outcomes. Responsibility for determining what customers value cannot be wholly delegated to the marketing department. Managerial leaders must engage in value determination and intimately know, understand, and own the results of such activity.

These leaders engage in a thoughtful, inquisitive, and collaborative investigation of how their customers use their products or services. Information gathering must be purposeful, planned, and extensive. Traditional methods that simply rely on engineered specifications are not adequate. Episodic, brief, unplanned, informal contacts will not suffice. Satisfaction or dissatisfaction surveys are not adequate. Reliance on customer complaints is inadequate, because complaints do not always accompany the failure of the product or service to meet customer needs or desires. Rather than complain, customers may simply switch suppliers.

To build a comprehensive body of knowledge about customer value, on-site visits and thorough analysis of customer applications, processes, and end use are required. Complex analytical approaches may also be necessary.

In addition, a competitive environment requires that managers *anticipate* the future needs of customers and not just react to customer surveys of expressed needs. Leaders must anticipate customer needs. This kind of information on customer needs may not come easily. Although some of this knowledge comes as intuitively obvious, or through imagination, much of it results from engaging in an arduous process of customer value determination.

Although managerial leaders should manage by facts and make informed decisions, they should not be paralyzed by analysis. They must know when to make a decision and when to defer a decision for further analysis. A judicious mixture of spontaneity and deliberation is most often required, and managerial leaders must determine when each ingredient is appropriate. Consider one example of a leader who has sought such a mixture. Burger King's CEO, Barry Gibbons, displayed decisive leadership in a turnaround effort when he "ignored roars of protest from his marketing department and launched a broiled-chicken sandwich without the usual 18 months of market tests." In addition to "going with the gut" when the time was right, Gibbons also formalized intelligence activities by setting up an information system to gather 80,000 "snapshots" of "value to the customer" every month. The methods of data collection include surveys and an 800-number hot line, to gather data from employees, suppliers, and customers on a regular basis. Displaying creativity, Gibbons also hired "mystery customers" to dine in every Burger King once a month and report their dining experiences (*Fortune*, July 16, 1990: 36-44).

Know the Various Constituents. Consumers of products and services are not the only environmental constituents with whom managers should concern themselves. During the years of deregulation of the airline industry, airline companies were thrust into a much more competitive market. Airline managers adopted many strategies to give their companies a competitive advantage. Several airline managers had the foresight to invest in a creative form of vertical integration between suppliers and customers through computerization. By providing computer reservation systems to travel agencies, an airline could use incentives and penalties to ensure that travel agencies complied with their quotas for reservations and tickets.

Constituents vary in their opinions about the value of the computer reservation systems. This creative and proactive system helps to secure market share for the airline, and thus serves the financial needs of stockholders and employees. However, the overall value to the flying public is less clear. Certainly, the travel agency may not always sell the least expensive ticket to the flying customer or arrange the most convenient flight. In addition, competitors not fortunate enough to have invested in these systems regard them as unfair. Investigating U.S. Senator John C. Danforth perceives these systems as unfair to competitors and the public and states that "it gives an airline a certain competitive advantage." This result should come as no surprise: deregulation was intended to establish competitive conditions. However, legislators threaten to force airlines to divest these computer reservations, which the airlines created in an attempt to adapt and compete, that is, to pursue a competitive advantage under freer market conditions. This illustrates that managers should attend not only to the needs of end users of their products and services, and stockholders, but also to those of other constituents, for example, regulatory bodies. The other constituents may perceive "value" differently and may assume responsibility for protecting their own and the public's interests. Even constituents within the flying public disagree about value. These diverse perceptions of value must be understood for managerial leaders to make wise strategic decisions about value offerings.

The auto industry provides another example of how companies often have to balance and integrate the demands of various external constituents with their long-term strategy. An automobile producer may continue to offer compact cars even though these offerings may bring little or no profit. The producer may decide to offer a full line of automobiles, including compacts and subcompacts to attract first-time buyers, to provide dealers with a full line, and to compensate for gas guzzlers and to maintain federally mandated corporate fuel economy averages (*Fortune*, February 26, 1990). Decisions about "value" for particular constituents require a lot of thought and should not be made independently.

Know the Systems. To produce and deliver value for customers, managers develop a profound knowledge of the systems and processes and understand the leverage points. The methods for developing this knowledge are discussed more thoroughly in this book by Carothers, Bounds, Sanders, Kirby, and Parr, and will not be repeated here. This responsibility for knowledge development of organizational systems joins the responsibility for value determination as a mandatory part of the managerial agenda.

With a basis of knowledge and understanding, managers can begin the continuous process of improving the value offered customers and the means by which value is created for customers. Thus, continuous improvement is the second theme that underlies the managerial agenda, and rests on the first theme, knowledge development.

Continuous Improvement Agenda

The Many Faces of "Control." Traditional approaches to management have emphasized control. However, the word "control" may be used to convey several meanings, for example, engineering control, statistical control, budgetary control, and control of variances. Managers may not consider the control they have over individuals through organizational systems, assuming that they have little control over their people. In contrast, managers have a great deal of "control" over the people who produce and deliver value for the organization's customers. This "control" exists because the managers, either knowingly or unknowingly, create the systems and culture within which these people work.

The systems of the organization determine the limitations and opportunities that employees encounter. For example, available technology influences operational practices; resources constrain actions; policies influence decisions; rewards induce behavior; flow design determines work patterns; and training and education determine knowledge and skill levels. These systems greatly impact individual behaviors, decisions, and activities.

According to classical management theory, "To control means seeing that everything occurs in conformity with established rule and expressed command" (Fayol, 1949). The classical control function implies staying on course, adhering to standards, and preventing change. Indeed, such control is a necessary part of organizational continuity. However, when control becomes a driving force, it precludes change.

Traditional approaches to control have relied on monitoring and reacting to unfavorable variances or deviations from standards and specifications. Certainly, a variance indicates departure from standard, which may be undesirable and not be allowed to persist. "But, the converse, i.e., that absence of a variance means all's well, 'ain't necessarily so'" (Juran, 1964). Furthermore, defining variance in terms of engineered or internally derived standards may be risky. These standards may permit more variation around targets than customers will tolerate, may encourage waste, or may be infrequently revised.

When the managerial agenda is unspecified, managers tend to "manage by walking around," responding to the most salient cues or red flags, which most often come in the form of "crises" or "today's alligator." Crisis management and recurrent problem solving can easily consume a manager's day. Crisis-driven activities distract a manager from system improvement. Frequent crises and recurrent problems represent a symptom that current systems are deficient or broken. The preoccupation with variances blinds managers to opportunity cost, that is, the loss of opportunity for improvement or breakthrough in the capability to meet improved standards. Managers have an alternative to blindly leading their organizations into corporate demise by chasing variances, while competitors rewrite and meet new standards.

Improve Systems for Customer Value. Managers have often pursued continuous improvement, but the focus has often been on one or a few dimensions of value, for example, cutting costs, increasing labor efficiencies, or increasing productivity. Costs, efficiencies, and productivity are important, but singular focus on one or a few dimensions of value may lead managers to ignore other dimensions. Thus, system improvement may not always involve doing things faster and with fewer people, although these measures are often important. Consider the following examples.

By emphasizing quality, Heinz managers stand conventional cost-cutting logic on its head. Heinz managers discovered that cost-cutting with the uncalculated swing of an insensitive ax can do a lot of damage. Conversely, they found that unconventional means such as *adding* workers and *slowing down* a production line can boost effectiveness. J. Wray Conolly [a senior vice-president at Heinz] estimates that these and other actions will save Heinz at least $250 million a year by the mid-1990s (*Fortune*, April 9, 1990).

Attempting to reduce the costs of operations, Heinz cut the workforce at its StarKist tuna canning factories in Puerto Rico and American Samoa by 5 percent. Faced with competition from low-wage rivals in Thailand, reducing labor costs seemed to make sense. However, the overworked fish cleaners who remained on the job left tons of meat on the bone every day. Conolly states: "We discovered that we had to add people, not subtract them. In the past, we just wouldn't have done that." StarKist slowed down the production lines, hired 400 hourly workers and 15 supervisors, retrained the entire workforce, and installed four more production lines to reduce the burden of each worker and to expand volume. These measures increased labor costs by $5 million, but it eliminated $15 million in waste, for an annual savings of $10 million.

Managers at Heinz's Ore-Ida potato processing plants discovered that declining sales in Tater Tots had resulted from years of cost-cutting that had changed the product's taste and texture. High-speed slicing machines sped the potatoes through the plant but also diced some of them too fine, which makes Tater Tots mushy instead of chunky. The Ore-Ida managers slowed down the production lines to churn out more uniform morsels. "Efficiency went down, but effectiveness went up. ... Tater Tots now taste the way they used to, and the increased sales volume – up 8.8% in the past year – has more than paid for the cost of going slow" (*Fortune*, April 9, 1990).

These examples illustrate that the interrelationships and tradeoffs among the components of value for customers, stockholders and employees, and other constituents must be carefully studied and understood. Management decisions also depend on the nature of the work required and the technology available, and many other aspects of the organizational systems that ultimately determine value for customers. Wise decisions require an enlightened management team, with knowledge based on intimate understanding of value and the means of creating that value.

The Multifunctional Nature of Systems. Managers must implement a systems improvement agenda. The task of systems management is challenging because of the interdepartmental and multifunctional nature of the systems that produce and deliver value for customers (Deming, 1986; Imai, 1986; Juran, 1964). These systems involve diverse activities from units such as product engineering, process engineering, accounting, marketing, logistics, procurement, maintenance, and production. Other chapters in this book seek to explain what it means to improve systems, how to start, and how to continue (e.g., those by Carothers, Toomey, Bounds, and Kirby). Such an agenda is purposeful and directed toward improving the means of creating value for the customer.

Attention, Thought, and Action Are Required. The nature of organizations is that they tend to grow; they also tend to decay if left unattended. Systems within organizations also change over time. Without managerial attention, systems may change for the worse and drift from their original intent. As mentioned earlier, system managers develop knowledge about how to produce and deliver value for the customer. This requires focused, purposeful attention to the details of operations. Analytical techniques familiar to statisticians and engineers may become increasingly necessary, for example, flowcharts, Pareto diagrams, cause/effect diagrams, statistical control charts. Not only should managers analyze existing systems to determine needed changes, but they must often create or synthesize new systems to improve customer value. Existing systems, which are inadequate or obsolete, have to be discarded in deference to newly created systems. As is true of the process of customer value determination, systems management is a cyclical and never-ending process. Managers are responsible for ensuring that their subordinates have been equipped with systems that work.

Reactive Management Is Deficient. The typical crisis-driven activity, wherein a manager spends a lot of time and energy responding to recurrent problems, or "firefighting," is symptomatic of the failure to successfully manage organizational systems. Hyperreactivity indicates system deficiency. The very existence of recurring problems and crises reflects the failure of managers to develop organizational systems. Management by walking around or simply monitoring outcomes is not adequate. There must be increased attention to the means of achieving outcomes.

Episodic, disjointed, and problem-driven managerial activity is not adequate nor is problem solving adequate. Problem solving is contingent on identifying a problem or an unacceptable deviation. For managers with a problem-solving orientation, absence of a problem breeds complacency, which breeds inactivity, and continuous improvement does not take place. With a problem-solving orientation, while looking for problems, managers may fail to see opportunities.

Problem solving and crisis resolution are two different events. Crisis resolution represents fixing the immediate situation, as in firefighting, just so normal operations can continue. For example, a sander belt may break and jam the sander machine. Removing the belt and unjamming the machine puts out the fire for now, but the fire may recur. Problem solving represents finding the cause of the problem and addressing the cause so that the problem does not recur. For example, problem solving may entail ensuring that the belt is of the right size and quality, and operated at the prescribed speed. Or it may entail repairing a malfunctioning sander that was causing breakage. Thus, problem solving involves removing the source of the fire, the smoldering embers. Note, however, that both crisis resolution and problem solving are prompted by deficiencies in the current system. By contrast, system improvement requires rethinking of the system. The system is not just repaired and maintained, but changed, perhaps by redesigning the system to eliminate belts or redesigning the part to eliminate the need to sand.

Problems and crises must certainly be solved. Resolving crises or addressing salient problems is not sufficient to remain competitive. Rather, proactively and continuously improving systems for customer value does enhance competitiveness. The work of managers may occasionally appear disjointed, fragmented, and crisis driven. However, managers should spend much less time responding to the needs of the moment, problem solving, and chasing variances. They should become less reactive and more proactive.

Improve All Types of Systems. Managers must continuously improve the means of providing value for the user of the products and services. The means are the strategic systems that produce and deliver value for customers. In the past, managers have tended to rely on technological innovations or capital expenditures to achieve breakthroughs. Technological improvements are important but not sufficient to keep up with changing customer expectations and competitors.

Fast food restaurants recognize the importance of change in remaining competitive. McDonald's Chief Executive Michael Quinlan states, "You simply have to be better today than you had to be years ago." McDonald's, which is facing stiff competition from other chains, mom and pop shops, and home microwave ovens, perpetually tinkers to improve on its original recipe for success – that is, "small menu, speedy service, consistent quality and good value." For example, the latest addition to the menu, pizza, required that McDonald's engineers work with oven manufacturers to devise an oven that would bake a pizza in less than six minutes, rather than the ten to twenty minutes for the average pie (*Fortune*, February, 26, 1990). The improved oven technology gives McDonald's the opportunity to render "speedy service" of pizza. But anyone who has stood in line for fifteen to thirty minutes for a strawberry shake at one of the many "fast food" outlets to discover that they only have chocolate shakes knows that "speedy service" also requires attention to staffing, work design, training, motivation of workers, flow of activities, and inventory management. The whole system for production and delivery of food should be managed aggressively and continuously improved.

In other industries, technological improvements are important, and often necessary, but not totally sufficient. For example, sophisticated equipment such as robotics, optical scanners, and computers can simply drive up costs of production, if conditions still exist such as line imbalances, or upstream variation in incoming raw materials and out of control proces-ses. Counteracting the effects of broader systems can negate any positive effect that might be derived from high technology. In addition to introduc-ing technological advances, managers must also improve methods, policies, practices, and any activities that compose the system or impinge on system outcomes. These issues are too frequently written off as un-avoidable "people problems" or "turf battles." Discounting these issues leads managers to avoid the interdepartmental and cross-functional work that will be required in systems improvement.[6]

The social dynamics of organizational culture clearly impact the production and delivery of customer value. Thus, in addition to improving the systems that provide valued products and services, improvements should be made in the managerial systems and social mechanisms that demand and sustain behavior, and ultimately affect these value providing systems. This managerial agenda for system improvement should be clearly prescribed in every organization. These managerial systems include authority structures, progress reporting relationships, performance ap-

---

6. For example, engineering and management within organizations have too often been treated as separable activities. In the future, management and engineering practices should be more integrated.

praisal and reward systems, information systems, and role definitions, perceptions, and relationships.

For example, organizational culture cannot be taken for granted. Schein (1985) conceives of culture as composed of three levels of depth: (1) artifacts and behaviors, (2) values and beliefs, and (3) basic underlying assumptions. In changing an organization, it may be easier initially to produce changes on the surface level of artifacts and behaviors. However, long-term sustained cultural change is most likely when the deeper levels are altered.

Researchers who have studied individual values and assumptions over time suggest that values and assumptions tend not to change. We may be tempted to conclude that since values and assumptions tend not to change easily, they are virtually impossible to change. Managerial leaders should not assume that these rudiments of culture are unchangeable. Many organizations will have to achieve purposeful and profound changes in underlying values and assumptions to effect change in managerial practices. When such interventions are attempted, observable changes in culture are possible. The organizational culture should encourage managers to continuously engage in the never-ending dynamic of continuously identifying user value and developing organizational systems that increasingly produce and deliver that value.

IMPLICATIONS FOR MANAGERIAL EDUCATION

For an approach to managing competitive organizations to adequately serve as a basis for managerial education, it must be proactively oriented, and directed toward knowledge development and organizational improvement to help managers cope with an increasingly competitive and dynamic future. Competing requires continuous improvement of organizational systems in order to increasingly contribute to customer or user value. Current organizational systems cannot be accepted as givens but as variables that determine user value. All practices, policies, methods, materials, processes, activities, inputs, and other components of organizational systems must be subject to reconsideration or change for an organization to compete. This type of managerial education requires a shift to a new competitive agenda for managers and for educators.

Educate for a Competitive Agenda

No longer can theorists contentedly describe managerial work. The question is not "What do managers do?" Rather, the question is "What should managers do?" Educators must learn about this prescribed agenda, and managers must experiment with it to learn through experience and experimentation.

Management training, in higher and continuing education, must be consistent with this new managerial agenda. As future employees, both managers and leaders, students need to (1) understand the importance of determining what their customers value and learn to assess current customer needs, (2) learn to anticipate the future needs of customers, (3) learn to look for opportunities for improvement and to think creatively, and (4) learn to identify, isolate, and measure the effectiveness of systems. This learning requires statistical and analytical skills to understand systems, identify opportunities for improvement, assess the effectiveness of continuous improvement activities, and manage in the presence of variation. Managers will need more training in quantitative methods of assessing system performance and improvement.

JOB DEFINITION: THE NEW MANAGERIAL AGENDA

A common definition of a manager is "one who is in charge of an organization or one of its specialized subunits." This definition accurately reflects the manner in which people are given responsibility and held accountable in organizations, that is, for their own unit. Assignment of ownership for a particular unit or chunk of the organization is frequently accompanied by the corresponding reward structures that encourage myopic pursuit of one's unit objectives. Collaboration across unit boundaries may not occur, and, in fact, fiefdoms may arise. Units may even become embattled, pursuing their own objectives to the detriment of the whole organization. Self-preservation and competitiveness may emerge when managers are appraised in terms of performance measures focused on unit objectives.

In the past, under these circumstances, managers have engaged in "improvement" activities. However, the effects have typically been short term or self-serving. For example, managers may employ techniques for short-term enhancement of profit, such as deferring maintenance, deferring R and D, deferring equipment replacement, and reducing product quality to get production out. Such actions may even result in rewards or promotion. While the numbers may look good in the short term, over time these practices diminish the competitive strength of the organization, and thereby jeopardize its long-term viability.

The definition of management changes in this new agenda. A manager should not be defined simply as one in charge of an organization or one of its specialized units. A manager is defined as one who works to improve organizational systems. Some managers will be designated as owners of systems, whose responsibilities and activities cut across boundaries of specialized departments and functional areas. These managers will become systems owners (knowers and improvers) with a specific agenda set by managerial leaders who identify what customers value. The diverse managerial activities required to compete through customer value are further discussed in Chapter 25 by Bounds and Pace.

The existing coordination mechanism of hierarchical organizations, that is, going up through the chain of command, will not be adequate in executing and integrating this work. Subdividing an organization into units and building control mechanisms on such a structure have encouraged a fragmented pursuit of individual or unit goals rather than organizational goals. Existing organizational structures and policies may impede managers from fulfilling their new roles as system managers, which expands managerial responsibility for systems that cut across contrived boundaries.

Managerial leaders assign personal ownership for system management and improvement to individuals, and teams of other managers assist and collaborate with the system owner. Such systems almost always cut across departmental and functional boundaries. Although this approach sounds like a structural fix for problems in organizational competitiveness, it is primarily a managerial fix. The leverage is in the change of managerial roles and responsibilities. Change in structure reflects and supports this change in management.

Several organizational mechanisms will have to change to support new managerial behavior. These mechanisms include rewards, appreciations, performance measurements, reporting relationships, communications, and selection and promotion criteria. These organizational mechanisms should be consistent with the redefined roles of managers. For example, managers should not be rewarded simply for firefighting and problem solving, but for system improvement. Human resourcing systems must recognize that the requisite skills are different for the system manager than for a manager in a traditional organization. Abilities and skills in collaboration, teamwork, and creativity will rise in importance, while skills in competing with colleagues, turf-protecting, and conflict managing will become less important.

A CAVEAT

We have warned against a reductionistic approach to management. The truth is that any approach to management, including the systems approach, must be reductionistic. We have to reduce our focus to some

manageable scope. The foregoing criticisms are based on the belief that
managers have in the past tended to manage their organizations through
too narrow a scope, for example, through functions or departments. The
unit of management chosen is critical. It may range from world economies,
to individual organizations, down to systems, functions, departments, and
activities and tasks of specific individuals within organizations.
Managerial leaders should be cautious when they pick a unit of management, because of interdependence and interactions among units within the
whole. The dangers of managing through so narrow a unit of management,
for example, functions or departments, have been addressed. Similar
dangers exist for managing through systems.

A group of organizational leaders, all of whom own their respective
systems, can easily become embroiled in the turf battles and internal
competitions for resources and managerial attention which often characterize functional managers. Thus, the unit of management through which
top managerial leaders manage must at least be the organization. The
systems within an organization will have overlapping boundaries, multiple
employee memberships, and perhaps at times incompatible agendas. Thus,
the managers who assume ownership for the improvement of specific
organizational systems must exhibit the maturity, teamwork, and collaboration that is often required of the innovative and autonomous self-
managing teams at the very lowest levels of organizations. They must
manage the organization, through systems, as a team. (The management
of systems by a team of leaders and managers is addressed in other
chapters.) Furthermore, the unit of analysis may even be extended beyond
the boundaries of the organization to include the length of the industrial
value chain, from suppliers, through distributors and individual consumers.
The task is formidable.

CONCLUDING COMMENTS

Planning, organizing, coordinating, commanding, and controlling are
behaviors that may have been adequate in the past when administering
existing systems and controlling employee behavior to meet traditional
standards allowed managers to maintain the status quo and retain market
share. In the dynamic and competitive world markets of today, managers
must go beyond these classical activities. Managers should execute the
agenda of knowing what customers value and improving organizational
systems that produce and deliver value for customers, in addition to
administering and maintaining current systems for stable performance.
Furthermore, rates of improvement should increase to ensure progress
relative to competitors.

Continuous improvement of any approach to management or any technology will always be required. Beware that those who once dared and succeeded often become those who now dare not. Always seek improvement, even in the content of this new paradigm. Do not become complacent with any approach to management or any technology. Push to the cutting edge, and challenge this new paradigm and improve it. These authors humbly request feedback on your efforts in this regard.

REFERENCES

Aronson, E. *The Social Animal*, 3rd. ed. San Francisco: W. H. Freeman and Co., 1980.

"Big Mac Attacks with Pizza." *Fortune* (February 26, 1990): 87-89.

"Can American Cars Come Back?" *Fortune* (February 26, 1990): 62-65.

Carroll, S. J., and D. J. Gillen. "Are the Classical Management Functions Useful in Describing Managerial Work?" *Academy of Management Review* 12 (1987): 38-51.

"Cost Cutting: How to Do It Right." *Fortune* (April 9, 1990): 40-49.

Deming, W. E. *Out of the Crisis*. Cambridge, Mass.: Massachusetts Institute of Technology, 1986.

Elliot, O. *Men at the Top*. New York: Harper & Brothers, 1959.

Fayol, H. *General and Industrial Management*. New York: Pitman, 1949.

Imai, M. *Kaizen: The Key to Japanese Competitive Success*. New York: Random House, 1986.

Juran, J. M. *Managerial Breakthrough*. New York: McGraw–Hill, 1964.

Katz, D., and R. L. Kahn. *The Social Psychology of Organizations*. New York: John Wiley and Sons, 1978.

Kotter, J. P. *The General Managers*. New York: Free Press, 1982.

"Manufacturing the Right Way." *Fortune* (May 21, 1990): 54-64.

Mintzberg, H. "The Manager's Job: Folklore and Fact." *Harvard Business Review* 53 (1975): 49-61.

"The New Turnaround Champs." *Fortune* (July 16, 1990): 36-44.

Pepper, J. E. "The Use of Total Quality Management in Driving Customer Satisfaction and Competitiveness in the Business Sector." Xerox Quality Forum II, August 1, 1990.

Peters, T. J. "Leadership: Sad Facts and Silver Linings." *Harvard Business Review* 57, no. 6 (1979): 164-172.

Schein, E. H. *Organizational Culture and Leadership*. San Francisco: Jossey-Bass, 1985.

Stewart, R. "A Model for Understanding Managerial Jobs and Behavior." *Academy of Management Review* 7 (1982): 7-14.

Zeithaml, V. A. "Consumer Perceptions of Price, Quality, and Value: A Means-end Model and Synthesis of Evidence." *Journal of Marketing* 52 (1988): 2-22.

CHAPTER 8

THE ROLE OF MIDDLE MANAGEMENT IN IMPROVING COMPETITIVENESS

GREGORY M. BOUNDS
Research Associate, Management Development Center
University of Tennessee

G. HARLAN CAROTHERS, JR.
Senior Lecturer, Institutes for Productivity
University of Tennessee

SUMMARY

Competing in today's markets demands new roles and approaches that emphasize the management of strategic systems for best net customer value. After a brief review of the evolution of middle management, we propose a new set of role activities for middle managers. These new middle management activities integrate and link the managerial activities of leaders and operators through standardization of strategic suprasystems. The cycle of activities composing operator activity management is discussed in light of these new linking activities by middle managers.

THE EVOLUTION OF MIDDLE MANAGEMENT

In many organizations the bridge between top managers and operators has become obsolete. Bridges built with structures like management by objectives, the science of traditional control theory, and the art of delegation are on the verge of collapse under the weight of global competition. This chapter builds a stronger bridge between the activities of managerial leaders and the activities of operators in managing systems. The bridge rests on the shoulders of those who fill the traditional hierarchical levels between managerial leaders and operators, the "linking pins" called middle managers. Middle managers provide a critical linkage between strategy and operations for customer value through standardization of strategic systems. To ensure this strategic linkage, the roles of middle managers must change from the traditional hierarchically dominated ones of the past.

Events marking the evolution of traditional middle management in U.S. business organizations are presented in Figure 1 (see Chandler, 1977, for further discussion). This chronology indicates that middle managers did not widely exist until the early part of the twentieth century. The railroads began the process of building what was then a new approach to management, that is, departmentalization. Subsequent geographic expansion, growth, and demands for efficiency by business organizations furthered the division of labor and specialization, and required additional managers to coordinate and administrate the work of functional supervisors.

Many of these organizations were led by entrepreneurs or owners well into the 1920s. Between 1920 and 1950 more businesses were led by the new subspecies of economic man, "salaried managers." This transition to salaried managers accompanied the changes brought on by the world wars and the growth strategy of diversification. Soon these salaried managers cloaked themselves in professionalism, and academics began to study "management" and describe the content of "managerial work."

This chapter discusses the content of the traditional middle management job within the hierarchical approach and then presents alternative roles for middle managers within a systems approach to managing for customer value. Systems theories have been around for decades (e.g., Bertalanffy, 1950). However, few theorists have operationalized systems theories into management practices.

The primary tenet of open systems theories of social organizations (versus closed systems) is that the organization is in constant flux with and depends on the environment for survival and prosperity. The management approach advocated in this volume operationalizes the systems view as the management of strategic systems (suprasystems and subsystems) for customer value. These strategic systems are the heart and driving force of the organization. Without customers to re-energize the organization with transactional inputs, the organization suffers entropy, decay, and loss of vitality. This chapter concentrates on the role of middle managers in this systems approach to management.

The suprasystems approach requires a new content for managerial jobs and for relationships among managerial leaders, middle managers, and operators. In this approach, the focus of managerial work and the criteria for assessing work progress and functional contributions to customer value are different from those in the hierarchical approach. As a result of changes

FIGURE 1
The Evolution of Middle Management

DATE	EVENTS
1840	Middle managers largely do not exist in business organizations. Other than the church and the military, no organizations require middle managers.
1850	The railroads decide that there is a demand for "a new system of management."
1860	The railroads begin functional departmentalization, the enunciation of the general principles of administration, flow of information and authority.
1870	New functional departmentalization demands increased administration; firms systemize the administration of functional activities and institutionalize diverse techniques to coordinate the flow of products through different departments.
1880	The formation of trust and vertical functional combinations requires additional administrative coordination and integration. The consolidation of decentralized functions to increase efficiency and decrease cost. Large decentralized consolidation demands volume to gain economies of scale; push toward forward integration. Some of the largest of the new enterprises become responsible for the administration of integrated multifunctional subsidiaries as well as single-function departments.
1890	Passage of the Sherman Antitrust Act.
1910	The Society for the Promotion of the Science of Management is established by Gilbreth. First courses in "factory management" and "decentralized management" at Harvard.
1920	Entrepreneur/owners still run businesses. The Administrative Management Association is founded. It will later become the American Management Association. Dupont is the first to adopt the first multidivisional (M-form) structure of organization. Diversity becomes the accepted strategy for accelerating business growth.
1920-1941	World wars accelerate the adoption of the M-form structure of organization.
1945	Mammoth world markets are available with limited business capacity to serve them.
1950	Salaried managers run the businesses. Businesses become multinational.
1960	Nearly all enterprises of size have adopted the multidivisional form of organization.
1965	Beginning of the era of intense international competition.

(Adapted from Chandler, 1977)

in managerial roles and the content and focus of managerial activities, organizational structure changes are implied.

THE CONTENT OF MIDDLE MANAGEMENT

According to Chandler, middle managers are those who supervise the work of other managers and in turn report to senior executives who themselves were salaried managers (Chandler, 1977). This statement defines middle management and implies the accompanying organizational structure, that is, hierarchy, which is one of the most prevalent organizational forms. By 1950, middle managers and hierarchical organizations became commonplace. A "salaried manager" heads this hierarchical organization. Other salaried managers report to the head, and still other salaried managers report to them.

Chandler's (1962) definition of strategy, that is, "the determination of the basic long-term goals and objectives of an enterprise, and the adoption of courses of action and the allocation of resources necessary for carrying out these goals," implies the core managerial job within the hierarchy, that is, setting goals and allocating resources. Hierarchical middle management thrives on "Getting things done through others." They "manage" through allocating resources, delegating, overseeing, and holding subordinates accountable for completing assigned tasks required to meet established goals. Specialized tasks and functions are overseen by specialists; for example, a senior engineer manages the engineering function. Functions and departments within functions are coordinated by layers of managers arrayed in a hierarchy.

The Likert linking pin model of middle management epitomizes this hierarchical approach. Figure 2 shows the linking pin function within the hierarchical organization. Likert argues that the work groups, shown within the triangles at each level, must function as a team, with lateral relations among all team members and not just vertical relations between superiors and subordinates. (For simplicity only three subordinates are indicated in the hierarchy.) Likert (1961) asserts that in regular staff meetings, held by the group leader to solve problems and make decisions, "Any member of his staff can propose problems for consideration, but each problem is viewed from a company-wide [or group-wide] point of view. It is virtually impossible for one department to force a decision beneficial to it but detrimental to other departments if the group, as a whole, makes the decisions."

Unfortunately, the linking pin role of middle managers does not necessarily ensure teamwork. The fact that organizations are currently spending many hours and resources (e.g., facilitators, task forces, ex-

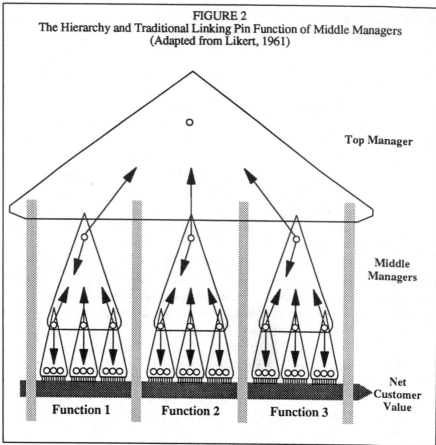

FIGURE 2
The Hierarchy and Traditional Linking Pin Function of Middle Managers
(Adapted from Likert, 1961)

Top Manager

Middle
Managers

Net
Customer
Value

Function 1　　　Function 2　　　Function 3

peditors) working on functional interfaces attests to the failure of the
hierarchy and the idealistic linking pin role.

This hierarchical approach to management relies on the linking pin
function of middle managers, that is, those who report to a manager and
have others report to them. The arrows pointing up and down from some
of the middle manager positions (in Figure 2) represent the linking pin
function. These arrows signify that effective group leaders must be able to
exert influence upward on his or her own boss as well as downward to lead
subordinates in their own work group. So middle managers are members
of two work groups, as a leader in one and a subordinate member in another.
According to Likert, when an individual middle manager fails in either the
leadership or the membership role, his or her subordinate group or groups
will not be linked into the organization effectively and will fail to perform
their tasks.

Although this hierarchical linkage approach attempts to incorporate
teamwork, coordination, and disposition toward the good of the whole

organization, it typically does not suffice. There are two primary reasons for its insufficiency: (1) the implied role of superior managers within the work group is inadequate, and (2) the hierarchical linkage fails to overcome functional barriers.

The Role of Superiors. Likert's model advocates that superiors within these work groups respond primarily to influence attempts and initiatives from subordinates. Thus, their "central problem" is conflict resolution. In this model the superior must ensure that individual goals are compatible with organizational goals. Conflicts and differences of opinion are always present among individuals and between individuals and the organization. Thus, superiors must be interpersonally skilled for the "constructive use of conflict," constructive interaction, and mutual influence to resolve the inevitable conflicts that emerge from subordinate attempts at upward influence.[1] This hierarchical role as mediator/facilitator is very different from the role of the managerial leader as suprasystem owner, architect, and improver. The owners of suprasystems and subsystems work primarily in concert to design effective resource usage and activity contributions of functions, rather than mediate conflict among functional initiatives.

The traditional hierarchical approach to management is inadequate in today's competitive markets. It falsely assumes that facilitating constructive conflict among the initiatives of subordinates ensures the good of the whole. In organizations, this theory too often translates into practices that result in bargaining for mediocre standards and objectives, political infighting, power brokering, and turf battles. The superior reacts to subordinate initiatives and plays the role as mediator of conflicts, arbitrator, and overseer of the various fiefdoms composing his subordinate domain. This activity distracts managerial leaders and managers from their task of continuously improving suprasystem and subsystem for customer value. Middle managers become antithetically entrenched as protectors and advocates of their function. They often place functional allegiance before customer value allegiance.

By contrast, the role of managerial leaders prescribed in earlier chapters requires a superordinate attitude among managers and employees

---

1. Conflict resolution should ideally yield synergistic solutions through the creative interplay of divergent positions or opinions. But too often the involved parties bargain for mediocre results. In some hierarchical organizations, functional disputes or incompatible initiatives of subordinates are treated as incriminating for the involved parties, that is, symptomatic of their failure to "cooperate" or "get along." Resolution may be delegated back down into the trenches, where there exists no real power to change the causes of the conflict. So, the involved parties either satisfice and strike a tolerable, yet suboptimal, agreement, or they continue to conflict.

throughout the organization, that is, disposes individuals toward suprasystem performance for customer value. As noted earlier, managerial leaders must be proactors, not reactors. They must set a customer value-focused agenda for subordinates and ensure that the roles of middle managers complement their own roles. This superordinate focus does not mean there should never be dissension, creative confrontation, or the interplay of diverse ideas. People should be encouraged to disagree, challenge one another and openly communicate.

Failure to Overcome Functional Barriers. Customers and others external to the organization may perceive the end product or service results from a horizontal stream of activities across the organization (see Figure 2). Top managers most often act as though cross-functional systems exist only at the lower levels of the organization, where value-adding activities take place. Personally detached from the horizontal flow, they assign cross-functional coordination roles to lower level supervisors or support staff, rather than redefine top managerial jobs in such terms. In contradiction to this horizontal flow, the managerial predispositions are vertically oriented, within functions. Functional distinctions often extend to the top of the organization, where vice-presidents spearhead the vertical extensions that are often disconnected from customer value.

At the bottom of the organization, the horizontal flow across the vertical hierarchy, which extends to the top of the organization, constitutes a fundamental incongruity. The hierarchical form predisposes managers toward functional allegiance, rather than suprasystem allegiance and customer value. This incongruity represents a profound organizational design flaw and contradicts the need to integrate functional activities to create and deliver customer value. Subordinates behave as though they regard their functionally oriented superiors as "the real customer," rather than regard the various users of their products and services as their customers. They adjust their response to customers within the constraints of their preferred, and economically reinforced, hierarchical relations with superiors.

Hierarchical organizations breed functional myopia and isolation, as implied by the walls in Figure 2. For example, Sales gets any order it can, Procurement buys the materials at lowest cost, and Production sets schedules to meet production quotas, fill orders, and meet efficiency standards.

Functions that extend to the top of the organization may disassociate managers from customers. Managerial leaders often attempt to overcome functional isolation and parochialism by building ad hoc horizontal linkages. They do so by overlaying the hierarchy with staff groups, ad hoc committees, task forces, expeditors, facilitators, coordinators or other communicative and integrative devices. These horizontal overlays absolve top managers of the responsibility to personally attend to integration of diverse activities for customer value. Top managers pledge "support" and "resources" for others to attend to cross-functionalism and personally disassociate themselves from it. This approach to management yields suboptimal results for customer value.

For example, in a consumer products organization, people at the various levels of the organization are drafted into cross-functional teams. However, bounded by hierarchical affiliations and allegiance, functional managers typically work across functional interfaces in ways that breed mediocrity. Those people with cross-functional assignments must constantly struggle against the vertical powerhouses. They have to bargain for arrangements that allow the involved functions to satisfice or achieve conditions and outcomes acceptable to the hierarchy, while the overall result for customer value is suboptimal because no one owns the customer value accountability.

These organizational overlays and patches are often temporary and relatively powerless in comparison to hierarchical authority.[2] These patches are remedial and actually reflect the underlying deficiency of the hierarchical structural form, that is, the lack of integration through suprasystems management. The hierarchical form fails to create the desired superordinate attitude for customer value. Without integration among the managerial leaders of the organization, programs that focus subordinate levels on internal supplier-customer linkages, functional interfaces, or cross-functional task forces will find disappointing limits to their success.

Productivity and quality programs and employee involvement efforts often start out with an upsurge in interest and motivation, then plateau in their accomplishments, and eventually suffer abandonment or apathy. These efforts fail, not because they are wrong or because they are not useful, but because without managerial leadership, they are inadequate. They are overwhelmed by the prevailing hierarchical organizational form. The top and middle levels of the organizational hierarchy are disconnected from the fundamental obligation to provide value to customers. Functionally oriented managers fail to personally participate in the management of strategic systems that are multifunctional.

---

2. The matrix organizational form represents the ultimate overlay and can become an enduring structure. The matrix form allots power among functional and project/product managers. Although the matrix form may cure some organizational illnesses, the hierarchical symptoms of parochialism and myopia may be embodied in product line managers or project managers. The matrixed organization may be viewed as consisting of two hierarchies, one vertical (by functions, and one horizontal (by product or project), with one hierarchy overlaying the other.

Lack of a pervasive and superordinate predisposition for customer value represents the fundamental shortcoming of the hierarchical approach. This lack arises because hierarchies, filled with functionally allegiant occupants, fail to assign ownership for the value-creating suprasystems and subsystems that span multiple functions. These systems are not simply the sum of functions.

Top managers are far removed, isolated by layers of hierarchy from these "unowned" suprasystems, which may exist by default at the lowest levels of the organization. Erroneously, hierarchical managers assume that by overseeing the functions through locally defined measures and controls the organization will competitively deliver customer value, through the flows they perceive to exist at the bottom of the organization. Perhaps this statement grants too much. Many managers do not even consider the resulting customer value. They simply manage toward specifications and standards within the functions.

In response to a *Forbes* (August 24, 1987, p. 33) question about GM's latest reorganization, General Motors' Chairman, Roger Smith, revealed some of the problems associated with hierarchical management and failure to manage "trans-functional" systems. *Forbes* calls the sickness "passing the buck." But the buck passing simply reflects underlying system deficiencies.

The reorganization intended to wipe out the Fisher Body Division and General Motors Assembly Division (GMAD), which seemed to slow the efforts to improve vehicle quality. Wondering why the reorganization is necessary, Forbes asks: "Couldn't you just call in the boss of Fisher Body and say, 'If I get one more complaint about your division, you and the top three guys are finished'?" Smith responds: "Okay, we could do that, and it's the way we used to do it. But he [the Fisher man] says, 'Wait a minute. I did my job. My job was to fabricate a steel door, and I made a steel door, and I shipped it to GMAD. And it's GMAD's fault.' So you go over to the GMAD guy and say: 'Listen, one more lousy door and you're fired.' He says, 'Wait a minute, I took what Fisher gave me and the car division's specs and I put them together, so it's not my fault.' So you get the Chevrolet guy, and you say, 'One more lousy door,' and ... 'Wait a minute,' he says, 'All I got is what GMAD made.' So pretty soon you're back to the Fisher guy, and all you are doing is running around in great big circles." GM had no system owners. So the buck was passed, but it found no resting place.

The alternative to this hierarchical approach is to create and provide customer value through the management of suprasystems. This alternative approach encourages and operationalizes a superordinate predisposition in managerial leaders, managers, and all other employees throughout the organization and not just at the lowest levels. Specialization and division of labor (which allow skill mastery and depth of knowledge) have been key ingredients of organizational success in the forgoing centuries, and appropriately managed, they will continue to be key ingredients. However, when these ingredients are taken to an extreme and embodied in a hierarchical organizational structure, they threaten flexibility, adaptability, and organizational success. Thus, the overarching concern in a suprasystems approach to management is integration of specialized knowledge and skills for customer value. Functional managers should not have the right to disassociate from the superordinate purpose of providing customer value. This new approach is shown in Figure 3.

There are two critical differences between the new approach in Figure 3 and the hierarchical approach in Figure 2. In the new approach, (1) customer value results from the management of suprasystems, composed of subordinate subsystem and functional contributions, and (2) functionalism resides in the organization *only* from the middle level down to the bottom and does not extend to the top of the organization. Top managers may have responsibilities for overseeing functional activities, but these are secondary.

These differences specify that the functions are subservient and disciplined toward contributing to the strategic suprasystems and subsystems of the organization. Integration of functional activities takes place because managerial leaders and managers enact prescribed roles as suprasystem and subsystem owners. The organization does not simply rely on cooperative cross-functionalism at lower levels of the organization, where operators and first-line supervisors or staff groups have been required to maturely bear the challenges of cross-functionalism. Rather, it also requires maturity at the top of the organization through transfunctionalism, for leaders to manage as a team. Transfunctionalism means transcending over and above, or beyond functions. Thus, functional activities are regarded as value contributing rather than value adding.

Tearing down functional walls to encourage communication, cooperation, and collaboration throughout the organization is important. However, building integration through the top of the organization, through suprasystem management, is most important to ensure that all functional contributions are complementary, that is, that the many parts complete the whole. Building such integration constitutes the transfunctional managerial job.

The competitive challenges of today's markets demand integration of the diverse activities throughout the organization to synergistically provide the best net customer value. The new roles of middle managers in meeting this challenge require a different type of linkage than the traditional hierarchical linking pin. These new roles are discussed below.

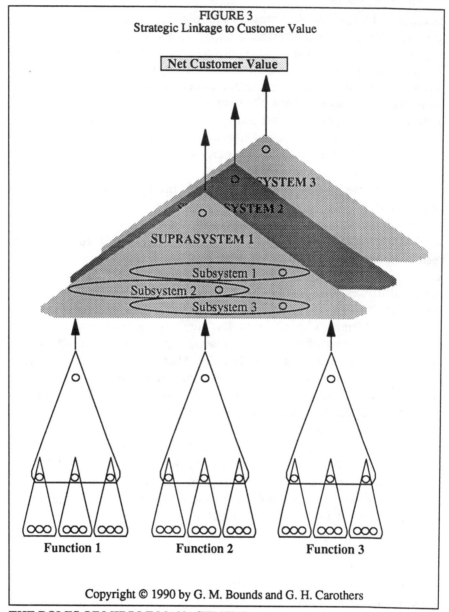

FIGURE 3
Strategic Linkage to Customer Value

Net Customer Value

SYSTEM 3

SYSTEM 2

SUPRASYSTEM 1

Subsystem 1

Subsystem 2

Subsystem 3

Function 1   Function 2   Function 3

Copyright © 1990 by G. M. Bounds and G. H. Carothers

THE ROLES OF MIDDLE MANAGEMENT

Traditional middle managers concentrate on managing functionally focused or specialized activities, for example, a marketing department, or they assume responsibility for administrative oversight of various functional departments. Functional expertise, specialization, and division of labor will remain important for competitive organizations in the future.

However, the manner in which functional activities are managed will be different from the traditional hierarchical approach.

The explicit role of middle managers in creating value for customers through suprasystem management is outlined below. This discussion does not comprehensively cover all duties, roles, and responsibilities that may fall to middle managers. However, the core of middle management activities consists of four critical roles shown in Figure 4: (1) assistants in the management of strategic suprasystems; (2) owners and assistants in the management of subsystems that are components of larger suprasystems; (3) owners and assistants in the management of functional contributions to suprasystems and subsystems; and (4) leaders of the operational activity of operators.

These roles will be distributed throughout the ranks of middle managers. Will every middle manager engage in these role activities? Not necessarily. These four roles of middle managers may not be played by every middle manager, although these roles must be fulfilled by middle management as a whole. Individual middle managers will engage in these four role requirements in varying degrees. Some middle managers will assume ownership (accountability and responsibility) for managing subsystems or for managing functional contributions to suprasystems. Yet others may assume multiple responsibilities for managing subsystems and functional contributions. Others may simply participate in subsystem management through limited task assignments or auxiliary support work and focus on ensuring their functional contributions to subsystems and suprasystems. Others will lead operational activities.

Before discussing these roles for middle managers, we will describe the complementary standardization requirements from managerial leaders. Managerial leadership must be established and behaviorally enacted for the complementary roles of middle managers to be appropriately linked into the organization. After discussion of these preliminary issues, we examine the roles of middle managers as shown in Figure 4.

Implications for Managerial Leadership

The above outlined roles of middle managers imply corresponding leadership roles for managerial leaders of the strategic suprasystems of the organization. Although managerial responsibility for subsystem and functional management may be partially delegated to subordinate middle managers, managerial leaders assume full accountibility for the architecture and output of the strategic suprasystems, subsystems, and functional activities. Managerial leaders may delegate some managerial activities, but they always retain accountability for subsystem and functional managerial

FIGURE 4
The Four-Part Role of Middle Management

Domain	Role	Role Contribution
Value determination and suprasystem management	Assistance	Assist suprasystem owners through individual and group task assignments in the execution of managerial leadership.
Subsystem management	Ownership and or assistance to others	Lead the management of subsystem contribution to suprasystems and/or assist other subsystem owners through individual or group tasks.
Functional activity management	Ownership and or assistance to others	Lead the management of functional contribution to suprasystems and subsystems and/or assist other functional owners through individual or group tasks.
Operator activity management	Leadership	Lead operators in the continuous improvement of operational activity and standardize the execution of operational activity.

Copyright © 1990 by G. M. Bounds.

activities (for demonstrated contribution to suprasystems). Managerial leaders must be accountable for what subordinates do; otherwise standardization of systems for customer value will never be accomplished.

It is imperative that managerial leaders not become detached and relinquish accountability for subsystem and functional contribution to strategic suprasystems. Integration of diverse activities within suprasystems requires complementary teamwork among managerial leaders and middle managers and will not exist if left to administrative oversight by leaders from afar.

Managerial leaders and system owners predetermine the rights and privileges of subordinates for changing subsystems and functional activities or processes. Managerial leaders grant such authority for change only when the subordinate is sufficiently skilled, motivated, and broadly knowledgeable to act in accordance with overall suprasystem purposes. Leaders bear the responsibility to develop subordinates for this work, because they will need help. However, at no time should managerial leaders become detached, and thereby unwittingly grant unbridled license and liberty to subordinates. Unawareness and detachment jeopardize the integration of the diverse subsystems and functional activities that comprise the suprasystems of the organization.

Managerial leaders are accountable for ensuring four principal outcomes. 1. The right components of value are focused on by all managers, for example, machinability of component parts for users. 2. Internal requirements for suprasystems, subsystems, and functional activities are aligned with external expectations in terms of range of performance on the variable selected for focus, for example, the degree of machinability of the parts offered is the same as what the customer wants. 3. Standardization demonstrates that activities throughout the organization do what managers say they have to do, which is an issue of having the right focus, stability, capability, reliability and being on target, for example, consistently produce the machinability of the parts the customer wants. 4. They change all the above through strategically directed research that finds the levers within the organization to create and deliver value.

Strategic Linkage Through Knowledge and Standardization

The activities of managerial leaders who manage suprasystems must be interlocked with middle management activities. This interlocking can be understood in terms of the managerial leadership model presented in earlier chapters, and represented in two of the cycles of activities of managerial leadership, that is, Value Determination and Suprasystems Management. The quadrant of activities in the Suprasystems Management cycle labeled STANDARDIZE represents one of the critical linkage points between managerial leaders and middle managers and all other members of the organization. Figure 5 illustrates these linkages among the primary roles of suprasystem owners, subsystem owners, functional owners, and operators.

As mentioned in earlier chapters, standardization of system architectures means managerial leaders verify the operability of suprasystems when used by others, prior to releasing them for use. It consists of providing suprasystems to enable organizational members to predictably create value for customers. Standardization is the necessary antecedent to empowerment of subordinates.

What Standardization Is Not. Unfortunately, the word "standardization" bears connotations that the worker has no discretion, no flexibility, no requirement for thinking, but only repeatedly and reliably executes a predetermined task. Although some tasks in a standardized

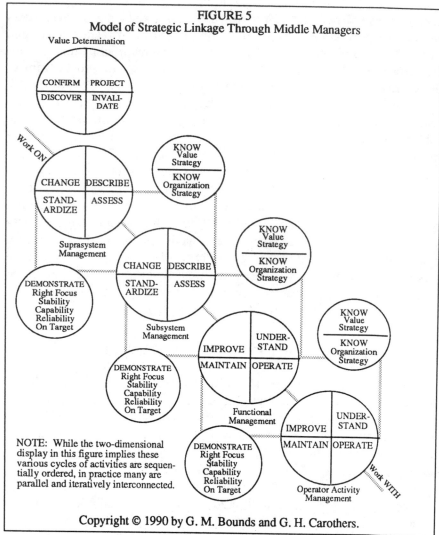

FIGURE 5
Model of Strategic Linkage Through Middle Managers

NOTE: While the two-dimensional display in this figure implies these various cycles of activities are sequentially ordered, in practice many are parallel and iteratively interconnected.

system may be perfectly scripted, others may require operator or managerial decision making and real time responses in dynamic situations, where not all contingencies can be anticipated. In predictable environments, predetermined rules and standard operating procedures may be in order. However, in unpredictable and changing circumstances, workers must demonstrate an understanding of the business and make decisions based on that understanding and the principle to provide customer value, rather than simply comply with the bureaucracy. For example, in a customer service position, a worker may have to autonomously make judgments about how to best serve a customer's needs, e.g., in billing, making referrals, providing information, or solving customer problems. Such worker autonomy and discretion is possible only when the worker knows the system and customer value strategy and is motivated to act accordingly.

Such dynamic jobs make it even more important that system owners ensure subordinates are (1) equipped through selection, job placement, training, education, knowledge of customer value strategy, knowledge of system architectures, knowledge of discretionary limits, rights and privileges, and (2) enabled through a well-standardized system of methods, materials, equipment, measures, heuristics, and assistants. As will be discussed later in this chapter and in Chapter 25 by Bounds and Pace, standardizing, routinizing, and maintaining strategic systems are far from mindless or monotonous tasks.

What Standardization Is. Standardization is a fundamental managerial responsibility designed to ensure strategic linkage for customer value. System owners should STANDARDIZE their system to ensure appropriately focused, stable, capable, reliable, and on-target system performance (see the linkage in Figure 5). In turn, this standardization provides a confident basis for directed and orderly system changes. Organizations must be prepared to flow continuously and constructively from standardization to change and from change to standardization, introducing and maintaining improved levels of system performance.

The managerial activities of STANDARDIZE require managerial leaders to transmit, educate, demonstrate, and institutionalize system architectures for customer value. The linkage between managerial leaders and middle management becomes evident when we answer the questions: Transmit what? Educate what? Demonstrate what? and Institutionalize what? The answers to these "what" questions are summed up as the architecture of suprasystem, subsystem, functional and operational contributions to customer value, which result from the managerial leadership activities.

STANDARDIZATION requires managerial leaders to impart to subordinates the suprasystem architecture, which is DESCRIBED and ASSESSED in prior managerial leadership activities. STANDARDIZATION operationalizes and establishes the means through which subordinate contributions to suprasystems will be managed. It is a translation exercise. Standardization requires managers to translate system architectures into operational tasks, activities, processes, or other means of achieving system performance expectations. The specific details for the subsystem and functional contributions are conveyed through means such as flow diagrams, justifications of system parts, operational definitions of practices and measures, confirmed measurement methodologies, data-gathering plans, relationship analyses, causal analyses, and capability analyses. This knowledge about system architectures is derived through the activities of the managerial leadership model (as discussed in chapter 5 by Carothers and Bounds).

As a precursor to STANDARDIZATION of the specific details of suprasystem architectures, and as a result of the ASSESS and DESCRIBE activities, managerial leaders ensure linkage to subordinate activities. They ensure this linkage through knowledge of (1) value strategy and (2) organizational strategy, as suggested in Figure 5 and defined in the following discussion. In relation to the interlocking of managerial leaders and middle management, this means that managerial leaders transmit, educate, demonstrate, and institutionalize the architecture of suprasystems, based on knowledge of value strategy and organizational strategy. Thus, the beginning point for middle managers must be general knowledge of value strategy and organizational strategy. Middle managers must KNOW these strategies to manage subsystem and functional contributions to suprasystems.

Complementary Knowledge Requirements

The knowledge requirements implied in Figure 5, and elaborated in Figure 6, suggest that managerial leaders must know that which is imparted to middle managers to ensure appropriate subsystem and functional contributions to suprasystems. The content of what must be known is discussed

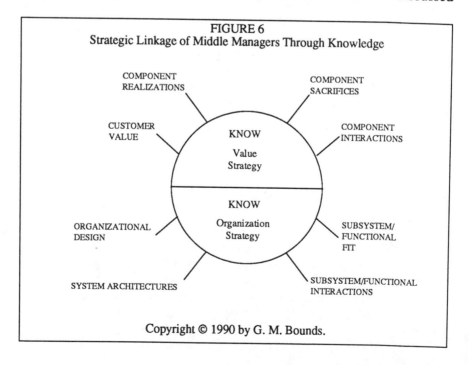

FIGURE 6
Strategic Linkage of Middle Managers Through Knowledge

COMPONENT REALIZATIONS

COMPONENT SACRIFICES

CUSTOMER VALUE

KNOW
Value Strategy

COMPONENT INTERACTIONS

KNOW
Organization Strategy

ORGANIZATIONAL DESIGN

SUBSYSTEM/ FUNCTIONAL FIT

SYSTEM ARCHITECTURES

SUBSYSTEM/FUNCTIONAL INTERACTIONS

next. This discussion is organized around the two domains of knowledge requirements: value strategy and organization strategy.

Value Strategy

Managerial leaders must be able to articulate and impart to middle managers the value strategy they have selected to pursue. As discussed in earlier chapters, net value is that which is realized by the customer of a product/service which justifies the sacrifice required. The net value, therefore, results from combining that which is realized and sacrificed. Managerial leaders must attend to each of these dimensions of customer value.

The value strategy represents that which managerial leaders have assumed responsibility to do for the customer, instead of the customer having to do it himself or herself. The value strategy indicates the value that will be produced and delivered for the customer, that is, what realizations will be provided and what sacrifices will be required in acquisition and use of the product or service. Any particular value strategy represents one of many potential strategies. A broad array of choices are available to managerial leaders.

For example, in creating value for customers who purchase automobiles, an automobile manufacturer may choose to emphasize fuel economy, low sticker price, high reliability for long-term usage, and an extended and comprehensive warranty to meet the needs of a particular segment of customers who want economic transportation. Clearly, an automobile manufacturer could pursue a multitude of other potential value components, for example, luxury, roominess, image, power, aesthetics, and diverse amenities. Just as the automobile manufacturer chooses among a multitude of value components that could be emphasized, other producers of goods and services must make similar decisions. The ultimate value strategy decisions should be based on the determination of what customers value and should be consistent with the organization's current and future capabilities.

Customer Value. The components of the selected value strategy should be imparted to middle managers to give them an understanding of the "big picture" in which they take part. Leaders should use discretion in painting the big picture for middle managers, who need all relevant information but do not need to be overwhelmed with irrelevant information. They do need to understand what customers value, in general, with enough details to allow them to appreciate the strategic thrust to create value for customers. However, for the particular subsystem or functional activities that the middle manager owns, specific details should be abundant, well articulated, understood, and validated.

Thus, as a result of their value determination and strategic suprasystems management activities, managerial leaders must understand how each of the subsystems and functional activities that make up their strategic systems impacts the components of value. This understanding is critical as a basis for the team efforts and mutual assistance among suprasystem, subsystem, and functional managers to ensure integration of these diverse activities. As shown in Figure 6, managerial leaders and middle managers must know the following about the components of value derived from subsystems and functional activities: component realizations, component sacrifices, and component interactions.

Component Realizations. Once an individual understands the whole, he or she is more prepared to understand the purpose of his or her particular part of the system. All middle managers must understand how the subsystem or function they own contributes to value by increasing that which customers realize. Middle managers must know what components of value are expected and delivered from the subsystem or function they own. They must also know how their component contributions impact value realizations throughout the broader strategic system. In order for middle managers to understand why their component contribution is important, both the intermediate and end users of their products and services must be identified. The results of the ongoing leader activities of value determination and suprasystems management should provide updated information and feedback on contributions to customer realizations of value.

Component Sacrifices. In addition to understanding what value they contribute, middle managers must understand how they detract from the value by requiring more sacrifice from customers. Value detraction may exist in the form of sacrifice for the customer, including difficulty of use, maintenance, waste, cost, and increased variation which impacts the rest of the system. Middle managers must know how their subsystem detracts from value, to ensure that value detraction does not occur.

Component Interactions. Leaders and middle managers must consider the interactions among value components, and not just the components singularly and independently. Middle managers within each subsystem and for functional activities must know complex tradeoffs and interactions among the components of value. Furthermore, these tradeoffs and interactions are likely not confined within organizational subsystem or functional boundaries. Components from one subsystem or function may interact with those of other areas. Leaders must address these broader interactions in their management of strategic suprasystems.

Organizational Strategy

In order to create value for customers, managers must use the socially contrived entity called organization. A value strategy means nothing without an organizational strategy for executing it. The organizational strategy consists of specific architecture of activities and resources through which leaders choose to create and provide value for customers.

For example, the automobile manufacturer may choose to engage in certain activities, such as body design, subassembly, final assembly, and marketing. Correspondingly, the automobile manufacturer may choose not to engage in other activities, for example, component parts design and manufacturing, distribution, and sales. These organizational decisions define the boundaries of the formal organization. Such organizational decisions, for instance, whether to outsource a critical component or to develop the capabilities for production of the component internally, are bound up with value strategy decisions.

Organizational strategy should be communicated to middle managers in sufficient detail to show them the big picture regarding the organization. Such an understanding provides a context for understanding how their particular subsystem or functional activity relates to the whole. This broader perspective provides a framework of understanding that should not only increase the meaningfulness of their work, but also encourage informed decision making for the good of the whole.

Thus, as a result of their supra-systems management activities, managerial leaders must understand the overall architecture of their suprasystems, including the subsystems and functional activities. This understanding must be imparted to middle managers. As shown in Figure 6, managerial leaders and middle managers must know the following about the components of organizational strategy: organizational design, system architecture, subsystem/functional interactions, and subsystem/functional fit.

Organizational Design. The organizational design conveys the totality of the organization. To understand the design, middle managers must know the activities that the leaders have chosen to execute internally and that have been relegated to outside suppliers, distributors, vendors, or other contractors. The design of the organization also encompasses the identified and owned suprasystems, and subordinate subsystems and functional activities of the organization.

System Architectures. In addition to knowing what users value and what part they contribute, middle managers must understand the whole suprasystems and subsystems of which they are a part. Middle managers must understand the perspective of other individuals within the systems.

A narrow perspective, focused on a single activity or function, breeds isolation. A broad understanding and an appreciation for the needs of others help dispose middle managers to contribute to suprasystems and make changes when necessary. Understanding system architectures requires middle managers to study the diagrams and documents generated by managerial leaders, for example, the justification for the parts of the system and the causal analyses. They must also understand the limitations and constraints imposed by broader systems.

While it is difficult to understand all the details of organizational design, middle managers must understand how their subsystem or function fits. Leaders should use discretion in imparting these details. For example, detailed charts showing reporting relationships, organizational authority structures, and system architectures may be shared as needed to ensure that middle managers know their context. However, learning extraneous details should not interfere with the more important jobs of learning personally relevant details about customer value and managing systems.

Subsystem/Functional Interactions. In order to avoid having middle managers work in isolation, either as functional specialists or as maverick owners of subsystems, they should know their interactions among suprasystems and with other subsystems/functions. The strategic suprasystems of the organization provide customer value best when the various activities composing these systems are integrated and complementary. Such integration does not come about simply by decree. Much hard work, collaboration, and interchange go into building integrated suprasystems. Middle managers must know how their subsystems and functional activity overlaps with, contributes to, detracts from, depends on, and is depended on by other activities. Such knowledge builds a foundation for collaboration and complementary actions that are good for the organization as a whole.

Subsystem Fit. Understanding the organizational design, system architectures, and subsystem/functional interactions helps middle managers understand the fit of their part. They must specifically understand how their part fits with the activity of others to contribute to or detract from customer value.

MORE ABOUT THE ROLES OF MIDDLE MANAGERS

Knowledge of value and organization strategies prepares and enables middle managers for one or more of the roles listed in Figure 4. Those four role domains are: value determination and suprasystem management, subsystem management, functional activity management, and operator activity management. Individual job responsibilities do vary across these four domains. Some middle managers will assist managerial leaders in value determination or suprasystem management. Other middle managers may be assigned the ownership for managing and improving of organizational subsystems. Others will be assigned the ownership for the management and improvement functions or functional departments. Still others may hold responsibility for both subsystem ownership and functional ownership. The four primary middle manager roles are discussed below.

Assistance in Value Determination and Suprasystem Management

As suggested in Figure 4, one role of middle managers is to assist managerial leaders in value determination and the management and improvement of suprasystems. (For more discussion on suprasystem management, see other chapters by Carothers and Bounds.) Just as the suprasystem owners, a subsystem owner may also lead a team of middle managers in improving a particular subsystem. Middle managers may participate, individually or in groups, by assisting a suprasystem owner or leader of a value determination process. They may assist through specific task assignments, investigatory activities, and analytical activities.

A suprasystem owner may assemble a team of middle managers, from various positions in the organizations, to assist in the management and improvement of a suprasystem. Nonteam members might contribute on an as-needed basis. While middle managers may assist managerial leaders in these tasks, managerial leaders must remain accountable, and remain directly involved and lead these activities.

Owners of systems, suprasystems and subsystems, alike, are much more likely than hierarchical managers to work as a team and make decisions for the good of the whole. This is true because system owners are accountable and responsible for activities that span multiple functions: their jobs are transfunctional. System owners are accountable for optimizing transfunctional performance, not functional performance. They are much more likely to be allegiant primarily to transfunctional purposes since functional distinctions do not extend to the top of the organization. Teamwork among the cadre of system owners is essential given the overlapping and interdependent nature of suprasystems and subsystems. Such teamwork should not be taken for granted. It requires attention.

Subsystem Management Activities

A subsystem represents a microcosm of a suprasystem, that is, a smaller version of a transfunctional system for providing customer value. Subsystems make up suprasystems. Functional activities, interchanges, and inter-actions make up subsystems. For example, a raw materials availability subsystem might be composed of activities spanning procurement, scheduling, accounting, and production activities. As suggested by the roles listed in Figure 4, in the domain of subsystems, the two roles of middle managers are ownership and assistance.

Ownership. The management activities for subsystems are essentially the same as those for managing strategic systems listed in the managerial leadership model (see chapter 6 by Carothers and Bounds). These activities include DESCRIBE, ASSESS, STANDARDIZE, and CHANGE (the DASC cycle), the details of which will not be discussed again in this chapter. Thus, the core job of middle managers in the management of subsystems can be summarized as in Figure 7.

Middle managers should continuously improve the subsystems they own and ensure that they contribute to the suprasystems for customer value. Subsystem activities must continuously be directed toward the strategic purposes of the larger systems. The integration of middle management activity represents a key to competing through customer value.

As subsystem owners, middle managers lead the contributions of functional activities to subsystems and suprasystems. They retain account-ability for confirming and standardizing the functional contributions that make up their subsystem. They ensure that subsystems are operable, that functional contributions are complementary, and that these contributions are maintained over time. Subsystem owners lead the improvement ac-tivities of functional managers to ensure they are appropriately focused for customer value.

Assistance. Although middle managers are responsible for managing and improving the subsystem they personally own, they also assist others with other subsystems and functions, as indicated by the roles listed in Figure 4. Just as is true of the suprasystem owners, a subsystem owner may lead a team of middle managers in improving a particular subsystem. As members of the team, these middle managers may participate, individually or in groups, by assisting the owner through specific task assignments, investigatory activities, and analytical activities. A middle manager may not be a member of a team but might contribute on an as-needed basis, to offer expert advice or make some coordinative change in his or her own function to assist a suprasystem owner. This assistance represents a critical activity of middle managers to ensure that the organization's diverse activities are integrated for suprasystem performance.

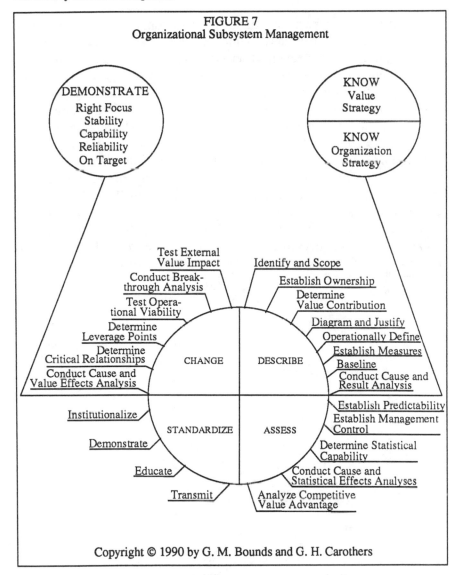

FIGURE 7
Organizational Subsystem Management

DEMONSTRATE
Right Focus
Stability
Capability
Reliability
On Target

KNOW
Value
Strategy

KNOW
Organization
Strategy

Test External
Value Impact
Conduct Break-
through Analysis
Test Opera-
tional Viability
Determine
Leverage Points
Determine
Critical Relationships
Conduct Cause and
Value Effects Analysis

Identify and Scope
Establish Ownership
Determine
Value Contribution
Diagram and Justify
Operationally Define
Establish Measures
Baseline
Conduct Cause and
Result Analysis

CHANGE   DESCRIBE

Institutionalize
Demonstrate
Educate
Transmit

STANDARDIZE   ASSESS

Establish Predictability
Establish Management
Control
Determine Statistical
Capability
Conduct Cause and
Statistical Effects Analyses
Analyze Competitive
Value Advantage

Copyright © 1990 by G. M. Bounds and G. H. Carothers

Functional Management Activities

Functional activities are organized according to the principles of task similarity, specialization, and division of labor. Typical functions within an organization include accounting, marketing, product/service design, process design, production, maintenance, procurement, distribution, and sales. As with subsystems, the two roles of middle managers in relation to managing functional activities and processes are those of ownership and assistance.

Ownership. As owners of functions or functional departments, middle managers often perform many of the traditional activities of allocating resources, overseeing specialized activities, and coordinating across functional or departmental interfaces. However, the primary job of functional managers is to ensure that functional activities contribute to subsystems and suprasystems (as shown in Figure 8). At first glance, Figure 8 summons thoughts about organizational structure, for example, who reports to whom, who has the right to hire, fire, and discipline whom, who does the performance appraisals of whom? These concerns should not cloud the primary message regarding the content of the managerial jobs implied in Figure 8. The management approach suggested in this figure has its foundation in managerial role definitions, and not organizational structure.

For managers of functional activities, their roles primarily require working *WITH* systems rather than working *ON* systems. Figure 9 summarizes the differences between working WITH a system as opposed to

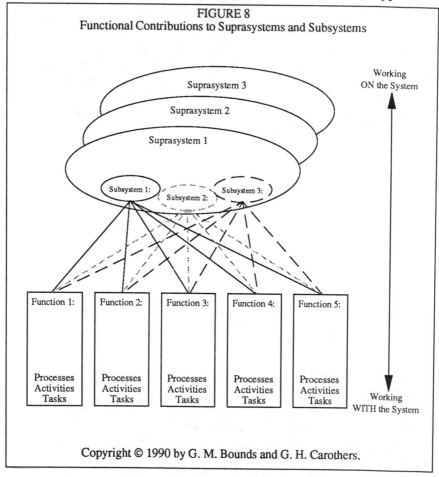

FIGURE 8
Functional Contributions to Suprasystems and Subsystems

Suprasystem 3

Suprasystem 2

Suprasystem 1

Subsystem 1:   Subsystem 3:
        Subsystem 2:

Working
ON the System

Function 1:   Function 2:   Function 3:   Function 4:   Function 5:

Processes   Processes   Processes   Processes   Processes
Activities   Activities   Activities   Activities   Activities
Tasks   Tasks   Tasks   Tasks   Tasks

Working
WITH the System

Copyright © 1990 by G. M. Bounds and G. H. Carothers.

FIGURE 9
Working ON the System Versus Working WITH the System

ON	WITH
Systemic focus	Problem/crisis focus
Determine customer relevant criteria	Work toward customer-relevant criteria
Improvement oriented: Change through creativity, innovation, and incrementalism	Maintenance oriented: Ensure stability by removing special causes, with limited incrementalism
Implement changes and test to confirm value improvement	Recommend relevant alternatives
Standardize and determine limitations, rights, and privileges	Routinize within the standardization instructions, demands, and constraints imposed by system owners

working ON a system. Working ON a system involves creating, innovating, and improving to change the system and standardize the change for better customer value in the future. In contrast, working WITH the system involves routinizing, maintaining, and executing the system to consistently produce and deliver customer value currently. Middle managers must work WITH broader systems and continuously direct functional activities toward the strategic purposes of the larger systems of which they are a part. The integration of middle management activity represents a key to competing through customer value.

The model of strategic linkage presented in Figure 5 suggests that the primary role activities of functional managers require them to work WITH the standardized system architecture, that is, to engage in UNDERSTAND, OPERATE, MAINTAIN, and IMPROVE (UOMI) activities. These activities are discussed more thoroughly in the following section of this chapter.

This role of middle managers in functional management consists of standardizing (operationalizing and translating) systems architectures into functional processess and activities. Functional owners must DEMONSTRATE functional contributions are the right focus, stable, capable, reliable, and on target. The primary and secondary emphasis of working ON and working WITH suprasystems, subsystems and functions is shown for each of the four domains of managerial roles in Figure 10.

Figure 10 suggests that the functional managers' secondary role is working *ON* subsystems and suprasystems that have been standardized by superiors (as elaborated in Figure 7, for the DESCRIBE, ASSESS, STANDARDIZE, and CHANGE activities or DASC cycle). The activities of strategic linkage in Figure 5 flow from suprasystem management, to subsystem management, to functional management, and to operator management. This flow implies a linear sequence of activities, when in reality these activities are often parallel and iterative.

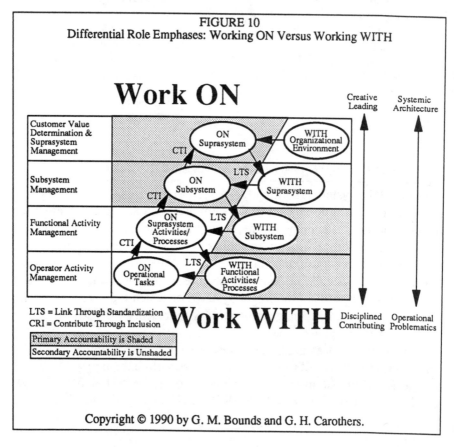

FIGURE 10
Differential Role Emphases: Working ON Versus Working WITH

LTS = Link Through Standardization
CRI = Contribute Through Inclusion

Primary Accountability is Shaded
Secondary Accountability is Unshaded

A subsystem is made up of various functional activities and functional interfaces and interactions, which are orchestrated by the subsystem owner. Subsytem and suprasystem owners cannot do all the improvement work needed, so they must enlist subordinates to assist. This means that to work ON (DASC) a subsystem will require a person to work ON (DASC) various functional activities in concert. Within the systems designed by superiors, and within defined limits, functional managers may work *ON* functional activities and processes to improve their contribution to customer value. So, functional managers may participate in working ON systems and processes (i.e., their secondary role: the DASC activities not shown for them in Figure 5) prior to working WITH systems (i.e., their primary role: the UOMI activities that are shown for them in Figure 5).

While functional managers may engage in the DESCRIBE, ASSESS, STANDARDIZE, and CHANGE (DASC) activities, they must do so in subservience to the subsystems and suprasystems of which they are a part. System owners may pull together a team of functional contributors to assist them. So functional managers participate in working ON systems as drafted and needed by system owners. Any changes in functional activities or processes are done in concert with subsystem owners and with other functional managers. Functional managers do not indiscriminately make changes that compromise subsystem and suprasystem performance.

Working ON the functional contributions coincides with system owners working ON subsystem and suprasystem architectures. These "working ON" activities are led by suprasystem and subsystem owners, who are accountable for the architectures they select. In time order, working ON precedes working WITH.

For the system owner, working ON is the primary job, whereas for the functional owner, working WITH is the primary job. The iterative inter linking of ON and WITH through suprasystems, subsystems, functions and operations is depicted in Figure 10. This figure must be interpreted in light of the foregoing figures, such as Figure 8, which shows the multiple and configural relationships among functions, subsystems, and suprasystems. Therefore, Figure 10 should not convey a simple hierarchical linearity from suprasystems down through subsystems and functions to operations.

While middle managers participate in working ON systems and functional activities and processes, their primary (most important) job is working WITH the systems that are standardized by suprasystem and subsystem owners. Once these system architectures are standardized, functional managers must fulfill their primary role in managing functional contributions, that is, working WITH the systems through UOMI activities.

Assistance. As mentioned above for subsystem managers, functional managers must often assist other functional managers in contributing to subsystem and suprasystem purposes.

Middle Management Leadership of Operational Activity

As a collective, operators are a significant part of the suprasystems that produce and deliver value for customers. Operators have to be included in the management and operation of strategic suprasystems and subsystems. Some middle managers are responsibile for leading the operational activities of subordinate workers. Just as managerial leaders improve and standardize the work of middle managers, so middle managers improve and standardize the work of operators. This managerial task is suggested by the STANDARDIZE quadrant in the System Management cycle. Through standardization the middle managers ensure the strategic linkage to operational activity, as suggested in Figures 5 and 10.

This work on operational activity is not just another operator-focused "program," but a strategically important complement to managerial leadership and strategic system management. Operator-focused programs have failed in the past because of the lack of integration into the strategic focus of organization.[3] Initial managerial support for operator-focused programs often erodes over time as managers encounter significant demands for resources and attention required to make operator programs "successful."

"Lack of managerial support" is widely regarded as the primary reason for the failure of operator-focused programs. However, even managerial "supportiveness" does not suffice to ensure operator contribution to strategic systems for customer value. In contrast to advocating managerial "supportiveness," the approach to management offered in this chapter suggests specific managerial activities that require operator inclusion in strategic activities.

Managerial Supportiveness Does Not Suffice

Outside the context of managerial leadership, and based on the assumption that "employee involvement" is the key to competing, many organizations have redefined managerial jobs to include words like facilitate,

---

3. In this chapter, the term *operator* refers to "nonsupervisory" employees who transform material, energy, and mental inputs into outputs (e.g., through physical manipulation, mental manipulation, or logistical movement) to provide value for customers. This definition does allow that operators may self-supervise, as individuals or as a team.

support, encourage, listen, and respond. Many functionally oriented managers, who are rewarded for meeting quotas and accomplishing functional objectives, for example, adhering to production and shipping schedules, have resisted these changes. Some middle managers perceive operators as usurping their power or as encroaching on their turf. Some may resist change, and relegate operators to strategically insignificant domains in an attempt to limit their power. Others may passively accept the change and incorrectly assume that they have no other job than to facilitate, support, encourage, listen, and respond to the initiatives and needs of the employee group.

In other organizations, operators participate in teams to address many aspects of their organization, for example, operation and maintenance, defects, recurrent cross-functional problems, costs, efficiency, product development, customer service, and productivity. These teams are often composed of people with diverse skills and knowledge. They may be charged to find ways to get around the bureaucratic bottlenecks and functional walls that typically keep people from cooperating. Local success may be quick and easy. However, sustained effort becomes difficult for these teams.

Problems eventually arise when the operator teams are given the responsibility to identify problems but not the authority to take corrective action, which is retained by managers. When managers are not responsive, operator motivation for such involvement dwindles. Managers may be nonresponsive for a number of reasons (e.g., personal detatchment from the findings, personal lack of authority over "cross-functional" issues, and lack of strategic importance of identified problems because the operators were not appropriately directed and focused).

When operators do get the authority to act, managers may feel threatened. They may resist and subvert such changes in authority, fearing the rumors about downsizing through cutting out middle managers. Such fears may even come true. Middle managers may actually be fired because they are regarded as bureaucratic fat in the age of the organizational crash diet.

Though organizations vary, in many cases the operator group eventually becomes frustrated, angered, demoralized, and/or apathetic toward the "involvement" program. The results occur either because of inadequacies stemming from (1) the relatively risk-averse program coordinators in a functionally dominated organization, (2) the politically powerless managerial steering committee members, (3) the recalcitrant middle managers who will not give up power and myopically strive to meet personal or functional objectives, (4) the facilitative middle managers who try very hard to "support" operators but ignore the broader systems that should be managed to require appropriate operator inclusion, or (5) the lack of suprasystem and subsystem ownership and improvement because so many managers were fired that the personnel for such transfunctional activities does not exist. Not only do operators suffer undesirable personal consequences under these circumstances, but also managerial leaders fail to optimize the wealth of contributions that are needed from operators for the organization to compete. These unfortunate consequences can be avoided by appropriately defining managerial roles.

OPERATOR INCLUSION DEMANDED

The approach to operator inclusion advocated in this chapter should prevent the unfortunate outcomes alluded to above. This approach suggests that managerial "supportiveness" should not be the primary managerial prescription for organizations to compete. More than support, demand is needed. Operator inclusion should be demanded because of the personal activities of managers in managing suprasystems for customer value. Middle managers have real and demanding roles that lead to operator inclusion. Middle managers should not be relegated roles as social facilitators.

Implementation of the managerial leadership model and roles for middle managers, as discussed in earlier chapters, creates a demand pull for operator inclusion. The term *inclusion* implies (better than the familiar term *involvement*) that there exists something with which to be included. That "something" is the managerial leadership and middle management behaviors, that is, ownership of systems, processes, and activities for customer value. Managers who lead by behavioral example and are accountable for managing systems for customer value will necessarily "demand" specific activities by operators.

Operator inclusion should be pulled into the managerial strategic effort, rather than pushed and supported as an end in itself. With the right orientation toward operator inclusion, managers can achieve all the humanistic objectives of enriching jobs, providing an outlet for human creativity, and meeting the needs of operators to engage in meaningful work. The managerial strategic focus, managerial task activities, and managerial culture must be in place before operator inclusion can be effectively implemented. If managers are appropriately equipped for and engaged in managing systems, then they may empower operators to contribute to customer value, for example, solicit suggestions, encourage operator problem solving, and grant specific autonomy to self-directing, self-supervising teams. However, empowerment without enablement through systems management yields suboptimal results.

THE MANAGEMENT OF OPERATOR ACTIVITIES

Discussion of the corresponding operator activity management cycle follows. These activities require operators to UNDERSTAND, OPERATE, MAINTAIN, and IMPROVE (the UOMI activities). These activities are similar to those prescribed for functional managers. However, they are performed on a narrower scope than functional managers, who are accountable for many operational activities and processes. Although narrower in focus, their primary activities are similar in that they are working WITH broader systems and processes to maintain the right focus, stable, capable, reliable, and on target operational contributions. Operators are a critical part of the broader systems to which they contribute.

Operator activity management is often done through or in conjunction with those in positions labeled first-line supervisors or foremen. In some cases, however, operators self-supervise or operate in autonomous work groups. In these instances, middle managers will work directly with operators in leading their activity management.

The middle manager role in leading operator activity management consists primarily of working *WITH* systems provided by superior managers. Although operators may be led to work *ON* operational activities for continuous improvement, these activities are monitored to ensure they complement the activities of others and are subservient to suprasystem and subsystem purposes. Figure 10 suggests (by the arrows flowing upward) that the work that is done ON subordinate subsystems, functional activities and processes, and operational tasks should contribute to the suprasystems which they compose. To make the fullest use of the creative and unique talents of all employees, managerial leaders should develop systems for including all employees. They should harvest the knowledge, experience and ideas of these people residing in the systems of the organization. All employees must be developed to make increasing contributions to suprasystems.

Perhaps not every operator will engage in all these activities, but in order for operators as a group to be included, some operators will have to perform each of the following activities. The four general categories of activities shown in Figure 5 comprise the core of the operator's role: UNDERSTAND, OPERATE, MAINTAIN, and IMPROVE. These activities require thinking as well as doing to ensure the systems standardized by their owners are routinized by operators. Standardization and routinization should demonstrate that operational activities throughout the organization do what managers say they have to do, which means the right focus, stability, capability, reliability, and being on target. Any traditional division between managers and operators as thinkers versus doers is inappropriate. Engaging in the operator activities for routinizing operator contributions to broader systems is intellectually challenging. The reader should be disabused of the notion that operators are simply "grunts."

The prescribed operator activities define operator inclusion in managing suprasystems for customer value. These activities assume that the managerial leaders have (1) determined what customers value, (2) formulated and articulated organizational strategy, and (3) assigned ownership for improving and standardizing suprasystems, subsystems, and functional processes and activities. The operator activities have little meaning outside the context of the roles prescribed for managerial leaders and middle managers. Each of the specific operator activities composing the UNDERSTAND, OPERATE, MAINTAIN, and IMPROVE quadrants of Figure 11 is discussed below.

Understand

Through their prescribed activities, managerial leaders generate knowledge about customer value and strategic suprasystems. They even-

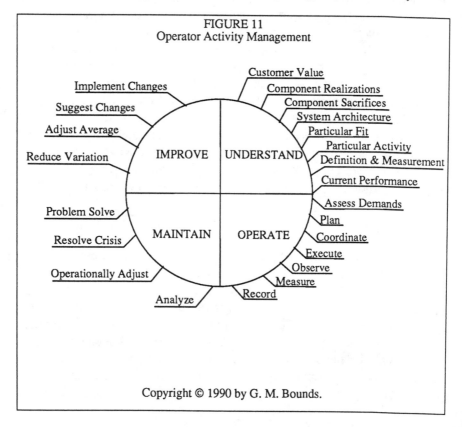

FIGURE 11
Operator Activity Management

Copyright © 1990 by G. M. Bounds.

tually impart relevant pieces of this knowledge to the operators within their system in order to standardize this knowledge into system performance.

Managerial leaders must standardize this knowledge and provide operators with systems within which they can work. This standardization role of managerial leaders implies that operators must UNDERSTAND (intellectually and operationally) what managerial leaders impart to them. This understanding requires translating of more general information about broader systems into specific operations, measures, criteria, and requirements for their particular work tasks, activities and processes, as suggested by the linkages in Figure 10.

Operators must UNDERSTAND the following: customer value, component realizations, component sacrifices, component interactions, system architecture, particular fit, particular activity, definition and measurement, and current performance.

As suggested in Figures 5 and 6, and as discussed earlier, subordinate contributors to suprasystems need to know general information about value strategy and organization strategy. The first few points on Figure 11, that is, customer value, component realizations, component sacrifices, and system architecture, suggest that the general knowledge be translated into terms personally relevant to and understood by operators. This understanding helps instill a superordinate disposition toward customer value in operators.

The managerial activities of customer value determination should provide a wealth of information. Operators cannot digest all this information and do not need all the details. However, they do need to UNDERSTAND what customers value and how the organization will produce and deliver that value through strategic systems, in general. Giving operators the big picture allows them to appreciate the strategic thrust for customer value. This operator understanding provides purpose (e.g., gives meaning to their work lives) and direction to their specific activities, that is, the personal and specific picture that deals with what they contribute.

When operators are aware of the whole system of which they are a part, they better UNDERSTAND the perspective of other individuals and their contributions within the system. Narrow perspective, focused on a single activity or function, breeds isolation and deprives the operator of meaning in their work. Broad understanding and appreciation for the needs of others help dispose operators to contribute to system purposes and collaborate when system changes are necessary.

To UNDERSTAND the big picture, operators should know the organization's value strategy, component realizations, component sacrifices, and system architectures, including suprasystems, subsystems, functional processes and activities and relevant interactions and interdependencies among these. Since these issues were discussed earlier, as introduced in Figure 6, such discussion will not be repeated here.

Particular Fit. Based on this general understanding of the big picture, operators must UNDERSTAND how their personal activities interact with other activities in the system for customer value. Understanding the system architecture helps operators UNDERSTAND the fit of their part and why their work activities are important to system performance. To fully appreciate their particular fit operators need to UNDERSTAND their immediate context in specific detail, for example, about interactions and relationships to proximal activities.

Particular Activity. Operators must master the knowledge and skills required for their own work tasks. They must know what their personal tasks are and UNDERSTAND the physical processes and operational definitions of their work activity, which explains what they do, and when and how. Checklists and decision rules may be useful in this regard. Operators must UNDERSTAND how to operate their machines and equipment, and know their limitations, capabilities, and needs for maintenance. All of this understanding of particular activity is essential for standardized operations.

Definition and Measurement. Operators must UNDERSTAND their particular impact on customer value and how that impact is defined and measured. Operators must UNDERSTAND data-gathering plans and measurement methodology to ensure they are appropriately focused. In addition, for operators to benefit from self-monitoring and feedback, they must UNDERSTAND the measurements of their value contributions. Besides understanding the definition and measurement of their particular activity, they should have some appreciation for the definition and measurement of system performance.

Current Performance. Operators must know how their part and the system currently perform, according to the prescribed measures. They must UNDERSTAND the discrepancy between what currently exists and what customers value, and where performance improvement is most needed.

Operate

Based on UNDERSTANDing, operators should be prepared to OPERATE the systems and processes provided to them by managerial leaders. The operators of these systems and processes execute the work tasks that transform material and energy inputs into valued products or services for customers. Execution of this transformation work is their primary task in operating the system. Prior to executing work tasks, however, operators may have to assess demands, and plan for and coordinate their work tasks. Upon executing the work tasks, operators must observe, measure, and record outcomes as needed to monitor, and subsequently study, their work.

The extent to which workers have to engage in the preliminary activities depends on the nature of the work, and on whether systems are in place to preclude their necessity. Operators may spend little time assessing demands, or planning and coordinating in a highly structured or invariant work environment. For example, the same product is always produced with constant demand and automated flow of materials.

Alternatively, these preliminary activities may be totally controlled by operators, as with self-managing work teams, or partially executed by supervisors or foremen. In some job settings, situational contingencies are not always predictable, which requires individual judgment and thought rather than execution of procedures and contingency plans. General solutions that apply to all organizations are not available, for example, autonomous work groups versus highly structured work tasks. Determining these details is best done by thinking managers, supervisors, and work teams. These people should create and standardize procedures and systems to fit their own circumstances and needs.

Each of the activities of the OPERATE quadrant is discussed below.

Assess Demands. Before executing work, operators should assess the demands for their output or contribution. They must determine what is needed from them and when it is needed. Assessment of demand is important to avoid starving downstream processes. Managerial leaders should build systems so that an operator can produce to demand, for the strategic purpose of customer value, and not produce to inventory just to look busy or to meet quotas.

Plan. Based on the assessment of demand, the operators should plan and schedule their work tasks. This planning may entail securing the appropriate tools, machinery, designs, and materials needed to execute the work. In preparing for the work, the operator may be equipped with checklists of procedures, prescribed steps for task execution, and/or skill mastery of the procedures to execute the work activity.

Coordinate. Before executing activity, operators may need to coordinate with other operators to ensure that their part of the system operates in harmony with the rest. Coordination may require verbal or written communication to synchronize activities or joint decision making to develop compatible schedules. For example, an operator may have to coordinate with the maintenance department to conduct routine maintenance while the line is down for a changeover to avoid unnecessary downtime.

Execute. Operators primarily do work tasks.[4] They execute to transform material or energy inputs into valued products or services. This work activity may entail tasks such as laboring skillfully to serve a customer, moving material to make it available to a customer, assembling subcomponents by hand or machine, or altering a material input into a useful form.

While operators bear the primary responsibility to execute the work tasks to contribute to customer value, they must also monitor the performance of their activity. Such monitoring may serve a number of purposes. They must monitor in order to ensure they competitively provided customer value, although the extent to which they monitor through formal means will vary with individual jobs.

Operators should seek to make their products and services consistently adhere to design targets. Monitoring allows operational adjustment and can also provide information needed by managers and operators for problem solving and improvement of work activities and systems. Monitoring may require operators to observe, measure, and record.

Observe. Operators can learn a lot about systems, processes, and activities simply by being attentive and noticing what happens as they OPERATE. Informally, operators may use their senses to gather information, with no means of formal measurement. Through conscious experience operators can gather much information about their work. Nonetheless, there are limitations to simple observation as a means of learning.

Measure. Formally measuring process and activity outcomes can provide information more pertinent to scientific inquiry. Useful operational definitions and measurement methodology help give meaning to physical occurrences. Although measurement methods may range from automated systems to manually operated devices, measurement activities should be based on confirmed operational definitions and on reliable, accurate, and strategically focused measures. Measurement provides information for making decisions about operational adjustments, reactive problem solving, and system improvement.

Record. An activity that complements measurement, and should most often accompany it, is to record the measurement, or make a permanent account in writing, print, or drawing. Data that result from measurement may be recorded in a variety of ways. For example, time-ordered charts

---

4. Each of the above preliminary activities can be seen as the special cases of the activity labeled "Execute." These activities are special cases of "Execute" when there are standardized procedures in place for knowing demands, for preparing and planning for the transformation of inputs into valued outputs, and for coordinating with other work centers and processes. Managers and subordinates must determine the extent to which these activities are systematized.

and histograms may be used to record quantitative data, and diaries or journals may be used to record qualitative information. Keeping a record of measurement results ensures that this history is preserved, and baseline information is available for subsequent use in analysis and decision making.

Maintain

The activities listed in this section are intended to MAINTAIN current performance. Maintenance is necessary because it provides a stable base from which to launch further improvements. In order to maintain current performance, operators must analyze data obtained through monitoring, and then operationally adjust, resolve crisis, and problem solve based on their analyses. These activities are discussed below.

Analyze. Raw data serve little use unless they are understood and have meaning for the person intending to use them. Once data are recorded, they must be interpreted and thought about to understand what the information reveals about activities, processes, and systems. Techniques such as Pareto diagrams, control charts, distributions, and other statistical procedures may be useful in analyzing recorded data. As a result of analysis, special events should be recognized, patterns identified, lessons noted, and the general state of activity, process, and system performance understood.

Operationally Adjust. Based on information gained through monitoring, operators will periodically find it necessary to make adjustments in operations in order to adhere to design targets and perform consistently. Operational adjustments do not entail changing systems or work activity procedures. They involve reacting to situational changes and acting within prescribed limits to maintain performance. Operational adjustment may be an ongoing responsibility for many operators. For example, over time tool wear may cause the performance of a sanding operation to drift away from thickness target, while simple adjustment of a dial on the equipment brings the thickness performance back to target.

Resolve Crisis. Periodically, special events will occur which jeopardize activity performance. These unpredictable, erratic, and disruptive occurrences must be repaired to return operations to normal and resolve the crisis. These "flare-ups" require people to engage in firefighting, a term used to characterize the expediting, overtime, rule-breaking, and hustling that is required to restore normalcy. On occasion, operators will have to take corrective action to MAINTAIN current systems.

Attentive monitoring will reveal these "fires" and lend clues to how to restore order. Operators are responsible for resolving crisis in their own work activity and may assist in resolving crises in recovering systems performance. Resolving crisis is necessary to ensure performance in the short term. Managers may occasionally have to lead crisis resolution. However, managers are not to preoccupy themselves with firefighting at the activity level. They are responsible primarily for improving and standardizing systems. Since crisis is a symptom of a broken system, managers should not spend their time attacking symptoms, but attacking their causes.

Problem Solve. Special events may tend to recur. Repetition of crisis indicates that the cause of the crisis was not removed, repaired, or improved. Stating that a problem has been solved implies that the root of the problem has been removed. Operators must solve problems in their work activity by determining what the causes are and by taking action on the causes that they control. Techniques such as the cause/effect diagram, and correlation and experimentation can provide clues about causes. Operators must assume responsibility for problem solving for their work activities to MAINTAIN current value contributions. By doing so, operators relieve managers for their primary responsibility as system owners. Although some problem solving will be necessary, managers are not to rely on problem solving to ensure that value is created for customers. System change is often required to meet and exceed changing value expectations.

Improve

Improvement implies that current performance is not only maintained but enhanced. Improvement in systems is the ultimate objective of all employees. Operator improvement activity must be disciplined to serve and contribute to the improvement activities of managerial leaders, in accordance with the rights and privileges granted by system owners. System owners determine the rights of subordinate operators to change parts of the system. Operators focus primarily on improving their work activities and on maintaining current systems. However, some participation in system improvement will be required.

Operators can IMPROVE operational proficiency through several activities. Operators will be required to reduce variation, adjust averages, suggest changes, and implement changes. These improvement activities offer operators opportunities to use their creativity and thinking ability to IMPROVE the strategic capability of their company. Managers must be aware of operator problem solving and improvement in activities, since changes in one part of their system may impact other parts of their system. Operators must seek approval for changes in work activity that might affect other system parts or outcomes.

Reduce Variation. In addition to resolving crisis to restore order and problem solving to maintain order, operators must change their work activities to reduce variation in their work outcomes. Reduced variation yields systemwide benefits, in terms of increased predictability, reduced costs, conformance to design target, and reduced sacrifice for a multitude of customers. Operators must engage in incremental and continuous improvement of their work activity to achieve reduction of variation in their work outcomes.

Adjust Average. Reducing variation is important. However, it must be reduced around a desired target (in terms of means and outcomes). Hitting the desired target may require adjustment of activities to move the average value so that the average of what is produced and delivered equals the target.

Suggest Changes. Given that operator work activity makes up a part of a larger system, problem solving and reduction of variation may not be possible without making changes in other parts of the system. Based on monitoring and their experience with crises, problem solving, and reduction of variation, operators may have a wealth of information and ideas about systems. The information and ideas from operators may be used to identify system problems and suggest changes in systems. Operators are not expected to be masters of systems, and so they may often perceive symptoms without fully understanding the underlying causes that reside in larger systems. In any case, operators should give information about symptoms and causes to managers, who are accountable for improving systems.

Implement Changes. All the foregoing steps in operator activity management (UOMI) should serve managers' efforts to manage strategic systems. Managers are responsible for creating and providing systems, with which operators can execute the transformational and logistical work that produces and delivers customer value. When managers change an existing system or create a new suprasystem to achieve breakthroughs in performance, operators must understand systemic changes. They must also implement the changes by ceasing to operate as they did in the old suprasystem architecture and by flexibly adopting the new ways of operating. The superordinate disposition should be manifested in operator willingness to implement system changes.

THE MANAGERIAL OBLIGATION

The foregoing discussion of the operator activity management cycle, composed of UNDERSTAND, OPERATE, MAINTAIN, and IMPROVE (UOMI), has little meaning or impact in an organization without managerial leadership and strategic system ownership. Before managerial leaders can legitimately require subordinates to engage in UOMI activities, they must participate in the management of strategic systems (suprasystems and subsystems). Managerial leaders must provide subordinates standardized systems within which they contribute to customer value. The responsibility for organizational competitiveness (or blame for the lack of competitiveness) must not be foisted on the backs of subordinates through abdication of managerial responsibility. Strategic systems management is a necessary antecedent to UOMI activities and managerial obligation to subordinates.

Pronunciation of the UOMI acronym suggests a credo for subordinate workers, that is, YOU OWE ME. Figure 12 suggests that there is a flip-side to requiring subordinates to engage in UOMI activities. Managerial leaders *owe* subordinates standardized systems. Subordinates should remind managerial leaders of this obligation by stating to them, "YOU OWE ME a system." Correspondingly, operators owe mangerial leaders disciplined contributions to this standardized system. Operators should complement their request for a system, with the pledge of I owe you contribution to customer value through working within that system. This is not a one-sided indictment of managers or a one-sided demand on operators. Adversarial relations among managers and operators should become a thing of the past since all have a vested interest in serving the customer. Together, managerial leaders, middle managers, and operators must be predisposed to customers and acknowledge that WE OWE THEM customer value.

CONCLUSION

The roles of middle managers described in this chapter are critical to ensure the integration of activity throughout the organization, ranging from the strategic activities of managerial leaders to the operational activities of operators. In this regard, middle managers contribute to the strategic linkage within competitive organizations. The relationships described in this chapter are not designed as an overlay for any particular organizational structural form, such as the hierarchical structure discussed in this chapter. These work roles and managerial relationships can be applied within a diversity of organizational forms.

To ensure the best net customer value, these strategic linkages must be ensured. The roles for middle managers outlined in this chapter provide the means of strategic linkage to ensure that customer value drives the activities of the organization. Value strategy formulation and implementation are thus linked through these roles.

Operators must be included in the management of systems for customer value. Without operator contributions, managerial leaders will not fully realize the potential competitive capabilities that reside within their or-

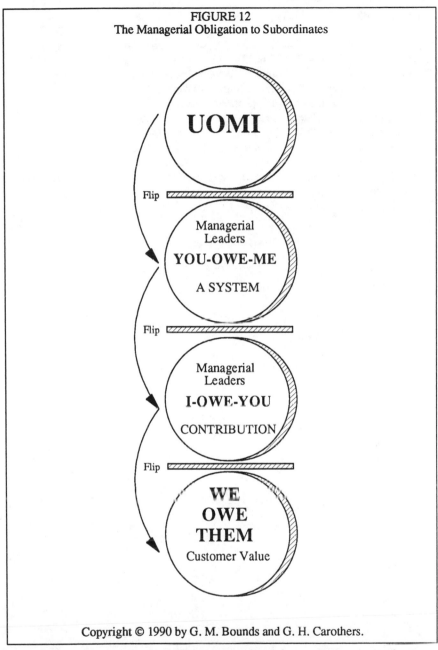

FIGURE 12
The Managerial Obligation to Subordinates

ganization. The cycle of activities prescribed for operators complements the prescribed activities of managerial leaders and middle managers. Including operators in the management of systems will help fulfill the strategic linkages needed throughout the organization to produce and deliver value for customers.

REFERENCES

Bertalanffy, L. von. "An Outline of General Systems Theory." *British Journal of Philosophical Science*, 1 (1950): 134-165.

Chandler, A. D. *Strategy and Structure: Chapters in the History of the American Industrial Enterprise*. Cambridge, Mass.: MIT Press, 1962.

Chandler, A. D. *The Visible Hand: The Managerial Revolution in American Business*. Cambridge, Mass.: Belknap Press of Harvard University, 1977.

"Fiddling with Figures While Sales Drop," *Forbes*, August 24, 1987, 32-35.

Likert, Rensis. *New Patterns of Management*., New York: McGraw-Hill, 1961, pp. 103-118.

Shafritz, Jay M., and Philip H. Whitbeck. *Classics of Organization Theory*. Oak Park, Ill.: Moore Publishing Co., 1978.

CHAPTER 9

THE ROLE OF THE EMPLOYEE IN IMPROVING COMPETITIVENESS*

LARRY A. PACE
Professor of Management and Marketing
Louisiana State University-Shreveport

GREGORY M. BOUNDS
Research Associate, Management Development Center
University of Tennessee

SUMMARY

This chapter begins with an exploration of some of the reasons why managers have implemented employee-focused programs to improve competitiveness. The authors then discuss several causes of the frequent failure of employee-focused programs. The role of the manager, the relationship of the manager and the employee, and the role of the employee are all shown to be critical both to the success of employee-focused programs and to the improvement of competitiveness. After discussing these roles and relationships, the authors turn their attention to ways organizations can create a "pull" for involving employees at all levels in improving the strategic suprasystems and subsystems of the organization.

*The authors are grateful to Mike Stahl, Bill Whyte, Harlan Carothers, and Richard Sanders for their critical and insightful comments on earlier drafts of this chapter.

OVERVIEW

Many organizations have responded to competitive crises by establishing employee-focused programs to improve productivity and quality. Managers in these organizations have adopted the view that employee-focused programs can unlock the creative potential and commitment of their subordinates. Such programs have varied in their scope and objectives. Implementation vehicles have included Quality of Work Life programs, Quality Circles, Team Building, Statistical Process Control, Work Group strategies, Organization Development, and Participatory Management, to list only a few of the most recognizable terms.

Although employee-focused programs have been touted as successful (see, for example, reviews by Zager and Rosow, 1982; and French, Bell, and Zawacki, 1983), the typical employee-focused program of the past two decades has proven to be band-aid therapy for a chronically ill patient. These programs have generally fallen far short of correcting the fundamental inadequacies of the organization to improve long-term competitiveness, and they often fail even to sustain themselves over time (Hoerr, 1987; Lawler and Mohrman, 1985). Other chapters in this volume deal more specifically with the role of the manager and the process of systems improvement. In contrast, this chapter focuses on the appropriate role of employees in improving organizational competitiveness within the context of managerial leadership. It is not the authors' purpose here to describe employee-focused programs in general, so the interested reader should consult other sources (Lawler, 1986, 1988; Pace, 1989).

REASONS FOR ESTABLISHING EMPLOYEE-FOCUSED PROGRAMS

Modern organizations are facing intense pressure for worldclass competitiveness. To achieve and maintain competitive advantage, organizations are looking for ways to increase the commitment and contribution of their employees. In the process of seeking explanations for poor productivity and quality, there is a natural human tendency to look outside oneself. This is nowhere more evident than in managerial attitudes. Managers have sought to blame lackluster performance on worker negligence and apathy, workers' bad attitudes, failure of workers to follow the correct procedures, or a diminution of the work ethic. Rather than focus on their own responsibility for creating and improving systems for customer value, managers have turned to employee-focused programs as ways to improve competitiveness. As these authors show, however, employee-focused programs, properly directed to the improvement of systems by managerial leaders, are only one ingredient in attaining higher levels of competitiveness.

The emphasis on employees per se as a key element of organizational success has origins in both the humanistic management tradition (e.g., Argyris, 1964, 1972; Likert, 1967; McGregor, 1960) and in our understanding of Japanese management practices.

The Humanistic Management Tradition

The humanistic management tradition asserts that workers should as a matter of principle and policy be involved in organizational problem solving and decision making. This involvement purportedly meets the worker's needs for job challenge and influence, it increases motivation, it unleashes human potential in the organization, and it improves morale and performance.

According to the humanistic view, workers are motivated to seek responsibility and to behave in the best interests of the organization if they are accorded respect and given the proper organizational setting. Such assumptions lead to organizations with few external controls and little direction. The employees in these organizations are supposed to manage themselves.

While there are many proponents of the humanistic management position, some managers attempting to implement a humanistic approach have been disappointed and even disillusioned. Productivity and morale improvements have not always followed the introduction of humanistic management (Schein, 1981).

It is obvious that employee-focused programs are capable of producing positive outcomes at the individual level. These positive outcomes, however, are not automatic. Furthermore, the positive individual outcomes that do obtain are not necessarily related to the organization's goals of increased competitiveness.

Japanese Management Practices

Hordes of inquisitors and observers have invaded Japan to learn the secrets of Japanese management. Each has returned with a different piece of the puzzle, and thus with individual interpretations lacking complete understanding. Two of the most commonly discussed "Japanese" practices, consensus decision making and Quality Circles, are discussed below.

Consensus Decision Making. Consensus decision making is a process in which group members discuss a problem or situation until they arrive at a position they all can support. Consensus is not necessarily unanimity or 100 percent agreement, but rather a fair, open process in which all group members have an equal opportunity to influence the group's direction. True consensus occurs when all group members accept and support the group's decision.

Drucker (1975) interpreted the intense face-to-face communication, informal discussions, and consultation that characterize the decision process in Japanese firms as bottom-up consensus. This, however, may be a misinterpretation of the Japanese management process. Others describe the decision process in most Japanese firms as a top-down consultative process, especially when long term strategy and planning are involved. The often lengthy and involved communication process is intended to reduce employees' uncertainty and increase familiarity with the decision, rather than to negotiate consensus.

Employees are allowed to offer their views and to identify impediments to implementing the decision, and they are given ample time to feel they have been heard. But the decision and any associated conflicts are handled by the exercise of authority and not by increased interpersonal involvement to achieve consensus (Hatvany and Pucik, 1981; Sullivan, 1983). The preceding discussion must not be misconstrued as an attack on consensus decision making in work groups. The authors recommend consensus decision making as an appropriate strategy for building commitment to a course of action that requires the support of the group. Consensus, though a time-consuming process, is an excellent device for resolving procedural issues and for problem solving at the work group level (no matter what level work group is considered). On the other hand, consensus may not be an appropriate strategy for all decisions; sometimes autocratic or consultative approaches may be necessary or desirable, depending on the situation.

Quality Circles. American managers implementing Quality Circles have often behaved as though the important focus was on the shop floor worker: Push Statistical Process Control to the lowest levels of the organization. The apparent assumption has been that since the Japanese have improved productivity and quality so dramatically and since the Japanese have been using Quality Control Circles since the 1950s (e.g., Ishikawa, 1985), the systemic improvements in Japanese organizations must have come from their Circle activities. This is both a naive and a dangerous view.

The view that Quality Circles by themselves have led to improvements in system performance is naive because the worker has little opportunity to impact the larger systems of the organization. These systems have been created and are maintained by management. Experts like Deming and Ishikawa attribute from 80 to 85 percent of the responsibility for performance variation in an organization to the management systems. The view that Quality Circles alone lead to system improvements is dangerous because it allows managers to give the impression to others, especially their own superiors, that they are doing something about productivity and quality without really doing much at all.

A senior executive recently stated to the first author that "Quality Circles are a bankrupt concept." That may be true in his and even in most American companies, but it certainly is not true in Japan. Japanese companies still invest in Quality Circles, and Japanese Quality Control experts routinely recommend Circles as an implementation device for Total Quality Management Systems. Clearly, Quality Circles have something to contribute. Just what they do contribute is a crucial question.

The manual *QC Circle Koryo: General Principles of the QC Circle* (JUSE, 1980), states three primary purposes for Quality Circles:

1. To foster study groups in which foremen and workers together study the magazine *FQC* (Quality Control for the Foreman).
2. To apply the results of this study in order to more effectively manage and improve the work environment.
3. To expand the "personality of the foremen and workers."

In Japan, effectively implemented Quality Circles serve several useful purposes. First, Quality Circles provide a social support mechanism for their members. In their own "humanistic orientation," the Japanese attribute QC Circle success to the "democratic process so suited to human nature, with which QC Circles were operated" (JUSE, 1980: iii).

Quality Circles also make a major contribution to the quality of the work lives of their members. By solving hygiene-related problems, workers can significantly improve their working conditions. In addition, by solving functional performance-related problems, workers can improve their contribution to the objectives of the systems of the organization. Rather than seeing these as mutually exclusive, as is sometimes the case in the United States, the *Quality Circle Koryo* unabashedly states that a goal of Quality Circles is "to respect humanity and build a happy bright workshop which is meaningful to work in" (JUSE, 1980: 21).

Finally, Quality Circles set the stage for implementing systems change. This stage-setting is an overlooked function of Quality Circles. Such activities conducted in the presence of management support and leadership establish a mindset of "routine change," or continuous improvement, and therefore enable Circle members to deal readily and constructively with system changes introduced by their managers. In our view, this is the most important advantage of a Quality Circle program.

Putting Two and Two Together

Western managers have been deeply affected by the humanistic management tradition and by the obvious accomplishments of the Japanese. Managers in the United States have come to believe both that it is an inherently good thing to involve employees and that the Japanese are doing it better than they are.

Whether the motivation is to emulate the Japanese or to implement a more humanistic management system, involving employees in problem solving, giving employees a say in the workplace, enhancing teamwork, responding to employee suggestions, and enriching jobs through delegation can have potentially positive effects on employee attitudes and behaviors and improve business outcomes. Likert's research on the adoption of his "System 4" management demonstrated these effects (Likert, 1967), and the performance of Japanese companies that have used worker participation is beyond question.

Clearly, all organizational members are unique and talented. For the organization not to take advantage of such a potential asset is both unwise and unfair. It is entirely possible to meet the humanistic objectives of according employees the opportunity to grow, contribute, and feel a part of the organization while simultaneously improving the firm's competitiveness. However, the effects of employee-focused programs on organizational competitiveness will be limited if the appropriate managerial roles, structures, and systems are not in place.

SOURCES OF FAILURE OF EMPLOYEE-FOCUSED PROGRAMS

Employee-focused programs are often initially successful and generate interest, activity, and enthusiasm among participants. Improvements may be made in such factors as productivity, quality, working conditions, or safety. Over time, however, such programs often lose energy, interest subsides, the initial promise fades, and the programs die. Initial successes within a work group or department seem easy to obtain, like picking low-hanging, easily accessible fruit.

Sometimes, even initial successes are minimal, as when employee groups are given little direction or support. Such groups may select a focus that is strategically inconsequential from management's perspective, for example, moving the water fountain or painting the stripes in the parking lot. These activities, while important from the employees' point of view, typically encounter managerial apathy because such activities bear no immediate relationship to critical business outcomes.

Even in the case of an initially successful group, the employee-focused program may eventually stagnate as employees encounter organizational limitations on their activities. Without the clear integration of employee programs with the strategic and tactical objectives of managers, employee programs are likely to suffer various situational constraints. These constraints include lack of job-related information, inadequate tools and equipment, insufficient materials and supplies, lack of budgetary support, restricted access to required services and help from others, time and task constraints, scheduling difficulties, transportation problems, authority conflicts, and an unsupportive work environment (Peters, O'Connor, and Eulberg, 1985).

The Importance of Context

The way to improve organizational competitiveness is not simply to "push Statistical Process Control to the shop floor level." Any program that focuses inordinate attention on the lowest levels of the organization will inevitably face the inherent limitations of such an approach and result in disappointment. Without the appropriate context of managerial leadership, an employee participation program is doomed to failure at worst and mediocrity at best when examined in terms of critical business outcomes.

Employee programs must be linked to the managerial activities intended to improve organizational systems that create value for the users of the organization's products and services. The compatible roles of employees and managers in improving competitiveness, and the relationships between these roles, produce just such a linkage. Outside this context, unfocused activity by employee participants and apathy by managers will result in frustration for employees and managers alike. Bitter experience has shown that such failures make very difficult if not impossible the subsequent reintroduction of employee-focused programs.

Unfortunately, employee participation programs have sometimes been used manipulatively to appease workers' desires for enhanced jobs or the right to influence the workplace (Parker and Slaughter, 1988). Manipulation eventually backfires, producing suspicion, mistrust, and resentment. Therefore, employees should participate in the improvement process only in appropriate, purposeful ways.

Achieving Success with Employee-Focused Programs

One tempting approach to ensuring the success of employee-focused programs is to dictate managerial support. But the answer is not simply to make the job of managers that of supporting employee programs. Rather, managers must seek to include employees in improving competitiveness as needed and appropriate. Team activities at the functional or departmental level may well be useful for process and job improvements that contribute to system objectives. Employees must also be prepared for *inclusion* in significant system changes introduced by management. Active engagement in problem solving in the workplace can develop positive attitudes toward continuous improvement and promote a psychological readiness for change. The so-called participation hypothesis states that employees support what they help create, that is, that their inclusion in system improvement will lead to their support for necessary changes.

Over the long term, however, it is not participation as an end in itself that is important from a business perspective. Rather, properly focused participation significantly contributes to important business outcomes. The criteria used to define appropriate inclusion thus become a key management issue.

In the following pages, the authors outline the appropriate participation of employees in improving organizational systems for value creation. The discussion begins with a brief synopsis of the role of the manager. Next, the authors discuss the role of the manager in relation to the worker and provide an explanation of the employee's appropriate role in improving competitiveness.

THE ROLE OF THE MANAGER: SYSTEM OWNER AND IMPROVER

The manager is fundamentally responsible for engaging in systems management. Collectively and individually, managers are accountable for the following:

1. To determine specifically what the customers of the products or services of the business actually value.
2. To select and specify the strategy of the business. This involves the development of a set of enterprise objectives that reflect the actual mission or purpose of the organization in serving external customers.
3. To identify the specific focus for systems work by managers to increase value for customers (including the desired business outcomes of systems improvement).
4. To clarify these outcomes: what is meant by the chosen organizational focus.
5. To identify the specific organizational systems that create these outcomes or impact the chosen organizational focus.

6. To describe, analyze, and improve these systems.

The work outlined above is the starting point in the management of systems. The systems improvement work of managers must receive the highest priority in the organization. The manager who "owns" each system should assume responsibility for seeing that the work of systems improvement gets done. Employee-focused programs within the context of managerial leadership in systems improvement will flourish. By continuously seeking to improve their own work activities, workers make a direct contribution to organizational competitiveness. In addition, this activity prepares employees for implementing system changes and routinizing these changes.

THE ROLE OF MANAGEMENT IN RELATION TO THE WORKER

In the push to become and remain competitive, organizations are downsizing, delayering, demassing, and dismantling hierarchies. Companies have eliminated levels of authority and decreased the numbers of supervisors. The result in many firms is an increased span of control for those who supervise others. In such systems supervisors can no longer keep close reins on all ongoing activities. Rather, the manager must shift responsibility to the worker. There is movement toward work teams and self-management at the operational level. This movement has led to changes in role for managers and employees alike.[1]

Managerial leaders are increasingly called upon to create and improve systems. To free up time for this critical activity requires that the worker be empowered to routinize and maintain these systems through individual and group activities. Managers who manage self managing employees are redundant and an expensive luxury organizations can no longer afford.

Managerial and employee roles in system improvement are shown in Table 1, which demonstrates both the contrast between and the compatibility of worker and management roles.

Many traditionally oriented managers fear that their power or status will be weakened if they allow workers to participate and make significant contributions to system improvement. This fear expresses itself in skepticism, cynicism, and even resentment toward employee-focused programs. As many observers have noted, this resentment is most likely to be found in the middle management ranks, where the jobs are most threatened.

---

1. The authors thank William Foote Whyte for suggesting this line of reasoning.

TABLE 1
Managerial and Worker Roles: Contrast and Compatibility

Managerial Roles	Employee Roles
Exhibit openness to employee suggestions and information.	Provide information on system performance.
Encourage workers' ideas and input into decisions.	Provide ideas and input into decisions.
Show genuine interest in workers and their concerns. Treat employees as customers.	Relate "customer requirements" to managers.
Identify and remove barriers to employee participation in systems improvement.	Participate in systems improvement. Implement systems changes.
Involve workers in identifying, analyzing, and solving work-related problems.	Participate in identifying, analyzing, and solving work-related problems.
Lead group problem-solving sessions.	Participate in group problem-solving sessions.
Openly communicate business information.	Respond to information provided by management.
Encourage development and application of employee skills in problem solving, decision making, and human relations.	Participate actively in skill development and the application of skills.
Give feedback, reward, and recognition for employee involvement in systems improvement.	Respond to feedback, reward, and recognition.
Integrate the involvement of workers in problem solving and decision making with the organizational focus and system improvement work.	Learn the broader organizational focus and support system changes that improve it. Participate in system changes as needed.

To reduce or eliminate this resentment and threat, top managers must demonstrate that systems improvement ultimately leads to success as the organization becomes more competitive. While some organizational theorists envision a vast reduction in or even the elimination of supervisory and managerial positions, we believe that the true shift is in the nature of managerial work. Managerial jobs are becoming more challenging as the emphasis moves from external control to that of integrating work activities for customer value.

System creation, improvement, and provisioning are the "new management" roles. Managerial jobs are shifting from reactive "firefighting" to a greater focus on system and process improvement as employees take on the role of functional problem solving and decision making. Delegation of problem-solving activity to workers need not be seen as a loss of power, but rather as a way of empowering the entire organization.

An illustration of this approach was recounted to the first author by Sidney Rubinstein. Two young engineers in the same organization were more productive than their more senior – and more traditional – counterparts. The hourly employees in their areas were satisfied and productive, and both engineers received high pay raises and swift promotions into managerial positions. When asked the secret of their success, both freely admitted that they had actively sought the involvement of hourly workers in the improvement of their work processes. Such involvement, they said, not only improved the operation of the organization's current systems, but it also allowed them to spend more time creatively, which led to significant breakthroughs in their work assignments. This stands in stark contrast to the typical view of the harried, overloaded, overworked manager.

To accomplish the transition to the new management role, managers must be given new skills and must be led by example. Reward and recognition systems must be changed so that the inclusion of managers and their employees in systems improvement produces positive outcomes for both of them.

THE ROLE OF THE EMPLOYEE IN SYSTEMS IMPROVEMENT

Within the context of managerial leadership, employees have several distinct roles to play in the organization devoted to systems improvement. These roles include operation of the current systems while improving performance, involvement in problem solving at the functional and workshop level, and maintenance and continuous improvement of existing functional activities as they relate to system objectives.

Employees must also report regularly and candidly to management regarding the performance of the current systems of the organization. Finally, employees play important roles as internal customers and suppliers.

These various employee roles are treated separately in the following paragraphs, but first an explanatory note is in order. All organizational members except the most senior executives and the front-line employees are *both managers and employees*. Therefore, from the first-level supervisor all the way to the corporate board room, most employees are responsible for fulfilling an employee role and for performing a managerial role.

As those who have tried to do both can attest, it is not easy. Therefore, the manager needs to ask periodically in which capacity he or she is serving at a given moment. The employee roles discussed are focused primarily on the shop floor level, but in reality the roles apply to anyone who is serving in a subordinate capacity at any level of the organization.

Operating, Maintaining, and Evaluating the Organization's Systems While Achieving Performance Standards

While the authors state emphatically that managers are fundamentally responsible for creating and improving organizational systems for customer value, it is just as true that employees are responsible for the work of the organization. That means producing the products or services of their organization while achieving cost, quality, and delivery schedule objectives.

Managers, of course, have the important role to play of provisioning the systems of the organization so that employees will have available the raw materials, equipment, training, and other ingredients necessary to perform their work. This empowering and enabling role is key to the success of any attempt to increase the employees' effectiveness in operating the systems of the organization.

Problem Solving and Decision Making

Within the context of managerial leadership, and always conscious of the objectives of the system, employees should be given wide latitude to identify and correct conditions within their control that affect the quality of their work and its outputs. In addition, employees must share with the work group or with management their knowledge of factors outside their control that are affecting the quality of their work.

Involvement in functional problem solving and decision making can and should occur at both the individual and collective levels, taking such forms as individual job enrichment, suggestion systems, Quality Circles, work group strategies, or even high involvement work systems (Lawler, 1986). For such involvement to be effective, employees must be trained in quality control, problem-solving and decision-making methods, and interactive skills. A good source for beginning worker education is Ishikawa (1982).

Maintenance and Continuous Improvement of Functional Activities

In addition to operating the current organizational systems and solving operational problems, employees should be trained to seek opportunities to improve the operation of their own systems.

This might involve efforts to improve efficiency, to reduce costs, to improve quality, to reduce scrap and rework, and to make changes and enhancements to the work process in order to reduce variation in process outcomes. System improvement activities should not be postponed until problems arise but should be engaged in continuously.

Participation with Management in System-Level Improvements

The GM-UAW Saturn plant and many other joint union-management projects have demonstrated the potential benefits of including functional employees in system-level changes that previously were solely the domain of management. Such inclusion has proved useful not only because people support what they help create, but also because functional workers provide a different perspective from managers. While some union leaders have resisted such inclusion for fear of cooptation or manipulation, others have welcomed participation in the economies of the firm because of its connection to job security for their members.

Candid Communication Concerning Current Conditions

Within an atmosphere of mutual trust and respect, employees must communicate frankly and truthfully to managers the current levels of performance of their systems, the problems encountered in doing the work of the system, and the conditions affecting the outputs of the system.

In addition, certain employees by the nature of their jobs interact with outside customers. Such employees include salespeople, bank tellers, service providers, and the like. These employees have an important additional responsibility: to provide feedback to management on what customers value and to relay customer perceptions of system performance.

Managers must learn to be nondefensive when such communication concerning the operation of the system and the views of customers occurs.

One of the chief results of implementing a Total Quality Management system is that it "opens up channels of communication within a company, filling it with a breath of fresh air. TQM allows companies to discover a failure before it turns into a disaster, because everyone is accustomed to speaking to one another truthfully, frankly, and in a helpful manner" (Lu, 1985).

Internal Customers and Suppliers

As Ishikawa has often stated, "the next process is your customer." Employees are responsible as internal suppliers to know the requirements of their internal customers.

Managers who "own" the systems of the organization are responsible for drawing the functional activities and employees of the organization into the service of system objectives. The establishment of internal customer/supplier linkages is ultimately, and necessarily, dependent on the requirements of external customers. Managerial leaders provide employees with information concerning what external customers value. Without a superordinate structure provided by system management, forcing employees to interact across organizational boundaries as internal suppliers and customers would be difficult at best.

While managers establish the necessary linkages between internal customers and suppliers in order to increase value to external customers, employees also play a critical role. As internal customers, employees are responsible for communicating clearly (and reasonably) their requirements for the products and services given to them by their internal suppliers. This implies an open communication process and establishing operational definitions and measures of the specifications of internal suppliers and the requirements of internal customers. Agreements must be negotiated as to what deliverables are to be produced for internal customers. Furthermore, concordance must be attained as to how the quality of these deliverables will be measured.

CREATING A "PULL" FOR INCLUSION IN SYSTEMS IMPROVEMENT – CONTEXT REVISITED

The managerial leadership role provides the appropriate context for employee inclusion in systems improvement. It was previously pointed out that many organizational constraints exist when employee-focused programs are not integrated with the managers' systems-improvement activities.

The effective performance of the roles and responsibilities discussed above sets the stage for a "pull" system of appropriate inclusion of employees. Rather than "push" employee involvement for its own sake or as an ideological end unto itself, managers must pull employees into system improvement by creating an environment where employees are routinely included in continuous improvement and are therefore prepared for implementing major system changes when they occur, rather than resisting them.

Such resistance is exemplified by the comment of a middle-level manager in a manufacturing organization who objected when corporate headquarters began implementation of a Total Quality Management process. The manager stated that his organization's TQM process was "like a freight train" bearing down on him and his organization.

In this case, an employee involvement program had been implemented several years earlier in the manufacturing organization as a bottom-up process without specific direction from the corporation. This process was focused primarily on Quality of Work Life issues rather than on system improvement. At the same time, the managers in the manufacturing organization were not consulted in the development of the corporation's strategy for TQM.

The result was a lack of integration as demonstrated in Figure 1. This lack of integration led to alienation and divided loyalties in the middle

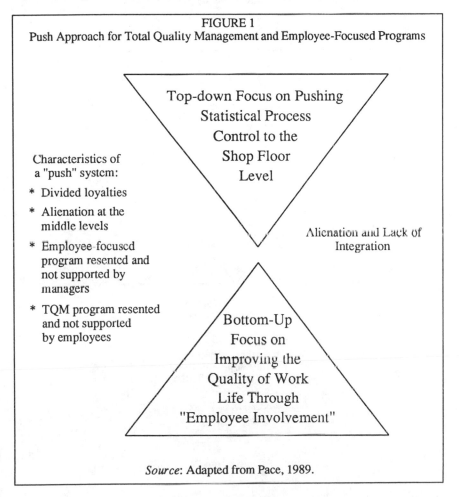

FIGURE 1
Push Approach for Total Quality Management and Employee-Focused Programs

Top-down Focus on Pushing Statistical Process Control to the Shop Floor Level

Characteristics of a "push" system:

* Divided loyalties
* Alienation at the middle levels
* Employee-focused program resented and not supported by managers
* TQM program resented and not supported by employees

Alienation and Lack of Integration

Bottom-Up Focus on Improving the Quality of Work Life Through "Employee Involvement"

Source: Adapted from Pace, 1989.

levels of the organization. Rather than create a pull system, the organization had "pushed" both employee involvement and TQM. The organization spent approximately three years integrating the top-down focus on continuous improvement with the bottom-up efforts to solve functional problems and improve the Quality of Work Life. A manager and his staff were given the specific, full-time responsibility of serving as integrators.

As demonstrated in Figure 2, a "pull" system will lead toward system integration without the necessity of establishing extra roles and processes for that integration. The approach outlined in Figure 2 shows that participation in system improvement is the job of everyone in the organization.

Managers who wish to create a demanding environment or a pull system approach for including employees in systems improvement should

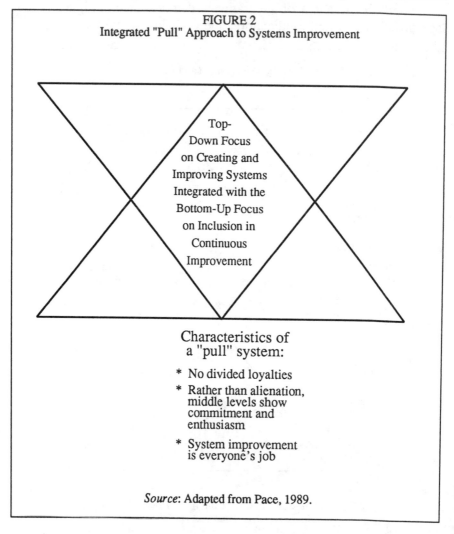

FIGURE 2
Integrated "Pull" Approach to Systems Improvement

Top-
Down Focus
on Creating and
Improving Systems
Integrated with the
Bottom-Up Focus
on Inclusion in
Continuous
Improvement

Characteristics of
a "pull" system:

* No divided loyalties
* Rather than alienation, middle levels show commitment and enthusiasm
* System improvement is everyone's job

Source: Adapted from Pace, 1989.

consider investments in the following areas: communication; training for all workers and managers in interpersonal skills and quality improvement; providing job-related opportunities for the use of tools and techniques of problem solving, decision making, and quality improvement; and the introduction of reward and recognition systems that motivate participation in systems improvement. In addition, managerial leadership via the establishment of effective role models, the effective implementation of system improvement activities, and a process for managing systemic change are vital. Finally, managers must implement periodic "process checks" to determine how much progress has been made and how much remains to be achieved.

CONCLUSION

Employees at all levels have a significant role to play in improving systems of work. Managers are fundamentally responsible for creating and improving the strategic systems of their organization. Employees at all levels must be equipped and motivated

1. To operate the current systems of the organization.
2. To identify and solve problems.
3. To improve continuously the work of their organization.
4. To communicate candidly the performance of the organization.
5. To learn and understand their roles as internal suppliers and customers in meeting system objectives.

The context of managerial leadership is critical to ensure the success of employee-focused programs to improve value creation for customers. If employee-focused programs are to contribute to organizational competitiveness, managers must create and maintain an internal environment that demands employee inclusion in systems improvement. Within this context, employees represent a powerful competitive advantage. Outside this context, the track record of employee-focused programs intended to improve competitiveness is likely to remain dismal.

REFERENCES

Argyris, C. *The Applicability of Organizational Sociology.* Cambridge, England: Cambridge University Press, 1972.
Argyris, C. *Integrating the Individual and the Organization.* New York: John Wiley and Sons, 1964.

Drucker, P. *Economic Realities and Enterprise Strategy*. In E. R. Vogel (ed.), *Modern Japanese Organization and Decision Making*. Berkeley: University of California Press, 1975.

French, W. L., C. H. Bell, Jr., and R. A. Zawacki. *Organization Development: Theory, Practice, and Research*. Plano, Tex./Business Publications, Inc., 1983.

Hatvany, N., and V. Pucik. "An Integrated Management System: Lessons Learned from the Japanese Experience." *Academy of Management Review* 6 1981: 469-480.

Hoerr, J. "Worker Participation Then and Now." In Rubinstein, S. (ed.), *Participative Systems at Work*. New York: Human Sciences Press, 1987.

Imai, M. *Kaizen: The Key to Japan's Competitive Success*. New York: Random House Business Division, 1986.

Ishikawa, K. *Guide to Quality Control*. Tokyo: Asian Productivity Organization, 1982.

Ishikawa, K. *What Is Total Quality Control? The Japanese Way*. Englewood Cliffs, N.J.: Prentice-Hall, 1985.

Japanese Union of Scientists and Engineers. *Quality Circle Koryo: General Principles of the QC Circle*. Tokyo: Author, 1980.

Lawler, E. E., III. "Choosing an Involvement Strategy. *The Academy of Management Executive*, 2, no. 3 (1988): 197-204.

Lawler, E. E., III. *High Involvement Management*. San Francisco: Jossey-Bass, 1986.

Lawler, E. E., III, and S. A. Mohrman. "Quality Circles after the Fad." *Harvard Business Review* (January-February 1985): 66.

Likert, R. *The Human Organization*. New York: McGraw-Hill, 1967.

Lu, D. Translator's introduction to K. Ishikawa. *What Is Total Quality Control? The Japanese Way*. Englewood Cliffs, N.J.: Prentice-Hall, 1985.

McGregor, D. *The Human Side of Enterprise*. New York: McGraw-Hill, 1960.

Pace, L. A. "Moving Toward System Integration." *Survey of Business* 25 1989: 57-61.

Parker, M., and J. Slaughter. "Managing by Stress: the Dark Side of Team Concept. - *Industrial and Labor Relations Report* 26 (1988): 19-23.

Peters, L. H., E. J. O'Connor and J. R. Eulberg. "Situational Constraint: Sources, Consequences, and Future Considerations. *Research in Personnel and Human Resources Management* 3 (1985): 79-114.

Schein, E. H. "Does Japanese Management Style Have a Message for American Managers?" *Sloan Management Review* 23 (1981): 55-68.

Sullivan, J. J. "A Critique of Theory Z." *Academy of Management Review* 8 (1983): 132-142.

Zager, R., and M. P. Rosow *The Innovative Organization: Productivity Programs in Action*. New York: Pergamon Press, 1982.

CHAPTER 10

MANAGING STRATEGIC SUPRASYSTEMS: THE NOBLESSE OBLIGE OF LEADERSHIP*

G. HARLAN CAROTHERS, JR.
Senior Lecturer, Institutes for Productivity
University of Tennessee

J. TOOMEY
Consultant for Harris Corporation

SUMMARY

It is likely that many organizations have no idea of their responsibilities as perceived by their customers. Self-interest and organizational strategic planning concepts have masked the understanding of managerial responsibility explicitly selected in the development of strategy. Inherent in the selection of organizational strategy are critical strategic (transfunctional) suprasystems. This chapter offers a new strategic orientation and a new methodology for discovering strategic suprasystems and includes examples of this new thought process, as they apply to commonly known organizations. Organizational implications, which may result from such a reorientation and their obligatory operational considerations, are discussed.

PURPOSE

This chapter has multiple objectives. The first objective is to consider some of the origins of modern-day organizational strategic planning and

---

*These authors would like to thank Richard Sanders and Bill Parr for their helpful comments and contributions in the development of this chapter.

their influence on organizational behavior. The second is to argue that inherent in the selection of organizational strategy are critical strategic (transfunctional) suprasystems. Such suprasystems are dictated by the self-love/interest *of those served*. These suprasystem expectations should describe specific organizational suprastructural form and content. The third objective is to suggest a methodology for identifying the strategic systems of an organization. The fourth objective is to consider the practical and theoretical implications of such a perspective.

INFLUENTIAL EARLY UNDERSTANDINGS AND POTENTIAL MISINTERPRETATIONS

Some individuals have significantly affected the way leaders of organizations think about the responsibilities of the business and the behavior of their leadership, their membership, and those that support their efforts. Adam Smith was one such individual. But as will be seen, Smith's perspective is often taken out of context and/or excerpted, perhaps for the manipulative purpose of legitimizing or rationalizing behaviors. Consider the case of Smith in some detail.

Adam Smith (note: "a moral philosopher," not an economist) justly deserves great credit for his insights into the effectiveness and efficiency of the division of labor, the underlying willingness of humans to "truck, barter and exchange," the concept of supply and demand, the fundamental definition of economic "value," and other tenets of modern-day economic theory. These ideas have helped promote the economic operational understanding of many within societies. It is perhaps wise, however, to remember the moral premise on which Smith drew his observations, the context within which he lived at the time, and even some of his other equally or perhaps even more profound realizations.

Smith lived at the dawning of the Industrial Revolution. It was a period of very limited industrial organizational development. Few organizations had more than a few hundred people, and for most businesses the number of industrial competitors was very small or nil. The highly competitive marketplace of the modern world did not exist.

In his renowned work, *The Wealth of Nations*, properly thought to be a thesis on social economics, Smith included the following:

> In civilized society he (meaning man) stands at all times in need of the cooperation and assistance of the great multitudes, while his whole life is scarce sufficient to gain the friendship of a few persons. In almost every other race of animals, each individual, when it is grown up to maturity, is entirely independent, and in its

natural state has occasion for the assistance of no other living creature. But man has almost constant occasion for the help of his brethren, and *it is vain for him to expect it from his benevolence only*. He will be more likely to prevail if he can interest their self-love in his favor, and show them that it is to *their advantage* to do for him what he requires. Whoever offers to another a bargain of any kind, proposes to do this: Give me what I want, and you shall have this which you want, is the meaning of every such offer; and it is in this manner that we obtain from one another the far greater part of those good offices which we stand in need of. It is not from the benevolence of the butcher, the brewer, or the baker, that we expect our dinner, but from their regard to their own interest. We address ourselves, not to their humanity, but to their self-love, and never talk to them of their necessities, but of *their advantage*. Nobody but a beggar chooses to depend chiefly upon the benevolence of their fellow-citizens. Even a beggar does not depend upon it entirely [Emphasis added].

In this passage, Smith appears to have given thought to the interdependency of humans. He suggests the constancy of this interdependency and says that one cannot be assured of the support of others based solely on the benevolence of the other. Rather, he states that the continued interest of the other must be maintained through the offering of "*their advantage*" to the other, that is, that which is offered must support the "self-love" of the other.

Set aside the underlying assumption of self-love for the moment. Note Smith's observation of the meaning of the exchange process: "Give me that which I want, and you shall have this which you want, is the meaning of every such offer." Smith specifically states that this was the "meaning of the offer," but did he intend "Give me that which I want . . ." as presented to be understood to be the appropriate orientation or orderliness of those engaging in the exchange process? Consider the contradiction of such an interpretation if we consider his arguments concerning the interdependency of humans and the offering of advantage to the other. We would, at a minimum, have to question "Give me what I want" coming first in the description of the "meaning of such offers." Is it possible, however, that the modern concepts of organizational strategic planning have erroneously followed the order of presentation without noting the contradiction. It is not uncommon for the managers of organizations to believe, first, we develop *our* mission statement, then *our* value statements, then we decide *our* goals and objectives, then describe market/products/services, and so on. Might the "*our*" advantage orientation distract organizations from a concern for "*their advantage*" and lead to inappropriate conduct? Furthermore consider the popularly described steps of modern-day organizational strategic planning: that is, (1) where are *we*?, (2) where do *we* want to be?, (3) how are *we* going to get there? To argue that Smith was wrong about the self-centeredness of humans flies in the face of such heuristics.

Immediately following Smith's perception on "the meaning of such offers," he reiterates the necessity of realizing that one must contribute to the other. He emphasizes that even a beggar should best not totally count on the benevolence of the other. This continuing argument of Smith would appear to reinforce the distinction to be made between the "meaning of the offer" and the appropriate orientation and conduct of those engaging in it.

Returning to the concept of self-love, Smith, who lived hundreds of years ago, has not been alone in the assumption of self-interest. In more recent times Abraham Maslow and others have supported the view that human motivation originates in the self, for example, self-preservation, self-esteem, self-actualization. These continued emphases on self may have warped the orientation of and shaped the conduct of many individuals and organizations that critically depend on the process of exchange for their very survival. Carried to its extreme, self-love, self-interest, limits full participation in a process which, in the final analysis, is predicated on reciprocity.

RECENT INFLUENTIAL THOUGHTS

Let us now leap forward from Adam Smith's time (1723-1790) and consider the influence that a self-interest orientation may have had on neoclassical organizational beliefs. In his seminal strategic management research book *Strategy and Structure,* Chandler (1962) presented his findings, that is, an organization's strategy causes its structure. In this work Chandler argues in favor of the interdependency of strategy and structure. Chandler worked from within the framework of his concept of strategy, which he defined as: "the determination of the basic long-term goals and objectives of an enterprise, and the adoption of courses of action and the allocation of resources necessary for carrying out these goals" (Chandler, 1962). Initially, his assertion of strategy as causal in determining structure was thought correct. Later Galbraith and Nathanson (1978) challenged this causal order. Their rebuttal suggested that a structure can influence (cause) the selection of strategy. Despite these different causal perspectives, agreement as to the interdependence of structure and strategy was furthered. While concern for causal order is important, what is most pertinent here is the substantiation of the interdependence. But what of the character of organizational strategies, organizational systems, and structures of organizations that originate with self-interest as an overarching premise?

A review of *The Visible Hand*, Chandler, 1977, an institutional histori-cal work, adds to one's concern. The author records the origin of the hierarchical structure of modern-day organization and the beginnings of what he refers to as a new "subspecies of economic man – the salaried manager." Close consideration of his study reveals the underlying motiva-tion of both. Chandler concludes:

> This study does more than trace the history of an institution. It describes the beginning of a new economic function – that of administrative coordination and allocation – and the coming of a new subspecies of economic man – the salaried manager – to carry out this function. Technological innovation, the rapid growth and spread of population, and expanding per capita income made the processes of production and the distribution more complex and increased the speed and volume of the flow of materials through them. Existing market mechanisms were often no longer able to coordinate these flows effectively. The new technologies and the expanding markets thus created for the first time a need for ad-ministrative coordination. To carry out this function entrepreneurs built multiunit business enterprises and hired the managers needed to administer them. Where the new enterprises were able to coor-dinate current flows of materials profitably, their managers also allocated resources for future production and distribution. As tech-nology became more complex and more productive, and as markets continued to expand, these managers assumed command in the central sectors of the American economy.

Originally, middle managers existed primarily for the purposes of coordination, control, and evaluation of geographically extended or highly vertically integrated organizations. Generations of "salaried managers" who have "assumed command," guided by dicta like "getting things done through others" (Mary Parker Follett, 1868-1933) and prescriptions like "planning, coordinating, organizing, controlling, and directing" (Henri Fayol, 1841-1925), may have contributed to the belief that organizational leadership consisted merely of macro extensions of their professionally prescribed administrative operational habits. The concepts of strategic planning, which evolved in the 1950s, (note the similarity of operational language selected; Fayol also used the word "planning"), may have been driven by the years of imbedded concepts. The context of rapid geographi-cal organizational extension, organizational size, and the need for administrative coordination modeled the content of neoclassical organizational strategy and strategist.

A review of just two of the significant seminal works in economics (Smith, 1937) and organizational management (Chandler, 1977) reveals some of the concepts or misconceptions that may have guided the thoughts, decisions, and operational behaviors of organizational leaders.

But new precepts and principles might offer considerably different thoughts, decisions, and operant behaviors.

DEFINITION OF NEW TERMS

A definition of new terms is required to provide a basis for logical argumentation.

Strategy is defined as: That valued product and/or service set for which an organization willingly chooses to accept responsibility for providing to a selected set of customers/users and for creating organizational strategic systems through which to satisfy the obligations of the enterprise. Obviously, this stated meaning flies in direct contradiction to many of those offered in classical strategic management literature (Ansoff, 1965; Chandler, 1962; Learned, Christensen, Andrews, and Guth, 1965). Its critical context is external to the organization; its social ethic and ethical orderliness, derived from its critical context, are explicit; its prescriptive order is not accidental. Some regard it as antithetical to past concepts of strategy, and it may be!

Strategic (transfunctional) suprasystems are defined as: Those systems derived from the strategic decision of an organization to willingly accept responsibility for providing certain customer-valued products and/or services. A unique set of strategic suprasystems is explicitly dictated by the specific previously self-held customer responsibilities for which the organization has chosen to accept full accountability. These accountabilities dictate the organizational suprasystems to be conceived, designed, operationalized, managed, and improved by an organization's managerial leadership. Strategic suprasystems demand the subordination and support of all other organizational functional unit subsystems, activities, processes, and tasks. Implicit in the management of strategic suprasystems is the assumption that the managerial leadership knows where the organization is and where it must go if it is to be assured its survival and its future. It is perhaps even more important that the leadership know the way to go.

Said Alice to the Cheshire cat, "Which way do I go?" Said the Cheshire cat to Alice, "That depends on where you are going." If we rethink the subtlety of the cat's response, interesting thoughts come to mind. We think we are lost only if we know where we intend to go. Or we may not know we are lost if we do not know where it is that we should be going. The second is the more unfortunate of these two alternatives. In the first alternative, we may be thought of as being caught in a maze, but despite confusion we believe ourselves to have some idea as to where we are and therefore where we are headed. In the second alternative; (i.e., those who don't even know they are lost), they are caught in the same maze but derive happiness from the fact that they are making decisions! They are feverishly active despite barriers: It matters little that they're not getting "there"; its the next windmill that counts, not whether we are getting "there." The first are puzzled; the second are fatally naive.

Many organizations are confused and misdirected by their own internal (self-love) organizational strategy and its implementation. Many have been victims of simplistic conceptualization. Consider: (1) where are *we*? (2) where do *we* want to go? (3) how are *we* going to get there? These classical questions in management planning exacerbate a dilemma. They have classically framed the organizational mission and the self-interest of the enterprise in the form of goals/objectives. Consider their revision to include: (1) what is there that is valued for which we are willing to commit to be responsible? (2) where would such willing responsibleness take us? (3) how might we go about fulfilling such accountability?

The strategic problem continues to be the resolution of the question "how." But when the "how" question, which is normally the last question, is framed by the reorientation of the enterprise sense of responsibility, it instead becomes the premier question. This would at first glance appear to be a contradiction in logic. It has always been presumed that we must know where we are going before pursuing how to get there. What has been missing is the new vehicular question: *What is there that is valued for which we are willing to commit to be responsible?* This new question is considerably different from either of the typical ones: what business are we in?, or what business do we choose to be in? These two queries have seldom carried the connotation of commitment to responsibility and declaration of willingness to be held accountable.

This new approach and orientation suggests a new way to conceptualize and operationalize organizational strategy. It also suggests a new way to identify the critical suprasystems of organizations. If operational strategy is the manifestation of the decision as to that for which an organization will be responsible and willingly be held accountable, then implicit in the choice are found the suprasystem(s) management obligations for which an organization coincidentally commits itself. Examples may provide insight and substantiation. The study of familiar organizations and their strategic commitments may provide conceptual clarification and aid in developing a methodology through which to discover critical transfunctional strategic suprasystems.

Consider the case of a common commercial bread manufacturer. As a result of its strategic choice, any organization that produces commercially available bread has accepted explicit responsibilities. The responsibilities include (1) the ability to successfully bake bread(s) upon demand; (2) the ability to replicate its bread(s); and (3) the ability to make available bread of the appropriate kind(s) and quantity to meet the desired consumption for purchase at customary points of sale. How might one draw such conclusions? Ask customers/users of bread, in particular about what they expect of a bread supplier. Almost all will respond: (1) the bread(s) must be available in the kind(s) and quantities where and when I desire it (them) at a reasonable price; (2) the bread(s) must be good (i.e., freshness, size, number of slices, not squashed, nutrition, moisture, texture, etc.); and (3) though often assumed – baked successfully when and where demanded.

Another way to find these explicit expectations may be by asking customers/users of bread: what is it that the bread manufacturer does for them, that if the manufacturer didn't do, they would have to do themselves? Here again, the consumer responses, given some thought, would be "the manufacturer of bread is relied on to (1) bake bread; (2) bake 'good' bread repeatedly; and (3) deliver (or make available) bread at the point of sale when it is desired."

At first glance the discussions with bread customers are hardly profound, but with further thought we realize that the customer/user's expectation might identify the critical suprasystem that must be managed, through which customer value is realized. Inferred in the bread customers' responses is the expectation that the bread manufacturer will have (1) a suprasystem for successfully baking bread to meet the customers' demands (cost and quality); (2) a suprasystem for insuring that the characteristics of the bread offered will be sufficiently consistent to allow the customer to be confident in each purchase, that is, not have to worry over extraordinary variation in the bread purchased from time to time; and (3) a suprasystem to insure the availability of bread at the point of sales when the customer desires bread in the quantity desired.

Looking through this reverse side of the classical strategic looking glass, we see something quite different from the overly simplistic question like "what business is the bread manufacturer in?" The superficial and clipped response to the question is too often, "They make bread." While this answer is true, it falls short of the perspective that a look from the other side of the glass might give. Perhaps this alternative view offers more information and even instruction.

Consider another example. Ask an individual with a volume of paper (too large to fax) who he or she will call on if the paper needs to be sent to a specific person in another city. The response may be Federal Express. In this case we are already on the other side of the strategic looking glass. So what is it that Federal Express provides the user of its services? What is it that the user would have to do for himself or herself were it not for the fact that Federal Express had accepted the responsibility for doing it? (1) Upon demand (normally a telephone call) Federal Express will respond by picking up the material or scheduling its pickup. (2) Federal Express will provide secure, informed, and timely movement. (3) Federal Express will see that the material is delivered into the hands of the intended recipient. (4) If it cannot complete the obligation of delivering the material to the person, or another agreed upon arrangement can be made, it is understood that Federal Express will return the material to the sender.

Users have come to expect Federal Express to have suprasystems for (1) responding upon demand to the individual's desire to have an item materialize in another's possession; (2) providing secure, informed, and timely movement of items; and (3) providing confident materialization of the item in the possession of the desired party. These unique suprasystems are the explicit derivatives of the strategy of Federal Express.

Selecting and fulfilling those responsibilities for which it willingly commits itself, Federal Express enacts how it will get to where it wants to go. It thereby sets out its strategy for moving forward from where it currently is to its desired future. Its degree of success is a function of two primary factors. (1) Are the responsibilities chosen valued and to what degree? (2) If so, how much more net value can it (Federal Express) produce for its users when compared with competitive alternatives? Net value is defined here as that which is realized by the user which justifies what he or she has to sacrifice.

Thoughtful consideration of an organization's explicit obligation to create and manage these suprasystems suggests that any compromise of responsibility may be met with rejection, particularly if others (viable competitors) exist.

These obligatory suprasystems *are not* the integrating suprasystem referred to by Bedeian (1980). He like many others before him has been preoccupied with coordinating the highly differentiated departments, functions, activities, processes and tasks of organizations. The suprasystems overarch all the elements of organization. They demand the subordination of all functional units of organization and serve as the undergirding suprastructure through which organizations attend to their superordinate obligations to the users of their products and/or services. They demand the integration of all functional organizational parts. Efficiency realized through managed differentiation, while necessary, must never compromise effectiveness brought about by managerially directed integration. The optimization of the whole must never be compromised by the suboptimization of parts. For if this were to exist the whole could never be greater than the sum of the parts. Optimization of the parts must never compromise the dedicated synergistic imperative.

Another example might be useful. Suppose that an organization suggests that it would willingly accept responsibility for defining, designing, and furnishing gravure print plates required in creating advertising art. Its obligations are innate in its promises. First, there is the expectation that it would have a suprasystem for insuring the expedient and appropriate definition of the product desired. Second, given the definition of product, there is a competent suprasystem for insuring the making of quality gravure plates in a timely manner. Third, there is the necessity to create and manage a suprasystem to insure the compatibility of the manufactured plates with the users' printing production process(es). This list of suprasystems may not be exhaustive. Such an organization may accept other responsibilities. This list attempts to capture only the primary suprasystems for which any organization with similarly selected responsibilities would find itself responsible.

Lastly, consider a public educational institution. Its willing acceptance of its responsibilities might lead to the expectation that there will be (1) a suprasystem for the development and/or assimilation of new knowledge; (2) another suprasystem for confident dissemination of knowledge, which might include both publication and educating; and (3) still another suprasystem for promoting and assisting in the application of knowledge in public applications.

IMPLICATIONS

For Practitioners

Customer/user-identified values determine the strategic purpose of an organization relative to its product and/or services. The organization's agreed upon purpose determines the critical management systems to be managed by an organization's leadership. Current organizational structures likely reflect local ownership of subordinate operational subsystems and/or processes that have been derived for the satisfaction of organizational goals/objectives. However, such subsystems and/or processes are not necessarily the descriptors of the strategic suprasystems of organization. The total membership of an organization must be led to the understanding that the strategic suprasystems expectations must direct, drive, and encompass the relevant subordinate functional systems and processes, regardless of the existing organizational structure. A strategic suprasystems management suprastructure will evolve. It is the rate of change to new systemic designs and their successful implementation which ensures the longevity of the organization. These strategically imposed organizational suprasystems will describe appropriate organizational structures, tasks, roles, relationships, and responsibilities.

For Theorists

Implied in these definitions of organizational strategy and their uniquely associated strategic suprasystems is a reexamination of classical and even neoclassical theories and concepts of organizational strategy, systems, and structure. Dramatic shifts will be required in organizational theory. For instance, division of labor (Smith, 1937), scientific management (Taylor, 1911), leadership stylist (McGregor, 1960) and modern sociotechnical concepts (Woodward, 1965; Walton, 1978) have fostered structural differentiation. Generally, differentiation has been conceptualized as preceding integration (Lawrence and Lorsch, 1967). The new customer/user value-based strategic suprasystems innate in the organizational strategy will serve as the constraining integrants of any and all structurally differentiated units and their distributed operational subsystems and processes. The assumption that unity of command provides unity of direction is false. Unity of effective direction must supersede. Unity of command is grossly inadequate.

Many organizations have sought improvement in the organization's performance through reorganization. Appropriateness of structure, tasks, roles, relationships, and responsibilities would appear to have been behind the organizational redesigner quests. Designers of structural reorganization have experimented with new structural models (e.g., brand management, matrix management, program/project management, strategic business unit, product line management). If the primary motive of these substructures was to improve "efficiency," could the forms of restructure have been limited by such a set of motives? The question at hand is: What might prove to be a more appropriate set of motives from which to design more "effective" organizations of the future?

CONCLUSION

In the past those who aspired to gain the respect of their followers (the nobility) were expected to earn that right by fulfilling their obligation to provide for their followers (serfs). The underlying precept was the deep sense and acceptance of responsibility: "the inferred obligation of people of high rank or social position to behave nobly or kindly towards others" (Webster's, 1980). If the leaders of organizations are to retain their desired right to be held in high regard, it may require a new realization of the inherent obligations to which they have inferred their agreement and accordingly consistent personal and organizational behavior.

REFERENCES

Ansoff, H. I. *Corporate Strategy: An Analytic Approach to Business Policy for Growth and Expansion.* New York: McGraw-Hill, 1965.

Bedeian, A. G. *Organizations: Theory and Analysis.* 2nd ed., New York: Holt, Rinehart and Winston, 1980.

Chandler, A. D. *Strategy and Structure.* Cambridge Mass.: MIT Press, 1962.

Chandler, A. D. *The Visible Hand.* Cambridge Mass.: Harvard University Press, 1977.

Fayol, Henri. *General and Industrial Management*, trans. Constance Sterns, London: Pitman Publishing, Ltd., 1949. (Original work published 1916.)

Follett, Mary Parker. *Creative Experience.* London: Longmans, Green and Co., 1924.

Follett, Mary Parker. *The New State: Group Organization the Solution of Popular Government.* London: Longmans, Green and Co., 1918.

Galbraith, J. R. and D. A. Nathanson. *Strategy Implementation*, St. Paul: West Publishing, 1978.

Lawrence, P., and J. Lorsch. *Organization and Environment.* Boston: Division of Research, Harvard Business School, 1967.

Learned, E. P., C. R. Christensen, K. R. Andrews and W. P. Guth. *Business Policy: Text and Cases.* Homewood, Ill.: Richard D. Irwin, 1965.

McGregor, Douglas. *The Human Side of Enterprise.* New York: McGraw-Hill, 1960.

Smith, Adam. *Wealth of Nations*, New York: Modern Library ed. 1937.

Taylor, Frederick W. *The Principles of Scientific Management.* New York: Harper and Row, 1911.

Walton, R. E. "The Topeka Story." *The Wharton Magazine* (Spring 1978): 38-48.

Webster's New World Dictionary. New York: Simon and Schuster, 1980.

Woodward, Joan. *Industrial Organization: Theory and Practice.* London: Oxford University Press, 1965.

CHAPTER 11

ORGANIZATIONAL CHANGE:
THE SYSTEMS APPROACH

KENNETH E. KIRBY
Professor of Industrial Engineering
University of Tennessee

SUMMARY

This chapter suggests that the study and improvement of organizational systems offers an effective means of providing strategic capabilities that are valued by customers. These desired capabilities form the basis for achieving long-term competitive position for an industry. Two approaches for addressing systems study are discussed – reductionistic and holistic; the holistic approach is proposed as offering the greatest leverage in providing a competitive rate of improvement.

Systems study should begin by analyzing the external environment. This analysis should discover those capabilities that are and will be valued by customers. Discovering valued capabilities leads naturally to identifying the critical systems of the organization. These systems are large, complex, and run horizontally across the organization. The organization's resources should be focused on these critical systems in contrast to solving "problems" as they occur. The chapter identifies and discusses capabilities currently valued by customers, describes how valued capabilities may change over time, and provides examples for translating valued capabilities into critical systems.

The chapter concludes by recommending a thirteen-step approach for analyzing and improving the critical systems of an organization. The success of the approach is heavily dependent on the assignment of responsibility for improving critical systems to top managers. The critical systems of most organizations currently have no owners. Systems owners are supported by other organizational members who typically represent functions or departments that significantly contribute to the desired capability provided by the system under study.

INTRODUCTION

During recent years U.S. managers have faced rapid changes in consumer demand for products and services. The demand for product quality has increased dramatically and shows no sign of moderating. Capabilities such as rapid after-sales repairs, reduced delivery lead times, production and shipment of smaller lot quantities, and fast introduction of new products and product derivatives are becoming accepted norms to secure a company's future. The instability in the marketplace, created by ever increasing customer expectations, is not a passing phenomenon. The dramatic changes in Eastern Europe and the Pacific Rim will only exacerbate the magnitude of change. These potentially huge markets offer tremendous opportunity for those companies with the ability to adapt to the new expectations.

Managers recognize that the rate of change in their external environment will continue to grow. Some of their responses are listed below:

1. Training employees in Statistical Process Control and exhorting them to strive for excellence, to be innovative, and to practice risk-taking.
2. Developing and communicating a vision and strategy for the organization.
3. Creating Quality Directors and charging them to conduct organizationwide quality and customer awareness campaigns.
4. Manipulating leveraged buyouts, downsizing and other forms of cost-cutting.
5. Identifying opportunities for automation in order to attack the labor portion of total cost.

These responses have undoubtedly had some impact, but they are insufficient. They offer only piecemeal "quick-fixes" that will not provide the basis for long-term organizational change. The majority of managers do not understand the variables that influence strategic organizational performance.

This chapter suggests that the performance of organizations can be dramatically improved when managers shed the constraining yoke of the traditional, vertical view of the organization. The traditional view is defined as one that perceives the organization in light of its structure, composed of several different departments or functions. Each function has identified responsibilities for the success of the company corresponding to the expertise residing within the function. Managers of several functional units manage those units individually. Goals for the functional units are set independently. Communication and interaction between the functional units are often limited to activity reports and infrequent meetings held for the purpose of informing organizational members of overall financial results. Decision making is held tightly by high-level managers. Conflicts between functions at lower levels rise to the top of the organization for resolution. Top-level managers, then, spend a significant portion of their time making tactical decisions; these decisions influence the internal organization but have very little influence on improving their competitive position in the external environment. Lower level managers often see themselves as mere implementors of upper level directives and assume little responsibility for results. Optimization within the functional units is achieved at the expense of organizational suboptimization.

The rate of change in both the environment and technology has proven the traditional view to be ineffective. This chapter suggests that managers must take on a systems view of the organization in better understanding how to invoke long-term change. They must recognize that the organization represents a transformation system that is comprised of a multitude of layers of subsystems that are interdependent and are put in place to provide what customers value. Managers are responsible for utilizing human, capital, technological, and raw material input resources effectively They must initialize the improvement effort by ensuring that an organizational system is in place to determine what customers most highly value. The current and future instability of the market in which those customers reside suggests that this accumulation of knowledge will not be a single event. The system must allow management to be aware of what is currently of value and what will be of value in order to proactively respond to changing needs. The rate of adaptation to changing value attributes will be the competitive differentiator.

Managers must recognize how work actually gets done in the organization through systems that cut horizontally across the entire organization. The effectiveness of these systems determines whether or not the organization is able to respond to changing customer values. Some of the systems are specifically directed at attributes highly valued by customers. Managers must focus their organization's resources on studying, improving, and designing systems that are robust to changing customer needs. This chapter provides insights that assist managers in focusing resources on those few critical systems that provide leverage in increasing the value of products/services for customers. It also offers recommendations for describing, assessing performance, standardizing, and improving those systems so that they will be adaptive to environmental change.

APPROACHES IN STUDYING SYSTEMS

The study of systems is extremely broad. Literature is available in practically every disciplinary area found in the library. There are a vast variety of things, ideas, and people that could be called systems. It would be fair to state that nearly anything that captures our attention could be called a "system." Since this chapter, however, deals primarily with organizational systems, a comprehensive definition for the specific type of system provided by Wright (1989) is given below:

1. An open social system of coordinated activities
2. that involves two or more participants
3. designed and managed to pursue a goal or goals
4. through subsystems that are internally consistent with each other and its goals,
5. while adjusting to maintain environmental consonance.

The above definition of an organizational system is taken from a conceptual framework that has existed for centuries. Only within the last thirty to forty years, however, was it formalized and did it gain increased emphasis. Note how the definition emphasizes the importance of the whole. It highlights the interrelationships of the component parts (subsystems), and it suggests that the whole is greater than the sum of the individual parts. It implies that changes in systems should take place only after a full understanding of the relationships between the parts. Addressing the study of systems giving due consideration and priority to a more comprehensive list of system traits similar to those listed above has been categorized as a *holistic* approach. A second approach focuses more on the component parts than the whole and has been identified as a *reductionistic* approach. The second approach appears to have been the choice of many who have involved themselves in the study and improvement of organizational systems in recent history. A further elaboration of each approach and summary comments are presented in the following sections.

The Reductionistic Approach

The period from the beginning of the Industrial Revolution until about 1950 has been described as the machine age (Ackoff, 1974). During this period there was a great emphasis on reductionism, the theory that everything in the world and every experience of it can be reduced to component parts. With physics, the indivisible parts become atoms; with chemistry, the parts are the basic elements; with biology, the parts are cells; with psychology, there are direct observables, basic instincts, drives, motives, and needs; with sociology, the parts become individuals and primary groups.

Reductionism gave rise to an analytical way of thinking of the world; of seeking explanations and gaining an understanding of it. With the analytical approach, something to be explained is broken into component parts. Next come the explanations of the component parts. Aggregating these partial explanations provides us with the explanation of the whole. As long as the parts are independent, this approach works reasonably well. The lack of independence, however, can generate much less than anticipated results.

The most lasting and damaging impact of thinking analytically was the effect it likely had on splitting the disciplines. Science separated itself from philosophy little more than a century ago. Next came the split of science into physics and chemistry. Chemistry, in turn, gave birth to biology. Psychology became a subset of biology. The social sciences became a subset of psychology. This much had occurred by the beginning of the twentieth century. Disciplines proliferated; the U.S. National Research Council now lists more than 150 of them.

This is not to imply that having a multitude of disciplines has not offered advantages. Disciplines are categories that theoretically allow us to file the content of science. Individuals with common interests have been allowed to share insights and gain an enhanced understanding of specific problem areas that could be improved by using some developed methodology. Each discipline, then, essentially developed its own body of knowledge, methods, principles, or views of how they collectively might improve the world. For years they have continued to expand their file. The problem is that nature is not organized in the way our knowledge of it is organized. The individual disciplines have not appreciated, and in some cases still do not (1) that the organizational systems truly worth addressing are complex and (2) that these complex systems require collaboration among several disciplines to design effective solutions. These systems require a great deal of time to study, and they often result in several potential solutions (no optimal solution) that must be evaluated. In essence, interdisciplinary integration is a necessary requirement to move away from the reductionistic/analytical approach in the analysis of organizational systems.

A perfect example of the reductionistic approach to systems study is the experience of many U.S. companies in coming to grips with the need to improve product quality within the manufacturing sector. During the 1980s, the organizational focal point for attacking the quality problem was at the manufacturing process level. The manufacturing function was assumed to have complete control over improving product quality. The collection of data and analysis at various steps in the process often revealed sources of waste and nonvalue-added activity that could be eliminated. Similarly, sources of variability in product quality were identified, changes were made in manufacturing processes, and quality did improve. Quality was significantly improved over a wide range of industries (Miller and Roth, 1988), particularly during the period from 1985 to 1988.

A reasonable proportion of those companies working diligently to improve quality, however, experienced a drop in the rate of improvement some one to two years after they had embarked on their "improvement" program. Invariably, unless the effort faltered and was discarded as the failed program of the year, the managers of these organizations would discover interdependencies between other organizational subsystems and the manufacturing processes that acted as constraints in continuing the current rate of improvement. The vendor subsystem was often identified as needing attention. The subsystem for planning and proactively scheduling "cost-effective" maintenance was often targeted. Moving away from the manufacturing site, the marketing subsystem, whose purpose was to provide feedback on product and service characteristics most valued by customers, was often ineffective and in some cases nonexistent. These represent only a few examples. One thing was certain: For those companies that did experience a loss of inertia, it became apparent that organizational subsystems were not aligned so as to continue the required rate of improvement. The lack of independence of functional activities was highlighted, and functional suboptimization became an issue. Managers began to speak of "functional silos." Those who continued to pursue their improvement effort began to sense a need to describe how functional activities must be coordinated to leverage their rate of improvement.

The Holistic Approach

General Systems Theory (GST) ultimately refocused attention on using a more holistic approach to study and improve organizational systems. GST was not developed in response to the need to address organizational systems, but rather to address a specific problem. There was no analytical methodology to explain organic biology. Similar to organizational systems, organic biology deals with varied principles and with systems at all levels. "Living" systems simply could not be studied effectively using the analytical-mechanistic approach.

The 1930s and 1940s passed with many researchers crying out for a more advanced, newer logic capable of addressing the study of both living and nonliving things. Nonliving systems could be addressed using closed-systems theory. In a closed system no exchange takes place with the outside. Studies of living things required open-systems theory. With an open system exchange does take place with the outside. It was generally felt that the exchange with the external environment brought with it complexity. As studies move from the physical and mechanical to biological, social, cultural, and ideological systems, they become progressively more complicated.

Ludwig von Bertalanffy, accepted as the father of GST, provided the rationale for studying living systems in 1950. The Society for General Systems Research was founded in 1954. GST can be regarded as a conceptual revolution. It has since been used in studying such varying applications as humanism, behavioral change, philosophy, curriculum, aeronautics, aesthetics, neurons, and organizational systems. Being extremely young and abstract, GST has little unquestionable doctrine. Its traits are many. The traits discussed below are those major benchmarks that should be given serious consideration when initiating an effort to study and improve organizational systems.

1. Goal seeking. The activities that take place within a system can be directed to achieving some goal or objective. The goal can be externally directed or internally directed to extend the life of the system.

2. Holism. A system is an inseparable entity. Attempts to break a system down and dwell on component parts will result in a loss of understanding of crucial relationships between those parts. GST suggests a field focus viewpoint; the field should consist of all the critical parts that interact with one another. We should first study the field and then narrow the focus to the component of concern.

3. Hierarchy. A system consists of subsystems that can be prioritized into a list in relation to their contribution to accomplishing the goal being sought.

4. Inputs and outputs. All systems require inputs. In closed systems the inputs are supplied before the system is sealed from outside influences. Their goal is simply self-maintenance, or the output is stored within the system. The most interesting and important systems are open systems. In these systems inputs or resources flow into the system, activity takes place in the use of these resources, and outputs are generated over the system life cycle.

5. Transformation. The activities that take place within a system are the means by which inputs are converted to outputs.

6. Energy. A system gathers and/or generates energy. Conventional forms of energy would include steam, gravity, electricity, and various fuels along with pumps, motors, and generators. But other types of energy are needed for human, social, political, and ideological systems. These other types might be, for example, assertiveness, influence, perceptions, or spirit from other people.

7. Entropy. A system tends to degenerate. Closed systems use up resources and wear out. Open systems have continuing supplies of resources and so the degeneration is not automatic. An open system uses resources in two ways: (1) to produce output and (2) to maintain itself. Thus, a system could become entropic if it used too much of its resources for self-maintenance that was not directly attached to its primary purpose or objective.

8. Equifinality. Open systems can reach their objectives in a number of ways. Unlike a closed system, an open system can change inputs, goals, or the efficiency of the transformation system in generating outputs. In effect, the tendency toward entropy can be delayed or totally avoided in open systems if they are effectively managed.

This new way of thinking has not been accepted unreservedly. Although it encourages us to take a broader view, it strongly recommends preliminary study before dealing with the details. This is not comforting to some. It forces us to understand the importance of relationships between component parts (subsystems) before changes are made to the components. This is particularly disturbing to those steeped in "causal thinking," which has been around for so long and has created enough success that it is almost generally considered as *the* scientific thinking.

But GST has several strengths that cannot be neglected. First, since it forces us to think more broadly, it offers specialists the opportunity to integrate their bodies of knowledge. The study of large, complex systems requires the expertise and perspectives of many specialists in order to generate a truly global improvement opportunity. To a degree, GST frees us from the parts-versus-whole dilemma. If we study the subsystems alone, we will lack knowledge of the whole system. If we stay at too high a level and study only the system without understanding the parts, we fail to achieve the necessary understanding to have an impact on incremental improvement of overall system performance.

Levels of Systems

There are many levels of systems. The levels are defined in accordance with the degree of complexity of the respective system. Kenneth Boulding (1956) is credited as having structured the most frequently cited hierarchy of systems, and this list is shown in the accompanying tabulation. Obviously, the higher the level, the more complex the systems.

Level	System Type
9	Transcendental
8	Social organization
7	Human
6	Animal
5	Genetic-societal
4	Open systems
3	Cybernetics
2	Clockworks
1	Frameworks

The lowest three levels include closed systems. Starting with level 1 we have the most elementary type, which are the static structures. Examples of these frameworks would be a skeleton, the set of stars, and a formal organizational structure. Frameworks would not constitute a system using the definition given earlier. As we move next to clockworks, the simplest of dynamic systems are found. Examples are machines, pendulums, and clocks. Movements within the system are predetermined by functional need. Clockworks are closed systems where the theories of physics and chemistry can be used to predict movement and/or change. As we move up to the third level, cybernetics, the systems are becoming more open. We begin to think about control mechanisms and closed loop control. The systems receive feedback from their environment. Examples would include thermostats, maintenance of body temperature, and mechanisms in organisms. These systems would be studied by the engineer, computer scientist, and biologist. Control theory and cybernetics would be relevant disciplines.

Open systems are addressed at level 4. These systems have the capability of structural self-maintenance by transforming material and energy. Elementary forms of life are introduced here – biological cells. Relevant disciplines that study these systems would include the biochemist. Level 5, genetic-societal, includes systems of lower organisms. Here we find the organized whole with functional parts, "blueprinted" growth, and reproduction. These systems have specialized cells and are structured with information receptors, although they cannot process and react to data received. Life stages are prescribed genetically. Relevant disciplines that would study these systems include the botanist. At level 6 we find the animal, an entity that is a living system, mobile, goal-directed, and self-aware. This system processes, stores, and responds to external information. It can determine certain goals and the means to those goals within bounds imposed genetically.

Next, we move to the human system. This entity can think about the future, set goals, and plan to reach them. Humans are self-reflective; they know they know things. Their world is further complicated in that they can communicate by images, symbolism, and language. As we move one step higher, the most complicated system that we will be able to affect is the social organization: social systems or systems of human beings. As noted earlier, the organizational systems that are the focus of this chapter are social systems that include subsystems; these subsystems, in turn, include and are influenced not only by the practices and procedures that have been established to achieve organizational objectives, but also by the values, norms, perceptions, and roles of the humans who are making use of them. The last system classification, transcendental, allows for future discoveries of the now unknown, the understanding of ultimate truths, and so on. This would allow us to understand, for example, the relationships that exist between the subsystems that support the system under study, regardless of how subtle or complex those relationships might be. For the immediate future, at least, we must be content to address our attention to social organizational systems and attempt to uncover the significant relationships between the subsystems that should be recognized.

GST has had much influence, but it has not really been concerned with practical systems analysis (Wood-Harper and Fitzgerald, 1982). It is more an attempt to come to terms with and understand the nature of systems. It offers a theoretical model-building capability for interpreting complex and diverse systems. Its generality makes it difficult to use and to develop a methodological solution. It is not a process that often recommends small incremental changes but one that more usually results in the complete reassessment of structures, roles, and behavior. Its contribution, therefore, is in providing some underlying principles from which practical approaches for analyzing and improving organizational systems can be developed. To be considered holistic, this approach, at a minimum, should possess the following traits or characteristics.

1. The organization should be perceived as a large transformation system. The activities that take place within the organization should be directed to some goal or objective.

2. An organizational system consists of many subsystems. Work should take place to understand how these subsystems interact with one another before focusing on improving an individual subsystem.
3. The major subsystems that interrelate to form a higher level organizational system should all be understood as to their (a) purpose and (b) contribution to the objective or goal being sought by the higher level system.
4. The major subsystems should be prioritized into a list in relation to their contribution to accomplishing the goal being sought.
5. Organizational systems directed toward specific objectives should be effectively managed to allow an organization to adapt to a changing external environment (equifinality).

In summary, managers must take a more holistic approach to study and improve organizational systems. The systems that are important to strategic survival produce results that are highly valued by customers. They are complex because they typically consist of subsystems that cut horizontally across the organization. The subsystems are interrelated. The output of one subsystem often acts as the input of another subsystem. Managers, then, must initially extend the boundaries of any system improvement effort to include the subsystems that contribute to the performance of the larger system under study. The importance of each subsystem in achieving increased value for the customer must be established in order to prioritize and coordinate improvement efforts. The establishment of subsystem importance is likely to be based on subjective rather than objective criteria. The performance of each important subsystem must be evaluated against its intended purpose and expected results. This evaluation provides the information on which to base subsequent work activity and to leverage improved performance. As is suggested in GST, this approach represents a field focus view. All critical parts that interact with one another are included in the field. After studying the field, the focus is narrowed to the component of concern. This approach is more complex and requires more initial planning and coordination effort before we can initiate changes in the system. It is necessary in order to avoid suboptimization and the attendant ineffective utilization of organizational resources.

The use of a more holistic approach does not preclude work on system improvement as part of functional managers' overall responsibility. Each functional manager has the responsibility to continuously evaluate the work performed under his or her responsibility so as to eliminate waste and nonvalue-added activity. The primary purpose of the functions, however, is to enhance the performance of the few systems that contribute to those attributes highly valued by customers. Functional managers must be assured that subsystem improvement within their respective units is not achieved at the expense of loss of performance for the larger system. Their work, then, must take place following a thorough knowledge of how their subsystem interacts with others that are major contributors to total system performance.

IDENTIFYING DESIRED CAPABILITIES AND OBJECTIVES

The Strategic Management Process

A rather new idea for U.S. managers has been identified as "policy management." The purpose of policy management is to integrate the systems of the organization to accomplish objectives (Sullivan, 1988). Sullivan suggests that policy management should take the form of a business plan that actually overlays an organization's systems and drives the management focus from emphasis on ultimate results to the systems that are used to achieve those results. Top management must initiate this plan by establishing company goals or objectives. The goals, objectives, and work activity of each division, department, and section are then aligned to ensure proper focus on these objectives.

The strategic management process, the vehicle for establishing company objectives, is a key step in initiating systems improvement efforts. The process results in a limited number of objectives to which management should dedicate the resources of the organization. Similarly, a limited number of critical organizational systems are the means by which these objectives are achieved. The approach for establishing these objectives, then, is worthy of some elaboration. The general steps as described by Thompson and Strickland (1978) are summarized below.

1. Definition of the business
2. Environment/Situation analysis
3. Strategy formulation
4. Strategy implementation
5. Evaluation and control

Further discussion of this approach is provided in Chapter 3 by Carothers and Adams. These authors suggest a reorientation of the strategic management process. They conclude that the current orientation focuses largely on the internal needs and wants of organizational members and other stakeholders such as stockholders. Rather than starting with questions like "what do we want?" and "how are we going to get it?", the process should be modified by positioning customers at the top of the list of stakeholders. Management must achieve an understanding of what customers value and commit itself to providing what is most valued. The authors state that marketing studies of customer satisfaction are insufficient. Managers must find the attributes of satisfaction/dissatisfaction, and they must then manage the delivery of these attributes. An alternative strategic management process is proposed and consists of the following components:

1. Determination of responsibility
2. Environmental analysis
3. Strategic organizational systems determination
4. Strategic systems management
5. Confirmation, correction, and change

Carothers and Adams elaborate on the proposed strategic management process and provide contrasts with the more traditional approach. A comprehensive comparison of the differences is beyond the scope of this chapter. The recommended approach, however, is complementary to our theme: that using a more holistic approach in the study of organizational systems represents a means of leveraging the rate of improvement of organizational performance. The more pertinent characteristics are summarized below:

1. Customers must be elevated over managers, employees, and stockholders in order to achieve the necessary external focus.
2. Emphasis should be placed on creating value for present and prospective customers instead of generating financial rewards for the firm.
3. The firm must intend to become increasingly preferred by customers when compared to alternatives.
4. The firm must have systems in place that will allow them rapidly to adapt to changing customer needs and competitors' improvements.
5. Managers must build detailed profiles of end users, channel customers, and competitors to assist in adapting.
6. Managers must identify the critical systems of the organization that will allow them to improve their capacity and capability to deliver what customers most value.
7. Managers must be assigned the responsibility of "owners" of the critical systems. Owners will be responsible for describing, assessing, standardizing, and improving the critical systems.
8. System owners must define expected levels of performance of the critical system and the subsystems that support it.

9. System owners must identify measures to quantify current and improved performance for their critical system and the major contributing subsystems that support it.

Items 8 and 9 above provide the integrating characteristics of policy management discussed earlier and the necessary linkage between strategy formulation and implementation.

Defining What Customers Value

Some authors suggest that a company can achieve competitive position within their industry by studying the external environment and selectively developing a strategy that includes achieving desired capabilities. These capabilities build on their strengths and their competitors' weaknesses. A general theme appears to be that a company cannot "be all things to all people." A company must decide what it should do best among several possible alternatives. This chapter reviews the thinking of those authors. It then suggests that, although an internal evaluation of the company and a study of competitors is necessary, the needs and valued attributes of customers must play a more dominant role in strategy formulation. An example is provided to highlight the benefits of identifying customer values and then focusing resources on systems improvement.

Michael Porter, in *Competitive Advantage* (1985), presents three generic strategies that can be used to achieve above-average position in an industry. First, there is cost leadership, in which a firm sets out to become *the* low-cost producer in its industry. A firm selecting this strategy typically has a broad scope, often serves many industry segments, and uses its breadth to achieve its cost position. A second generic strategy identified is differentiation. In this case a firm attempts to be unique in its industry by providing some service that its customers value highly. This differentiation could be based on the product itself, such as having high quality or a high degree of reliability. It could be based on having a delivery system capable of achieving fast and dependable deliveries. Other differentiators could involve after-sales service, spare parts availability, an exceptional dealer network, and so on. A firm must truly be unique at whatever is selected or be perceived to be unique if it is to demand a premium price. The differentiation strategy offers more variety in routes to competitive position if customers value a number of attributes. The third generic strategy is focus. In this case a company selects a segment or group of segments in an industry and directs its attention to serving their needs. The intent is to achieve a competitive position in a narrow market segment, even though the company may not have a competitive position overall.

With a focus strategy, a firm can decide to compete on cost or differentiation within that narrow market segment.

In *Restoring Our Competitive Edge* (Hayes and Wheelwright, 1984), the authors propose that developing a manufacturing strategy, and assuring that it is compatible with the strategy developed by other components of the organization (product development, product design, marketing, sales), will essentially define organizational objectives and provide the basis for achieving long-term competitive position. Their definition of manufacturing strategy is that it consists of a pattern of decisions that, over time, enables an organization to achieve desired structure, infrastructure, and a specific set of capabilities. Thus, they suggest that strategy formulation involves identifying structure, infrastructure, and a set of desired capabilities that are eventually stated in the form of objectives.

Defining structure involves four components: capacity, facilities, technology, and vertical integration. Capacity decisions have to do with the amount to be installed, the timing of increases, and the type (large blocks versus small incremental). Facility decisions include the size of plants to be built, the location of plants and distribution centers, and the specialization of the plants relative to breadth of product lines. Technology decisions involve whether new equipment will utilize existing versus new technology, the level of automation planned for existing and new equipment, and how closely equipment will be tied together. Finally, vertical integration decisions encompass the direction of integration (forward versus backward), the extent of integration, and the balance of internal versus external capabilities.

Defining infrastructure also involves four components: workforce, quality, production planning and control, and organizational structure. Workforce decisions include establishing the planned skill level for employees, determining how skill level will influence wages, and firming practices for handling employees during swings in the business cycle. Quality decisions encompass selecting between prevention, monitoring, and intervention as the basis for providing the desired level. Production planning and control decisions involve deciding on sourcing policies (limited number versus low bid), selecting between centralized versus decentralized procurement practices, and establishing decision rules for meeting commitments on delivery dates. Organization decisions include establishing a formal structure, defining the level in the organization that selected decisions are to be made, formulating the role of staff groups, and effectively communicating the reward system for recognizing outstanding performance.

Hayes and Wheelwright note that the above decision categories are highly interrelated. Once made, decisions that fall under the structure section are difficult and expensive to reverse. Decisions under the infrastructure section can be more easily changed, but can also be very expensive if change is required. Therefore, once made, changes in any of the eight categories change very infrequently. Most organizations, however, will make at least one major decision that falls into one of the eight in any given year. The key is to maintain consistency. Are the decisions made in a given category consistent with decisions made at other points in time? Are the decisions made in a given category consistent with decisions made in other categories? We must be sure that all eight over time cumulatively result in the desired set of capabilities.

Maintaining consistency in the pattern of decisions will provide improvement in competitive position, given the firm's choice of priorities. A firm, again according to Hayes and Wheelwright, basically has four competitive dimensions: cost, quality, dependability, flexibility. Lower cost is the more common competitive priority and needs no further elaboration. Quality is achieved by providing higher product reliability or performance in a standard product or by offering unique features unavailable in competing products. The market must obviously be willing to pay any additional price required if additional costs are incurred to achieve the higher quality level. Dependability can consist of several different desired capabilities. The product can be dependable by working as specified. Dependability can take the form of on-time delivery or of being able to quickly and effectively mobilize resources to correct any failures that occur after delivery. Flexibility can take two forms: product flexibility and volume flexibility. Product flexibility requires the ability to handle difficult, nonstandard orders and to take the lead in product innovation. Volume flexibility requires that a firm be able to accelerate or decelerate production very quickly and to rearrange orders so as to meet demands for unusually fast delivery.

Hayes and Wheelwright suggest that a company must give different emphasis to each of the competitive dimensions. In essence, those who decide to be all things to all people end up being (as a best case) second best in all areas. The route to competitive position, therefore, is to excel in one of the dimensions and to be competitive in the others. Prioritizing the dimensions will allow the organization to define desired structure and infrastructure and to resolve any conflicts that might occur.

The acceptance of the above set of competitive priorities by manufacturing companies has been confirmed to a degree by a research report of the Boston University School of Management (Miller and Roth, 1988). The conclusions in this report are based on approximately two hundred usable surveys, with the typical respondent being the vice president of manufacturing for a division with sales of $150 million. The results were tabulated by the following industry categories: (1) Basic Industries, (2) Consumer Packaged Goods, (3) Electronics, (4) Machinery, and (5) Industrials. It is important to note that managers for these companies identified what they regarded to be their competitive priorities. No mention was made of confirmation from customers being served for the different industry categories. A ranking of competitive priorities for North America for the years 1986 and 1987 are shown in Table 1. Although the priority has been slightly modified over the two-year period, quality and delivery performance remain the competitive priorities that are receiving maximum attention. The data in the table represent an overall summary for all industry categories provided above. Quality and delivery topped the list of desired capabilities in all industries for 1987; the ranking of other capabilities varied by industry.

In summary, the current literature shows that an organization should study the external environment to determine what is of value to customers. Managers must assess the strengths and weaknesses of the organization in relation to competition and select a set of capabilities to enable their organization to achieve and retain a leading position. The capabilities selected are used to design and manage the components of structure and infrastructure of the organization. The general desired capability categories for a manufacturing organization are quality, cost, dependability, and flexibility. Note that the capabilities of Table 1 are further attributes derived by segmenting the four major categories. Some authors suggest that managers must choose among the set of attributes valued by customers. In essence, priorities must be developed to handle any conflicts incurred while implementing the strategy. To attempt to be all things to customers results in being second best in all the general categories. After deciding

TABLE 1
Competitive Priorities – Manufacturing, 1986 and 1987

1986	1987
1. Consistent quality	1. Conformance quality
2. High-performance products	2. Dependable deliveries
3. Dependable deliveries	3. High-performance products
4. Low prices	4. Fast deliveries
5. Fast deliveries	5. Rapid design changes
6. Rapid design changes	6. After-sales service
7. After-sales service	7. Low prices
8. Rapid volume changes	8. Broad product line

Source: Adapted from 1987 and 1988 Executive Summary of the North America Futures Survey- Research Report of the Boston University School of Management Manufacturing Roundtable.

among the available capabilities that are valued, objectives are established for those that have been selected. Managers are to ensure that systems are put in place to achieve the derived objectives. The activities of all functional units within the organization are then aligned to support the objectives.

As with the strategic management process, a reorientation of emphasis in selecting strategic capabilities is proposed. The selection of strategic capabilities directly impacts the identification of critical systems. Management's ability to anticipate how the value of those capabilities might change over time affects the way systems are studied and designed.

The importance of identifying what customers value was discussed earlier but deserves reemphasis. Understanding what customers value is a much more complex undertaking than selecting between subsets of quality, cost, dependability, and delivery. Understanding desired quality characteristics by itself is a monumental task. As noted by Garvin (1988), quality is a multidimensional capability. Quality will mean different things to different customers. The meaning will depend on how the product is used, the idiosyncrasies of specific manufacturing processes that may be used, and a host of other considerations. Understanding what customers value requires an aggressive effort to discover the detailed needs of specific customers. Visits, observation of the product being used, and discussions with managers, supervisors, and operators are needed to accumulate the required knowledge. It is appropriate initially to project what customers value. But as discussed in Chapter 5 by Carothers, Bounds and Stahl, it is insufficient. Projection must be followed by an exhaustive investigation to attempt to invalidate what is projected, to discover what is truly valued, and to confirm the discovery. This activity should best precede the identification and improvement efforts on critical systems. As a minimum, however, it must occur simultaneously in order to effectively utilize valuable resources.

The benefits of taking an aggressive approach to identify what customers value and to concentrate on a few select capabilities are clearly highlighted in a recent article by Sirkin and Stalk (1990). These authors describe the experiences of a paper company during the mid-1980s. The story begins with a recently acquired papermill losing more than $1 million a month. Top managers initially responded by shutting down part of the facility. They then developed a plan to use capital to improve quality and delivery performance. After careful consideration, that plan was rejected because of the length of implementation.

Management ultimately developed a strategy to increase the volume of profitable products while deleting those that were unprofitable. They made this transition by enhancing their capabilities in the areas of quality and service, service taking the form of reliable deliveries. They further decided selectively to identify higher leverage opportunities for improvement, focusing on those areas that would be very highly valued by customers such that improvements would be recognized in a short timeframe. To ensure that efforts were properly focused, the CEO structured product teams for the profitable products. One other team was to handle the transition away from the other product lines. These teams were headed by the product-line salespeople to reinforce the focus on customers and included one representative from each of the key functional areas. The CEO charged each team to spend the first few weeks talking with customers to learn their needs (what was most valued) and developing plans for responding.

The results of the product teams, when armed with first-hand knowledge of what customers most value, were impressive. They found out that many of their current practices, some of which could be easily changed, were creating significant problems with their customers. They uncovered the root causes of their quality and service problems and implemented permanent changes to systems to eliminate them. They identified a way to offer customers lower basis-weight product that competitors could not provide, providing them with a strategic advantage. With experience, they discovered new combinations of raw materials and additives that permitted them to make lower cost varieties that they had not been able to make before. The bottom line, however, is that direct contact with customers, gaining an understanding of what was valued, and focusing resources so as to improve their ability to provide that which was valued resulted in a fourfold increase in the volume for one of their more profitable product lines. The number of employees required did not change. The mill became the number one supplier for all remaining products in two and one half years. When management initiated the improvement effort, the mill was dead-last among the five available suppliers.

The above example reinforces the position that managers are taking a short-term view in identifying what is valued by customers. Short-term financial success remains their major focus. Moving beyond the projection phase of identifying what customers' value requires a significant investment of resources to accumulate the required knowledge. Many top managers make grand statements about their company being "customer-driven," but few have provided the resources to bring that desire to reality.

It is also ill advised for managers to select naively among the four general categories (or subsets of those categories) of generic capabilities. Managers cannot afford to design systems that can effectively deliver quality but not flexibility, cost, or delivery. Many will find their company must be capable of excelling in most of the generic strategies if they are to increase market share. See Table 1 which lists the competitive priorities provided by the two hundred or so companies. Note that the top priorities for North America in order of highest importance are consistent quality, high-performance products, and dependable deliveries. This same survey was sent to Japanese managers. Their results were low prices, rapid design changes, and consistent quality, in that order.

We propose that Japanese managers have recognized that customer values change over time. It is well known that the Japanese made quality the number one strategic objective during the 1970s and well into the 1980s. They have now achieved a reputation for offering products of exceptional quality in relation to international competition. Their strategy is undoubtedly to offer product derivatives (rapid design changes) with additional features valued by customers that are high in quality at attractive prices in order to retain their competitive position. We propose that Japanese managers were simultaneously improving their capability to rapidly deliver additional features at the same time they were continuing to improve on the system to deliver valued quality. Thus, managers must be working on those systems that deliver the capability that customers most value today, they must anticipate those capabilities that will be valued tomorrow, and, as much as possible, they must build robust systems that can deliver a variety of capabilities as needed.

One way that companies with multiple plant sites are establishing a variety of capabilities is through strategic allocation of products. Some plants are assigned products in the infancy of their product life cycle. Managers at these locations are primarily responsible for product and process development and for manufacturing a broad product mix in small-lot quantities. A critical system at these sites would likely be the development and delivery of innovative product and process technology. Another critical system would involve their manufacturing capability. Their manufacturing system would require flexibility so that they could react rapidly to changing product mixes. Their success would be heavily influenced by the system that identifies what customers value. A system to identify the need for new products and new and revised processes to satisfy current and future customers would be critical.

As products grow in volume and as processes to manufacture them are fine-tuned, they are allocated to another manufacturing site. That site would have a narrower product mix. Product volumes would warrant dedicating specific processes to given product lines. The increased volume and reduced variety would likely result in a critical system for achieving low cost. Dedicated processes would tend to become more automated in order to drive cost down and retain control at the higher output rates. Achieving consistent quality would likely be another critical system. A system for achieving dependable deliveries would be another candidate for a critical system.

To summarize, managers must recognize that the effective identification of desired strategic capabilities is heavily influenced by taking an aggressive approach in understanding what customers value. An aggressive approach is one that moves beyond managers projecting what they think customers value. It involves first-hand contact with customers/users of the product. It involves accumulating detailed information about specific customer problems in using the product or service and identifying what customers are currently sacrificing. Managers must also recognize that those attributes valued by customers are likely to change over time. Top management, then, must build systems that allow them to provide a variety of capabilities valued by customers in order to formulate a strategy that is capable of rapidly adapting to a changing external environment.

ANALYSIS AND IMPROVEMENT OF CRITICAL SYSTEMS

Establishing desired strategic capabilities as discussed in the previous section essentially identifies the critical systems of the organization. A critical system must be in place to provide each capability. We have found that an organization rarely has more than five or six critical systems. As already noted, these systems are large and complex. To have a greater number would dilute the organization's resources. The critical systems are interdependent. Parts of a critical system may act to support more than one strategic capability. A recommended approach for analyzing and improving critical systems is identified in Figure 1 and discussed in the following sections.

FIGURE 1
Analyzing and Improving Critical Systems

1. Identify a system owner and team members for each critical system.
2. Describe the system under study.
3. Identify all subsystems that contribute to the critical system.
4. Define the interdependencies of the subsystems.
5. Prioritize the subsystems as to their contribution to the critical system.
6. Develop a detailed "as is" description of the critical system. This includes identifying interfaces between all system components as well as expanding the level of detail for major contributing subsystems.
7. Identify obvious system deficiencies.
8. Identify possible causes of system deficiencies.
9. Establish "baseline" measures for system and major subsystem(s) performance.
10. Assess the performance of system and major subsystems.
11. Develop a "should be" description of the system and subsystems.
12. Recommend changes to improve system and subsystem performance.
13. Make changes to specific subsystems and confirm that the changes generate improved performance.

General Comments Regarding Approach

The proposed approach is not provided without precedence. Successful results have been reported by both Japanese and U.S. companies using similar approaches. The general management practices of the Japanese as described in *Kaizen* (Imai, 1986) and *What Is Total Quality Control?* (Ishikawa and Lu, 1985) have been most influential. For example, in a typical, large Japanese manufacturing organization, top management formulates its annual policies or goals on the basis of its long-range plans and strategies. There are two major goals categories: (1) goals related to such factors as profit, market share, and product mix; and (2) goals related to overall improvements in the company's systems and so-called cross-functional activities. Reference to cross-functional activities corresponds directly to what we have identified as critical systems. Although achieving the results targets associated with the first category takes priority as the primary goal for managers, the goals to strengthen and improve the organization and its systems are no less important. The latter is, in fact, described as a "self-generated move for improvement in corporate culture, chemistry, and overall competitiveness" (Imai, 1986, 127).

The goals of the second category are identified as "superordinate" goals and are directed at quality, cost, and schedule (quantity and delivery). All other management functions such as product planning, design, production, purchasing, and marketing are regarded as secondary. Cross-functional goals and measures are determined prior to departmental goals, either by top management or by a cross-functional committee. A cross-functional committee is organized at the top manager level for each critical system, and these committees are second in importance only to the board. Each consists of about ten members and is headed by a senior manager appointed by the president. Thus, a specific top-level manager is assigned responsibility for a given critical system. A given cross-functional committee is responsible for defining the kinds of activities and functions each department should provide in meeting the respective goal.

Select Systems Owners and Team Members

The previous section described how many Japanese companies assign top managers the responsibility for improving cross-functional or critical systems. Brache and Rummler (1989) also describe the widespread use of assigning top managers the responsibility for managing critical systems. They refer to this as managing the "whitespace" of the organization. Their proposed criteria for selecting systems owners are summarized as follows.

- Holds a senior management position.
- Holds a position that has the most to gain if the system is improved.
- Manages the largest number of people working in the system.
- Understands the entire system.
- Has an overall perspective of the effect of the environment on the system and the effect of system performance on the business.
- Has the personal ability to influence decisions and people outside of his or her line management responsibilities.

Rummler and Brache note that the assignment of responsibility for improving the performance of critical systems to specific top managers is the single most important step in achieving organizational change. A systems owner is provided a team of individuals to assist in improving critical systems. These team members are typically selected from each of the functional units having the greatest impact on the performance of the critical system.

Describe the System Under Study

The first major step of the team selected to improve a given critical system is to describe the system. This description should establish system boundaries; it should identify all inputs, outputs, and transformations that take place within those boundaries; it should define the purpose of the system. What strategic capability is to be achieved? It should identify all internal and external customers of the system. The team should tentatively identify how system performance can be evaluated. How can the system owner determine whether progress is being made?

Identify the Subsystems That Contribute to System Performance

The subsystems that contribute to system performance should first be identified on a macro basis. For example, the subsystems that would likely interact to support a strategic capability directed to reducing the total time to provide new or revised products (Product Development System) are as follows.

1. Product ideas
2. Customer needs projection
3. Product technology selection and development
4. Process technology selection and development
5. Final product definition

6. Product design and evaluation
7. Manufacturing system design
8. Product manufacturing

These subsystems need not be attached to specific functions at the initial stage of identification. They represent the basic building blocks of work activity that must take place in the system under study. It is worthwhile to describe what should take place rather than what does take place in order to avoid missing disconnects that exist in the present system. The attachment to functional units and a description of the current system can come later. Each subsystem receives inputs, utilizes resources to perform transformations, and generates outputs for either internal or external use. After identifying these subsystems, the system owner and team members should attempt to define the inputs, transformations, and outputs of each subsystem. They should identify the functional units that currently receive the inputs, transform the inputs, and generate the outputs for each subsystem. They should also identify those subsystems that are part of another critical system other than the one being addressed by their team. This additional information allows the team to develop the interactions and interrelationships between the total set of critical systems and the functions. In essence, the contribution of the functional units to the total set of critical systems can be defined and study can be coordinated accordingly.

Define the Interdependencies Between the Subsystems

A flowchart of the system is useful to define the interdependencies between the subsystems. A flowchart for the Product Development System using the subsystems listed earlier is shown in Figure 2. Note again that the initial flowchart to describe the relationships between the subsystems is best structured at the macro level. It graphically portrays the flow of outputs from one subsystem to another. Each output must be further defined. Specific outputs must be attached to each of the arrows shown on the flowchart. What form do the outputs take? Which functional unit currently supplies the output? Which functional unit currently receives the output? How does the receiver (customer) operationally define whether the output received is acceptable? How can the performance of each subsystem be measured? How can we identify whether the output is being improved over time? Which of these outputs have the greatest impact on total system performance? The study of subsystem outputs as to their importance to overall system performance and their current level of performance provides direction in identifying system leverage points.

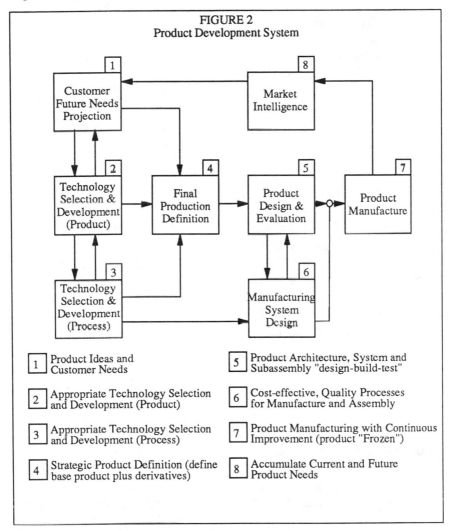

FIGURE 2
Product Development System

1. Product Ideas and Customer Needs
2. Appropriate Technology Selection and Development (Product)
3. Appropriate Technology Selection and Development (Process)
4. Strategic Product Definition (define base product plus derivatives)
5. Product Architecture, System and Subassembly "design-build-test"
6. Cost-effective, Quality Processes for Manufacture and Assembly
7. Product Manufacturing with Continuous Improvement (product "Frozen")
8. Accumulate Current and Future Product Needs

Prioritize the Subsystems

The management process at the Toyota Motor Company is used to describe how subsystems that support a given cross-functional system can be identified and prioritized. The specific cross-functional system addressed is the quality assurance system. Toyota defines that system to be the one that "assures that the quality of the product is satisfactory, reliable, and yet economical for the customer" (Imai, 1986, 135). The horizontal flow of cross-functional activities from product planning to sales are described as falling into one of the following eight steps. These steps compare to what we have identified as subsystems.

1. Product planning
2. Product design
3. Product preparation
4. Purchasing
5. Full-scale production
6. Inspection
7. Sales and services
8. Quality audit

Each of the eight steps is considered individually. For each step the following information is accumulated:

1. Specific activities performed within each step that contribute to the cross-functional system.
2. The manager responsible for the performance of each subsystem.
3. The priority of each activity.
    a. Critical importance, and downstream alteration impossible.
    b. Influential but downstream alteration possible.
    c. Of little consequence.

In summary, activities within a subsystem (transformations) generate output that contributes to total system performance. These outputs can be prioritized in accordance with their impact on downstream parts of the total system as described above. These priorities, coupled with an evaluation of the current performance level of specific subsystem outputs, can be used to focus resources for improvement. Those critical outputs that are not performing well should obviously receive immediate attention. If measures for subsystem outputs have not been put in place, then attention should initially be focused on those outputs that have been classified as critical.

Develop an "As Is" Flowchart for the Present Critical System

The prioritization of subsystem outputs discussed in the previous section provides direction for focusing on specific subsystems that are most important. Before zeroing in on a particular subsystem, however, it is useful to develop a detailed flowchart of the total system. Each subsystem should be explored so as to describe in greater detail the work currently being done and who is responsible for doing it. The symbols defined in Figure 3 are often helpful in developing detailed flowcharts.

The flowchart is also more useful when specific tasks are assigned to the functional units responsible for performing the work. In essence, a

FIGURE 3
Symbols for Flowcharting

Symbol   Description

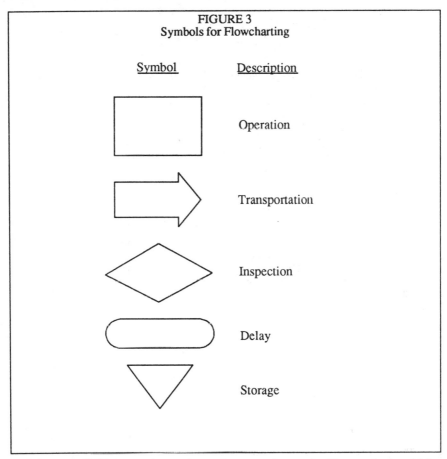

Operation

Transportation

Inspection

Delay

Storage

task/responsibility matrix such as the one shown in Figure 4 should be developed.

The functional interfaces are particularly important. Work passing between functions represents a point where measurements may be important. In this case functions act as customers of other functions. The function receiving the output of another function should be given the opportunity to assist in establishing operational definitions for the output being received. Operational definitions consist of (1) a written statement (and/or a series of examples) of what it takes for a product or some other output to conform to requirements that arc communicable, (2) a decision criterion by which an item, group, or other output can be judged to conform to requirements, and (3) the ability to make a clear yes or no decision on the basis of the statement of requirements and the decision criteria. System disconnects are often found at functional interfaces. Detailed flowcharts should also identify redundant inspection points. They should identify recycle loops and other forms of waste (see Functions A, B, and D in

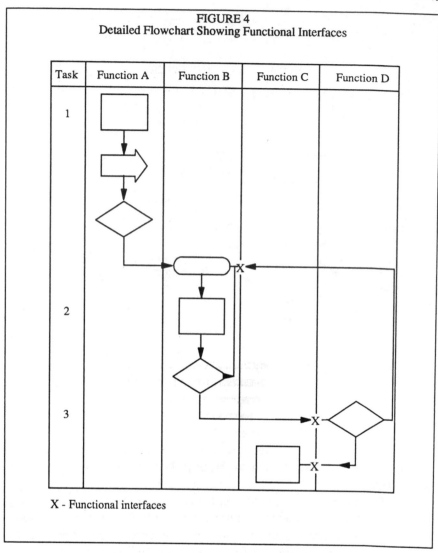

FIGURE 4
Detailed Flowchart Showing Functional Interfaces

X - Functional interfaces

Figure 4). The level of detail required for a given subsystem is dependent on its importance relative to total system performance.

Identify Obvious System Deficiencies

Following the development of the detailed flowchart of the system, the team should attempt to identify obvious system deficiencies or disconnects. Are there missing, redundant, or illogical inputs, transformations, or outputs? Is there an obvious failure to carry out efficiently or effectively a given step in a particular subsystem? Is waste being created by work cycling back and forth between functional units because of ineffective communication or lack of assignment of responsibility? Are there excessive delays at certain steps in the system because selected information is not available in a timely fashion? Is incomplete work being passed between the functions, only to be returned later, in order to satisfy some measurement that prompts undesired organizational behavior? In essence, each step in the various subsystems should be questioned and investigated. All system weaknesses should be identified but not resolved at this point.

Identify Possible Causes of System Deficiencies

Following the analysis of the system flowchart, the "as is" system as described by the team members should be verified by in-depth discussions with individuals working within the current system. A cause and effect (C/E) diagram to identify the potential causes of each system deficiency should be developed. The structuring of these C/E diagrams can be assigned to team members from the various functions and subsequently reviewed by the entire team. The focus of future work activity on specific subsystems will depend on the magnitude of system disconnects discovered within and between subsystems, along with the priority of subsystem output as defined earlier.

Establish Baseline Measures

System measures are necessary to improve systems. In essence, you cannot manage what you cannot measure. Measurements for the output of the critical systems are required, along with measurements for each of the major subsystems to be studied and improved. Measurements for the critical systems will often require some feedback from the customer since these systems should focus on improving capabilities that they value. These measurements may be generated slowly over time and may take the form of surveys along with direct contact by representatives of the company.

The Product Development System discussed earlier is used as an example to demonstrate establishing system and subsystem measures. Under the assumption that the company is developing both new products and product derivatives, there would likely be a need to develop general categories for product development projects. A product derivative would likely take less time to move through the development cycle than a totally new product. Similarly, a product that essentially uses current product and process technology would require less time on the average than a product that requires new product or process technology. Given comparable product categories, we could measure the time for future product development cycles compared to historical product development cycles for like categories to evaluate total system performance.

Assuming Marketing/Sales had the responsibility for projecting future customer needs, we could measure the timing and quality of the forecasts. Was the need identified in a time-frame conducive to bringing the new product through the development cycle within the window of opportunity? We could measure the time available compared to the estimated time to complete the development cycle. Marketing/Sales could be measured as to the accuracy of projected product volumes. Both product and process development depend very heavily on that forecast. We could measure the number of times that product requirements change. Inadequate market intelligence concerning product requirements often results in changing requirements well into the development cycle, creating unnecessary delays.

Research and Development would likely be responsible for product development (one subsystem identified earlier). Manufacturing Engineering would likely be responsible for process development (another subsystem identified earlier). These two groups working jointly would typically develop a project plan for a given product introduction. The plan would identify all tasks required, the estimated time to complete each task, and the sequence in which the various tasks would be performed. Individual tasks would then be assigned to specific groups or individuals. We could compare actual completion times against estimated completion times for specific tasks or logical groups of tasks assigned to each subsystem to measure the effectiveness of these two subsystems.

Performance against plan could be used as a "lessons learned" approach to improve performance on future projects. What was done right? What went wrong? What types of work activity deviated significantly from the plan? What could be changed to reduce deviation in the future? Which tasks were performed sequentially when they could have been performed simultaneously? Which type of tasks seems to dictate the total length of the development cycle?

Similarly, measurements could be developed for the manufacturing subsystem. What were the cycle times on "first of a kind" or R and D runs? How many suppliers did not perform as anticipated? The appropriateness of this measure would depend on whether or not manufacturing had the responsibility for qualifying suppliers. What timeframe was required to qualify suppliers in comparison with the estimated time included in the plan? How many changes were made in the process plan to achieve desired quality levels?

In summary, measures must be put in place to establish performance levels for each critical system. Each major subsystem to be studied must also have measures. A "baseline" or current level of performance is required in order to evaluate the effectiveness of subsequent changes in systems to improve performance.

Assess Performance of System and Subsystems

The measures discussed in the previous section, coupled with the prioritization of the subsystems, provide the basis for directing effort to specific subsystems. If system and subsystem performance cannot be properly assessed from historical data available (lack of operational definitions, lack of historical data, etc.), then efforts should be focused on the basis of the number of disconnects found within the various subsystems along with the priority rating developed. Measures should be initiated as soon as possible and used for focusing resources on future system study.

Develop a "Should Be" Description of the System and Subsystems

The detailed flowchart developed for the "as is" system can be used as the starting point for developing the "should be" system. In building the proposed system, we should assume that no constraints exist to systems change. We should ask the question, "how would we structure the system if we had complete freedom to design it without being biased by what currently exists?" Some changes may not prove to be economically viable, but they should not be excluded initially. Developing an "effective" system should be given first priority. This means the system should be doing the right things. When system elements are missing that dramatically impact system performance, those parts of the system must be designed so as to fill in the holes. After the team is comfortable that all necessary system parts have been structured, then the focus should move on to improving system "efficiency." This means the system should be doing the necessary things as well as possible. Some possible questions that can help improve efficiency are: (1) Can activities/tasks be eliminated because they do not contribute to value? (2) Are certain activities unnecessarily duplicated? (3) Are activities fragmented? Are they performed in a number of areas when they could be performed more efficiently if focused in one area? (4) Could certain activities be performed in parallel rather than in sequence to reduce elapsed time? (5) Can some activities be automated when there is no question that the activity is truly needed? (6) Are there areas of complexity that can be simplified? (7) Are there layers of inspection points and other waste that could be eliminated if work responsibilities were reassigned?

Recommend Changes to Improve System and Subsystem Performance

After identifying system disconnects, identifying possible reasons for the occurrence of these disconnects, and evaluating each step in the major subsystems to improve effectiveness and efficiency, a large number of possible system changes could likely be made. A word of caution is in order. The impact of changes in systems must be confirmed. It should be validated that they have resulted in improvement. System changes should not be made until there is general agreement as to how the impact of these changes is to be validated. Furthermore, implementing numerous changes simultaneously complicates the ability to determine which change resulted in improvement. Obvious changes that fill current voids in the system should be made as soon as possible. Other changes should be prioritized in accordance with their impact on performance and implemented so as to be able to confirm their contribution.

Make Changes and Confirm Improved Performance

The system and subsystem measures should be used to confirm that changes have generated improvement. As noted earlier, these measures provide managers with the ability to manage system improvement.

CONCLUSIONS

This chapter suggests that for managers to generate the rate of improvement necessary to maintain or achieve competitive position for their company, they must use an effective approach for continuously improving organizational systems. An approach that is characteristically reductionistic, one that requires each functional unit to be responsible for improving their respective organizational systems, independent of the remainder of the organization, will be insufficient in the future. Companies must use a more holistic approach. This approach will study not only the parts (subsystems) but how these parts interact with each other to create the whole. The holistic approach will require more direct involvement and guidance on the part of the top managers of the organization. Top managers must provide the focus to ensure that resources are being used effectively. They must direct their attention externally in order to formulate this focus. If the company is to be customer-driven, then systems must be in place to determine those attributes of product or service that their customers most value.

Managers must establish a desired set of capabilities that are based on what customers now value and will value in the future. The critical systems that provide these capabilities must perform well and be continuously improved as the external environment changes. Instead of the results being the focus, as with management by objectives, these critical systems become the focus. Since the critical systems have subsystems that are found in the functional units, a top manager must be given specific responsibility for improving each critical system. Unless this responsibility is assigned, no one has responsibility and the rate of improvement is constrained because of lack of attention. The manager assigned responsibility for a given system must then identify every subsystem throughout the organization that contributes to system performance. Not only must these subsystems be identified, but the importance of each in contributing to the objective of the critical system must be prioritized. This priority allows the manager to focus the resources of the organization. Finally, the assigned manager must describe the system, assess its current level of performance by establishing system measures, and coordinate all work activity in improving the system.

The assigned manager must also recognize that some of the subsystems contained within his or her critical system will also support other critical systems. This implies that system managers must coordinate their improvement efforts with other system managers. Changes made to improve one critical system should not negatively impact the performance of another critical system.

This chapter has concentrated on the need for top management to direct and guide the effort in improving organizational systems. It is hoped that the message has been made quite clear. The intent, however, is not to imply that the role of other employees is to be reduced. Achieving strategic competitive position requires the effective involvement and use of all organizational resources. Resources, however, will continue to be scarce. Managers must assume the responsibility for identifying what customers most value and for mobilizing and directing the members of the organization to create what is valued more effectively than others. In essence, effective use of lower level employees will not take place until top managers exert the necessary leadership role in acquiring sufficient knowledge about the needs of the external environment in order to properly focus the resources under their direction and control.

REFERENCES

Ackoff, Russell L. "The Systems Revolution." *Long Range Planning* (December 1974).

Boulding, Kenneth. "General Systems Theory: The Skeleton of Science." *Management Science* (April 1956).

Brache, Alan P. and Geary A. Rummler. *Improving Performance: How to Manage the WhiteSpace on the Organization Chart*. San Francisco: Jossey-Bass, 1989.

Garvin, David A. *Managing Quality: Strategic and Competitive Advantage*. New York: Free Press, 1988.

Hayes, Robert H., and Steven C. Wheelwright. *Restoring Our Competitive Advantage: Competing Through Manufacturing*. New York: John Wiley and Sons, 1984.

Imai, Masaaki. *Kaizen: The Key to Japanese Success Competitive*. New York: Random House, 1986.

Ishikawa, Kaoru, and David J. Lu. *What Is Total Quality Control?: The Japanese Way*. Englewood Cliffs, N.J.: Prentice-Hall, 1985.

Miller, Jeffrey G. and Aleda V. Roth. "Manufacturing Strategies: Executive Summary of the 1988 North American Manufacturing Futures Survey," A Research Report of the Boston University School of Management Roundtable, 1988.

Porter, Michael. *Competitive Advantage: Creating and Sustaining Superior Performance*. New York: Free Press, 1985.

Sirkin, Harold and George Stalk, Jr. "Fix the Process, Not the Problem." *Harvard Business Review* (July-August 1990).

Sullivan, Lawrence P. "Policy Management Through Quality Function Deployment." *Quality Progress* (June 1988).

Thompson, A. A., and A. J. Strickland. *Strategy and Policy: Concepts and Cases*. Dallas, Tex.: Business Publications, 1978.

Wood-Harper, A. T., and G. Fitzgerald. "A Taxonomy of Current Approaches to Systems Analysis." *The Computer Journal*, 25, no.1 (1982).

Wright, Robert. *Systems Thinking: A Guide to Managing in a Changing Environment*. Dearborn, Mich.: Society of Manufacturing Engineers, 1989.

CHAPTER 12

MANAGING IN THE PRESENCE OF VARIATION

RICHARD D. SANDERS
Associate Professor of Statistics
University of Tennessee

MARY LEITNAKER
Associate Professor of Statistics
University of Tennessee

GIPSIE RANNEY
General Motors

SUMMARY

During the past decade, managerial practice in the United States has undergone an increasing level of questioning and criticism. The critiques have had several major themes dealing with theoretical, technical, and behavioral aspects of management and leadership. This chapter addresses only one of those themes: managing in the presence of variation in the inputs, outcomes, processes, and systems of the organization. The aim of this chapter is to focus attention on variation and to consider how that variation affects and is affected by managerial theory, practice, and purpose.

Several chapters in this volume consider various aspects of the responsibility of management to identify the critical, cross-functional systems of the business. In addition to identifying critical systems, there are responsibilities to develop an improved understanding of how the current system functions, to establish output predictability, and to work on improving system performance in fulfilling its purpose. Knowledge of variation is critical to effective execution of those responsibilities. A conscious recognition of variation, an informed interpretation of the messages it contains regarding managerial practice and the organizational system, and an understanding of the effects variation has on system performance imply adoption of different practices and analytical processes by the manager engaged in systems management.

CURRENT PRACTICES AND INTERPRETATION OF VARIATION

Monitoring business unit performance by using several monthly indicators is an accepted practice. For example, the management of a manufacturing organization with multiple plant sites typically uses reports for various indicators by each plant. Numerical indicators might include monthly throughput values per direct labor hour, cost of purchased materials per unit of production, dollar amount of all goods in inventory, scrap, budget variances, and number of lost time accidents. These numbers are meant to serve several purposes at the corporate, division, and site levels. Comparison against previous periods or over longer periods helps reveal positive or negative trends in overall business activity, performance, and efficiency. Comparisons from one site to another are often used to gain an appreciation as to superior performance or suggestions for changes at other sites. Management also uses the results to decide where to put emphasis in order to affect changes or improvements in the business. It is customary practice to use these monthly indicators as a means of monitoring the business as well as a basis on which to act.

Any manager who has been required to report such results or who has chosen to use them to understand the current position of the business knows that they fluctuate, or exhibit variation, over time and locations. The manager understands that the recorded numbers are the results of numerous activities and decisions, many of which he or she has little ability to influence. The manager also understands that usually more than one option is available for affecting changes in the numbers. That is, the manager understands something about the sources of variation in these numbers. At issue is the depth of understanding regarding the reasons why the results vary and the range of viable choices the manager has for affecting the outputs measured. Because the range of potential choices for affecting the outputs will broaden as this understanding increases, knowledge of the nature of the variation in these numbers, the causes or sources of that variation, and the effect that different management behaviors would have on these numbers might be useful in realizing how improvement in the numbers might be affected.

In evaluating business results through the use of monthly indicators, two contexts often used for making judgments are the relative size of the result in question when it is compared to (1) some value established as a forecast, goal, or some other type of expectation or prediction or (2) a result of the same kind observed in a previous time period. In both contexts, the evaluation does not take into account that the particular result being evaluated is usually one in a series of similar results produced by the organizational system week to week, month to month or year to year. Omission of the historical perspective by focusing on evaluating one result at a time limits the range of potential questions regarding the fluctuations in the entire series of numbers and therefore restricts the learning and understanding that might be had from the numbers. A purpose of evaluating results must be to learn something about why it is that the numbers behave the way they do. It is in this learning that guidance can be found for selecting and taking appropriate actions to change those things that in turn change the numbers. The appropriate actions and the selection of what to act on depend on management intention and are not likely to be found in the numbers themselves. By treating the current result as a member of a series of results and by making judgments in light of the variation exhibited by that series, useful information for evaluating current and past practice and for assessing degree of belief in forecasts of future results can be gained.

A powerful perspective of the variability in a series of results is expressed in terms of a model which relates that variability to sources, or causes, identified as common and special causes of variation. Common causes are those system sources that affect each and every result in the series. Figure 1 is a plot of how measurements subject only to common

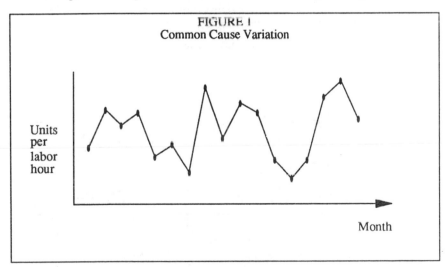

FIGURE 1
Common Cause Variation

Units per labor hour

Month

cause sources of variation might fluctuate. Statistical limits for common cause variation, if calculated for this series, would support the preceding statement. Although the most recent value in the series shows a deterioration when compared to the previous value, the most recent value is within the boundaries of variation seen in the historical series. It does not represent an exceptional case, and it is the result of the interaction of multiple causes. This insight into the behavior of the series is useful, because efforts to react to the most recent result without understanding the cause system that generated the result may not have the intended effect.

According to a somewhat simplistic interpretation, special causes of variation are those that act at isolated times or locations to produce variation in addition to that produced by common causes. Given both the level and degree of variation in the earlier values of the series plotted in Figure 2, the most recent value plotted is exceptional. If statistical limits of common cause variation were established for that series of results, the most recent value would lie outside those limits, indicating the existence of special cause. It should be possible to identify the cause of that unusual result. Special causes are behavioral, methods, material, equipment, or environmental variations that are beyond the usual experience.

When defined, the concept of common and special cause variation appears simple and straightforward. Use of the concept requires study, elaboration, and insight, however. Understanding the possible sources of variation becomes essential because the analysis of variation is meant to serve as a means of identifying where and on what to work in order to affect changes according to managerially selected criteria. The concept and interpretation of common and special cause are meant to be used as guidelines to help identify and eliminate sources of erratic variability, as well as to provide support for focusing on and working to improve the

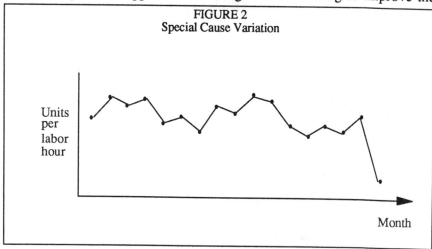

FIGURE 2
Special Cause Variation

Units
per
labor
hour

Month

underlying system. A system subject to only common causes is not interpreted to be the ideal or perfect system; it simply produces a predictable level of variation. (In the following, a system that produces predictable variation is referred to as stable.) It is the manager's job to systematically revisit and reevaluate the existing system and make judgments concerning changing that system to improve its future performance.

Numerical indicators of performance often are reported each month along with a standard that indicates what is currently expected of the system. Figures 3 and 4 are plots of the same time series depicted in Figure 1. The line drawn on each plot indicates a standard that defines acceptable performance for a plant. Without awareness of the concept of stable variation about a steady average, each deviation from the standard is taken to be a separate measure of the performance of the system. The

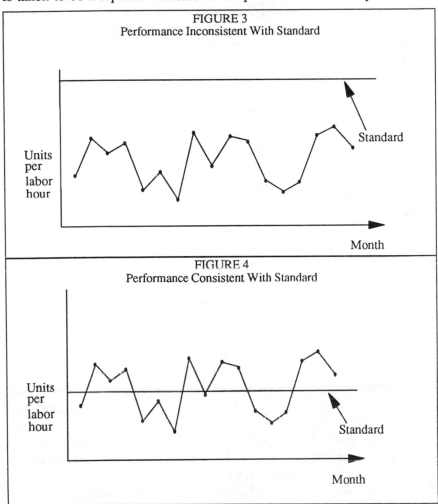

FIGURE 3
Performance Inconsistent With Standard

FIGURE 4
Performance Consistent With Standard

concept that the system might be acting in a similar fashion over all recorded outcomes is missing. Interpreting the results compared to the standard would be different when viewed in light of the concept of stable variation. Examining the most recent and earlier results in comparison to the standard shown in Figure 3 would lead to the conclusion that the process that generated those results could only rarely meet the standard. The capability of that process is insufficient to meet the standard, and there will have to be changes in the way the work gets done and supported in order to have any reasonable chance of meeting the standard. In Figure 4, the conclusion to be drawn by viewing the results in light of stable, common cause, variation is that the standard cannot be met all the time. Exceeding the standard or falling short of it in any given month appears to be about equally likely. Only changes in the design of the process will make it possible to raise the process level sufficiently to consistently meet or exceed the standard. From the graph, it is obvious that the more variability there is in the system, the higher the average will have to be raised in order to consistently meet the standard. The data themselves provide a commentary on the capability of the process or system generating the results; the mere existence of the standard does nothing to change that capability.

The idea of using a standard to judge current performance is prevalent in many industries. Typically, a manager required to report such performance measures will also be asked to explain deviations from the standard. Of course, explanations will be sought and found, but the usefulness of this activity is questionable. Standards are set for a number of different reasons. In some instances, they are meant to describe the results of best practices. In other cases, they are meant to serve as a goal or an aspiration. In yet other cases, they are simply translations of a forecast or planning number. In evaluating current results against standards, the purpose of the standard and its definition must be known, be operative, and be used in the evaluation. Furthermore, the organization's capability must be considered. If the establishment of the standard has not been based on the known capabilities of the system, but possibly on the hope that setting a high standard will give the business something to aim for, then explaining each deviation misdirects attention from examining the system to explaining differences that may have little to do with the system's performance and much to do with the means used to set the standard.

There are additional dangers in using deviations from standard as a management signal that must be recognized and addressed by immediate action. The need to act promotes hasty analysis and the tendency to treat the current deviation as a one-time occurrence. If each result is considered a one-time event, disconnected from the history contained in the series of previous results, it becomes difficult to appreciate the concept that work is a process. Yet, work as a process, a contributor to the system that delivers the goods or services of the organization, is a necessary point of view, because this view provides a means for interpreting the interrelationships among the practices, principles, and behaviors by which the organization functions. Without a process point of view, results will remain one-time events, providing little insight into the behavior of the underlying processes.

A further limitation of viewing a deviation from standard as a one-time event is that there is no awareness that the observed deviation is only one observation from an array of possible values that could be produced by that system. Consequently, there is no awareness of the largest or smallest values that might have been observed for the deviation, and so there is no means by which to judge whether the standard is within the range of results that define the capability of the system. In addition, the manager is in no position to judge the specific deviation as being either exceptional or produced by the collection of causes that are common to all results. Without this information, it becomes difficult, if not impossible, to identify causes of the deviation in question with any confidence in the correctness of the identification. Without that confidence, the implications of actions that might be taken can only be guessed. Furthermore, there is no strong incentive to analyze and improve the system that actually produced the deviation; indeed, the manager may not appreciate that possibility. Without the concept of a predictable range of results produced by the system in existence, issues regarding system variability and average are not considered. Without the analytical view of the system and its components as generators of results and the recognition that actions to change average and variation can produce sustained change in future results, only weak actions that are likely to produce transient change are available as managerial options.

The manager with system responsibility has to be able to measure and analyze variation. By measuring variability at moments in time, the manager can know the magnitude or size of the variation and can track that measure over time, over a variety of changing conditions, and know something about the stability of the variation. Knowledge as to stability or instability provides information as to priority and opportunity for useful work. Tracking system variation is not only for the purpose of controlling and moderating the system, although that may be a valuable correlate. The purpose is to learn about the cause and effect relationships that exist in critical system activities.

UNDERSTANDING THE EFFECTS OF VARIATION

Variation results from the interactions of procedures, people, material, and equipment used in creating a product or service; variation of a given magnitude is a consequence of a particular way of doing business. In the same way that symmetry is imparted to the vase by the artisan's vision, knowledge, skill, and intention, variation in the product or service is created by the organizational system. Obviously, an organization or its leadership would not deliberately create variations in results. Of course, the causes of the variation are not always known or appreciated. For example, variation in the cost or performance of a complex mechanical or electrical product may be partly due to manufacturing and assembly capability, but largely due to the actual design itself, the selection and implementation of the manufacturing process, or the specification and procurement of materials and parts. Knowledge as to the effects of the variations, in terms of cost, capability, or performance, would be essential in deciding if improvements were necessary or potentially beneficial. Perhaps because variability is always present, the effects of variation are not always well known or understood. With this difficulty in mind, several examples are presented to provide some experience in thinking about the possible effects of variations.

Fill weight for a granular product shipped in containers with a given label weight provides a straightforward example for considering the impact of variation. There is a target value for container content. The target has been set based on a lower specification and recognition that fill weights vary from container to container. If the filling process were managed to produce stable variation in fill weights, then managers could confidently determine the target, taking into account the existing, known magnitude of variation in fill weight. When this knowledge is lacking, target selection must be influenced by the organization's lack of confidence in its ability to perform in a predictable fashion over time. Because a minimum value must be maintained, erratic, unpredictable variability generally means that a larger target value is set in order to assure that the lower specification is met. Known, stable variation provides knowledge concerning an appropriate target value and supplies information for arriving at a firmer assessment of the cost associated with a given level of variability. Predictable variation opens the opportunity to consider the possible benefits from working to reliably reduce the variability. Decreased variation in fill weight gives management the possibility of lowering the targeted fill weight, thus reducing costs and increasing efficiency and throughput. All these possibilities are made available by developing knowledge of the cause and effect relationships of process factors and output results.

The advantages of predictable and decreased variation in fill weight are easy to recognize. The preceding discussion also implies certain types of analysis and actions by process managers. Process managers should be measuring and analyzing variability in actual fill content. In order to be able to affect sustained improvement, managers would have to know those operating practices, as well as those material, equipment and environmental properties that affect variation and its stability over time, and would have to be willing to act on that knowledge. They would have to accept that it is their job to do so.

Large, though predictable, variation in net content means a financial loss owing to the practice of overfilling to maintain a lower specification. Thus, some of the financial implications of variation are readily apparent in the preceding case. The relationship of variation to costs and benefits is not always as easily understood. Gelatin capsules, widely used in the pharmaceutical industry, have a product characteristic that offers a different perspective on what variability might mean to management. Wall thickness is an important property of gelatin capsules. The current target value for wall thickness has been specified in order to provide the material in the capsule with the necessary protection from the environment and to insure the capsule's compatibility with the customer's filling equipment. There is no need to change average wall thickness; indeed, there are strong reasons for not changing the average. Because average wall thickness must remain unchanged, there is no opportunity to lower the average and save material after achieving decreased variation in wall thickness. However, suppose that current process variability consistently produces capsules with wall thickness outside of specifications. This large variability has several consequences; the capsules must be sorted to remove those of an incorrect size. Thus, additional material is used to manufacture capsules that cannot be shipped, and machine capacity and other resources are employed to produce products that cannot be used.

The costs associated with these losses are neither easily identified by current cost accounting practice nor recognized as being a part of current management practice. The process may be on budget because standards allow for a given amount of waste. If the costs are not seen to exist, then the benefits may also not be recognized. However, decreased variability can provide some tangible internal benefits. After reduced variation has been documented and proven replicable, there will be less inspection and cycle times will be reduced. The financial gains may appear to be modest, but other, possibly more significant, benefits are to be found external to the business. With shipments of capsules having known, predictable values within a specified range, the customer can have greater assurance that a shipment of capsules will run on his or her equipment without machine stops, leading to higher equipment utilization and improved cycle times with attendant economies. This assurance in high efficiencies provided by verified reliability of material properties can yield competitive advantage. In addition, there may be competitive advantage in having gained process knowledge; development of process knowledge is a method and a result of work to reduce variation. The ability to reduce variation demonstrates improved process knowledge. This improved knowledge allows the manufacturer of capsules to respond better to new information on customer needs and to become a valued supplier to the customer.

It is significant that the benefits of decreased variation in wall thickness do not result in an immediate, visible return to the manufacturer of capsules. In order to pursue reduction in variation, managers must understand the implications of variation for this characteristic. Narrow interpretation of costs and benefits will not lead to uncovering opportunities for gaining new customers or securing old ones. In this instance, the management group needs more than process knowledge. They must know what their customers might value or where diminished penalties incurred in use would offer potential gains to the customer with consequent benefit to themselves. They must be able to connect attributes valued by the customer with internal systems, and they must assume responsibility for stabilizing and improving those systems. Because of the complexity involved in thinking about and considering the effects of variation, it is imperative that a manager develop an understanding of the impact of excessive and erratic variation on fulfillment of system responsibilities. These system responsibilities include continuing to learn about customer needs.

Experience indicates that financial analyses usually focus on the more narrow, internal evaluation of costs and benefits. Complete reliance on financial analyses as the means of developing strategies and making decisions directs attention away from the range of possibilities created by decreased variability and system improvement. Reliance on existing financial models will not identify the financial gains that may be had by managing the variation in the systems which provide value to the customer. For a particular system, the manager must determine the costs or disadvantages associated with variation. By beginning to understand the effects of variation, the manager can make an objective analysis regarding the benefits of reducing variability.

CHANGING PRACTICES

Variation must be understood in the context of a particular system. It is necessary that the manager understand clearly why the system exists. Without this knowledge, the manager is in no position to make informed judgments about variability and the benefits of its reduction, movement, or translation to other forms. Understanding the sources of variation and the effects of variation in the context of system analysis will affect how a manager approaches his or her work. Understanding the sources of variation in results is only one part of the story. There must be a motivation for developing and using that understanding. Working to achieve stability follows from knowing that achieved stability is a responsibility of the manager. Decreased variability results from system change and incremental improvement. These results follow only after management understands that this is its work.

Consider a situation in which an increased throughput rate is desired. The rationale for that objective is not questioned here; rather, the needed increase will serve as a starting point for a short discussion on tactics for obtaining the increase. Increased throughput could be attained in a variety of ways. It is the selection from among the alternatives and the rationale for choosing an alternative that forms the centerpiece of this simple example. Typically, the expectation that throughput be increased is expressed forcibly to a plant. However, in defining the expectation management may not have considered how the requested gains might be achieved. Some tactics for achieving the increase may be stated very specifically, such as working to eliminate a known bottleneck or requiring that the throughput rate of each unit in the facility be increased.

The expressed focus may not be consistent with the actual system sources that influence current throughput levels. An overemphasis on the result itself, increased throughput, may promote practices contrary to other requirements and needs of the business. For example, under pressure to increase throughput, a department may release poor quality material. By choosing that alternative, the measured throughput rate may increase while actual yield stays the same. Under pressure to attain or surpass schedule, equipment may be run without adequate maintenance, having an impact on quality and future plant performance and well-being. Shifts, treated as if they are independent production units, may be goaded toward quota. The effect may be to delay appropriate maintenance or to set aside the opportunity to better choose when to perform maintenance. If each shift is pressured to achieve a certain production quota, the effect is often to set one shift working against the others. Production knowledge is hoarded; work is shifted to other locations or shifts by a variety of means. Each shift concentrates on getting its own quota, often emptying the line of all work in progress in order to achieve the objective. Thus, a larger start-up job is left for the next shift. The idea of running the operation in a smooth, consistent fashion over the different shifts is not considered, nor are the benefits in improved throughput that might result.

As a further consequence, the opportunity to achieve sustained improvement in throughput by increasing the ability to consistently produce high-quality products at each stage of operation is foregone by concentrating on the schedule rather than on other system factors. There may be no sustained experience in working to improve process and product quality; therefore, there is no assurance that the approach will yield appreciable benefits. There is no confidence that working systematically on the input side will result in improved throughput capability. There may be other losses. The capability of the people has not been increased because no process knowledge has been gained. The management group has not been strengthened by acquiring different behaviors and new knowledge by which to manage in the future.

A different practice for working to improve throughput levels would involve understanding the sources of variation that contribute to the level and variability in throughput rates, evaluating those sources, and selecting where and when to make changes to improve the existing system. This statement implies that there exists a multitude of sources of variation which affect each other as well as combining to affect throughput rate. With the different approach, the idea of searching for one, or the most prevalent, cause of deviations from a standard is replaced by the idea of understanding system behavior and the variation in components of the system which affect throughput levels. In examining the total system for making product, management might begin to look at specific activities with an expanded viewpoint, finding opportunity for improvement in places previously unexamined. Numerous setup changes and within-run modifications to accommodate raw material variation reveal that the procurement subsystem may not be effectively connected to the production subsystem. At least two issues surface. There is the obvious impact of frequent setups and modifications on productivity and efficiency. There is also evidence of system breakdown between the procurement and production subsystems. Examining the interface between procurement and production has the potential to create large returns.

Another simple example to illustrate the contrast of past practices with practices that recognize variation and its implications is tool quality. Inconsistent tool quality leads to erratic and frequent tool changes with a consequent effect on throughput in terms of quantity and quality. Poor tool quality indicates that management has not paid attention to developing knowledge about tool requirements, to understanding why the tools vary in their performance characteristics, and to working with vendors to prevent those same issues from resurfacing, year after year, product after product. The existence of variation evidenced by frequent and unpredictable tool changes may initially be characterized by the physical properties of the tools themselves. At a more fundamental level, these sources are seen to result from management practices and behaviors that fail to address the issues of developing adequate requirements and knowledge of sources of variation and providing an effective mechanism for working with vendors.

Working on sources of variation can be focused in a variety of ways within an organization. One focus is at the operational or functional level. Although this focus is necessary and desirable, it leaves unaddressed many of the most valuable opportunities for improvement. For example, work on improving throughput might lead to noting the different capabilities of several machines that are performing the same operation. Different capabilities might mean that the products of the different machines are different, thus creating product variation that must be accommodated further downstream. Alternatively, different capabilities in terms of throughput rates would imply downstream actions to absorb variation in rate of supply. Improvements in the process would be realized by identifying this source of variation and then making changes to bring all machines into similar operation. Because operational improvements are both useful and necessary, the focus for working on variation may be limited to this level of the organization. In fact, a previously espoused role of management has been to empower the personnel involved with this work to investigate and implement such changes. However, this role by itself is inadequate to address many of the practices that might be the larger drivers of variation.

Working to insure that all machines operate in a consistent manner may provide a valuable improvement, but perhaps it is more important to address the management actions that allowed the machines to operate inconsistently. No system may have existed to bring new machines on line to be consistent with the other machines. Indeed, those who design, procure, install, and maintain processing equipment may not recognize that they have a responsibility to avoid introducing variation into the production system. Those with broader responsibility for design, procurement, and operation of the production system are responsible for seeing that potential sources of variation and complexity are recognized and addressed in plans and practices. Perhaps there exist no procedures in this or other operations for ongoing study of the effects of these types of differences, nor processes for developing and adhering to standard operating procedures. It is possible that machine differences could be addressed by changing maintenance practices. Again, it is management's role to understand the sources of variation manifested in operations and to address them.

The manner in which management addresses functional interdependencies is also important. Just as the role of empowering people is not sufficient to manage the variation in the business, neither is the role of serving as a facilitator of improvement work across functions. Although it would be inappropriate to conclude that this approach has not provided valuable improvements, the role of facilitator is not adequate to address the issues confronting management. The ability and responsibility to address issues that involve functional interdependencies and to optimize the system as a whole lies with upper management. The content of the work of management is enhanced by knowledge of the existence, stability, magnitude, and effects of variation. The context within which this work takes place is the systems management approach.

A SYSTEM PERSPECTIVE OF MANAGING VARIATION

The preceding examples of what variation might mean to a manager are relatively obvious. More general examples, requiring a system view, are presented in the following paragraphs. These examples offer more general reasons for studying variation, and they appear to require the system view, a more comprehensive and useful perspective for the manager. They also involve variability and the need to know the magnitude, predictability, and sources of variation, as well as developing an understanding that the system must be addressed in order to effectively confront issues that manifest themselves in the form of variation.

The view that results can be usefully managed by examining deviations from standard has a number of limitations. Often accompanying this view is the perception that the observed deviation is the result of one cause. Actions taken from these particular points of view, and without system knowledge, are likely to have unintended consequences. By identifying and acting on only one cause, other causes do not get addressed, either wholly or in part. This in turn may have the consequence of moving variation from one part of the business to other parts, perhaps in a different form and possibly at a different time. That may be an appropriate strategy, but it may also have unintended and negative effects on other system parameters which may impair performance in terms of cost, quality, or delivery. Another result, one that generally goes unnoticed, is that no new knowledge has been accumulated to support system change or improvement or to support future decisions.

Acting on a single type of result can have unintended effects when potential effects on other results and on the cause system that generates the collection of results are not taken into account. As an example, consider a situation in which shipping dates are not being met. Deviations from committed dates are observed, attention is drawn to these deviations, and a program to improve those results is initiated. Performance to shipping dates will improve, at least until attention turns to other concerns. What really happens depends on the method used to affect change and the people and departments involved. Shipments may leave on schedule after the program goes into action, with its attendant publicity, because materials of questionable quality are shipped. Or overtime is incurred, or additional crews are added, or more capacity is available because maintenance is delayed or canceled. All these actions are likely to be unintended. It might also be that shipping dates are manipulated through an ongoing series of negotiations with customers. These dates could be met and performance improved on this single dimension, but perhaps real customer needs with respect to timing, quality, and quantity are not being addressed. Thus, improvement of one type of result has been accomplished by methods that will contribute to the discredit of the business in the future.

A system viewpoint by management would indicate that the issue of improving organizational results and the means by which that is accomplished must be considered more deeply than simply deciding to better meet promised shipping dates. The underlying system issues concerning why there are difficulties in meeting shipment schedules would have to be addressed. Causes of difficulties may be found to be quality or assembly problems, which in turn may be related to design, equipment capabilities or maintenance, or material purchases. Inability to meet scheduled shipping dates may also be due to the process used for assigning a particular order mix to the plant, or possibly to the lack of criteria for deciding which products to produce first for which customer. If the potential effects on other results such as labor cost, future equipment performance, quality, and future sales were not considered and attempts were made to manage, by directly affecting, performance to shipping schedules, the outcome could be damage to current and future business performance.

As another example, consider a manufacturing firm that incurs a large fraction of direct cost in the acquisition of raw materials, components, or piece parts. Since management is surely aware of these costs, attention quite naturally becomes focused on purchase of incoming supplies. Pressure to reduce materials costs results in searches for low bid price. However, gaining a reduction in purchase price may result in variation in other costs, many of which may not be directly linked to the purchasing function and thus may go unnoticed as a result of the effect of purchase on low bid. For example, quality of incoming material may suffer, leading to internal sorting and rework, thus resulting in an increase in production costs. Inferior materials can easily decrease productivity because of difficulty in working, forming, or assembling purchased parts. The resulting complexity of materials handling and attendant recordkeeping consumes labor hours and increases the opportunity for errors and confusion. The difficulties of meeting schedules are increased by the difficulties encountered in working with inferior materials. There are any number of other ways in which the acquisition of raw materials, components, or piece parts can contribute to system deficiencies. Costs, of course, must be decreased; that is a fact of managerial life and a necessity for continued success. But which costs, against what criteria, and achieved by what means are not generally addressed from the organization's perspective. If the guidelines for managing costs are established function by function, then functional optimization may move the variation and attendant waste from one part of the organization to another with no overall benefit to the business.

This discussion makes clear that a prerequisite for successfully managing variation is to have knowledge regarding its sources. Variation, of course, manifests itself in open and visible ways in products and services. It is also revealed in an organization's ability to deliver these results. Variation that affects the organization's capability to execute can be particularly difficult to recognize, understand, and overcome. The sources of this variation are often found in organizational practices, affecting and affected by the organizational culture. The budgeting process affords an instructive example. The practices of budget construction and use, supported by wide knowledge of accepted and possible behaviors, form the cultural methodology of the budgeting process. The budgeting process affects managerial and nonmanagerial behaviors, and these behaviors critically influence and affect organizational effectiveness and capability.

From a theoretical and a practical viewpoint, one presumed intent of developing a budget is to plan for the orderly allocation and management of resources across an organization's functions. By its nature, budget development should be transfunctional, supporting the coordinated work that must go across functions to successfully manage business systems. Yet, typical practices surrounding the development, use, and evaluation of a budget deny this elementary necessity. Management usually intends for the budget to serve several purposes. At one level, management expectations, combined with a forecast of business conditions, serve as a basis for planning acquisition and investment and for allocating resources in support of the organization's strategies. At another level, budgets serve as an expression of a goal, conservatively or optimistically stated, for what individual business units are expected to produce with the resources provided. As a deployment instrument, the budgeting process becomes a powerful motivator and guide for behavior among middle managers and other employee groups with the potential for harmful as well as positive conduct. Budgets are taken to be goals that influence planning and decisions at lower levels, and they become the standard by which performance is judged. Thus, the multiple purposes of budgets are put into effect at different times. What was initially a forecast or planning figure is transformed into a goal or objective to be met and a standard for evaluating and judging performance.

Multiple budget purposes can become a source of variation in personal conduct and execution as the one instrument cannot serve all needs. If there are multiple expectations of the budget in its formulation, multiple criteria, possibly contradictory, ones, will be used in review and evaluation. A confounding factor is that budgetary purpose is not clearly and uniformly understood among those who collectively compile and use the budget document. In exercising managerial control, misunderstanding regarding the intent of the budget and its capability for delivering precise and accurate information becomes crucial and often leads to inappropriate conduct. Depending on managerial perspective, a budget deviation may be taken as providing information on a crucial attribute or on managerial performance. In fact, frequently, the reasons for budget deviations are hopelessly confounded among themselves. The process by which budgets are created may compromise the purpose of having and using a budget and complicate the understanding of budget deviations.

Budgets are typically determined by a circular process during an annual budgeting period. Budget revisions cycle upward and downward as middle management searches for what senior managers will accept as the right answer for the frequently unasked question or unarticulated strategy. This activity detracts from the need to settle on what will be necessary at various levels to begin to fulfill the business strategy. Because rewards and punishments are thought to be meted out on the basis of performance to budget and explanations may be sought for deviations, managers learn to protect themselves from variation. Initial budgets are padded so that expected reductions during the revision process can be absorbed with a relatively small risk of being caught without the means to make the final budget or of damaging the ability to deliver expected results of other kinds. In many organizations, line items and departments are allocated financial resources as quasi-independent entities with little regard for the correlated and coordinated behavior necessary for successfully practicing systems management. The departmental budgeting structure often dictates functional conduct with unsatisfactory system results. Implications for introducing variation into the system are obvious. In addition, the actual budget formulation is often guided by the historical uses of the budget in the review stage rather than by current and future business needs.

In passing from the planning and deployment phase of the budgetary process to the review stage, difficulties are encountered as the budget evolves into a standard by which to judge performance. In the review process by more senior management groups, individual departments are reviewed as though they were independent businesses. The review and evaluation process in which senior managers are expected to participate does not build in them an appreciation for the organization's systems, nor does it require that they accept responsibility for those systems. This is a crucial behavioral practice that requires close questioning and deserves reform. Other issues intrude. The line items in the budget itself may not reflect the requirements of the critical systems that cut across departments or functions. There is no structure in the review process to support an analytical evaluation of how systems are consuming resources or to allow determination of whether the collective activities that comprise critical systems are funded at the appropriate level. The point is not that the budget is an imperfect instrument; rather, the point at issue is that variation is perpetuated and induced throughout the organization because budget deviations are misinterpreted and misused. This activity does not promote improvement by identifying and removing sources of variation; it does, however, promote actions that may create unintended variation.

Typically, performance to budget is evaluated by identifying important deviations. In judging the degree of deviation of actual results from budget, differing methods are used. For example, a deviation of actual result from budgeted result of a given magnitude, perhaps a certain percentage, may be arbitrarily established, with all larger deviations being subjected to close scrutiny. Alternatively, the array of all deviations is arranged by order of magnitude, and the most unfavorable are intensely questioned. Deviations from budget may exhibit either predictable or unpredictable variation. If deviations were varying predictably, similar to the pattern depicted in Figure 1, there would be no basis for deciding that the system of causes of deviations was operating any differently during the most recent period than during any other period included in the data history. Unusual deviations might be revealed by data patterns indicating unpredictable behavior, as in Figure 2. However, interpretation is not likely to be straightforward. If a given deviation in the time series were to indicate the influence of a special cause, that information by itself provides no knowledge about what that cause might be, or what action might be taken in response to the unusual deviation if, in fact, action were appropriate.

A deviation from budget for a business unit may not be descriptive of the performance of that unit, independent of all others, since budget variances are a function of the interaction of various systems, each being transfunctional and subject to interdependent causes. Nevertheless, functional or departmental managers faced with the responsibility of providing explanations for deviations from budget will surely provide an explanation and, in rationalizing the explanation, act accordingly. These explanations may or may not be correct; the issue is that results are not likely to be evaluated with respect to the formal and informal systems of the department or organization. Reactive measures in response to a single result or its explanation will very likely have unanticipated effects at later times in different places. Imposition of a benchmark deviation as a basis for managerial intervention is likely to lead to unproductive activity at best, with overcontrol a possibility, an outcome known to create increased variation in results.

The knowledge that some budget variances will be selected for critical examination and the actual selection of some variances for further scrutiny has a cascading effect upon the organization. Managers may maintain a contingency bank to cover unexpected upsets in the revenue-cost balance. Potential improvements to reduce cost or improve market position may be deferred until they are needed to offset unfavorable results. Such deferrals have the effect of maintaining variation in current products or services and the accompanying waste in the processes that produce them. During the budgeting period, early deviations from the forecast may go unreported as a matter of choice, and the magnitude of results that must be had to meet the annual budget becomes more rigid and formidable later in the cycle. At the end of a budget cycle, spending and shipments are deferred or accelerated, depending on the current position relative to the budget. These behaviors have the effect of not addressing variation sources in a timely and correct manner. Budget review and evaluation carried out in this manner provoke behavior that can introduce cost and quality variations into the system.

Business units may be treated as independent entities and be compared to one another in terms of budget performance. Because apparently favorable performance depends to some extent on being able to manipulate cost and revenue in the short term, costs are shipped on to other units and revenue is recorded by dumping products on other units when necessary to improve budget performance. The effect is to promote confrontation, to militate against cooperation for organizational benefit, and to induce variation in the cross-functional systems. A few iterations of such a cycle lead to increased levels of padding, deferrals, changes in spending rates, and internal competitive games among business units. Budgets suffer diminished credibility as variation is introduced into revision, use, and interpretation. As the budget becomes a less useful aid to planning and evaluation, fiscal responsibility departs the ranks of line managers to be replaced by games of fiscal manipulation. Heavy reliance is placed on the financial function, and financial personnel take on the role of managing the business. The customer, the marketplace, and future business needs are forgotten in the competition for reward and in actions to avoid penalty.

The preceding discussion of the budgeting process focused primarily on evaluating deviations of realized costs from budgeted costs. A more useful analysis might consider how the budgeting process may place limitations on the organization's growth, improvement, and ability to meet customer needs. If managing the budgeting process becomes a part of a specific system responsibility, these issues have a context within which to be addressed. In the typical budgeting process, both in its formulation and in subsequent evaluations, there is an implicit assumption that managing the budget is equivalent to managing the business and its systems. The financial value assigned to a line item or department is taken to define and represent a series of behaviors, procedures, and activities that will promote business success, if fulfilled. These assumptions should be regularly questioned. This use of the budget results from a human need to make things simple and clear. In this instance, however, the search for a simplification procedure is a miscarriage of the complexity of organizational systems. Examination of the budget, as it is currently constructed and used by most organizations, will not substitute for gaining system knowledge. When there is managerial failure to understand budget content and intent and its relationship to transfunctional responsibilities, inappropriate interpretation and misuse will occur. Current organizational structure and practice, with its functional responsibilities and loyalties and its reward systems, encourage middle managers to engage in behavior that reinforces the misuse and misunderstanding engaged in by senior managers. The consequences include a large potential for inducing variation into the system by direct and indirect influence from managerial behaviors and by the timing and execution of decisions.

Of course, managers bring more sophistication to review and analysis than what is implied here. The budget is not set in concrete; revisions are made. Deviations are not judged absolutely. There is informal forgiveness and understanding; there may be implicit recognition that circumstances changed in unanticipated ways. But there will be inconsistent and inappropriate use of budget deviations, and this inconsistency results in consistent, possibly inappropriate, behavior by junior management. With these difficulties in mind, what alternative strategies might be considered? The management group can begin to differentiate between results-oriented criteria and process-oriented criteria for evaluation and place a greater emphasis on process. As long as the focus of review and discussion is on results as shown in various indicators, there will be limited understanding that the generators of results lie in the daily work of the organization. The planning and deployment process represented by the budget cannot be set aside; that exercise provides a necessary and valuable service. However, use of budget deviations as a device for exercising managerial control should be carefully limited. The characteristics, positive and negative, of any performance indicator should be examined, with particular attention paid to the positive and negative behaviors likely to be induced by use of the indicator in evaluation. The sources of variation in the realized values of any performance indicator should be explored. Indicators must be thoughtfully used with a deep understanding of their purpose and limitations. Finally, the content of interaction of any manager with his or her subordinates can be changed to include collaborative analysis of systems and processes with the intent of identifying opportunities for improvement. Expected behaviors by subordinates are most effectively reinforced by seeing them modeled by their superiors.

CONCLUSION

Variation is a complex and subtle phenomenon. Identifying the organizational system as the source of variation is correct, but the identification is perhaps too general to be persuasive or useful. Nonetheless, it will be necessary. Sources of variation are often thought of too narrowly, being found typically in technology, in equipment, in material, and in methods as practiced by nonmanagement groups. The influence of management behavior and practice then goes unrecognized. The understanding and execution of organizational purpose, derivative of leadership content and conduct, have their impact on output characteristics, whether those characteristics be in materials or services or in economic results. The education and competence of manager and nonmanager alike exert an effect on the organization's capability of delivering product or services to an expectation. For these reasons, managers will find it expedient and necessary to adopt a complex mentality when considering sources of variation and will resist the temptation to classify these into several small, unrelated boxes.

As part of his or her job the manager must demonstrably know system capability for measurable parameters and judge the suitability of that capability. The stability, average, and variation of those parameters must characterize the results of decisions and process or system structure and operation. Evidence of system instability indicates to the manager that either unmanaged sources of variation are impacting system performance or that management activity has an inconsistent effect on performance. This in turn suggests to the knowledgeable manager that certain managerial behaviors are required to address, remove, and prevent such occurrences. Evidence of system stability sends other signals to the manager and necessitates a different management mode with a different judgmental structure. While the average performance strongly dominates the description of what the system can typically produce, it is an outcome different from the typical result that reflects the existence of variation. Thus, it is the variability that confuses and misleads, perhaps generating inappropriate activity. It is necessary to understand that the magnitude of the variability and the consistency with which that magnitude is repeatable is a measure of system capability. Consistency by itself has some virtue; however, that consistency must be measured against what is needed. If system capability is inadequate to deliver what is needed in the near term and in the future, that inadequacy is the responsibility of managers to address.

CHAPTER 13

UNDERSTANDING CAUSE AND EFFECT RELATIONSHIPS FOR SUPRASYSTEM IMPROVEMENT: DESIGN OF EXPERIMENTS AND BEYOND*

WILLIAM C. PARR
Professor of Statistics
University of Tennessee

SUMMARY

Managers traditionally think of the design of experiments (DOE) as a tool whose primary applications involve the improvement of production processes and the development of new products and processes. Genichi Taguchi (1987) has shown that DOE can also be an effective tool for developing of robust products and processes. Robust products, in Taguchi's sense, are products designed so that their performance and manufacturability are insensitive to difficult or impossible to control variabilities in manufacturing process inputs or manufacturing process variation. Robust processes do not vary appreciably, in spite of variability in process inputs. These extensions of the concepts of experimentation and causal investigation, due to Taguchi, are quite welcome. However, modern managers need even more ambitious extensions to enable them to function in the new managerial leadership paradigm. Specifically, owners of strategic organizational suprasystems need tools to work causal issues

*This author would like to thank Harlan Carothers and Richard Sanders for their substantial contributions to the thinking in this chapter through a long series of thoughtful conversations. Steve Martin generously provided the author with access to two examples of his work, which have found their way into this chapter.

arising in system description, assessment, standardization, and change. This chapter briefly discusses the use of the design of experiments as a tool for robust product and process design. Then, it outlines specific tools as they apply to the task of organizational suprasystems management. The result is the documentation of a toolbox for managerial leaders – a comprehensive methodology for causal investigation. This chapter integrates a variety of ideas on inference about cause and effect relationships. The treatment, though only broadbrush for some areas of suprasystems management, provides a useful map for future research efforts. This chapter includes a description of some of these efforts.

Our treatment of tools for causal studies falls into two basic categories. The first category consists of use of experimentation for process improvement and robust process and product design. The second discusses tools for owners of suprasystems.

The first material contains the most technical discussion in the chapter. Readers with primary interest in the management of suprasystems may skip to this section as desired without loss of continuity.

PRELIMINARY CONSIDERATION

At this time, it is appropriate to address briefly one simple question: Why should a manager, much less a senior manager, be interested in understanding cause and effect relationships? This author envisions three basic categories of reasons for a manager to seek a profound understanding of cause and effect relationships: (1) to achieve breakthrough improvement of an existing system, (2) to define a control and recovery system for an existing system, and (3) to enable a system under development to be translated into organizational practice. These three reasons are depicted in Figure 1.

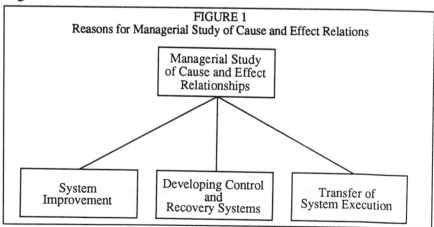

FIGURE 1
Reasons for Managerial Study of Cause and Effect Relations

Managerial Study of Cause and Effect Relationships

System Improvement

Developing Control and Recovery Systems

Transfer of System Execution

The first reason (breakthrough improvement) is perhaps the best understood of the three. This reason reflects the desire to capitalize on an increased understanding of causal factors to improve a system by reducing the variability of some key output or by better targeting the average of that output to what is externally valued. Into this category of effort fits much current effort at using design of experiments to improve processes. In particular, this is a major thrust of so-called Taguchi methods.

Unfortunately, the second definition of a control and recovery system is less well understood. If a system is to be standardized (turned into organizational practice), those executing the systems must understand how they can recover if the system runs amok. To understand this concept, it is helpful to pursue a simple, mundane example. To truly put a manufacturing process in the hands of those who are executing the process, those responsible must define an understanding of how to recover the original process performance if the variability increases or the mean moves off target. This is best facilitated if there is a definition of those variables that can be used to adjust the mean and those that might affect the variance. This knowledge will have a twofold application: (1) for adjustments of the mean, and (2) for diagnostic work, to enable those executing the process to quickly detect which of a multitude of possible factors has moved and driven thereby a change in system or process average or variability. Hence, the knowledge of factors likely to affect the mean and variance, in prioritized order, will be a powerful tool in the hands of those who maintain and execute the system. It will permit quick diagnosis of system breakdowns and simple adjustments of the system as needed.

The third reason (transfer of a new system into operations) overlaps in concept with the first and second reasons. Those transferring a new system into operations have a responsibility to give those accepting the new system more than a "recipe" for the new system (that is, a flowchart and specifications). They must also give knowledge of those variables that can be used for system adjustment and recovery as discussed above, and hence of those variables that should be studied as part of the improvement work on that transferred system.

In summary, managers will need to understand the tools for causal inference as part of managing in the future. The following material gives a brief introduction to the causal toolbox for modern managerial leaders.

CAUSAL TOOLS FOR PROCESS IMPROVEMENT AND ROBUST PROCESS AND PRODUCT DESIGN

Use of the design of experiments (DOE) as a tool to understand causal relationships is best established in the area of process improvement. The early roots of DOE are in the dual areas of agriculture and chemical processes. For agriculture, DOE has proven to be a key tool in the advance of American agriculture to the forefront of the world. Much of the early research work in this area was done by two British researchers, Ronald A. Fisher and Frank Yates. Much of the subsequent evolution of these tools into powerful tools for industrial application can be attributed to George E.P. Box. Those interested in the history of DOE should read Hahn (1982).

This chapter discusses these two major categories of applications of DOE – process improvement or troubleshooting, and design of robust processes and robust products, through one example devoted to each. The purpose of this treatment is not to instruct in the technical detail of the methodology, but instead to give an overall initial glimpse into the power of the analytical methodology of DOE.

Process Improvement and Troubleshooting at BCI

The use of DOE to fathom causal relationships in order to improve or troubleshoot processes is best explained through the device of an example. (This case study is highly fictionalized to protect confidentiality arrangements.) In this situation, an organization that will be termed BCI (a fictional name) manufacturing bulk chemicals had been working with the paradigm discussed in this book, defining suprasystem owners for the following strategic organizational suprasystems: (1) product availability, (2) make, (3) human capability, and (4) technology development and application.

BCI produces bulk chemical products for companies across the United States. Customers value high purity of product, frequent and reliable deliveries, low total cost, high reliability (assurance of no contamination), and availability of technical consulting help. Since BCI's customers participate in highly volatile markets, it is important that BCI have the capability, on extremely short notice, of ramping up production or developing new bulk chemical products to meet customer needs. It is also critically important that it sustain its customers by offering technical help on short notice. At the time of the incidents described in this chapter, the organization was committed to making technical help available to their customers on less than 24 hours notice. This, in addition to the emphasis on frequent deliveries and low total cost, had driven the organization to pursue a strategy of locating small plants close to customers. (Note here the explicit implications for the organizational and managerial behavior of understanding what customers value for organizational suprasystems, and for capital decisions.)

A number of these plants have been operating from several years to a couple of decades. A new plant, located in South Dakota to serve an emerging customer base there, exhibited severe problems: a particular filtration cycle, which consumed a large fraction of the total product lead time, took roughly 1.5 times as long as the older, more established plants. Investigation revealed that seven changes had been made in the process of transferring the operations to South Dakota. The organization located the new plant in South Dakota as a result of explicitly considered customer values. These values specifically enable (1) lower total cost (through logistics improvements), (2) faster response to changing volume needs (through the closer location), and (3) faster provision of technical consulting help from the plant. They have also implemented the process changes mentioned above under the (possibly mistaken) impression that they were enhancing value to be delivered to the customer and reducing sacrifice. (Specifically, they thought they would reduce cost and cycle time while sustaining a marginal improvement in purity.)

Table 1 presents a summary of the variables that were changed and of the values that these variables took at the older plants (labeled "old") and at the new South Dakota plant (labeled "new"). The water supply source and the raw material origin were changed as a result of the plant location. The other five changes were the result of research work done in the lab to identify possible process improvements.

A typical troubleshooting approach might have been pursued in the attempt to identify which one or more if any of these seven changes from the configuration at the old plant was responsible for the deterioration in cycle time performance. Such an approach might involve experimenting with all variables at the levels they were assigned in the old plants, and then systematically changing variables one by one until an improvement (reduction) in cycle time was observed. There are several drawbacks with

TABLE 1 Variables Studied By BCI			
Variable	Letter	Low Level (-1)	High Level (+1)
Water supply source	A	New	Old
Raw material origin	B	New	Old
Temperature	C	70 (new)	80 (old)
Recycling device	D	Absent (old)	Used (new)
Rate of addition of caustic soda	E	Low (new)	High (old)
Type of filter cloth	F	New	Old
Length of holdup time	G	Less (new)	More (old)

this "one variable at a time" approach, three of which we discuss in the following paragraphs.

One drawback is that such approaches often miss the opportunity of major improvements that can arise by taking advantage of interactions. [1] George Box has provided a useful and easy to understand example of an interaction: If we intend to understand the causal relationship between the presence of rabbits and the making of baby rabbits, we might be tempted to try a one factor at a time approach. (See Figure 2.) If we do this, and put a female rabbit in the empty pen and wait, we obtain no baby rabbits. If we then take out the female rabbit and put a male rabbit in the pen and wait, we again obtain no baby rabbits. The one factor at a time approach has failed! The problem is that an interaction (pleasant for the rabbits and fiscally useful for the rabbit-raiser) between the male and female rabbit must occur in order for baby rabbits to be produced. Only if the experimenter happened to put both rabbits in the pen at the same time would the intended result occur. No amount of experimentation with the two rabbits individually will produce baby rabbits.

A second drawback is that one factor at a time approaches typically fare poorly in environments characterized by high variability in response variables. (In the example under consideration, the response variable is filtration cycle time.) This is because only individual results are compared in the one factor at a time approach, instead of averages as in a DOE-based

FIGURE 2
Interaction

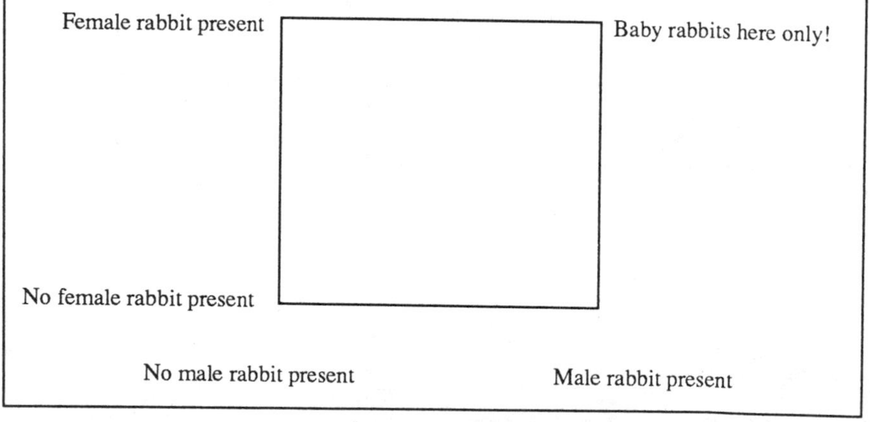

Female rabbit present   Baby rabbits here only!

No female rabbit present

No male rabbit present   Male rabbit present

---

1. Statistically, an interaction arises when the impact of increasing both variable A and variable B is different from the sum of the impacts of individually increasing A while holding B constant, and the impact of increasing B while holding A constant.

approach. Since averages are less variable than individual results, comparisons based on averages are inherently more precise and more reliable than comparisons based on individual results.

A third drawback, perhaps more important than those previously mentioned, is that the one factor at a time approach lacks structure when compared to the DOE approach. Approaches lacking structure run the risk of leading to confusion and to the collection of much data while generating little insight. A major contribution of the thinking process that underlies DOE is the maximization of the amount of knowledge and insight (and hence improvement) generated, while minimizing the requirements in terms of time, finances, and data collection.

By way of contrast to the one factor at a time approach, DOE provides a structured way of studying a process or a system even in the presence of substantial variation, and still have a chance to understand interactions. Fortunately, in typical cases it is not necessary to consider all possible combinations of the variables being manipulated to spot simple interactions. For instance, there are 128 possible combinations of the seven variables being studied in the BCI example under examination. Using the statistical theory outlined in Box and Hunter (1961a, 1961b), the managers picked a small subset of the 128 combinations and still obtained meaningful information to guide them in improving the filtration process. Using this theory, they ran the sixteen selected combinations listed in Table 2 in a pilot plant setup, with the observed filtration cycle times listed. The sixteen selected combinations were run in random order in the pilot plant.

In this chapter we do not review or even attempt to outline the theory behind the selection of which sixteen combinations to run but simply refer the interested reader to the above references or to Box and Draper (1987). For an expository treatment that is more accessible to the general reader, Wheeler (1988) is an excellent reference. Here we seek to acquaint the practicing manager with the potential benefits of using tools such as DOE for causal investigations, not to instruct in the technicalities of those tools.

From these data, it is possible to isolate the (average) main effects of each of the seven manipulated variables. Further study of these data would enable the analyst to assess roughly the possible size of interactive effects.[2] Table 3 gives a quick summary that enables us to determine those variables with the largest effects on the average filtration cycle time. Here, an

2. We note for the statistically sophisticated reader that unique and unambiguous estimates of the interactive effects will not be possible. In fact, the two-way interactions are aliased in sets of three (see Box and Hunter, 1961a, for details); hence, the determination of which if any interactions are active is not definite. Nonetheless, process knowledge and other clues from the experiment (including which variables appear to have larger main effects) usually suffice to disentangle the ambiguity.

TABLE 2
Chosen Runs And Results For BCI

Water Supply Source	Raw Material Origin	Temperature	Recycling Device	Rate of Addition of Caustic Soda	Type of Filter Cloth	Length of Holdup Time	Filtration Cycle Time
new	new	70	absent	low	new	less	80
new	new	70	used	low	old	more	82
new	new	80	absent	high	old	more	70
new	new	80	used	high	new	less	70
new	old	70	absent	high	old	less	70
new	old	70	used	high	new	more	71
new	old	80	absent	low	new	more	81
new	old	80	used	low	old	less	80
old	new	70	absent	high	new	more	53
old	new	70	used	high	old	less	52
old	new	80	absent	low	old	less	64
old	new	80	used	low	new	more	62
old	old	70	absent	low	old	more	63
old	old	70	used	low	new	less	64
old	old	80	absent	high	new	less	53
old	old	80	used	high	old	more	55

TABLE 3
BCI Results

Factor Name	-1	+1	Effect
Water supply source	75.5	58.25	-17.25
Raw material origin	66.625	67.125	0.50
Temperature	66.875	66.875	0.00
Recycling device	66.75	67.0	0.25
Rate of addition of caustic soda	72.0	61.75	-10.25
Type of filter cloth	66.75	67.0	0.25
Length of holdup time	66.625	67.125	0.50

"effect" for a variable is defined as the difference between the average filtration cycle time when that variable is at its high (+1) level and the average filtration cycle time when that variable is at its low (-1) level. The larger the effect, the more substantial the difference that can presumably be produced by changing that variable. Figure 3 provides a quick and informative graphical display of these results. This line graph presents the

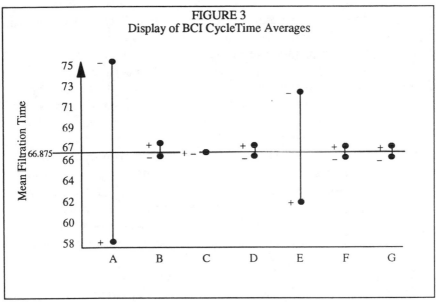

FIGURE 3
Display of BCI CycleTime Averages

averages at the high and low levels for each manipulated variable. Hence, the length of the line segment connecting these two averages indicates the size of the effect of that variable.

Figure 3 readily shows that the "old" water supply leads to substantially shorter cycle times than the "new" water supply and that the higher rate of addition of caustic soda is similarly preferable. Both preferred levels are different from those chosen for the South Dakota plant.

The water supply finding presented the managers with a dilemma: It was obviously impractical to bring water in from the old plant locations. Thus, in order to get to the root cause, they directed an investigation of the water chemistry. The managers quickly determined the significant difference in the water to be due to chemical content which could be economically and quickly altered by a simple preprocessing of the water at the South Dakota plant. The finding on the rate of addition of caustic soda led to increasing the rate to that at the older plants. Some exploratory runs revealed that further increases in this rate led to adverse effects on product quality, in spite of producing even further decreases in the filtration times. Further investigation of this phenomenon might well lead to even more gains.

The finding with regard to the water supply deserves a slight commentary: It is never sufficient merely to find a "cause" that produces an "effect." To achieve economic advantage based on their knowledge, the managers of BCI had to drive the causal link further back and find out the nature of the difference between Atlanta and South Dakota water. A superficial response of trucking Atlanta water to South Dakota would obviously be rejected. However, it would not be at all unlike a typical managerial response of quickly finding a band-aid solution, instead of probing the root cause. Such typical band-aid responses might have included insertion of an extra expensive process step, expansion of plant capacity to respond to decreased throughput, or other resource-consuming system alterations.

What might have happened if the managerial group had worked without the analytical tools of DOE? A typical scenario would have involved the plant management and the suprasystem owners for make, technology development and application, human capability, and product availability in a long series of acrimonious meetings, characterized by the taking of positions and high ratios of talk to data and argument to knowledge. DOE gave management a method for quickly isolating those critical few variables for detailed concern, and working on them in an organized fashion that made possible an open discussion, debate, and implementation.

Examples abound of using DOE for process improvement. An excellent source of industrial case studies is Snee, Hare, and Trout (1985). Technical detail regarding DOE is found in Box and Draper (1987) or, at a lower technical level, in Wheeler (1988). Since causal investigation for process improvement or troubleshooting is not the entirety of our interest in this chapter, we now turn our attention to the use of causal investigations for robust process design.

Design of Experiments for Robust Process Design

One outstanding contribution credited to Genichi Taguchi (1987) has been the concept of using DOE for what he has termed parameter design. Succinctly put, parameter design is a method for using DOE to quickly identify choices for process variables that lead to low variability and on-target process output, in spite of the possibility of highly variable process inputs. Taguchi's insight was that suitable process design choices could lead to transfer to production of processes insensitive to difficult (or expensive) to control process inputs. Consider a typical Taguchi experiment for parameter design. In such a case, the investigator has several design parameters. These represent possible choices to be made by a process or product designer. They are termed design parameters. In mechanical design, they might be lengths and widths. In circuit design, they could be the nominal lengths and widths of resistors, or nominal capacitance values. The noise factors, another set of factors considered in the experiment, represent, in a circuit design context, the natural variations to which the manufacturing process is subject. In a typical application, of course, there might be a large number of design parameters (typically more), and there might be a similarly large number of noise factors.

All these ideas are easier to understand in a specific context. Next, we consider an application of Taguchi's ideas of parameter design in process development or improvement through a specific example in integrated circuit (IC) manufacturing. This example arose in a process development application in the Semiconductor Sector of the Harris Corporation. The actual numerical results (and levels of factors) have been altered to avoid disclosure of any confidential data, while preserving the essence and ideas of the work.

In integrated circuit manufacture, silicon wafers are coated with a photosensitive material that is then selectively exposed. This photosensitive material is termed photoresist. After exposure, etching steps are used to define metal lines. The thickness and uniformity of thickness of the photosensitive material are critical parameters that help to drive the uniformity of the final significant characteristics of the metal lines, including width and profile. These characteristics are critically related to customer-valued product attributes, such as speed of the integrated circuit. In addition, these characteristics are linked to yield, which drives both predictability of delivery time and cost.

Analysis of existing control chart data on the resist thickness on coaters for processes currently being run in manufacturing revealed that most of the variability was within a wafer. It was decided to run an experiment to determine which of several variables might influence the variability. These variables are displayed in Table 4.

Using statistical technology like that used in the BCI example and documented in Wheeler (1988), a sixteen-run design was selected. For each variable combination selected for inclusion in the design, one wafer was randomly selected, the indicated treatments were applied, and five thickness readings were obtained across the wafer. The range and average were

TABLE 4
Variables Manipulated In Photoresist Study

A: Spin speed – rpm during drying cycle
   Levels: 2500, 3000
B: Acceleration – how fast final spin speed is reached
   Levels: 50%, 70%
C: Dry time – Length of time at spin speed
   Levels: 4 seconds, 20 seconds
D: Dispense time in seconds
   Levels: 1 second, 1.5 seconds
E: Bake time – time of hot-plate soft bake
F: Bake temperature – temperature of soft bake
   Levels: 90, 110

recorded for each wafer/treatment. In this way, the experimenter was able to capture in the range the variability across the wafer, and to capture in the average the "typical" or usual thickness. (See Table 5)

Thus, in this example the design parameters are the variables spin speed, acceleration, dry time, dispense time, bake time, and bake temperature. The noise factors are not specifically identified, with the exception of position on the wafer. The ranges reported are those of five positions measured on each wafer, according to a standard and widely accepted sampling convention. The other noise factors (not controlled by the experimenter) are in fact those factors that cause different wafers coated using the same recipe to have different thicknesses. The noise factors are exercised by running the production process in this case. No need exists to carry out any specific activity to make these factors vary. This is in sharp contrast with other possible experiments in which the experimenter might explicitly vary the noise factors.

(The experimenter would be delighted to know of a way to stop them from varying in production! In fact, the entire purpose of this experiment is to discover a process in which the thickness of the photoresist does not vary appreciably in response to these factors that cause variability at present. Such processes are termed robust processes.) Analysis of these data follows the same lines as analysis of the data in the BCI example, with one significant twist. Two separate analyses must be performed. First, an analysis is carried out using the variable "range" as the response. This analysis has as its purpose the determination of which of the six process

TABLE 5
Photoresist Runs and Data

Spin	Accel	Dry Time	Dispense	Bake Time	Bake Temp.	Range	Mean
2500	50%	4	1	45	90	191	21,481.6
3000	50%	4	1	60	90	164	18,655.0
2500	70%	4	1	60	110	402	20,331.0
3000	70%	4	1	45	110	123	17,985.0
2500	50%	20	1	60	110	211	17,858.8
3000	50%	20	1	45	110	117	16,298.0
2500	70%	20	1	45	90	199	18,550.0
3000	70%	20	1	60	90	136	16,921.8
3000	70%	20	1.5	60	110	190	16,245.4
2500	70%	20	1.5	45	110	214	17,968.2
3000	50%	20	1.5	45	90	131	16,868.8
2500	50%	20	1.5	60	90	324	18,526.0
3000	70%	4	1.5	45	90	50	18,642.2
2500	70%	4	1.5	60	90	295	21,278.0
3000	50%	4	1.5	60	110	211	18,002.4
2500	50%	4	1.5	45	110	252	20,721.0

variables have a major effect on the within-wafer variation. Once this determination is made, the appropriate levels of these variables having a major effect on the within-wafer variation will be chosen, and the variables set to those levels.

As can be seen from Table 6 and Figure 4, the variables that have a large impact on the range of the photoresist thickness are the spin speed and the bake time. The levels of these two variables producing improved uniformity are a spin speed of 3000 rpm and a bake time of 45 seconds. These variables are termed control factors in the language of Taguchi and are set at these preferred settings to produce reduced process variation.

Then, a second, parallel analysis is carried out using the variable "mean" as the response. The purpose of this analysis is to identify at least one variable that can be used to adjust the mean of the process without causing the variability of the process to increase. Taguchi calls such a variable a signal factor.

As can be seen from Table 7 and Figure 5, the variables with greatest impact on the average thickness are spin speed and dry time. Spin speed is clearly being used already to improve uniformity, according to the results of the analysis that used the variable "range" as the response. Hence, the process engineer in this case was left with attempting either to use dry time as the signal factor or to determine a signal factor using independent

TABLE 6			
Table Of Averages For The Range Of Thickness			
Factor	Level	Average Range	Effect
Spin speed	2500 (-1)	261.00	-120.75
	3000 (+1)	140.25	
Acceleration	50% (-1)	200.12	1.00
	70% (+1)	201.12	
Dry time	4 (-1)	211.00	-20.75
	20 (+1)	190.25	
Dispense time (sec.)	1 (-1)	192.88	15.50
	1.5 (+1)	208.38	
Bake time	45 (-1)	159.62	82.00
	60 (+1)	241.62	
Bake temperature	90 (-1)	186.25	28.75
	110 (+1)	215.00	

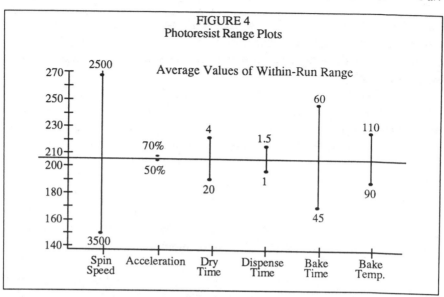

FIGURE 4
Photoresist Range Plots

TABLE 7
Table Of Averages For The Mean Thickness

Factor	Level		Average Range	Effect
Spin speed	2500	(-1)	19,589.32	-2,137.00
	3000	(+1)	17,452.32	
Acceleration	50%	(-1)	18,551.45	-61.25
	70%	(+1)	18,490.20	
Dry time	4	(-1)	19,637.02	-2,232.40
	20	(+1)	17,404.62	
Dispense time (sec.)	1	(-1)	18,510.15	21.35
	1.5	(+1)	18,531.50	
Bake time	45	(-1)	18,564.35	-87.05
	60	(+1)	18,477.30	
Bake temperature	90	(-1)	18,865.42	-689.20
	110	(+1)	18,176.22	

process knowledge. In this particular case, the second course was chosen for ease of application, and the amount of photoresist applied was used to adjust the average thickness. This is in keeping with the rather typical experience that experimenters often already know signal factors. DOE is needed as a tool to identify control factors that can be used to reduce

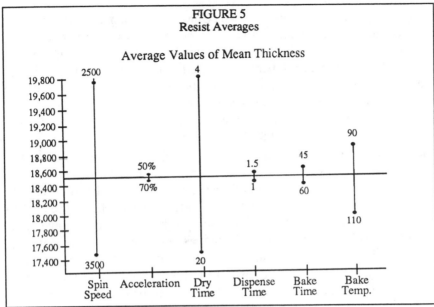

FIGURE 5
Resist Averages

variability, while ordinary knowledge of first-order effects suffices to identify signal factors. The analysis of which factors affect the mean merely serves either to verify what is already known or conjectured, or sometimes to help the experimenter discover a new relationship of interest. Additional examples of robust process and product design can be found in Dehnad (1989), to which we refer the technically minded reader interested in a more detailed treatment.

Probably the most significant tool for investigating cause and effect for systems and processes admitting a quantification is the ordinary Shewhart control chart. This tool is discussed in detail in the chapter by Sanders, Leitnaker, and Ranney included in this volume (Chapter 12). It is an extremely versatile tool for quickly sorting out varying sources of dispersion in system or process performance. Here we merely mention and briefly discuss the control chart as a tool for sorting out variation; for a more complete discussion, the interested reader should consult the above reference.

For the sake of simplicity, this chapter mentions the ordinary Xbar and R chart pair. This chart pair is much more profound than the simplistic description of the mechanics of the chart pair might suggest. Specifically, any application of a control chart involves two major critical determinations. The first of these critical determinations is the choice of which variable to chart. This choice is significant. It reflects managerial purpose in the choice of a measurement point in the process or system that is likely to lead to uncovering interesting patterns of causal relations, often termed assignable causes. This purpose must be an expression of an understanding of what measurement points will enable the manager to learn better about how realization and sacrifice are created by the suprasystem being studied. Useful choices of measurement points lead to increased understanding of the suprasystem, and hence to the ability to improve the ability of the suprasystem to deliver best net customer value.

The second choice, that of the subgrouping scheme, deserves further discussion. In the Xbar and R chart pair, the manager in determining the subgrouping scheme chooses the subgrouping to separate out potential sources (causes) of variability into two categories – those which vary within subgroups, and those that vary between subgroups. When the control charts are used to check for "common causes" versus "assignable causes," they in fact enable the manager to examine the validity of his or her conjectures regarding which of the potential sources of variability are operative. "Assignable causes" being found means that some of the causes that were categorized as between subgroups were active. In such a case, the manager is able to determine the need for further work to isolate the cause for the observed effects, based on narrowing down the possible causes to those that operate at the between-subgroup level. See Chapter 12 for a more detailed discussion of the concepts of common and assignable causes, and the role of the control chart in sorting out these causes.

Causal Tools for Suprasystem Managers: Suprasystem Description

W. Edwards Deming speaks of the need for "knowledge about the interaction of forces, including the effect of the system on the performance of people. We need understanding of the dependence and interdependence between people, groups, divisions, companies, industries, countries... We must be aware of dependence and interdependence, and the effect that it has on our work, our product, our service, our quality; otherwise we shall have no protection against the hazard of suboptimization" (quoted in Neave, 1990, pp. 265-266).

This author can think of no more eloquent summary for the need for the owner of a strategic organizational suprasystem to understand causal and interactive relationships. In the absence of understanding what causes the creation of value or sacrifice, the suprasystem owner will be unable to avoid suboptimization. Suboptimization is what naturally happens when "improvements" are pursued on various subsystems and system parts without careful consideration and understanding of the effects these "improvements" will have on the performance of other subsystems, system parts, and the system as a whole. The purpose of considering a system is to understand and seek to optimize the whole rather than suboptimize the parts. Figure 6 illustrates the dilemma of the suprasystem owner who either does not understand the relationships between the owned suprasystem and value and sacrifice created for the customer, or who does not respond to that understanding by improving the suprasystem's ability to deliver best net customer value.

A key difference between suprasystem description and the causal investigations discussed earlier is that the discussion is inevitably "softer." Suprasystem-level issues are much less amenable to hard experimentation than are those issues at the process level. This leads to consideration of a different toolbox for the suprasystem owner. In the DESCRIBE phase of suprasystem management, the reader already begins to see several of the major tools for causal investigations at the system level which will reappear throughout the suprasystem management cycle. For the sake of brevity, we will discuss these tools in greatest detail at their first or most crucial mention, and only comment on them briefly as they appear elsewhere in the cycle.

The first major tool for understanding causal relationships at the suprasystem level is the cause and effect diagram. This should be no surprise since the cause and effect diagram is perhaps the best known tool for quickly capturing what is known about causal relationships. It has been popularized as one of "Ishikawa's seven simple tools," and it is rightly regarded as one of the most critical simple tools for improvement.

The concept of the cause and effect diagram, discussed in Ishikawa (1982), is quite simple. It is founded on quickly capturing what is thought

FIGURE 6 Suprasystem Owner Responsibilities		
	Suprasystem owner does not improve suprasystem's creation of value and limitation of sacrifice.	Suprasystem owner improves suprasystem's creation of value and limitation of sacrifice.
Suprasystem owner does not understand impact of suprasystem on customer value and sacrifice.	1 Natural State	2 Serendipity or Instinct
Suprasystem owner understands impact of suprasystem on customer value and sacrifice.	3 Suprasystem Owner Abdication	4 What Must Be

to be true about causal relationships, saving verification or disproof of these relationships for a later step. As such, it is an ideal tool in system description for quickly summarizing the current state of knowledge regarding how the suprasystem respectively causes creation of value and sacrifice for the customer. At least one cause and effect diagram (or similar summary) should be constructed for each primary value or sacrifice, to document the known relationships between the system and the values and sacrifices.

The benefits of this construction are multiple. First, merely thinking about the relationship of suprasystem performance to value and sacrifice may suggest insights that have not previously been obtained. Second, a major corrective to the temptation to suboptimize is obtained. The managerial responsibility to determine what causes creation of value or creation of sacrifice is one that demands that the manager not participate in or allow tampering with the system in the interest of some local improvement, unless that system change also leads to improvement in the creation of best net comparative value.

An informative example of a cause and effect diagram is provided by Figure 7. The organization under consideration produces customized gravure cylinders for use in printing packaging for consumer products. The organization, engaged in the Strategic Value Determination and Organizational Suprasystems Management cycles, had made a preliminary determination (Projection) of those things realized and sacrificed by the customers and users of their products and services. This has led them to focus on the key realization or value of rapid response (short lead times). Three suprasystems identified by the organization included Product Definition, Human and Technological Capability and Resources, and Make/Deliver. In order to understand the impact of the Make/Deliver suprasystem on the key customer realization of short lead time, the owner of Make/Deliver created a cause and effect diagram with "Service Lead Time" as the box on the right-hand side, and those potential causes that contributed to short or long lead times (or to variability in lead times) listed as branches on the cause and effect diagram. This diagram enabled the owner to capture quickly the existing knowledge of things affecting service lead time, as well as to organize thoughts and future efforts at better understanding the relation of Make/Deliver to delivery of this value. This diagram gives the suprasystem owner the ability to further focus improvement efforts on selected causes (branches of the cause and effect diagram), or alternatively to test the validity of the current conjectures regarding which causal inputs are most influential regarding creation of value for the customers of the organization. For an excellent and straightforward discussion of the construction of cause and effect diagrams (also known as

FIGURE 7
Cause and Effect Diagram for Service Lead Time

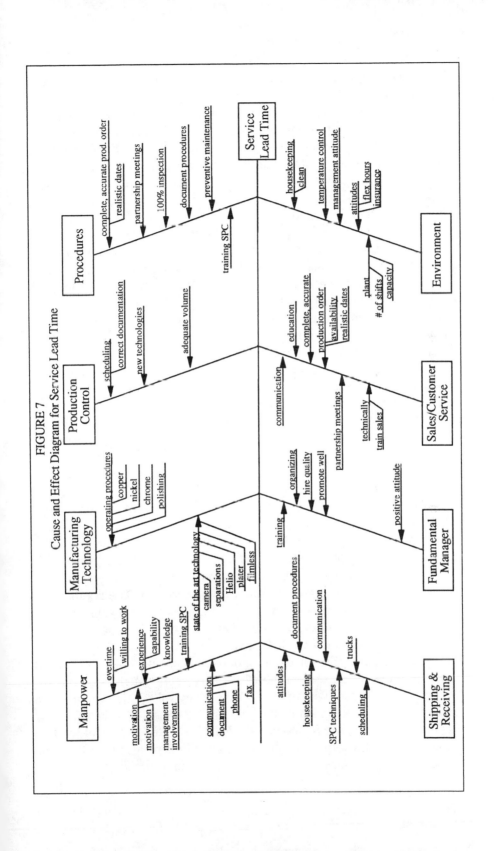

fishbone or Ishikawa diagrams), see Ishikawa (1982) or Wheeler and Chambers (1986: pp. 288-293).

A second major tool that enters at this point is the relations diagram. This tool is discussed in Mizuno (1979) as a prime tool for clarifying intertwined causal relationships in complex situations in order to obtain an understanding of the best way to improve the situation. The tool is also one of low structure, highly suitable for use in a brainstorming context. It will typically be most useful in situations where the current knowledge is highly conjectural or anecdotal, and little or no quantification has occurred.

Essentially, a number of parts of the system are displayed on a page, along with a number of "values" and "sacrifices." Arrows are used to delineate known cause and effect or objectives-means relationships. Typically, such a diagram must be drawn up and revised several times in order to confirm the understanding. For an example of a relations diagram used in the early attempts to understand the nature, structure, and priority of a suprasystem in the System Description cycle, we turn to work done at the Management Development Center (MDC) at the University of Tennessee, under the leadership of Steve Martin, associate director of the MDC. The MDC is an organization that provides an integrated set of learning experiences and collaborative support to organizations seeking to operate in the new paradigm discussed in this volume. In an attempt to improve our understanding of the systemic elements related to delivery of value to customers of the MDC, Display 1 was constructed. This is the beginning of a relations diagram. It contains a list of the conjectured (Projected) aspects valued by customers of the MDC, and a number of "events," "process outcomes," or other items thought to be related to those things that are valued. This list is displayed in unstructured form, being the result of a brainstorming session of the management group. This is a typical first step in constructing of a relations diagram.

The second step was to discuss and consider key causal relationships among the items on the page, as currently understood. The result is the drawing of arrows to reflect currently understood causal relationships, leading to Display 2. Display 2 was then used to better understand the "Relationships" system at the MDC, which deals in developing relationships with participants, companies, and major accounts. It led to a careful reconsideration of the true purpose of many suprasystem components. Nonclassroom contact was found to have a key role in determining the strength of future relationships between the customers and the MDC, as was the quality of first contact with the MDC. This led to careful work to orchestrate nonclassroom contacts such as common meals to facilitate the building of relationships. It also led to a wholesale overhaul of the process

DISPLAY 1
What Is Valued by Our Main Customers?
(Participants, Companies, Major Accounts)

First Contact

Caring Staff

First Impressions

Referrals

Ease of Dealing with MDC

New Knowledge Creation

Nonclassroom Contact
(Hilton, breaks, meals,
hospitality, shuttle,
faculty availability)

Logistics Perfect

Front End Contact

Caring Faculty

Relationships with Faculty

Relationships with MDC

Post-course Contact

Relationships with Other Participants

Quality of First Contact

Receiving New Knowledge

First Call to MDC

While Here

Ease of Access to Us

Reputation of Course Content

Arrival in Knoxville

Arrival at Hilton

Easy Registration

Sunday Night Activities

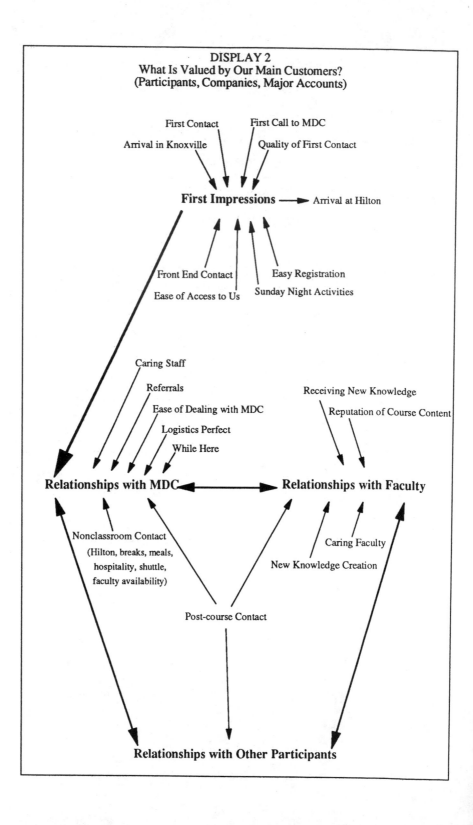

DISPLAY 2
What Is Valued by Our Main Customers?
(Participants, Companies, Major Accounts)

First Contact   First Call to MDC

Arrival in Knoxville   Quality of First Contact

First Impressions ⟶ Arrival at Hilton

Front End Contact   Easy Registration

Ease of Access to Us   Sunday Night Activities

Caring Staff

Referrals   Receiving New Knowledge

Ease of Dealing with MDC   Reputation of Course Content

Logistics Perfect

While Here

Relationships with MDC ⟷ **Relationships with Faculty**

Nonclassroom Contact
(Hilton, breaks, meals,   Caring Faculty
hospitality, shuttle,   New Knowledge Creation
faculty availability)

Post-course Contact

Relationships with Other Participants

for dealing with initial calls to the MDC to better begin the critical relationship building system at the first possible contact.

The third and last tool we discuss at this time for System Description is the time-honored flow diagram. The flow diagram is a picture of a system or process, with the intent of revealing the temporal and flow relationships that currently exist in the system or process.

For a simple example of use of a flow diagram, this chapter returns to the company mentioned above which produces gravure cylinders for the printing of packaging for consumer products. Figure 8 presents a flow diagram for the entire Make/Deliver system of this organization. We note in passing that this is a variant of the flow diagram, sometimes determined a deployment flowchart. It now contains only ordinary flow diagram information, but it also indicates where the organizational responsibility lies for the "boxes" in the flow diagram by displaying these boxes underneath a designation of the organizational responsibility provided at the top of the page. Figure 8 illustrates the complexity which is quickly seen in even an initial flow diagram. This particular flow diagram has been expanded multiple times, as further detail and knowledge were needed to guide improvement of the Make/Deliver suprasystem.

For an example of the use of a flow diagram to determine system parts that do not contribute value and only add sacrifice, we turn again to the Management Development Center at the University of Tennessee. In study of the system for relationships (a strategic organizational system for the MDC), it was decided to study the registration process, which had major impact on the forming of relationships. Figure 9 portrays the registration process as it existed at one point in time. The boxes and portions of the flowchart which have the diagonal slashes through them are portions of the flow which were deleted as the result of a study of the registration process as it contributed to the relationships system. These boxes were eliminated after it was determined that they only caused sacrifice in terms of time, inconvenience, and cost to customers, and added nothing.

Further details regarding the construction of flow diagrams can be found in Wheeler and Chambers (1986: pp. 297-300).

Causal Tools for Systems Managers: Suprasystem Assessment

Suprasystem assessment is the second quadrant in the fundamental Organizational Suprasystems Management cycle found in the managerial leadership model in Figure 2 of Chapter 5. As such, it constitutes a critical point in the cycle. The DESCRIBE quadrant has involved extensive work in determining the nature of the suprasystem as it now exists, through tools such as cause and effect diagrams, flow diagrams, relations diagrams, and

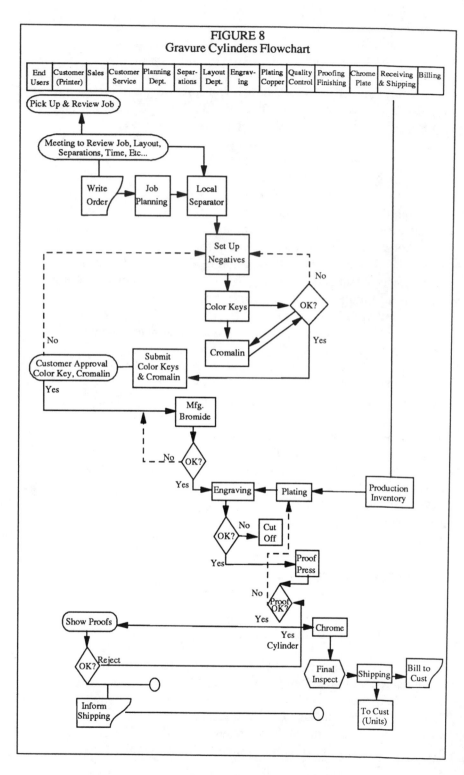

FIGURE 8
Gravure Cylinders Flowchart

End Users	Customer (Printer)	Sales	Customer Service	Planning Dept.	Separations	Layout Dept.	Engraving	Plating Copper	Quality Control	Proofing Finishing	Chrome Plate	Receiving & Shipping	Billing

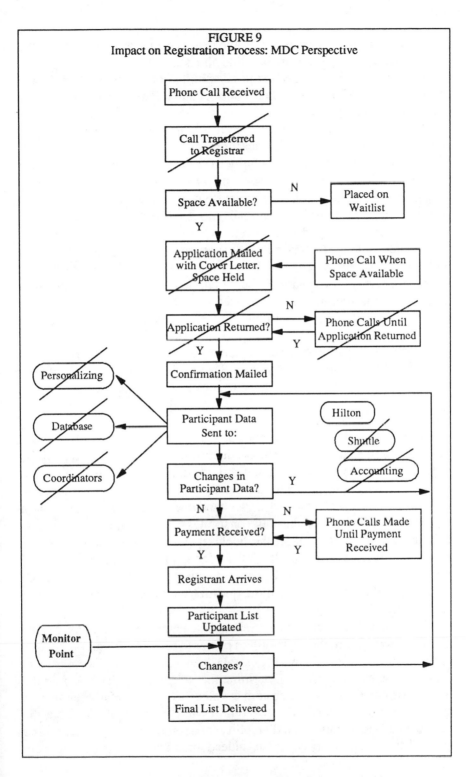

FIGURE 9
Impact on Registration Process: MDC Perspective

Phone Call Received

Call Transferred to Registrar

Space Available? — N → Placed on Waitlist

Y

Application Mailed with Cover Letter. Space Held ← Phone Call When Space Available

Application Returned? — N → Phone Calls Until Application Returned
Y

Y

Confirmation Mailed

Personalizing

Database

Coordinators

Participant Data Sent to:

Hilton
Shuttle
Accounting

Changes in Participant Data? — Y →

N

Payment Received? — N → Phone Calls Made Until Payment Received
Y

Y

Registrant Arrives

Participant List Updated

Monitor Point

Changes?

Final List Delivered

299

definition of systems measurements and results measures. At this time, the managerial leader begins to baseline the suprasystem to establish an understanding of the stability and predictability of the suprasystem. Tools involved in this effort will include control charts, Pareto charts, capability analysis, and histograms.

The control chart is a fundamental tool at this point. The suprasystem owner begins to collect results measures (measures of the desired results of the suprasystem in terms of ability to create realization and minimize sacrifice to the customer and user) and systems measurements (leading indicators of the ability of the suprasystem to deliver the desired results measures, and hence the desired realizations with minimized sacrifice to the customer and user). A critical determination to be made is whether the suprasystem is stable in its performance with respect to the results measures and the systems measurements. The primary tool for this investigation is a control chart, with the variable being charted either the results measure or the systems measurement of concern. The managerial leader will subgroup first by time, to determine whether the suprasystem is stable over time. Further investigation will lead to alternative subgroupings by interesting causes conjectured and documented in the cause and effect diagrams constructed in the DESCRIBE phase. These subgroupings might separate the data by plant, by manager, by shift, or any other interesting grouping of the suprasystem which might lead to insight into sources of unpredictability of the suprasystem.

As mentioned earlier, the control chart is a primary tool in these investigations. One reason for this is the (technically) simple nature of the tool. From a technical standpoint, it should not require detailed training in sophisticated technical tools for the managerial leader to begin to successfully use the control chart to understand the predictability of system performance. As a result, this tool constitutes the "jackknife" of suprasystems investigation. It is seldom the "ideal" method for an investigation, but it is quite often appropriate. It is also a far safer tool in the hands of the nonstatistician than technically more sophisticated tools that demand more mathematical depth and leave more questions answered at the expense of addressing a focused question.

The control charts of the systems measurements and the results measures will permit the suprasystem owner to baseline the suprasystem's performance. This will make possible later comparisons "before" and "after" changes are made, to determine that they have indeed been in the interest of creating best net customer value. As such, this baselining of suprasystem performance via the control chart is essential. Without the control charts to document predictability (or unpredictability) and level and variability (if the suprasystem is indeed predictable), the suprasystem owner will be left adrift, not knowing if efforts have led to improvement or have merely amounted to useless roiling of the suprasystem's waters.

In cases where the systems measurements and results measures are predictable, the suprasystem owner will use the tools of capability analysis (for numerically quantified measures) to study the suprasystem's ability to deliver the realization demanded by the customer and to limit the sacrifice. A suprasystem might be quite predictable and yet totally fail to deliver best net customer value. A detailed discussion of capability analysis and capability study can be found in Wheeler and Chambers (1986: pp. 125-147). Although their discussion is carried out at the process analysis level, their methods and strategies are entirely appropriate for suprasystems management.

Another tool used in the ASSESS quadrant is the Pareto diagram. This tool is one of the basic methods for determining priorities and focus. An example of a Pareto diagram is provided in Figure 10. Here, we see a display of one of the key systems measurements for the Make/Deliver

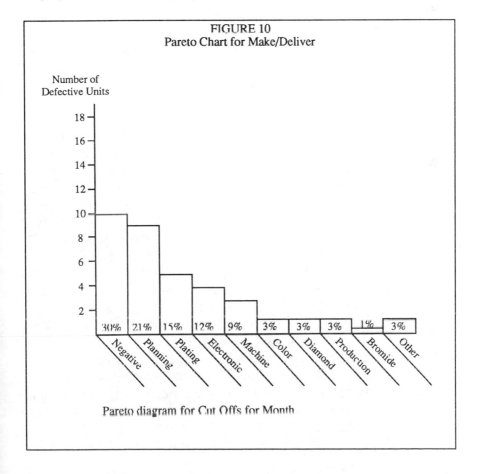

FIGURE 10
Pareto Chart for Make/Deliver

Pareto diagram for Cut Offs for Month

suprasystem of the gravure cylinder manufacturer mentioned above. This simple diagnostic tool, used in the ASSESS phase of suprasystems management, enables the manager to prioritize investigations in the pursuit of defining suitable standardization and improving of the suprasystem.

It might be thought that "customer satisfaction surveys" would constitute major tools for revealing the causes of deficiency in realization or increase in sacrifice. Unfortunately, these surveys as commonly executed are woefully inadequate for this purpose. At best, they can simply alert management to a discontented customer base. Seldom will they help the manager to determine how to deal with this discontent. For this purpose, systems analysis and improved knowledge of what is valued and what would be of more value are required. Ultimately, positive or negative results on a customer satisfaction survey will not lead the manager to discover the root cause or to determine why customers and users make the choices and evaluations they do make. Much less will customer satisfaction surveys help the manager know what will be of more value in the future.

Causal Tools for Systems Managers: Suprasystem Standardization

System standardization, the third quadrant of the Organizational Suprasystems Management cycle, involves the suprasystem owner in a new set of obligations. See Carothers and Bounds, "Customer Value Determination and System Improvement Cycles," Chapter 6 in this volume, for a detailed discussion of the concepts of this quadrant.

Kaoru Ishikawa (1985: pp. 62-65) has spoken eloquently concerning standardization: "Determining a method equals standardization. This may at first sound strange. But what I mean is this: if a person determines a method, he must standardize it and make it into a regulation, and then incorporate it into the company's technology and property. What I am suggesting is that the method to be established must be useful to everyone and free of difficulty. It has to be standardized for that reason." Standardization is not trivialization or routinization. Instead, it is determination of best practice, education of those participating in the suprasystem in how to execute the best practice, demonstration that the education has been successful, and institutionalization of the system.

The key tools for causal investigation at this juncture are control charts, before and after the "determination, education, demonstration, and institutionalization." Evidence of constructive standardization will be improvement in system performance through reduced variability between shifts, operators, managers, divisions, or any other groupings that may have heretofore done things "their own way." In the words of Ishikawa (1975:

62), "An individual may choose to do things his own idiosyncratic way, and it may prove to be the best method for him. But an organization cannot rely on a method thus derived. Even if it were a superior technique, it would still remain the specialty of one individual and could not be adopted as the technology of the company or workplace."

A key choice to be made in the STANDARDIZE quadrant is the choice of those suprasystem aspects on which to concentrate the efforts. Means of verifying appropriate choices here will include examining cause and effect diagrams for nodes of the system which are critically related to realization or value and Pareto analysis of suprasystem failures owing to inadequate standardization to determine those system nodes most strongly in need of work.

Other than control charts, the other primary tool for the actual standardization investigations will be operational definitions. Operational definitions are discussed in Ishikawa (1975) and in Carothers and Bounds' Chapter 6 in this volume. Establishment of clear operational definitions will be verified by the ability of those using those definitions to consistently and predictably apply them. Control charts will be the longitudinal means for this verification.

Causal Tools for Systems Managers: Suprasystem Change

The tools for the suprasystem owner at this stage are already familiar to the reader of this chapter. Control charts that compare the systems measurements and the results measures before and after changes are a key method for verifying (or disproving!) that a change has improved net customer value. DOE is a superb tool for determining system changes that will yield improvement in net customer value. The reader is referred to the first section of this chapter for an overview of DOE at a nonmathematical level and to the references cited therein for more technical information.

This chapter has presented a brief survey of the tools that belong to the practicing managerial leader of the future. The managerial leader will require analytic capability for understanding causation which will go far beyond that required of his or her predecessors. The educational challenges involved in equipping the managerial leaders of the future are immense. They pale, however, before the challenge of defining the understanding and exploitation of causal relationships as a requirement for managers. This definition and the move to the new paradigm of managerial leadership and managerial responsibility will eventually happen, however. Those organizations whose managers refuse to assume these responsibilities will die out in the competitive environment of the future.

REFERENCES

Box, George E.P. "Science and Statistics." *Journal of the American Statistical Association* 71 (1976): 791-799.

Box, George E.P. and Norman R. Draper *Empirical Model-Building and Response Surfaces*. New York: John Wiley & Sons, 1987.

Box, George, and E. P. Hunter. "The 2^{k-p} Fractional Factorial Designs. I." *Technometrics* 3 (1961a): 311-351.

Box, George, and E. P. Hunter. "The 2^{k-p} Fractional Factorial Designs. II." *Technometrics* 3 (1961b): 449-458.

Dehnad, Khosrow. *Quality Control, Robust Design, and the Taguchi Method*. Pacific Grove, Calif.: Wadsworth & Brooks/Cole, 1989.

Fisher, Ronald A. *The Design of Experiments*. 8th ed. Edinburgh: Oliver and Boyd, 1966.

Fisher, Ronald A. *Statistical Methods for Research Workers*. 13th ed., Edinburgh: Oliver and Boyd, 1963.

Hahn, Gerald J. "Annotated Bibliography of Books on Experimental Design." *Quality and Reliability Engineering International* 4 (1988): 193-197.

Hahn, Gerald J. "Design of Experiments: Industrial and Scientific Applications." *Encyclopedia of Statistical Sciences*, 2, ed. S. Kotz and N. L. Johnson, New York: John Wiley and Sons, 1982.

Ishikawa, Kaoru. *Guide to Quality Control*. Tokyo: Asian Productivity Organization, 1982.

Ishikawa, Kaoru. *What Is Total Quality Control? The Japanese Way*. Englewood Cliffs, N.J.: Prentice-Hall, 1985.

Kackar, R. N. "Off-line Quality Control, Parameter Design and the Taguchi Method." *Journal of Quality Technology* 17 (1985): 176-188; 189-209.

Mizuno, Shigeru. *Management for Quality Improvement: The Seven New QC Tools*. Cambridge, Mass.: Productivity Press, 1979.

Neave, Henry R. *The Deming Dimension*. Knoxville, Tenn., SPC Press, 1990.

Snee, Ronald D., Lynne B. Hare, and J. Richard Trout. *Experiments in Industry: Design, Analysis, and Interpretation of Results*. Milwaukee, Wis.: American Society for Quality Control, 1985.

Taguchi, Genichi. *System of Experimental Design: Engineering Methods to Optimize Quality and Minimize Costs*. White Plains, N. Y.: UNIPUB/Krause International Publications, 1987.

Wheeler, Donald J. *Understanding Industrial Experimentation*. Knoxville, Tenn.: Statistical Process Controls, 1988.

Wheeler, Donald and Chambers, David. *Understanding Statistical Process Control*. Knoxville, Tenn.: Statistical Process Controls, 1988.

C. IMPLEMENTING NEW MANAGERIAL

AND ORGANIZATIONAL ROLES

CHAPTER 14

ASSESSING PROGRESS IN MANAGING FOR CUSTOMER VALUE

GREGORY M. BOUNDS
Research Associate
Management Development Center
University of Tennessee

H. DUDLEY DEWHIRST
Professor of Management
University of Tennessee

SUMMARY

To compete, an organization must increasingly create value for customers. Quick fixes and partial approaches to competitiveness doom an organization to mediocrity, at best. Competing globally requires comprehensive managerial attention to many factors in the organization. These factors include individual, cultural, and management system considerations. To maximize their competitive impact, leaders must ensure these relevant factors are complementary and congruent. Doing so requires a lot of managerial thought, attention, and hard work. Managerial leaders must identify these factors and track progress for improvement within their organization. This chapter provides a framework and method for doing this work to improve organizational competitiveness through managing for customer value.

INTRODUCTION

> We know now that it will not suffice to meet the competition; that
> he that hopes only to meet the competition is already licked
> (Deming, 1986: 149).

The ability of U.S. firms to compete effectively in world markets
became a salient issue in the 1980s. Global competitiveness will likely
remain an issue during the 1990s and beyond. Competing in global and
domestic markets will require managers of an organization to provide
superior value to customers. To competitively provide value to customers,
managers must increase that which is realized and reduce that which is
sacrificed by the customer. They must improve quality, reduce cost, and
ensure delivery of needed products and services. For convenience, we
label such an approach to management "managing for customer value."

Organizations, of course, use many tactics to competitively provide
value for customers. These range from research and development for
innovative and/or less costly products, to moving production offshore to
lower production costs. This chapter does not address strategic decisions
like the introduction of dramatically different products and services or the
wholesale replacement of production facilities. Instead, we focus on the
assessment of initiatives to improve the value of existing types of products
and services.

The importance of managing for customer value will increase in the
1990s, owing to more intense global competition and the growing awareness that improved value is a potential source of competitive strategic
advantage. International comparisons point out the challenge for increased
competitiveness in customer value. For example, many United States
firms have been shocked by hard evidence that foreign competitors,
especially Japanese firms, manufacture products with fewer defects than
U.S. firms (Abernathy, Clark, and Kantrow, 1981) and by the growing
perception of U.S. consumers that U.S. products are inferior to those of
foreign manufacturers (Garvin, 1988).

This chapter briefly reviews the concept of managing for customer
value. Relevant academic and popular literature is used to explain this
concept and provide the basis for an assessment questionnaire. The
questionnaire measures organizational progress in managing for customer
value in terms of several organizational and managerial attributes. Suggestions are offered for the use of the questionnaire to guide and periodically
assess organizational competitiveness in providing customer value.

Continuous improvement enables an organization to more competitively provide value for customers, when the right things are improved. With

regard to customer value, the "right things" are the strategic systems of the organization, as determined by thorough analysis and understanding of customer value.

WHAT IS MANAGING FOR CUSTOMER VALUE?

Managing for customer value exists in an organization when it is being managed for the competitive provision of value for customers, in accordance with the framework presented in Figure 1. This framework for managing for customer value reflects the change philosophy developed and taught at the University of Tennessee's Management Development Center.

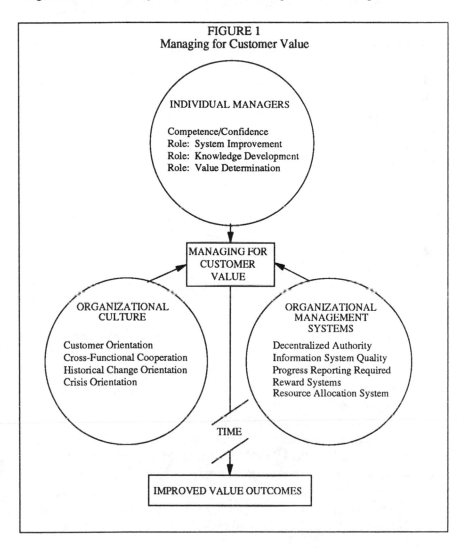

FIGURE 1
Managing for Customer Value

INDIVIDUAL MANAGERS

Competence/Confidence
Role: System Improvement
Role: Knowledge Development
Role: Value Determination

MANAGING FOR CUSTOMER VALUE

ORGANIZATIONAL CULTURE

Customer Orientation
Cross-Functional Cooperation
Historical Change Orientation
Crisis Orientation

ORGANIZATIONAL MANAGEMENT SYSTEMS

Decentralized Authority
Information System Quality
Progress Reporting Required
Reward Systems
Resource Allocation System

TIME

IMPROVED VALUE OUTCOMES

The basis for the development of this framework is fourfold: (1) the writings of four respected authorities on competitive improvement, (2) organizational change and development theory, (3) an exploratory investigation by Carothers (1989), and (4) the authors' observations of organizations attempting to change.

The four selected authorities are Deming (1986), Imai (1986), Ishikawa (1985), and Juran (1964). These authorities were selected because of their popular stature, historical significance, and influence on the development of the approach we call managing for customer value. Although it is often believed that these four authors simply address the application of statistical process control tools, this is clearly not the case. They are more concerned with managers and organizations than with statistical techniques.

BROAD FOCUS OF MANAGING FOR CUSTOMER VALUE

Managing for customer value requires broad and integrated efforts to improve the organization. Disjointed programs and projects do not suffice. Managing for customer value enhances competitiveness best when the organizational elements shown in Figure 1 are complementary and aligned with a customer value strategy. These authors have observed that many firms attempt to improve competitiveness by working on a single element. For example, one firm might build its knowledge base by hiring a quality control manager or by training first-line supervisors in statistical methods. Another firm may attempt to change its cultural orientation by sending employees to visit customer work sites. Yet another may change its performance appraisal system so that "quality" receives more emphasis. Although all these actions are helpful, each one alone is insufficient. A major cause of the disappointment experienced by many managers is that they attack only one of the necessary elements. Such narrow programs are rarely successful.

Narrow initiatives fail because virtually every aspect of an organization is intertwined with all other aspects. Managers should not attempt to change one part of the organization in isolation. All the parts have to work together if an organization is to sustain competitive improvement. Consider the following example.

The manager of a manufacturing plant wants to improve quality and consistency of parts supplied to the big three automakers. He decides that implementation of Statistical Process Control (SPC) is necessary. Machine operators and first-line supervisors are trained in SPC techniques. The training emphasizes continuous improvement philosophy and effectively provides the trainees with the competence to construct and use control charts. Numerous processes are found to be out of control, and the technical staff begins to work on process control. Workers and supervisors pitch in to learn more about process variables and help solve problems. However, production sags temporarily as the process control problems are addressed.

As they are accustomed, the plant manager and the group vice president carefully review the monthly production report, which provides data on productivity, labor efficiency, material efficiency, indirect and direct labor costs, scrap rates, machine utilization, shipments, profit/loss, and so on. Both managers see declines in efficiency, increased scrap rates, increased indirect labor costs, and lower profit. These declines are due in part to random variation and in part to the more intensive efforts to investigate, experiment, understand, and ultimately improve production processes. However, both the group vice president and the plant manager are in the executive bonus plan, which is based on productivity, efficiency, and profit. Both men are concerned.

The group vice president calls the plant manager to suggest that he would like to see those numbers get better by next month. The plant manager, himself already concerned, needs no further encouragement. He calls a meeting of his top management team and lays down the law that "those numbers will get better next month."

After the meeting, managerial interest and effort devoted to learning about production processes through experimentation and study wane. Interdepartmental collaboration within the plant diminishes as managers and supervisors refocus on functional objectives. Making the departmental numbers becomes "JOB 1" for the next month.

The above example is instructive on several counts. First, there exists a conflict between the SPC program initiated by management and the systems of measurement and control over operations, owing to a failure to engage top managers in needed changes. Second, there is a time lag between the first improvement efforts and the capability of conventional control systems to reflect improvement.

If change is to become institutionalized and accepted as "the way things are done around here," the various elements must be congruent and not in conflict. Many improvement programs, such as SPC initiatives, training programs, and Quality Circles, have not been effective because managers have failed to change many of the elements that are critical to success in improving organizational competitiveness. In the above example, steps taken to improve managerial competence and to change role perceptions were in conflict with organizational control and reward systems. The data gathering, learning, and problem solving encouraged by the SPC training were in conflict with the emphasis of the control system on this month's efficiency, productivity, and profits. This conflict doomed the "quality initiative" to fail. Changing other organizational elements could have improved the odds of success in quality improvement.

Quality initiatives, improvement programs, and SPC are generally doomed if they are not done in the appropriate context. For example, an organizational culture that encourages change, or a highly competent management team, might have enabled the SPC activities to continue, in spite of the negative pressures emanating from the control system. Obviously, the probabilities of success are highest when all the organizational elements encourage, support, and reward those activities that improve systems to create customer value.

In the above example, top managers had not decided to work on all systems of the organization. The plant manager and the group vice president failed to personally engage in continuous improvement of all systems in the organization important to their strategy. A strategy of system improvement for customer value was not formulated and implemented. The control system was not changed. In this context, programs and initiatives that are focused on isolated parts of the organization or specific production processes within plants will enjoy limited success.

Avoid the Quick Fix. To assure success, managers must personally engage in improving strategic systems to enhance their competitiveness in customer value. Overemphasis on short-term efficiency and productivity can torpedo improvement initiatives. Managers cannot just watch the bottom line. Neither can managers delegate responsibility for competitive improvement by initiating programs and projects and retreating from involvement. Plant and corporate managers must personally engage in improving all the systems that impact and determine strategic outcomes.

Problem-solving activities focused on production processes are not sufficient. SPC may serve as useful tools or components in this broader way of managing, but SPC alone does not suffice. "Quality" cannot be worked in isolation to ensure competitiveness. Quick fixes and partial solutions will be disappointing. Managers need a comprehensive program. The systems that determine the realizations and sacrifices in quality, cost, and delivery are intertwined and must be worked in an integrated fashion to provide value for customers.

ORGANIZATIONAL ASSESSMENT THROUGH QUESTIONNAIRE

Organizations are increasingly challenged to change. Employees must adapt to the changing internal and external conditions. Survey information is one way for managerial leaders to gather information, prompt discussion and communication, and identify areas that need attention and modification or total change.

The questionnaire presented in the Appendix of this chapter provides a means of assessing progress in changing these organizational elements shown in Figure 1. The assessment questionnaire measures three types of organizational elements, namely, individual managers, organizational culture, and organizational management systems.

The information in Figure 1 suggests that if the organizational elements all demand, encourage, support, and reward the appropriate managerial behavior to improve value-providing systems, eventually the effects will be observed in outcome measures. This improvement should be reflected in measures of customer value. Bottom-line measures such as market share and profitability should reflect improvement in customer value. However, there is a time lag involved. Top managers must be patient and persistent, recognizing that time is required to change the elements shown in Figure 1.

New behavior by managers leads to changes in operating processes and systems, which leads to improved customer value and ultimately to better numbers on the bottom line. The time lag required to improve systems for customer value makes periodic assessment worthwhile to assure continued progress. Through this assessment managers focus their attention on the aspects of individual managers, organizational culture, and organizational management systems, as shown in the figure, which may act as barriers to improvement.

Changes in those elements precede the permanent, long-term improvement in bottom-line results. How long is the time lag? It depends on the nature of the production or service processes and on the beginning state or starting point. It may take a minimum of six months to a year before positive bottom-line results can be seen, and even longer to notice improvement in competitive market position. It should be noted that organizations such as Xerox and Milliken (winners of the 1990 Malcolm Baldrige Award) required a decade of hard work before emerging as top organizations in the highly competitive global marketplace. Improvement in bottom-line results also depends on competition. So, the rate of progress through time must exceed that of competitors to provide preferred value alternatives. Market share will improve more slowly, or not at all, if competitors improve value at a greater rate.

The central idea that individual, organizational culture, and management systems are critical to providing value for customers is elaborated below. In the following discourse, the general terms manager and management are used for convenience and to show that these ideas apply to various levels of organizational management and leadership.

INDIVIDUAL VARIABLES

The primary building blocks of organizations are individual people and their behavior. Since managerial behavior determines organizational reality (Hambrick and Mason, 1984), the forces that shape managerial behavior are critically important to managing for customer value. Two forces that reside in the individual are competence ("can do") and role perceptions ("what to do"). Competence and role perceptions have been recognized for their impact on behavior, effort, and persistence (e.g., Graen, 1969; Hackman and Porter, 1968). Managerial competence and managerial role perceptions are potentially powerful leverage points on managerial behavior and performance.

Managerial Competence ("Can Do"). The competence of individual managers is fundamental to their successful performance in managing organizational systems for customer value. Competence results from individual aptitudes, attributes, abilities, and skills. The relationship between these components of competence and job performance has been demonstrated in a variety of job settings (Ghiselli,1966, 1973) and through managerial assessment centers (Bray, Campbell, and Grant, 1979; Thornton and Byham, 1982). Clearly, individual competence inherently limits or enhances performance once an individual decides to "perform." Under equal circumstances, for example, systems and resources, more skill outperforms less skill.

Ability is important but not sufficient. The powerful effects of motivation on performance should not be overlooked (Vroom, 1964). Competence affects performance through both ability and motivation. Motivation to perform results from one's beliefs, desires, self-concept, self-perceived abilities, and perceptions of environmental demands and potential inhibitors. These motivational forces form the basis for psychological processes of behavioral choice, that is, the decision to expend effort and to persist in the face of obstacles and aversive experiences. Bandura (1977) summarizes the effect of belief systems and behavioral choice: "The strength of people's convictions in their own effectiveness is likely to affect whether they will even try to cope with given situations. ... People fear and tend to avoid threatening situations they believe exceed their coping skills, whereas they get involved in activities and behave assuredly when they judge themselves capable of handling situations that would otherwise be intimidating" (p. 193).

If managers perceive themselves to be incapable or incompetent for the work of determining what customers value and improving organizational systems, they may avoid it. Managerial skills, abilities, knowledge, and understanding are important in managing for customer value and should not be taken for granted. These managerial resources must be ensured through selection, placement, education, coaching, development, and practice.

The specific competencies that are important will vary according to the organization and the managerial position. The diverse competencies that may be important include statistical understanding of variation, investigatory skills, analytical skills, creativity, fortitude, social skills, technical and engineering knowledge, leadership abilities, abstract thinking, and risk tolerance. Avoidance of the prescribed managerial role may reflect the lack of managerial self-confidence or competence.

Managers of all hierarchical levels should be equipped with the competencies required to fulfill their prescribed role in managing for customer value. These authors disagree with Juran's (1964) suggestion that managers rely on staff for particular breakthrough activities. Reliance on staff or delegation of responsibility can be a dangerous practice, because it may allow managers to excuse themselves from the responsibility to personally develop particular skills. Furthermore, managers relieved of personal involvement may be less inclined to "own" the results. Such detachment fosters lack of understanding and undermines decision making.

The reader should note that there is clearly a conceptual difference between competence and self-confidence. Self-confidence is realized through self-perceptions of competence. However, when we measure both of these through self-reports (as with the questionnaire presented in this chapter), measurement distinction becomes blurred. These authors make no attempt to tease out the difference between self-reported competence and self-confidence by measuring them separately.

Self-perceptions of competency are integral determiners of managerial behaviors; however, there are other important considerations. The competence of the individual must be considered in relation to the specified role requirements of managers.

Role Perception ("What to do"). Katz and Kahn (1978) defined human organizations as role systems and gave the concept of "role" a central place in their theory of organizations as the "summation of the requirements with which the system confronts the individual member" (p.186). Role theory suggests that associated with each position in an organization is a set of activities or expected behaviors. These activities constitute the role to be performed, at least approximately, by any person who occupies that position. Furthermore, roles help integrate the behaviors of a diverse set of individuals and channel their activities toward desired objectives.

Formal roles represent prescribed or standardized forms of activity, in which the rules defining the expected interdependent behavior of individuals are made explicit. Formal roles may originate in the formal task requirements of a particular position and are frequently expressed in the form of a job description. However, job descriptions are typically skeletal descriptors of how individuals actually perceive and enact their roles. The usefulness of job descriptions decreases with the increased flexibility demanded of people involved in managing for customer value.

Informal, unwritten role systems also define the behavioral expectations for individuals. When an individual enters a position, a dynamic process of "role making" ensues. The particular properties of the organization, interpersonal relations, and attributes of the person, for example, skills, competencies, knowledge, values, and self-perceptions, interact to form the context and constraints within which role expectations develop (Graen, 1976; McGrath, 1976).

Role expectations evolve from an individual's beliefs about this context. Jobs are elaborated and often primarily consist of the last item listed on job descriptions, which reads: "Other tasks as necessary." Thus, enacted roles may only remotely resemble job descriptions. The particular content of role perceptions and individual competencies important to managing for customer value are discussed below.

Role Perception – System Improvement. The strategic systems (suprasystems and subsystems) of the organization must be improved to obtain better business outcomes for customers. Systems are composed of interdependent patterns of activities that organizations use to assure desired outcomes, and include processes, functions, activities, tasks, and various material inputs, which cut across departmental and organizational divisions. These strategic systems are the means of producing goods and services for customers.

Customer value is not improved simply by stating goals. Managers must take action on the system of causes, the means of providing value for customers. Standards are not to remain constant but are to be continuously revised and improved. System improvement should be a major part of a manager's ordinary job, and not a sideline activity. Managers must perceive their primary role to be system improvement. These authors disagree with Juran (1964), who emphasizes the use of committees to guide the work of staff assistants in system improvement activities. Managers should take specific responsibility for improving the strategic suprasystems and subsystems of their organization. This improvement should include continuous incremental improvement, such as reduced variation, and discontinuous improvement, such as breakthrough innovation.

Role Perception – Knowledge Development. Action to improve a system must be based on thorough knowledge of the system. Managers must be personally involved in the knowledge development process. This knowledge of the system includes an understanding of variation in systems and the causal relationships among the system's inputs, processes, and outcomes. We cannot take appropriate action to improve the system without such knowledge of causal relationships, special causes, and common causes. Therefore, managers are responsible for knowing the details of systems.

This knowledge comes about through the hard work of observation, investigation, data collection, statistical analysis, and synthesis of information. To improve competitiveness, managers must have a personal knowledge base to improve value-providing systems for customers. Managers must not rely exclusively on staff assistants as data gatherers and analysts but must engage in learning themselves.

Role Perception – Value Determination. Managers must understand what customers value in order to guide system improvement. To understand what customers value in products and services, managers must understand the way the customer uses the product. The knowledge required to design and produce better products and services cannot come from information provided by customer satisfaction surveys, and certainly not from customer complaints alone. This knowledge results from direct dialogue, observation, investigation, and testing. Managers must learn about the current and future needs of customers, in specific detail, and then translate those needs into measurable characteristics for design of valued products and services.

To determine what customers value, managers must leave their office and go to where the customer uses the product or service. Once managers determine what customers value in terms of quality, cost, and delivery, they must determine how to create value through organizational systems. The knowledge development and system improvement activities mentioned earlier must be directed toward creating this value for the customer.

Although managerial competence and role perceptions are important determinants of managerial behaviors, boundary conditions affect the relationship between the forces of managerial competence and role perception and ultimate behavioral performance. Organizational contingencies, rewards, structures and climates make less predictable the translation of individual beliefs about roles and competencies into individual behavior. People may not actually do what they say they are capable of or what they are inclined to do.

Organizational factors intervene between the intention to behave and the actual manifestation of this intention as successful role performance (Peters, O'Connor, and Eulberg, 1985). Impediments or constraints may thwart the best of intentions. Therefore, other forces, such as organizational culture and management systems, must be considered as direct inhibitors or facilitators of role performance, as well as shapers of role perceptions.

ORGANIZATIONAL CULTURE VARIABLES

Defining culture is difficult because of its intangible nature. Culture has been defined as dominant values (Deal and Kennedy, 1982); guiding philosophy (Pascale and Athos, 1981); the climate conveyed by an organization (Taguri and Litwin, 1968); and as the "social glue" that holds the organization together (Morgan, 1989). Schein (1988) suggests three levels of culture: (1) visible artifacts and behavior patterns, (2) testable values and beliefs, and 3) basic assumptions that are so taken for granted as to be invisible. For our purposes, the cultural values of Schein's three-level model are of interest. We focus on a few central cultural values important in managing for customer value.

Although respected authorities may disagree on the exact definition of culture, there is consensus on its importance. Its impact on organizational effectiveness is widely recognized in both popular and academic literature. Deal and Kennedy (1982) found that most high-performing firms had strong cultures (clearly articulated values, well understood throughout the organization). Schein (1988) argues that "Organizational cultures are created by leaders, and one of the most decisive functions of leadership may well be the creation, the management, and–if and when that may become necessary–the destruction of culture" (p. 2).

Thus, strong cultures are a two-edged sword. Culture's long-term benefit to an organization results from its being matched to strategic needs. Conversely, a strong culture can be disadvantageous if the values it espouses are no longer appropriate in a changing environment. Managers seeking to implement strategic change in their organizations often have difficulties because of a well-entrenched existing culture that supports the status quo.

There are many potentially relevant cultural values. The following are among the most important cultural values necessary to implement system change for customer value: Customer orientation, cross-functional cooperation, crisis orientation, historical change orientation.

Customer Orientation. A strategy to improve the value of products and services for customers obviously requires that producers listen to their customers and respond to their needs. It is, after all, the customer who makes the ultimate value assessment. Nonetheless, customers are often neglected and their needs left unattended. Most organizations have nice-sounding slogans that trumpet the importance of the customer. Unfortunately, many of the slogans for meeting the customer's needs are routinely forgotten when fulfilling the promises in the slogans requires hard managerial work for lasting change or incurs costs or is otherwise inconvenient.

Customer orientation means first and foremost, listening to the voice of the customer. When it is well done, it is a continuous rather than an episodic activity. Customer orientation may be difficult because the customer's elaboration of unmet needs tends to make managers uncomfortable and defensive. But the most difficult aspect of customer orientation, as Ishikawa (1985) points out, is the cross-functional nature of the task. Customer orientation is not the responsibility of marketing alone. It requires the attention of managers responsible for design, manufacturing, sales, delivery, and service – and it requires their mutual collaboration.

Cross-Functional Cooperation. Cross-functional cooperation is absolutely necessary to enable the integration of the various functions for customer value. The reason is obvious: efforts to enhance customer value require sharing information, collaboration, and integration of activities. The critical systems that provide customer value and enable continuous improvement are largely cross-functional systems. In segmented functional organizations, there is no one who "owns" these important systems. Thus, in the important tasks, the functions are mutually interdependent. Among competitive improvement experts, Juran (1964) places the most emphasis on cross-functional cooperation. He suggests that all important problems are cross-functional in nature. His logic is that problems within the complete control of a single functional unit will get attention and will, if truly important, be resolved. The responsibility for such problems is crystal clear. Thus, the only important problems remaining are the cross-functional ones – those that no single functional manager owns and can solve alone.

High levels of cross-functional cooperation are difficult to achieve owing to functionalism. The natural tendency of functional managers is to talk mostly among themselves and to concentrate on their own functional objectives. This tendency is reinforced by conventional control and reward systems in the majority of organizations. The combination creates what Kanter (1983) terms "segmented organizations" in which managers focus their attention on meeting short-term functional efficiency and output goals.

The presence or absence of cross-functional cooperation indicates whether the cross-functional systems of the organization are owned and managed. Lack of such cooperation is a symptom of system deficiency. The answer does not lie in forcing cooperation at functional interfaces, but in drafting functional activities into system participation. Such integration into superordinate systems makes cross-functional cooperation a natural byproduct.

Crisis Orientation. By nature, human organizations become complacent and cling to established methods, standards, and approaches to problems. Even in the face of changes in the competitive arena, many organizations find it difficult to face the fact that what was satisfactory – even superior–in the past is no longer good enough. It is well established that people are more likely to accept, support, and participate in innovation and to change if they perceive that a crisis exists.

Crisis, literally defined, means turning point. Turning an organization toward providing customer value in a significant way is aided if there is a widespread perception of threat from a changing competitive environment. There may be a need to disconfirm the present in order to provide motivation and momentum for change. The starting point for improvement is recognition of the need for change. Cultures that support complacency will destroy the motivation needed to undertake the difficult and demanding tasks.

Historical Change Orientation. Organizations are most often constructed to be "in control." That is, authority structure, job descriptions, measurement systems, procedures, standards, controls, rewards, and so on, all serve the purpose of encouraging organizational members to behave in prescribed and predictable ways. Most organizations reward managers who meet established standards. Those who fix problems that threaten standards – or get systems back in control – are typically seen as good managers and as candidates for promotion.

Organizations vary greatly in the degree to which their cultural values are "in control." At the extreme, organizations with cultures that highly value control become very mechanistic. The operating principle is: "If it ain't broke, don't fix it." While all organizations must have some degree of control emphasized in their culture, excessive value placed on control prevents the experimentation, risk-taking, innovation, and change that are required to create continuous improvement. There needs to be a cultural value that supports and welcomes change. Managers must value that relentless hunt for systems improvement that will enhance customer value.

ORGANIZATIONAL MANAGEMENT SYSTEMS

The final type of elements important to managing for customer value, in the classification system of Figure 1, is organizational management systems. Organizational management system variables consist of a set of relatively enduring systems and processes that direct, guide, and control the behavior of individual organization members. As such, organizational management systems shape, but do not fully determine, the role perceptions of managers. Performance measurement or control systems, reward systems, information systems and authority systems are examples of organizational systems.

These systems are important because of the need for a fit between an organization's strategy (e.g., a customer value strategy) and its structure and systems (Miles and Snow, 1984). Without fit, organizational success is less likely. Galbraith and Nathanson (1978) identified several critical organizational design variables as making an economic difference in organizational performance. These include structure, reward systems, and information and decision systems.

While scholars use somewhat different terminology and may differently emphasize particular systems, it is clear that such systems do guide and direct the behavior of individual organizational members. These systems account for a significant portion of the variance in organizational performance. The primary purpose of such systems is to provide stability and predictability in the organization. Behaviors become institutionalized through systems.

The fact that organizational systems become institutionalized over time often creates barriers to change. Control systems that measure and reward managers on the basis of traditional departmental goals often provide incentives for managers to resist change (Hayes and Jaikumar, 1988). For example, measuring the purchasing manager's performance on the basis of least "cost" may inhibit the implementation of Just-in-Time manufacturing. The use of a few suppliers willing to meet the required delivery schedules and capability requirements may raise the price of purchased materials, so these suppliers are rejected. Selected lower price producers may not be able to consistently meet schedule and capability requirements. Thus, there are "costs" for the system other than purchase price.

In a similar way, the degree of decentralization or delegation to a particular hierarchical level in the organization becomes institutionalized. When system changes are necessary, a structure wherein all authority for change resides at the top may be inapproporiate. There may develop a bottleneck on decision making. Organizational inflexibility, bureaucratic constraints, and reporting and authority systems may impede managers' efforts to change systems.

The organizational management systems addressed below can become powerful tools to implement change. These include decentralized authority structure, information system quality, progress reporting requirements, reward system, and resource allocation system.

Decentralized Authority Structure. Providing value for customers requires an authority structure that is decentralized in some regards. There are several reasons why decentralization is necessary. Most importantly, managers' primary task is the improvement of systems. Therefore, managers must be free to experiment, to try new methods, and to make changes. They cannot do this if every decision must be approved by several levels of management. Leaders cannot do everything; they need help. Subordinates must be developed for this work. To this end, managers and workers within the broader systems must be allowed to learn through experience and to make mistakes. Fear of making mistakes can preclude learning for improvement. In learning, mistakes are allowed, but repetition of mistakes should be avoided through improvement.

Having a decentralized authority structure does not imply that managerial improvement activities are disjointed and not integrated with organizational strategy. Clearly, upper management must clarify strategy and objectives, provide helpful advice, participate in learning and improvement, and define limits of authority for subordinates. Top management must also retain responsibility for the systems they own, which cannot be adequately managed by subordinates. For example, systems that cut across plants and involve corporate procedures, practices, and policies cannot be managed by a plant manager who does not have the appropriate authority. Similarly, a foreman cannot adequately manage a system that cuts across departments of purchasing, production, maintenance, shipping, and billing within a plant. Perhaps only the plant manager or superintendent has the authority, knowledge, and skill for managing a plantwide system.

Corporate leaders, plant managers, department heads, supervisors, foremen, and workers are each qualified for ownership of systems, processes, and activities that vary in scope and complexity. Once these appropriate responsibilities are determined, superiors must delegate more and control less. What is required is freedom, not license. What provides discipline for the middle manager is the personal responsibility for improvement that managers must be made to feel. Decentralization makes the individual factor of managerial competence extremely important. Training, education, and development must be ensured. Additional direction results from real time feedback from operating systems as managers gather and analyze process data in their quest for improvement.

At another level, managers must delegate routine operations to subordinates. Deming (1986) points out that the emphasis on control has robbed workers of the pride of doing their jobs. Furthermore, the use of statistical methods allows, in fact demands, that workers be allowed more autonomy since they have the real time information that provides the basis for appropriate decisions.

Information System Quality. Given the initial focus of the Japanese quality movement on statistical process control and the use of control charts, it is not surprising that high-quality information is an essential ingredient of value-providing systems. The minimum requirements for information system quality are that accurate information be obtained and that information be widely and freely shared.

The type of information needed to support continuous improvement is different from that generated by most U.S. firms' information systems. There must be more emphasis on process measures as compared to outcome measures. Outcome data suffer from two flaws. They are after the fact, and they tell you only that you have a problem without suggesting what is wrong. By contrast, process data can be analyzed on a real time basis and often provide the basis for direct attacks to improve systems.

That is not to say that information systems should ignore output measures. By contrast, value-providing organizations will likely see improvements in efficiency and costs over time. But "results" depend on how these outcomes are defined and measured. Managers also need to focus more on quality measures as compared to cost and throughput measures. This focus provides an additional basis for progress reporting requirements, discussed below.

Progress Reporting Requirements. If continuous improvement and providing customer value are to be taken seriously by organizational members, then progress toward these objectives must be required of managers. Typical corporate reporting systems focus management's attention on short-term volume and profit measures. Deming (1986) is particularly outspoken in his disdain for the "management-by-objectives" type of programs which do not include objectives for quality improvement.

It is clear that control systems do direct managers' attention and effort to whatever is being measured. Therefore, progress toward systems improvement and measures of quality must ultimately become integrated into corporate controls and reporting systems. Juran (1988) has proposed that organizations prepare a standardized package of quality reports, comparable to standard financial reports. Presumably, these reports would be included alongside balance sheets and income statements in annual reports.

Reward System. Even more powerful than control systems in influencing managerial behavior, are reward systems which should focus on systems improvement and progress in providing customer value. Managers attend with great interest the kind of behavior and results that are rewarded in organizations. The minimum requirement for reward systems is that the criteria on which rewards are based must be consistent with continuous improvement of systems. Otherwise, as is far too often the case, initiatives designed to improve customer value (e.g., Quality Circles) are often ineffective and eventually fade away because the behavior they need for success is not rewarded.

In addition to rewarding improvement and progress toward goals, reward systems should encourage risk-taking. Innovation and improvement will frequently require trial and error, and controlled experimentation. Not all trials will succeed; nevertheless, effort should be encouraged. It is especially damaging if conscientious but unsuccessful efforts result in punishment or withholding of rewards.

Reward systems must be designed and implemented with great care. Deming (1986) argues that many incentive pay systems that reward workers on the basis of output are both ineffective and unfair. This is because output is a stochastic process, often out of the control of workers and managers alike. In Deming's view, this is akin to rewarding people on the basis of the number of red beads they draw from a bead box (that is, a completely random process).

Resource Allocation System. The resource allocation system must provide support for managing for customer value. One should not believe that "customer value is free." It requires investments in training, supporting equipment tools, and supplies. It also often requires capital investment or the sustained aid of staff groups or consultants. Most importantly, managers must invest time and hard work. Juran (1964) points out the frequent dilemma faced by middle managers who, subjected to constant crises and the "treadmill of control," focus exclusively on short-term output and have no time to work on improving systems.

APPLICATION OF SURVEY INSTRUMENT

The remainder of this chapter presents the purpose of the survey instrument, a sample profile analysis, suggested steps in using the survey, and caveats for its use.

Purpose

The two purposes of the questionnaire are to assist managers with education and to provide information.

Education. The questionnaire can be used to begin the progress of education for the group of participating managers. Through the process of data collection, individuals read each item on the questionnaire. As they respond, they think about the relevance of the content of the item to their organization. The respondent has to think about the meaning of the item and to project that meaning into the context of his or her own organization.

Through this forced mental activity, the process of responding to the questionnaire items serves an educational function. As a means of increasing awareness, survey participation prompts thinking that might not otherwise occur. It raises issues that may not otherwise be considered. It also suggests to the respondents the breadth of factors involved in managing for customer value, informing them of the many factors involved in implementing a strategic managerial agenda.

Information. The primary purpose of any survey instrument is to provide managers information. In an age of information explosion, managers must weed through the abundance of available information and the infinity of potentially relevant information. They must focus their limited resources on strategically important information. The survey instrument proposed in this chapter provides information focused on a very specific strategic managerial agenda (i.e., improving the strategic capabilities of the organization to provide value to the customers of its products and services). These strategic capabilities entail the managerial competencies, role perceptions, cultural values, and management systems discussed earlier.

Ideally, the questionnaire should be used in conjunction with a change initiative intended to ensure that managers engage in the prescribed activities of determining what customers value and improving systems to provide that value. In this context, the questionnaire can be used to:

1. Provide top managers with information about managers' perceptions of the organization, in terms of the thirteen variables discussed in the previous section;
2. Establish a baseline understanding of current management practices and compare the baseline with norms;
3. Feed back results to participants to encourage communication and interaction regarding needed changes;
4. Facilitate discussion and interaction between and among participating managers on the content of the questionnaire;
5. Assess progress over time.

A Sample Profile Analysis

The questionnaire shown in the Appendix uses forty items to measure the thirteen variables discussed above. Responses to questions related to the same variable are combined to create scores on each of the thirteen variables.

As discussed above, the questionnaire can be used to determine a baseline measure of the present state of an organization. Used in this way, it provides managers with information on how their organization compares with a broad sample of over eight hundred managers from a wide variety of organizations, including a number of the top Fortune 100. This is done by comparing average scores from the sample group with those of the eight hundred managers in the comparison group.

Consider the examples presented in Figure 2. The managers, supervisors, and foremen of two plants that produce products for both consumer and industrial use responded to the questionnaire prior to a training and change program. Responses from each plant were averaged to produce the profile of scores on each of the thirteen variables listed in Figure 2. These plants are in the same division of a corporation and produce similar products for different geographical areas. In addition to responding to the questionnaire, each participant was interviewed by these authors.

The structured interviews were conducted to learn about the managerial practices. After the interviews, these authors summarized these managerial practices in terms of role perceptions, and how managers determine what the users of their products and services valued, develop knowledge about systems, assess system performance, use data, problem solve, and improve systems. Furthermore, this managerial group was also characterized in terms of cultural and interpersonal conditions such as teamwork, cooperation, communication, trust, change orientation, autonomy, and reward orientation. Analysis of the summarized information about managerial practices in these two plants led us to suspect that Plant A was more prepared than Plant B for accepting and successfully implementing the content of the training and change program.

The questionnaire data also confirmed our opinion that Plant A may be more prepared. In Figure 2, the profiles of these two plants are plotted against the norms based on eight hundred managers. The scores are expressed in percentile form. A variable score for a plant plotted at the sixtieth percentile indicates that the average plant score was higher than 60 percent of the managers in the comparison group.

The profiles for the two plants indicate the major points of both strengths and weaknesses perceived and expressed by managers in their responses. The profile for Plant A suggests that managers believe they are weakest on customer orientation. That Plant A produced primarily generic "off the shelf" products for public consumers contributed to this relatively weak orientation toward customers, while their sister Plant B produced more for industrial users. The profile for Plant B shows that managers are weakest on cross-functional cooperation. The low score on decentralized authority structure for Plant B reflects the rather authoritarian control exercised by the plant manager to hold together a volatile collection of warring factions. The questionnaire and interview processes provide potentially useful information that might otherwise remain hidden for trainers, educators, change agents, and managerial leaders.

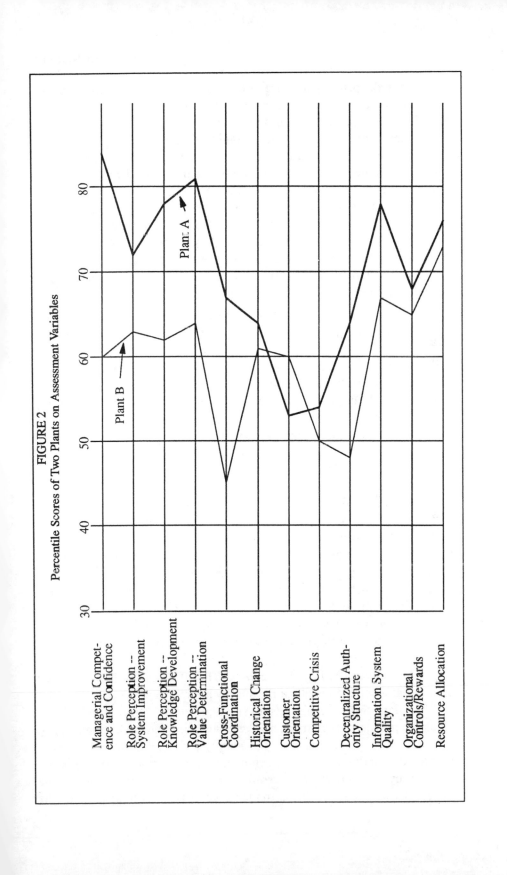

FIGURE 2
Percentile Scores of Two Plants on Assessment Variables

Plant A

Plant B

Managerial Compet-
ence and Confidence

Role Perception --
System Improvement

Role Perception --
Knowledge Development

Role Perception --
Value Determination

Cross-Functional
Coordination

Historical Change
Orientation

Customer
Orientation

Competitive Crisis

Decentralized Auth-
ority Structure

Information System
Quality

Organizational
Controls/Rewards

Resource Allocation

30 40 50 60 70 80

Although the primary purpose of the survey is to provide information, the ultimate objective is to facilitate changes in the organization that will lead to increased competitiveness in customer value. The survey should provide useful information about managing systems for customer value. The survey may be used to improve the organization's strategic capability by engaging in the following steps. Each step increases the informational benefits to the managers of the organization.

These steps include administration of the questionnaire; feedback of survey results to management and to respondents; dialogue with respondents to learn more about the meaning of the survey responses; further exploration of the current conditions of the organization; and action to improve the organization. Lastly, these activities must be continuously revisited, since continuous improvement never ends.

Steps in Using the Survey

Step 1: Administration of the Questionnaire. To get information that adequately represents the organization, many people, in different work situations, should complete the questionnaire. Managers in diverse positions and levels should be surveyed. The appropriate unit of analysis should be defined, at either plant, division, or corporate levels; and all managers and supervisors in the unit should complete a questionnaire. Worker levels may also be sampled. This broad sampling reduces the chance that the results will be biased toward any unique or narrow perspective. The data should be collected in such a manner that managers may remain anonymous, which encourages honesty by respondents.

This first step provides both informational and educational benefits to those completing the questionnaires. However, the benefits of this first step of data collection are only one-directional, exposing participants to the concepts. Information flows from the questionnaire designers to the respondents, pointing to general issues and factors involved in managing for customer value. Data collection initiates the flowback of information from respondents, but this flow remains incomplete if it does not reach the managers.

Step 2: Feedback to Top Management. The information flow becomes bidirectional when the results of the survey are fed back to upper management. The data must be analyzed and summarized into a meaningful form, such as the profile shown in Figure 2, before being fed back to managers. Once analyzed and summarized, the survey provides information about perceptions of individuals in the organization. Perceptions are important because they are powerful determinants of attitudes and how people behave. The feedback informs management of the current state of the organization, as perceived by the respondents, in terms of the factors important to managing for customer value.

These authors have discovered that the perceptions of top managers or general management positions are often quite different from those of managers in other positions. Top managers tend to have a more positive view of the conditions of their organization. They often appear blind to conditions within their organizations which act as barriers to managing for customer value. There are several plausible reasons for these perceived differences or "blindness" by top managers, including:

1. Ego involvement. Personal responsibility for organizational conditions leads top managers to deny deficiencies to protect their egos.

2. External orientation. Top managers may tend to be more attentive to external relationships, for example, with stockholders, government regulators, competitors, customers, or corporate superiors. Internal conditions may be less salient.

3. Subordinate filtering. Subordinates protect top managers from bad news. Subordinates do so in order to avoid being "killed as the messenger" or because of unwillingness to reveal their failures in managing internal affairs, which may have been delegated to them by the top manager.

4. Different orientation. Top managers may simply have a different point of view and may attend to a different set of stimuli. Top managers may tend to observe outcomes and may be attentive to process issues only when crises or problems demand. By contrast, subordinates live with process issues on a daily basis, captives of the systems created by top managers. The phenomenal experience of those working within the system can be quite different from those observing the outcomes of the system.

5. Time constraints. Top managers are simply too busy to attend to internal affairs that do not have immediate or salient profit/loss implications.

Feedback on the questionnaire responses can be a useful means of bringing reality to the typically optimistic view of top managers. The profile analysis and feedback lead managers to a more honest appraisal of organizational conditions and encourage exploration of organizational conditions. Initial feedback of the survey information may also provide managers a baseline against which to measure future progress.

Step 3: Feedback to All Respondents. In Step 3 the same survey results are fed back to those who provided the data. This feedback could be part of a structured learning experience within a training or educational program initiating a change effort. One potential danger needs to be pointed out. Feeding back results to participants may raise expectations about what will be done to remedy deficiencies or to redress enduring, recognized problems, which have now been confirmed with data. Making public this information may send the signal that managers intend to "do something about it." On the one hand, raised expectations may lead to disappointment and resentment when the expectations are not met. On the other hand, raised expectations may lead to inspired action and commitment to change when the expectations are met. Leaders should be prepared to pursue the issues further, to inspire managerial behavior change, or to be prepared for a demoralized set of subordinates.

All too often, organizations have initiated a survey methodology and never made it past step 2 or step 3. Awareness of perceived deficiencies is created, but nothing is done. One manager lamented to one of these authors that "Surveys always say the same old thing. They tell us how screwed up we are. So, what's new? Why should we do another survey to hear the same old story?" This manager heard the same old story from surveys because he apparently did not attend to the message conveyed by the survey data, that is, that the systems of the organization are deficient and need improvement. Rather than do harm to the organization, for example, raising and then dashing expectations, managers should boldly decide to pursue continuous improvement.

Leaders must realize that the above two steps of survey feedback represent only the starting point in a change process. Feedback information tells managers a summary picture or profile of "where our unit stands on these issues," in terms of data distributions and average responses on the familiar 1 to 5, agree-disagree scales. These profiles increase managerial awareness and indicate perceived problems, strengths, confidence, and complacency. But the information provided by survey feedback is seldom conclusive; thus, leaders must investigate further to achieve more understanding. The specific details needed for real improvements are not provided in survey feedback. The power and opportunity for change lie with these details. Managers must work out these details within the organization, in light of individual, environmental, and organizational needs. The profile provides a framework and directs managerial attention to initiate a focused investigation and learning process, which is discussed below.

Step 4: Further Exploration of Current Conditions. Top managers should conduct a series of meetings to delve into the meaning of the responses to get a better understanding of the current state of the organization. Top managers should initiate a dialogue with respondents to learn how they interpreted the questions on the survey. They should ask the question: What components of the organization, practices, structures, policies, behaviors, and constraints came to mind when you answered the question?

Top managers should go beyond just learning what came to mind when respondents read the items. They should also learn why the participants responded as they did and how existing conditions impact customer value. This exploration might begin with brainstorming to identify what is currently in place for each variable on the survey. Ask the questions: What practices, structures, policies, behaviors, and constraints are in place to ensure that the organization provide value for customers? What impact do these components have on strategic objectives? How do these components interact? What behaviors do current conditions encourage? What might be done to improve deficiencies in organizational conditions? Such dialogue builds mutual understanding and support for the ultimate changes in these organizational factors. Managerial leaders should seek to confirm their initial learning by further investigation and observation. They should seek the detailed understanding.

In seeking continuous improvement and in using the survey, leaders should avoid the trap of the traditional controls. Survey profile and dialogue reveal deficiencies as perceived by organizational members. However, they do not necessarily lead to creative development of new approaches, structures, or cultures that go beyond current concepts.

The judgments of the respondents are made relative to some internal standard or frame of reference. People probably use multiple frames of reference to judge their organization. These include current perceived needs, future needs, conditions in peer organizations, dream of an ideal organization, past organizations, their personal situation, and demands of competition. Failure to continuously improve the frames of reference of individuals, through education and continuous learning about customers and competitors, can lead to false self-perceptions and to a self-sealing process ensuring the status quo. The individual respondent may be unaware of changing conditions that will require improvement by the organization. Thus, individuals may not perceive the need to change simply because they do not know any better.

The nature of the survey profiles presents managers with this problem. The results of the survey may be summarized in distributions, statistical averages, and standard deviations on a 1 to 5, agree-disagree scale. The extremes of the scale implicitly identify the ideal conditions. If the profile indicates that the organization is doing well on a particular attribute and implies no deficiency, by traditional control theory, there will be no impetus for managers to try to improve that particular aspect of the organization. This reactive, "if it ain't broke, don't fix it" orientation is deficient for an organization to remain competitive in the long term. Even if the survey results and subsequent dialogue reveal no perceived deficiencies, the managers must still seek improvement.

Managers must go beyond simply reacting to perceived deficiencies. They should ask the questions: What can be done to proactively improve beyond those conditions considered adequate? What other opportunities are there to improve our capability for managing for customer value? The various factors reflected in the content of the questions may usefully point to areas that managers must consider, but the creativity and innovation must come from the heads of managers. There is no substitute for vision and creativity.

Step 5: Action to Improve. As a basis for designing an action plan, managerial leaders may start by defining what they would consider ideal conditions. Then they can compare the ideal to the current conditions discovered in Step 5 and highlight the gaps or deviations from ideal. They should conduct these activities in accordance with the activities of the managerial leadership model. The survey is a useful tool for managerial leaders to pursue their agenda to provide value for customers.

The factors in this framework for managing for customer value should be considered with regard to their impact on customer-valued outcomes. Action must be taken to improve these organizational conditions by either retaining, eliminating, remediating, recreating, or creating systems and system parts. Change must be based on detailed understanding. The effects of organizational changes should be followed over time.

Step 6: Continued Assessment. The survey should be periodically repeated as a part of ongoing improvement efforts. The improvement process never ends. The survey can provide managers with information about progress, or lack of progress, in managerial processes and individual and organizational conditions pertinent to managing for customer value. Repeated assessment through the survey can help pinpoint elements that retard progress. Repeated assessment also reminds managers of the important elements in managing for customer value. Managers should periodically cycle back through the above steps to further investigate and improve organizational systems.

For example, the questionnaire and interview processes were repeated for Plant A. In Figure 3, the profiles of Plant A are presented. Two profiles are presented for Plant A. The data for both profiles were collected at the time of the followup. Participants were asked to respond to questionnaire items by describing what their plant conditions were like before the training and change program, "Then," and what their plant conditions were like currently, "Now." The two profiles for "Then" and "Now" are presented

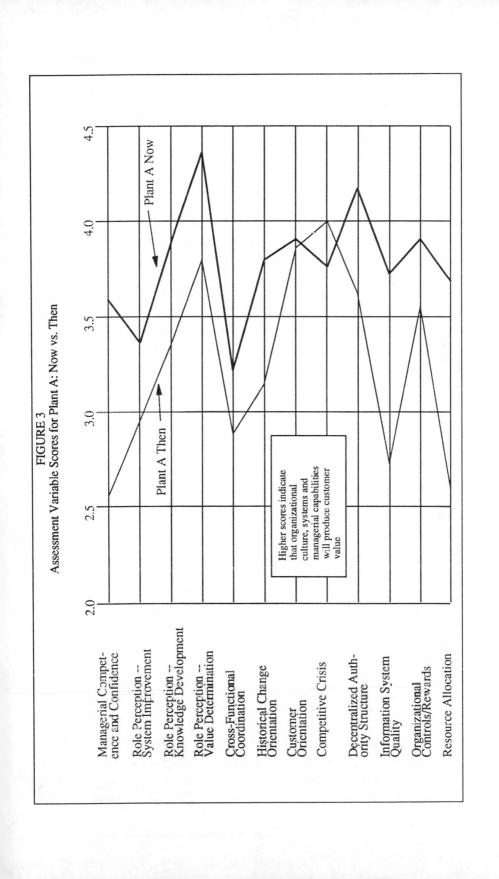

FIGURE 3
Assessment Variable Scores for Plant A: Now vs. Then

in the figure. The difference between the "Then" and "Now" scores reflects the amount of perceived change. (Note that Figure 3 data are plotted on an absolute scale and are therefore not comparable to data from Figure 2 which is plotted on a percentile basis.)

These profiles indicate that the managers perceive positive changes associated with managing for customer value, with the exception of customer orientation. However, the interview responses suggest that perhaps the nature of their orientation toward the customer has changed. These managers appeared to be more proactive in seeking feedback and in meeting customer needs, rather than reactive in responding to customer complaints, problems, and crises.

All other perceived changes in the remaining variables were statistically significant and in the direction of "improvement." These changes reflected the changes in managerial behavior and the cultural and interpersonal conditions investigated through interviews. In addition, the plant manager reports that the changes in management and the resulting system improvements for customer value are already being reflected in the financial indicators of performance. He states, "it has made us money this year, and will continue to do so in the future."

Caveats for the Use of the Survey

The preceding discourse indicates the recommended steps in using the survey instrument. To be successful with any tool or method managers must adapt it to their own needs and capabilities. Similarly, the survey and framework for managing for customer value should be used creatively to improve organizational competitiveness. To ensure success in using the survey, managerial leaders should also address the following two issues: measuring change and the extent of use.

Measuring Change. As mentioned earlier, individual respondents make use of various frames of reference for making the judgments reported on the survey. These individual frames of reference or standards do change over time. As the standard or frame of reference of the individual changes, so do the responses. Thus, responses to the questions must be interpreted in light of the organization's context and the individual predispositions. Repeated measurement and analysis of survey results over time require methodological adjustments to consider changes in individual frames of reference.

Extent of Use Should Vary. Not all management groups are prepared to execute all the steps outlined above. In using a survey to provide information pertinent to managing for customer value, managers should consider the following: Higher levels of use of the instrument are more taxing in terms of personal challenge, responsibility, and time and energy required. Higher levels of use require a higher price, but the benefits are also higher, with increased information afforded and greater potential for enhancing organizational strategic capabilities. The extent of use of the survey instrument must be in accord with (1) top management's commitment to a customer value strategy and (2) top management's belief in the instrument, methodology, and process.

The extent of involvement and use of the survey must be determined based on a number of other considerations, including voluntary participation; willingness of managers to engage in the increasingly demanding levels of use; psychological readiness to address issues; belief in the method and procedures; readiness to listen to potentially threatening information; readiness to consider personal and organizational shortcomings; acceptance of responsibility for current conditions; acknowledgment of problems; readiness to envision alternatives; resolve to act on findings; and resolve to continue pursuit of the issues. Success with the survey method ultimately relies on managerial willingness to actively participate in evaluating, responding to, and taking action based on the results of the survey.

The Appeal to Manage for Customer Value: Just Do It

The theme of this chapter on assessment of progress is that providing value for customers requires attention to many aspects of management and organization. Changing to this approach to management presents a formidable challenge for many leaders. Accomplishing enduring change to managing for customer value requires change in the variables identified in the framework of managerial competence and role perceptions, organizational systems, and organizational culture.

The challenges of global competition require bold action by managerial leaders. Quick fixes, programs, partial solutions, and part-time attention to providing value for customers will result in failure to compete. The competition has already gone beyond these half-hearted measures. If you intend only to invest just enough in managing for customer value to meet and keep up with the competition, you will forever be chasing an accelerating target. Competing requires time, attention, hard work, thought, and a comprehensive approach to continuous improvement. Your rate of progress must continually improve. The framework presented in this chapter offers you a place to start and a guide for how to continue.

REFERENCES

Abernathy, W. J., K. B. Clark, and A. M. Kantrow. "The New Industrial Competition." *Harvard Business Review*, 59, no. 5 (1981): 68-81.

Bandura, A. "Self-efficacy: Toward a Unifying Theory of Behavioral Change." *Psychological Review*, 84, 191-215.

Bray, D. W., R. J. Campbell, and D. L. Grant. *Formative Years in Business: A Long-term AT&T Study of Managerial Lives.* Huntington, N.Y.: Robert E. Kriegor Publishing Co., 1979.

Carothers, G. H., Jr. "Managing the Managers of Competitive Strategic Change: An Exploratory Study of Variables of Organizational Context and Individual Managerial Personnel in Four American Manufacturing Business Units." A doctoral dissertation, College of Business Administration, University of Tennessee, 1989.

Deal, T. E., and A. A. Kennedy. *Corporate Cultures.* Reading, Mass. Addison-Wesley, 1982.

Deming, W. E. *Out of the Crisis.* Cambridge, Mass.: Institute of Technology, 1986.

Galbraith, J. R., and D. A. Nathanson. *Strategy Implementation: The Role of Structure and Process.* St. Paul, Minn: West Publishing, 1978.

Garvin, D. A. *Managing Quality.* New York: Free Press, 1988.

Ghiselli, E. E. "The Validity of Aptitude Tests in Personnel Selection." *Personnel Psychology*, 26 (1973): 461-477.

Ghiselli, E. E. *The Validity of Occupational Aptitude Tests.* New York: John Wiley and Sons, 1966.

Graen, G. "Instrumentality Theory of Work Motivation: Some Experimental Results and Suggested Modifications." *Journal of Applied Psychology*, Monograph, 53, no. 2 (1969).

Graen, G. "Role-Making Processes Within Complex Organizations." In M. D. Dunnette (ed.), *Handbook of Industrial and Organizational Psychology.* Chicago: Rand McNally College Publishing Co., 1976.

Hackman, J. R., and L. W. Porter. "Expectancy Theory Predictions of Work Effectiveness." *Organizational Behavior and Human Performance*, 3 (1968): 417-426.

Hambrick, D. C., and P. A. Mason. "Upper Echelons: The Organization as a Reflection of Its Top Managers." *Academy of Management Review*, 9 (1984): 193-206.

Hayes, R. H., and R. Jaikumar. "Manufacturing Crisis: New Technologies, Obsolete Organizations." *Harvard Business Review*, 66, no. 5 (1988): 77-85.

Imai, M. *Kaizen: The Key to Japanese Competitive Success.* New York: Random House, 1986.

Ishikawa, K. *What Is Total Quality Control? The Japanese Way.* Englewood Cliffs, N.J.: Prentice-Hall, 1985.

Juran, J. M. *Juran on Planning for Quality.* New York: The Free Press, 1988.

Juran, J. M. *Managerial Breakthrough.* New York: McGraw-Hill, 1964.

Kanter, R. M. *The Change Masters.* New York: Simon and Schuster, 1983.

Katz, D. and R. L. Kahn. *The Social Psychology of Organizations.* New York: John Wiley and Sons, 1978.

McGrath, J. E. "Stress and Behavior in Organization." In M. D. Dunnette (ed.), *Handbook of Industrial and Organizational Psychology.* Chicago: Rand McNally College Publishing Co., 1976.

Miles, R. E., and C. C. Snow. "Fit, Failure and the Hall of Fame." *California Management Review*, 26, no. 3 (1984): 10-28.

Morgan, G. "Corporate Culture and Core Values." In G. Morgan (ed.), *Creative Organization Theory*. Newbury Park, Calif. Sage Publications, 1989: 157-158.

Pascale, R. T., A. G. Athos. *The Art of Japanese Management*. New York: Simon and Schuster, 1981.

Peters, L. H., E. J. O'Connor, and J. R. Eulberg. "Situational Constraints: Sources, Consequences and Future Considerations." *Research in Personnel and Human Resources Management*, 3 (1985): 79-114.

Schein, E. H. *Organizational Culture and Leadership*. San Francisco: Jossey-Bass, 1988.

Taguri, R., and G. H. Litwin (eds.). *Organizational Climate: Exploration of a Concept*. Boston: Harvard Graduate School of Business, 1968.

Thornton, G. C., III., and W. C. Byham. *Assessment Centers and Managerial Performance*. New York: Academic Press, 1982.

Vroom, V. H. *Work and Motivation*. New York: John Wiley and Sons, 1964.

APPENDIX
Questionnaire Items

1. The authority structure here makes it difficult to get needed changes accomplished.
2. Learning the details of what our customers value is an important part of my job.
3. At performance appraisal time managers are evaluated according to the extent of improvement in their systems and processes.
4. Managers at my level invest effort in learning the details of how systems actually work.
5. My formal unit objectives require me to demonstrate that I have made changes to improve our quality/cost competitive position.
6. Managers in this unit share information readily.
7. We are close to our customers.
8. This unit has a history of changing in anticipation of the future it desires.
9. I am required to report my progress in making continuous improvements.
10. System improvement is the job of managers at my level.
11. The need to improve quality/cost/delivery is a crisis in this unit.
12. This unit is too compartmentalized to expect any significant changes in cross-functional systems.
13. The way to be a hero in this unit is to successfully manage competitive strategic change.
14. My manager expects me to formally provide information on systems performance improvements.
15. Managers at my level do not understand what is needed to make competitive strategic change.
16. A high number of approvals are required to implement significant systems changes.
17. Managers at my level believe it important to learn about system functioning.
18. Managers in other functional areas of this unit willingly provide information needed to institute system changes.
19. This unit tends to react slowly to changes in external environmental situations.
20. Information needed to diagnose system problems can be obtained easily.
21. Historically, this unit has proactively altered systems to improve our competitive position.
22. Managers at my level believe it important to learn about the specific uses of our products and services by customers.
23. Resources are available for activities that will yield long-term benefits.
24. Managers at my level believe that making continuous improvements in organizational systems is a part of their job.
25. Cooperation between functional areas is good.
26. We keep close watch on how satisfied our customers are with our products or services.
27. The pressures of increased competition and environmental change are intense for this unit.
28. Managers at my level do not have the skills that are required to manage continuous improvement.
29. The quality of information available to managers instituting change is good.
30. A major criterion considered in promoting managers is their demonstrated ability to improve the competitive strategic posture of the unit.
31. Learning the details of how systems work is an important part of my job.

32. Managers at my level are confident in their ability to manage competitive strategic change.
33. Managers are kept informed as to how our products are performing in the hands of the customers.
34. This unit is decentralized to allow managers to implement system changes.
35. Managers at my level invest effort in learning specifically what customers value.
36. The information system of this organization provides managers with reliable data.
37. Resources needed to implement changes are available to managers at my level.
38. In this unit, making changes in systems to improve our long-term competitive position is part of every manager's job.
39. Managers perceive a crisis regarding our position relative to the competition.
40. Resources are available for the systems improvement work of managers.

CHAPTER 15

MANAGERIAL LEADERSHIP AND CULTURAL TRANSFORMATION*

LYLE YORKS
Professor of Management Science
Eastern Connecticut State University

GREGORY M. BOUNDS
Research Associate, Management Development Center
University of Tennessee

SUMMARY

This chapter presents the necessary changes to organizational culture which are driven by managerial leadership. The dimensions of organizational culture are reviewed, the cultural context of the managerial leadership model is presented, and critical issues in changing organizational culture are discussed in detail. Specific attention is given to assessing organizational culture and positioning the change effort in order to successfully develop an organizational culture supportive of managerial leadership.

INTRODUCTION

At one time discussion of culture evoked images of tribal communities portrayed on a National Geographic special, narrated by an erudite, sloppily dressed anthropologist. During the 1980's, however, the concept moved uptown and traded its field jacket for corporate pinstripes. The notion that culture is important for both understanding and changing

---

*The authors thank Richard Sanders for his contribution to this chapter.

organizations is not new. Eliott Jacques productively utilized the concept in this context nearly forty years ago in *The Changing Culture of a Factory*, (1951). Only in the past decade, however, has culture become a central topic in organization and management theory (e.g., Deal and Kennedy, 1982; Pettigrew, 1979; Schein, 1985). Very quickly, however, it became a popular concept in the management community, making *Business Week's* list of "what's in" in business fads in 1986 (January: 20). A survey of chief executive officers by Gardner (1985: 59-63) reported that a majority believed that organizational cultures exist. Forty percent of them thought that it was important to "deal with culture of a company in a serious manner."

Like many concepts that become part of the popular management literature, the term *culture* has come to blend many heterogeneous phenomena. Almost any and all organizational phenomena have been described as "cultural" by managers. "Culture" has become a catch-all phrase used without full appreciation for the richness of the concept. Fortunately, the study of culture and its application to the task of changing organizations continue to be refined (for example, Duncan, 1989; Ott, 1989). Both field experience and research indicate that culture is important because organizational change can be reinforced and sustained by it. Therefore, culture is an important consideration in assessing the degree of difficulty an organization will have in digesting a given set of changes and can help inform the change strategy. In this chapter we address the issue of cultural change in relation to managerial leadership and organizational competitiveness in creating value for the users of the organization's products and services.

ORGANIZATIONAL CULTURE AND ITS RELATIONSHIP TO MANAGERIAL LEADERSHIP

What is organizational culture? How do you describe or measure it? How do you change it? In practice, these are difficult questions for an organization contemplating change. The type of change we are interested in is the implementation of an approach to managing organizational systems for continuous improvement and the provision of valued products and services for the customer. The following definition of culture advanced by Schein (1985) is useful in this regard:

a pattern of basic assumptions – invented, discovered, or developed by a given group as it learns to cope with its problems of external adaptation and internal integration – that has worked well enough to be considered valid and, therefore, to be taught to new members as the correct way to perceive, think, and feel in relation to these problems.

Recall the definition of managerial leadership and its discussion by Carothers, Bounds, and Stahl earlier in this volume:

Managerial leadership consists of continuously knowing what is currently of value to users, discovering what will be of increased value to the customers of its products/services, and creating, providing, and continuously improving strategic organizational suprasystems which, when used by the organizational members, ensure the creation of value for the customers of its products/services (Chapter 5).

Note that the two components of managerial leadership, continuous organizational systems improvement and customer value determination, parallel the problems of internal integration and external adaptation in Schein's definition of culture.

As we would expect, a host of cultural factors will exist in any company centered around the patterns of "internal integration and external adaptation." These factors will have emerged through years of practice. These cultural influences justify the traditional ways of doing things and work against establishing new behavior patterns consistent with the managerial leadership model. Before delving into the importance of culture in this context, an elaboration on the concept itself is useful. We ask the practical-minded reader to indulge us in this brief exercise. The issues raised below are germane to the effective establishment of the managerial leadership model.

Culture Revisited

A plethora of definitions of culture exist in the management literature. Most of them define culture as a system of shared meaning, largely taken for granted, through which people come to a rather complex understanding of their world. Inherent in this definition is that culture is a stabilizing influence on human interactions. It provides for socialization into a given group by defining "how things are done around here." Culture is a source of structure for people's lives as they come to know what is expected of them and others. Hence, it is a force for social control. The stronger an organization's culture, the less the need for more explicit and direct forms of control. Culture frames the interpretation of the present in terms of the

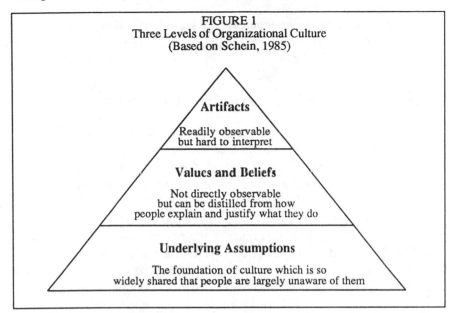

FIGURE 1
Three Levels of Organizational Culture
(Based on Schein, 1985)

Artifacts

Readily observable
but hard to interpret

Values and Beliefs

Not directly observable
but can be distilled from how
people explain and justify what they do

Underlying Assumptions

The foundation of culture which is so
widely shared that people are largely unaware of them

past. In doing so it allows for communication and mutual understanding, and prediction of the behavior of others.

Schein (1981, 1984, 1985) has postulated three levels of organizational culture (see Figure 1). The first level, *artifacts*, consists of the "behavioral patterns and the visible, tangible, and/or audible results of behaviors" (Ott, 1989: 59) including written and oral language (including jargon), office layouts, dress codes, rituals, and the like. Artifacts are the observable manifestation of the other levels and are "easy to see but hard to interpret without an understanding of" levels two and three (Sathe, 1985: 10). Level two consists of the *values and beliefs* rooted in the ideologies, moral codes, and attitudes shared by people. Not directly observable, values and beliefs can often be distilled from how people "explain, rationalize and justify" (Sathe, 1985: 10) their actions. Level three is the *basic underlying assumptions* which are so fundamental to the value and belief systems and so widely shared that people are largely unaware of them. These assumptions form a collective unconsciousness which binds people together and is virtually never articulated and/or debated.

Of course, organizations do not exist in a cultural vacuum. They constitute subcultures of the larger cultures in which they are embedded. Furthermore, since complex organizations are themselves comprised of several subunits (divisions, departments, work groups, etc.), they contain several subcultural variations as well. Some of these subcultures may be *enhancing subcultures*, which embrace the dominant organizational culture even more fervently than the rest of the organization does; *orthogonal subcultures*, each of which accepts the values of the dominant (organizational) culture as well as a nonconforming set of values that it considers its own; or a *counter culture* which challenges the values of the dominant culture (Duncan, 1989: 234).

Cultural Context of the Managerial Leadership Model

What will an organization driven by the managerial leadership model feel like culturally? Based on our experiences, it is possible to project certain cultural characteristics. Although the following description is not exhaustive, we suggest some of the cultural characteristics of an organization driven by managerial leadership.

The culture is primarily reflected in the permissive behaviors and language challenging the status quo. While not cavalier toward past success, the phrase "if it's not broke, don't fix it" is not given popular currency. Rather, "if you are standing still, you are losing ground" is the popular expression. People seek to improve both products and processes on a regular basis. These efforts are grounded in ongoing efforts to test and supplement intuitive and experiential knowledge by seeking more thorough understanding and empirical support. Suggestions for improvement are welcomed, discussed, and tested. Furthermore, this type of behavior is rewarded.

While the above observations sound like popular managerial homilies, they become points of conflict when managers seek to transition their organizations. We must develop an ear for cultural resistance, since it is often subtle and well intended. For example, in an organization with which one of the authors is currently working, some managers are asking for a specific definition of maximum effectiveness so "we will know when we achieve it." The request is both sincere and reflective of the traditional culture of the old organization. They were earnestly seeking a new status quo. The idea of them personally defining and revising effectiveness measures against a "receding horizon line" of continual performance improvement is so foreign to them that they are struggling to grasp it. Theirs is an organization in which managers manage to meet standards, and not to continuously improve.

In addition, in the managerial leadership culture, the focus of managerial behavior is horizontal as well as vertical. Time is spent in cross-functional discussions with colleagues and associates in which the conversation centers on system performance. Managers are often conversant with the work of individuals throughout the organization who are part of these systems.

Conversations between people are infused with specific references as to what customers value. This is perhaps one of the most telling cultural indicators. In many organizations today lip service is paid to customer focus, but discussions within the organization center on criteria important to the organization itself. Managers still focus on the functional imperatives of their departments rather than on how the relationships between functional areas contribute or detract from specific aspects of customer value.

Another characteristic of the managerial leadership culture is that people throughout the organization identify with customers, not products. One indicator of this is the extent to which product innovation is resisted. For example, in one organization long-term employees were very resistent to accepting replacement products, even though the new product lines would provide more customer value. Comments like "these [the traditional products] got us where we are" were common. This resistance was a significant measure of just how little the culture of the company was focused on the customer. Conversely, in another organization product innovation was met by intense questioning of information regarding customer value. This questioning was directed toward insuring that innovations went far enough in providing such value, a subtle but impressive indicator of the managerial leadership culture.

In a managerial leadership culture, performance improvement discussions center around process improvement rather than people. Subtlety abounds here. Many organizations run training course after course on "dealing with the problem employee" and "corrective performance counseling." While training in such areas is still necessary, under cultural conditions supporting managerial leadership, more emphasis is placed on providing employees and managers with tools for improving systems and processes. An implicit assumption on the part of members of the organization that performance problems are process, not employee, based is reflected in the response of supervisors and managers to performance problems. Initial questions center around process measurements as opposed to "who's at fault."

Senior executives should be identified with suprasystems rather than functional areas. Ultimately, one of the sources of problems in many organizations is that senior managers identify with their "functional team." People working under them are reluctant to appear disloyal to their function. Accordingly, their people are hesitant to work collaboratively with other functions unless their own functional interests are well protected. One indication that the managerial leadership model has taken hold culturally is when in their minds employees associate senior people with suprasystems and seek direction from them on transfunctional concerns.

Such behaviors take on meaning within the context of a number of specific values and beliefs important in transitioning to the managerial leadership paradigm. These values include:

1. The value of continuous improvement versus working to specification or adherence to the status quo.
2. The importance of experimentation for knowledge and openness to new information.
3. The importance of determining what users value as opposed to what we think they need.
4. A customer versus an organizational focus.
5. A long-term as opposed to a short-term time frame.
6. A focus on process measures related to customer value rather than maximizing functional end results.

Impact on the Organizational Change Process

Typically, the idea for adopting a management program (as many will undoubtedly, and mistakenly, view the managerial-leadership model) is enthusiastically brought into the organization by an upper- to middle-level executive, who "sells" it to his or her superiors. Alternatively, a very senior executive encounters stories of success based on the idea and assigns a subordinate to determine how to import it into the organization. In either case a manager in the middle of the organization is given the assignment of assessing the concept's validity, demonstrating it within the organization, and then diffusing it throughout the appropriate parts of the company with the nominal support or approval of senior management. The initial hope is that the idea will transform the organization in some positive and fundamental way. This scenario rarely succeeds in producing transformational change. After an initial period of enthusiasm and some organizational success stories, the effort usually runs into obstacles and eventually dies. Or it becomes codified into a training course that is conducted by a management development department. Without the sustained involvement of top management, the organization is not transformed.

Effective implementation of the managerial leadership model requires nothing less than a transformation of the organization in terms of structure, systems, and ultimately its culture. Indeed, organizational transformation is equated with cultural transformation, since by transformation we mean that major organizational systems have been altered in such a fundamental way that the changes are sustainable in the sense that, even if the major advocate went away, the changes would remain. It would take as much of a sustained effort to replace the systems as was required to establish them in the first place. They simply represent the "way things are done around here." By definition, they have been built into the cultural fabric of the organization at all three levels.

The implications for change are clear. To the extent that the assumptions and normative implications of the managerial leadership model are counter to the dominant culture in an organization, the existing culture represents an initial obstacle to the change process. Later, if the model is taking hold, new cultural influences that reinforce the behaviors required by the model will emerge. The emergence of these new influences signals the institutionalizing of managerial leadership in the organization.

Another implication is that accomplishing such change is a prolonged process. Research by one of the authors suggests that it may take five to seven years to get changes similar to those being discussed in this volume sufficiently institutionalized to be largely sustainable. We are not suggesting that it takes this long to see measurable progress. However, the process of building the changes into an organization's culture does require patience.

Because culture provides the context through which people in the organization interpret events, efforts to change it are fraught with the potential for well-intended missteps. For example, in a company with a somewhat paternalistic culture, decisions by management which are intended to ease the impact of the transition on employees may be viewed as evidence that nothing is really changing. In another company, senior management has a long history of not delegating important decisions. Furthermore, the operating committee, which was comprised of senior management, made virtually all decisions on a consensus basis, a practice that often led to long delays and indecision. In order to streamline the decision-making process as part of a strategically driven transformation effort, several committees were formed to make operating decisions. Each committee was chaired by a senior executive but was comprised largely of managers from one and two levels lower in the operating structure. Senior executives, other than the chair, were also members of these multilevel committees. Occasionally, senior executives sent key subordinates in their place to committee meetings because these people had more expertise on a given issue. This was also seen as a developmental/motivational assignment. They were empowered to exercise their judgment on the issue in question. Many people throughout the organization viewed it as an effort to deemphasize the committees and force decisions back to the operating committee. They interpreted it as a sign that nothing was changing. Simply put, early in the transition process employees are likely to interpret management's efforts at change through the prism of the old culture.

Efforts at organizational transformations require employees to undergo psychological transitions of similar magnitude as the organizational one. Psychological transition is a gradual process through which individuals and groups reorient themselves to a significantly changed situation (Bridges, 1988). This transition is often inhibited by denial as people resist acknowledging that they will indeed have to adjust (Yorks, 1989). This denial is reinforced as people focus their attention on behaviors and events that can be interpreted as evidence of things not *really* changing and that this too will pass. Furthermore, quite independent of denial, participants will naturally see the events of the change process itself through the looking glass of the existing culture. There is no other possible frame of reference.

During a meeting of first-line supervisors and managers being facilitated by one of the authors, a supervisor raised her hand and quite sincerely asked, "when will this be over?" This was several months into the effort in this particular work unit. The author asked what she meant by "over." "Every two years or so we do something like this," she replied. "Several years ago we did sensitivity training, then we did MBO, then team building, then job enrichment. I just wanted to tell my people when this will be over." Reactions by several other participants suggested she was not alone in her assumptions. Even though this process had been emphasized as an ongoing one and not as a management "program," the same had been said of most of the others as well. The cultural level three assumption held by members of the organization was that "processes" are programs that end. Thus, people were not making a full psychological commitment to the effort. If unaddressed, this lack of commitment would prevent the new approach from being institutionalized.

CHANGING ORGANIZATIONAL CULTURE IN SUPPORT OF THE MANAGERIAL LEADERSHIP MODEL

Organizational culture is a product of many factors, including the broader culture of the society of which the organization is a part, the beliefs, values, and actions of the founders and other dominant actors in the organization's history; and the nature of the industry and business environment. These influences combine with the complex interactions of the systems, processes, and behaviors through which the work of the organization is done to produce its culture. Culture is not managed (and certainly not designed), as much as it is produced or generated by the social structure and behaviors it supports. There is an interactive relationship between social structure and culture. Social structure and behavior lead to culture, which in turn serves to reinforce (and occasionally help the evolution of) those structures and behaviors that have helped produce it. Management has little control over societal culture, its industrial task environment, or, in most instances, the behavior of the founders. This leaves the current management behavior, systems, and processes as the major levers of change.

Organizational development professionals have had to wrestle with a "which comes first, the chicken or the egg" type question during the past several years: Does management focus on structure or culture during the early stages of change? Our experience suggests that both must be given attention. The way management produces cultural change is through intense, focused, and prolonged attention to the managerial leadership task. This includes establishing those structures and systems necessary for the managerial leadership task to be performed effectively. These structural and system changes, along with the behaviors they support must drive the change process. However, in devising a strategy for doing this, managers must assess the current culture to anticipate how the process itself should be leveraged and how certain tactics are likely to be interpreted by the majority of people in the organization. Furthermore, reactions throughout the change process should be monitored both to learn more about the culture itself (insight into many level three assumptions becomes apparent only after the change process is underway) and to recognize how the changes are being interpreted in the organization. Finally, an ongoing sensitivity to culture is important to insure that those elements of the managerial leadership model which management is seeking to institution-alize are indeed being integrated into the dominant culture.

Assessing Organizational Culture

Developing a profile of an organization's culture is a delicate task involving the use of multiple research methods. Through such varied methods as observation, personal interviews, archival research, and questionnaires, a number of data sources that have a bearing on an organization's culture can be tapped. The most useful methods for assessing organizational culture are summarized in Figure 2. This figure also demonstrates the need for multiple assessment methods, since no one method successfully taps all three levels of organizational culture.

Because of the nature of the phenomena itself, the process will involve a number of judgment calls. An executive seeking to describe his or her own company's culture can easily find what he or she wants to find. Even for those trained in the behavioral sciences, the process can be difficult with data lending themselves to different interpretations. The difficulty in interpreting the meaning of observed data has led some researchers like Schein (1984, 1985) to argue that culture can be determined only through a clinical or helping process.

We can more accurately describe and learn from the culture through experience with the change process itself. Hence, where a formal change process is underway, assessing the organization's culture should be part of

FIGURE 2
Summary of Methods for Assessing Organizational Culture

Method	Level of Culture Studied
1. Observation	Artifacts
2. Personal Interviews	Values and Beliefs, Confront Underlying Assumptions
3. Archival Research	Artifacts, which can provide insight into Values and Beliefs
4. Questionnaires	Values and Beliefs
5. Collaborative Involvement with Organizational Change	Values and Belief Confront Underlying Assumptions
6. Data Feedback and Processing of the Information Gathered through the Above Activities (Action Research)	Confront Underlying Assumptions

an ongoing action research process in which inside participants of the culture and trained observers work as colleagues, jointly deciding which data are relevant and working to understand their meaning. These trained observers may be outside collaborators, staff specialists of the organization, or a combination of the two. The point is that those too closely involved in the culture may fail to raise critical questions regarding the level three values and assumptions that underlie organizational practices, because they, too, implicitly share them. On the other hand, it is impossible for a nonparticipant to understand the meaning of certain events and practices without becoming intimately involved with participants and repeatedly testing his or her interpretations.

Careful observation of the physical environment which the organization creates for itself is a good beginning point for studying organizational culture. So, too, is the observation of behavior and rituals by a trained nonparticipant observing, inquiring, sitting in on meetings, and becoming immersed in the feel of the organization. Norms can be inferred from behaviors and rituals. Accumulating these level one data is a good starting point for assessing organizational culture. They must be supplemented, however, by level two data on beliefs and values.

Tapping into the value structure of an organization presents a challenge. As Ott (1989) has noted, unlike norms, inferring beliefs, values, and ideologies from behaviors is risky since intervening factors may obscure the relationship between behavior and these factors. A well-constructed questionnaire, such as that described by Bounds and Dewhirst in Chapter 14 in this volume, is a valuable tool for measuring these elements of an organization's culture, especially if supplemented by interviews and participant observation methods. This instrument can provide an assessment of critical values, beliefs, and attitudes in a very efficient manner. The resulting statistical profile can also be utilized as a baseline measure against which changes in this important intermediate level of corporate culture can be monitored through subsequent administration of the instrument.

Any survey instrument is limited in that it only provides measures of the specific constructs on which it is based. The value structure of a culture can be conceptualized in terms of a variety of different frameworks. Bounds and Dewhirst have specifically designed their assessment instrument in terms of dimensions that link culture to the managerial leadership model. More specifically, the survey includes individual, cultural, structural, and control variables useful for diagnostic purposes. Other methods will identify additional cultural factors important to understanding the organization. Hence, while adminstration of a questionnaire is a useful tool for tapping level two data, it is critical that it be combined with other methods. For example, it is virtually impossible to arrive at level three insights by such a single method.

Questionnaire data provide a statistical profile that can be used not only for gaining insight into the culture, but as an instrument of the change process as well. Indeed, administering questionnaires is an obtrusive process that may alter subsequent data-gathering activities (Ott, 1989). Completing a well-structured instrument requires that respondents confront beliefs and values that may be somewhat suppressed. This will often trigger a recognition of level three assumptions and make data gathering on this difficult level more fruitful. For this reason relatively unobtrusive participant observation work should be initiated prior to implementation of a questionnaire and formal interviewing. Use of the questionnaire should precede interviews focused on gathering level three data.

While problematic for purposes of more academic inquiry, we suggest that the consciousness-raising impact of the survey process be utilized as a vehicle for facilitating the change process. During data feedback sessions, participants provide those conducting the cultural assessment additional data by examining more critically the level three assumptions implied by the data. They also begin the process of "unfreezing" some of their thinking patterns by becoming more aware of the organizational culture that frames their organizational perspectives. Either during the same session, or at workshops soon after, links can be drawn between behaviors contrary to managerial leadership observed during the first phase of the data gathering and the value system embedded in the organizational culture. Descriptions of behaviors counter to the managerial leadership model can focus attention on dysfunctional practices in terms of customer value. The data-based profile of cultural values and beliefs raises the question of why they behave this way.

Identifying the level three assumptions presents the most formidable problems for analyzing an organization's culture. It is also very important since these assumptions are at the core of the organizational culture. Collaboration between a trained outsider and knowledgeable insiders increases the chances for success. As described above, data gathering can take place during data feedback sessions on the results of the questionnaire. Similarly, iterative interviewing of key people is part of the data-gathering process. Part of the problem is learning which questions to ask. Each interview often suggests new questions.

Happily, this process can be integrated with the change process itself. As the organization pursues the managerial and organizational tasks suggested by the model, critical assumptions can be surfaced and discussed.

It is hoped that the reader has been left with the impression that assessing an organization's culture is not a casual task. On the other hand, for the organization truly committed to revitalizing itself, these data-gathering activities are not burdensome. They become part of the change process as organizational learning about its culture is part and parcel of making progress in becoming more competitive. Full discussion of the methodological issues involved could be a chapter unto itself. For the reader interested in taking the next step in learning about these issues, Duncan (1989) is a readily accessible reference. Ott (1989) provides a more extensive, but very readable, discussion of methods.

Positioning the Change Effort Relative to Culture

Earlier in this chapter we stated that the way management produces cultural change is through sustained and intensive attention to the managerial task. This includes creating appropriate work structures, reward systems, accounting methods, and management practices as detailed in other chapters in this volume. As these changes are designed and put in place management must decide how to position them within the cultural context of the organization.

Because the managerial leadership model represents a dramatic shift in how we look at organizational structures and processes, it has counter-culture implications. However, most corporate cultures are highly resilient and can coopt new managerial systems and process. For example, people in the organization can adopt new buzz words, but continue to function largely as before. Staff groups can take over responsibility for new systems, asserting themselves as experts. Line managers can treat the new approaches as the domain of the staff experts, thus removing primary responsibility for results from themselves. Gradually, new initiatives become slotted into the existing bureaucracy so that change takes place in only a very superficial way. The end result reflects the old saying, "the more things change, the more they stay the same."

For transformational change to take hold, it must be clearly and convincingly linked to the core strategic issues of the organization (Nadler, 1988). The managerial leadership model should not be presented as an end in itself but as a framework for addressing strategic imperatives. As suggested above, in an action research mode, assessment of culture can be linked to the early stages of change. Managers and employees need to be challenged to identify the values, beliefs, and suppressed assumptions that support the existing organization. In the process, dysfunctional elements of the culture must themselves be examined.

This suggests that cultural issues cannot be addressed out of the context of competitive ones. Cultural assessment must be linked to concurrent assessments of the competitive issues that confront the organization, the strategic response to those issues, and the degree of fit between the existing organization and this response. A general vision of the new organization must be consistently promulgated from the top, with lower level managers involved in the process of shaping that vision through the development of specific applications of the managerial leadership model. Where cultural factors inhibit change, they must be explicitly addressed. This may occur within the context of workshops, working meetings, and personal encounters. Through the change process the organizational members' understanding of their culture becomes more refined.

What we arrive at is a conception of cultural transformation as an ongoing, interactive process, beginning with the initial assessment and continuing throughout the implementation of change in organizational structures and processes. This is in contrast to approaches of involving the organization in an elaborate "culture design" project. Drawing on field data, Beer (1988: 24, 31) has described how setting out to change the culture of an organization prior to implementing changes in structure, systems, and process fails "to stimulate significant change, despite top management's involvement in examining the old culture and defining the new one."

The change process should be driven by the managerial leadership model, with managers putting in place those systems and processes that embody it. A cultural change will be a natural outcome of this behavior change. Managerial leaders must recognize their role in shaping culture (Hambrick and Mason: 1984) and in ensuring the actualization of the managerial leadership model in management actions. They must drive the change process, by playing an instrumental, as opposed to purely inspirational, role (Beer, 1988: 39). This instrumental role is summarized in Figure 3 and is discussed below.

The change agenda must be linked to operative goals. Operative goals "designate the ends sought through the actual operating policies of the organization; they tell us what the organization actually is trying to do, regardless of what the official goals say are the aims" (Perrow, 1961: 855-856). Management will often make pronouncements about the organization being committed to continuous improvement and customer value, but the actual operating policies imply different goals. For example, managers are rewarded for maintaining quotas, or product modifications with strong customer value are resisted because implementing them would be disruptive to existing operating procedures and require investment of resources.

Sensitivity to operative goals is fundamental to assessing organizational culture. They tend to persist and become the standards around which decisions are made (Hall, 1987: 271). Thus, they reflect choices between competing values that may impede change. Changing operative goals through consistent and persistent practices and actions is basic to sustaining organizational change.

In an interesting study, Blackler and Brown (1980) demonstrate how an effort at organizational transformation failed in part because the new philosophy of management was inconsistent with the operative goals and the reward structure of the organization. A recent study of successful organizational transformation by Yorks and Whitsett (1989: 94-95) il-

---

FIGURE 3
The Instrumental Role of Managerial Leaders

Link the Changes in Operative Goals Through:

1. What management attends to, controls and measures.
2. Reactions to critical incidents and organizational crises.
3. Role modeling and coaching.
4. The criteria used for the allocating rewards
   and status.
5. The criteria used for recruitment, selection, promotion,
   retirement, and isolation.

lustrates the importance of linking the change agenda to operative goals. Each of the remaining behaviors or practices is tied to or reflects operative goals.

What Management Attends to, Controls and Measures. That the structure of most accounting and control systems may be inhibiting competitiveness (Kaplan, 1984) is an idea slowly gaining currency in the U.S. business community (*Business Week,* June 6, 1988: 100-115). A comment by a finishing foreman in one organization illustrates the problem. "The bottom line, unit costs, is driving production to run things poorly. The rules about running things are not followed. They put anything they have into the 'widget' without regard to quality, just to get the 'widget' out the door. The foreman will tell people to do things wrong just to get production out." The plant manager in the same plant stated he is supportive of improvements when "financially feasible." Culture cannot be shaped in directions not supported by the cost management system of the organization. Accordingly, the proposals advanced in the following two chapters are critical to the change process.

Subordinate managers and workers are very sensitive to what higher management emphasizes. In one organization, meetings at which supervisors were to address a number of quality-related issues were canceled because management wanted to minimize costs during the fourth quarter. In another organization, emphasis was placed on hitting production quotas once market demand for their product started to strengthen. This was done regardless of the impact on factors valued by the customer.

Reactions to Critical Incidents and Organizational Crises. For the past decade popular management writers have been fond of observing that the Chinese character for crisis is a combination of the characters for danger and opportunity. The point is well taken with regard to the implications of how key executives respond to organizational crises. Every crisis represents an opportunity for disavowing dysfunctional practices, values, and assumptions, while reinforcing the values and assumptions inherent in the managerial leadership model. Failure to do so sends a strong message that management is not serious about the changes and that it is 'business as usual.' This failure not only retards the change process, but in most organizations actually represents a regression by reinforcing the traditional expectations of people. The change process is viewed as just another superficial program that is little more than rhetoric.

A few years ago one of the authors was touring an automotive engine assembly plant. During a downturn in the economy the plant had been modernized. Each assembler had some control over the pacing of work. All were trained in statistical process control (SPC) and received regular data on their work. Management and the union had jointly agreed on innovative procedures focusing on quality. The author remarked how impressive all this was, to which an employee stated, "we haven't yet experienced capacity demand. Once the market comes back and we can sell everything we produce; then we'll see whether they are serious about all this." This employee, like most of his colleagues, was enthused but cautious, adopting a wait and see attitude. It is during times of crisis, when push comes to shove, that operative goals are made explicit and, in turn, cultural factors are either reinforced or changed.

Role Modeling and Coaching. Role modeling and coaching is at the heart of the leadership issue. Research consistently points to role modeling as a significant factor in defining managerial style, especially among the young, ambitious managers who represent the future of the organization. Imitation is how most of us cultivate our managerial styles.

During periods of change, managers and supervisors become unsure about how to act in certain situations. Unsure of the proper behavior, they carefully take their cues from the behavior of more senior executives. It is not enough to talk the new values. Leaders must demonstrate them; in the popular terminology of today, one must be able to "walk the talk."

Consider an example from a division of a diversified consumer products company that was making gradual but effective progress in changing its managerial culture in the direction of the managerial leadership model. A lot of respect for top management was expressed in interviews. One person spoke of a superior in the following way: "We need someone to help us learn and not just judge us by what we do wrong. Like (name of the manager), he takes men and gives them work. He lets them proceed their way and analyzes to instruct them in a more efficient way and does not just come down on them for not making the numbers."

The Criteria Used for Allocating of Rewards and Status. It hardly comes as news that people shape their performance according to the organization's reward structure. Many years ago a classic article on management expounded on the folly of rewarding A while hoping for B (Kerr, 1975). Apart from shaping behavior, rewards are a method of communication. They are one of the clearest expressions of what an organization values.

In an interview with a manager in a leading consumer products company which explored the relationship between measurement systems (discussed above) and the allocation of rewards, the manager told one of the authors, "If your rewards are set by your functional manager, whose goals are cost containment and your business needs quality improvement, what are you going to work on? You will work on cost containment."

The Criteria Used for Recruitment, Selection, Promotion, Retirement and Isolation. One of the most effective ways of changing an organization is through staffing decisions (Porter, Lawler, and Hackman, 1975: 442). Seeding the organization with managers who demonstrate the behaviors of the managerial leadership model is fundamental to diffusing the tenets of the model. Yorks and Whitsett have reported data that demonstrate the impact of seeding on the change process (1989: 69-70, 93, 150, 159-160). Indeed, positioning people throughout the organization who share one's values and goals is the time-honored, pragmatic way of gaining control of an organization. (See Halberstam, 1986 and Katz, 1987, for excellent examples of this process.) Reluctance to do so is one sign of lack of commitment to change.

Too much indiscriminate rotation of managers is disruptive to the change process, especially when it is linked to counterproductive criteria. In one organization we were told, "people are rotated every one to two years and are rewarded on what they come in and change to immediately yield a result. Later a manager comes in and changes it back to the way it was."

Another person in that same company told us, "I don't know of one person in our company who has been promoted and progressed through the organization by working on these things [continuous improvement]." Yet a third stated, "Maybe the formal performance appraisal criteria are in line with T.Q. [total quality], but I've never seen anyone promoted based upon those criteria. Working in the informal structure of the old culture is what gets you ahead."

Using the Past Constructively

Many of the cultural supports of the new culture will be counter to the prevailing one in the organization. However, where possible, the managerial leadership model should be linked to values long held by the organization. In this fashion those aspects of the traditional culture which have continuing value can be positioned as enhancing the new paradigm.

Even when there is little opportunity to enhance past values, rarely should the past be denigrated. It is a strong part of the current organizational culture (Wilkins and Bristow, 1987) which may have been appropriate at the time and therefore is a fundamental part of the personal identity of those who comprise the company. Past success and strengths should be acknowledged, while it is made clear that the globally competitive environment mandates change. Only when the past involves unethical behavior or suffers from problems of legitimacy with the bulk of the members of the organization should it be denounced. It is easier for people to accept the future if they don't have to give up their past. They have to "let go" of the past and accept the new approaches and methods, but letting go does not always require rejecting or disavowing one's past. Therefore, early in the change process, cultural targets should be chosen selectively.

Periodic Disconfirming Experiences

Those driving the change process must create a degree of disorientation to inhibit the tendency of some people toward denial. A disconfirming experience is an event created through management action whose implications are significant and highly countercultural. Members of the organization cannot be sure how to interpret it. This uncertainty creates a degree of psychological chaos and opens a window of opportunity, during which a significant part of the organization is trying to redefine what is happening. Employees pay particular attention to management behavior, and rapid progress can be made on implementing new systems. More than one such experience may be required as the organization makes its transition.

The regional executives of a large insurance company were told to develop plans and budgets for implementing a set of changes which were a radical departure from the conventional methods used in the company. They were told the plans would be approved as submitted with no negotiation, although most of the regional heads did not believe this would be the case. They expected their budgets to be reduced.

"Corporate management did exactly what it said would be done: the plans were approved and sent back with instructions to go to work. There was no negotiating, no justifying individual items; they just sent the plans back approved as submitted. Many in field management were stunned. The company meant what it said; it was going to do this. For some it was an exciting, confirming experience. For others, especially skeptics, it was disorienting" (Yorks and Whitsett, 1989: 121).

Additive Change and "Inclusive Redefinition"

Cultural transformation requires time. In our experience management tends to seriously underestimate how long and difficult the pathways of cultural transformation can be. Even once progress is underway to implement various new structures and systems, the organization will not be significantly different culturally. If management is not prepared for a sustained campaign, focus will be lost and the transformation effort will atrophy.

Progress seldom seems linear and in proportion to the degree of effort that is expended by advocates of change. Efforts in different organizational units rarely proceed in symmetrical fashion. Success in one part of the organization may not lead other parts to emulate the new approach. Instead, managers threatened by the changes may seize on any emerging problem as reason for delay. Furthermore, managers and employees may experience confusion as they seek to understand new systems while not fully divorced from their past cultural frame of reference. In this context it is important to avoid the implementation of competing "programs" that promise to be panaceas. Nor should people be overloaded by management implementing too much too soon. The transformation process must be characterized by phases, with past progress being periodically consolidated as the basis for the next initiative. What has been learned from initial efforts is integrated into the next impetus for change, revitalizing the change effort. Throughout the process the focus is on organizational learning and development, not on imitating other companies.

In one company too much emphasis had been placed on SPC per se. Those responsible for the SPC training had become isolated, and line managers denied responsibility for the effort. Change was viewed as an extraorganizational move rather than as part of the company's operational strategy. The effort was subsequently redefined, with SPC part of a more inclusive effort involving additional elements of a Total Systems Quality concept.

An organization may have to go through three, or even four, of these consolidations, with each one involving more of the managerial leadership model. We refer to this process as inclusive redefinition, which reaffirms the essential thrust of the process rather than displaces it. If we view each phase as a new generation of the change effort, we can assert that cultural transformation is a multigenerational phenomenon.

Toward Unconscious Competence

Management must continue to drive the change process using the levers described above and explicitly tying success to the critical values and beliefs of the managerial leadership model. Symbols of these values should become increasingly part of the internal organizational environment by design. Over time, additional symbols should emerge on their own. It is only after people come to interpret events in a way consistent with the new systems and are looking toward the future making assumptions consistent with the new paradigm that the cultural transformation is completed. Employees are no longer asking themselves "what if" questions: They have internalized a new logic in approaching their jobs.

This internalized new logic represents an unconscious competence. When confronted with problems or opportunities, they no longer have to hesitate or be coached through the customer-oriented responses. Rather, they respond in the appropriate manner.

CONCLUSION

Unhappily, there are many examples of failed efforts toward corporate transformation and the pattern of failure is now evident. An organization will become involved with one or two aspects of the managerial leadership model at the lowest levels of the organization, for example, SPC and employee involvement groups. Between twelve and twenty-four months later the early successes have been won but need to be sustained. It will be evident that one or two techniques will not revolutionize the company's competitive position. Nor will the unintegrated applications of any number of techniques suffice. More needs to be done. Further progress threatens to be more difficult. Having gotten things started, senior management will direct its attention elsewhere. Perhaps management will be disappointed that progress has not been more rapid. It is precisely at this critical point that many organizations lose focus in the transformation process.

Conversely, companies successful in managing the transformational process recognize the extended nature of the process. They build on initial success.

The change process puts additional burdens on everyone in an organization. In addition to the ongoing work of the business, tasks associated with the change process must be completed (e.g., planning for the changes, redeployment of people, training, and designing new systems). This change process must be driven by the managerial task. Leadership must be instrumental in providing a structured path for the change effort which has realistic resources for the task at hand (Beer, 1988).

The focus of the managerial leadership model must be at the highest levels of the organization. Otherwise well-intentioned, but disjointed, programs and techniques will fail to produce satisfactory results. As a consequence, the organization's competitive position will be less than it could be.

REFERENCES

Beer, M. "The Critical Path for Change: Keys to Success and Failure in Six Companies." In R. H. Kilmann and T. J. Covin (eds.), *Corporate Transformation. Revitalizing Organizations for a Competitive World.* San Francisco: Jossey-Bass, 1988.
Blackler, F. H. M., and C. A. Brown, *What Ever Happened to Shell's New Philosophy of Management?* Westmead, England: Saxon House, 1980.

Bridges, W. *Surviving Corporate Transitions*. New York: Doubleday, 1988.

Deal, T. E., and A. A. Kennedy. *Corporate Cultures: The Rites and Rituals of Corporate Life*. Reading, Mass.: Addison-Wesley, 1982.

Duncan, W. J. "Organizational Culture: 'Getting a fix' on an Elusive Concept." *The Academy of Management Executive*, 3, no. 3 (1989): 229-235.

Gardner, M. "Creating a Corporate Culture for the Eighties." *Business Horizons*, 28, no. 1 (1985): 59-63.

Halberstam, D. *The Reckoning*. New York: William Morrow and Co., 1986.

Hall, R. H. *Organizations. Structures, Processes, & Outcomes*. 4th ed. Englewood Cliffs, N.J.: Prentice-Hall, 1987.

Hambrick, D. C., and P. A. Mason, P. A. "Upper Echelons: The Organization as a Reflection of its Top Managers." *The Academy of Management Review*, 9, no. 2 1984: 193-206.

Jacques, E. *The Changing Culture of a Factory*. London: Tavistock Institute, 1951.

Kaplan, R. S. "Yesterday's Accounting Undermines Production." *Harvard Business Review*, 62 95-101.

Katz, D. R. *The Big Store. Inside the Crisis and Revolution at Sears*. New York: Penguin Books, 1987.

Kerr, S. "On the Folly of Rewarding A, While Hoping for B." *Academy of Management Journal*, 18 (1975): 769-782.

Nadler, D. A. "Organizational Frame Bending: Types of Change in the Complex Organization." In R. H. Kilmann and T. J. Covin (eds.), *Corporate Transformation: Revitalizing Organizations for a Competitive World*. San Francisco: Jossey-Bass, 1988.

Ott, J. S. *The Organizational Culture Perspective*. Chicago: Dorsey Press, 1989.

Perrow, C. "The Analysis of Goals in Complex Organizations." *American Sociological Review*, 26 (1961): 854-866.

Pettigrew, A. M. "On Studying Organizational Cultures." *Administrative Science Quarterly*, 24 (1979): 579-581.

Porter, L. W., E. E. Lawler III, and J. R. Hackman, *Behavior in Organizations*. New York: McGraw-Hill, 1975.

Sathe, V. *Culture and Related Corporate Realities: Text, Cases, and Readings on Organizational Entry, Establishment, and Change*, Homewood, Ill: Irwin, 1985.

Schein, E. H. "Does Japanese Management Style Have a Message for American Managers?" *Sloan Management Review*, 23 (1981): 55-68.

Schein, E. H. "Coming to a New Awareness of Organizational Culture." *Sloan Management Review*, 23 (1984): 3-16.

Schein, E. H. *Organizational Culture and Leadership*. San Francisco: Jossey-Bass, 1985.

"The Productivity Paradox." *Business Week*, June 6, 1988, 100-115.

"What's In – And Oust." *Business Week*, January 20, 1986, 52-61.

Wilkins, A. L., and N. J. Bristow. "For Successful Organizational Culture, Honor Your Past." *Academy of Management Executive*, I, no. 3 (1987): 221-229.

Yorks, L. "Organizational Transformation in Total Systems Quality." *Survey of Business*, 25, no. 1, (1989): 51-56.

Yorks, L., and D. A. Whitsett, D. A. *Scenarios of Change. Advocacy and the Diffusion of Job Redesign in Organizations*. New York: Praeger, 1989.

CHAPTER 16

MANAGERIAL PERFORMANCE MEASUREMENT*

GREGORY M. BOUNDS
Research Associate
Management Development Center
University of Tennessee

JAMES M. REEVE
Associate Professor of Accounting
University of Tennessee

KENNETH C. GILBERT
Associate Professor of Management
University of Tennessee

SUMMARY

Performance measurements are critically important managerial tools. They may be poorly designed and misused to the detriment of organizational competitiveness in creating value for customers. Alternatively, performance measurements may be used to encourage continuous improvement in systems that provide value for customers. This chapter reviews the shortcomings of traditional performance measurement and controls systems, and proposes alternatives. The shortcomings of traditional systems include the assumption that optimization of local objectives results in optimization of system objectives, ignorance of variation, measurement of what's easily available, and internal orientation. The proposed alternatives emphasize broader system measures, external orientation, and

*We thank Dudley Dewhirst, Mike Ehrhardt, Jack Evans, Joe Lesher, Charlie Quiek, Harry Roberts, and Lyle Yorks for helping us improve this chapter.

a cascading set of measures for continuous improvement. Guidelines for making changes to these proposed alternatives emphasize managerial behavior change.

INTRODUCTION

Managerial leaders are challenged to orchestrate the knowledge, skills, competencies, and energies of employees toward organizational objectives. In doing so, they may use performance measurements to leverage these individual human resources. However, if these measures are poorly designed or improperly used, individual efforts can be counterproductive for the organization as a whole. To their chagrin, leaders often get what they request through these measures. A popular adage states: "Tell me how an individual will be measured and I will tell you how that individual will behave."

Consider an anecdote from the world of sports. Tommy Henrich played baseball for the New York Yankees during the 1940s. He was nicknamed "Old Reliable," because of his apparent ability as a clutch player and a cleanup batter to help his team score. However, his individual batting statistics belied his value to the team. When his rather ordinary statistics were brought up in a discussion of his salary, he brilliantly articulated the inconsistency between individual performance measures and organizational goals: "What do you want, a higher batting average for me personally or value to the team? Every day, every at-bat, I do what's good for the team, I move runners around, and I knock runners in. But if you want batting average I'll give that to you next year. It'll weaken the team, but you can have what you want" (Halberstam, 1988). Fortunately, the Yankee management preferred a winning team to impressive individual statistics, and Henrich was granted a generous $2000 raise.

Baseball must be considered the consummate individualist team sport; that is, the sum of individual contributions approximates the overall performance of the team. However, even in baseball, pure individualism and reductionist management can diminish team performance. Whether Henrich was really a clutch hitter or whether he simply enjoyed a popular misconception of him as "Old Reliable," his comments illustrate the tension between individualism and teamwork.[1] Unfortunately, many other organizations are still basing decisions on performance measures that do an

---

1. In his review of this chapter, Harry Roberts of the University of Chicago questions the evidence that Henrich was "really" a clutch hitter. He notes an important lesson: there is a tendency in sports [and in management] to "overfit" the data–to read assignable causes into chance variations or to form lasting impressions from a few vivid examples.

even poorer job than batting averages in bridging individual (and group) performance to organizational purposes.

The Managerial Change

The globally competitive markets alluded to throughout this book demand changes in management approaches, which have been discussed in more detail in other chapters. While profitability and organizational prosperity are important outcomes in both of these contrasting approaches to management, the suggested means to these ends are very different than they were in the past. The traditional approach to management emphasizes the hierarchical management of individuals, subunits, and functions through a "divide and control" approach to meet standards or to achieve preset financial goals. A new approach emphasizes continuous improvement of systems to produce and deliver customer value.

These changes in management must include changes in performance measurement systems. The traditional performance measurements and control systems typically suffer the following shortcomings, which should be avoided: (1) They assume that optimization of local (functional or departmental or individual) objectives directly translates into optimization of overall (organizational or system) objectives; (2) they ignore the issues of statistical variation and the understanding of sources of variation; (3) they are internally oriented toward engineered standards and financial goals; and (4) they encourage measuring what is easily available.

These shortcomings in performance measurements are important because they are so often tied to formal and informal evaluations, self-appraisals, rewards, appreciations, promotions, role perceptions, and other cultural values, beliefs, and practices that impact organizational competitiveness through effects on individual behavior. To help managers avoid these pitfalls, we propose alternatives to these traditional systems in order to suggest what managers should approach in changing their performance measurement systems.

An alternative to traditional performance measurements and control systems is characterized by (1) transfunctional performance measurements that capture a broader span of the value-providing system, to encompass and capture interactions among diverse parts of the organization ("trans-" means above and beyond or transcending functions), (2) study of variation in means measures (i.e., measures that reflect the means to improved results), (3) integration of the internal performance criteria with external criteria to encourage competitive customer value provision, and (4) a check point/control point type of structure, wherein the performance criteria are interrelated and cascade throughout the organization. (Criteria are measures of value or indicators of progress in producing and delivering value to customers.)

Both the traditional and the alternative performance measures are discussed in more detail below. The purpose of this discussion is not to suggest a laundry list of measures that should or should not be used by an organization pursuing continuous improvement in customer value. Rather, these authors suggest (1) some general characteristics of the measures that should help an organization become more competitive, and (2) a process for making the change to put these measures in place. If implemented, these suggestions should help you determine the appropriate measures to guide your organization toward competitiveness in providing customer value. Cookbook recipes for success are not offered. These ideas must be implemented by thinking managerial leaders who adapt to the needs and contingencies of their customers, employees, other constituents, and available technologies.

TRADITIONAL PERFORMANCE MEASUREMENT SYSTEMS

The shortcomings of traditional performance measurement systems listed above are discussed in the following section.

Local Optimization and Overall Optimization

Organizations are typically differentiated and divided according to tasks and functions, with narrow job descriptions for diverse operator, supervisory, and managerial positions. To control these operations, managers attempt to monitor diverse activities and ensure their integration toward organizational objectives. Controlling becomes increasingly difficult as organizations grow larger, more diverse, and more complex. Therefore, performance measures are tailored for each organizational subunit, to allow managerial oversight of diverse operations.

The practice of narrowly defining performance measures is legitimized by the widely accepted cultural principle that personal accountability should match personal responsibility. For example, this principle dictates that the production manager should be evaluated on the basis of performance of the production department over which he or she has "control." Under this pressure, normal self-interest and conscientiousness lead managers to attend to their "own" objectives. This traditional approach assumes that if each individual attends to his or her own business, the business of the whole will be ensured.

Unfortunately, the sum of the local optima does not necessarily produce a global optimum. For example, a marketing group may be expected to maximize sales. Sales promotions represent the "Old Faithful" of the marketing manager, who seeks the predictable and pronounced, yet temporary, upswing in sales. Yet a major cause of variation in demand is periodic sales promotions by marketing. The production scheduling and inventory control costs resulting from these variations in demand may outweigh the benefits of the promotions. One company in the consumer products industry regularly experiences overtime, more inventory, poorer delivery, and reduced product quality owing to the variation introduced by periodic promotions. However, the marketing group is measured only in terms of sales and shows no interest in these "production problems." Similar problems exist within other functions. For example, a machine operator who seeks to maximize his or her production efficiency measures may create waste by making unneeded inventory.

Consider the interaction effect of raw material procurement policies on downstream production processes. If leaders evaluate procurement on the basis of purchase price variance, then the department has an incentive to optimize on this performance measure. Procurement may minimize purchase price for "in spec" material and maintain multiple vendors in order to maintain price competition. Unfortunately, the systemic impact of this behavior can be expensive. The facility will be subject to vendor-to-vendor variation, which degrades overall system performance. Furthermore, procurement will take advantage of quantity discounts to reduce price and purchase in quantities greater than needed. The resulting raw material inventories add cost to the system in terms of remnants, carrying charges, and material management.

Managers must appreciate the interdependent nature of the various parts that make up an organization. Decisions made in one place influence others throughout the organization. As indicated above, optimization of local performance may detract from overall system performance. These authors acknowledge that organizations vary in the extent of integration, interaction, and synergy needed. For example, an organization of basic researchers, with each working on different projects, may require little interaction among researchers. The performance of the whole aggregate of researchers largely reflects the sum of individual performances. However, every type of organization can derive some benefit from collaboration, mutual assistance, and integration of efforts toward common concerns for customers. This is true for loosely integrated firms, such as basic researchers, and particularly true for the types of organizations that have taken a hierarchical approach to managing functional interdependence.

Statistical Control and Variation Ignored

Traditional performance measures and controls implicitly assume that the individual or group being evaluated totally causes the observed performance. When managers assume that factors under the control of the individual completely determine performance, they tend to overlook the inherent nature of both input and process variability. Managers must recognize that most processes are subject to many sources of variation. A baseball player who bats .300 will occasionally get no hits in five turns at bat. This does not mean his skills have deteriorated or he is not trying. Similarly, he will sometimes get three hits in five turns at bat. This does not mean his skill or effort has improved. His performance may be in a state of statistical control.

What Is Statistical Control? Central to understanding variation is the concept of a "state of statistical control." A process "in statistical control" is stable and predictable; that is, there is a predictable range of variation around a predictable average. The sources of variation in such a process are constant from observation to observation. These sources of variation, which are part of the system, are referred to as common cause sources of variation.

A process that is out of control is unstable and unpredictable owing to the presence of "special cause" sources of variation, in addition to the common cause sources of variation. Special cause sources of variation are those sources that vary from observation to observation or appear unexpectedly, briefly, or sporadically, such as shown during Period 1 in Figure 1. For example, workers in a system differ in their ability. If a new and poorly trained worker filled in for another during his or her absence and created an out of control situation, this phenomenon would be a special cause of variation. Improvement in a process that is out of control is achieved by first removing the special causes of variation to achieve a stable process, such as shown in Period 2 in Figure 1. A stable process reveals the level of variability inherent in the process which is due to common causes. Common causes are addressed to improve the system, for example, reduce variation as shown in Period 3 in Figure 1.

Most variation in performance is due to common causes or the enduring system (Deming, 1986). Managers often fail to understand the sources of variation because traditional control systems focus on variance in aggregate measures over relatively long time periods.

Aggregate Period Variances. Traditional control systems are based on a model that assumes resources are input to a process for transformation into a measurable output. Ideally, the transformation is assumed to be deterministic, that is, what goes in determines what comes out, just as

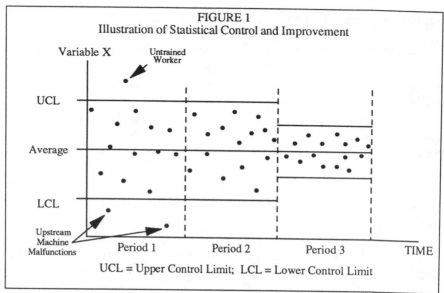

FIGURE 1
Illustration of Statistical Control and Improvement

UCL = Upper Control Limit; LCL = Lower Control Limit

planned. A measure of performance, such as efficiency of the transformation process, may be determined by a transformation equation based on
engineered standards. Period efficiency reports reveal the gross variance
over a period of time between standard output and actual output for the
inputs used. Small repetitive losses in efficiency, otherwise undetectable,
become visible through accumulation over time and are reported in period
variances to reflect aggregate deviations from standards. The aggregate
variance number serves as a signal for management attention. Unfortunately, the signal provided management is deficient as a guide to
managerial action for several reasons.

These control systems lead managers to react to aggregate period
variances and to ignore variation within the period. It may appear nonsen-
sical that a means of control that is based on "variances" can be accused of
ignoring "variation." However, period variances are quite different from
variation within the time period. The period variance (an accounting term)
is an aggregate number that simply sums up what happened over a time
interval, in terms of a deviation, on the average, from an engineered
standard. Forever hidden in this number is the variation (a statistical term)
that occurs during the time interval, from day to day, hour to hour, minute
to minute, or second to second. (For further understanding of the deficiencies of engineered cost centers, see Reeve, 1990. More complex issues of
engineering process control are discussed by Moore in Chapter 19.)

The following shortcomings are associated with these traditional performance measurements: untimeliness, loss of time order, encouragement
of results orientation, encouragement of complacency, discouragement of

experimentation, constraint of strategy, underestimation of the systemic impact of variation, and unfairness of appraisal. These shortcomings are discussed below.

Untimeliness. The periodic, infrequent and untimely nature of these reports (e.g., monthly) limits their value as a feedback mechanism. By the end of the period the events have transpired. Managers cannot take action to change the operating characteristics of the process in time to prevent the losses, which are subsequently reported as inefficiencies. Furthermore, to avoid recurrence of unfavorable variances, managers must rely on memory to figure out the causes of the reported variances. Untimeliness of data disallows understanding of causes, because the data arrive too late for effective root cause analysis.

Loss of Time Order. The most serious shortcoming of period variances derives from aggregating time-ordered data. The time order of the individual data points is lost in an accumulated variance used in accounting control systems. Period variances ignore variation as it occurs over time within the period. Evidence on the causes of process outcomes remains a mystery, subject only to conjecture. For example, with efficiencies, there is no way to discern whether any loss in efficiency during the period occurred gradually over time or immediately or whether it was due to a single, nonrecurring event. Potential causal influences such as material lot, fatigue, shift effects, machine wear, ambient temperature, and personnel assignment cannot be associated with process events. The choice of how to aggregate data and preserve the time order of data bears critical implications for learning and improvement.

By destroying the time order, there is no way to determine whether the system is stable or predictable, that is, in a statistical state of control. The reader must again sort through the semantic confusion. How is it that a "control system" does not tell whether a process is in "statistical control?" These two uses of the term *control* are very different conceptually and practically.

The traditional concept of control revolves around meeting engineered standards. A department manager told one of the authors, "Yes, we're almost always in control. We meet standards every month." However, after real time statistical sampling and SPC (statistical process control) charting of data (see Figure 2), this department manager discovered that production efficiency varied erratically from hour to hour and day to day. Efficiency was not predictable or stable over time, although on the average, over a period of a month, the department met engineered standards. For example, the manager frequently recognizes a projected shortfall in production numbers near the end of the month. He then makes a long production run, a "gravy run," of an "unneeded" but easy to run part to get

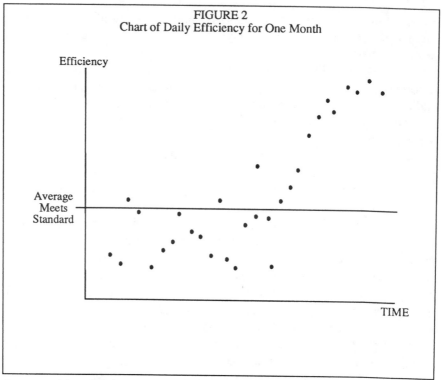

FIGURE 2
Chart of Daily Efficiency for One Month

the monthly efficiency up to standard. Standards were met, but the production efficiency was not statistically in control, that is, stable and predictable over time.

Instability and variation in production outcomes are important because of the ripple effects throughout the organization. Thus, a department may meet standards for accounting control, as aggregated over the period, and yet be out of statistical control, within the period, to the detriment of overall system objectives.

Encouragement of Results Orientation. By ignoring real time variation, period variances are no more than historical reports or end-result measures. This traditional control mechanism suits the managerial proclivity for a "results-oriented style," wherein the manager simply oversees operations. However, it provides little useful information for the analytical manager interested in managing the means, learning about operations, identifying causes, and taking corrective action to improve the process for better future outcomes. Furthermore, this traditional system does not encourage continuous improvement to reduce variation.

Essentially, all measures document end results and outcomes. Any measure must be regarded as historical, recorded after the fact. However, it is important "how historical" the measure happens to be. Specificity of the measure and time lag between the event and the recorded measure determines the usefulness of the measure. With a big time lag, operational adjustment and statistical control becomes less effective. The lack of learning through association with surrounding events and circumstances encumbers continuous improvement. Furthermore, the focus of measurement on outcomes that are pure results, for example, a burnt egg, may give less information for actions than focus on outcomes that directly reflect the process, for example, temperature of the grease in the frying pan. Real time process measures and observations provide hints and opportunity for action to improve results.

Encouragement of Complacency. The traditional control mechanism allows the complacent attitude that one can "just meet specifications or standards." Consider the description of the basic control processes, in Figure 3, that have traditionally been taught in introductory management textbooks (Stoner and Wankel, 1986: 575). Traditional control processes encourage reactive management, that is, reaction to problems or failure to meet standards, and complacency when standards appear to have been met. This attitude is "particularly harmful when the standard cost system builds waste into the standard, and thereby conceals the improvement potential." To illustrate, consider that "a major wood products firm decomposed their

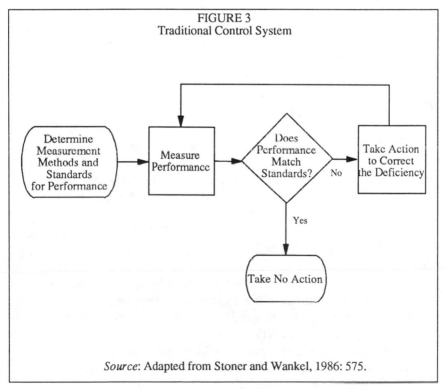

FIGURE 3
Traditional Control System

Source: Adapted from Stoner and Wankel, 1986: 575.

material standards only to discover that there was a 20% material waste built into the standard transformations from raw material to finished board. This amount represented a very significant dollar savings potential. Management was completely surprised by this discovery" (Reeve, 1990). If standards are infrequently revised, continuous improvement does not exist.

Discouragement of Experimentation. Not only do traditional control systems distract attention from the study of variation, but they insidiously discourage any attempt at experimental manipulation of variation. Experiments purposefully designed to generate specific new learning are integral means of reducing variation and improving systems. Even though strict control, with emphasis on production quotas and monthly costs, impedes experimentation, some defiant souls do it anyway. They simply bury the costs in operating budgets and overhead. Managers should not have to waste their creative energies circumventing bureaucracy, in search of ways to do what is best for the company despite the company.

Constraint of Strategy. Control tends to become an end in itself, snuffing the flames of creative change. Standards convey expectations and norms on which managers assess performance, make decisions, and build systems. For example, traditional budgetary control and accounting practices encourage investment in depreciable hardware rather than in human capabilities. Managers absolve their conscience of the need to improve "humanware" based on the incorrect assumption that investment in high technology and automation allows deskilling of the workforce. To the contrary, such complexity often requires increased skill to operate, maintain, and integrate high technology equipment.

Standards and budgets tend to become fixed and self-preserving mechanisms that rigidly constrain organizational strategy. Rather than being driven by strategy, these fixtures limit the ability of managers to adopt and implement improved strategies for customer value. For example, managers too often assume that money should be budgeted based on past budgets, tempered by such factors as replacement costs for worn out equipment. Thus, budget increases or decreases are executed across the board, to simplify decision making and ensure "fairness." Strategic issues, such as diverting and channeling resources to build improved strategic capabilities, are thus overlooked.

Underestimation of the Systemic Impact of Variation. Managers tend to underestimate the impact of local variation on the rest of the system and, as a result, frequently tolerate variation. Consider the following example of the impact of ignored variation.

A consumer products company fills containers with product at the end of the process. The labeled net weight for the product is 16 ounces. The amount of variation in net fill weight is severe (see Figure 4). As a result of variation in net fill weight, the process must be centered at 16.5 ounces, in order to protect the lower specification limit from underfill. Notice that the variation in net fill weight translates into higher average levels of fill. Over a large volume of production, an average overfill of 3 percent, as in this case, could represent substantial loss. If the variation were less, the average level of fill could drop to nearer the lower specification limit.

The financial losses from variation only start with the material losses from the additional average fill of 0.5 ounces above the lower specification limit. Since each package has, on the average, an additional 0.5 ounces, the size of the package must be larger in order to accommodate the statistically determined largest fill. Therefore, direct packaging costs are higher. The filling machines must work a little longer on average in order to pack an average package 0.5 more ounces. The labor and capital cost of the packing department is wasted for the extra time to pack the additional average 0.5 ounces. The storage, handling, and freight costs are all higher, since the same number of packages at 16.5 ounces are heavier and take more space than packages packed at 16 ounces.

This example illustrates two important general principles about variation. First, variation translates directly into the levels of performance observed, and, second, the impact of variation is far reaching through the organization. These lessons apply to many situations in material-intensive organizations, such as processing times, delivery times, setup times, and repair times, and other types of organizations, ranging from job shops to services.

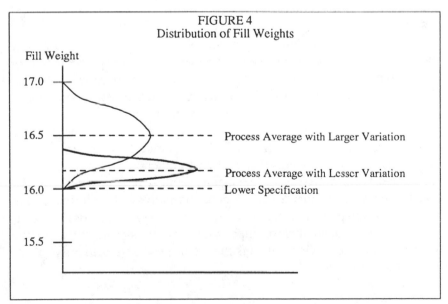

FIGURE 4
Distribution of Fill Weights

Fill Weight

17.0

16.5 – – – – – – – – – – – Process Average with Larger Variation

– – – – – – – – Process Average with Lesser Variation

16.0 – – – – – – – – – – Lower Specification

15.5

Clearly, the failure to investigate and understand variation results in an inability to learn and improve. An understanding of variation is central to monitoring processes, to revealing the impact of process changes, and to improving processes. Returning again to the baseball player who bats .300, we see that distinguishing the random variation in his performance from variation that is due to special cause represents a fundamental issue. Only then would it be possible to monitor his performance and evaluate the effects of changes in his technique or his effectiveness against right-handed pitchers versus left-handed pitchers.

Unfairness of the Appraisal. Performance measurements that ignore statistical control and variation are often used to evaluate individual performance. Managers must consider the potential unfairness to those appraised. It is obviously unfair, demoralizing, and undesirable to hold individual managers, supervisors, and operators accountable for outcomes over which they have little or no control. This is precisely what happens when individuals who are performing within the predicted range of variation of the system are ranked and rewarded based on the observed variation between individuals.

Deming (1986) addressed this problem and pointed out the unfairness of rewarding and punishing on the basis of individual performance within a system created by higher management. The individual may have relatively little control over variation in work outcomes. Primary control resides with the system, which encompasses the training, equipment, information, work environment, materials, organizational demands, and methods provided the worker. Rewarding and punishing those within the system who are not statistical outliers is tantamount to flipping a coin to decide who gets rewarded and who gets punished.

Performance measurements that encourage local optimization may lead to great frustration for managers unable to fully control the results of their own unit's performance. For example, a manager of a manufacturing department may work diligently to ensure the department's efficiency. However, the performance of this department may be more a function of actions in other areas, such as procurement, training, maintenance, capital acquisition, and scheduling. It seems inappropriate to hold this manager solely accountable for results that depend on others.

Furthermore, in striving to meet locally defined measures, this manager may behave in ways that lead to acceptable individual performance but diminish system performance. Individual stress may result from the negatively affected social relationships with other managers, or from the inconsistency of behavior with personal values and desires to do a "good" job for the company.

Internal Orientation

Traditional performance measurement and control systems tend to be only internally focused, and thus deficient. These traditional control systems tend to be based on internal definitions of "standard." This internal focus encourages comparison against one's self, often not even one's ideal self, but an engineered self, historically expected or theoretically derived. Furthermore, this internal focus is based on only one aspect of value for the customer, that is, cost. Managers often ignore other aspects of the customer's needs and perspective. They also generally ignore how they are doing relative to the competition. These issues are discussed below.

Emphasis on Cost. Traditional financial and accounting paradigms tend to encourage a focus on cost, for example, through efficiency and utilization measures. Cost is important to the customer because of the implications for purchase price, and for the company because of the implications for operating margins and profit. Achieving financial and accounting objectives is certainly necessary in order to stay in business. Organizations must contain costs, get return on their investments, and maintain cash flows in order to remain competitive. But simply focusing on these objectives may take attention away from the changing demands and needs of customers, and may lead managers to pursue courses of action that are financially attractive in the short term but strategically deficient in the long term.

Furthermore, customer needs are more than one dimensional. Cost, and ultimately purchase price, is only one component that determines the value of products and services to customers.

Traditional cost accounting systems often emphasize efficiency and utilization as measures of performance. Efficiency compares the actual time to produce a part to a predetermined standard time. Utilization measures how intensively a resource is being used. These measures encourage managers to reduce the labor time and the machine cost to produce a part, and they are presumed to be linked to organizational financial performance. However, efficiency and utilization measures may encourage managers to defer maintenance, to produce whatever is easy, to build inventory, and to make things quicker while ignoring quality. Depending on how they are used, these measures can trigger dysfunctional actions and encourage managers to maximize individual functions instead of optimize the performance of the total system. These managerial behaviors may yield an array of questionable performance patterns over time.

Consider a plant wherein during each reporting period supervisors act out of normal self-interest. They work in isolation to meet their standards for time and cost, oblivious to the needs of other departments. These supervisors run large batches of products. The work-in-process inventories of some items grow, while there are shortages of others. Bottlenecks are created because supervisors use only their most efficient machines, allowing less efficient machines to sit idle, to keep efficiencies high. Downstream operations are severely affected, with huge backlogs of work at some, and shutdowns due to shortages at others. The work schedule is poorly executed. Overall system performance suffers. Shipping falls further and further behind schedule.

As the end of the month approaches, the plant manager takes charge in reaction to the crisis. The local performance measures are temporarily overridden by more global performance measures. The shipping goals for the reporting period become the top priority. All energies are focused on expediting and problem solving and crisis management. The partially finished orders are hustled together to boost shipping and income numbers. Workers earn overtime pay. Priorities in scheduling and batching of work are altered. Even the inefficient machines are used. More orders are completed, and shipments increase. Once the crisis is over and the reporting period ends, the plant returns to the local measures. The cycle repeats in the next reporting period. This pattern has been called the End of Month Syndrome (Umble and Srikanth, 1990). A graphic display of the pattern resembles a hockey stick (see Figure 5).

This example illustrates the danger in picking performance measures. You might get what you ask for. People may make operating decisions

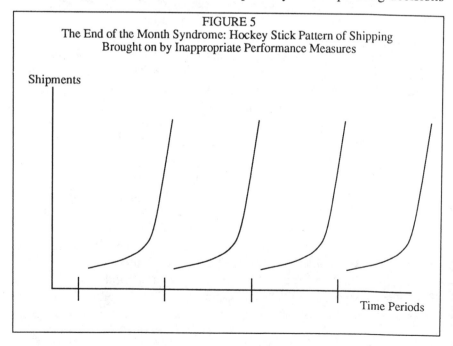

FIGURE 5
The End of the Month Syndrome: Hockey Stick Pattern of Shipping
Brought on by Inappropriate Performance Measures

inconsistent with overall objectives. Thus, the choice of what to measure is critical. The measure chosen may be the cause of the problems observed, especially when the numbers are used inappropriately, for example, to control individuals through performance evaluation rather than for continuous improvement of customer value.

Customer Taken for Granted. Without external focus on the customer, distracted by internally derived standards, management may not adequately attend to the relationship with customers. Customers may be treated as pawns to be manipulated, or as competitors to be outwitted in a profit contest, rather than as partners in a collaborative and mutually beneficial relationship. Much like a marriage, this collaborative relationship requires social maintenance, equitable exchange, mutual provisioning of needs, mutual adaptation, flexibility, and mutual dependability. The needs of both partners must be met for the relationship to prosper.

We are not inferring a pervasive, malicious intent on the part of those who blindly pursue traditional objectives. Rather, managers often mistakenly believe that the standards they pursue adequately or competitively ensure customer value, while the customer believes management is doing an inferior job. In rare cases, individuals may actually be maliciously negligent, self-serving, or more interested in reducing frustration in their own lives than in their customer's lives. Others may even assume they know the needs of the customer better than the customer himself. Still others do not assess customer satisfaction because they are afraid the results will dictate a remedy. However, most cases are not cases of abuse, but misunderstanding. The fault lies with managers who fail to make explicit connections between customer value and internal performance measures.

Competition Overlooked. Even if managers do attend to more than the cost dimension, and they do create value for customers, they may not do so better than competitors. Thus, the other aspect of external focus may include an understanding of performance relative to competitors. Internal focus and failure to conduct specific comparison to one's best competitor as an external "standard" can be a mistake. Failing to compare to competitors, managers may remain ignorant of strategic deficiencies, and strategic opportunities, in their capability to create value. Competitors may make advances that remain undetected. Managers may lose market share and not know why.

Measuring What's Easily Available

Traditional performance measurements tend to emphasize those things that can be most easily measured, which is evident in several persistent biases in measurement. These biases include (1) emphasis of short-term goals at the expense of long-term goals, (2) emphasis of tangibles at the expense of intangibles, and (3) encouragement of competition rather than collaboration among individuals and internal groups.

Short Term Versus Long Term. One bias favors short-term performance measures over long-term performance measures. It is obviously easier to measure this quarter's profit than to measure the impact of this quarter's activities on the competitive position of the organization ten years hence. Although the long-term impact is more important, the short term gets more emphasis because it is easy to measure. In addition, the short term is clearly more salient and naturally commands more attention.

Tangibles Versus Intangibles. Another bias is emphasis of "tangibles" at the expense of "intangibles," or more remote, less measurable outcomes. It is not surprising that cost per unit, dollar sales, throughput, machine uptime, and other easily quantifiable measures often show up as performance measures. Neither is it surprising that outcomes more directly related to customer satisfaction and more difficult to measure, such as service, delivery, and product quality, show up less often. With the emphasis of the more tangible over the less tangible, a biased decision-making pattern results. For example, managers may systematically compromise product quality in order to reduce standard costs. Be aware that the word "intangible" implies undefinable and unmeasurable. Although it may be difficult, managers should not excuse themselves from devising creative means of measuring these important "less tangible" outcomes.

Competition Versus Collaboration. A third type of bias encourages people to compete rather than collaborate. It is often easier to measure individual performance than it is to measure individual contribution to the team. For example, it is easy to measure an individual's sales volume. It is much more difficult to measure the individual's effectiveness as a coach and mentor to junior salespersons or the creation of goodwill among members of the organization. Hence, the individuals frequently are measured and rewarded on the basis of sales dollars. This practice emphasizes individual achievement at the expense of organizational goals. The organization also loses opportunities to pass accumulated learning to others.

The Inadequacy of Traditional Approaches: An Example

Local objectives that are defined in terms of relatively narrow tasks often appear to be logically related to overall organizational objectives. In practice, however, when performance measures encourage relentless pursuit of local objectives, overall system objectives may be compromised.

Furthermore, a results-oriented management style may have unexpected and undesirable side-effects when combined with heavy emphasis on control through performance measurements.

The following excerpt reveals some of the problems associated with managing by a "divide and control" approach, which emphasizes administrative oversight of subunit results, rather than integrated and proactive management of systems. This excerpt was adapted from an unpublished Organizational Assessment Report by Gregory M. Bounds. Structured interviews were used to baseline the managerial behaviors and cultural practices of an industrial products manufacturing plant.

The Case Of The Misguided Control System

The managers of this plant experience various problems in delivering a competitive product, including: unpredictable variation on important measures, 10 to 15 percent downgrade and scrap, long lead times, and "frequent" failure to meet scheduled commitments.

In the work environment there exists a lot of fingerpointing and passing of the buck, resulting in high levels of stress and poor morale. Although there is general acknowledgement of what the next process needs, some of the managers appear unconcerned about the problems of others. The attitude toward internal customers seems to be "I'll do my job, let them worry about theirs." A quote from a maintenance supervisor characterizes the tension with production, "My customers are the managers above me, I don't pacify the supervisors, especially those on the production side."

Although there are exceptions, the teamwork in the plant appears to be pretty poor. Managers do not cooperate. Tension, jealousy, and blaming abound. While some people communicate and cooperate fairly well, the general case is that each manager worries about his or her own operation with modest regard for others. In the words of one manager, "people do not have a lot of respect for each other." Levels of trust appear low–"it is every manager for himself." Managers acknowledge a need for collaboration on quality problems, but see no one responsible for overall operations or systems.

The management style contributes to the organization's problems. The top managers delegate operational responsibilities. They manage by watching the daily production numbers and by "reacting" when things get out of line, even though they admit to mistrusting all the numbers. A quotation from the plant manager reveals this "results oriented" management: "the first thing I do in the morning is get the production report, review the numbers, and assess who to call in and what to attack." The "attack" resembles a good old fashioned tongue lashing more than a constructive search to understand causes.

"Firefighting" prevails. Problem solving and system improvement are more infrequent. There is a lot of pressure to "improve," but improvement is defined as "better production numbers," without direction and assistance on the means of improving the numbers. This pressure appears dysfunctional and creates a lot of stress and activity, but not much in the way of results. Good results seem to be accidental, yet applauded. The top managers are not highly respected, perhaps because of their "find the culprit" style.

The pervasive conflict between maintenance and production lends a clue to a cause of the problems in this plant. While maintenance and production often have stressful relations in any manufacturing operation, the conflict here is abnormal. A quotation from the maintenance foremen reveals the stress. He states, "I don't give a damn about making [widgets], my job is to keep the machines running." A closer look at the management control system reveals an overemphasis upon departmental measures of performance. The control system assigns responsibility for the production line being down and measures each department manager on this unscheduled downtime.

It seems only logical that in order to meet the production quota, the machines must be kept running. And reducing downtime by holding the responsible parties accountable for downtime seems logical. Operators should be careful not to cause stoppages, and maintenance people should keep the machines in good repair and fix them quickly when the line does stop. However, the system of control in this plant is dysfunctional and discourages continuous improvement.

Downtime meetings are held to assign blame for line stoppage and, ideally, to figure out what slows down the production. But the meetings stray from their original purpose. Managers do little problem solving to remove the causes of the downtime incidents. Meetings degenerate into arguments. Needless to say, the quibbling and fighting over who is really responsible for the downtime is not only fruitless, but it distracts them from their jobs.

They fail to collaborate on improving the system of production. Maintenance people are reluctant to stop the line for requested repairs because they fear being held accountable for the downtime. The quality of the product suffers until the next scheduled shut down. Afterall, maintenance is not responsible for making "good quality" product. That is Q.C.'s and Production's responsibility. Right? Knowing no better, these managers continue to manage these tensions, divisions, and crises, aware of the difficulties, yet convinced that this approach is necessary for success.

The situation used to be tolerable when this producer could sell everything they could make. However, customers are demanding reduced variation from part to part, and from shipment to shipment. Deliveries are requested just in time. Additionally, costs must be reduced to remain price competitive. Value must be delivered to the customer for this plant to remain competitive, but there are no owners of the systems which create value. There are only owners of the various local pieces of the hodgepodge systems.

An alternative to traditional performance measurement systems is presented below. The differences between the traditional approach and this alternative approach can be seen in Figure 6.

ALTERNATIVE PERFORMANCE MEASUREMENT SYSTEM

Customers seek products and services that provide the best net value, that is, more realized and less sacrificed. Conventional performance measurements only weakly relate to these concepts. Competitiveness requires a performance measurement system that is customer focused and captures the firm's ability to provide the right product, at the right time, in the right quantities, of the right quality, at the right price, at the right sacrifice, and so on. This capability represents the ultimate competitive

---

FIGURE 6
Traditional Versus Alternative Performance Measurements

Traditional	Alternative
1. Assumes focus on localized performance measures yields system performance.	1. Encourages focus on cross-functional system performance measures.
2. Ignores sources of performance variations.	2. Encourages study of variation in the means to system performance.
3. Internally oriented toward engineering standards and financial goals.	3. Externally oriented toward customers and competitors.
4. Measures what is easily available.	4. Measures interrelated criteria cascading from customers.

weapon: not simply low cost or differentiated product, but an ability to provide customer value better than any competitor in the world. Performance measures must operationalize the firm's ability to provide net customer value.

A performance measurement system that unduly focuses on financial measures of performance, market share, ROI, and cost efficiency will petrify managers into a narrow view and mission. Such a firm will constantly seek higher ROI but be unable to achieve such. The financial measures of performance are ends, which result from competitive strength. Certainly, profitability helps renew the next generation of the organization for competitive strength. However, an exclusive focus on financial measures of performance distracts the organization from its fundamental obligation to create and provide value for customers.

Do not misconstrue the message. Cost and financial performance are critically important. Without performance on these dimensions, a company will not survive and prosper. Profit provides continued investment and revitalization for the future. Without achieving profitability, the reinvestment and the provisioning of the next generation of organizational systems is jeopardized. However, managers must pay attention to continuous improvement of the means of achieving profit. For example, cost reduction can be achieved through improving other components of customer value, like quality and consistency of operations. Furthermore, higher market share and financial performance can be achieved by improving customer value and generating customer loyalty based on best net value.

In complex and fast changing markets, the performance measurement system of a globally competitive organization must promote change and vision. Such vision must be customer oriented, wherein lies the source of competitive strength. The measures of performance must be directed toward those product and service features that are of value to customers. Each of the characteristics of the alternative approach presented in Figure 6 is discussed below.

Transfunctional System Measures

Ideally, all employees should internalize a superordinate disposition or be disposed toward needs and concerns that are broader than their own local or personal pursuits. This disposition embodies a culturally valued orientation toward system objectives and the good of the whole organization. Measures that focus individual attention on system objectives help to cultivate this disposition. Exclusive reliance on individualized and local criteria do not encourage individuals to focus on the needs of others or the broader system. System measures will encourage teamwork and collaboration for system objectives, rather than single-minded pursuit of local objectives.

For example, consider a corporate division wherein collaboration between plants would result in better response time to customers and reduced costs. This collaboration might take the form of sharing customers when one plant is full to capacity, unable to respond quickly to an order, and another plant, with slack capacity, could quickly respond to fill a customer need. In this case, applying broader system measures would mean measuring plants on the basis of improvement in divisional service to the customer and division profitability rather than plant profitability. Further forms of collaboration would consist of sharing information about improvements in methods and technologies, rather than hiding discoveries to obtain a relative advantage over sister plants. Individual contributions should be complementary and should fit to form an integrated whole. Managers and workers should not be competing over how big a slice of the pie they are going to get, but, rather, collaborating and mutually complementing one another's contributions to make the pie bigger for all.

As another example, rather than measure design engineers simply for the timely release of product designs, to be tossed over the wall to the process engineers, their attention should be broadened to encompass design for manufacturability and ultimate value to the end user of the product. The entire product life cycle must be considered during each phase of product life, rather than narrow criteria for functionally dominated, discrete phases.

Study of Variation in Means Measures

Emphasizing transfunctional and broader performance measures does not preclude the use of indicators of progress at the level of functional activities or job activities. Indicators of progress at local levels are important, because improvement in local contributions can add to overall success. There are means measures (micromeasures) at local levels that are important for guiding and directing the improvement activity. But simply focusing on means measures within functions does not suffice. There must also be attention to the interplay and interactions among team members within the broader system. Means measures, within and across functions, can serve as yardsticks of progress toward system objectives.

An analogy from the sport of basketball illustrates the distinction between a focus on means and a focus on results. The coach of a basketball team knows that the number of points scored is the critical determiner of success. These results determine who wins, but they lend no clue as to how to win. To learn about how to win, the coach must watch the team play, in practice and in the game. While the coach may occasionally glance at the scoreboard to take note of the results, he intensely scrutinizes the plays of the game to determine weaknesses, strengths, strategies, and tactics.

Statistical charting of processes can be a useful means of improving system outcomes. However, when the means become ends in themselves, which happens when these measures are formalized in performance evaluation, their use can be dysfunctional. In most cases these means measures must be decoupled from the evaluative context wherein performance appraisals determine rewards and punishments. This decoupling encourages managers not to optimize on these measures, but to study variation in order to continuously improve and use their best judgment to rein processes and diverse activities for the good of customers. These measures should be emphasized as a means to improvement, and not be turned into a traditional evaluative and control device that is externally driven by a superior.

Some people may argue that the motivational effects of evaluative criteria, as broad as overall system performance, are far removed and ineffectual for people toiling in the bowels of the organization. However, if the suggestions of this chapter are properly implemented, this objection disappears. Proper implementation requires that managers come to rely on other means of motivation than traditional carrot and stick approaches, for example, need for achievement, intrinsic motivation, job enrichment, superordinate attitudes, information feedback, self-appraisal on improvement in means measures, and social recognition. Statistical charting to monitor and study variation enables continuous improvement of the means. It also provides feedback that can be motivating and intrinsically satisfying, and give individuals a sense of accomplishment.

External Orientation

Performance measurement should be externally oriented by encouraging managers to know what the customer values to improve net customer value. Awareness of competitor capabilities for value provision represents another component of this external orientation.

Competitive Benchmarking. Comparison against one's best competitors helps identify the organization's competitive position regarding strategically important capabilities. Simply improving productivity, quality, cost, or timely delivery does not ensure competitive provision of value. Managers must improve value provision at a rate faster than the competition. Failure to improve at a competitive rate can jeopardize customer relationships, even though those relationships have been symbiotic in the past. These authors know of a high technology company that discontinued business with an "improving" sister division because another supplier demonstrated more commitment to improvement, and actually improved more than the sister division.

Competitive benchmarking assumes tremendous insight into what customers value. For benchmarking to be useful, managers must choose the right focus. For each of the factors selected to benchmark, managers must know the significance and relative importance to customers to set priorities. A company can be the best in the world on a product feature that is irrelevant to the customer. Thus, in selecting what to benchmark, managers must first do their homework on what customers value.

Benchmarking can provide motivation for improvement if you are a follower. It helps to eliminate complacency. It focuses managerial attention on clarification of strategy and identification of deficiencies and opportunities in strategic capabilities. However, simple reliance on benchmarking can be a mistake. Managers should seek to understand the strategy of competitors and implications for comparative advantage. However, they should not simply react to competitor actions. They should seek to lead rather than to follow competitors, to exceed the standards of even the best competitor. One way to avoid complacency, and be a market leader, is to focus on customer value.

Providing Value for Customers. Managerial leaders must ensure that system objectives and performance criteria are closely aligned with customer needs and organizational strategy. System objectives should be motivated by the strategic resolve of managers to provide value to the customer and be tempered by considerations of profitability and enhancement of future strategic capabilities. Leaders should compete to provide the best net value for customers.

The readers should beware of those who advocate any one set of performance measures to fit all organizations. Few measures are universal.[2] In general, measures should vary with the organization's strategy and should be determined through much thought and study of customers by management.

---

2. There are several criteria that will always be useful guides to improving organizational competitiveness. Any work by any employee to improve on these criteria will be welcomed, particularly when such improvement does not require sacrifice on other criteria. These criteria include improved design to meet customer needs, reduced variation in conformance to design, reduced lead time in production and delivery, reduced costs, and reduced sacrifice required by the customer. Managers must be sensitive to the interactions, relationships, and tradeoffs among these criteria.

Cascading Structure of Measures

To ensure the connection to customer value, leaders should start with a consideration of organizational strategy and then determine the transfunctional, superordinate systems (e.g., the suprasystems that provide value for customers), which the managers will manage and improve. Managerial leaders bear the responsibility for determining which customers will be served and what these customers value. They must also articulate this knowledge and organizational strategy to others. The criteria selected for the critical systems should be used in determining the criteria for subsystems, functional activities, processes, and tasks that are components of the larger system.

The work of subordinate managers should be gauged and guided by criteria that indicate progress toward the objectives of the critical system. The subordinate criteria should cascade throughout the organization, from broad critical systems to processes and activities. This structure sounds like a management-by-objectives (MBO) approach, but there is a critical difference. The MBO approach focuses managers on achieving negotiated goals and objectives. By contrast, this approach focuses managers on continuous improvement toward customer-valued criteria. This approach also requires that managers clarify causal relationships between means and ends. These issues are discussed below.

Continuous Improvement. An MBO program typically erodes into a bureaucratic paper chase, steeped with red tape and characterized by gamesmanship in negotiating obtainable and unchallenging goals. By contrast, this approach emphasizes continuous improvement and not just meeting specific, preset, target objectives for productivity or financial performance. The criteria of subordinate functions and processes are linked to system criteria, and performance should be continuously improved as indicated by these criteria. Compare the simple model of this approach in Figure 7 with the traditional "if it ain't broke, don't fix it" approach in Figure 3. The improvement activity never ends as in problem solving. When improvements are made, subsequent complacency is not encouraged.

Clarifying Causal Relationships. System-level criteria are the indicators of system outcomes or results that should reflect success in providing value for customers. These system criteria are derived from organizational strategy and selection of the critical systems. Then, subsystem criteria are identified which are causally related to the system criteria. Next, criteria for subordinate activities are likewise identified as causally related to subsystem and system-level criteria. The process continues down to individual jobs, until a cascading set of criteria are developed

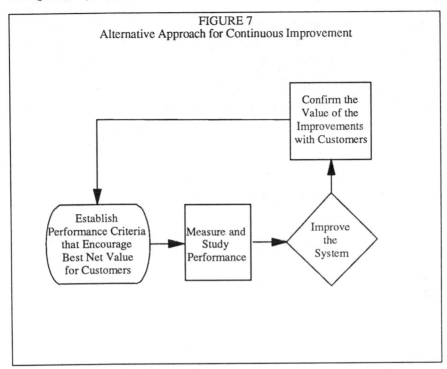

FIGURE 7
Alternative Approach for Continuous Improvement

throughout the organization which are subservient to strategic system objectives.

The resulting cascading structure of measures integrates the various subsystem, functional, departmental, and individual activities in subservience to strategic system objectives. To this end, pertinent behavioral activities of the managerial leadership model include determining causal relationships and leverage points in system diagnosis and analysis.

Within the cascading structure, there may be a host of operating factors or causal factors (means) that are managed in order to improve criteria (ends). The means at one level of strategy deployment may represent the ends at the next layer of the cascade. These informal means factors may be determined through causal analyses and experiments by local or system managers.

If the strategy is appropriately deployed throughout the organization, and the appropriate interactions are addressed, then improvement of cause factors at local levels should be reflected by improvement in system criteria. Putting this system to work also implies a measurement system, with corresponding operational definitions, measurement methods, and sampling strategies for each of the criteria.

Leaders must also prioritize and determine which criteria are the most important means to the desired strategic ends. They must determine which criteria will be considered for continuous improvement and which will be monitored for maintenance and stability. These priorities will likely change over time. This system of measurement should help managers focus their limited resources on strategically important criteria for improvement.

Superordinate Focus. The performance measurement system should encourage collaboration of various organizational units toward accomplishing superordinate system objectives, rather than competition among units to optimize local and focused, intermediate objectives. Superordinate criteria should capture the interactions among the various units and individuals required to collaborate in meeting system objectives. The means measures for achieving superordinate objectives should cascade throughout the organization and be causally linked to the accomplishment of system objectives. People should understand these linkages to know the purpose of their activities.

An example of superordinate focus through strategic transfunctional system management comes from the particle board industry. A particle board consists of wood particles bonded by chemical agents and has various industrial and construction applications. Furniture manufacturers represent one of the industrial users of particle board. For example, particle board is used for table tops and shelving. Furniture manufacturers typically laminate the surface of the particle board to give it a finished look.

The managerial leaders in a particle board company determined that their customers increasingly value smoother surfaces across a board and from board to board. Consistency in smoothness of surface of the particle board reduces variation in the lamination process, which yields higher quality, reduced scrap, less downtime, reduced costs and fewer headaches for the furniture manufacturer, and a better product for the consumer. The consumer gets a product that lasts longer, looks better, and costs less.

These leaders quickly discovered that achieving a smoother surface is a result of more than just the activities of one department like the sanding operation in the finishing department. Smoother surface results from the actions of departments throughout the plant. The actions compose the transfunctional system that must be managed at the plant level to achieve smoother surface.

The transfunctional system spans activities, processes, and tasks from the front end of the plant to the back. Raw materials procurement must ensure "consistent" wood chip "quality." Milling must produce the "desired" quality of fiber. Drying must achieve moisture content "appropriate" to the resin (bonding agent) properties. "Inappropriate" resin application may result in surface blemishes and defects. Blending and forming must ensure an evenly distributed mat (layered, unpressed wood particles) for the heat-pressing operation. In pressing, the board must be "cooked" under the "right" conditions, temperature, pressure, and time. Finishing must trim and sand the board to ensure a "quality" surface and board edge. Shipping must ensure "secure" delivery of smooth surface to the user. Maintenance must ensure the "effective" operation of equipment and machinery throughout the plant in the interest of smoother surface.

The challenge to the strategic system manager is to operationally define outcomes like consistent, quality, desired, appropriate, right, and effective. These outcomes must be managed simultaneously, for they interact to determine the resulting surface of the board. Causes of the outcomes must be determined and controlled. Managing such a mix of processes can be done more effectively when all these processes are in statistical control and variation is reduced. Measures and activities must be operationally defined. Decision criteria, methods, and procedures must be standardized. Furthermore, interrelationships among outcomes must be investigated. Reliable measurement methodologies must be established. Functional, departmental, and individual activities must be subservient to the transfunctional system for improving the smoothness of surface for the user.

Organizational policies and reward structures must also be consistent with strategic system objectives. For example, the procurement manager must not be rewarded simply for holding down raw materials cost, buying cheap chips without regard for wood chip "quality." Similarly, evaluating maintenance on machine downtime may discourage preventative maintenance and repair, while surface "quality" suffers. The strategic system manager must be personally responsible for the inputs, outputs, processes, procedures, and policies that transcend departmental boundaries and provide customer value. The system manager's perspective and system responsibility may even reach beyond traditional organizational constraints.

The demands of system management extend beyond the plant level to encompass the activities within the corporation. Consider the effect of activities and decisions of the marketing function. In consumer products manufacturing, promotional campaigns and issuance of coupons may create higher short-term demand, reaping havoc for plants that strain to push the abnormal load through the doors. Quality and costs may suffer, while profits do not appreciably improve by the temporarily inflated sales volume. Corporate accounting procedures also impact the plant outcomes. The required reports and evaluative measures impact managerial decisions and actions on maintenance policies, capital upgrades, raw material expenditures, and other operating expenses.

The production outcomes at the plant level are determined by strategic transfunctional systems that extend far beyond the control of any one departmental manager. (See Figure 8 for an illustration.) Someone must

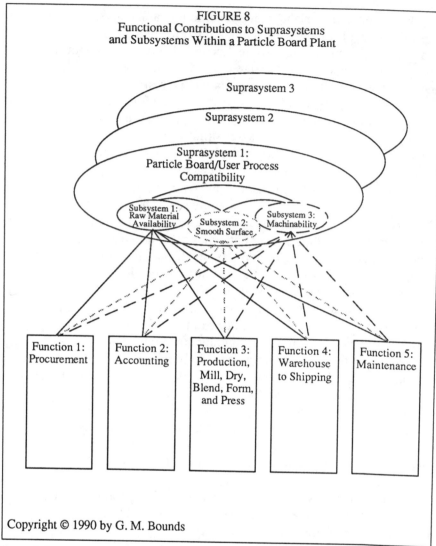

FIGURE 8
Functional Contributions to Suprasystems
and Subsystems Within a Particle Board Plant

"own" the suprasystems and subsystems and manage them for the provision of value for the customer. Performance measurements must direct the attention of managers in all positions toward improving strategic systems for customer value. Left unattended, uncoordinated, and unmanaged, the many functional activity and process architects construct a loosely connected, hodgepodge system that produces value-deficient outcomes.

The following discussion outlines the final characteristic of this alternative system: making a change to emphasize managerial behavior. Without this final component, full understanding and implementation of the forgoing suggestions is impossible. Putting in place a performance measurement system requires development of behavioral skills and understanding.

MAKING THE CHANGE

Managers must attend to the many aspects of customer value, and not just a few. They must move from a "short-term, hit the numbers this quarter, and run the existing system as hard as you can" orientation to a "long-term, provide value for the customer, and build and continually improve systems" approach. Managers must become investigative and creative thinkers. For many organizations, transformation is required not only in performance measures but also in managerial behaviors. Competing globally requires more than reliance on reactive problem solving, firefighting, administration, overseeing, and results-oriented managing.

Anyone who has attempted organizational change recognizes it is an incredibly complex task. It is difficult to reverse old habits. Resistance pops up; inertia is evident; people are threatened; insecurities abound; uncertainty arises. Most people prefer to have some direction and structure when experiencing the ambiguity and uncertainty that often arise during organizational transformation. If given no structure, they seek it and find it in the existing structures that encourage the status quo.

How do you change habitual managers to thinking managers? You can't simply point at the ideal model, continually tell them to run toward it, and scold them when they fail to progress. Nor do you simply eliminate the existing structure with which they have become so familiar, while providing no alternative structure. Removing familiar structures disturbs people during a period of transformation.

Just as you can't immediately take a baby directly from crawling to running the four-minute mile, you must be sensitive to people's needs for guidance in progressing from current state to ideal state. This is perhaps one reason why organizations have had such difficulty successfully "doing Deming." Managers need a transformational strategy with incremental progression from where they are to where they ought to be. What form does this direction take? The answers for managerial leaders are suggested in Figure 9 and are discussed below.

Leaders Provide Direction

Longstanding habits provide security and predictability, yet discourage thinking, analysis and creativity. How do managers change from managing through traditional control systems to managing collaboratively to

---

FIGURE 9
Suggestions for Leaders Making the Change

1. Leaders provide direction.
2. Change manager and leader behavior first.
3. Ensure consistency of behaviors and measures.
4. Avoid premature selection of new measures.
5. Treat the measurement system as an outcome.
6. Emphasize human development rather than evaluation:

    a. Change the criteria of judgment.
    b. Control systems, not people.
    c. Know and understand the behaviors required.
    d. Teach the behaviors.
    e. Role-model expected behaviors.

---

pursue superordinate system objectives for organizational competitiveness? Will the simple education of people allow them to fight the tide of the powerful forces, habits, and systems already in place? No. However, if the education takes place among the formal and informal leaders of the organization, broader managerial change is more likely.

The people at the top of the traditional organizational hierarchy are in the best position to alter organizational forces, to align them with the mission of providing value for the customer. This means CEOs, presidents, and vice presidents on a corporate scale, and divisional and plant managers on a local scale. The key is to emphasize behavioral measures in the initial stages of transformation, to monitor, and to expect behavioral change. To institute an alternative performance measurement structure like that described above, managers must engage in the appropriate managerial behaviors. Leaders must take the first bold steps to change managerial behavior by introducing new expectations and new performance measures.

Change Manager Behavior First

Subordinates have often been frustrated by demands from superiors for change, while superiors hypocritically allow existing control systems to remain. The demands, rewards, punishments, incentives, disincentives, recognitions, and appreciations administered through existing control systems, which are determined by managerial leaders, may prevent change. This means that behavioral change must come first and should begin at the top.

Change must start at the top because of two conditions: (1) the cascading nature of performance measures, that is, leaders set the focus for others, and (2) the necessity to base performance measures on knowledge of customer value, which is a leadership responsibility.

Prior to requiring behavior change at subordinate levels, managerial leaders must engage in the appropriate behaviors themselves. Failure in this leadership explains why a lot of organizations fail to successfully implement programs of change. Improvement projects may proliferate at subordinate levels, with no direction or integration from leaders. To avoid this lack of direction managerial leaders must determine what customers value. They must set and communicate strategy and identify related system criteria. This behavior change generates a knowledge base for the improvement activities of all employees.

These activities must be reiterated throughout the organization, as a part of the managerial leadership model. Leaders should convey the importance of continuous improvement and seek to have managers internalize this model of management as a part of their cultural values.

Ensure Consistency of Behaviors and Measurements

Once the managerial leaders initiate behavior change, they must quickly focus measures on customer value, to overcome the opposing and stagnating effects of the traditional control systems. They must engage managers in developing an alternative to the existing performance assessment and control systems. Otherwise, the existing system of controls will thwart the motivations of managers and divert attention and allegiance from traditional objectives. Participation in this learning and criteria development builds understanding and commitment among managers.

Some people defy the traditional controls left in place by leaders and do what they know is best for the organization. However, organizations should not rely on individual backbones to increase their competitiveness. Performance measures must reinforce a focus on customers and sustain the behavior change. Regular reviews should attend to these behavioral means as well as outcome measures. In addition, managers must eliminate any self-defeating practices. Old systems, structures, and roles must be replaced.

Avoid Premature Selection of New Measures

By necessity, managerial leaders must first determine which customers they will serve and what value they will create. Managers cannot just put in an entirely new set of performance measures without doing this homework. Otherwise, managers may initially choose the wrong measures at various levels of the organization, that is, measures that unexpectedly run counter to the organization's strategy by not being linked to customer-valued outcomes.

While leaders should not act prematurely, neither should they procrastinate or be petrified by fear of making a mistake. Leaders may make initial changes to reorient their organization toward customers, but these measures should not be regarded as fixed and unchanging. As leaders, anticipate that you will make mistakes and be prepared to make adjustments. This flexible attitude can help you get started.

If you attend to the framework and suggestions provided in this chapter and book, your performance measurement systems may be greatly improved. However, there will always be room for improvement. Changing performance measures represents only the beginning. The appropriateness of selected measures must be confirmed repeatedly over time.

As managers continue to engage in the activities of the managerial leadership model, the performance measures may be altered to reflect the most recent learning. Leaders must recognize that strategically relevant performance measures result from establishing the right behaviors. Without the appropriate managerial behaviors, the wrong performance measures will likely be selected, and the organization will be misguided. Thus, behavior change must accompany and lead changes in performance measures.

Treat the Measurement System as an Outcome

The installation of an alternative performance measurement system should be viewed as an outcome of appropriate managerial activity. The outcome is a system of measurement characterized by transfunctional and broad system criteria, strategic linkage with customer valued outcomes, competitive benchmarking, and a cascading structure of interrelated criteria. Furthermore, both behavioral criteria and results criteria are tied to the objective of increasing organizational competitiveness through customer value.

Emphasize Human Development Rather than Evaluation

Managerial leaders should move toward emphasis on developmental feedback and deemphasize evaluation for evaluation's sake. There is danger in linking formal performance evaluation to merit pay and bonuses.

The split roles of the evaluator, that is, counselor versus judge, are often incompatible and make difficult the continuous improvement process and personal coaching, mentoring and training.

We have seen and heard of managers who bang the table, rant and rave, and kick the chair when performance results fluctuate unfavorably; we have also seen them celebrate the upward fluctuations, inexplicable improvements. These reactions do no good if the means of improvement are not addressed. The "means" start with managerial behavior. In order to emphasize human development rather than evaluation, managerial leaders must change the criteria of judgment, control systems and not people, know and understand the behaviors required, teach the behaviors, and role model the behaviors.

Change the Criteria of Judgment. Judgments of behavioral performance, though distasteful to some people, will have to be rendered as an inherent part of determining developmental needs for managerial behavior. Judgment of performance will be placed in the developmental context, and not an evaluative, blame-casting atmosphere for determining who is at fault. The performance of workers within the system ultimately reflects the performance of the leaders and system owners in training, educating, coaching, enabling, provisioning, resourcing, and building systems. All employees must be taught the requirements of their job and be coached in learning through experience. Furthermore, leaders determine the criteria that form the basis for judgment.

In order to capture the attention of managers, a significant emotional event, such as an immediate change in criteria, helps to transform habitual managers into thinking managers. People become calloused to the table banging. They come to expect that the system will not be changed and that they must endure the consequences of fluctuations in system outcomes.

By contrast, upon a change in the criteria, they become nonhabitual, thinking, and inquisitive, attempting to discover the contingencies of the new situation. People are accustomed to inspection and evaluation; however, the emphasis has traditionally been on results rather than means. The old structure of inspection and evaluation should be initially recast with a focus on behavior, rather than simply bottom-line results. The tone of these "inspections" should be developmentally focused, that is, with the content focused on the behavioral prescriptions set forth in this volume. Leaders must make this bold move to change behavioral expectations.

Managerial leaders and managers should engage in a structured process for developing instruments for performance feedback and assessing developmental needs. These instruments should be anchored in the behavioral requirements of the managerial leadership model. Traditional performance appraisal instruments, such as graphic rating scales and forced distributions based on generic attributes, are deficient. Rather, these behavioral instruments must be descriptively robust, reliable, understandable, tailored to the organization, and appropriately focused. Methods are available for tailoring these instruments.

Control Systems, not People. Managerial leaders must seek to develop people who can control systems (in a statistical sense) and improve systems by reducing variation and consistently delivering what customers value. Managerial leaders should deemphasize control of people through evaluation and appraisal. Performance measurement should be used to develop individuals for continued learning and thinking and other appropriate behaviors. This change of emphasis may appear superficial or simply semantic to some, but it represents a significant attitude change.

Know and Understand the Behaviors Required. Emphasizing behavioral criteria and the development of human strategic capabilities imposes strict requirements on managerial leaders. Managerial leaders must be thoroughly knowledgeable of the behavioral requirements imposed on subordinates in order to be actively involved in behavior management. Managerial leaders must be attentive, involved, observant, and inquisitive regarding behaviors. The nature and content of questions asked by leaders gives clues and direction to others about expected role requirements.

Teach the Behaviors. Begin with training and education and guidance on the specific behaviors in which managers should engage, that is, knowing customer value, translating into operational definitions, and building systems that are capable of creating that value. Technical training may be necessary, but it will not suffice. People must develop the abilities of thinking, analysis, synthesis, creativity, adaptation, and continual self-renewal. People must be taught. The real test of whether leaders know the behaviors is whether they can teach the behaviors.

Periodically review, give feedback, and coach on individual progress on the means of attaining results, and not simply the results. Expect more and more from subordinates as they develop the capacity for improving systems. Do not expect people to instantly make the behavioral and mental shift to the ideal model. Acknowledge where they are initially and persist for change.

Leaders must regard human resources and capabilities as critical inputs to their systems and as a means to strategic advantage. They must continually improve the organization's capacity for providing customer value. The multiplier effects of investment in human resources should prove to be long lived.

Role-Model Expected Behaviors. Managerial leaders must clearly articulate and demonstrate the expected behaviors in their own actions. Actions scream louder than words.

BALANCE CHANGE WITH CONTINUITY

In managing organizational transformation, managerial leaders must be sensitive to the need to deliver current production promises and to run existing systems. Without continued transactions with customers and suppliers to continuously energize and provision existing systems, no transformation will be possible. Managerial leaders must be able to balance the need for continuous change and improvement and the need for predictable performance and maintenance of current system performance. There is no cookbook method for this balancing act. One must exercise judgment. The implications are that managerial leaders must attend, investigate, and be incredibly attuned to their systems and operations.

Indicators of progress, or bottom-line results, may suffer short-term drops, which often occur during periods of experimentation and transformation. However, over time improved outcomes should appear. They typically lag behind process or managerial behavioral changes (see Figure 10). Improved results may not be immediate. Persistence and gut-wrenching endurance may be required.

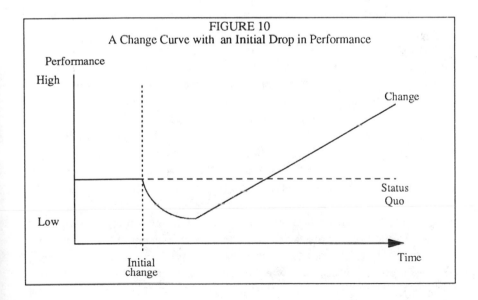

FIGURE 10
A Change Curve with an Initial Drop in Performance

CAVEAT EMPTOR

Let the buyer beware. Those who buy the notion that the performance measurement is a critical tool for management must be aware of an unresolved issue. We offer no solution but acknowledge the issue implied in this question: Is it possible to measure performance without creating undesirable behavior? Measurement is dangerous, since the act of measuring influences the results now and in the future. Even when measures are not employed in formal evaluation of individuals, measurement directs behavior.

The dynamic impact of performance measurement makes it even more important to pick the right measures. However, even when measures are appropriately picked, optimization at a local level may lead to suboptimization of system performance. To minimize the undesirable and unexpected effects of measurement, managers must remain intimate with the means of production of goods and services. Managers cannot remain competitive by just watching results and reacting to period variances or violation of specifications.

Some aspects of system performance may not show up on the selected measures. Complex interactions within the system must be anticipated and understood. Thus, managers must confirm system performance with customers.

Leaders must not regard performance measurement as a panacea. Do not assume that putting in place a performance measurement system will ensure that the appropriate behaviors will automatically result. Even if a person wants to fulfill performance expectations, he or she cannot do so without the knowledge and skills for the appropriate activity, or without the systems and resources, or without the direction and understanding of where and how to take action. Performance measurement remains ineffectual without action to improve the means of performance.

Danger lurks even in emphasizing behavior as a criterion. Specific managerial activities have been spelled out and prescribed in other chapters of this book. The authors of this book defined specifically required behaviors with some trepidation. First, there will be some practitioners who will go by "the recipe," lacking heart and spirit for the task, and excuse themselves from disappointing outcomes, and point to others as scapegoats. Second, upon reading this book, critics will likely emerge with rejoinders such as the following: management jobs cannot be operationalized; writing such specific "job descriptions" for managers is wrong because there is no "one best way" to do a managerial job. Such criticism rings with truth. These prescriptions should not be considered simple recipes for success in competitiveness. Competition precludes such simplicity. Furthermore, "thinking" by individual managers is a necessary ingredient that these authors cannot provide.

Because of intense competition, many managers in the field have recounted to these authors that they are "convinced that they have to do something differently," but they are "not sure what to do or how to begin." The behavioral activities outlined in this book provide a basis for beginning.

Beginners at this new approach to management should find these behavioral prescriptions a useful guide for their managerial activities. Those more advanced should find these behavioral prescriptions to be a firm foundation on which they can build and from which they can experiment to improve the foundation. Individual styles should usefully elaborate these basic activities, just as the artistic architect adds beauty to a functional building design. Most importantly, the prescriptions in this book should be executed by those who have internalized the purpose, are disposed to compete through customer value, and fully intend to succeed.

CONCLUSION

Creating an alternative approach to managerial performance measurement as outlined above provides direction and clear expectations to all employees. It also ensures that the existing system is eliminated, by replacing the existing performance evaluation and control system. Many organizations have attempted to work on improving customer value provision or continuous system improvement as a parallel activity, while not changing the existing rewards and performance evaluations. The results have not been adequate. Existing systems prevail in the long run. Thus, efforts to revise performance measurement and control systems must be given priority on the managerial agenda. Specific ownership for systems, processes, and tasks must be assigned, and corresponding continuous improvement must be behaviorally prescribed. Ideally, such revisions are supported and demanded by all facets of the organization.

REFERENCES

Deming, W. E. *Out of the Crisis*. Cambridge, Mass.: Massachusetts Institute of Technology, 1986.
Halberstam, D. *Summer of '49*. New York: Avon Books, 1988.
Reeve, J. "The Impact of Variation on Operating System Performance." In P. Turney (ed.), *Performance Excellence in Manufacturing and Service Organizations*, American Accounting Association, 1990, pp. 75-90.

Stoner, J. A., and C. Wankel. *Management (3rd ed.),* Englewood Cliffs, N.J.: Prentice-
    Hall, 1986.
Umble, M. M., and M. L. Srikanth. *Synchronous Manufacturing: Principles for World
    Class Excellence.* Cincinnati, Ohio: South-Western Publishing Co., 1990.

D. THE NEW ROLE OF TRADITIONAL FUNCTIONS

CHAPTER 17

ACTIVITY-BASED COST SYSTEMS FOR FUNCTIONAL INTEGRATION AND CUSTOMER VALUE

JAMES M. REEVE
Associate Professor of Accounting
University of Tennessee

SUMMARY

Organizations are asking questions such as, are all products profitable, should we accept this order, should we continue to do business with a customer, and what is the cost impact of process waste and improvement? These questions imply that organizations need to know the cost of product, process, and serving customers. Without such information firms are unable to establish direction with regard to product and customer strategies. These questions cannot be answered under traditional costing frameworks. Activity-based costing provides a methodological breakthough that can help supply operational and strategic knowledge.

INTRODUCTION

A metal machining company executive used the latest numerical control machine tools, control charts to lower variation in measured dimensions on parts, design of experiments to identify causes of scrap, and JIT techniques to eliminate waste in the process. Yet this executive didn't know his costs. *Knowing* cost is an important part of managing cross-functional processes. In this volume we have discussed the importance of process knowledge as a prerequisite to managing process improvement for purposes of increasing customer net value. Without process knowledge, all work is just a matter of opinion and guesswork. Similarly, strategic knowledge must be a prerequisite to strategic improvement. Without strategic knowledge of relative profitability and cost, decisions become just a matter of opinion, guess, or power to influence. Questions like the following must be answered with reliable economic data.

> What are the economic dynamics of process interactions as I engage in continuous process improvement?
> Should I outsource this part?
> Which customers and customer segments are my most profitable?
> What should I bid for this order?
> Are my pricing strategies in line with my costs?
> What will happen if my volume changes?
> What are my cost drivers, and how do they behave?

The machine tool executive was improving processes by making the firm flexible, low cost, and responsive to customers. Yet, without knowledge of cost position this firm was unable to translate this work into competitive strength. For this firm poor choices in bidding and accepting orders led to unprofitability. This company won bids that it thought it should have lost and lost bids that it thought it should have won. The jobs it won later turned out to be jobs it regretted ever bidding. Something was wrong.

What was wrong was an incomplete understanding of the cost drivers in the organization. Managing toward customer value involves making decisions with reliable data – whether data are about customers, process knowledge, or products. Without data work becomes unfocused or misdirected. Knowledge of cost and profit can help a firm unveil hidden profit opportunity and eliminate hidden losses.

Unfortunately, conventional accounting systems appear to be constructed solely for the purpose of obscuring the true cost of decision alternatives. Conventional internal accounting systems reflect a hierarchical organizational approach that is rapidly becoming obsolete. The old philosophy of optimizing and directing narrow spans of control must give way to a new philosophy based on cross-functional flexibility. A conventional accounting system, designed around a cost center mentality, assigns cost to department and cost center managers. The shortcomings of this model center around three false assumptions. First, cost is best controlled at the point of incurrence. Second, optimizing the performance of each center of control (department) will lead to global optimization. Third, costs are related to products based on volume of output.

With respect to the first false assumption, the point where cost is incurred may have little to do with cost elimination and control. Organizations are much more complex than the simple financial model would imply.

This is known, yet the financial system continues to fail. Consider the conversion cost of a machining center. The processes that interact with this machining center probably account for 80 percent of the variation in cost efficiency for this center. Processes such as upstream machining, the tool replacement system, the equipment maintenance system, the raw materials procurement system, the machinist training system, and the part design system all interact to impact the performance of the machine work center. The cost is incurred and accounted in the machining operation, yet decisions made in other systems impact the performance of this system. Correcting this shortcoming is by no means easy, yet a focus on the critical *activities* of the firm is a first step toward cross-functional cost analysis.

The second false assumption assumes that optimization in the functional areas will result in the complete system being optimized. There are many reasons why this is not so. The interrelationships between functional areas are complex. Frequently, cost interactions make it very reasonable to incur cost in one area in order to obtain greater offsetting benefits in another. For example, there are many interactions between material price and downstream activities. One firm discovered that a higher quality and higher priced raw material would cause a lower rate of residue buildup. As a result, the cleanout frequencies decrease substantially. The point is that simplistic focus on the purchase price variance report in the procurement function would prevent this firm from discovering a strategy that lowers total cost. The strategy only becomes apparent by comparing across multiple activities.

The third flawed assumption relates to traditional product costing techniques that incorrectly treat overhead costs as variable with unit volume. This assumption is incorrect when there are significant overhead activities unrelated to unit-level volume. As a result of heavy reliance on volume-based cost drivers, such as direct labor or direct machine hours, low-volume products will appear highly profitable (when they are not), whereas high-volume products will appear unprofitable (when they are not). Moreover, there is some question if the product is the appropriate final cost object, as assumed under most conventional systems. The customer and major customer channels are the true final cost objects. Conventional systems fail to account for costs incurred outside the factory and, therefore, fail to reveal the cost to serve customers. Firms need to know not only about product profitability, but also about customers and customer segment profitability.

This chapter presents a new costing framework, known as activity-based costing, to address the false assumptions outlined above. The activity-based architecture represents a significant improvement over conventional costing approaches. However, we must remember that no costing system will explain the organization perfectly. Cost numbers are ends measures that can be subject to severe measurement error. Deming rightly calls some figures unknown or unknowable. Activity-based systems can make some of what was previously unknown more knowable.

CROSS-FUNCTIONAL INTEGRATION

Business leaders recognize their enterprise's need for greater cross-functional decision making, coordination, and integration of activities. In pursuing these objectives senior managers have reduced the number of levels in the organization, engaged in team-based management, and become managerial leaders. Along with organizational changes adjustments must be made in the information system to support cross-functional decision making. Activity-based costing represents such a change.

Consider the typical framework found in many organizations (see Figure 1). Manufacturing is separated from marketing/sales, in terms both of organization and financial responsibility. Manufacturing is given the responsibility for cost. The basic assumption is that the cost is controlled at the point that it is incurred. Since most cost is incurred at the point of manufacture, the cost system is focused on, and manufacturing is given the responsibility of, controlling and reducing cost. This philosophy is driven further down into the plant through subdividing reporting and cost control to the operating departments.

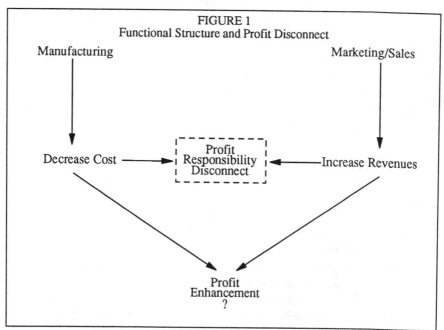

FIGURE 1
Functional Structure and Profit Disconnect

The marketing/sales organization usually has a very different mission. This part of the organization is responsible for sales volume and market share. The tools used to impact volume and share include new product introductions, promotions, cash-back offers, merchandising efforts, and advertising. Therefore, revenue responsibility lies with marketing/sales, while cost responsibility lies with manufacturing. Will optimizing behavior inside manufacturing with respect to cost and inside marketing with respect to revenue necessarily lead to enhanced profitability? There is no reason to believe so. The problem lies with the interdependencies between decisions made at one place on the performance of another.

In marketing, not all decisions that result in increased revenues are profitable. Marketing may attempt to respond to a decline in sales by engaging in promotional efforts. Along with increasing revenues temporarily, these promotional efforts may add artificial demand variability that may have substantial cost impacts owing to production surging. Another example is accepting orders from marginal customers. Not all customers are the same from a profitability perspective. Some customers demand more activities from the organization than others. Small orders from customers requiring many activities may not be profitable. Only an activity-based cost system can indicate this.

Similarly, manufacturing decisions that appear to reduce cost may in fact be unwise from a global system perspective. Manufacturing product in long runs or delaying a switchover may improve efficiencies and unit costs, but such behavior causes the logistics system to be unresponsive to customers. As a result, revenue can be lost owing to the inability of manufacturing to respond quickly to customer needs.

What is needed is a system to explicitly link the organization by assigning profit responsibility for the complete product delivery system. In this way, revenues and costs no longer remain separated in responsibility but are formally brought together. Therefore, decisions with both revenue and cost impacts can be evaluated in terms of profitability and not on the basis of just one side of the equation. However, for this to be successful the profitability must be determined from the activities of the firm.

An activity-based cost (ABC) system allows the firm to engage in cost management inside the plant and profit management from the marketing organization. The accompanying table lists potential uses of ABC for improving decisions.

Manufacturing-Cost Management	Marketing-Profit Management
1. Product/package design	1. Pricing and bidding
2. Evaluation of economic tradeoffs	2. Product profitability analysis
3. Elimination of waste	3. Customer profitability analysis
4. Investment justification	4. Segment profitability analysis

The sections that follow focus on the advantages of activity-based cost systems in addressing these issues.

THE ACTIVITY-BASED COST (ABC) SYSTEM STRUCTURE

Activities form the foundation of an activity-based cost system. Examples of activities include moving, inspecting, receiving, shipping, processing orders, selling, and merchandising. Figure 2 provides a conceptual diagram of an activity-based system. Activities consume resources and are traced to cost objects. Possible cost objects include vendors, products, and customers. The decision capabilities of an activity-based cost system are illustrated by the dotted lines in the figure. Knowledge of the cost of activities, in and of themselves, supports efforts to improve processes. Once activities are traced to cost objects then additional strategic insight is made available. The following sections discuss the major components of the structure illustrated in Figure 2.

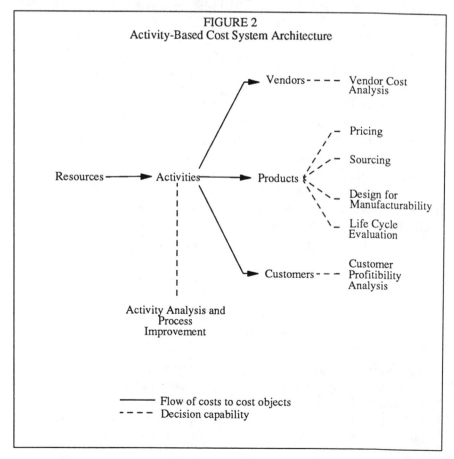

FIGURE 2
Activity-Based Cost System Architecture

ACTIVITY ANALYSIS AND PROCESS IMPROVEMENT

Cost information can help continuous process improvement in three ways: identifying financial leverage, making tradeoffs, and selecting alternatives. For example, are all continuous improvement efforts the same, or do some have more financial leverage than others? Must tradeoffs within the plant be made, and if so, would it be useful to understand the economic dynamics of the tradeoff, and finally if there is more than one continuous improvement strategy, which one is the best strategy? All these questions beg for an economic answer.

Leverage Points

When an organization embraces continuous improvement, the first question that usually arises is where to begin. There is a tremendous temptation to engage in a shotgun strategy of working on many systems simultaneously. Without coordination and prioritization, many improvement efforts are likely to be of trivial significance. The questions are, would a rifle shot strategy make more sense? Are some improvement efforts likely to provide more leverage than others, and how are these opportunities identified?

In the face of limited financial and time resources, the priorities must be established for identifying those continuous improvement efforts that are likely to yield the largest benefits. Making such a determination can be aided through the support of financial analysis. For example, are all setup improvement projects equal? The stated imperative of improving setups may be misplaced if the requirement is to treat all setup improvements equally. For example, setups on nonbottleneck resources should have a lower priority than those on bottleneck resources.

In a defense plant an activity analysis indicated that significant resources were invested in engineering changes. This process was a major cross-functional system that operated across the functions of material management, procurement, marketing, and engineering. The activity analysis led to focus on reducing the number of occasions that engineering change orders (ECO) were implemented on released drawings and improving the underlying process of each implementation. The objective of continuous improvement is to eliminate the impact of engineering change intensity on newly released drawings. This could be communicated to engineering by budgeting an amount of engineering support based on the cost driver, the number of ECOs. The purpose would be to provide an incentive to begin bundling engineering changes on recently released parts. In this way, a variety of changes could be incorporated simultaneously rather than discretely. Design engineers sensitized to the cost per change would avoid incorporating changes one at a time. The activity-based cost system would modify behavior toward this continuous improvement result.

A building products manufacturer makes asphalt shingle products. The nature of this process requires that tar be applied to the shingle base before the exterior granules are applied. The critical control condition is the temperature of the tar. The temperature operates within a given level of variation. The cost of the temperature being too low is vastly greater than the cost of the temperature being too high. When the temperature is too cool, unscheduled downtime is required to perform a very difficult cleanout. In contrast, when the temperature is too hot, the tar exhibits poor adhesive quality for the granules and, therefore, results in high scrap. The relative costs of scrap versus cleanout, combined with the natural variation in the temperature, are used to determine the optimal nominal temperature value for this process. Moreover, the savings potential for removing temperature variation can be estimated from these relationships – namely, if variation in temperature can be reduced, the amount of scrapped shingles will be reduced. As a result, temperature variation was targeted as a critical continuous improvement objective.

One study evaluated the significant cost drivers in a papermaking operation.[1] The objective of the study was to determine the most important contributor to material waste cost in this operation. The study evaluated cost drivers such as shift effects, crew effects, crew change, grade, and grade change. The study determined that grade change was a significant contributor to yield variation and that papermaking improvement efforts should focus on making grade changes costless. In addition, the significant material and equipment losses suffered during grade changes were causing the firm to produce in long runs, thereby increasing the lead time to customers. The activity study revealed an important source of waste and targeted improvement effort in the plant.

A major electronics firm uses the output of activity analyses to build financial measures of waste.[2] The largest sources of waste prioritize the continuous improvement work. In one application the sales order process was determined to produce wasted resources when customer orders were returned. The cost of returned orders included the direct and indirect costs of the firm, plus the direct and indirect costs of the customer and the firm's

1. T. L. Albright and J. M. Reeve, "The Impact of Material Yield Related Cost Drivers on Process and Product Cost," unpublished working paper, University of Tennessee, November 1990.
2. F. T. Fuller, "How to Construct and Use a Productivity Loss Index," *National Productivity Review* (Spring 1988): 99-113.

vendor. These costs included the costs of freight, shipping and receiving personnel, salespersons' time, documenting, packing, and repacking. The total cost of each return multiplied by the number of returns (the cost driver) provided a measure of lost value.

Financial analysis is not always required to begin continuous improvement efforts. Sometimes, the size of the problem is obvious to all, and there is no financial guidance required. However, continuous improvement should result in improved quality and lower cost. If this is not the case, then effort could be better invested.

Analysis of Interactions

Most continuous improvement strategies involve some sort of process interaction. The cost in one area offsets greater savings in another. Without cost numbers the interaction frequently involves comparisons of numbers in different measurement units. For example, the reduction in batch sizes will increase the frequency of material moves, purchase part receipts, shipments, and the like. How far should the production lot size be reduced within a given manufacturing capability? Furthermore, what impact would anticipated changes in that capability have on lot size reduction? The physical activity of the facility should be translated to common terms, such as dollars, so that a rough estimate of the interaction can be determined.

An aluminum can manufacturer faced an interaction between purchasing raw material with a higher tin content against reducing the cost of an enameling operation. The enameling operation was very energy intensive. The interaction analysis evaluated the impact of less enameling-related cost against greater raw material cost. In this case, the total cost of the operation was reduced if expensive raw material with higher tin content was used in the process. Again, the reasonableness of this strategy is not obvious on the front end. Only after "working the numbers" does the engineer have a sense of the relative attractiveness of engaging this strategy.

Another example of an ABC system supporting difficult interaction analyses is in the area of developing optimal maintenance and machine component replacement strategies. The critical costs of activities that enter into this analysis are the cost of an on-line failure and the cost of an off-line replacement. These represent cost drivers related to process activities and not to products. For example, maintenance-related activities are driven by the number of processes, not by product strategy (usually).

We would expect the cost of an on-line failure to be greater than an off-line replacement in most situations. A formula has been derived to find the optimal time to replace a component, given that one wishes to minimize the frequency of off-line replacement and completely avoid costly on-line failures. There is a unique cost minimum which is the interaction between these two activities that gives the optimal replacement frequencies.

Many companies are beginning to evaluate the cost dynamics of the extended customer value system as part of their continuous improvement effort. The objective is to share cost savings with system participants by reducing the cost drivers of services. As an example, a customer of a major consumer goods company wishes to enjoy preferential pricing by providing accurate forecasts of product needs. Accurate forecasts reduce the logistical complexity of the consumer goods company and, therefore, reduce their costs. The analyst needs to estimate the amount of savings that are related to accurate forecasts to form the basis of benefit sharing among the producer and customer. These savings will emanate from reductions in surge-related activities (overtime, excess capacity, warehouse moves, etc.)

Operational Improvement Tactic Selection

One of the clear uses of ABC in continuous improvement is aiding the team in selecting one improvement tactic from an array of seemingly reasonable alternatives. Without activity information, the selection criteria break down into argument based on conjecture rather than argument based on fact.

A consumer electronics assembly plant conducted an activity analysis of its procurement system. Purchased parts were divided into an A, B, C classification based on the significance of the part in assembly. The A & B parts represented 5,000 invoices for $80 million of purchased value. The C parts represented 15,000 invoices for only $6 million of invoiced value. Clearly, the C parts were requiring a much greater activity intensity than their value to the organization would seem to imply. This company used an activity-based system to evaluate three possible alternatives toward improving the process of purchasing C parts. The three alternatives were (1) purchase each C item once a year, (2) purchase each C item twice a year, or (3) use a Kanban replenishment system with a single vendor for all C items.[3]

These three choices all solve the problem in one way or another. Choices 1 and 2 involve difficult tradeoffs between additional inventory storage and carrying costs, against fewer activities related to purchasing/receiving. As mentioned previously, the activity-based cost system is expressly designed to evaluate these tradeoffs. Moreover, the activity-

---

3. This example comes from a discussion with Peter B. B. Turney.

based system can be used to model the overall cost consequences of each alternative and to identify the optimal choice. In this case, selection 3 was the most optimal. C parts were replaced on visual inspection by the vendor. This vendor provided a monthly invoice for all C parts. Therefore, counting, receiving, moving, unloading, and stocking activities were eliminated, while keeping inventory at a minimum.

A consumer products company was faced with three alternatives for reducing the amount of overpack in a packaged good. The overpack problem could be significantly reduced by purchasing a higher grade of raw material, increasing the residence time in an upstream mixing operation, or doing more frequent pack head cleanouts. The tactical selection was not obvious. For example, doing more frequent cleanouts involved more than just the cost of labor and lost time on the packing line for doing the work. More frequent cleanouts required much more supervisor attention, more frequent moves of finished product to the stores area, and greater complexity in scheduling the facility upstream. As a result of the activity analysis, it was determined that greater residence time in the mix area was the least costly solution to the problem.

Activities of enterprises can be used to assess improvement priority, evaluate complex cross-functional interactions, and aid in operational tactic selection. The next sections discuss the use of ABC to support strategic evaluations with respect to vendors, products, and customers as illustrated in Figure 2.

VENDOR AS THE COST OBJECT

A cost object is a final attachment point of cost. Activities consume resources, and cost objects consume activities in the ABC framework. The most common cost object in most enterprises is the product. In an ABC system the cost object is the focal point for activities. Activities are related to the cost object by way of cost drivers. Cost drivers are physical measures that relate the cost of the activity to the cost object. For example, an activity might be incoming inspection. The cost driver for this activity could be the number of purchased goods receipts. Every receipt may need to be inspected. By dividing the cost of the inspection activity by the number of receipts, an inspection cost per receipt is determined. This is the cost driver rate. The cost per activity unit can then be traced to a cost object by linking the activity to that object.

If the vendor is the cost object, then an organization can determine the extended system cost of various vendors. Very few companies have attempted to do this, but the idea is to expand the understanding of the cost of purchased material beyond purchase price. For example, one vendor may have processes that are in demonstrated control; therefore, our incoming inspection activities are reduced. By contrast, another vendor's quality performance forces the firm to inspect 100 percent of incoming parts. These two vendors' costs to the firm are influenced by their different activity demands. The activity-based cost system gives an opportunity to combine purchase price information with extended system costs in order to evaluate total vendor cost performance.

In this case the cost per driver unit, such as number of inspections, is traced to one vendor but not the other. The vendor with the 100 percent inspection will be attributed cost from the inspection-related activities at the appropriate rate. The vendor without inspection will not accumulate these driver units, therefore, the cost traced to this vendor will be less. The result is a management report that shows the total cost of vendors, decomposed by activity intensities.

PRODUCT AS THE COST OBJECT

The most traditional cost object is the product. For obvious reasons organizations need to know the cost of product. Therefore, one is not surprised to discover that most activity-based cost systems designed to date have been designed around the product as the cost object. Conventional systems are designed with a fundamental flaw. They assume that cost can be divided into two basic types, fixed and variable. Variable costs are conventionally defined as costs that change in relation to increases and decreases in units of production. This definition does not capture manufacturing reality. Activity-based systems take a more sophisticated perspective.

Levels of Product Cost

Figure 3 illustrates product costing under activity-based approaches. Activities consume resources in at least four distinct ways.[4] The first relationship is the conventional approach. Activities consume resources in direct relationship with units of production. So, for example, machine and direct labor resources are expended in incremental units of production. In this case reasonable cost drivers to trace activities to products are direct labor hours or machine hours to make a product.

---

4. The concept of different activity levels was first introduced by Robin Cooper, "Cost Classification in Unit-Based and Activity-Based Manufacturing Cost Systems," *Journal of Cost Management* (Fall 1990), pp. 4-14. He identified unit, batch, product, and process level activities. In addition, there are customer, channel, and project level activities.

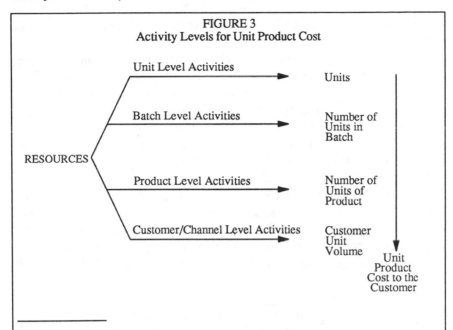

FIGURE 3
Activity Levels for Unit Product Cost

The second major relationship between activities and products involves batch level drivers. Batch level activities relate to the processing of batches of product, not individual units. There are many transactions of this type. To illustrate, consider the within-plant logistical system. Raw material is received in batches, inspected in batches, and moved to raw material stores in batches; production is scheduled in lot sizes; work in process is transferred by batch; shipping is done by order size; production scheduling is for batch runs; machines are set up for a lot size; and so on. The point is that these activities relate more to the batch than they do to individual units. For example, receiving does not receive individual units but batches of units.

Separate identification of batch level activities is important from a product-costing perspective, because the cost system should be sensitive to batch size diversity within the facility. Batch size diversity means some products may be manufactured in small lot sizes, while others in large lot sizes. The batch level costs relating to each run may be the same, but the number of units in each batch different. Therefore, the batch level costs should be divided by the number of units in the batch in order to determine the correct unit cost. As a result, products manufactured in small lots will end up absorbing greater unit cost than those in larger lots for a given level of batch level cost intensity.

To illustrate, consider costs related to activities such as billing, order receiving, shipping, changeovers, material moves, and inspections (first piece). These costs may be incurred equally for an order for 1,000 units as for an order of 10 units. If this is the case, then the unit cost for the order of 10 is really much greater than the unit cost for an order of 1,000. An activity-based cost system captures this reality by attaching cost at the order level for activities consumed by orders, as opposed to assuming that all activities are proportional to the labor (or machine) time per unit. To continue, if the cost per order was determined to be $1,000 from the ABC system, then an order of 1,000 units would have a cost impact of $1 per unit. An order of 10 units would have a cost impact of $100 per unit. Under the conventional approach, overhead is associated to product by direct labor (or machine) hours. As a result, the unit costs in the 1,000 unit and 10 unit orders would be the same, because each unit takes the same number of direct labor (machine) hours to manufacture. This can be a dangerous misconception, because the activities listed above are associated not with manufacturing units but with manufacturing batches of product.

Not only are there batch level activities, but there are activities that relate only to the complete product line, and not to either batches or units of product. These are product level activities. Examples of product level activities include engineering activities on products and part numbers, procurement activities to establish vendors for specific part numbers, numerical control (NC) programming costs to machine a particular part, advertising activities for a particular product, and dedicated machinery for a particular product. These activities must be divided by the volume of production in the product line in order to determine an appropriate product unit cost.

With respect to product level costs, the existence of both activity diversity across products and/or total volume diversity across products gives rise to a need for an activity-based system as will be illustrated below. Activity diversity means that the amount of dollars dedicated to a particular product is different across the product line, such as different engineering support levels. Volume diversity is when the total production volume across the product line is different. Volume diversity is not the same as batch diversity. A facility can possess very little batch diversity and still have total volume diversity by manufacturing in very small lots under a JIT philosophy.

For an example of the product level costs, suppose a discrete parts manufacturing facility manufactures a component that is common to many product applications (producing 10,000 per year) and also manufactures a component that is used in only special situations (producing 100 per year). If the engineering costs and NC programming costs for each component part total $15,000, then the cost per unit is different because of the different volumes. The common component has a cost of $1.50 per use, while the special component costs $150 per use. It is important to notice the incentive effects of such a cost system. The cost of noncommonality in component design is now visible. This information can be used to change the behavior of engineers toward designing products with common components. There is a cost penalty for designing products with unique components. The use of activity-based systems to support design for manufacturability is discussed in more detail in a later section of this chapter.

Recognition of unit, batch, and product level activity relationships changes traditional thinking with regard to volume changes. The classical approach is to segregate fixed and variable costs, and then conduct cost-volume-profit analysis from these data. The problem is in the definition of variable costs. As discussed above, costs are variable with activities other than unit changes. Under activity-based accounting, costs are variable with units, batch activity, and product code diversity. This distinction can help a firm understand cost behavior with much greater confidence.

For example, consider three firms facing a decline in volume. In one firm the decline in volume is characterized by customers purchasing as frequently as in the past but with half the order size. The second firm loses half its customers (representing half its volume). A third firm loses volume by dropping products that represent half its sales volume. The cost consequences of each of these scenarios are entirely different. The first scenario is the worst. Loss of half the volume by losing half of each order size does nothing to eliminate batch or product level costs. There will be the same number of batch level activities, but just spread over fewer units per batch. Therefore, the first scenario will result in the most adverse profit situation.

In the second scenario, the batch activity is halved with the unit volume. This is because half the orders are lost, and therefore half the batch activities triggered by orders are also eliminated. As a result, there is opportunity for greater cost savings. Similarly, the third firm has halved product level costs because the product line has been reduced. Again, cost savings are possible in the product level activities. In a more realistic situation the loss in volume will be combinations of unit, batch, and product changes. Only an activity-based system would be able to analyze the sensitivity of cost to such complex volume changes.

A fourth level discussed later in this chapter involves customer level activities. These activities are related to customers and not products.

Product Strategy

In the case of product strategy, the activity-based cost system allows management to assess the consequences of product line proliferation. Excessive variation in the product line occurs when decisions are made to expand it unprofitably beyond a level valued by the marketplace. The strategic consequences of such a strategy have not been well understood, since the cost of complexity introduced by such a strategy has not been documented in most firms. The cost of complexity can represent excess resource commitments in the form of product changeovers, production control, inventory management, inspections, material movement, and the like. Without information on the cost of activities, the cost consequences of product line complexity are averaged across the complete product line. As a result, firms have unwittingly allowed product lines to expand to the point where 20 percent of the line contributes 80 percent of the revenue, and must therefore support the remaining 80 percent of the line that may be unprofitable.

A manufacturing facility responsible for manufacturing a wide variety of products in which there is a great deal of batch size and product level diversity will frequently be subjected to significant cost burdens. In traditional accounting systems complexity costs are frequently hidden by spreading the cost across all products through the burden rate. These systems erroneously assume that all costs are consumed by the activity of machine or direct labor hours. As a result, the cost system reports the cost per unit of low-volume products as nearly the same as large-volume products, since they take similar hours to produce per unit. The manufacturing reality is often counter to this.

An example is the case of a precision machining company. Representative product costs for seven products are shown in Table 1. In the third column are the product costs under a system based on the traditional machine hour. The fourth column is the product costs determined under the activity-based cost system. The ABC system assigned order-related, setup, inspection, and machine downtime costs to the products in the proportion that they were consumed by products. Therefore, small runs had very high costs relative to what was traditionally thought. The diversity in the product line caused this firm to operate at three shifts, while equipment ran at only 40 percent of capacity. The low-capacity utilization was due to excessive setup time, material loading time, and waiting for inspectors at each production run changeover. All the small-lot runs required setup-related costs, first piece inspection, bar stock moves, shipping, and order processing at the same rate as larger lots.

TABLE 1			
Product Costs: Traditional Versus Activity-Based Cost System			
Representative Products	Annual Volume	Traditional Unit Cost	Activity-Based Unit Cost
A-101	5,000	$4.50	$3.95
X-002	150	$11.50	$125.80
D-400	15,000	$8.50	$7.50
X-505	650	$15.00	$78.20
X-050	450	$22.00	$130.70
A-201	8,000	$16.80	$16.30
A-301	10,000	$12.50	$11.30

The product cost report illustrated in Table 1 changed management's policy of accepting all orders over $50 to one of accepting only orders in excess of $5,000. The report revealed that the old strategy caused misuse of capacity. Under the new strategy, management was able to increase shift throughput by reducing the amount of product line complexity. Moreover, the product cost report demonstrated the importance of investing in flexibility. The new order acceptance policy was coupled with investments in direct numerical control technology and operator training in statistical process control in order to reduce the opportunity cost of idle equipment.

Activity-based systems in environments characterized by a short cycle and other worldclass manufacturing capabilities have a role to play.[5] One might erroneously conclude that activity-based systems will promote large batch production, which is counter to a short-cycle philosophy. The move to short-cycle manufacturing is expressly designed to remove the economic impact of batch level activities. The objective is to produce and sell an order of one unit at the same unit profit as an order of 1,000. This can be accomplished only by removing the cost of batch level activities such as setups, inspections, moves, and receiving. JIT strategies attack these activities by driving setups down, placing adjacent processes in close geographic proximity, and eliminating inspections through use of statistical process control. As a result, a whole class of cost driver is eliminated, namely, the batch level cost. Therefore, from an activity-based design perspective many batch level drivers will lose their significance; however, product level drivers, super-unit drivers, and customer level drivers will remain. These last two are discussed in the following sections of this chapter.

---

5. For an extensive discussion of these issues, see Peter B. B. Turney and J. M. Reeve, "The Impact of Continuous Improvement on the Design of Activity-Based Costing Systems," *Journal of Cost Management* (Summer 1990), pp. 43-50.

Discrete Part Manufacturers Versus Continuous Processors

The design of an activity-based cost system is influenced by whether an operation is discrete part or continuous/batch processing.[6] Figure 4 illustrates the difference between these two types of manufacturing. Discrete part manufacturing involves managing part number diversity, such that the right part arrives at the right place in the right quantities with the right quality. The high level of complexity gives rise to significant coordination-related overhead in the form of quality control, material management, production control, material movement, and procurement activities.

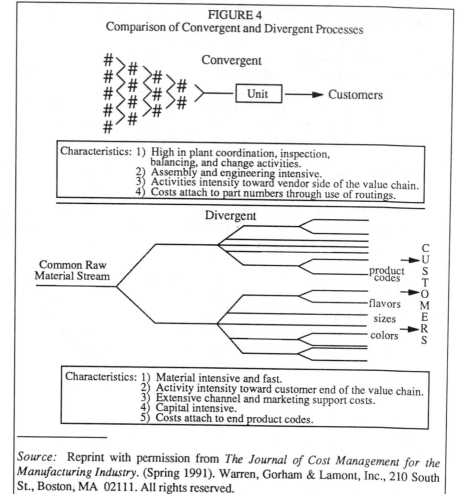

FIGURE 4
Comparison of Convergent and Divergent Processes

Characteristics: 1) High in plant coordination, inspection, balancing, and change activities.
2) Assembly and engineering intensive.
3) Activities intensity toward vendor side of the value chain.
4) Costs attach to part numbers through use of routings.

Characteristics: 1) Material intensive and fast.
2) Activity intensity toward customer end of the value chain.
3) Extensive channel and marketing support costs.
4) Capital intensive.
5) Costs attach to end product codes.

Source: Reprint with permission from *The Journal of Cost Management for the Manufacturing Industry.* (Spring 1991). Warren, Gorham & Lamont, Inc., 210 South St., Boston, MA 02111. All rights reserved.

6. For an extensive discussion, see J. M. Reeve, "Cost Management for the Continuous Process Environment," *Journal of Cost Management* (Spring 1991), forthcoming.

The discrete part manufacturer is focused on the vendor side of the customer value system. Not surprisingly then, many of the original examples of activity-based costing are in the discrete part manufacturing environment to explain traditional in-plant overhead costs more accurately.

In contrast, the continuous and batch material processors exhibit the greatest complexity toward the customer end of the customer value system. Common raw material streams are changed through the addition of color, additives, size change, specification changes, flavors, and the like to produce a large end-product code variety. This end-code variety drives the complexity-related costs in these environments. The complexity occurs in the line switchovers near the end of the manufacturing process, the post-plant-logistics system, and marketing-related costs. Unlike the discrete part manufacturer there is very little relative activity investment in production control, procurement, and material management. The materials requirements planning (MRP) system has an inverted bill of materials and is relatively easy to manage. The activity intensity is greatest in the post-plant logistics systems. Therefore, the activity-based cost system should be oriented toward channel sales and logistics-related costs. Cost drivers such as the number of invoice lines shipped become important.

Design for Manufacturability

One objective of a worldclass manufacturing organization is to produce product variety at low cost. A tension emerges between the marketing and manufacturing organization in terms of how much product variety can be accommodated without introducing excessive complexity costs. One way to minimize the impact of complexity is to promote functional diversity through use of process commonality. The manufacture of different product combinations using similar processes causes economies of scale on those processes and, therefore, will promote economies of scope (variety) across the product line. The activity-based system can promote behaviors consistent with product diversity through process commonality.

Value engineering reduces non-functional differences between products that are unrelated to critical customer-defined product requirements. Products may be redesigned, for example, to eliminate nonstandard components and subassemblies that do not add features required by the customer. As a result, hundreds of individual parts may be eliminated from a product by imposing commonality of design.

As another example, package goods manufacturers produce goods in a number of size varieties. These size varieties are customer-driven requirements. The package design engineer, however, can impose uniform packaging specifications by using common rounds. Common rounds refer to the diameter of the container bottom. The key is to accommodate size differences in the height of the container, not the diameter. The reason is because package lines must be set up for a given diameter. Size changes by diameter will result in expensive line changeovers, whereas size change by height is relatively simple. The cost driver is not the number of different package sizes, but the number of different bottom diameters. An activity-based cost system that attributes cost on the basis of the number of bottom diameters will lead the organization to minimize the number of bottom diameters.

One difficulty of design engineering is incorporating difficult design tradeoffs in order to achieve customer performance requirements. This is especially the case when the product is designed for custom application by the customer. In this environment a worldclass cost system needs to accomplish two objectives: to support design engineering for low cost, and to support sales/marketing in bidding jobs for custom products. Activity-based cost systems are now being designed to address these two needs through the use of "super-unit" cost drivers. A super-unit cost driver is one in which the cost is attributed to the product on the basis of product attributes. This is radically different than attributing cost on the basis of process characteristics such as direct labor hours or machine hours.

As shown in Figure 5, cost can be managed through process cost drivers and product attribute drivers. Process cost drivers have been discussed previously. Product attributes such as the number of colors, number of holes, perimeter dimension, number of additives, and number of insertions are examples of product attributes on which cost drivers can be based.

A simple example is a small company that manufactures designed T-shirts. The critical aspect of the operation is the number of colors printed on the shirt. Each color must be silk-screened separately, have a unique silk screen template, be mixed and prepared, and be cleaned out before the next run. Therefore, the number of colors on the shirt is a significant cost driver. The cost system can be designed so that the salesperson can quote a bid based on the size of the order (since the order is the other major cost driver to capture batch-size effects) and number of colors. This change in the cost system away from direct labor hours helped this company compete intelligently for new business.

In a much more complex setting, a circuit board manufacturer uses a very sophisticated cost driver system based mainly on the product attributes of printed circuit boards.[7] This facility must be able to produce a high variety of custom circuit boards for many different customers in many

---

7. R. Cooper, and P. B. B. Turney, *Powell Electronics: Printed Circuit Board Division*, Harvard Business School Case, 189-054, 1989.

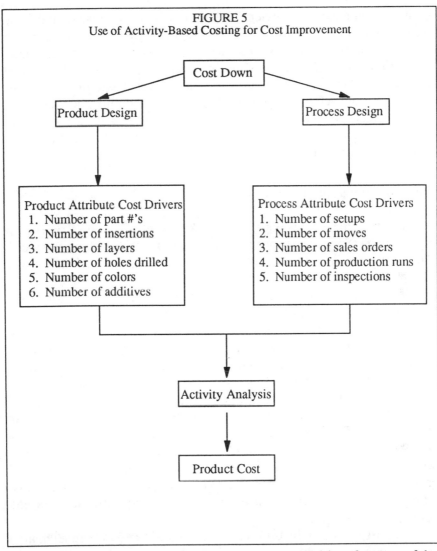

FIGURE 5
Use of Activity-Based Costing for Cost Improvement

different batch sizes. As a result, sales order is a cost driver for most of the batch-related activities in the facility. In addition, this company uses super-unit cost drivers such as the number of layers, board perimeter, number of holes drilled, number of points masked, board square feet, and number of tests. These super-unit drivers replace the traditional direct labor and machine hours in order to support job quoting. In addition, the design engineer can use this cost system to determine the cost of various board design alternatives before the board is ever produced. For example, this cost system has the capability of determining the cost differences between different sizes of drilled holes for different stack heights (thicknesses) of PC board.

In another example, Hewlett-Packard is able to use super-unit drivers in the printed circuit board stuffing operation.[8] Hewlett-Packard uses a number of different methods for inserting components on bare PC boards. The options available include auto dip insertions, hand insertions, axial insertions, and robotic insertions. Super-unit drivers based on the number of insertions of each type can be used to determine optimal board design. As a result, an engineer can determine the tradeoff between a single hand insertion against multiple robotic insertions to achieve the same functionality for the customer.

THE CUSTOMER AS THE COST OBJECT

The co-editors of this book have spoken of building cross-functional systems that are managed to provide value to users of products and services. These cross-functional systems will frequently be customer oriented rather than product oriented. A product orientation is how the firm sees itself, but this is not how the customer sees the organization. The customer's relationship with the organization may cut across many different products. As a result, there can be confusion in providing consistent value-contributing service to customers, when internal systems are organized by product.

This realization has important implications for the cost management system. Figure 6 illustrates the scenario. The plant is focused on product. Within the plant are the unit, batch, and product level drivers used to determine product cost. The activity-based cost system cannot remain narrowly focused on only plant activities. The product cost is the platform on which a new cost relationship is formed. This new relationship adds post-plant customer and channel-related costs to the unit, batch, and product levels identified in the plant. The new relationship captures customer level activity. Customer level activities are unique to customers, and not to products.

The post-plant activity differences are related more to channel than to product; therefore, a channel orientation is necessary to complete a profit understanding of the system. A hardware product looks the same to the consumer in the local hardware store as it does in a high-volume warehouse store, except the activities beyond the plant to support that product are quite different in these two channels. The firm would lose strategic insight to channel profitability if channel activities were averaged for the hardware product across the channels.

---

8. D. Berlant, Reese Browning, and George Foster, "How Hewlett-Packard Gets Numbers It Can Trust," *Harvard Business Review* (January-February 1990): 178-183.

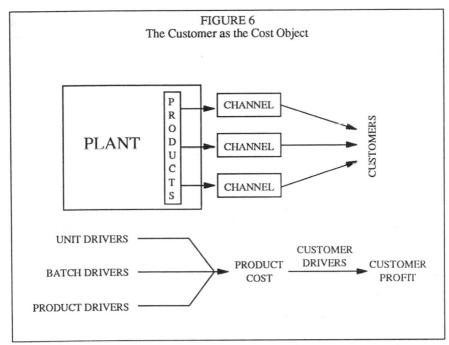

FIGURE 6
The Customer as the Cost Object

An example of channel diversity in the consumer goods area is tissue products. These products can be sold to a convenience store, high-volume club store, grocery store, or commercial market. The focus extends beyond the product to the channel. A focus on product may well lead to averaging channel differences across the product line. This averaging hides the various opportunities for profit within channels. Each channel represents different activity demands on the company. The cost system should reveal the margin opportunities in each channel by tracing the costs of activities to those major channels.

Let us now consider the different activity demands of the channels listed above.[9]

Convenience store: many shipments in small volumes, small sizes, small run lengths, greater warehouse effort to break bulk shipments, some smaller than truckload shipments, large merchandising and sales support per sales dollar volume.

Club stores: special packaging, special palletizing, high volume, long runs, direct ship, full truck load, no merchandising, low sales support per sales dollar volume, no break bulk.

---

9. From J. M. Reeve, "Cost Management for the Continuous Process Environment," *Journal of Cost Management* (Spring 1991), forthcoming.

Grocery stores: standard packaging, high variety (all sizes), full truck load, high sorting per truckload, high merchandising effort, cash incentives, purchased shelf space, high sales support per sales dollar volume.

Commercial: heavy use of brokers, greater receivable collection problems, more invoice adjustments, full truck load, some direct ship to major brokers, no marketing support, no merchandising support, minimal sales support.

As can be seen from above, each channel has significantly different activity demands once the product leaves the mill. The significant contribution of activity-based cost systems will be to highlight the margin opportunities of each customer segment (including major single customers) so as to support marketing strategy.

This basic idea can be extended beyond major channels down to the customer level itself. When the product being sold is highly customized, the channels become specialized to the customer. The cost system must attach costs down to the customer level. Unique levels of engineering support, inventory stocking, receivables levels, freight, and order related costs should be traced to the individual customer level. In this way orders can be subjected to margin analysis. One firm conducted a profitability analysis by order and was much dismayed to discover that an important customer was using the firm as a secondary supplier for small-lot, hard-to-manufacture parts. This customer demanded fast turn capability for very unusual items at unpredictable intervals. A tracing of activity costs to the customer level identified this particular customer as highly unprofitable. As a result, the firm's pricing policy with regard to this customer was adjusted. Much to this firm's surprise, the customer did not react unfavorably to the price adjustments. Apparently, this customer viewed the value received as exceeding the additional price.

CONCLUSION

Activity-based costing can provide both tactical and strategic information for the firm and can aid cross-functional decision making. Understanding the cost of activities is the first step in conducting intelligent analysis of interactions in environments characterized by complex interdependencies. Tracing the cost of activities to vendors, products, and customers gives the organization additional strategic insight. Capturing the relative activity demands placed on the firm by vendors and customers can allow the firm to address the costs of the extended customer value system. Expressly, the firm can react to the cost and margin differences that exist across major supplier and customer channels. The activity-based cost system provides the framework for addressing the cost pieces of the strategic customer value systems, and it offers a methodology for addressing interactions within the system.

REFERENCES

Albright, T. L. and J. M. Reeve. "The Impact of Material Yield Related Cost Drivers on Process and Product Cost." Unpublished working paper, University of Tennessee, November 1990.

Berlant, D., Reese Browning, and George Foster. "How Hewlett-Packard Gets Numbers It Can Trust." *Harvard Business Review* (January-February 1990): 178-183.

Cooper, R. "Implementing an Activity-Based Cost System." *Journal of Cost Management* (Spring 1990): 33-42.

Cooper, R. "The Rise of Activity-Based Costing–Part Two: When Do I Need an Activity Based Cost System?" *Journal of Cost Management* (Fall 1988): 41-48.

Cooper, R. "The Rise of Activity-Based Costing–Part Four: What Do Activity-Based Cost Systems Look Like?" *Journal of Cost Management* (Spring 1989): 38-49.

Cooper, R. "Cost Classification in Unit-Based and Activity-Based Manufacturing Cost Systems." *Journal of Cost Management* (Fall 1990), pp. 4-14.

Fuller, F. T. "Eliminating Complexity from Work: Improving Productivity by Enhancing Quality." *National Productivity Review* (Autumn 1985): 327-344.

Fuller, F. T., "How to Construct and Use a Productivity Loss Index." *National Productivity Review* (Spring 1988): 99-113.

Miller, J. G., and T. Vollman. "The Hidden Factory." *Harvard Business Review* (September-October 1985): 142-150.

O'Guin, M. "Focus the Factory with Activity-Based Costing." *Management Accounting* (February 1990): 36-41.

Ostrenga, M. R. "Activities: The Focal Point of Total Cost Management." *Management Accounting* (February 1990): 42-49.

Reeve, J. M. "Cost Management for the Continuous Process Environment." *Journal of Cost Management* (Spring 1991), forthcoming.

Reeve, J. M. "The Impact of Variation on Operating System Performance." In Peter B. B. Turney (ed.), *Performance Excellence in Manufacturing and Service Organizations*. American Accounting Association, 1990, pp. 75-89.

Reeve, J. M. "Product Costing and Performance Measurement in Flexible Manufacturing Environments." In H. R. Parsaei et al. (eds.), *Justification Methods for Computer Integrated Manufacturing Systems*. Elsevier Science Publishers 1990, pp. 222-233.

Roth, H., and A. Faye Borthick. "Getting Closer to Real Product Costs." *Management Accounting* (May 1989): 28-33.

Shank, J. K. and V. Govindarajan. "Transaction Based Costing for the Complex Product Line: A Field Study." *Journal of Cost Management* (Summer 1988): 31-38.

Turney, P. B. B. "Accounting for Continuous Improvement." *Sloan Management Review* (Winter 1989): 37-47.

Turney, P. B. B., and J. Reeve. "The Impact of Continuous Improvement on the Design of Activity-Based Cost Systems." *Journal of Cost Management* (Summer 1990): 43-50.

CHAPTER 18

IMPROVING THE PRODUCT DEVELOPMENT PROCESS

CLEMENT C. WILSON
Professor of Mechanical and Aerospace Engineering
University of Tennessee

MICHAEL E. KENNEDY
Graduate Student, Mechanical and Aerospace Engineering
University of Tennessee

SUMMARY

This chapter outlines some essential elements for improving the product development process. These elements are extracted from case studies of leading U.S. companies that are competing successfully against worldclass competitors, particularly those from Japan. These studies span the entire product development process, from product conception through manufacture, and are developed from direct interviews with participating expert engineers, project presentations, and supporting product history documentation. The "essential elements" presented in this chapter are part of a comprehensive effort to build an integrated product development methodology that can be practiced successfully by product development teams.

The chapter is divided into four articles to simplify the discussion. Article I, entitled "Some Essential Elements for Superior Product Development," provides an overview of the entire product development process. Article II, "Some Essential Elements for Product Technology Selection and Development," focuses on the critical technology selection and development phase of the product development process. The third article, "Quantification of Critical Product Characteristics for Superior Product Development," discusses the identification and effective use of product performance and quality measures throughout the product development process. Finally, Article IV, "Some Essential Elements for Superior Product Manufacture," examines the development of superior manufacturing processes.

PURPOSE

The primary purpose of this chapter is to initiate a discussion of the product development process. The successful future of U.S. engineering and manufacturing depends on the substantial improvement (or, in some cases, overhaul) of our product development, manufacturing, and business systems. As shown by a persistent trade deficit, U.S. industry is no longer the leader in developing worldclass products. In comparison to the call for a "manufacturing revolution" in the United States, relatively little attention has been focused on the critical need to improve the product development process. Superior product development methodologies are needed to assure that the most effective engineering methods available are used at the most effective time during the development process. This chapter provides an initial step toward formulating a superior product development methodology. The effectiveness of these "elements" depends both on *how* they are used and *when* they are used in the development cycle.

RESEARCH NEED – THE U.S. PRODUCT DEVELOPMENT DILEMMA

During the last twenty years, leading Japanese firms have repeatedly demonstrated the ability to develop and manufacture almost any product they select, with the best performance, lowest cost, and highest quality in the world.

Leading Japanese firms have integrated engineering with manufacturing and have formed long-term partnerships with subsidiaries and vendors. They have simplified their manufacturing processes, which enable them to understand, control, and manage their processes more effectively. Japanese managers understand their product, processes, and employees. Japanese product development engineers generally have broader knowledge of manufacturing requirements than their American counterparts, since Japanese engineers usually start their careers in manufacturing. Japanese firms emphasize employee involvement, which has broadened the factory worker's responsibilities and has dramatically reduced the need for the indirect professionals that are so apparent in U.S. organizations.

Many U.S. firms are abandoning their manufacturing processes because they cannot meet their parts manufacturing cost and profit requirements. To protect their short-term profits, these firms are contracting with Japanese companies to manufacture U.S.-designed products or are resorting to marketing Japanese products under their U.S. labels. As these manufacturing and product development activities move overseas, U.S. firms are losing their ability to design and manufacture products. As this transfer continues, the U.S. trade deficit will worsen, and U.S. engineering and manufacturing competitiveness and employment will decline.

Some U.S. companies are responding to the challenge; the firms that have responded first are those that compete directly with the Japanese. Operations in these responding companies are not "business as usual"; in some cases, radical changes to the corporate organization have been required. In all cases, the technical and managerial leadership of the project was a conscious, focused effort to improve product development and manufacturing. This type of technical and managerial leadership must be enhanced if U.S. industries are to regain leadership in product development.

RESEARCH APPROACH

Studies of successful product development cases reveal common themes that contribute to the superior attributes of a product.

While the term *successful* may be interpreted in several ways, the term is used here to contrast these product development results with those of "failed" cases, where the development effort is either abandoned before the product is completed or the product is "completed" only to fail miserably during customer use. These "failed" product cases may occur because the product does not work properly, cannot be manufactured successfully, costs too much, and/or cannot be developed on schedule. In addition, "successful" products may often be recognized by their commercial success, technical innovation awards, and other indicators.

The essential elements described in this chapter have been extracted from twenty actual product development case histories that involved the development of complex, innovative products. In many of these cases, significant technology development was required before the products could be designed and manufactured. Many of these case studies were developed and presented by participating engineers in graduate engineering courses taught by the senior author at two different universities (see References).

During our collective twenty-eight years of experience in U.S. product development organizations, we have found that certain fundamental approaches, when applied at the correct time during the development process, can prevent serious problems that might occur later. Indeed, the avoidance of serious problems late in the development process is necessary to develop a new product on schedule with the lowest possible cost.

Some members of the engineering research community have recognized the need to improve the design process and are working to develop new design methodologies that can be used to design products more effectively. Such design methodologies and tools that are developed from these efforts can be important and can impact the product development process. Indeed, design methodologies such as Design-for-Assembly (DFA) can be important in achieving successful product development.

Many other methodologies are being championed to improve product manufacturing processes and product quality. Design-for-Manufacturing (DFM), Early Manufacturing Involvement (EMI), Total Quality Culture (TQC), Quality Circles (QC), Quality Function Deployment (QFD), Taguchi/Experimental Design Methods, Computer-Aided-Design (CAD), Computer-Aided-Engineering (CAE), Computer-Aided-Manufacturing (CAM), and Just-In-Time Manufacturing (JIT) have joined an ever growing list of purported solutions to U.S. product development problems. However, these methodologies can be followed perfectly, and still the product may fail. The ability of these individual methodologies to improve U.S. product development is limited unless powerful product development factors, such as appropriate technology selection, strategic product definition, adequate testing, product reliability/life evaluation, product quality control, and manufacturing are assured.

Thus, we propose that design methodologies, manufacturing methodologies, technology management, and the like must also be considered within the broader context of a product development methodology, whereby the goal is not merely superior design and so on, but the goal becomes superior design, manufacturing, and management to create a superior product. Based on this broader context, the ultimate goal of the essential elements research is to create an integrated product development methodology that can be practiced successfully by product development teams.

Not all the essential elements that are required to develop a superior product can be covered adequately in one discourse; indeed, this chapter provides only a foundation toward understanding and improving this very complex process. Thus, the essential elements discussed in this chapter should be considered to be necessary, but not sufficient for superior product development. Most importantly, the essential elements must be implemented appropriately throughout the product development process, and not merely discussed at some point along the way.

STRATEGIC AND OPERATIONAL IMPLICATIONS

Many U.S. firms have identified a strategic need to reduce new product development time and to improve the overall quality levels of their products and processes. To accomplish these improvements, the product development process must be considered as a prime strategic weapon in the fight to remain competitive in world markets. Indeed, one U.S. study has indicated that the leading Japanese firms are not beating U.S. firms with high technology, but rather with basic engineering and design processes and practices (Bebb, 1989). The essential elements presented in this chapter, then, can be considered to be operational philosophies and methods that can be used to achieve the strategic goals of development time reduction and product quality improvement.

ARTICLE I: Some Essential Elements for Superior Product Development

ARTICLE SUMMARY

Some essential elements for superior product development apply to the overall product development process, whereas others apply specifically to particular phases of the process. A composite diagram of the product development process for an innovative product is presented to provide a platform from which the elements can be discussed. The process and essential elements described here can be used as a basis for structuring a development process for a specific product.

THE PRODUCT DEVELOPMENT PROCESS

We have constructed a composite diagram (Figure 1) of the development process for an innovative product. An innovative product is a relatively complex product containing new technology and features that provide additional customer value when compared to currently available products. In the diagram, the development process flows from left to right through eight major phases, originating with product ideas and concluding with product manufacture. Product and process technologies are developed concurrently, as are product and process design, as shown in the figure. Each development phase has milestone goals that define the completion of that phase, as indicated by the numbered "flags" on the figure.

Even at this very general level of consideration, there are some fundamental essential elements that greatly affect the outcome of the development process. Some of these essential elements apply to the entire

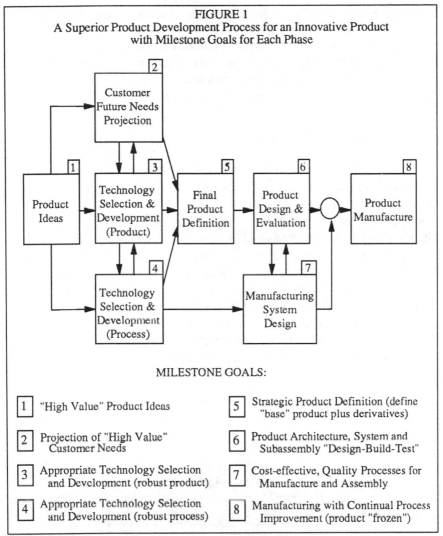

FIGURE 1
A Superior Product Development Process for an Innovative Product
with Milestone Goals for Each Phase

MILESTONE GOALS:

1 "High Value" Product Ideas

2 Projection of "High Value" Customer Needs

3 Appropriate Technology Selection and Development (robust product)

4 Appropriate Technology Selection and Development (robust process)

5 Strategic Product Definition (define "base" product plus derivatives)

6 Product Architecture, System and Subassembly "Design-Build-Test"

7 Cost-effective, Quality Processes for Manufacture and Assembly

8 Manufacturing with Continual Process Improvement (product "frozen")

development process, whereas others apply specifically to particular phases and enable the phase milestone goals to be met. Some of these essential elements prior to product manufacture are discussed in this article; essential elements for the product manufacture phase are presented in Article IV. Although they are discussed in separate articles, all the essential elements must be integrated into one consistent methodology to be most effective.

Essential Elements That Affect the Entire Development Process

Three essential elements are so fundamental that they affect the entire product development process. These overall elements integrate the many diverse product development activities into a coherent, focused process. These elements are summarized in Figure 2 and are discussed below.

Control by a Single Team (single leader with authority)

The element with the most far-reaching effects is the selection of a single development/manufacturing team to control the project from technology selection through the first six months of manufacturing. The Xerox Corporation uses a product delivery team that reports to a chief engineer (Hadden, 1986). When IBM could not produce a personal computer within its formal product development system, it commissioned a small team with complete autonomy called an Independent Business Unit to develop the machine. Hewlett-Packard used the team approach to develop its color "Paintjet" printer (Baker et al., 1988). These major companies, which are competing directly against the Japanese, have found that matrix organizations, with their accompanying "turf battles," "nonconcurrences," and lack of responsibility for the product, are not competitive when pitted against

---

FIGURE 2
Some Essential Elements Affecting the Entire Product Development Process

Control by a Single Team

      * Integration of Broad Skills
      * Team Controls All Aspects, from
          Technology Selection to Manufacturing

Projection of Customer Future Needs

      * Team Participation
      * Customer Input to Team

Information Convergence at Product Definition Phase

      * Early, Simultaneous Consideration
      * Common Goals and Plans

Japanese cooperative systems. Figure 3 illustrates how the parochial interests of the traditional matrix organization cause the product to be broken by the very people who are supposed to be ensuring its success. Xerox's Lyndon Hadden (1986) states: the previous product delivery system was a "system created to prevent errors . . . but almost prevented product delivery." Thus, the single development/manufacturing team (illustrated in Figure 4) is an essential element (if not the most essential) for superior product development.

If the single team is to be responsible for the product throughout the development process, it must contain the proper skill "mix" and experience to complete its job effectively. Various team members need to have the design, manufacturing, marketing, testing, and other skills that are necessary to develop the product successfully. The most effective teams have a single leader with the authority to control all aspects of their project, including product definition and specifications, product evaluation, vendor

FIGURE 3
The U.S. Product Development System "Inaction"

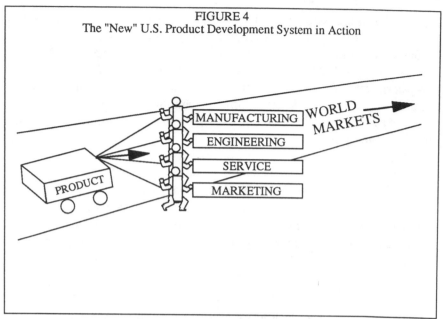

FIGURE 4
The "New" U.S. Product Development System in Action

selection, and procurement, from the technology selection phase through the first six months of product manufacture.

Projection of Customer Future Needs

The second essential element affecting the entire development process is the proper determination of customer needs. In a product development context, proposed products must provide a competitive solution to customers' needs over a FUTURE time period, starting with product introduction and continuing at least until product development costs are recovered. The customer needs projections that are developed from this analysis are then used during the product definition phase to establish product design and process specifications.

Figure 5 illustrates how customer needs are projected into the future to develop a competitive product. Figure 5a depicts a situation in which the competition currently has superior capability and an improved product is needed to catch up. If only "today's" competitive information is considered, we might be led to believe that just a relatively small product improvement is required.

When the development time, the product's projected life, and future improvements in the competitor's products are considered (Figure 5b), however, the product improvement that is really required to create a superior new product is much larger than what today's information would indicate. Consequently, the product development team must think beyond

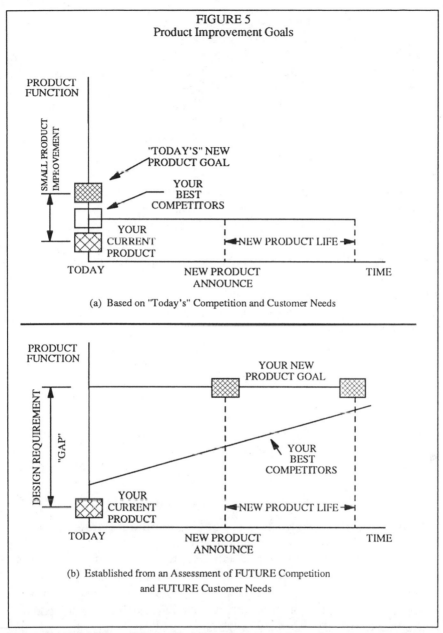

FIGURE 5
Product Improvement Goals

(a) Based on "Today's" Competition and Customer Needs

(b) Established from an Assessment of FUTURE Competition
and FUTURE Customer Needs

being "market driven" by today's customer needs, and must extrapolate to the customer's FUTURE needs to assure that the new product will have adequate customer value.

Selecting the proper combination of product features to meet customers' future needs is an exceedingly difficult task. Often, some less important current market requirements must be ignored in order to make the significant product improvements that will be required to meet future needs. The team must exercise careful judgment while assessing the product design tradeoffs that are involved. In the functional organization, in which the marketing function provides "market requirements" to the design organization, the product feature selection process can create major contention between functional groups and can impede the product's development. One of the most ineffective "needs analyses" is the extensive marketing list that details every feature and statistic of every competitor's product, along with demand that the new product exceed all the items on the list.

To ensure that customer needs are met most effectively with the new product, the team should participate directly in the customer needs analysis and determination. In several of the studied cases, teams performed their own analyses by interacting directly with customers. Team participation can enhance team members' creative contributions by enabling them to "see" opportunities that they might not see by merely reading a report from a distant market analysis group.

For example, one data storage firm established a Customer Advisory Board to provide direct customer input to the design process. The board is composed of technically astute customers, such as data center directors and systems engineers. New product designs are discussed with board members to provide them with advance notice of new products and to solicit suggestions for product changes and improvements. Design engineers attend these meetings to answer questions and to receive direct feedback from customers. In one specific product development case, the board was able to identify two problems that would have adversely affected the marketability of the product. The product was modified to eliminate the problems (Abbott, 1988).

Information Convergence at the Product Definition Phase

The convergence of marketing, engineering, and manufacturing information is essential to creating an adequate product definition. This convergence is shown in Figure 1 by the three input arrows that lead into the product definition phase of product development. The information convergence that occurs during this phase assures that marketing, engineering, and manufacturing issues are considered simultaneously as the product is defined.

Early simultaneous consideration of these issues enables the project leaders to agree on a common set of product goals and action plans. This agreement, in turn, enables parallel product and process development to occur with minimum conflict. If common goals and plans are not developed, the "simultaneous engineering" of product and process will likely diverge, resulting in major product and process rework late in the development process, lengthy project delays, and/or project failure.

Some Essential Elements Affecting Specific Phases of the Product Development Process

Many of the essential elements apply specifically to particular phases of the product development process. These "specific phase" elements emphasize the use of the most appropriate engineering methods at the most appropriate time and aid in discovering problems at the earliest possible phase of the development process. These elements are summarized in Figure 6.

Some Essential Elements Affecting Technology Selection and Development

While the technology selection and development phase is discussed much more extensively in Article II, we should provide an introduction to some essential elements for this phase, as this phase can be critical to the success of the overall development process.

Technology Feasibility Evaluation. An essential element for the technology selection and development phase is to evaluate the ability of a selected technology to accomplish its intended purpose. Failure to assure the feasibility of a technology can lead to a poor technology choice, which, in turn, can result in marginal product performance or failure.

Discovery of the critical variables that control the technology's output is the first evaluation task, for initially little is known about a new technology. Depending on the technology, these variables may be certain part dimensions, temperature, current, or a myriad of other factors. Once the critical variables are known, an operating space for the technology is to be demonstrated. The term operating space, which may also may be known as operating range or operating window, can be simply defined as the parameter zone "where everything works" (Voit, 1988). As the operating space is developed, any limitations of the technology also need to be discovered.

Before beginning the product design phase, it is important to be sure that an adequate operating space exists and that technology limitations are understood since these items define critical product design requirements, tolerances, and other important factors. For example, inkjet printer engineers discovered that a minimum ink drop velocity was needed to attain acceptable print quality. Ink drop velocity, in turn, was found to be affected

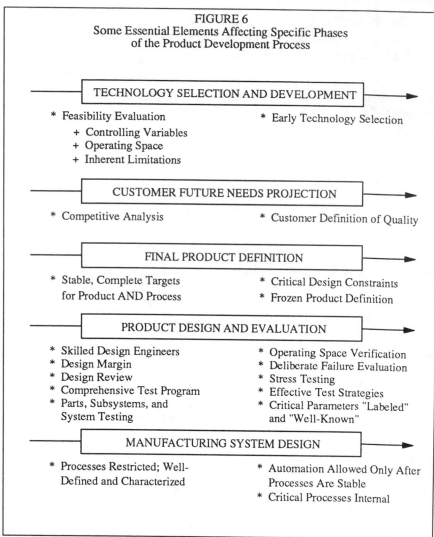

FIGURE 6
Some Essential Elements Affecting Specific Phases
of the Product Development Process

by the voltage applied to the jet, so a minimum inkjet voltage specification was defined to assure acceptable print quality for the printer (Figure 7). These engineers also learned that the inkjet tended to clog after the printhead was not operated for several minutes. This technology limitation dictated the subsequent design of a "spittoon" for the printer so that the clog could be cleared from the jet nozzle without adversely affecting print quality (Baker et al., 1988).

Early Technology Selection. In most of the cases studied involving a new technology, the technology selection process revealed the need for other related technological developments. Thus, each new technology needs not only to be evaluated to reveal these additional technology needs,

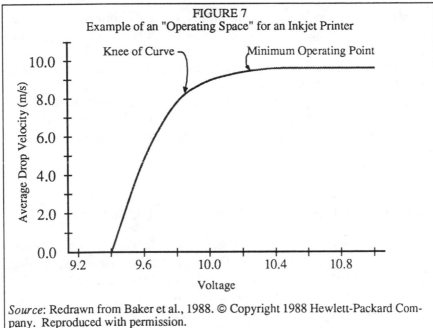

FIGURE 7
Example of an "Operating Space" for an Inkjet Printer

Source: Redrawn from Baker et al., 1988. © Copyright 1988 Hewlett-Packard Company. Reproduced with permission.

but also to be selected early enough in the development program to allow sufficient time for the additional technological development. For example, successful development of a resistive ribbon typewriter required not only the development of resistive ribbon technology, but also advances in tungsten manufacturing technology so that the resistive ribbon printhead could be manufactured successfully (Voit, 1988). The technology dependency noted above can be avoided *only* by making a conscious decision at the start of the program to use only "established" technologies in the new product.

Some Essential Elements Affecting Customer Future Needs Projection

Competitive Analysis. While certainly not a new technique, an effective competitive analysis is an essential element for determining a customer's future needs. An effective competitive analysis can provide the development team with a good understanding of competing products, their best features, and likely product trends.

The most effective competitive analyses not only assess a competitor's products, product substitutes, and industry trends, but also evaluate a competitor's product development capabilities, manufacturing ability, costs, and speed. For example, when one U.S. company's "Competitive Benchmarking" process revealed that Japanese competitors were developing superior products in one-half the time and cost, the company was forced to change its products *and* its development process to be competitive (Hadden, 1986).

Customer Definition of Quality. A comprehensive understanding of customer quality perceptions and expectations is essential to develop superior product designs. A variety of techniques are available to assess customer needs, and the case study teams used several different techniques to determine their customers' quality expectations. Some methods for effective determination and measurement of customer's quality expectations are explored in Article III.

Some Essential Elements Affecting Final Product Definition

Stable, Complete Product and Process Targets. The product definition, also known as the product specification or product requirements, provides the basis for the product design. In the successful case studies, stable, comprehensive requirements and goals were developed for both the product and the processes used to manufacture the product.

Superior product definitions contain all elements that are needed to create a complete product. In addition to features, they address product and process quality goals, target cost, development schedule, human interface design, and product performance. Effective use of (accurate) information gathered in the technology selection and development and customer future needs projection phases is imperative to create a successful product definition. The product definition should be established before detailed product and process design activities start.

Critical Design Constraints. Product definitions also include any required "special" items, methods, guidelines, or features. Design for assembly goals such as "no screws allowed" were established for one popular, low-cost printer (Galatha, 1988); for another printer, the printhead was to be designed as a disposable module (Baker et al., 1988). Other requirements such as the ability of the design to be used as a basis for a "family" of products or design standard requirements (such as UL), were listed as necessary on successful product definitions. In many of the cases, design targets were prioritized depending on the importance of the particular goal.

Frozen Product Definition. Product definitions should be "frozen" once they are approved. Freezing the product definition performs several functions: it constrains the ability to change or lower the product specification as a way to "solve" design problems, and it eliminates a "continuous redesign" process that results from numerous definition changes. Experienced product developers list unstable product requirements as a major cause of product development schedule delays. However, freezing the product definition dramatically increases the importance of establishing the proper definition the first time and completing the project on schedule. A product plan that incorporates a series of derivative products, each with an incremental improvement, can continue to stimulate the market with new features while still allowing the base product definition to remain "frozen."

Some Essential Elements Affecting Product Design and Evaluation

The product design and evaluation phase is the heart of the engineering activity that is required to assure successful product function. In the case studies, the emphasis during the product design phase was on ensuring reliable product function rather than on minimum parts cost. Product cost was minimized by simplifying the design and by reducing manufacturing and service times.

Skilled, Experienced Design Engineers. To achieve a superior design, the development/manufacturing team includes experienced design engineers who have extensive knowledge of current parts manufacturing and assembly practices. In the case studies that utilized a "design-for-manufacturing" approach (Abbott, 1988; Baker et al., 1988; Galatha, 1988; Hadden, 1986), the design engineers worked closely with parts vendors to assure that part designs were optimized for manufacturing processes. The design engineers also received additional training in manufacturing techniques.

Design "Margin." Words like "margin," "safety factors," and "safety zone" appear frequently in the literature for the successful technologies and products that were studied. Products with "margin" operate properly with "worst-case" parts and in the worst possible environment. Margin generally does not occur by accident; rather, it requires knowledgeable design decisions based on a thorough understanding of the product environment, use, and failure modes. "Designing beyond specification" and redundancy are two methods that can be used to provide design margin.

For example, the hot-roll fuser operates in an operating space "box," surrounded by a "safety factor region" (Figure 8). This extra margin allows the copier to operate acceptably even if some unusual event (such as a temperature measurement shift) should cause the fuser to operate outside its normal temperature range.

A tape cartridge library design team used the term *derating components* to describe their "conscious effort to ensure that all components – are effectively overdesigned for the job" (Barrett, 1987). Components were "overdesigned" from two to six hundred times expected life (and even more

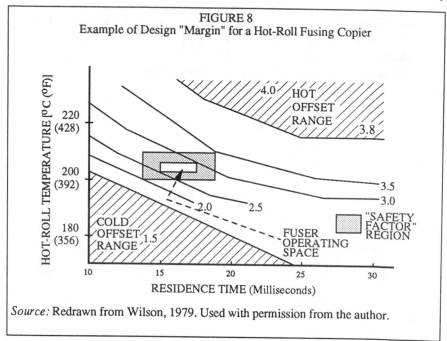

FIGURE 8
Example of Design "Margin" for a Hot-Roll Fusing Copier

Source: Redrawn from Wilson, 1979. Used with permission from the author.

in a few cases), depending on how well engineers could predict loading conditions and other factors (Barrett, 1987).

Design Review. Concentration on a single project can lead to "tunnel vision," where the design team can no longer see certain problems because they are too close to the work (Barrett, 1987). Design reviews solve the "tunnel vision" problem by serving as "the official second guess" for the development of a product.

All the projects studied used a design review as part of the development process. The design review was often performed by members of other related product teams (Hewlett-Packard, 1987a). Even if no major problems are revealed during the design review, reviews are still useful because, in the words of a veteran engineer, "New people can successfully improve on old design, even GOOD old design" (Galatha, 1988). In many companies, design reviews are mandatory (Xerox Corporation, 1988).

Comprehensive Test Program. Most systems involve complex interactions among parts, assemblies, and the environment that cannot be modeled analytically. Thus, part, subassembly, and system testing are required to assure that the product operates as desired under actual customer conditions. Testing was a prominent feature in all the successful projects that have been studied.

Parts, Subsystems, System Testing. Component, subassembly, and system testing is one of the longest and most expensive tasks in the development process. In the haste to reduce development time and costs, development leaders can be pressured to trim the test effort. In the cases studied, however, these development leaders required thorough characterization and verification of designs through testing. Corrective action times were reduced by having development teams test their own components and subassemblies.

Operating Space Verification. One key requirement is to assure that the product design operating space corresponds to the previously developed technology operating space. Performance confirmation may involve considerable effort. For example, thousands of inkjet printheads had to be produced to satisfy characterization and reliability testing requirements (Baker et al., 1988).

Deliberate Failure Evaluation. Tests-to-failure are imperative to verify sufficient design margin. For example, aircraft parts were "scientifically destroyed" to determine their margin in structural strength (Wilkerson, 1988). However, it must be noted that prototype destruction is not necessarily called for; failure may be defined in many ways, like inadequate print quality (for a copier) or excessive signal loss (for a communications device). Failure mode prediction, evaluation, and effect analysis are key techniques.

Stress Testing. Stress testing is used selectively to assure that the product will operate as expected when used by actual customers. Inkjet resistors were tested at "worst-case" product overpower conditions (Baker et al., 1988). When hot-roll fuser engineers discovered that solid white and solid black zones caused the worst problems, copiers using the hot-roll fuser were tested using both solid white and solid black sheets (Wilson, 1979).

Resistive ribbon systems in typewriters were evaluated using a "stress-pak" of papers; twenty types of very "difficult to print on" paper were run through the machine to assure that quality type would be printed on all the different papers (Voit, 1988). An inkjet printer "BEST" test subjected the product electronics to temperature cycles of 10°C per minute and to vibration levels that were four times higher than the product specification (Baker et al., 1988). These tests were designed to attack serious, dominant failure modes that can be stimulated during normal product use.

Effective Test Strategies. While some differences were noted across the case studies, all the successful teams had a carefully defined and elaborated test strategy for their development efforts. One company stresses what it calls "early system integration," which entails the earliest possible building and testing of a complete system (Hadden, 1986). Another company's product teams have expressed a strong commitment to a "bottoms-up" approach, with parts tests leading to subassembly tests leading to system tests (Abbott, 1988). Both methods, as well as combinations of methods, have proved effective when thorough design characterization was the goal. Of course, test strategy selection can be affected by the relative cost of the product. In addition, early system testing is indicated when the product's subsystems are comprised of highly interactive technologies.

Critical Functional and Manufacturing Parameters "Labeled" and "Well known." The discovery of critical variables was listed previously as an essential element for the technology selection and development process. As the product is designed, the technology requirements are converted to subassembly functional requirements and then to design requirements. In the successful case studies, these critical design features were well known to all members of the design team, including the manufacturing personnel.

One design element that requires improvement in even the successful cases is the description of critical product variables in "official" product documentation. In many projects, the most valuable information about critical technology, design, and manufacturing factors resides only with the product team members (often hidden in engineering notebooks). The formal project documentation rarely denotes critical design dimensions, manufacturing controls, and related features that are needed for successful product manufacture. If the members of the original product team are no longer available (through retirement, transfer, etc.), this information is lost. Later, if product or process changes are contemplated, the information has to be redeveloped, often at considerable cost, or "blind" choices are made, with possibly disastrous results. A solution to this problem will eliminate many product quality problems that currently appear during the manufacturing phase. One simple method for denoting these critical items is presented in Article IV.

Some Essential Elements Affecting Manufacturing System Design

Processes Restricted, Well-Defined, and Characterized. Proper process technology development is a critical prerequisite to achieve this essential element. This essential element restriction is described best by the engineers who stated, "Use standard, well understood processes. Historically, when we have strayed from this concept we have suffered low yields, cost increases, and many engineer hours of process support and characterization" (Baker et al., 1988).

Automation Allowed Only After Processes Are Stable. In the successful projects, automation development was performed *after* the critical manufacturing processes were demonstrated successfully using a manual procedure. This essential element was so important to one product development team that they included the warning, "Don't automate until feasibility is proven," in their development phase goals (PaintJet, 1987).

Another team assured that their automated processes were feasible by modeling the automated process in the laboratory. Only after the automated process was demonstrated successfully in the laboratory was it installed on the production line. As side benefits, the demonstration information was used to balance the automated production line flow, and design refinement ideas were provided to the development team (Deaton, n.d.).

If automation is pursued before manufacturing processes are stable, manufacturing process changes may cause a "continuous redesign" of the automated process. Substantial changes in automation programming and/or equipment may be necessary if the "old" automation is not compatible with the "new" processes.

It is significant that the above project examples were designed specifically for high-volume, automated assembly. In some cases, automation efforts still may not be successful even if manual assembly methods are demonstrated. Application of the letter template for a popular keyboard was a manual procedure in an otherwise automated process, because "no existence theorem" existed to automate that process (Pollard, 1988).

Critical Manufacturing Processes Performed Internally. In all of the successful cases, processes involving critical technology or design parameters were controlled internally by the company or were controlled *very* closely with preferred vendors. The hot roll for one copier was manufactured in-house to assure control of critical material, thickness, and other parameters of the part (Wilson, 1979). One printer team developed proprietary (in-house) processes to assure that all print quality standards would be met during product manufacture.

CONCLUDING REMARKS

This article defines some essential elements for superior product development as a basis to develop a product development methodology and to structure a superior product development process for a specific product. Use of these essential elements throughout the product development process will enhance the ability to produce a product superior in customer satisfaction and quality. Development schedules can be planned and maintained by combining the product development process milestones (Figure 1) with the essential elements; the elements can be used to identify appropriate (necessary) activities, while the milestones may be used to define phase goals and completion dates. The essential element of "control by a single development/manufacturing team" links the developing product to customer needs, as well as to functional and manufacturing requirements, by assuring continuous cross-functional integration and coordination throughout the product development process.

The elements also serve as a platform for discussing detailed techniques which are a subset of this product development methodology. The subsequent articles will consider the individual processes in more depth using the essential elements concept.

ARTICLE II: Some Essential Elements for Product Technology Selection and Development

ARTICLE SUMMARY

The competitive need to shorten development cycle times has made the technology selection and development process critical to the timely development of superior quality products. This article identifies some essential elements for product technology selection and development that allow the project to be planned and executed with the appropriate emphasis on technology selection, development, and verification. This article represents the second part of a comprehensive effort to build an integrated product development methodology that can be practiced successfully by product development teams. It should be recalled throughout this chapter that, although they are presented in separate articles, all the essential elements must be used as one consistent methodology to be most effective.

TECHNOLOGY'S IMPACT ON THE PRODUCT DEVELOPMENT PROCESS

Since it occurs very early in the product development process, the Technology Selection and Development Phase significantly impacts the outcome of the product development process. As shown in Figure 1, the Technology Selection and Development Phase "feeds" the rest of the product development process. Product and process technology results are combined with customer needs information to establish the product definition, the product is designed and tested, manufacturing systems are created, and the product is manufactured. Thus, the proper selection and development of technologies are imperative to develop a superior quality product.

GOAL: A "ROBUST" TECHNOLOGY

A properly selected technology meets customers' value expectations, works properly in a product environment, and is manufacturable with high yields. Process technologies are controllable and capable of producing high quality products. Thus, the primary goal of the technology selection and development process is to select and develop "robust" technologies that are capable of meeting these requirements. A "robust" technology performs as intended even when subjected to operational and environmental variations, manufacturing or process tolerances, and other unfavorable conditions. Significant parameters affecting the performance of the technology are understood and controlled.

CONSEQUENCES OF A "FRAGILE" TECHNOLOGY

Very severe product quality problems and development schedule delays may be created if a machine is designed with a "fragile" technology that is not under control or is not understood adequately. Although short development schedules are a high priority, "rushed" technology selections that are made before the technology is well understood often set the stage for spectacular design failures, perplexing manufacturing problems, and lengthy development schedule delays.

The consequence of rushing a "fragile" technology into a product design is well illustrated by a recent effort to accelerate the development and manufacture of new-technology composite wings for a military aircraft. The new composite technology was "rushed" into the design phase. Then, with the design 40 percent complete, the first wing model ripped apart in a wind tunnel test. To correct the design, plastic sheets were added to the composite. Later, assembly workers could not attach the wing parts together because the new plastic layers separated around the bolted connections. To fix this problem, special shims were designed and rushed into the manufacturing process. After 29,000 bolts were installed, engineers discovered that the new shims made the bolts too short. All 29,000 bolts were inspected and 4,000 were replaced. One development manager summarized the effort: "We took shortcuts trying to meet the schedule, and we failed. We were trying to do things so fast that we ended up shooting ourselves in the foot as we walked along." The new wing now costs two times as much as its "current technology" counterpart and is, in the words of a military manager, "way behind" schedule (Carley, 1989).

Thus, while proper technology selection and development can improve the quality and pace of product development significantly, poor technology selections and inadequate technology development can lead to lengthy project delays, large development cost overruns, and/or project failure. The essential elements described in this article are designed to assure the selection and development of "robust" technologies that enable superior product and process development.

THE TECHNOLOGY SELECTION AND DEVELOPMENT PHASE

The technology selection and development phase of the product development process consists of three basic tasks: evaluation of technology alternatives, technology selection, and technology development/verification (Figure 9). The time and effort required to complete this phase will be different depending on whether an existing or an alternative ("new") technology is selected for the product.

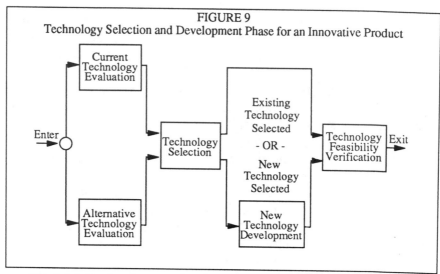

FIGURE 9
Technology Selection and Development Phase for an Innovative Product

The initial technology evaluation generally encompasses both existing and alternative ("new") technologies, as shown in the figure. All the technology candidates are evaluated for a limited time, after which the most promising one is selected for additional development and verification. If a "new" technology is selected, it must be developed during the new technology development stage. Finally, the ability of the selected technology (either existing or new) to meet the proposed product requirements is verified during the technology feasibility verification. Some essential elements that affect this activity are discussed below, and a summary of these elements is presented in Figure 10.

SOME ESSENTIAL ELEMENTS FOR TECHNOLOGY EVALUATION

Evaluation is a crucial, recurring activity during the technology selection and development phase. Several prospective technologies are first evaluated so that the most appropriate one can be selected. If a new technology is selected, development ideas must be evaluated. Finally, the

---

FIGURE 10
Some Essential Elements Affecting the Technology Selection and
Development Phase of the Product Development Process

TECHNOLOGY EVALUATION

* Discovery of Critical Variables
* Demonstration of an "Operating Space"
* Discovery of Inherent Technology Limitations

TECHNOLOGY DEVELOPMENT

* Customer Criteria Use in Selection
* Early Selection
* Consideration of Several Candidates
* New vs. Existing Technology Considerations

TECHNOLOGY FEASIBILITY VERIFICATION

* Critical Variables Defined, Quantified, and Targeted
* Critical Requirements Demonstrated
* Technology Feasibility Statement

---

completed technology is evaluated (verified) for its proposed product or process application during the technology feasibility verification stage.

Three common factors, derived from the case studies, apply to all evaluation activity throughout the technology selection and development phase. These three essential elements also help to integrate all technology evaluation activity into a focused and coherent effort.

Discovery of Critical Variables. The first essential element is to discover the critical variables that determine or control the output of the technology. This element is especially important when contemplating selection of a "new" technology, since few facts are available with which to perform an evaluation (Voit, 1988). Both analysis and experimentation are useful to determine those factors that are critical to the desired operation of the technology.

Demonstration of "Operating Space." Once the controlling variables are discovered, an operating space for the variables of the technology must be demonstrated. The term *operating space* is defined in Article I as the parameter zone for the technology "where everything works" (Voit, 1988).

The technology team needs to be able to project that an adequate operating space for the critical variables can be developed before starting the product design; otherwise the technology must be rejected as too fragile. The product or process design is to be capable of controlling all critical variables within the technology's operating space. Statistically designed experiments are particularly valuable in quantifying the operating space for controlling variables.

For example, engineers working to develop a hot-roll fuser copier technology discovered that fuse quality was affected by the hot-roll temperature and paper residence time. A "fuse quality rating" of 2.5 to 3.0 was desired. When combined with a tradeoff between minimum hot roll temperature and minimum residence time, the operating space was determined as shown previously in Figure 8. This determination established copier design requirements to assure that the hot-roll was maintained within the specified temperature range, and that paper was fed to the hot roll within the specified rates (Wilson, 1979).

Discovery of Inherent Technology Limitations. Any inherent technology limitations need to be discovered during the technology feasibility study, as these limitations constrain the technology's ability to meet product requirements or otherwise impose additional technology or product design requirements. For example, a resistive ribbon technology development team for a new typewriter learned that two adjacent resistive elements had to be "on" to assure acceptable print quality. This technology limitation dictated a limit for the minimum print width of the typewriter (Voit, 1988).

SOME ESSENTIAL ELEMENTS FOR TECHNOLOGY SELECTION

The success of the technology selection and development phase ultimately depends on whether the appropriate technology is selected. To make the best choice, correct and timely information about the technical objectives of the project is necessary. The essential elements below are fundamental to making a proper technology selection.

Customer Criteria Used in Selection. In the successful projects, technology selection and evaluation criteria were strongly based on customer needs for performance, quality, reliability, and cost. Technology team members had a good understanding of customer needs for which the technology was being developed. (Customer requirements may not be very familiar to some technology developers.) A technology's cost was used only to the extent that proposed customers were perceived to consider cost as important; quality and reliability of the technology generally were emphasized more than cost. The teams used customer criteria not only for selection, but also during the technology feasibility verification stage to assess how well the developed technology met customer needs. Some ways to assess a technology's ability to meet customer expectations is discussed in Article III.

Early Technology Selection. As discussed in Article I, the new technology development process often reveals the need for related technological developments. Thus, each new technology not only must be tested to reveal these additional technology needs, but also must be selected early enough in the product development program to allow enough time for the additional technology development and machine design that is required.

Consideration of Several Candidates. Systematic evaluation of several technology candidates increases the probability of selecting the most appropriate technology and restricts the tendency to "over-pursue" the first potential concept (avoids the "eureka" syndrome). Usually, both current and new technologies should be considered, as shown in Figure 9. Hardware developed during this activity may be known as a concept demonstrator and is built primarily to assess the ability of potential technologies to meet "basic" requirements. (A successful "concept demonstrator" should never be considered as the end to the technology selection and development phase.)

The alternative technologies are developed only enough to enable a proper technology selection; the time required to accomplish this must be balanced with the need to make an early technology selection. Subsequent effort then is focused solely on developing and verifying the selected technology.

New vs. Existing Technology Considerations. The technology selection and development phase can be affected dramatically by whether new or existing technology is selected. As shown in Figure 9, selecting a new technology requires that it be developed so that the technology can function properly in a product or process environment. Issues related to this difference between new and existing technology selection must be considered.

The first issue to be considered is that new technology development and verification usually takes much longer than does the verification of a current technology. Thus, "fast-track" projects with accelerated product development schedules should avoid selecting new technologies when sufficient time is not scheduled for the necessary technology development. In one case study, a successful product had to be developed quickly to save a company from bankruptcy liquidation. To minimize development time, a conscious decision was made at the start of the program to use only "established" technologies in the new product. The selection of appropriate, established technologies enabled the development team to meet its accelerated schedule and deliver a highly profitable Automated Magnetic Tape Cartridge Library (Abbott, 1988).

Inherent limitations for *both* existing and new technology alternatives are to be assessed carefully. The effort needed to demonstrate a new technology may be considerably less than what will be necessary to make the new technology feasible for use in a product.

Technology problems must be considered as much more serious than machine design problems. In complex machines, new technologies may interact adversely with other new and existing technologies used elsewhere. Therefore, a new technology's compatibility with other technologies should be evaluated early. Failure to assure that all selected technologies are compatible during the technology phase may result in an unwelcome surprise when the machine design is completed.

SOME ESSENTIAL ELEMENTS FOR NEW TECHNOLOGY DEVELOPMENT

If a new technology is selected, it must first be developed to a feasible state for design and manufacture. Three essential elements greatly enhance the quality of new technology development.

Optimization of Operating Space. The primary task of the new technology development step is to expand and optimize the operating space so that the technology is adequately robust. Values for the controlling parameters are found to allow the widest possible variation while still obtaining the desired output. These values are then used as engineering targets for the machine design. Multivariate statistical testing procedures, such as design of experiments or Taguchi methods, can be very useful tools for this task.

Variability Minimization. Maximum use of the available operating space can be attained by minimizing the variability of the controlling variables. For example, the hot-roll fuser technology was enhanced by developing a precise temperature measurement and control system accurate to 1° C. Accurate temperature control helped to assure reliable copy fusing, even though the fuser functions properly only within a narrow temperature range (Wilson, 1979).

Simultaneous Product-Process Technology Development. New product technology development often necessitates the development of new process technologies to manufacture the new product hardware. Moreover, because requirements and limitations of one affect the other, product and process technology development must be closely interrelated.

The success of a manufacturing system design is predicated largely on its ability to control critical manufacturing processes. This control capability must be initiated during the technology selection and development phase. Indeed, problems caused by new process control difficulties can cause long delays in the development of a new technology product. Thus, new process technologies should be developed simultaneously and in conjunction with new product technologies. For example, an inkjet printer project not only involved inkjet printhead development, but also required a new sealing technology to eliminate printhead air gaps (Boeller, 1988).

While the emphasis of this article is directed toward product technology development, the same essential elements apply equally to process technology development. Successful new technology manufacturing processes are "capable," controlled, and characterized. Key process technology attributes are quantified and well understood; they are not "black art." Limitations of selected manufacturing processes are known. These elements are the same as those necessary for successful product technology development.

SOME ESSENTIAL ELEMENTS FOR TECHNOLOGY FEASIBILITY VERIFICATION

After selection and development, the final task is to verify that the technology indeed is "ready" for the product or process design phase and to assure that all requirements are achieved. Exiting the technology selection and development phase before completing this verification step can be a large technical risk; the composite wing example presented earlier shows that failing to verify a technology before design can be very expensive in both development time and cost.

Critical Variables Defined, Quantified, and Targeted. All operating factors related to the technology are known, quantified, and targeted. Operating spaces are defined. All necessary design and performance data are available to accomplish a complete product and process design.

Critical Requirements Demonstrated. All technology requirements related to performance, quality, life, and reliability are demonstrated successfully with prototype hardware. Materials and manufacturing processes critical to successful technology use are identified and developed if necessary. The prototype hardware has all relevant controls, instrumentation, and features that are necessary for proper technology operation. Development results compare favorably to the goals that were established to begin the project.

The Technology Feasibility Statement. The technology feasibility statement is a formal assessment of the capabilities, requirements, and limitations for the selected technology. It summarizes the technology effort. The statement includes a recommendation as to whether to proceed with product design. If "go," it provides the necessary technical data to utilize the technology in a product design, especially information related to the two elements noted above.

For example, the hot-roll fuser technology team constructed a technology feasibility statement to conclude its technology effort. Along with a recommendation to proceed with a copier design, the statement included design and performance information, special material selections and manufacturing methods, and a life estimate. A working configuration, with the necessary instrumentation and controls, was shown to have a sufficiently large "operating space" for acceptable quality. In short, the technology was verified for use, and necessary design requirements were provided (Wilson, 1979).

CONCLUDING REMARKS

The technology selection and development phase is critical to the timely development of superior quality products. Some essential elements for product technology selection and development are described in this article to enable the correct selection, proper development, and adequate verification of product (and process) technologies.

The most effective technology developers strive to create robust products and processes. They carry technology experiments beyond a fragile "gee whiz" stage to characterize and control the technology. They discover critical parameters, establish an operating space, and find any technology limitations.

The technology selection can dramatically affect the product development process. If a new technology is selected, personnel, resources, and time must be allocated for new technology development. In all cases, deliberate engineering action and leadership are imperative to demonstrate the feasibility of a technology.

ARTICLE III: Quantification of Critical Product Characteristics for Superior Product Development

ARTICLE SUMMARY

The proper quantification of critical product characteristics is a vital part of a superior product development process. Well-conceived product performance and quality measures can be used effectively throughout the entire development process to assure that the developed product indeed meets customer needs. These measures provide consistent means by which various technology and design alternatives can be evaluated, and also help optimize the product design.

This article discusses some key features of effective quantitative measurements for critical product characteristics. Three case study examples are utilized to show that effective quantitative measures can be developed for even subjective characteristics.

THREE EXAMPLES

Three actual industrial examples illustrate how proper development of quantitative measurements for critical product characteristics contributes to successful new product development. In this article, the term *critical product characteristics* refers to those features, performance levels, and quality attributes that contribute significantly to the product's customer value. Quantification implies that an objective, repeatable, numerical measure is used to assess the level or amount of that characteristic.

In these example cases, quantitative measures were developed to assess the critical product characteristic of "print quality," a highly subjective but important feature for machines such as copiers, typewriters, and printers.

Quantification of Color Inkjet Print Quality

Print quality quantification played a crucial role in the new technology and product development of a new color inkjet printer. Almost a full three years before product introduction, the color inkjet printer development team undertook a two-pronged effort to measure print quality. A marketing assessment identified potential customers and competition for the printer, while the engineering group developed about thirty measurable print quality characteristics. A vision system was created to measure inkjet print quality characteristics such as ink spot size and shape, media/ink interaction, and mechanical alignment (Figure 11).

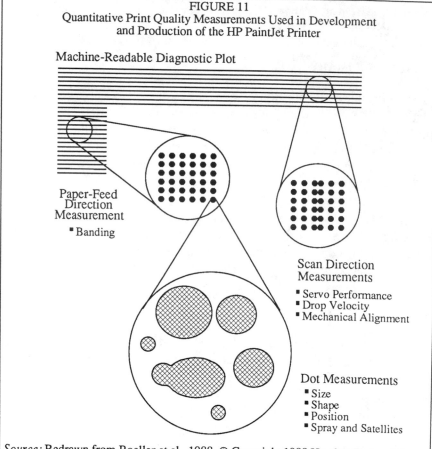

FIGURE 11
Quantitative Print Quality Measurements Used in Development
and Production of the HP PaintJet Printer

Machine-Readable Diagnostic Plot

Paper-Feed
Direction
Measurement
▪ Banding

Scan Direction
Measurements
▪ Servo Performance
▪ Drop Velocity
▪ Mechanical Alignment

Dot Measurements
▪ Size
▪ Shape
▪ Position
▪ Spray and Satellites

Source: Redrawn from Boeller et al., 1988. © Copyright 1988 Hewlett-Packard Company. Reproduced with permission.

A special inkjet machine was built to create print samples containing various inkjet printing errors. Samples produced by this machine were distributed to potential customers to survey how the different error types affected customers' print quality perceptions. The survey results were utilized in several ways: to set limits for the color inkjet technology's critical variables, to establish product performance specifications, and to set engineering design targets. Later, the survey results were used again to define printer production quality standards (Beamer et al., 1988).

Production test equipment was designed to perform the critical print quality measurements during product manufacture. The equipment is used not only to measure inkjet print quality, but also to qualify design and manufacturing process changes. A comprehensive, integrated engineering and manufacturing team effort was necessary to maximize the usefulness of the quality measurement tools.

Quantification of "Hot-Roll" Fusing Quality

Print quality quantification was also very important to the new hot-roll fusing technology development for a high-speed copier. The process of "hot-roll fusing" utilizes a heated roll to apply heat and pressure to affix ("fuse") thermoplastic toner to paper. Because dry hot-roll fusing was a new technology, the print quality characteristics of a hot-roll fuser were unknown.

To develop the hot-roll fuser for the new copier, methods were needed "to keep score" on copier print quality. Two characteristics of the hot-roll fuser technology were found to affect copy quality greatly: (1) toner abrasion resistance, and (2) the amount of "background" toner on white areas.

Toner abrasion resistance is an important copy quality characteristic because it indicates how well the toner is adhered to the paper. The development team first attempted to develop an analytical test to measure abrasion resistance, but was unable to correlate any of the proposed tests to customer print quality perceptions. Eventually, the team settled on an empirical, subjective "fuse grade" scale of 1.0-4.0, as judged by a five or six member "fuse committee." Committee members used their own abrasion test techniques, then rated the copy abrasion numerically using the scale definitions (1.0 = Unacceptable to 4.0 = Excellent). After a "calibration" period, the committee grading values provided a consistent and reliable means of quantifying abrasion resistance.

A special laboratory version of the hot-roll fuser (with adjustable fusing temperature, pressure, and speed) was built to produce copies of varying quality. Project managers, secretaries, and others rated these copies as "acceptable" or "not acceptable." These "customer" ratings were then correlated to the fuse committee's numerical ranking to establish quality limits for the fuse grade scale. The fuse committee and scale were used throughout the development process to define the fuser technology's operating space, to establish copier quality objectives, and to optimize the fuser design.

Background toner in white areas is also an important copy quality characteristic because background toner creates "black spots" or a "gray" appearance in the white areas of the paper. A light reflectance test was created to measure the amount of this background toner. The reflectance of the paper was measured before and after being run through the fuser. Customer testing indicated that background reflectance decreases of less than 1 percent could not be detected, so this level was established as the upper allowable limit. This test was also used throughout the copier development to assure proper operation of the fuser and related systems (Wilson, 1979).

Quantification of Resistive Ribbon Print Quality

A resistive ribbon technology and typewriter development team also needed to develop reliable print quality measures to develop a new "resistive ribbon" typewriter. The resistive ribbon technology uses forty tiny, current-carrying wires that contact an electrically resistive ribbon. Current from the wires travels through and heats the ribbon, which melts a thermoplastic material. Pressure from the wires presses the melted material into the paper.

Fast, reliable measures were needed to assess the quality of the resistive ribbon printing. Since the new typewriter was to reproduce traditional, well-defined type styles, the basic quality measurement approach was to compare the printed characters to the ideal characters stored in the typewriter's memory.

A scanner device was set up to measure two printed type parameters that had a large effect on perceived print quality: printed character area, and printed character perimeter. Two nondimensional indexes, a normalized area index and a geometric index, were established from both measured and ideal values of area and perimeter to create simple print quality indicators.

Type characters of various area and roughness were graded visually to determine acceptable values for the normalized area and geometric index indicators. Normalized area limits were biased slightly to account for customers' preference for very bold, dark type. Geometric index limits were set to control rough edges, stripedness, and voids.

These type quality measures were developed during the technology development phase so that they could be used to establish the resistive ribbon technology's operating space. The measures were also used to optimize machine variables such as printing speed and to assure that acceptable type quality could be attained on many different paper types (Voit, 1988).

ROLE OF QUANTIFIED MEASURES IN THE PRODUCT DEVELOPMENT PROCESS

The case study examples demonstrate the importance of proper quantification of critical product characteristics to successful product development. Thus, the way these measures affect the development process and the significant features of sound quantitative measures need to be well understood.

As discussed in Article I, the goal of the essential elements is to integrate the many diverse product development activities into a coherent, focused process and to emphasize the use of the most appropriate engineering methods at the most appropriate time in the process. In particular, several of the essential elements in Articles I and II emphasize the need for good methods for assessing how well the new product meets customers' quality and performance expectations. Thus, the development and use of effective, quantitative measurements for critical product characteristics are keys to successful implementation for many of the essential elements for superior product development.

The need for reliable, customer-oriented product measures arises very early in the development process, during the technology selection and development phase. Quantitative measures are required to establish the operating space and to assure the feasibility of a new technology. In the hot-roll fusing example, the development team needed to find and to optimize an operating space for fuser temperature, pressure, and speed that produced good quality copies. The abrasion resistance and background toner measurements were indispensable methods for evaluating fuse quality during this effort.

As shown in Figure 1, a customer future needs projection is performed at the same time as the technology selection and development. Defining customer needs in terms of quantified measurements provides useful tools to measure product performance versus customer requirements. The inkjet team, for example, performed a survey to determine customer sensitivity to different types of inkjet printing errors. The survey results were used to determine which inkjet characteristics were most important to customers, and to set customer-based, quantitative limits for inkjet print quality measurements. In all three cases, quantitative measurements for customer needs were developed at the start of the development process so that customer-derived limits could be used to verify technology and product performance throughout the process.

Product specifications are set during the final product definition phase (Figure 1), after the technology is verified and customer needs are established. Quantitative values for critical product characteristics, based on the measures developed earlier, are set as targets for the product (and process) design. In the resistive ribbon typewriter example, the team put numerical limits for the normalized area and geometric index indicators into the product definition. Quantified print quality targets were an integral part of the final product definition in all three examples.

The quantified measures are used during the product design and evaluation phase to assess the evolving product's ability to meet the product definition requirements. In the fuser project, strict fuser temperature control was necessary to maintain adequate copy quality. Fuse grade measurements were used during the copier's design and evaluation phase to assure that the fuser temperature was controlled adequately.

When the product enters the product manufacturing phase, the measures are used again for product audit testing and may even be used in production to verify that the production-level product meets customer requirements. The color inkjet project used the same equipment and tests developed during the technology development phase for manufacturing quality assurance testing.

As the above discussion indicates, quantitative measurements of critical product characteristics are used throughout the entire product development process. Some of the ways that these measures can be used in the various development phases are illustrated in Figure 12. The selected product development phases shown are extracted from Figure 1.

ESSENTIAL ELEMENTS FOR EFFECTIVE MEASUREMENT OF CRITICAL PRODUCT CHARACTERISTICS

The selection and development of suitable measures for critical product characteristics is a difficult task. Since product characteristics vary widely, measurement criteria and techniques also differ. However, some common elements among the best product characteristic measures clearly distinguish them from other, less effective measures. These essential elements of superior product characteristic measures are discussed below and are summarized in Figure 13.

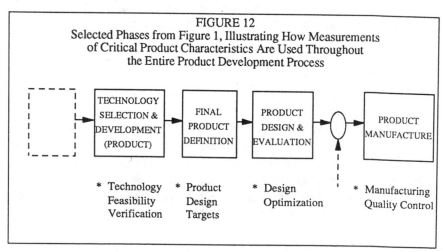

FIGURE 12
Selected Phases from Figure 1, Illustrating How Measurements of Critical Product Characteristics Are Used Throughout the Entire Product Development Process

---

FIGURE 13
Some Essential Elements of Superior Product Characteristic Measures

* Measures Are Customer Oriented

+ Measure Characteristics Important to Customers
+ Limits Are Customer-Based

* Measures Developed at Start of
Product Development Process

* Measures Have Multiple Uses
Throughout Process

+ Product Quality "Scorekeeping"
+ Measure Team Progress

* Measures Are Simple, Easy-to-Use

* Measurement Development:
A Planned, Deliberate Activity

The preceding case study examples were selected to illustrate many of these essential elements for superior product characteristic measures. The best measures are customer oriented in at least two ways: (1) the measures quantify characteristics that are important to customers, and (2) acceptable values for these measurements are based on direct customer input. Even subjective characteristics are measured, as necessary, if those items are important to the customer. In the presented cases, measurements for the important, subjective characteristic of "print quality" were developed. Customer surveys and evaluation were used to establish print quality requirements for the products.

The most effective quantitative measures for critical product characteristics are developed at the start of the product development process. The measures are then used for multiple purposes throughout the entire process, from technology selection to manufacturing. In particular, the measures enable product quality "scorekeeping," so that the development team can evaluate its own progress throughout the process. In the case study examples, the print quality measures were used to verify technology feasibility, to define product design targets and specifications, and to set production quality requirements. The respective development teams used their measures to assess how well they were doing throughout the entire product development process.

The most effective measures are simple, effective, and easy to use. Because of the considerable time and effort that is necessary, the development of suitable product characteristic measures is a planned, deliberate activity. Good product measures improve the product development process by providing essential evaluation and quality data that are needed to develop the product. In the case studies, development teams expended considerable effort to develop, verify, and simplify measurement equipment and procedures. Although the measurement development required some time, overall product development times were not adversely affected because the measures provided fast and accurate feedback to the development team throughout the development process.

CONCLUDING REMARKS

The proper quantification of critical product characteristics is an important component of a superior product development process. Good product measures can be used throughout the entire process to assure that the product meets customer needs. Even many subjective product characteristics can be measured quantitatively.

The three industrial case study examples can be used to generate ideas, to improve their use of product measures, and to "benchmark" their product measures against those of worldclass product development teams. The essential elements for effective measurement of critical product characteristics can be used as a guide for creating, verifying, and using effective quantitative measures.

ARTICLE IV: Some Essential Elements for Superior Product Manufacturing

ARTICLE SUMMARY

The competitive need to shorten the product development process and to improve product quality makes the product manufacturing process critical to the timely introduction of superior products. This article identifies "some essential elements" for superior product manufacturing that enable a product development project to be planned and executed with the appropriate emphasis on the manufacturing process. A method for formalizing the transfer of critical product information to the manufacturing process is also presented. Appropriate implementation of these essential elements is imperative to achieve superior results.

PRODUCT MANUFACTURE PHASE OF PRODUCT DEVELOPMENT

For discussion purposes, it is convenient to divide the product manufacture phase of product development into parts manufacture activity and system assembly activity, as shown in Figure 14. Before presenting the essential elements for superior product manufacture, we examine some significant manufacturing-related problems in American industry today. The development teams in the case studies successfully avoided these problems.

SOME PROBLEMS IN PRODUCT MANUFACTURING

The management structure of a typical large U.S. company is functionally based, consisting of many separate departments performing specialized tasks. Largely autonomous marketing, manufacturing, procurement, distribution, engineering, finance, pricing, plans and controls, and service departments (to name but a few) each perform their particular functions utilizing their own management systems and controls.

Within this functional structure, a new product is transferred from the engineering and design departments to manufacturing through a formalized release-to-manufacture checkpoint procedure. To pass through the checkpoint, product functional testing has been completed successfully, final engineering drawings and specifications have been prepared, and the product is ready for full-scale manufacture. Theoretically, the release-to-manufacture checkpoint assures that the product engineering and design

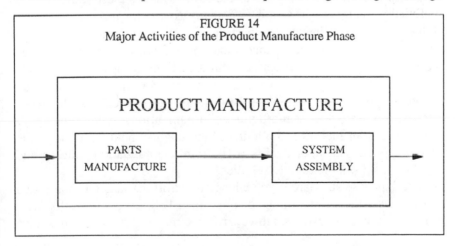

FIGURE 14
Major Activities of the Product Manufacture Phase

PRODUCT MANUFACTURE

PARTS MANUFACTURE → SYSTEM ASSEMBLY

functions are 100 percent complete, so that the manufacturing organization merely has to procure parts and replicate the product.

In reality, the checkpoint procedure can fail to detect significant problems, such as expensive-to-manufacture parts and flawed system assemblies. Because engineering and manufacturing are separate functions, and are often further separated by a procurement organization and perhaps long distances, product designers and engineers have little incentive to consult with manufacturing, other than that required to complete the release-to-manufacturing procedure. Design and engineering errors that slip through the release checkpoint then become manufacturing department problems, regardless of cause. Many manufacturing personnel have become so dissatisfied with the release procedure that they refer to it disparagingly as engineering "throwing the product over the wall" to the manufacturing organization.

Some firms, cognizant of the problems inherent with the release-to-manufacture system, advocate an early manufacturing involvement concept, whereby manufacturing staff personnel (but not the actual parts manufacturing personnel) participate in the product design process. However, this "involvement" can easily degenerate into a continuous manufacturing "veto" process, where any potential design that might create even the least bit of a manufacturing challenge becomes subject to needless controversy. The undesirable design compromises and schedule delays that can result from this kind of involvement may result in delayed and uncompetitive new products.

In addition, many U.S. firms have large "materials" or "commodities" organizations to manage the increasingly complex parts bidding, purchasing, and delivery systems. As these groups attempt to reduce product cost by bidding repeatedly for minimum parts cost, an increasing number of vendors bid and/or supply parts to the firm. Having these multiple and continually changing part suppliers in many diverse locations exacerbates problems related to inadequate part design, miscommunication through drawings and specifications, inadequate manufacturing process control, and vendor errors. Computer and communications companies contribute to this problem by suggesting that problems caused by multiple-site, remote manufacturing can be solved simply by increasing electronic information transfer. Manufacturing organizations have repeatedly demonstrated an inability to maintain high-quality manufacturing while being supplied with poor-quality parts from a continually changing and largely uncontrollable remote supplier base.

The Japanese standard of excellence in world markets has magnified tremendously the shortcomings of traditional U.S. product development and manufacturing systems. However, some major U.S. companies have responded successfully to this competition by changing their product development and manufacturing processes. In many cases, these leading U.S. firms have studied Japanese companies and methods and found them to be superior; the essential elements for superior product manufacture that have been adopted by these firms have much in common with well-established and successful Japanese methods.

SOME ESSENTIAL ELEMENTS FOR SUPERIOR PRODUCT MANUFACTURE

Some essential elements that are fundamental to the manufacture of superior quality products have been extracted from the case studies. The concepts presented are not new; many people working in product development and manufacturing are familiar with these essential elements. However, success in the studied cases was not based on mere awareness of the essential elements; rather, it was predicated on how well the essential elements were implemented throughout the product development and manufacturing processes.

Single-Product Development/Manufacturing Team. Although this element is presented in Article I, the single-development/manufacturing team merits repetition, as it may be the single most influential essential element affecting the entire product development process. The most successful teams in the case studies controlled all aspects of their projects, from technology selection through to manufacturing.

An obvious advantage to the single team structure is that all product design *and* manufacturing decisions become the responsibility of a product-dedicated team with a single leader. Since the team is staffed to have expertise in the many diverse skills needed to develop a product successfully, including manufacturing skills, the team is quite capable of managing all the manufacturing aspects of the project.

The team management responsibilities create an enormously broad technical demand on the chief engineer (project leader), who must manage everything from technology selection to modern manufacturing methods. Today's specialized environment makes it difficult to find people capable of managing concurrent development of both complex products and complex manufacturing systems, on the shortest possible schedule. A deliberate management effort is required to assure that the talented people within the organization obtain the broad technical and managerial experiences necessary to become effective, capable chief engineers.

Product Manufacture – Assembly

Several of the essential elements apply particularly to a company's internal system assembly processes. They are discussed below and are also listed in Figure 15.

Product Team Responsible for First Six Months of Product Manufacture. Under the single-team approach, the development/manufacturing team is responsible not only for the product design, but also for pilot product manufacture. The traditional release-to-manufacture checkpoint is replaced by a proof of manufacture point that occurs about six months after the start of production. This manufacturing requirement is established at the beginning of the project, when the team is formed.

In the case studies, the team approach to manufacturing is quite different from that for a functional structure. The ultimate objective of each project is to complete pilot manufacturing, including product delivery to the customer. Thus, all the project goals are geared to successful product manufacture rather than just to release to manufacture. When product designers in the team share responsibility for successful product manufacture, the design emphasis is changed from "getting the design finished to give it to manufacturing" to "completing a design that can be manufactured with the highest quality and lowest cost."

Critical Manufacturing Processes "in-house." In many of the case studies, selected parts and assemblies critical to the product are specially designed and manufactured to give the product a distinct competitive advantage. These advantages are achieved by advancing the state of the art

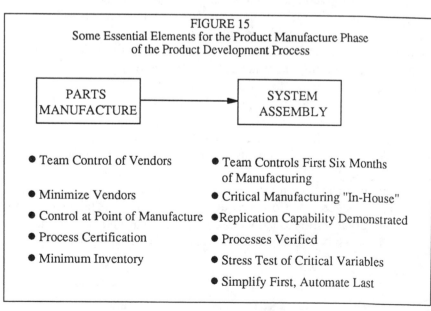

FIGURE 15
Some Essential Elements for the Product Manufacture Phase
of the Product Development Process

| PARTS MANUFACTURE | → | SYSTEM ASSEMBLY |

- Team Control of Vendors

- Minimize Vendors

- Control at Point of Manufacture

- Process Certification

- Minimum Inventory

- Team Controls First Six Months of Manufacturing
- Critical Manufacturing "In-House"
- Replication Capability Demonstrated
- Processes Verified
- Stress Test of Critical Variables
- Simplify First, Automate Last

for important product features and their associated manufacturing processes.

In most of these cases, the manufacturing process advances are developed in-house and kept proprietary to preserve the competitive advantage and to maintain maximum quality control and improvement. In other cases, very close partnerships with specialty vendors are established to achieve the advance.

A pen plotter development team formed a partnership with an innovative plastic molder and die maker to develop advanced molding techniques for their disposable plotter pens. The new techniques enabled the pen parts to be made to extremely small tolerances, which allowed fast automated pen assembly and improved pen performance. Based on this experience, the firm now has designated single sources for all its plastic parts from one of three designated molding vendors. When a new project team is formed, die maker and molding firms are selected to work with the team (and its parts designers) throughout the entire project (McLeod et al., 1989).

Replication Capability Demonstrated (by Pilot Run and Test), prior to Starting Full-Scale Manufacturing. Manufacturing processes developed in the studied cases were tested thoroughly to assure that they were capable of replicating the new product assembly. The teams conducted full-scale tests to assure that their processes were capable of making defect-free products in the production environment. Some companies used the terms *pilot run* or *manufacturing verification test* to describe this activity. Controlled ramp-ups were used to verify production capability in an orderly manner. One firm not only requires a manufacturing scale-up to full production, but also mandates customer testing of pilot-run produced products before any product can be introduced to the general market (Xerox Corporation, 1988).

Manufacturing Processes Verified. The importance of using characterized, verified processes in manufacturing is stated by a color inkjet team: "Use standard, well-understood processes. Historically, when we have strayed from this concept we have suffered low yields, cost increases, and many engineer hours of process support and characterization" (Smith et al., 1988). In the case studies, the primary manufacturing goal was to assure the quality and reliability of their processes. Development teams met this need by limiting manufacturing processes to those that were well understood and characterized. These characterized processes, then, were verified as being capable of meeting the product engineering specifications.

Obviously, process verification is dependent on the quality of the process design. For one advanced manufacturing firm, process verification begins in the manufacturing system design phase of product development (Figure 1). Their manufacturing system design plan includes several key requirements. First, each process must be "verifiable"; that is, methods must exist to ascertain that "you did it right" (Hewlett-Packard, 1987b). Next, no "black art" processes are permitted; "all key performance attributes must have quantifiable PPMs part-per-million failure rates" (McLeod et al., 1989). In addition, processes must be engineering-free; that is, processes must function without ongoing support from engineering.

Stress Testing of Critical Variables. A most difficult assessment for some products is to determine whether the assembly process adversely affects the reliability of critical machine functions. Short-duration functional check tests demonstrate only one-time, nominal operation, and provide no indication of the function's reliability (unless its reliability is so poor that it fails the functional tests). Without a manufacturing reliability assessment, products that pass factory functional tests may be shipped to customers, only to fail as soon as the product experiences a slight variation in operating conditions. To address this problem, manufacturing stress testing (screening) was used in selected cases to verify that the functional operating space of the product was not compromised during product assembly.

For example, high-speed copy machines are stress tested to assure document handling reliability after initial system assembly. A paper "stress pak," consisting of many different paper thicknesses and types, is used to test the document handler's ability to process the wide variety of papers that might be used in the copier. Because the document handler's operating space includes all of the stress pak paper types and thicknesses, manufacturing test failures indicate an incorrect assembly or a faulty part and thus signal the need for corrective action. No copier is permitted to be shipped without passing this test error-free. The use of this stress screen preserves the design reliability of the document-handling function through the assembly process.

A manager of a popular automated tape cartridge drive system attributes "the early improvement in the drive . . . to the early implementation of stress screening." However, management support and rapid corrective action were required for successful implementation, since stress screening substantially affected initial production yields as latent defects were uncovered (Abbott, 1988).

The need for management support and rapid corrective action during the implementation of stress screening must not be underestimated. The use of a manufacturing procedure that deliberately imposes production limitations (i.e., stress testing and its resulting product failures) may be considered an unnatural act to a manufacturing organization that is measured by production quantities. A potential conflict is created when factory production volume is deliberately sacrificed to prevent a potential customer failure. The management of the production measurement system must prioritize the elimination of field failures over the volume shipment of supposedly error-free products that actually have a latent defect.

A stress screening strategy is greatly affected by technology, materials, and design decisions, and thus has to be formulated specifically for each product. To be effective, the stress test needs to attack important product failure modes and must test the product at a sufficient stimulus level while the product is operating. Provision must be made for product failure diagnosis and repair (Burcak, 1986). Although stress testing is controversial and must be managed properly to be effective, it is important enough that one major company in 1983 established a worldwide corporate strategy to incorporate systematic stress testing during product design and manufacturing (Hayes and Wheelwright, 1984).

"Simplify First, Automate Last." Several teams developed their product and manufacturing systems concurrently. Products in several of the case studies were designed for automated robotic assembly. Product assembly time and complexity were reduced dramatically by minimizing the number of parts and by using "snap-together" techniques in the product's design.

In these cases, the need for robotic assembly was brought into question after the design was completed, since human assembly of the simplified design was trivial and virtually error-free. In one case where robots had already been purchased and installed, robotic assembly methods were implemented as planned. However, when the product assembly was later transferred to another manufacturing location, the robots were left behind and human assembly was used instead, except for a few select operations. The change was made because robot setup and maintenance costs were found to be excessive when compared to simple human assembly. The lesson learned is this: simplify the product design as if a robot were going to assemble it; then carefully choose what operations are worth the investment of robotic assembly (Janssen, 1988).

Product Manufacture – Parts

Control of the parts manufacturing process in the case studies was found to be critical to achieving product quality objectives. Thus, parts acquisition and control were not delegated to other organizations. Some essential elements affecting parts manufacture are discussed below.

Team Responsible for Vendor Selection and Coordination. In most of the studied cases, vendor selection was controlled completely by the development/manufacturing team, and not by an independent functional organization. This approach required a change in management practices so that the team controlled the organization's procurement practices, not a materials management or procurement organization. Vendor decisions were based on assuring continuous flow of quality parts and assemblies with a minimum of scrap, rework, and service costs.

In a few cases, the overall functional management structure was unchanged, but a procurement member was assigned to, and located with, the development/manufacturing team. Where the procurement organization was utilized, the procurement organization understood that the development team was to select and control vendors, not the bidding process. Development team managers in the case studies considered vendor selection based on capability, and not "low bid," as an extremely important element in the project's success. No other subject evoked such intense feelings as did the control of vendor parts. Virtually every group had previously experienced serious quality problems based on parts obtained via the "low-bid" process.

Minimization of Number of Vendors. All the companies studied have striven to reduce parts quality problems by minimizing the number of vendors and by establishing certification programs for their parts manufacturing processes. They have reversed the "vendor roulette" process that has maximized bidding, increased the number of vendors, and created major quality and cost problems.

One major company uses single sourcing with early vendor identification to control the manufacturing process. Single sourcing is used exclusively, unless domestic-content laws require that a percentage of the product be manufactured in the same country in which the product is sold. This single-source strategy enabled the company to reduce its "forward product" vendor base from five thousand to three hundred firms (Bebb, 1989).

Process Control at Point of Manufacture. Volumes have been written about Statistical Process Control (SPC) techniques to control manufacturing processes, so these methods will not be discussed here. However, the most effective use of SPC requires that it be used at the point of manufacture, by production personnel, to stop the creation of bad parts at their sources. Therefore, the essential element of process control includes the words, "at the point of manufacture." An example of process control of critical variables at the point of manufacture is presented later in this chapter in Figure 16.

Process Certification Required. Process control at the point of manufacture was equally important for vendor-produced parts as well. The selected single-source vendors were required to certify process control for each part number by sending the process control information with every parts shipment. These vendors were not "blanket certified," but instead

FIGURE 16
The Trail of Critical Product Characteristics

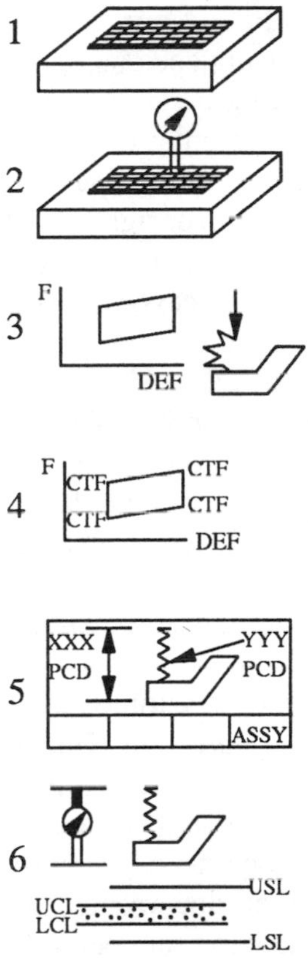

	ACTIVITY	PHASE
1	CHARACTERISTICS IDENTIFIED (CUSTOMER INPUT)	CUSTOMER FUTURE NEEDS PROJECTION
2	CHARACTERISTICS QUANTIFIED	TECHNOLOGY DEVELOPMENT
3	MECHANISM DESIGNED TO ACHIEVE CHARACTERISTICS	PRODUCT DESIGN AND DEVELOPMENT
4	ACHIEVABLE CHARACTERISTIC DOCUMENTED IN ENGINEERING SPECIFICATIONS AS [CTF]	PRODUCT DESIGN AND EVALUATION
5	PROCESS CONTROL METHODS SELECTED AND DIMENSIONS IDENTIFIED AS PROCESS CONTROL DIMENSIONS [PCD]	PRODUCT AND MANUFACTURING SYSTEM DESIGN
6	POINT-OF-MANUFACTURE STATISTICAL PROCESS CONTROL IMPLEMENTED IN CAPABLE MANUFACTURING PROCESS	PRODUCT MANUFACTURE

were certified on a part-to-part basis. Vendors became partners in the manufacturing process and were rewarded with long-term contracts for their efforts. This long-term contract partnership provided an incentive for continual parts quality improvement, which reduced long-term parts costs by reducing scrap and rework (McLeod, 1989).

Minimum Inventory. The studied companies understand the Japanese axiom of inventory is the enemy and are acting to reduce it. Eliminating multiple vendors, lowering parts inventory, and reducing bidding require significant organizational changes and thus encounter considerable resistance. The materials management and procurement bureaucracies are so entrenched in many American companies that it is difficult to implement the necessary changes. However, the companies in the case studies are overcoming these barriers and are improving their manufacturing processes by making these changes.

FORMALIZING THE DEVELOPMENT/MANUFACTURING CONNECTION:
The Trail of Critical Product Characteristics

The structure of many current U.S. functional organizations makes it difficult to assure that important information related to critical product characteristics (product functions, important part dimensions, etc.) are transferred to and understood by the manufacturing organization. The single development/manufacturing teams in the case studies literally "carried" this critical product information into the manufacturing phase, since the team was responsible for manufacturing system design and pilot manufacturing. However, even in most of these cases, the transfer of critical product information to the manufacturing process was still an informal activity, and the effectiveness of this transfer was entirely dependent on the actions of the particular individuals involved.

One team in the case studies was able to define a formal method for transferring critical product characteristic information to the manufacturing process. This transfer formally connects development to manufacturing and serves as an outstanding example as to how product quality can be improved by integrating the essential elements throughout the development process. This method is described below and is also illustrated in Figure 16.

The keyboard's "touch" is an important product feature for a typewriter and is often the deciding factor in a new typewriter purchase. Therefore, the force-deflection characteristic for the keys, which controls their "touch," is a critical product characteristic for the keyboard design. Steps 1 through 3 of Figure 16 illustrate how the characteristic is identified, quantified, and designed. The characteristic is then documented in the product engineering specification as a critical-to-function parameter (CTF) that must be controlled (Step 4 of Figure 16). Part dimensions and features that affect the critical-to-function parameter are subsequently identified as critical-to-function (CTF) dimensions on the engineering drawings. In Step 5, some of the critical-to-function dimensions are designated as process control dimensions (PCDs) to be used for manufacturing process control. Statistical process control (SPC) is implemented in manufacturing (Step 6) using the process control dimensions (PCDs) to assure that the process is stable and capable of making a product that will meet all engineering specification requirements. To assure manufacturing adherence to engineering specifications, any off-specification permit for any CTF dimension requires the written, signed approval of the third-level manufacturing manager.

The PCDs may not always correspond one-to-one with the CTF dimensions. For example, a keyboard's "touch" characteristic is not only determined by key spring force-deflection characteristics, but may also be affected adversely by guide surface binding. The guide plate, a long plastic part that supports all the keys, must be flat and free from warpage to prevent this binding.

Thus, precise control of the guide plate molding process is necessary. After testing the molding process, a specially defined PCD, extending diagonally across the length of the guide plate, was added to the drawing just for process control. As long as this sensitive PCD stays within its control bounds, the individual key guide surfaces will not cause binding. This cleverly defined process control dimension (PCD), along with the spring force-displacement control, is used to ensure the quality of the critical-to-function (CTF) force-displacement "touch" characteristic for the keyboard (Pollard, 1989).

We propose that this method of converting CTF parameters into process control dimensions (PCD) for statistical control of the manufacturing process is a powerful technique that should be emulated by other manufacturers. It is a documented, formal method for transferring the necessary information so that critical product characteristics can be controlled properly throughout the entire product development process.

CONCLUDING REMARKS

Case studies of innovative product development indicate that some major American companies are changing their product development and manufacturing processes significantly to be competitive. In the successful cases, engineering, manufacturing, and parts vendor organizations are combined into single teams that value the successful production of a high-value product over all other functional objectives. These teams function as small vertically integrated organizations that include all necessary engineering and manufacturing functions.

The essential elements for superior product manufacture form a basis for integrating the parts manufacturing and system assembly operations into one functioning whole. These elements recommend methods for effective control of both the parts manufacturing and system assembly processes. They also help to assure that the critical-to-function variables of the product are controlled properly during the manufacturing process.

A specific case study example was presented to illustrate a formal method for transferring critical product characteristic information from development to the manufacturing process. The authors recommend this approach as an effective method for improving and controlling the quality of manufactured products.

REFERENCES

The material in this chapter is adapted from four technical papers that have been published and presented to the following major engineering conferences:

Wilson, C. C., and M. E. Kennedy. "Some Essential Elements for Superior Product Development." Presented to ASME Winter Annual Meeting, San Francisco, Calif., December 1989.

Wilson, C. C., and M. E. Kennedy. "Quantification of Critical Product Characteristics for Superior Product Development." Presented to ASME Winter Annual Meeting, San Francisco, Calif., December 1989.

Wilson, C. C., and M. E. Kennedy. "Some Essential Elements for Product Technology Selection and Development." Presented to Second International Conference on Management of Technology, University of Miami, Miami, Fla., February 1990.

Wilson, C. C., and M. E. Kennedy. "Some Essential Elements for Superior Product Manufacture," Presented to Manufacturing International '90 (MI'90), Atlanta, Ga., March 1990.

Case Study References

Abbott, T. "Improving the Product Development Process." Notes from ASME Short Course. "Case Studies of Engineering and Manufacturing Methods for Superior Results," Atlanta, Ga., April 18-19, 1988.

Abbott, T. Storage Technology Corporation. Letter to C. C. Wilson, dated August 30, 1989.

Baker, J. P., et al. "Design and Development of a Color Thermal Inkjet Print Cartridge." *Hewlett-Packard Journal* (August 1988): 6-15.

Barrett, D. "Designing for Reliability." Working paper from Course ME 597, "Investigations of Design Methodology for Superior Products," University of Colorado at Boulder, April 22, 1987.

Beamer, D., et al. "Print Quality and Pen Development." *Hewlett-Packard Journal* (August 1988): 14.

Bebb, B. "Quality Design Engineering, the Missing Link in U.S. Competitiveness." Presented at National Science Foundation Design Theory Workshop, University of Massachusetts, June 1989.

Boeller, C. A., et al. "High-Volume Microassembly of Color Thermal Inkjet Printheads and Cartridges." *Hewlett-Packard Journal* (August 1988): 32-40.

Burcak, T. "Application of Stress Screening to Commercial Products." Proceedings, Institute of Environmental Sciences, pp. 317-320.

Carley, W. M. "Wing Flap: Contractor's Mishaps in New Technology Made the Navy Seethe." *The Wall Street Journal*, January 11, 1989, pp. A1, A6.

Deaton, F., et al. "The Proprinter Story." IBM Corporation, Charlotte, N. C., no date.

Galatha, M. "Design for Automation – The IBM Proprinter." Notes from lecture at the University of Tennessee, Knoxville, April 14, 1988.

Hadden, L. L. "Product Development at Xerox: Meeting the Competitive Challenge." Notes from presentation to Copying and Duplicating Industry Conference, February 10-12, 1986.

Hayes, R. H., and S. C. Wheelwright. *Restoring Our Competitive Edge.* New York: John Wiley and Sons, 1984.

Hewlett-Packard. "Lab Project Phases." Working Document from HP PaintJet team, San Diego, Calif., 1987a.

Hewlett-Packard. "PaintJet Manufacturing Goals." Working Document from HP Paint-Jet team, San Diego, Calif., 1987b.

HP Checkpoint Objectives. Hewlett-Packard Working Document. San Diego, Calif.

Janssen, D. "A Diskette Drive Design for Automatic Assembly." Course Notes from ASME Short Course. "Case Studies of Engineering and Manufacturing Methods for Superior Results," Atlanta, Ga., April 18-19, 1988.

Kennedy, M. E. "Quality Programs: Structure and Implementation." Working paper from Course ME 5990, "Investigations of Design Methodology for Superior Products," University of Tennessee, May 26, 1988.

McLeod, G., et al. Hewlett-Packard Plotter Pen and PaintJet teams, Interviews. San Diego, Calif., May 1989.

PaintJet Manufacturing Goals. Working Document. Hewlett-Packard Corporation, San Diego, Calif., September 1987.

Pollard, E. "IBM Keyboard Development." Notes from lecture at the University of Tennessee, Knoxville, May 5, 1988.

Pollard, E. "IBM Typewriter Keyboard Design." Notes from case study presented at the University of Tennessee, Knoxville, September 26, 1989.

Smith, J. C., et al. "Development of a Color Graphics Printer." *Hewlett-Packard Journal,* Palo Alto, Calif., August 1988, pp. 16-20.

Voit, W. "Resistive Ribbon Technology." Notes from case study presented at the University of Tennessee, Knoxville, Tenn., April 14, 1988.

Wilkerson, H. J. "Boeing 747 Testing." Notes from lecture at the University of Tennessee, Knoxville, Tenn., April 12, 1988.

Wilson, C. C. "A New Fuser Technology for Electro-photographic Printing Machines." *Journal of Applied Photographic Engineering* (Summer 1979): 148-156.

Wilson, C. C. "Investigations of Design Methodology for Superior Products." Proceedings – American Society for Engineering Education Zone II Meeting, Louisville, Ky., April 9-12, 1988.

Xerox Corporation. "Product Delivery Process Overview (PDP)." Business Products and Systems Group, Webster, N.Y.

CHAPTER 19

A NEW ROLE FOR ENGINEERING PROCESS CONTROL FOCUSED ON IMPROVING QUALITY

CHARLES F. MOORE
Distinguished Service Professor of Chemical Engineering
University of Tennessee

SUMMARY

This chapter discusses technical and organizational issues related to engineering process control. Traditionally, engineering process control has been responsible for the design of automatic control systems. It is time, however, to broaden the role of engineering process control to include a more long-range perspective on manufacturing operations: one that is focused on eliminating as well as compensating for the presence of operational disturbances.

Details of the operation and control of process units may seem far removed from customer value. However, there should be many important relationships between engineering process control and customer satisfaction. Engineering process control can help improve the consistency and uniformity of the product shipped to the customer, as well as the efficiency, reliability, and flexibility of a manufacturing operation. Product quality, dependable shipments, lower price, and flexibility to changing customer needs are all valued by the external as well as the internal customers. The new role of engineering process control is one that works much more closely with other functional groups in addressing such customer sensitive issues.

The traditional role of engineering process control has been the design and implementation of automatic systems to monitor and control manufacturing processes. Such systems are often essential for safe, consistent operations; yet, manufacturing quality would be better served if the need for these systems were reduced. Engineering control systems are effective in compensating for variation; nevertheless, they often address only the symptoms of more fundamental problems. Poor process design, equipment malfunction and failure, and sloppy process operations are all potential sources of variation that can be eliminated. Clearly, it is important to identify such fundamental problems and, where economical, to correct them.

The new role of engineering process control focuses on managing variation beyond designing and implementing compensation systems. This chapter discusses a broader role of engineering process control that includes studying variation and how it affects quality. Several cross-functional liaisons are suggested that could provide important new perspectives to both understand and manage variation. The technical and organizational issues presented in this chapter are particularly salient to the continuous process industries; yet, they also apply to any industry that operates continuous or semicontinuous process equipment.

ENGINEERING PROCESS CONTROL AND THE QUALITY REVOLUTION

A quality revolution is occurring throughout manufacturing. In the United States that revolution started in the automobile industry and is now beginning to influence other areas of manufacturing. The experiences in the automobile industry generally provide a framework for quality improvement in other areas. In the continuous process industry certain differences need to be considered in the design of quality improvement initiatives. One important difference concerns the role and function of engineering process control.

In discrete manufacturing the prevailing attitude is that feedback control systems should be avoided. The experience on assembly lines has been that automatic adjustments are a potential source of variation and tend to obstruct and confuse studies that focus on variation. In continuous manufacturing, however, engineering process control plays a more essential role. The nature of continuous processes and of the environment in which they operate usually requires the presence of engineering control systems. These systems monitor critical process variables and must continually make fast and subtle adjustments to the material and energy flows to insure safe and dependable operations. The demand for such systems is increasing. The evolution of process design has been toward more complex plants. Emphasis on energy efficiency and production flexibility has resulted in process designs that are inherently more difficult to operate. New process designs also include environmental safeguards that tend to add to the complexity of the process and to increase the need for well-designed engineering control systems.

Quality improvement programs in the continuous process industry (especially those that are based on models from discrete manufacturing) must come to terms with engineering process control. In continuous manufacturing it is naive (and indeed unsafe) for quality programs to insist, in the name of quality improvement, that all feedback control systems be turned off. Most continuous processes will not operate without some level of automation. In the continuous process industries, such engineering control systems are not only a fact of life but also an important tool that, if properly understood, can be used effectively to help improve quality.

On the other hand, engineering process control cannot exist in a vacuum. We, who design and oversee automatic control systems, must come to terms with the goals of these quality improvement programs. We must realize, with respect to quality, that considerable room for improvement exists in the present generation of control system designs. We must also realize that engineering process control must play a vital role in defining the focus of these quality improvement programs.

To fully participate in quality improvement, engineering process control must take some of the myth, magic, and math out of its speciality. Historically, engineering process control has been wrapped so tightly in its own highly technical language that communication with other functional groups has been difficult. In its new role such cross-functional communication is vital. Engineering process control must be responsible for finding ways to clearly communicate important quality-related issues without using such highly specialized jargon.

QUALITY IMPROVEMENT

Before considering a new quality oriented role for engineering process control, it is important to understand the nature of quality in the continuous process industries. Programs that use the automobile industry as a model for quality improvement can miss aspects of quality that are more important in the continuous process industries than in discrete manufacturing. The use of quality improvement models developed from experiences in another industry provides a useful framework. But thoughtful care should be taken to adapt and adjust those models for the differences between industries and between processes within each industry.

As indicated in Figure 1 there are two broad components of quality: product quality and production quality. Both are concerns in continuous and discrete manufacturing; yet, the nature and relative importance of each vary from industry to industry and from application to application. It is important to quality improvement programs that both components of quality be clearly understood for each application.

```
┌──────────────────────────────────────────────────────────────────────┐
│                              FIGURE 1                                  │
│              Dimensions of Quality in Continuous Manufacturing         │
│                         Product Quality                                │
│                          ● Uniformity                                  │
│                          ● Consistency                                 │
│                          ● Purity                                      │
│                         Production Quality                             │
│                          ● Efficiency                                  │
│                          ● Flexibility                                 │
│                          ● Reliability                                 │
│                          ● Productivity                                │
│                                                                        │
└──────────────────────────────────────────────────────────────────────┘
```

Product Quality: The factors that characterize product quality can be complex and confusing. The quality of discrete consumer products (i.e., automobiles, stereos, laundry detergent, house paint) may be difficult to quantify and can be influenced (in the short term, at least) by marketing strategies. In the continuous process industries, however, most products are intermediates and/or commodities whose quality standards are measurable and clearly defined by the market.

In such cases product quality primarily concerns the purity, uniformity, and consistency of the products shipped to the customer. In the continuous process industries improving uniformity and consistency is typically more important to the customer (internal or external) than improving purity. A product that has a higher purity than defined by the customer costs more to produce and does not necessarily contribute value to the customer. When further processed, an increase in purity may be disruptive to the customer. It is more important to the customer for the materials to be uniform and consistent with respect to specifications and to be delivered on a dependable schedule.

Production Quality: Improving the production operation is fundamental to quality initiatives in both discrete and continuous manufacturing. One objective of a focus on the process is to detect and correct problems early. Problems anywhere in the manufacturing chain can eventually affect the quality of the final product.

Improving production quality to enhance product quality is important, yet there are other production issues. How much rework is necessary to meet the customer requirements? How much off-spec product must be sold at a discount rate because it can't be reworked? Particularly important in the continuous process industries are issues such as efficiency, flexibility, reliability, and productivity of the processing units used to make the final products. These factors are important considerations in determining the cost of production, and the cost of production influences both market position and profits. How much energy and material are required to make a salable product? How flexible is the process equipment for adjusting to changes in the market? How reliable is the process equipment with respect to unscheduled shutdowns and lost production? What is the capacity of the plant and where are the bottlenecks that limit capacity? In both discrete and continuous manufacturing, the customer's needs must be understood and met; yet, the profits invariably go to the company that can consistently and faithfully meet customer needs while effectively reducing the costs of producing the product.

There is also an important long-term objective for the focus on production quality. In today's intensely competitive world markets there can be no status quo. Companies must continually be working on new products and new processes. The knowledge necessary to substantially improve that next generation of process equipment can only be obtained from careful and thoughtful studies of the problems with the current operation.

COST OF PROCESS VARIATIONS

Quality improvement programs typically focus on measuring and managing process variation. In discrete manufacturing the concern is primarily that process variations are the root cause of product variation and therefore must be systematically identified and eliminated. In the continuous process industries there is an increasing concern for process variation in a much broader context. Process variation often causes product variation, but it can also impact the basic efficiency and productivity of the process units and affect how well the process operation can be studied.

The direct and indirect costs associated with process variation in the process industries are listed in Figure 2. An understanding of each of these costs and the relationships they have to quality improvement is important to establish a new role for engineering process control.

FIGURE 2
Costs of Process Variation

- Reduced Product Quality
- Higher Energy Costs
- Lower Production Rates
- Unfocused Picture of Operation

Reduced Product Quality: The effect of process variation on product quality is becoming an increasingly important concern in the process industries. Most sale contracts now include statistical performance measures with the more conventional product specification. The mean and the standard deviation and performance measures such as Cp and Cpk are increasingly being used to document product quality. Performance with respect to these quality measures can largely decide the duration of a customer-vendor relationship. Customers of the continuous process industry realize that the quality of the materials they purchase affects the quality of their manufacturing operation. They increasingly demand and expect consistent quality from their vendors.

With respect to improving product quality, it is important to identify and eliminate those process variations that reduce the quality of the product. It is also important to design process systems in which the product quality is not strongly affected by inherent variations in the process. Engineering process control should have an important role in both activities.

Higher Energy Costs: In the process industries the ramifications of process variations on manufacturing quality go well beyond the direct effect they have on the product quality. They can also impact the basic cost of producing the product. For example, consider the acetic acid distillation column shown in Figure 3. The purpose of the distillation column as a process unit is to remove water from a dilute acid feed. If variations exist in the feed composition and/or feed rate, those variations will propagate through the column to affect the acid product purity. Besides product purity, such variation will also affect the energy consumption that is necessary to produce a salable product.

Consider the relationship between product purity and the energy consumption shown in Figure 4. If variations are present in the acid product purity, the column must be operated at a higher energy level to insure that the minimum purity specification is not violated. Figure 4 shows the relative energy cost for the column operating at three different levels of variation: No Variation; Low Variation; and High Variation. The difference in energy cost among these three is significant. Distillation columns, and most other processing equipment used in the continuous process industries, are highly energy intensive. A typical column may consume several million dollars a year in steam. Process variations can inflate that amount by as much as 100 percent.

Since many products manufactured in the continuous process industries are fluid in nature, product specifications are often met by blending. It should be realized that blending does not eliminate the additional costs of energy. Figure 5 shows the energy costs associated with a blended

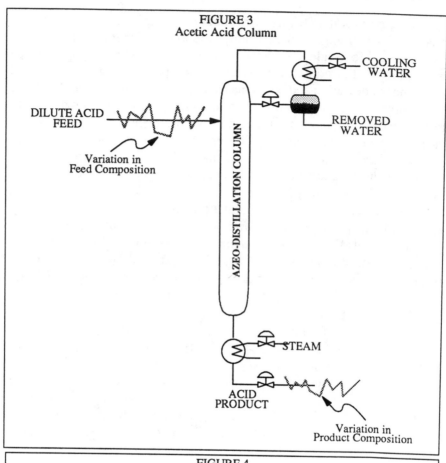

FIGURE 3
Acetic Acid Column

COOLING WATER

DILUTE ACID FEED

Variation in Feed Composition

AZEO-DISTILLATION COLUMN

REMOVED WATER

STEAM

ACID PRODUCT

Variation in Product Composition

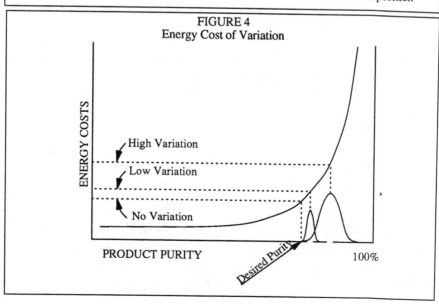

FIGURE 4
Energy Cost of Variation

ENERGY COSTS

High Variation

Low Variation

No Variation

PRODUCT PURITY

Desired Purity

100%

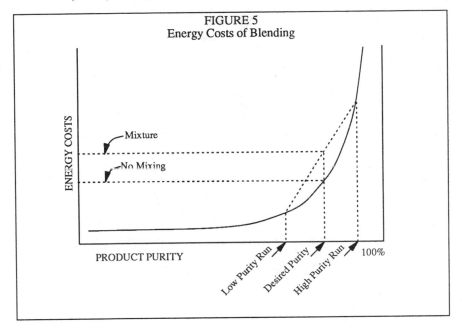

FIGURE 5
Energy Costs of Blending

product compared with the ideal cost of producing the product with no variations. The energy costs of the blended product will always be higher.

Lower Production Rates: Process variation can also lower the production capacity of a process unit. For example, consider the effect of process variation on the capacity of the acid column. Figure 6 shows that as the energy requirements increase the production capacity decreases. This is true of most complex continuous processes with constraints and bottlenecks. Process variations tend to lower the production capacity by limiting how close to a constraint a process can be operated. This is a serious problem for a plant that can sell every pound of product that is produced. Reduced production capacity can represent a significant reduction in the return on capital investments.

Unfocused Picture of Operations: Process variation has yet another, more subtle, effect on manufacturing quality. The state of the individual process variables indicates the state of the overall manufacturing operation. If critical process variables contain variation it is much more difficult to determine the actual state of the process. Variations in the key process variables make the otherwise clear picture appear fuzzy and unfocused (see Figures 7 and 8). With a fuzzy picture of process operation, it becomes difficult to understand what is really going on in the process. It becomes harder to make sound management decisions about the day-to-day operation or to plan changes and modifications that would improve the long-term operation.

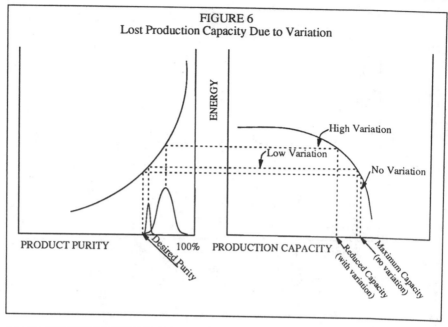

FIGURE 6
Lost Production Capacity Due to Variation

MANAGING PROCESS VARIATION

Fundamental to improving the quality of manufacturing operations in the continuous process industry is a wise and thoughtful policy for managing process variation. There are two general components to a sound variation management policy, and engineering process control should play an important role in both. As indicated in Figure 9, the two components are the transformation and the elimination of variation. The transformation of variation is a short-term, high frequency focus that is often necessary to maintain safe, dependable operations. The elimination of variation is usually a more long-term focus. It is a focus that is necessary to any quality program dedicated to continual process improvement.

Transformation of Variation: The traditional role of engineering process control concerns managing short-term variation. A typical continuous process operates in an environment in which the material and energy balance is constantly changing. Engineering process control is concerned with monitoring those changes and automatically making adjustments that compensate for the changes. The objective of the adjustments is to transform variation in critical process variables to more benign locations.

For example, consider the simple heat exchanger shown in Figure 10. In the exchanger, steam provides the energy that heats a liquid feed for further processing (i.e., the heat exchanger could serve as a feed preheater for the distillation column described in Figure 3). Here, the process

FIGURE 7
Fuzzy Picture of the State of the Process

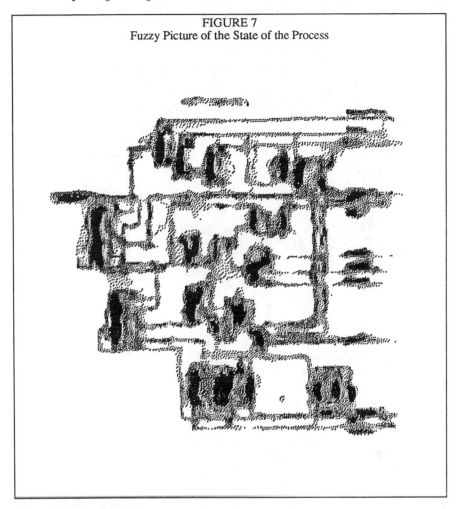

variations include changes in the feed flow rate, the feed temperature, and the ambient air temperature that surrounds the exchanger. These variations are normal and are somewhat harmless in themselves; yet, they can cause, with no feedback correction, a significant variation in the outlet temperature. Such variations would be passed on as a disturbance to the next processing unit. (For the acetic acid column example, feed temperature variations would be yet another source of variation in the acetic acid product stream.)

The resulting excursions in outlet temperature could be reduced by implementing an engineering control system as indicated in Figure 11. The engineering control system has a temperature sensor and transmitter (TT) on the outlet stream, a control valve on the steam flow, and a temperature controller (TC) that connects the two. The temperature controller compares

FIGURE 8
Clear Picture of the State of the Process

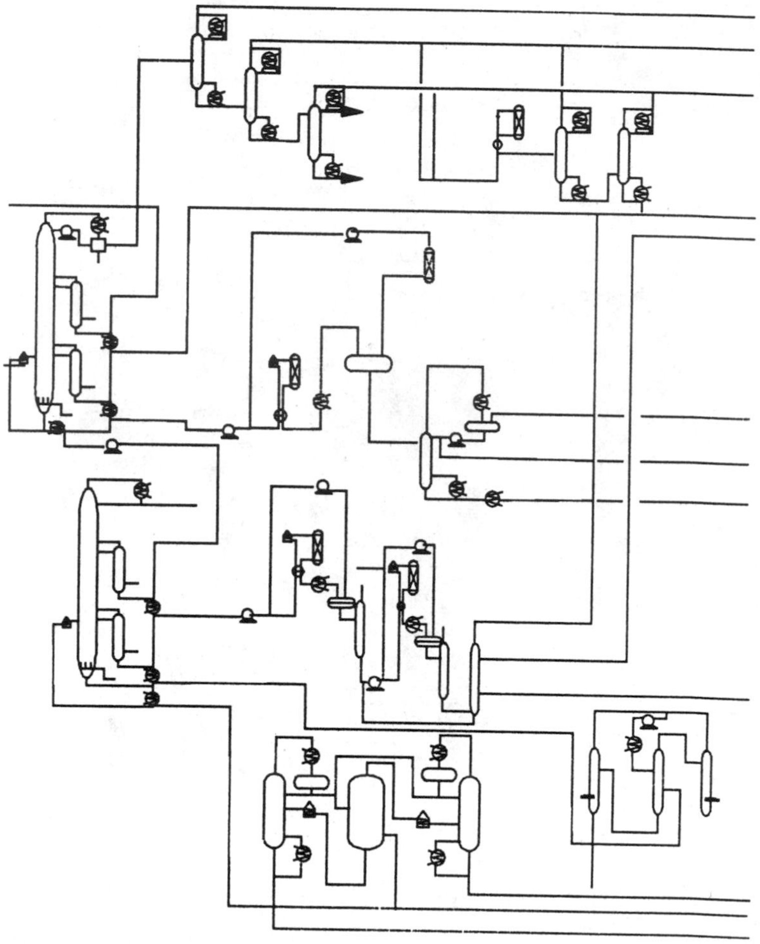

FIGURE 9
Managing Process Variation

- Transformation of Variation

    - Using control systems that transform variation from critical
      process variables to variables more benign with respect to quality

- Elimination of Variation

    - Implementing studies that identify the root cause of process
      variation and determine a course of action that eliminates the
      variation at the source

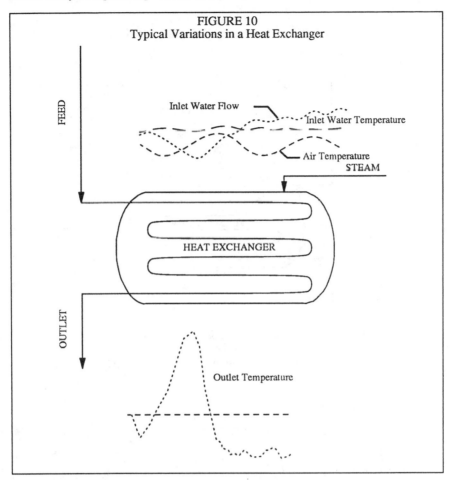

FIGURE 10
Typical Variations in a Heat Exchanger

the measured temperature to a target temperature and adjusts the steam flow rate according to the error. Note that, as shown in Figure 12, if designed and implemented properly, the engineering process control system transforms the variation from the outlet temperature to the steam flow. The steam flow is a much less harmful place for the variation to occur. Variations in steam flow affect only the energy balance of the heat exchanger, whereas variations in the outlet temperature can potentially affect all downstream process units. Automatically adjusting the steam flow to maintain the desired outlet temperature isolates the effects of local heat exchanger variations. This prevents them from propagating to other more critical parts of the process.

Elimination of Variation: A long-range focus on variation is one that attempts to identify the root cause and determines a course of action that could eliminate the variation at the source. But determining the root cause

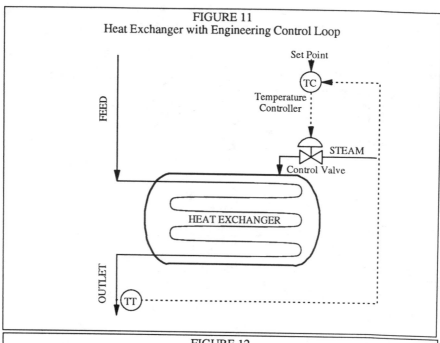

FIGURE 11
Heat Exchanger with Engineering Control Loop

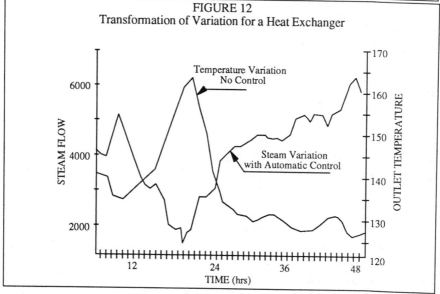

FIGURE 12
Transformation of Variation for a Heat Exchanger

of process variation is seldom a simple task. Continuous processes are characteristically complex, convoluted plumbing systems in which materials and energy move as fluids. Variations tend to propagate through these systems much likes waves, the origin of which is difficult to figure out, especially if there is more than one source. Local engineering control systems are essential for damping and isolating the effects of variations;

yet, the total quality interests are better served if the fundamental source of the variation can be identified and removed.

A Question of Economics: Managing variation is seldom simply a choice between elimination and transformation. The basic question of economics must also be considered. The process and engineering changes that are necessary to eliminate a source of variation are never free. Modifications cost money and time, and such costs should be compared with the expected benefits as in any economic analysis.

Figure 13 shows that the wise decision may be to eliminate the source of variation only partially. Consider the aforementioned heat exchanger (Figure 12). One source of variation is the ambient condition. The heat loss varies with the air temperature, with the exposure to the sun, and with the presence of wind and rain. This environmental source of variation could be totally eliminated by constructing an air-conditioned shelter around the unit. However, such a solution would be difficult to justify based on quality improvements. A much more reasonable choice would perhaps be to add a couple more inches of insulation. The insulation would not completely remove the variation, but it would improve the operation at a reasonable cost.

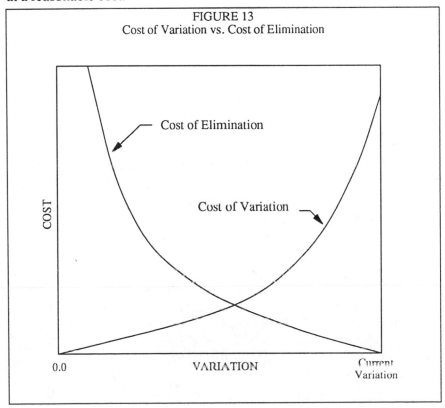

FIGURE 13
Cost of Variation vs. Cost of Elimination

Cost of Elimination

Cost of Variation

COST

0.0   VARIATION   Current Variation

The same economic analysis should also be applied to engineering control systems. Engineering control systems also are not free. They vary in cost, sophistication, performance, and difficulty of operation. The control system shown for the heat exchanger (Figure 11) is simple and straightforward, and effectively and economically eliminates the impact of such variations on manufacturing quality. Yet, this is not always the case. Consider, for example, the distillation column shown in Figure 3. Here, a simple measurement and control system will not be as effective in compensating for the variations that affect product quality. Direct on-line composition measurements are tricky and expensive to make. In addition, the multivariable, dynamic nature of the distillation column makes automated adjustments difficult and complex. A good engineering control system for this application may require a process control computer and a sophisticated model-based control strategy. Such control systems are costly and probably will not completely remove the effects of variation on process and product quality.

Solving the Variation Puzzle: A rational, quality-conscious program for managing process variation should not consider the question of transformation versus elimination to be an either-or proposition. Process variation is a fact of life in the continuous process industries. It is not possible, even with careful study, to eliminate all variation that detracts from manufacturing quality. There are too many sources, some of which cannot be physically avoided. It is also not possible, using engineering control systems, to transform all variation to harmless locations. There are not enough locations insensitive to variation, nor are there enough degrees of freedom in the operation of a typical process to compensate for all the detrimental variation that does exist. Managing process variation is a puzzle that can be solved only by making wise decisions about where to focus improvement efforts, and, within each improvement effort, by making sound economic judgments about the mix and match between engineering process development and engineering process control. Wise decisions can be made only by developing a clearer understanding of the process operation and how that operation relates to issues of process and product quality.

Putting the pieces of the puzzle together is a management challenge in organizations today. There is no traditional speciality with a background large enough to solve these problems. It is a solution that requires the perspective and cooperative input of many different specialities. As indicated in Figure 14, quality improvement requires many cross-functional teams. If properly focused, engineering process control can bring a unique and important perspective to these teams.

FIGURE 14
Improving Quality Requires Many Perspectives

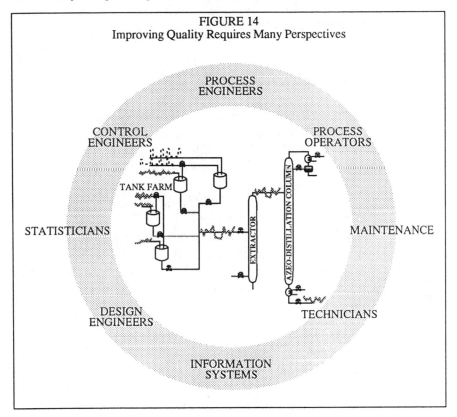

NEW CROSS-FUNCTIONAL ROLES FOR ENGINEERING PROCESS CONTROL

Traditionally, engineering process control has been concerned primarily with the design and implementation of automatic control systems. It is time for those companies dedicated to continuous quality improvement to broaden that traditional role. Engineering process control has a unique perspective on the operation and control of continuous and semicontinuous processes. Historically, engineering process control has viewed and understood processes as a system of dynamic causes and effects. This is an extremely important aspect of the operation and behavior of a continuous process that is not generally considered by other traditional functions. Such a perspective can be important in piecing together the quality improvement puzzle if properly integrated with other organizational units. Statistical process control, process design, process operations, management information systems, and training programs are a few of the traditional organizational units that should be teamed with engineering process control. Such liaisons could provide cross-functional insights into the quality puzzle that are not generally present in a traditional company organization.

STATISTICAL PROCESS CONTROL

With the emerging concern for quality, perhaps one of the most urgent areas to establish a cross-functional working relationship is the one between engineering process control (EPC) and statistical process control (SPC). Statistical process control has been active in discrete manufacturing for many years; yet, it is a somewhat new functional area in the continuous process industries. Currently, for many organizations, the two areas appear to be either in direct conflict or in a state of confusion. The misunderstandings arise from both territorial disputes over who is in control and confusion with the technical language used by the two disciplines. There is much to be gained by resolving the problems and establishing a healthy cross-functional relationship: one that works cooperatively toward the common goal of improving manufacturing operations.

SPC vs. EPC Feedback Control Strategies: Two principal concerns of statistical process control are short-term process adjustment and long-term process improvement. Both concerns are important to the interface between SPC and EPC; however, the question of short-term adjustments seems to cause the most serious (albeit, misplaced) conflict. Each discipline has its own philosophy and set of strategies to perform such adjustments. At times these strategies seem to clash; yet, in the continuous process industries each has a role and a place. Figure 15 presents some important considerations in choosing the appropriate strategy for each application.

The distinctions made in this chapter between SPC and EPC feedback control strategies have more to do with automation than with the procedure used for control. In an SPC feedback loop, the human operator has the responsibility for implementing feedback correction. He or she may also be responsible for collecting the sample, analyzing it, and plotting the results on a control chart. In an EPC feedback loop the data collection, analysis, and action function are all fully automated. It is also possible to automate an SPC strategy in a computer-based control system, but, in such cases, the human operator is no longer part of the control loop. An automated SPC strategy becomes, for all practical purposes, yet another EPC control algorithm. Such statistical-based algorithms can be effective for some feedback control applications; however, they lose the important human element present in a conventional SPC implementation.

Study of Variation and Its Cause: The design of both automatic and operator-implemented feedback strategy is important to both EPC and

---

FIGURE 15

Choosing Between SPC and EPC Strategies for Feedback Control

- *The Type of Process*: Process units that mix, react, and separate fluid materials continuously are the most common type of process found in the continuous process industry. The designs of such systems usually lend themselves quite well to control by an engineering feedback control system. However, batch and semibatch processes are also frequently used as steps in the manufacturing operation. These units have many of the same operational and control characteristics as found in discrete manufacturing and can benefit from the prospective and historical experiences of statistical process control.

- *The Class of Process Measurements*: The process measurement system used by the control system can also be either continuous or discrete. Measurements such as temperature, pressure, flow rate, and level can be continually measured using reliable and relatively inexpensive sensors and transmitters. Such measurement systems lend themselves well to engineering process control systems. On the other hand, measurements such as compositions, density, and viscosity are more difficult and expensive to measure online. Often such measurements are determined by using a laboratory procedure on a sample taken from the process. Such measurement systems present discrete data to the control system and lend themselves well to SPC feedback strategies.

- *The Speed of Response*: The speed of response concerns how fast the process reacts to disturbances and to the corrections made by the feedback control system. For continuous processes the response time of individual control loops can vary from seconds to hours. Such process characteristics are important in selecting an appropriate feedback control strategy. EPC strategies provide much more flexibility in dealing with differences in response speeds than do SPC strategies. EPC incorporates such differences in the basic design and tuning of the feedback strategies while SPC is rigidly limited in its control response to the frequency of the chart. Limits on human resources and patience typically dictate that control charts maintained by a human operator can only be run at rates no higher than one or two control actions each hour. Processes that react considerably faster than that chart frequency may operate for long periods of time in need of a control action. Processes that respond much slower than chart frequency can result in an SPC strategy that overcontrols.

- *Complexity of the Control Action*: Control actions vary in complexity and in the degree of intelligence required. In the continuous process industries most control loops are rather mundane. They are well defined and can be successfully executed by a simple feedback algorithm. However, there are also many situations that are not so simple and straightforward. There may be several control actions possible, that and the choice of which feedback correction to use may require intelligent judgment. The intelligent judgment may require a broader view of the process than is reflected in the measurement of the control variables. It is possible, to some extent, to implement such considerations using advanced engineering feedback control strategies; however, such sophisticated systems are difficult to develop, and complex in implementation, and require close technical attention. In such cases, the SPC alternative, may be attractive because of its simplicity. The SPC approach deals with the need for intelligent judgment and a broader view by placing a well-trained human operator in the control loop.

SPC, although the area in which a cross-functional liaison between the two groups could have the most benefit concerns the study of variation. Such studies attempt to identify, systematically, problems that disturb the process operation and to seek solutions that fix, rather than compensate for, the basic problems. Such studies are the heart and soul of most successful quality improvement programs.

The study of variation for long-term process improvement is one of the primary functions of statistical process control, but it is a functional activity that cannot be performed by statisticians alone. It also requires the insight and perspective of engineers and technicians with a working knowledge of the process. SPC provides a framework and set of statistical tools for studying variation; however, technical knowledge of the process, essential to understanding variation, must come from other traditional functions. The nature of variation in the continuous process industry is broad and difficult to study without the perspectives of both SPC and EPC.

Figure 16 lists some important considerations in any study of variation. One consideration concerns the potential sources of variation for each application. Figure 17 lists general sources of variation typical for the continuous process industry. These different sources tend to mix and mingle and propagate like waves into a sea of confusion. One important cross-functional activity provides some order to the confusion by identifying for each application the most probable sources of variation. This can

---

FIGURE 16
Considerations in Studying Variation

- Sources of Variation
- Cost of Variation
- Location of Measurements
- Frequency of Focus

FIGURE 17
Sources of Variation

- Measurement Noise
- Changes in the Material Balance
- Changes in the Energy Balance
- Process Dynamics
- Interaction Between Process Units
- Shift and Personnel Changes
- Equipment Malfunction and Failure

only be done by a detailed study of the process and of the systems (human and machine) that operate and control the process.

Another fundamental consideration in a cross-functional look at variation is understanding the relationship between each component of variation and quality. Some types of process variation are costly with respect to quality; others are relatively insignificant. Consider, for example, the liquid-liquid extractor shown in Figure 18. Variations in the tank feed rate propagate through the system affecting the level in the tank, the feed to the column, and finally the product purity. Clearly, the variation in product purity is costly with respect to quality, although the variation in the other process variables may not be altogether bad. In this case, variation in the tank level actually improves the operation. The tank inventory, if allowed to float, can serve as a shock absorber to changes in production rate. This tank would also serve as a shock absorber to changes in the feed composition and temperature. The study of variation should also include the identification of useful variation.

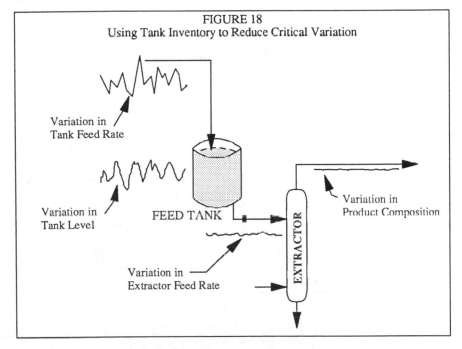

FIGURE 18
Using Tank Inventory to Reduce Critical Variation

It is not practical to study all process variation. In a typical continuous processing plant there may be thousands of variables, and a study of variation must narrow the focus to only a reasonable few. Such decisions require an appreciation for the most probable source of variation as well as some understanding of cause and effect in the process systems. One potential problem is that engineering feedback control systems typically focus on the most important process variables. The concern of statisticians (largely an artifact from discrete manufacturing) is that these control loops tend to get in the way of the study of variation by masking the effects of variations. The argument is that problems cannot be corrected if they cannot be detected. Control engineers should realize, however, that the place to monitor variation on a process controlled by an EPC system is at the controller output. Consider again the heat exchanger shown in Figure 11. Monitoring the outlet temperature with a statistical control chart would be of little value since the temperature control system adjusts the steam to maintain a desired outlet temperature. Still, the process variation is in the system and can be monitored by focusing on the steam flow as indicated in Figure 19. The steam flow now contains the variation that would have been in the temperature before the feedback transformation.

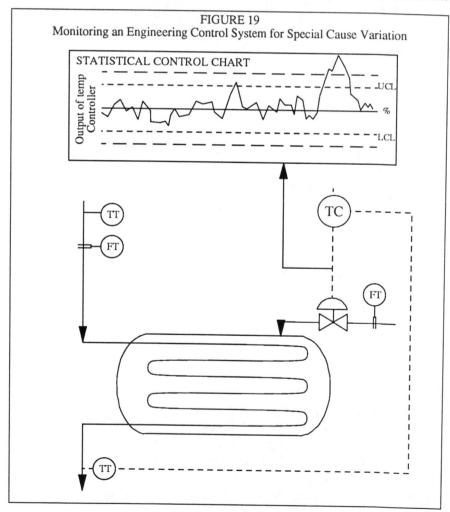

FIGURE 19
Monitoring an Engineering Control System for Special Cause Variation

The location of the variation has been transformed from the temperature to the steam flow. In this location the variation is much less harmful, however, it can still be measured and studied.

Frequency of focus is another important issue in studying variation for which engineering process control can play an important role. In order to unravel the mystery of variation it is crucial to realize the importance of time. Each source of variation has its own characteristic rhythms and frequencies. These differences can be very confusing if ignored, but, if properly considered, they can also be helpful in separating the multivariable nature of the problem. Moreover, each process unit is a dynamic system that reacts to disturbances and propagates them to other parts of the process in strange but predictable ways. The issues concerning such time-related factors are critical in the study of variation in the continuous process industries. Engineering process control provides a framework and a know-how to consider questions of dynamics that no other traditional function provides.

PROCESS DESIGN

Another important cross-functional liaison with engineering process control is process design. Historically, the design of continuous process systems has been concerned primarily with steady-state operations. Very little consideration has been given to how a proposed process design will operate when the material and energy balances are in a state of change. As a result, many unexpected operational and control difficulties can occur which might have been avoided through better design. With respect to improving quality, it is important that engineering process control become much more involved with the traditional process design function to help address such problems. Engineering process control can help in evaluating the dynamics of proposed designs. In a more general sense, the role of engineering process control in this cross-functional liaison helps to develop a clearer perspective of the complex relationships between process design and manufacturing quality.

Evaluation of Preliminary Process Designs: Process design includes the following phases: functional design, mechanical design, instrumentation design, and control system design. These phases are usually sequential, and typically the functional process design is rigidly fixed before the control system design phase begins. In such cases, the control system designers have little choice but to deal with inadequate process design by the addition of overly complex control systems.

This practice would be inconceivable in the aerospace industry. It would be absurd to separate the control system design of an airplane from the functional and mechanical designs. An aircraft designed in such a way might have enough lift to become airborne, but it would be limited, at best, in performance capabilities. In the continuous process industries far too many designs suffer from similar performance limitations.

In the long run, a process design that is difficult to control may be more costly than one that considers both the steady-state and dynamic performance. To avoid such costly problems, it is important that issues related to the operation and control of the process be included in the preliminary functional design phase. Figure 20 lists some of the operational and control

---

FIGURE 20
Operational and Control Issues
Important to the Functional Process Design

* *Location and Type of Sensors*: The selection of the sensor and measurement systems is critical to the performance of a process control strategy. The locations and type of sensors set the perspective of the automatic control strategy. A proper sensor perspective is far more critical to the performance than is the choice of feedback strategy. The measurement system is important to the preliminary process design only in that it must be specified before the controllability of a proposed design can be evaluated.

* *Location of Actuators*: The actuator systems are also critical to the performance of a control loop. The characteristics of the actuators and their range and sensitivities are important to the control system design; yet, the issue most important to the preliminary process design is the location. Establishing the location of the actuators helps establish the fundamental degrees of freedom in which the process can be operated and controlled.

* *Actuator-Sensor Response Characteristics*: Once the actuator and sensor locations have been set, the relationships between actuation and sensor response need to be considered. Both the dynamic characteristics and the steady-state sensitivity affect the performance of the control system and help establish the complexity of the control system design required to meet the desired performance objectives. Such studies are necessary before a preliminary process design can be fully evaluated.

* *Location and Size of Process Inventories*: Process inventories are an important control system design issue that is usually set during the preliminary process design phase. If properly sized and located, these inventories can serve as natural shock absorbers for variation. They can help with local control problems as well as provide a broader degree of freedom for the plantwide control focus.

* *Disturbance Rejection and Propagation of Variation*: The fundamental plant design also defines the sensitivity of a process to unavoidable disturbances. It is becoming increasingly important to consider the natural disturbance rejection capabilities of a proposed design. It is also important to consider how variation will propagate through a proposed process system. Subtle process design changes may well be all that is necessary to improve the variation picture. Such changes are relatively simple to justify during the preliminary process design; yet, they can be prohibitively expensive once a design becomes fixed in concrete and steel.

issues that are important to consider during the functional design phase. At present the only functional group capable of answering such important questions is engineering process control, and such questions need to be addressed early in the process design.

Evaluation of Existing Process Designs: The biggest challenge of the liaison between process design and process control concerns the evaluation of the design of existing processes. Once fixed in concrete and steel, design problems are often difficult and expensive to correct; yet, they should at least be identified. In many cases the resulting improvements may well justify the cost of modifying the existing design. Identifying and under-standing such problems on an actual process can have an even broader payback. A retrospective evaluation of a process design establishes a clearer perception of the basic problems. It is important to learn from existing designs to establish a better understanding of the complex and subtle relationships between process design and manufacturing quality. For future processes it is important not to repeat the same design mistakes over and over again, simply out of ignorance.

A Case Study: Modifications of an existing process are not always costly. Dramatic improvement in operation and control can come from relatively simple process changes. Consider the acid recovery plant shown in Figure 21. Acid feeds of various concentrations and flow rates are pumped from a number of external sources to storage tanks. From the tanks

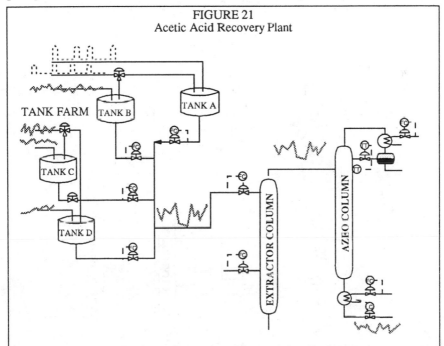

FIGURE 21
Acetic Acid Recovery Plant

the acid is fed through a common header to a separation plant. The separation consists of extractive and azeotropic distillation columns designed to remove water and other impurities. The final product is an anhydrous grade acid.

As indicated in Figure 21, the product purity is strongly affected by many upstream variations. Local engineering systems help stabilize the columns to insure that the product meets minimum market specifications. These variations result in higher energy consumption and lower production capacity (see earlier discussions). At times, large variations can disrupt the column operation to such an extent that it is necessary to shut down and restart. The fundamental source of such variation can be easily traced to variations in the rates and concentrations of the many feeds that are pumped to the tank farm. In this case, as a recycle facility, it is not practical to negotiate with the suppliers for more consistency in the raw materials. There is little choice but to take the recycled acid as it comes, variation and all.

There is a possibility, however, of reducing the magnitude of the problem by modifying the process and control system designs to be less sensitive to such unavoidable upstream variations. Consider the modification indicated in Figure 22. The plumbing of the tank farm is changed to make better use of the capacity of the inventory to reduce the magnitude

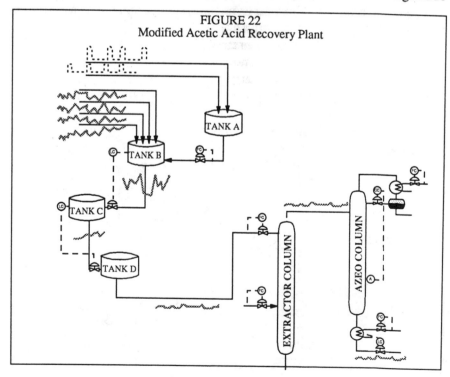

FIGURE 22
Modified Acetic Acid Recovery Plant

and the frequency of the variations seen by the columns. All the low concentration streams are fed to Tank B and then must flow through and mix with the contents of two other tanks before reaching the separation columns. All the intermittent, high-concentration streams are collected in Tank A and then fed to Tank B at a constant rate. Such an arrangement eliminates the dramatic problems in variation that such feeds caused in the original design.

The control systems on the tank farm were also changed. Level controllers were added to Tank B and Tank C to insure that inventory remained sufficiently high to insure that mixing would reduce the magnitude and frequency of the compositional variation passed on to the separation units. The levels of tanks A and D are allowed to float, under the operator's supervision, so that variations in flow rate can also be dampened. The control system on the distillation column was also modified. A detailed analysis of the column design indicated that the control system would be much more responsive if sensor type and location were changed. Note that a composition analyzer replaces the temperature transmitter and that the location has been moved closer to the bottom of the column.

It is important to note that when the project to reduce variation in the acid recovery plant was first initiated, it was anticipated that this could best be accomplished by a more sophisticated engineering control system. The plan was to develop a complex computer-based control system to route flows to and from the tank farm to minimize variations in composition and flow felt by the separation units. The obvious solution was not realized until dynamic process design studies were initiated. Then it became clear that better results could be achieved at much lower cost by making a few simple changes to the process.

Changes in the process design that improve the operation by decreasing the need for engineering control systems are not always so inexpensive and impressive. It is important, however, that an organization committed to improving quality look for such opportunities. In its new role, engineering process control needs to work closely with process design. All control studies should review the basic process design and consider both simple and far-reaching changes that could improve the control problem. This can only be done by a healthy liaison between engineering process control and engineering process design.

MANAGEMENT INFORMATION SYSTEMS (MIS)

Most companies in the continuous process industries are building large management information systems (MIS). These systems are designed to collect, store, and provide friendly access to operating data, both current and historical. An active liaison between engineering process control and the group responsible for the design and implementation of these systems is important to the new role of engineering process control. Such MIS systems offer a powerful platform from which to study and manage variation. If used properly, it should play an important future role in the efforts to monitor and improve manufacturing quality.

In most companies there is already an active relationship between engineering process control and management information systems. In the continuous process industries the process control computer often provides the interface for all the on-line process data and is itself an integral part of the total management information system. The two groups have already had to form a liaison to address problems such as networking the process control computers to the central management information computer, integrating their separate databases, and providing reliable security for both computer systems. These concerns have more to do with hardware and software issues than with managing variation. It is time for that liaison to move to a more mature focus – one that is more concerned with the use of the historical database than with the details of the design of the system in which they are stored.

Structuring the Database: Using the management information platforms to help in the study of variation requires the presence of a well-focused perspective in the database. This focus generally cannot be adequately addressed by a database that includes only the primary process variables and only one sampling frequency. As indicated in Figure 23, the database should include obscure process variables (such as valve positions) as well as variables that are calculated to represent some specific aspect of process performance. Furthermore, the database should be structured to represent adequately the frequency at which variation originates and propagates through the process. This can be done either by selecting the proper sampling frequency for the study or by including the results of a routine frequency analysis as calculated data in the standard low frequency log.

System Cultivation Analysis: Structuring the database is an important part of the new liaison between engineering process control and management information system; yet, a more important concern is the development of data analysis schemes and their reporting structures. Even the best designed management information systems are of little value if the database is not properly analyzed. If the results are to be effective they must be presented in clear, well-focused reports and summaries. It is in this system cultivation area that engineering process control and management information systems have the greatest opportunity for improvement. At

---

FIGURE 23
Structuring the Historical Data Base for the Study of Variation

* *Selecting Process Variables*: The variable selections should reflect a perspective appropriate for the study of the origin and propagation of variation. It should include the *primary process variables*. These are the variables that measure the state of the process as well as the product. Ideally, they should include the product quality as well as the information necessary to define the energy and the material balances around and in each process unit. In addition to these primary process variables the database should also include a number of select *intermediate variables*. Intermediate variables, such as valve positions, controller status, and controller tuning, can provide subtle but important clues in studying variation.

* *Defining Performance Variables*: A database designed for studying variation should also contain performance variables. Such variables are useful in focusing a study of variation. Such variables can sometimes be measured directly; yet, they most often need to be calculated. They can include simple statistical performance measures, such as mean and standard deviation, or they can be more sophisticated measures such as power spectral densities. Steady-state performance measures, such as Cp and Cpk, should be determined from the historical database; however, dynamic performance measures should be calculated before being logged in the database. Performance measures determined before entry in the database are much more representative of the minute-by-minute performance of the process. Performance measures determined at the frequency of the database typically are more representative of the hour-by-hour operation of the process.

* *Selecting Sampling Frequencies*: The frequency of focus is important in the study of variation. The frequencies that provide the most revealing insight into the study of variation are usually much higher than the frequencies captured in the standard low frequency logs. For some studies, higher frequency data logs may be essential. For others, the higher frequency information can be quantified and included in the low frequency log. (That is, a Fourier analysis of the high frequency data would yield the strengths of dominant frequencies of the variation. This information could be included as a record in the database). Yet in other cases, it may be necessary to design high frequency, high density data traps. These traps (each a self-contained historical log itself) would be logged into the database on either a time- or an event-driven schedule.

* *Designing the Analysis and Reporting Structures*: A database is of little value if the data are simply stored in a historical log and not used. Strategies and algorithms need to be developed that monitor the process through the broad focus of its historical database. These algorithms should be designed to detect abnormal operations and, when possible, identify the root cause. These algorithms could be simple SPC strategies or be based on more advanced pattern recognition techniques. The reporting structure of such algorithms is also important. It is important, if the results are to be actually used, that they be clear and well focused. Many of these reports should also be included automatically as parts of the standard daily or shift summary reports.

---

present, little is done other than automating simple control chart functions. It is possible to implement much more sophisticated analyses (i.e., pattern recognition techniques, model-based data reconciliation, etc.) that would more precisely detect problems and pinpoint the most probable cause.

UPDATING THE TRADITIONAL ROLE OF ENGINEERING PROCESS CONTROL

The perspective of engineering process control should be broadened to include programs designed to identify and remove sources of variation. It is not likely, however, that such long-term programs would ever eliminate the need for engineering control systems. Such systems provide a short-term focus on variation that is usually necessary for safe, reliable operations. In most cases, correcting problems that cause variation simply improves the regulatory performance of the engineering control systems already on the process. In its broader quality-oriented perspective the traditional role of designing automatic control systems is still the most important function of engineering process control. This traditional role, however, needs to be reviewed and updated.

Computer technology is rapidly changing the nature of engineering control systems. Computer-based control systems make it practical to consider many advanced control strategies and algorithms that were simply not possible a few years ago. The possibilities increase as the basic technologies involved rapidly change. Computer control hardware is improving in size, speed, reliability, and costs; computer control software is becoming more user friendly and more flexible; advances in the area of numerical computation and mathematical modeling are greatly enhancing the ability of control system designers to capture knowledge of the process in their designs; and developments in expert systems and shells for artificial intelligence are expanding the framework in which advanced control can be implemented. Engineering process control needs to greet these new developments with a cautious enthusiasm.

By better managing local variation, advanced control strategies can dramatically assist the pursuit of quality improvement. Their applications, however, need to be well selected. Complexities in a control strategy have both direct and indirect costs that can be justified only in terms of significant improvements in operations. Today, the biggest indirect costs are the personal impacts on the operators and engineers who must use the system. The more complex the design, the more difficult it is for these personnel to understand the strategy well enough to assume responsibility for the system. It only takes a few surprises before an advanced control strategy (as well as the engineer who designed it) can lose all credibility with the operator responsible for the unit.

With the inevitable increase in the number of applications of advanced engineering control strategies it is even more important to keep the overall objectives of process control in mind. The broad objective is to improve process operations. Although improving the control strategy is important, in the continuous process industries, the biggest leverage is in the process and with the people who operate this process. Improving the design of the process and improving the basic understanding of the problems of operation can have a far greater impact on quality than the implementation of a more advanced engineering control loop.

TRAINING PROGRAMS

Engineering process control should become significantly more involved in plant training programs in two areas: process dynamics and process control. The purpose of involving engineering process control in training is to provide better foundation in the plant community from which to understand and discuss operational problems that are dynamic in nature.

Process Control: The first area concerns engineering process control systems. Although control engineers systematically design control systems, they often do a poor job explaining their operation to the personnel who must use them. The details and mathematical subtleties of a control system design are not important subjects to be taught outside the engineering process control group; however, the operational philosophies and the rationale for the design of the control systems need to be clearly understood by all personnel involved with the operation of process equipment. A better working knowledge of process control systems at this level would not only help engineers and technicians understand existing control systems, but would also facilitate the broader perspective necessary to improve plant operations.

Process Dynamics: Engineering process control is the only functional group in a manufacturing operation that formally deals with the dynamic nature of processes. These characteristics of a process are important to the design of control systems, but they should be equally important to all functional groups that relate to the operation of the process. An understanding of the process that considers only steady-state operations is very limited and often confused. In its new role, engineering process control has a responsibility not only to explain more completely the control systems, but also to introduce other groups to the dynamic perspective of operations.

Common Language: Language is one of the primary problems facing the training role of engineering process control. The language of process dynamics has historically been defined in math symbols and abstract concepts that are beyond the working knowledge of all but the process control specialists. As a result, process control specialists only talk to other process control specialists, when the greater need for conversation is typically with the plant operations. The engineering process control community needs to find a language that is more appropriate for such conversations. Process control training programs aimed at the nonspecialist can be helpful but not if the focus is on the mathematics of control. The focus needs to be on specific problems and on using a language that is understood by anyone who is familiar with the process.

Working simulations can provide an excellent framework to discuss process dynamics and control without using mathematical rhetoric and symbols. Instructive simulations can be presented almost entirely in the same language as commonly used to discuss the process. Simulations can illustrate points more clearly than explaining a set of differential equations. Demonstrations based on simulations are more to the point than abstract arguments and are more likely to be used to further self-study.

Process modeling and simulation are part of the traditional role of engineering process control. Such models are used to evaluate and tune control system designs, and they are used as components in the model-based control strategies. It would require some additional effort to package such simulations in a form more suitable for use outside the control group; however, the benefits in terms of communication would be invaluable.

CONCLUSION

Outlined in this chapter is a broader focus for engineering process control – a focus that includes the elimination of, as well as the compensation for, operational disturbances. This more global view of managing variation and controlling processes requires that engineering process control establish active liaisons with the other functional groups. Improving quality requires many perspectives, and in the continuous process industries the perspectives of engineering process control are vital.

The recommendations presented in this chapter, if taken literally, would require organizational changes and a significant increase in allocation of resources to the engineering process control group. Presently, such groups are already understaffed with backlogs of projects waiting to be considered. Broadening the role of engineering process control to include active liaisons with process design, statistical process control, management information systems, and plant training programs without additional personnel would even further dilute the capacity of this group. It is important for management, in allocating resources, to realize such limitations. It is even more important for control engineers to realize that many of the changes cannot wait for management. The changes need to start on an individual basis. We, in process control, need to obtain a better understanding of our roles, individually and collectively, in improving manufacturing quality. We need to understand the need for both formal and informal liaisons as well as our responsibility to communicate more effectively with other functional groups. If the individuals who are concerned with engineering process control clearly understand these points, the organizational changes necessary to support effective cross-functional work will follow more naturally.

It is also important for management to realize its responsibility in defining a new role for engineering process control. Certain changes need to be made to facilitate the formation of cross-functional liaisons that can only be done by management. The current organizational structure of most companies neither provides nor encourages liaisons of the depth and degree suggested in this chapter. In addition, the reward and incentive policies of most companies are a deterrent for the teamwork implied in cross-functional liaisons. Job performance ratings that are based primarily on individual achievements discourage the team perspectives necessary to improve the operation and control of a manufacturing operation. Management must play the lead role in changing the organizational culture so that the cross-functional relationships described in this chapter can more naturally exist.

CHAPTER 20

CLOSING THE GAPS IN SERVICES MARKETING: DESIGNING TO SATISFY CUSTOMER EXPECTATIONS

JAMES H. FOGGIN

Associate Professor of Marketing, Logistics and Transportation
University of Tennessee

SUMMARY

The year 1988 was a milestone year in the quality movement. Three manufacturing firms won the nation's first quality award – the Malcolm Baldrige Award. In the following year, 1989, two more manufacturing firms won the award.

The Baldrige Award also has a service category. Unfortunately, until 1990, when Federal Express was declared a winner, no service firm was considered good enough to win, although several applied. All the other winners were manufacturers, yet only about 18 percent of the U.S. gross domestic product (GDP) is in manufacturing. Not only is the service sector a major portion of the GDP, but also many companies are beginning to recognize the importance of providing a high level of quality in the services that support the products they make. These firms are striving to give better total value to their customers. They are failing in spite of their efforts.

QUALITY AND VALUE

Value and quality are discussed elsewhere in this book. The definitions used in this chapter will be consistent with them, but somewhat simplified.

A number of definitions of quality are in use today. A discussion of how to improve it should begin with a definition of what it is.

Crosby's definition is very simple and easy to remember: "Quality is conformance to requirements" (Crosby, 1979: 15). By this definition a Volkswagen made to the requirements specified for the manufacture of a Volkswagen has quality. Conversely, a Jaguar that does not meet all the requirements of a Jaguar lacks some measure of quality. The definition deals with the requirements set forth for the product, not aesthetics. This definition lacks something. It lacks that something which makes the well-made Jaguar more appealing to some than the well-made Volkswagen.

Garvin provides a thorough discussion of what quality is. He categorizes definitions of quality into five groups:

- Transcendent – some form of "innate excellence."
- Product-based – measurable based on attributes of the product itself.
- Manufacturing-based – for example, Crosby's definitions.
- User-based – quality is "in the eyes of the beholder."
- Value-based – defined in terms of price and/or cost (Garvin, 1988: 36-68).

The last-named group often looks at the use to which an item may be put and compares it to the cost of the item. One way of looking at this matter is to consider the value in terms of the cost and the benefit to the consumer. But this view is too simplistic; "value" may not be so easily quantifiable.

The Xerox Corporation (a 1989 Baldrige winner) has adopted a definition that encompasses the user-based and the manufacture-based definitions noted above. "Quality is conformance to customer requirements" (Xerox Corporation, 1986: 3).

A very innovative approach to defining quality is that of Lew Lehr, former CEO of 3M. He defines quality as "the consistent conformance to customers' expectations" (Anderson, 1988: 2-3). This approach, according to a 3M spokesman, makes quality dynamic. When quality is simply a matter of meeting specifications or requirements, it becomes static. If we treat quality as a matter of meeting expectations, then it forces management to seek continuous improvement.

And what of value of services? What is it? Nearly two decades ago, in a British library journal, Orr discussed value and quality in very simple, deliberately obscure terms (Orr; 1973: 317-318). He referred to quality and value in terms of "goodness." Quality, he said, relates to the question "How good is the service?" Value relates to the question "How much good does it do?" The customer assesses quality in terms of meeting a need. Value is assessed in terms of the beneficial effects from using the service, by those who incur its cost.

Extending this reasoning, we deduce that quality and value are related but are not the same thing. A service may have quality without having much value. A customer may recognize some aspect of a service as being very good but does not believe it to be important. For example, the doorman at one hotel may open the door, say hello, and come to attention. At another, the doorman may simply open the door and say hello. The additional formality may be viewed by a guest as "quality," but it may not be very important – it may not have very much "value." It may not have much impact on the decision of the hotel's guest to stay at one over the other. Quality alone will not be enough to make the decision. Quality is a necessary but not sufficient element of value. It is value that affects the purchase decision.

The firm's task, then, becomes one of answering two basic questions.

•   What do my customers value most?
•   How must I design my process to give them what they value?

This chapter address these two questions.

THE IMPORTANCE OF CUSTOMER SERVICE

Service, in addition to being a major sector of the U.S. GDP, is part of every product sold. In fact, service is often the determining factor in whether a product sells at all. The Marketing Mix model explains how service affects the sale.

Figure 1 shows that the Marketing Mix consists of the Four P's of Marketing Price, Product, Promotion, and Place. This is the total package that a customer considers when making a purchase.

Using Price as a competitive tool implies that it should be low enough that customers will be willing to pay it. Obviously, if the other parts of the mix are the same for two products, a customer will buy the product with the lower price.

Promotion implies stimulating sales by using advertising, personal selling or sales promotions. Promotion's purpose is to inform the customer about the product or provide some other incentive to make customers want to buy the item.

The concept of the Product is more complex. The term may refer to providing more features than the competition, or giving it some image that the customer wants. Or, it may mean a high level of quality built into the

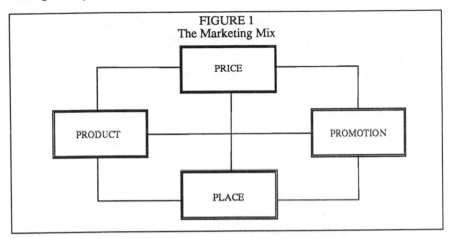

FIGURE 1
The Marketing Mix

PRICE

PRODUCT

PROMOTION

PLACE

product. The term may also incorporate additional facilitating services such as repair, guarantees, and a variety of after-sales services that the customer views as important. Finally, it may refer to the service itself, if there is no tangible "product" offered. A haircut is an example. The customer does not carry anything out of the barber shop. The product was the service.

Place in this simple model refers to delivery, which results from Logistics Customer Service. Some authors now refer to this fourth "P" as Physical Distribution, the outbound component of logistics. The quality of the service which the logistician provides results in the customer receiving the good at the right place, at the right time, in the right condition, and so on. Under the Kai'zen philosophy, this element is a cross-functional activity referred to as scheduling or delivery (Imai, 1986).

The problem with applying the model in the real world is that only in a few instances are "all other things equal." Each customer has a mix of things he or she is willing to pay for. One may want higher quality and be willing to pay more for it than another. Another may be willing to settle for a somewhat lower quality level if they are assured of a supply when they want it (i.e., Place). Complicating the problem is knowing that the several elements have value, but not knowing which has the *most* value. Yet, this complication can be overcome.

Unfortunately, knowing the value of each element of customer service and providing the required level of that element are not the same. Designing a system to provide the right mix of service elements desired by customers is very difficult. The balance of this chapter will discuss how this may be done.

Designing a service system from scratch is an extremely difficult thing to do, if we wish to do it well. There are simply too many options open to the designer to select from for it to be simple. One need only consider the problem of delivering to the customer. A number of transportation modes are available to the "average" shipper. Warehouses may be located in a few or in many cities. Orders are placed by sales personnel, by telephone, by mail, or are sent in directly using Electronic Data Interchange (EDI). The firm may stock inventories or may attempt to move everything following a Just-in-Time (JIT) philosophy. In addition, some customers may prefer different service options than others.

The question then is, how can we design a system that does what the customer wants at a cost the firm can afford?

It sounds difficult, and it is. But so too is designing a product that the customer likes from the myriad of possible designs.

It is the same problem that design engineers have faced for many years. They are learning to do this better in American industry today. They have learned much from the Japanese who seem to have been managing it well for quite some time. The techniques and tools used in product design engineering can very readily be applied by service system designers.

A MODEL OF SERVICE QUALITY

Parasuraman, Zeithaml, and Berry have performed a series of studies on service quality. They describe a closed loop model of service and explain how failures can occur in a system designed to provide services to consumers. These studies address consumer services, but they apply to product-related support service as well (Parasuraman *et al.*, 1985).

These authors reported on the findings of a limited literature search, findings that are more germane to consumer research but that have application to other kinds of service delivery. One is that service quality is more difficult for the consumer to evaluate then goods quality. This makes sense intuitively. Services are not tangible. Unless service parameters are measured while they are taking place, there is no easy way to compare the actual to the expected. Such is not the case with products. The product is tangible, can be seen, touched, tested, and picked apart. The service occurs and is gone. There may be a remnant of some sort, such as something repaired or a shipment delivered, but other aspects may be forgotten.

Another of Parasuraman's, *et al.* findings is that a customer's service quality perceptions result from a comparison of their expectations with actual service performance. If the descriptors involved in service expectations are vague, the comparison may not be favorable. For example, assume that a package service advertises "overnight" delivery. The customer may believe "overnight" means "early the next morning" while the provider means "before the close of business the next day." Note that these findings support the 3M definition – quality is the consistent conformance to customers' expectations.

Parasuraman *et al.* developed a model (Figure 2) of a customer service system. It is a closed loop model and shows the process of service delivery, from management's perception of a need by the customer, to the completion of the service and the customer's perception of it. The most significant aspect of the Parasuraman *et al.* study is their description of a set of key discrepancies or "gaps" that exist in this model. These gaps can be major

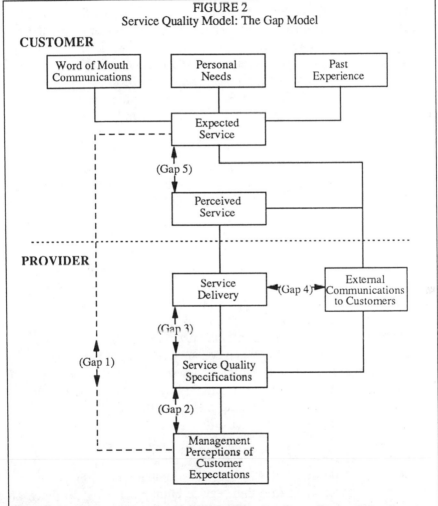

FIGURE 2
Service Quality Model: The Gap Model

Source: Reprinted with permission from A. Parasuraman, Valarie A. Zeithaml, and Leonard L. Berry, "A Conceptual Model of Service Quality and Its Implications for Future Research," *Journal of Marketing*, 49, 4 (Fall, 1985), pp. 41-50, published by the American Marketing Association.

hurdles in attempting to deliver a service that consumers would perceive as being of high quality.

These gaps exist for a number of different reasons, but, together, they cause the service rendered to the customer to be other than what the customer wants. These gaps are as follows:

Gap 1: The gap between what the customer expects and management's perception of those expectations. This is the result of a misinterpretation of what the customer wants. The authors' research showed that small firms were perceived as providing better service than large firms. This is logical. Management in smaller firms should be closer to the customer.

Gap 2: The gap between management's perception of what the customer wants and the designed capabilities of the system they develop to provide the service. The authors attribute this to a number of causes including market conditions and lack of resources. Other reasons they did not mention would be poor planning capabilities or the size or complexity of the design problem.

Gap 3: The gap between the service the system is designed to provide and what it actually does provide. This is essentially a control problem. The authors attribute this to standards that are not always easy to maintain. Other reasons could include poor operating instructions to employees, or inadequately training them to run the system properly.

Gap 4: The gap between the service the system provides and what the customer is told it provides. This may be the result of management not knowing how good or bad the system actually is, and not informing the customer of the true level of service.

Gap 5: The gap between the expected service and the perception of that service. The quality that a consumer perceives is a function of the size and direction of the gap between expected service and perceived service. This gap is a simple function of the other four gaps mentioned above. Eliminate them and this fifth gap simply goes away (Parasuraman *et al.* 1990: 35-50).

The authors have developed a set of questionnaires to determine if these gaps exist. Called SERVQUAL, the questionnaire is administered to customers, managers, and first-line service employees. The existence of gaps is readily apparent when the questionnaire results are compared (Parasuraman *et al.*, 1990: 175-205).

The model is an effective way of describing what can go wrong in how a supplier designs a process to provide a service. Each of the gaps may result in small deviations from what was developed in the previous step but can collectively result in a significant difference in Gap 5. Conversely, it is entirely possible that there may be some very significant deviations in each of the first four gaps, but they are such that they cancel one another out. For example, the service in question may be a delivery service. The customer wants to receive a delivery on the third morning after order placement. The supplier erroneously believes the customer wanted first morning delivery. They try to develop a system to deliver on the first morning, but the system they devise can do no better than the second. They fail to control it adequately, and deliver on the third. Furthermore, they make no effort to tell the customer anything about the system's capabilities. The customers are happy; they are getting the service they wanted. The supplier, however, is wasting effort (and cost) trying to provide a service greater than what the customer wants.

The model that Parasuraman described leaves out one very important aspect. It does not show the competition and market, and what these contribute to the customer's expectations. Figure 3 illustrates this aspect, which is critical to what follows.

The model described above leads us to a single major theme – the task of the services manager is to design a system to close the gaps.

The way the manager can do this is as follows:

Gap 1: Learn what the customer values, and values most. Among the tools to accomplish this objective is appropriate market research. Benchmarking and competitive analysis will also be helpful.

Gap 2: Design a proper system. This is perhaps the manager's most perplexing problem. Many tools have appeared over the years. A recently developed tool called quality function deployment is valuable in ensuring that proper design is achieved.

Gap 3: Control the process. Traditional quality control approaches such as inspection often fail, particularly in services. Statistical process control techniques provide quantitative tools that are very useful for control.

Gap 4: Provide accurate information. The information on system performance provided in controlling the process will help close this gap. Appropriate use of failure information will also be very helpful.

Gap 5: Measure the results. If Gaps 1 through 4 close, then Gap 5 closes. It is a function of the other four.

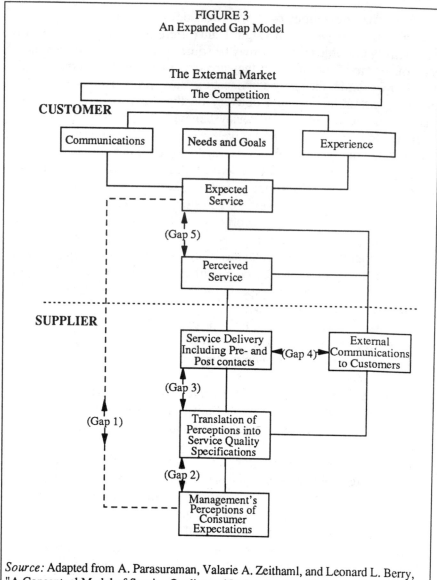

FIGURE 3
An Expanded Gap Model

The External Market

The Competition

CUSTOMER

Communications | Needs and Goals | Experience

Expected Service

(Gap 5)

Perceived Service

SUPPLIER

Service Delivery Including Pre- and Post contacts ◄(Gap 4)► External Communications to Customers

(Gap 3)

(Gap 1)

Translation of Perceptions into Service Quality Specifications

(Gap 2)

Management's Perceptions of Consumer Expectations

Source: Adapted from A. Parasuraman, Valarie A. Zeithaml, and Leonard L. Berry, "A Conceptual Model of Service Quality and Its Implications for Future Research," *Journal of Marketing,* 49, 4 (Fall, 1985), pp. 41-50, published by the American Marketing Association.

The specific tools and techniques mentioned above will close the described gaps. Each is explained in some detail in the following sections. How the tools fit in the design process is illustrated in Figure 4.

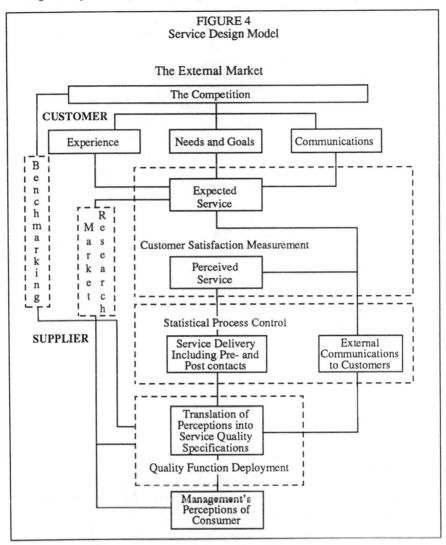

FIGURE 4
Service Design Model

CLOSING GAP 1: LEARNING WHAT THE CUSTOMER WANTS

As everyone knows, market research is supposed to tell management what customers want. The main problem is that, although managers may know what the customer wants, they often don't know what the customer wants *most*.

One effective way to help management learn what the customer wants most is to have the customer make choices during an interview or on a questionnaire. The interview involves determining the relative importance of many elements in the marketing mix. Once the most important elements are determined, management then prepares a tradeoff analysis to ascertain

FIGURE 5
Examples of a Forced Ranking Matrix

MATRIX ONE
BEFORE FILLING IN
SERVICE QUALITY

FOOD QUALITY	SUPERB	EXCELLENT	GOOD
SUPERB	1		
EXCELLENT			
GOOD			9

MATRIX TWO
ILLUSTRATING A MODERATE PREFERENCE
SERVICE QUALITY

FOOD QUALITY	SUPERB	EXCELLENT	GOOD
SUPERB	1	2	4
EXCELLENT	3	5	7
GOOD	6	8	9

MATRIX THREE
ILLUSTRATING A VERY STRONG PREFERENCE
SERVICE QUALITY

FOOD QUALITY	SUPERB	EXCELLENT	GOOD
SUPERB	1	2	3
EXCELLENT	4	5	6
GOOD	7	8	9

which of these are more important than the others. An example of this trade off analysis is shown in Figure 5.

Figure 5 shows three matrices. The first matrix is a blank one that might be given to a customer of a fine restaurant. The customer is being asked to evaluate the relative importance of the quality of the food and the quality of the service. We will assume that the customer has already stated a preference for food quality. But a simple ranking does not show the strength of that preference.

The upper left-hand cell of matrix one shows the best performance of both variables, whereas the lower right-hand cell shows the worst performance of both. The value of "1" and "9" in these cells reflects what any reasonable buyer would prefer as the best (1) and the worst (9) combinations. The customer is asked to fill in the rest of the cells with the numbers 2 through 8 to show his or her preferences for the balance of the cells. Ordinarily, the labels for the columns and rows are defined more specifically than in this example.

Trade off matrix two shows the matrix filled in. This matrix shows a moderate preference for food over service. The third matrix shows a very strong preference for food over service. When combined with matrices for service versus price and food versus price, the researcher will be able to determine the relative strength of the customer's requirements as well as a simple rank order. The technique used to analyze the data is conjoint analysis (Johnson, 1974: 121-127).

By using this form of analysis, management can develop value-oriented service and marketing strategies. It certainly should allow management to determine the relative importance of the variables under analysis.

Sterling and Lambert used the methodology to identify which customer service components of the overall marketing mix contributed the most to the share of the business received. They developed a questionnaire listing between 82 and 99 variables (depending on the targeted respondent) related to price (16 variables), product (22-23), promotion (15-28), and place (29-33). Their questionnaire consisted of four parts: (1) importance rankings of the marketing service variables, (2) expected service performance or standards, (3) evaluations of suppliers' services from part 1, and (4) demographics of the respondents. They used multidimensional statistical analysis to determine the relative importance of the variables in the particular industry under study. They then tested the results of the customers' evaluation of several firms in the industry against the market share of these same firms to determine the contribution each made to the selling firm's market share. They found a relationship between the variables tested and market share (Sterling and Lambert, 1987: 1-30).

The relevance of the above work is as follows. It shows that management can determine which variables of the marketing mix affect sales and how service components affect product sales.

Another critical aspect of market research is to determine the customers' perceptions of how the firm is doing in providing the level of service or product quality that they have ranked. In addition, the customer is asked to rank the firms' competition for the same factors. These data are critical to the next phase of the design process.

Once the customers' requirements and perceptions of the important factors have been determined, then the firm needs to find out how well the firm actually is doing relative to the competition. This is not a perceptual evaluation; it is a factual one.

The technique used in this step is called benchmarking. Much of the landmark work in benchmarking was done by the Xerox Corporation in the early 1980s (Camp, 1989). Xerox defines benchmarking as "the continuous process of measuring our products, service, and practices against our toughest competitors or those companies recognized as the leaders" (Xerox Corporation, 1988: 3).

Benchmark data, when combined with customer importance ratings and competitive perceptions, help the firm to design products and services that will have the greatest impact on the firm's market share. How this is done is described in the next section.

By using appropriate market research and benchmarking, *Gap 1 can be closed.*

CLOSING GAP 2: DESIGNING THE PROCESS

Perhaps the hardest part of the quality implementation program is to design the process to be sure that the service provided consistently meets the specifications that management has developed from the customer's requirements. Yet, the evolution toward using quality as a strategic weapon demands effective design efforts.

In the last decade, Japanese management devised a tool for use in designing a manufacturing process called Quality Function Deployment, or QFD. It offers a way of designing a product that develops measurable standards during the design process. Fortuna's definition of Quality Function Deployment is "a systematic means of ensuring that customer . . . demands (requirements, needs, wants) are accurately translated into relevant technical requirements and actions throughout each stage of product development" (Fortuna, 1988: 23-28). The American Supplier Institute is a principal supplier of QFD training. It defines QFD as "a system for translating consumer requirements into appropriate company requirements at each stage from research and product development to engineering and manufacturing to marketing/sales and distribution" (American Supplier Institute, 1987).

One weakness of the several definitions of QFD that are in use is that they make no mention of how the QFD process prioritizes customer requirements to gain the greatest level of customer satisfaction. The implication of most of the definitions (and even the articles published on QFD) is that one must carry out a complete design of the product or system. Such is not necessarily the case. It can be used to identify the most critical elements that must be redesigned to satisfy the customer's most important requirements. Although it is a tool itself, it also requires the use of the other common quality tools, for example, the checklists, flowcharts, fishbone diagrams, etc.

The QFD team proceeds through a series of steps, creating charts that convert the data of one step into the requirements of the next (Eureka, n.d.). These steps include:

1. *Customer Requirements.* The customer requirements are listed in terms of what the customer has said he or she wants. This is "the voice of the customer." This step is frequently the most difficult, "because it requires obtaining and expressing what the customer truly wants – and not what we think he or she wants" (Sullivan, 1986: 40). The voice is recorded in nontechnical terminology. An example of the voice of the customer might be "stays hot" for a carry-out cup of coffee.

2. *Design Requirements.* Design requirements are the voice of the customer translated into technical and measurable terms. There may be more than one design requirement for a customer requirement, and vice versa. A design requirement for the cup of coffee might be, "loses no more than 5 degrees every ten minutes." Design requirements can be tested by panels of customers to determine if they are satisfactory. They are also called "substitute quality characteristics."

3. *Part Characteristics.* Part characteristics are technical features that the item must have to achieve a design requirement. For the temperature loss above, this could be a particular R factor for the cup used. Part characteristics do not usually apply to services.

4. *Manufacturing Operations.* These are the manufacturing processes that will achieve the part characteristics just described. For the service sector, or product-related services, it involves achieving the design requirement of Step 2.

5. *Production Requirements.* This step involves determining the critical control requirements necessary to be sure that all the previous critical requirements are met. These are the measurements that the firm will take and to which they will apply SPC techniques.

Properly done, QFD is a systematic process for making sure that customers get what they want.

QFD has three features that make it different from traditional design techniques. The first feature is the way the design team is organized.

QFD ensures that the firm delivers a product or service to meet what marketing has determined the customers' requirements to be. From a philosophical point of view, the concept is not new. Marketing supposedly developed over the years as a discipline to identify customer requirements, and then see that the product offered by a firm was what that customer

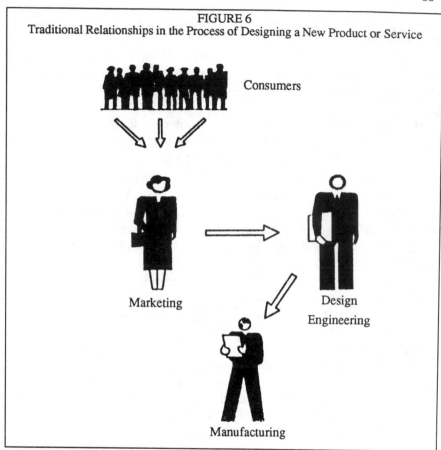

FIGURE 6
Traditional Relationships in the Process of Designing a New Product or Service

Consumers

Marketing

Design
Engineering

Manufacturing

required. But this was not always the case. Marketing has not always had the technical expertise required to design products or services, and did not speak the language of the design engineer.

Figure 6 is a simplified illustration of the traditional approach in a graphic manner. The process involves a one-way flow of information, beginning with customers telling marketing what they desire. Marketing takes that information, interprets it, and passes it on to the design engineer. The design engineer takes the interpreted information, designs the product or service, and then tells manufacturing how to make it. There is no mechanism for feedback or questions.

Figure 7 illustrates the normal structure of a QFD team. Representatives from marketing, design engineering, and manufacturing are each on the team. The team remains together throughout the design process. No member signs off on any portion of the project. Marketing leads in the effort of deciding what the customer wants, but the design engineer and the manufacturing representative are involved at this step. They can see

FIGURE 7
QFD Team Relationships in the Process of Designing a New Product or Service

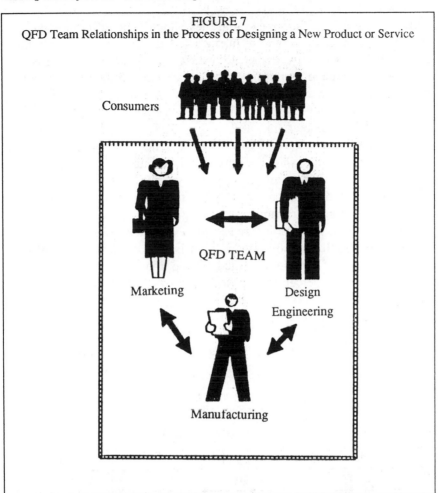

the requirements of the customer and interpret how it will impact on what they do. Similarly, the marketing representative helps design the final product and can be sure that it meets the customer's requirements.

The second major feature of QFD is the manner in which it takes the customer's requirements in the customer's own words and from these words designs a product or service and the process to fulfill those needs. As part of this design process, it also specifies the measurements that will be used in the control process.

Translating the voice of the customer is not as easy to understand as it may sound. The author worked with one company that was losing customers. These customers told the company they were no longer buying from the company because of "late delivery." Since it was possible to serve the portion of the market in question in three days under good conditions, the firm interpreted this to mean that they should deliver in three days or less. When their customers were interviewed, the consensus of customers indicated that a *ten-day* order cycle time was adequate, with twenty-one days being about the worst they would stand for. Subsequent analysis indicated that 15 percent of their customers' orders were not even being shipped within twenty-one days. The firm had gravely erred in translating the voice of the customer.

The final major feature of QFD is the manner in which priorities are set. It uses the data that were collected to close Gap 1 to determine which customer requirements to attempt to satisfy first. It does not necessarily involve working on the one that customers feel is most important. The information in Figure 8 demonstrates this point.

Once again the hypothetical restaurant example is being used. Market research data are illustrated in the top matrix. The customer requirements are in the customer's voice. Included are the importance ratings for each and the customer's perception of how the firm and the competition compare. The bottom matrix shows the customer's requirements after they have been converted into substitute quality characteristics. Hypothetical priorities have been calculated. The details of how these priorities were calculated are not shown here; however, the reader should be aware that they are calculated from the importance rating and the strength of the

FIGURE 8
An Example of Setting Priorities in QFD

MARKET RESEARCH RESULTS

CUSTOMER WANTS	IMPORTANCE	FIRM	COMPETITION
Superb Food	9.0	9.0	7.5
Superb Service	7.5	6.2	6.4
Reasonable Price	5.0	6.0	6.0

Note that these are in the customer's own words.

BENCHMARKING RESULTS

SUBSTITUTE QUALITY CHARACTERISTICS	PRIORITY	FIRM	COMPE-TITION	IMPROVEMENT DIFFICULTY
Taste Jury Evaluation	1	8.0	6.5	7*
Service Jury Evaluation	2	6.0	6.0	5
Price per Meal	3	5.5	7.0	8

Key: * High numbers are more difficult to improve.

relationship between the customers' wants and the substitute quality characteristic.

These two matrices seem to suggest that the restaurant should put its first efforts into how the food tastes. This is not the case, *even though it is ranked as most important.* The reason why is that:

- The firm's food quality is already perceived to be higher than the competition's.
- Service is perceived to be essentially the same for both firms.
- Making improvements to service will be less difficult than food improvements.

Consequently, the element to improve will not always be the one that ranks the highest. QFD helps the firm interpret the voice of the customer so that differential value is maximized.

QFD in this country is widely used in the automotive industry. There are also examples of how QFD has been applied to services. One firm, for example, applied QFD to designing an employee benefits package.

QFD is not easy to do. Many companies that have tried it have expressed a great deal of frustration in applying it. Others have successfully done so, however, and have demonstrated significant product or service improvements.

Gap 2 can be closed.

CLOSING GAP 3: CONTROLLING THE SYSTEM

The key to closing Gap 3 is to control the process effectively. Fortunately, the tools and methodology to provide control are readily available and have been for some time. One tool is statistical process control, or SPC (sometimes called statistical quality control, or SQC). SPC is discussed elsewhere in this book and need not be elaborated upon here.

SPC involves taking precise measurements of samples of a product or a service while it is still in the process to be sure that the process is performing as designed rather than inspecting the product or service after it is complete. SPC stimulates immediate correction of any problem as soon as the problem occurs, and not trying to correct it long after the error occurs.

Yet, SPC alone is not enough to guarantee that a product the customer wants is what he or she gets. It only ensures that the product meets the specifications that were designed into it, not that the product was designed to meet the customer's requirements. Sullivan observes that Japanese companies concentrate more on what the customer likes, while U.S. manufacturers pay more attention to fixing what the customers don't like.

Fortuna suggests that SPC is the second generation in the evolution of quality activities, with inspection being the first, and designing the customer's quality definitions into the product during development as encompassing the third. He refers to QFD as "taking SPC upstream" (Fortuna, 1988: 23-28).

These measurements are defined using the terms developed during the design function. The process can be controlled as it was designed to be controlled.

Gap 3 can be closed.

CLOSING GAP 4: THE INFORMATION GAP

Parasuraman *et al.* describe two major reasons for the existence of Gap 4. One is the propensity to overpromise, and the second is a failure within the firm to communicate horizontally (Parasuraman *et al.*, 1990: 117-28). In other words, Gap 4 may result for the following two reasons:

- Not all the firm's employees know what the system provides.
- Some of the firm's members promise more than the system can provide.

There are other reasons why Gap 4 may exist. They relate to failures that may occur intermittently, but that may have a disproportionate impact on the customer's perception. These are:

- The firm is unaware of some problems that the customer has experienced.
- The customer has experienced a problem, but the firm chooses not to correct and discuss it with the customer.

In these latter two cases, the firm may be telling the customer about its overall service level, which may be normally true, but it ignores instances of failure. The firm may need to tell the customer its true level of service to avoid problems of recency of service failures.

A primary benefit of using SPC is that it makes available precise information. When given to a knowledgeable customer, an SPC report will usually be accepted by that customer as an accurate and reliable report of the quality of the process. In other words, SPC can close the fourth gap as well as the third. For the uninitiated customer, the sales and marketing staff can interpret the reports in a format the customer may understand.

What the firm has to be careful about is ensuring that the customer is consistently told the same thing. It is very possible that an overzealous employee may tell the customer that the firm will do something it cannot. *Gap 4 can be closed.*

CLOSING GAP 5: MEASURING THE RESULTS

The several gaps discussed above can be closed. With market research, benchmarking, good design, adequate control, and good information feedback, Gap 5 should disappear with the others.

The effort involved at this stage involves measurement of customer satisfaction. Measuring to see if this gap is closed helps the firm verify that all the gaps are closed.

- Gap 1 – can only be measured indirectly.
- Gap 2 – measured internally.
- Gap 3 – measured internally.
- Gap 4 – measured internally for what the firm is aware it has told the customer; the firm cannot always be certain that every employee has told the customer the same thing.

Measuring Gap 5, and knowing that Gaps 2, 3, and 4 have been accurately measured and closed, implies that Gap 1 is closed.

Timing is a critical issue in measuring Gap 5. Obviously, since one cannot always be pestering the customer asking about the service, then the firm must space these measurements. But the firm must not simply assume that snapshot measurements taken over time represent the totality of the customers' satisfaction. Satisfaction may vary according to the most recently experienced level of service.

Setting the Stage: Implementing Quality

This chapter has attempted to show how some of the principal tools of quality can be used to ensure that the service offered to a customer is consistent with what the customer wants and values. It shows the sequencing of the tools and why each is used.

Implementing quality improvement involves a number of important considerations. These include, but are not limited to, gaining top management commitment, changing the corporate culture, and building employment involvement. These issues are addressed elsewhere in this book. But even if these other issues have already been resolved, it remains for management to develop a process to improve the service that is being offered to the customer, that is, to close the gaps.

REFERENCES

American Supplier Institute. *Quality Function Deployment: Implementation Manual for Three Day QFD Workshop. Dearborn, Mich.: American Supplier Institute, 1987.*

Anderson, Douglas N. *Quality, A Positive Business Strategy.* [Pamphlet]. St. Paul: 3M Quality Management Services, 1988.

Camp, Robert. *Benchmarking.* Milwaukee: ASQC Press, 1989.

Crosby, Philip B. *Quality Is Free.* New York: New American Library, 1979.

Eureka, W. E. "Introduction to Quality Function Deployment." *Quality Function Deployment: A Collection of Presentations and QFD Case Studies.* Dearborn, Mich.: American Supplier Institute, undated.

Fortuna, Ronald M. "Beyond Quality: Taking SPC Upstream." *Quality Progress* 21, No. 6 (June 1988): 23-28.

Garvin, David A. *Managing Quality.* New York: Free Press, 1988.

Imai, Masaaki. *Kaizen, the Key to Japan's Competitive Success.* New York: Random House Business Division, 1986.

Johnson, Richard M. "Trade-off Analysis of Consumer Values." *Journal of Marketing Research* (May 1974): 121-27.

Orr, R. H. "Measuring the Goodness of Library Services: A General Framework for Considering Qualitative Measures." *Journal of Documentation* 29, No. 3 (September 1973): 317-318.

Parasuraman, A., Valarie A. Zeithaml, and Leonard L. Berry. "A Conceptual-Model of Service Quality and Its Implications for Future Research." *Journal of Marketing* 49, No. 4 (Fall 1985): 41-50.

Sterling, Jay U., and Douglas M. Lambert. "Establishing Customer Service Strategies Within the Marketing Mix." *Journal of Business Logistics* 8, No. 1 (1987): 1-30.

Sullivan, Lawrence P. "Quality Function Deployment." *Quality Progress* 19, No. 6 (June 1986): 40.

Xerox Corporation. *Competitive Benchmarking: The Path to a Leadership Position.* Stamford, Conn.: Xerox Corporation, Training Manual #700P90261, 1988.

Xerox Corporation. *Concepts of Quality: Workbook.* Stamford, Conn.: Xerox Corporation, 1986.

CHAPTER 21

THE PRODUCTION AND INVENTORY CONTROL SYSTEM

KENNETH C. GILBERT
Associate Professor of Management
University of Tennessee

SUMMARY

Improvements in production and inventory control translate directly into customer value through better product quality, cost, and delivery. This impact dictates that the production and inventory control system must be a focal point in a manufacturing firm's strategy to compete through customer value. The inability of many firms to achieve good production and inventory control stems from fundamental deficiencies in certain organizational systems. The role of management must be that of identifying and improving those systems. Unless management accepts this role, implementation of MRP, Kan Ban, or any other technique for coordinating production will, at best, result in marginal improvements.

INTRODUCTION

The president of a microcomputer company that filed for Chapter 11 bankruptcy in 1986 was quoted as saying, "I learned a new oxymoron for the computer industry. It's called 'inventory control.'" This statement reflects two realities of manufacturing. First, the manner in which a company manages (or mismanages) its production planning and inventory control system is of vital importance to its survival. Second, good production and inventory control is an elusive goal, for such an accomplishment requires fundamental changes in the way a company is managed.

Good production and inventory control is characterized by a synchronized flow of materials through the production process with a minimum of idle inventory. It is also characterized by short manufacturing lead times and productive use of the available work capacity and materials. Improvements in production and inventory control translate directly into customer value through better product quality, cost, and delivery. This impact dictates that the production and inventory control system must be a focal point in a manufacturing firm's strategy to compete through customer value.

Inventory is a barrier to improvement in customer value. The purpose of inventory is to insulate each step of the production process from the other steps and to protect the production process from the suppliers and the customers. Although this protective barrier may make life easier in the short run, it is an obstacle to understanding and improving the systems involved.

If an easy method of achieving good production and inventory control existed, it would be like the philosopher's stone – capable of creating gold from base metal. Unfortunately, there is no quick fix. Certainly, effective production and inventory control cannot be accomplished by simply installing new production scheduling software. Ironically, the period from 1966 to 1980, in which most U.S. manufacturing companies installed computerized inventory control systems, was a period of rising inventories.

What is required, however, is improvement in those systems whose deficiencies give rise to the problems. A major theme of this book is the role of managers in improving systems as opposed to that of controlling and maintaining the existing systems. In the production and inventory control area, the distinction between these two roles is vividly illustrated.

THE COST OF INVENTORY

As recently as 1984, one automobile manufacturer was measuring its production and inventory control improvements in terms of inventory holding cost (which had been reduced to one-fourth the 1982 level). Today, improvements are more typically discussed in terms of inventory turns, manufacturing lead times, and buffer times. Many companies have gone far beyond the point where the potential reductions in inventory holding cost, as traditionally computed, are used to justify continuing improvement efforts. These companies are realizing gains in increased productivity, better quality, and improved delivery, in addition to a reduction in holding costs.

Inventory as a Barrier to Improvement

Inventory holding costs, as traditionally measured, are so incomplete in their representation of the real cost of inventory that they are misleading. The real cost of inventory, stemming from its role as a barrier to improvement, is the waste caused by these hidden problems. Inventory is used to cope with the symptoms of problems, for example, unpredictable product quality. However, its effect is to make these same problems less visible and much more difficult to track.

For example, consider two consecutive steps in a manufacturing process in which defects in items produced in the first step cannot be detected until the items are used in the second step. In the absence of inventory between the two steps, defects will interrupt production, thus making the problem very visible. The absence of inventory will also permit defects to be discovered as they occur. This facilitates tracking the causes of defects, so that process improvement becomes easier. Thus, any inventory between these two steps is a barrier to improvement, and a cost of inventory is incurred.

Inventory makes it possible to live with machine breakdowns, unreliable vendors, inaccurate inventory records, unpredictable yields, long and unpredictable setup times, absenteeism, unreliable forecasts, long and unpredictable lead times in processing customers' orders, poor quality, and poor scheduling. (It has often been said, not completely in jest, that every evil known to manufacturing manifests itself in some form of inventory.) These problems are very costly, but they are sometimes difficult to see and impossible to solve in the presence of large inventories.

There is a popular analogy relating inventory to water in a river and the problems to the rocks below the surface. Each rock is a hazard to navigation. In order to cope with the rocks, one can add more water (increase inventories) or attempt to navigate around the rocks (use a more expensive and complex production scheduling system). These methods of coping with the rocks are the more expensive ways. The rocks can only be discovered and removed by gradually lowering the water until they are exposed.

Inventory as Lead Time

Work-in-progress inventory increases manufacturing lead times. This fact is often counter to intuition. Typically, the response to a demand for shorter customer lead times is to increase inventory levels. However, inventory located upstream from an operation represents a waiting line through which each order must pass. The longer the line, the longer the order will take to get through the system.

For example, if a manufacturing process has six weeks of work-in-progress inventory, then materials released at the first step of the process will exit as finished goods, on average, six weeks later. This means that in order to produce to customers' orders, the customer lead time must be six weeks, that is, orders must be placed at least six weeks in advance. If the customer lead time is to be shortened without reducing the work in progress, the production schedule must be developed from a forecast that may be very unreliable. Either alternative is costly.

The Illusory Benefits of Inventory

Traditional models for inventory overestimate the benefits of inventory. The assumed benefit of work-in-progress inventory is that it provides protection against idle work center capacity. Long production runs of similar items and the resulting inventories reduce the frequency of downtime for setups. Buffer stock inventories between work centers protect each work center from the variation at other steps that could cause downtime owing to starvation and blockages in the work flow. This variation may be due to unpredictable yields, unscheduled downtime, unreliable vendors, unpredictable run times, unpredictable quality, inaccurate inventory records or absenteeism.

The assumption of such benefits ignores two important facts. First, the production system is amenable to improvements that can reduce the time required for setups and reduce the sources of variation. Thus, there are alternative means of eliminating wasted capacity. Second, lost capacity will necessarily result in lost productivity only if a work center is a bottleneck (i.e., an operation that restricts the production rate of the process) needed at 100 percent capacity. For example, the time saved by eliminating a setup at a work center that is not needed at full capacity becomes either idle time or, even worse, time used to produce unneeded inventory.

THE BIAS TOWARD HIGHER INVENTORY

Many manufacturing firms hold an excessive amount of inventory, as much as a third of their total assets. One reason for such large inventories is that firms have not undertaken the improvement efforts eventually required in inventory reduction. Even so, most firms hold more inventory than is necessary, even in the absence of these improvements. Indeed, a reduction in inventory is typically a needed first step in the improvement process.

Since most manufacturing organizations do not have a policy of intentionally holding excessive inventories, there is an obvious question as to why high inventories consistently evolve. There obviously must be organizational biases toward higher inventories. The most fundamental reason, discussed in the following section, relates to the way managers perceive their role in organizations.

Solving the Wrong Problem

A theme of this book is that the job of managers is to improve systems, rather than to control existing systems. Nowhere is the distinction between these two roles more vividly illustrated than in the area of production and inventory control. The fact that many managers in this area have until recently chosen the inventory control role is illustrated by the focus of the tools that have been emphasized in the past.

These tools reflect an attitude that the manager's role is to optimize the performance of the existing system, rather than to improve the system. For example, there is a major focus on tools for coping with variation, such as safety stock formulas (or, equivalently, safety lead time formulas), input and output control systems, and closed loop material requirements planning systems. These tools are designed to provide a cushion against variation or to make continual corrections to compensate for variation. There is little focus on reducing the variation. Similarly, lot sizing has focused on determining the best lot size, given a setup time required, rather than on reducing the time required for setups. There has been a similar focus on developing long-term forecasts of demand (a typically futile undertaking) rather than on reducing lead time so that production can be planned from customers' orders.

The Role of Human Nature

There are human tendencies to emphasize the tangible over the intangible, the visible over the invisible, and the short term over the long term. These tendencies produce consistent biases toward higher inventories. It follows that an important role of the manager is to create systems to overcome these biases.

People commonly believe (erroneously) that commercial air travel is more dangerous than automobile travel and (also erroneously) that murder is more common than suicide. These beliefs reflect the fact that plane crashes and murders are more likely to be reported in the news than are automobile wrecks and suicides. A similar distortion occurs with inventory. When a machine is shut down owing to a stockout, it is immediately and clearly visible. Furthermore, the resulting drop in utilization shows up as a tangible "cost" in the monthly utilization and efficiency reports. On the other hand, the costs of having too much inventory are more insidious. For example, the cost of losing customers owing to poor quality and long lead times is not immediately visible and certainly not recognizable as inventory holding cost. Hence, a "better to have inventory and not need it, than to need it and not have it" mentality evolves.

The Performance Measurement System

Traditional means of performance measurement tend to bias the decision-making process in the direction of higher inventories. These means include the cost accounting system as well as the local measures of performance used on the floor.

The following scenario could occur in a multitude of industries: An order is received for five hundred pieces of a certain item. A 100,000-piece production run is made. One year later most of the extra pieces produced have still not been sold.

The reasons why this seemingly irrational waste of raw material and capacity has occurred lie in the performance measurement system. First, the performance of the plant is measured in pieces (tons or square feet) produced, not in pieces shipped or sold. The 100,000 items contributed to production for the month, even though they did not lead to comparable shipments and, in fact, may have delayed shipments of other orders.

Second, the plant allocates overhead costs based on direct labor content. Thus, a setup for only five hundred units would have resulted in a heavy penalty in overhead cost allocation. By making the longer production run, the standard cost per unit was reduced.

Third, the work centers involved in the production of the items are evaluated on efficiency (standard hours/actual hours worked) and utilization (direct time charged/clock time scheduled) for machine time and labor time. Small lot sizes increase the amount of machine time and labor devoted to setup and cause these performance measures to decline.

Fourth, throughput is measured in tons (or in square feet, cubic feet, or linear feet). In terms of the number of tons that could be produced per shift, this item was better than other items on order. Hence, the second shift decided to make a "gravy run" of 100,000 of these items in order to make the throughput look good.

This example illustrates four common problems of the performance measurement system that penalizes low buffer stocks and small lot sizes:

1. In measuring production, no distinction is made between items produced for inventory and items to be sold to customers. Thus, the accumulation of inventories of items that are convenient to produce is encouraged.

2. Fixed overhead costs are treated as variable costs that increase in direct proportion to labor content, machine time, or some other similar factor. Therefore, standard costs increase as lot sizes are reduced since more time is devoted to setups.

3. Local optima are assumed to produce a global optimum; that is, maximizing the production of individual work centers will maximize the production of the entire process. Hence, decisions are based on local measures such as work center efficiency and utilization. This assumption ignores the fact that most production processes do not have completely balanced capacities. Maximizing the output of the work centers that are not bottlenecks only produces excess work-in-progress inventory.

4. The units used to measure performance do not make sense. Most manufacturing operations do not produce a single, immutable product. Attempts to combine different products in a common unit of measure of production volume are most likely biased toward certain products. That is, when certain products are being produced, the performance measures look better than when other products are being produced. This bias distorts the decision making process. (In the past, the USSR established production quotas for production of trucks in tons. Predictably, the truck factories produced very heavy trucks.)

An impact of the performance measurement system is often observed in the "end-of-period" syndrome. Normally, the attempts to optimize local measures of productivity (e.g., utilizations, efficiencies, and production volume) and standard costs predominate, resulting in accumulation of high levels of inventory. As the end of the financial reporting period approaches, financial measures become the focus of concern, and the need for actual shipments becomes urgent. Thus, the pattern of shipments is flat for most of the period and abruptly curves upward near the end of the period as an all-out effort is made to ship as many orders as possible.

The Functional Silos

Many of the problems caused by the suboptimization of the various units of the functional silos show up as inventory. For example, the

variation in demand that makes inventory control so difficult is often due
to periodic price reductions used by the sales department to stimulate sales
to the retailers. In evaluating the effectiveness of these sales promotions,
the cost of the promotions in overtime and inventory holding cost are not
taken into account. Similarly, purchasing policies used to procure raw
material are developed without taking into account the impact that the
policies may have on the rest of the production process. The commission
structure may encourage sales people to push items that load bottleneck
operations rather than those items that use capacity at operations with
excess capacity.

VARIATION, CAPACITY, AND INVENTORY

The popular perception of inventory control focuses on the relationship
between capacity utilization and inventory levels. This view overlooks the
central role of variation in production systems.

Inventory control is typically viewed as a process that makes tradeoffs
between high inventory costs and low utilization of capacity. This tradeoff
is an important aspect of all production scheduling techniques. For example, material requirements planning relies on long predetermined lead
times between operations that create buffer stocks as cushions against
variation. Just-in-Time systems use less-than-capacity scheduling of
equipment (in conjunction with worker flexibility). The slack capacity and
the ability of the workers to do more than one job serve as a cushion against
variation. The drum-buffer-rope approach of Goldratt and Fox (1986) uses
buffer stocks to protect bottleneck operations and less-than-capacity
scheduling at nonbottleneck operations.

The Impact of Reducing Variation

The problem of inventory control should not be viewed as one of simply
making a tradeoff between the evils of wasted capacity and the evils of
excess inventory. This tradeoff is necessary because of variation in the
process. Inventories can be reduced and capacity utilization can be improved simultaneously through a reduction in variation.

Analytic studies of waiting lines have consistently shown that in the
presence of variation when the workload of an operation approaches
capacity, the expected number of units waiting in queue becomes very
large. For example, an operation whose workload is 90 percent of its
capacity may typically have twice as much work in queue as an operation
whose workload is at 80 percent of capacity. However, the point at which

this growth in the queue becomes significant is directly dependent on the amount of variation in the system.

The solid line in Figure 1 shows the relationship between the upstream buffer inventory of an operation and the capacity utilization in the presence of variation. The total variation seen by the system consists of both variation in the rate at which work arrives at the work center and variation in the rate of production at the work center. This system variation stems from variations in yield, run time, scrap, up-time, and many other factors.

The horizontal axis shows the utilization factor for the work center, that is, the amount of work scheduled through the work center as a fraction of the total capacity of the work center. The vertical axis represents the upstream buffer stock required to achieve this level of utilization. The solid line illustrates that, in the presence of high variation, low levels of buffer stock and high utilization of capacity are mutually exclusive.

The broken line shows how the relationship between upstream buffer inventory and utilization changes when the variation is reduced. A reduction in variation permits buffer stocks and idle capacity to be reduced simultaneously. As the variation gets smaller and smaller, the line moves closer and closer to the horizontal axis, illustrating that lower inventory and higher capacity utilization can be realized as variation is reduced.

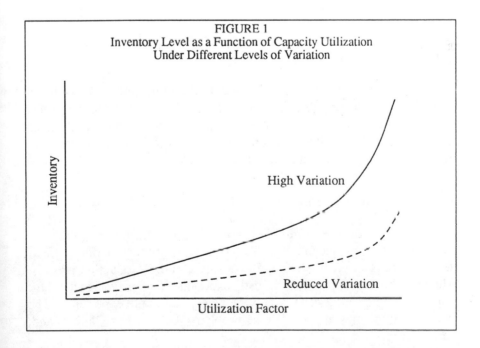

FIGURE 1
Inventory Level as a Function of Capacity Utilization
Under Different Levels of Variation

High Variation

Reduced Variation

Inventory

Utilization Factor

Variation and Production Scheduling

Variation is the key obstacle in the development and execution of a well-coordinated production plan. Consider the following question: If a production process produces 10 percent defective parts, how many parts should be produced if 100 are needed? Or, if a process produces one good part every cycle, but is down 10 percent of the time, how much time should be allocated to ensure that 100 good parts can be produced?

If the variation is not in a state of statistical control (i.e., neither stable nor predictable), there is no way of answering such questions. Even if a state of statistical control is assumed, we are still faced with a dilemma. One possible answer to the first question would be to make 111 parts, since subtracting 10 percent defectives from 111 leaves about 100 good items. Unfortunately, the solution is not this simple. Although producing 111 items would, on the average, result in about 100 nondefective ones, the actual number would usually be either less than 100 or greater than 100. If 111 items are produced, the three standard deviation range of variation for the yield of good items would be from 91 to 109.

It would be necessary to produce 123 parts in order to be relatively certain (three standard deviation protection) of obtaining 100 good parts. Of the 123 items produced, on average, 111 (90 percent) would be nondefective. Thus, the variation makes it necessary to accumulate, on average, the additional inventory of eleven extra good parts and to waste nearly a fourth of the capacity.

THE IMPACT OF PRODUCTION AND INVENTORY CONTROL ON PRODUCT QUALITY

Reducing inventories and achieving a synchronized flow of material through the production process enhances the ability to detect and track quality problems. Conversely, improving product quality reduces the need for "just in case" inventories and padded production schedules as protection against scrap losses and unpredictable yields.

Visibility of Quality Problems

Elimination of inventories makes quality problems more visible. For example, in the absence of buffer inventories, the production of a batch of defective parts may cause a shutdown of the entire production process. Although this may appear to be a costly experience (and may be in the short run), in the long run it can actually be a very profitable experience. The shutdown may draw attention to the problems that cause the defects and, therefore, lead to the problems being fixed. In fact, the knowledge that a batch of defective parts can shut down the process may be sufficient to stimulate proactive efforts to improve quality.

On the other hand, when large buffer stocks are present, a batch of defective parts may simply be scrapped while the production process continues uninterrupted. Thus, the problems that caused the defects remain invisible and unsolved while losses resulting from poor quality accumulate. These losses may, in the long run, far exceed the cost of a shutdown.

Earlier Detection of Problems

An obvious impact of reduced inventories on product quality is quicker detection of quality problems. In many production processes, defects introduced at one step of a process may not be detectable until a later step of the process. If there is a week's worth of buffer inventories between these two steps in the process, the possibility exists for a week's worth of defective inventory to be produced at the former step before the problem is detected at the latter step. Even if such an extreme problem is unlikely, other equally expensive (in the long run) problems may exist. Problems occurring at the first step will be detected, at best, one week later. By this time the events that caused the problem are typically forgotten. The same problem occurs repeatedly, but its causes are never isolated and corrected.

Facilitation of Quality Improvement Efforts

A less obvious but very important impact of improved production scheduling and inventory control is the facilitation of statistical process control activities. The essential focus in these efforts is achieving an understanding of the sources of variation in quality attributes. Among the potential sources of variation are the materials, methods, equipment, people, and environment. Identifying the sources of variation is difficult when it is not possible to identify for a given item the conditions encountered at each upstream step of the process. This identification is impossible when items sit idle for long periods of time between steps of the process or when the production order of the items becomes scrambled between steps in the production process. On the other hand, it is much easier when items that exit the process together not only have gone through each upstream step of the process together, but have done so very recently.

A key sampling concept in statistical process control is that of a rational subgroup. This concept is based on the fact that the control chart has the maximum power to identify sources of variation when each subgroup is homogeneous with respect to the potential sources of variation. For example, if temperature is a potential source of variation, then all items within a subgroup should have been produced at the same temperature setting. It is often assumed that a rational subgroup can be achieved when subgroups consist of consecutive parts from an operation. However, this may not be true when the potential sources of variation are encountered at upstream operations and haphazard production and inventory control is practiced.

SCHEDULING MECHANISMS

No production scheduling system will in itself solve the problems of inventory control. For example, variation will result in either large inventories, wasted capacity, or both, regardless of the production scheduling mechanism used. If the performance measurement system is biased toward high inventories, then there will be high inventories. However, the production scheduling mechanism used will have an impact on the ability to locate systemic problems and implement improvements. It can be instrumental in exposing the sources of variation or the bias in the performance measurement system.

Production scheduling systems can be classified into three categories: push systems, pull systems, and drum-buffer-rope. In push systems, for example, material requirements planning (MRP), production is coordinated through a detailed (normally computer-based) production schedule. The items are pushed through the system by this schedule. In pull systems, items are produced in response to downstream consumption of that item. Thus, items are pulled through the system in response to downstream demand. The operations are linked through physical devices, such as containers or Kan Bans (cards). Drum-buffer-rope systems focus on building detailed schedules at certain critical points, for example, bottlenecks and points where raw material is released into the process.

Push Systems

The logic of push systems is simple. Scheduling begins with a master schedule, which is the planned weekly production of finished products, for several weeks into the future. This schedule is converted into gross requirements for level one items (items used directly to make the finished product). The existing inventory and scheduled receipts of these level one component items are then subtracted from the gross requirements to determine the weekly net requirements. These weekly net requirements are offset by an estimated lead time (consisting of queue time, setup time, run time, and move time) to yield the weekly production levels for the level one component items. This production schedule for the level one items is then used to develop a schedule for items two steps removed from the finished product, or level two items. This process is repeated at successively higher levels until weekly production schedules for all manufactured items and weekly planned order releases for raw materials have been obtained.

Push systems, in using this predetermined schedule to coordinate operations, have an inherent weakness in dealing with variation. For example, even though a particular operation may be behind schedule, the MRP schedule continues to push inventory toward that operation. Enhancements such as closed loop MRP and input-output control are reactive mechanisms that make periodic adjustments to the schedule, in an attempt to compensate for variation. (As feedback loops, these mechanisms are supposed to reduce variation but have the capability of increasing variation if improperly used.)

These systems also ignore capacity constraints, or, in the case of finite loading MRP, they only deal with them in an ad hoc manner by making heuristic adjustments to the master schedule. Thus, the schedule derived may load some operations beyond capacity (i.e., the schedule may not be feasible). In practice, such problems are often managed by building extra lead times into the schedule, so that the inevitable delays at various overloaded operations will not disrupt the overall schedule. However, these long lead times translate into high inventories.

A benefit of push systems is that they focus attention on the need for accuracy of the inputs – inventory records, customers' orders, forecasts, bills of materials, and yield formulas. Thus, companies that have gone through the implementation of these methods tend to have a more complete database, a higher level of data integrity, and a better ability to monitor the inventory flows in the production process. These capabilities are useful in understanding and improving systems.

Pull Systems

In pull systems the production of component items is triggered by downstream demand. A predetermined schedule is developed only for the finished product. A system of standard containers or, alternatively, cards are used to coordinate operations. For example, production items may be moved to downstream usage points in standard containers each of which holds twenty pieces. When a container is emptied at a usage point, it is sent back upstream to the operation where the item is produced. An empty container acts as a work order requesting the production of twenty more pieces of the given item. Similar coordination is achieved with a card system in which cards attached to production items are passed back upstream when the items are used.

Pull systems have several advantages. One is that the pull systems respond immediately to variation, that is, variation in the production rate is immediately communicated to upstream operations. Pull systems also facilitate deliberate reduction of inventory (by simply reducing the number of cards and containers), which is necessary to expose problems and improve systems.

The applicability of pull systems is obviously greater in processes producing high volumes of similar products. The ideas for waste reduction used in conjunction with these systems are generally applicable: setup time reduction, better quality control, flexibility of workers, and flexibility of the production process.

Drum-Buffer-Rope

The drum-buffer-rope approach was developed by Dr. Eliyahu A. Goldratt (see, for example, Goldratt and Fox [1986]). The drum refers to the fact that the schedule is built around the bottleneck operations. This schedule becomes the drumbeat for the entire production process. The buffer refers to the fact that bottleneck operations are protected by an inventory buffer to ensure that the bottleneck will keep working at all times. The rope refers to the coordination of the release of raw materials into the system with the actual progress at the bottlenecks, in order to prevent excessive inventory buildup.

Consider a process in which some of the operations have excess capacity. The excess capacity at these operations can be profitably used for inventory reduction through smaller lot sizes and reduced buffer stocks. With excess capacity the machine time used for extra setups does not reduce the overall production rate of the process and is, therefore, virtually free. Similarly, since the work center can use its excess capacity to recover from disruptions to its schedule, it can also accommodate periodic starvation caused by upstream disruptions. Hence, an upstream buffer may not be necessary.

On the other hand, any lost production at bottleneck work centers translates into lost production for the entire process. Thus, the scheduling should focus on ensuring that the bottleneck operations remain productive at all times.

As an example, consider a process having only one bottleneck operation and a single point at which raw materials are released into the production process. Two things are important in scheduling this process: (1) ensuring that the production time at the bottleneck is not wasted, and (2) ensuring that the materials released into the process do not bury the process in inventory. These two goals can be achieved by close coordination of the bottleneck operation and the raw materials release point.

The bottleneck operation will have a detailed schedule planned from customers' orders (the drumbeat). The release point will stay far enough ahead of this schedule to ensure that the bottleneck is never starved for work (the buffer), while also guaranteeing that production at the release point will never increase so greatly that an excessive amount of inventory is accumulated (the rope). Suppose, for example, that there is an average of six days of flow time between the release point and the bottleneck. Then the release point might attempt to stay ahead of the bottleneck's schedule by perhaps nine days. This would allow, on the average, about three days of inventory buffer to accumulate at the bottleneck. The other work centers would simply work on jobs as they arrived.

The drum-buffer-rope approach differs from other scheduling methods in several important aspects. Scheduling priorities are determined by the capacity constraints. Lead times for each operation are not predetermined (whereas in MRP lead times are specified before the schedule is derived). Process batches are broken down into smaller transfer batches in order to allow the operations on the batch to overlap in time. Lot sizes are not fixed but vary from time to time and from operation to operation.

The drum-buffer-rope approach assumes that the process has a small number of operations that are actually bottlenecks and that these bottleneck operations do not change with the normal variations in the order mix. The method also assumes that it is possible to identify these bottleneck operations and to accurately specify setup times and run times so that realistic schedules for the bottlenecks can be developed. Obviously, these assumptions are not valid for all manufacturing processes.

CONCLUSION

Few manufacturing organizations deliberately plan a competitive strategy based on excessive inventory levels and long customer lead times. Yet many end up with these results. These problems stem from deficiencies in the organizational systems and can be solved only through a process of systems improvement.

Without this improvement effort that removes the fundamental causes of high inventory levels, improved scheduling approaches will at best achieve only marginal improvement. New scheduling techniques are particularly doomed if they are applied as a tool to improve the results (inventory levels, lead times, and production rate), rather than as a mechanism for improving the means to those results, for example, exposure and resolution of deficiencies in the system.

REFERENCE

Goldratt, Eliyahu M. and Robert E. Fox. *The Race*. Croton-on-Hudson, N. Y. : North River Press, Inc., 1986.

CHAPTER 22

ACHIEVING CUSTOMER VALUE THROUGH LOGISTICS MANAGEMENT

C. JOHN LANGLEY, JR.
Professor of Marketing and Logistics
University of Tennessee

MARY C. HOLCOMB
Research Associate, Marketing and Logistics
University of Tennessee

SUMMARY

The logistics area encompasses unique opportunities to create value for the customer. Defined as "the management of product and information flows from original source to final customer in a manner which contributes value to the external customer," logistics represents a key bundle of resources that can be applied successfully to the task of providing best net value for the customer.

In the interest of focusing attention on the new role of logistics management, this chapter discusses four propositions that seem to be valid and relevant. The first is that of the logistics concept itself, and the proposition that it represents a comprehensive process that is of strategic importance as well as boundary-spanning in terms of significance. Second, logistics provides unique and meaningful opportunities to create customer value. Third, a number of contemporary tools and approaches validate and facilitate the effectiveness of logistics to the task of value creation. Fourth, logistics is well positioned to take advantage of the new strategic management process discussed earlier in this book. In fact, there is considerable justification to think of logistics as one of the key strategic suprasystems responsible for providing certain customer-valued products and services.

This chapter provides a perspective on logistics that should help us to understand its current and future role as a principal creator of value for the customer. In order to take advantage of the available opportunities, it will be helpful to learn even more about the value-creating properties of logistics, as well as the key means to facilitate achieving customer value through logistics.

ACHIEVING CUSTOMER VALUE THROUGH LOGISTICS MANAGEMENT

In their continuing quest for new ways to establish and maintain a competitive edge, many leading companies are recognizing the unique and meaningful types of customer value which can be contributed through logistics management. This is certainly true today at firms such as Xerox, L. L. Bean, Frito-Lay, and McDonald's. While these companies would surely agree that product quality and consistency are of exceptional importance, they would argue that the elements of logistical service also create significant value for their customers. This viewpoint is in sharp contrast to the traditional, yet fast-changing, marketing paradigm relating to the importance of the tangible product form itself.

In recognition of the new emphasis on providing the best net value for the customers, logistics represents a key bundle of resources that can be applied successfully to this end. In effect, this formally recognizes the fact that customer value can be created by providing elements of customer service such as product availability, timeliness and consistency of delivery, and ease of placing orders. The net impact is that logistical service is becoming recognized as an essential element of customer satisfaction in a growing number of product markets today.

A fundamental premise of this chapter is that logistics provides certain types of products and/or services that create value for the customer. Thus, it is accurate to think of logistics as one of the strategic suprasystems responsible for creating customer value. Although this premise should be of interest to people who are involved with logistics on a daily basis, it will also serve to highlight some of the value-creating properties of logistics for the benefit of others throughout the organization.

In the interest of focusing attention on the new role of logistics management, the following four propositions have been formulated around key issues that need to be addressed. Responses to these propositions will serve as focal points for the major sections of this chapter.

1. Logistics represents a *comprehensive process*, one that not only incorporates a wide range of activities, but that also evidences key linkages with other strategic suprasystems. The logistics function is changing rapidly as firms apply significant resources to effective management in this important area.

2. Logistics provides unique and meaningful opportunities for achieving *best net value to the customer*. A high priority is also placed on satisfying the needs of customers which are internal as well as external to the firm.

3. A number of *new tools and approaches* have emerged as proactive elements of the logistics response to the task of creating value for the customer. Included are the emphasis on management of the supply chain, provision of logistical customer service, and the development of strategic alliances.

4. Logistics is well positioned to take advantage of the *new strategic management process* discussed earlier in this book. A significant area of research priority in the 1990s will focus on how to take maximum advantage of this concept in the logistics area.

DIMENSIONS OF CONTEMPORARY LOGISTICS PROCESSES

In order to provide a springboard for the remainder of this chapter, this section defines what is meant by logistics and discusses the types of activities that are normally associated with logistics. Following the identification of several trends that are emerging with respect to logistics, the section concludes with a commentary on how logistics creates value for the customer.

The Concept of Logistics

In general, logistics may be defined as "the management of product and information flows from original source to final customer in a manner which adds value to the external customer" (Langley, 1986). The essence of this concept is captured in Figure 1, which illustrates the comprehensive nature of the logistics process. Representative logistics activities include supply chain management (including inventory and materials management), transportation, and customer service. Linkages with other areas of the firm such as marketing and production/operations management are prevalent and meaningful. Issues related to cross-functional coordination and integration will be dealt with specifically at a later point in this chapter.

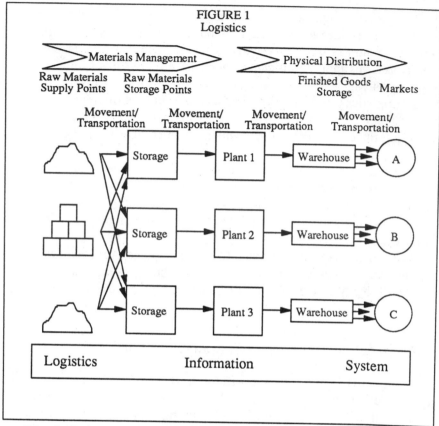

FIGURE 1
Logistics

The logistics process has several unique characteristics. First, it is comprehensive, extending from the original source of raw materials to the location of the final customer. In fact, the logistics process can, and does, span organizational boundaries in terms of encompassing very comprehensive, industrywide channels of supply and distribution. The second characteristic is that it pertains to the flows of both product and information, and considers each as essential to the value-creating process. This concept has received broad acceptance and acknowledges the critical role of logistics in the overall area of information processing and management. Third is that logistics represents a viable means to satisfy and create value for the external customer(s) of the firm and/or the channel of distribution. It is this dimension that truly justifies the recent attention directed toward the new role of logistics management.

FIGURE 2
Activities Included in Logistics Organizations

Activity	Percentage of Respondents Indicating Inclusion of Each Activity[a]
Outbound traffic	93
Finished goods warehousing	84
Inbound traffic	90
Plant warehousing	73
Finished goods inventory management	68
Proprietary transportation	75
Customer service	64
Order processing	65
Purchasing	52
Production planning	50
Raw material in-process inventory management	36
Packaging	40
Sales forecasting	41

[a]Percentages indicate the proportion of study respondents who included each activity in their firm's logistics functions.
Source: C. John Langley, Jr., Stephen B. Probst, and Roy E. Cail, "Microcomputers in Logistics: 1987," a presentation at the Annual Conference of the Council of Logistics Management, September 1987.

Representative Logistics Activities

Based on a study of one hundred U.S. business firms across a broad range of industries, Figure 2 provides data concerning the specific activities included within the firms' logistics areas (Coyle, Bardi, and Langley, 1988). Of particular note is that logistics activities center around the "move-store" functions of transportation, inventory, and warehousing. Recently, however, there have been noticeable trends toward the greater involvement of logistics in the areas of production scheduling (evidencing a broader "move-make-store" orientation), order processing, and purchasing. Finally, as evidenced by the attention being directed to the area of customer service, it is clear that logistics is being recognized more and more as an essential element in the overall process of creating customer value. This topic is discussed in much greater detail later in this chapter.

Emerging Trends in Logistics

First, and perhaps the most significant trend, is the growing recognition of logistics as a means to creating customer value. Whereas the concept of logistics was still somewhat unfamiliar in the early and middle 1980s, it is now better understood and more frequently acknowledged. Although the logistics literature certainly lends substance to this statement, business firms are taking an increasing number of initiatives to capitalize on the customer value created by logistics. Examples of industries where considerable progress has been made include chemicals, pharmaceuticals, and food products.

It is also noteworthy that the Council of Logistics Management recently revised its definition of logistics to encompass this broader context, as well as to acknowledge formally that the logistics process pertains directly to the customer's requirements. The net effect of this change was to assist the process of shifting logistics from a "reactive" to a "proactive" mode, and to do so in full consistency with the needs of the customer (LaLonde, Cooper, and Noordeweier, 1988). So far the results in this direction have been encouraging.

A second observation is that business firms are directing greater resources toward logistics and that the senior logistics executive is becoming more visible and involved on a firmwide basis. It is not unusual today, for example, to identify vice-presidential-level logistics executives in major business firms. Examples where this is the case include Quaker Oats, Dow Chemical, Bergen Brunswig, Limited Stores, Campbell Soup Company, and Land O'Lakes, to name but a few.

Third, considerable attention has been directed toward the integrative aspects of logistics, and the fact that the length and consistency of the customer "order cycle" is emerging as a key concern of firmwide interest. In effect, the integrative aspects of logistics (to be discussed subsequently) have qualified this area to be a major contributor to the creation of customer value. As a result, logistics managers have been actively repositioning their efforts in the interests of facilitating cross-functional coordination in order to best serve the customer. It is encouraging to see logistics managers work closely and consistently with their counterparts in areas such as marketing, manufacturing, finance, and general management. This type of activity is a significant factor in helping to eliminate the so-called functional-silo syndrome that has been so negative and characteristic of the past.

A fourth emerging trend and one to be discussed in more detail later is the development of partnership arrangements with suppliers, customers, other channel members, and external third parties in the interest of achieving desired results in logistics. It has become apparent that a "holistic" view must be adopted, one in which the "win-win" paradigm is recognized as being valid. Logistics has become a frontrunner in this regard among the various corporate functions. The overall impact of this trend is that customer service policies, as well as the wide range of logistics sourcing and procurement suprasystems, have been overhauled and modernized in meaningful and productive ways.

Logistics as a Value-Creating Function

Although the next section addresses the topic of customer value in greater detail, it is useful at this point to recognize the three generic ways through which logistics creates customer value: effectiveness, efficiency, and differentiation.

Effectiveness refers to the issue of performance and whether the logistics function meets customer requirements in certain critical result areas. An excellent example of the focus on effectiveness is evidenced at L. L. Bean, which has identified seven customer service "key result areas" (KRAs). The specific KRAs include the following: product guarantee; in-stock availability; fulfillment time (turnaround); convenience; retail service; innovation; and market standing (image) (LaLonde, Cooper, and Noordewier, 1988).

Efficiency refers to the organization's ability to provide the desired product/service mix at a level of cost that is acceptable to the customer. This concept implicitly identifies the need for logistics to manage its resources wisely and to leverage expense into customer value whenever possible. The interests of efficiency are well served, for example, by the current interest in and trend toward the use of activity-based cost management systems.

Differentiation manifests itself in the ability of logistics to create value for the customer through the uniqueness and distinctiveness of logistical service. For example, the ability of the Limited Stores Distribution Division to mark and tag all merchandise prior to store delivery creates value for the company-owned retail stores within its overall system. The unique ability of the Frito-Lay driver/salesman to provide product integrity at the store level translates to customer value for the independently owned retail stores. A final example of uniqueness through differentiation is exemplified by Federal Express's PartsBank operation in Memphis, that maintains inventories of repair and emergency parts for firms that may have an immediate need for shipment of such items to locations throughout the world.

LOGISTICS AND THE CREATION OF CUSTOMER VALUE

The 1980s introduced a significant amount of technological and environmental change in logistics systems. Yet through all these changes, the focus in logistics has remained on customers and the firm's need to provide best customer net value through effectiveness, efficiency, and/or differentiation of services.

This has not always been the case. Just a few decades ago, most managers involved in logistics had operational responsibility for a single function such as inventory, order placement, or transportation. As customer requirements became more complex, however, the integration of physical distribution and materials management took place. The coordination of activities under the logistics umbrella resulted in increased organizational effectiveness and responsiveness to customer needs and requirements.

The traditional concept of value added by logistics has been viewed as that of cost efficiency versus competitive service levels. This tradeoff reflects a customer-oriented philosophy that integrates all elements of the customer interface with a predetermined optimum cost service mix (La-Londe and Zinszer, 1976).

The scope and role of logistics has evolved to the extent that many firms now believe that a strategic logistics orientation is required to create customer value and sustainable competitive advantage (Bowersox and Murray, 1987). The proposition that logistics can add value to a firm's product and service offerings is a simple and intuitively appealing statement that firms have increasingly come to accept. However, implementation of a value-added logistics process can represent a challenge for firms because it involves a changing and repositioning of perspective and strategic outlook. Based on the premise that value is created when customer satisfaction is achieved, logistics has evolved to mean much more than simply having the "right product, at the right place, at the right time, in the right quantity, and in the right condition."

Strategic logistics distinguishes itself from the traditional perspective through its ability to coordinate, as well as integrate, a number of interdependent activities in a simultaneous fashion across major functional areas, thereby providing various additional dimensions and ways in which logistics can create further value. Within this context, customer value is enhanced by adopting a total channel perspective of the logistics function. The integration of attributes such as customization, flexibility, innovation, and responsiveness results in highly valued and expected levels of service that become the new standard for competitive advantage.

Value can be created in two ways: externally and internally.

External value creation can be planned for by conducting customer surveys, preferably using a third-party, blind survey method. The survey results can be used as a basis for determining the values customers seek. Business reviews, or "previews," should then be developed to identify and specify ways in which the firm can meet or exceed customer requirements (Langley, Rosen, *et al.*, 1989).

Emphasis should be placed on having a specific understanding of the needs and requirements of the many and varied customers of the logistics function. An implied and essential part of creating external value involves the firm's willingness and capability to become a "better" supplier in the coming period. Aside from achieving a one-time understanding of customer needs and requirements, some mechanism to regularly monitor and be aware of the changing priorities of the customer should be instituted. While internal resources may be directed to such a task, this type of activity may justify the use of an outside consultant or service to provide objective information on a regular basis.

While significant attention is usually focused on the customer service needs of the firm's external customers, it is equally important to identify the needs of the firm's internal customers/users as well. Alternatively, internal value creation involves concentrating on how the organization can function more effectively and efficiently for all its constituents, both internal and external to the firm. A first step is to get employees to understand whether the next customer in the pipeline is internal or external to the organization, even though this distinction should make no difference in terms of the quality of service offered.

For example, the business needs of those involved in production/operations, marketing, and financial management should be recognized by those in the logistics area, and suitable initiatives should be taken to facilitate accomplishment of those needs. At companies such as Land O'Lakes, the issue of internal value creation is dealt with through the institution of interdivisional task forces that identify problems from customer service surveys, customer inquiries/complaints, and day-to-day operations. The task force is a cross-functional group that spans all relevant areas (Langley, Rosen, *et al.*, 1989). Although the task force approach has been quite successful at Land O'Lakes, experience at other firms has sometimes evidenced a number of limitations as well as advantages to this type of initiative. In addition, the notion that "task-forcing" should be a principal responsibility of managers all the time is worthy of scholarly as well as pragmatic deliberation.

The task of needs identification is not always straightforward and obvious. It is often complicated by issues surrounding "perceived" versus "real" value, and basic needs versus value-added expectations. To this end, customers can be surveyed to validate their perception. In addition, by ranking various aspects of the defined logistics service, it will be possible to distinguish basic needs from value-added expectations (Selin, 1988). More often than not, however, the process of needs identification entails considerable scrutiny and judgment as logistics searches for new and innovative ways to serve the needs of the firm's internal and external customers.

Management focus in logistics is expanding beyond the existing company structure to involve suppliers and vendors. Progressive firms regard the role of suppliers and vendors as essential to achieving satisfaction for the firm's external customers. Historically, however, many firms treated their customers with respect and dignity, while simultaneously bearing down hard (and frequently unmercifully) on their suppliers and vendors. This type of action is counterproductive to a truly value-added perspective. By spending more time interfacing with suppliers and vendors, interorganizational alliances/partnerships are evolving which enable a firm to willingly commit performance capabilities to customers in advance, and then perform to expectations.

Specific case studies can be used to further clarify the value added through integrated and strategic logistics management. For example, a chemical manufacturer found that its customers did not view the corporation's product offerings the way the organization had assumed. To correct this perceptual difference, a corporate level function was created to handle customer service and orders. This group was supported by a highly sophisticated information system. The resulting change in service level focus from plant to customer provided the firm with the information necessary to increase control over shipments and performance. It also provided the necessary basis for integrating transportation and production scheduling.

Some companies have found that by reevaluating logistics activities, improved efficiencies can be gained by outsourcing essential services. In particular, an industrial equipment manufacturer converting to Just-in-Time found that by using a third-party provider for regional cross-dock operations, both dock congestion and inventory in the system could be reduced. The benefits of integrating resources through supply chain management help to produce total pipeline efficiency which translates to creation of customer value. Properly planned and implemented, this type of approach can produce desirable results without losing competitive capabilities.

In general, there are three related areas of focus for the firm with regard to value creation. First, objectives should be set to achieve customer satisfaction. This involves finding out exactly how customers perceive the organization as a whole, and not just the perspective of a single product or product line. Second, the firm must determine and assign responsibility for systems and processes that are necessary for creating and sustaining customer value. In many instances, the responsibility will span traditional functional boundaries. Third, the basics of marketing must be incorporated into the process of logistics delivery, transforming these basics into benefits that yield value.

Thus, the concept of value creation requires training ourselves not to focus on the individual business firm or its functional components. Rather, it involves addressing the entire supply chain and enhancing efficiency, effectiveness, and differentiation throughout the entire pipeline. This can range from refining internal operations to developing new information systems. The key to successful management of the logistics function as a value-creating operation is to recognize that a firm is viewed from many different perspectives and that each of these perspectives must be taken into account if logistics is going to contribute to achieving best net value for the customer.

NEW LOGISTICS TOOLS AND APPROACHES

In its continuing quest for new ways to create customer value, the logistics area has evidenced the development of a relatively wide range of tools and approaches that are suited to this task. Among the more prominent and comprehensive of these are emphasis on logistical customer service, management of the supply chain, and the development of strategic alliances. Each will be discussed in the paragraphs below.

Emphasis on Customer Service

As defined in a recent study for the Council of Logistics Management, customer service may be thought of as "a process for providing significant value-added benefits to the supply chain in a cost-effective way" (LaLonde, Cooper, and Noordeweier, 1988). In effect, this definition encompasses the notion that customer service in a logistical sense creates value for the entire supply chain and, in so doing, for the end customer as well. This same study identified a number of representative measures of logistical customer service. Included were product availability, order cycle time, distribution system flexibility, distribution system information, distribution system malfunction, and post sale product support.

One of the popular ways to view customer service is that it represents a key link between the traditionally defined marketing function and the

FIGURE 3

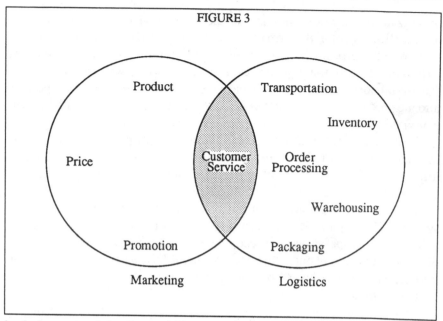

logistics area of the firm. Although a much newer and more progressive view of marketing is presented elsewhere in this book, Figure 3 has a degree of validity in that it helps to explain how customer service can be an important and effective linkage between these two important areas of the firm. A high priority should be attached to assuring that the focus of both marketing and logistics efforts is identical, that being on the creation of value for the customer.

The Council of Logistics Management study identified a number of prevalent trends in customer service, such as the following:

- Firms are becoming very proactive in how they approach the area of customer service. Considerable attention is focused on how to provide the customer with value-creating service prior to, during, and after the product itself is delivered.
- Much of the change is in response to aggressive customers who are beginning to insist that suppliers take formal steps to identify the customer's needs and to provide the value that is desired.
- The ability to effectively manage information flow is viewed as a key to providing breakthrough levels of customer service.
- There has been a significant trend from transactional to contractual-driven systems. Buyers are valuing the longer term relationships with fewer suppliers, rather than treating each purchase or acquisition as a discrete event.

- Pressures to create value through enhanced customer service are increasing, and as a result, capable firms are evidencing an ability to achieve sustainable competitive advantage.

An encouraging observation relating to customer service is that firms are enhancing their understanding of specific logistics attributes such as on-time delivery, damage-free shipments, and in-stock availability. They are also moving toward the development of more holistic and comprehensive measures of customer satisfaction. Actually, this represents a key area in which research is needed to identify critical issues and appropriate logistical responses.

Recent research reported by Pisharodi and Langley (1990a) has suggested a perceptual process model that can be used to enhance understanding of customer service. Shown in Figure 4, the model explains customer response in terms of the industry comparison levels and the actual levels of customer service as perceived by both buyers and sellers in a

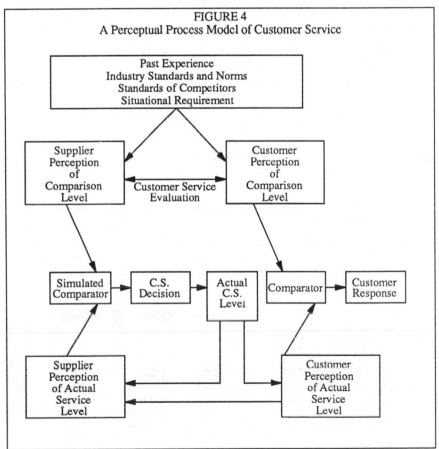

FIGURE 4
A Perceptual Process Model of Customer Service

channel of distribution. The basic premise of the model is that customer response is related not only to the actual customer service levels and those identified as norms for the industry, but also to the gaps between the perceptions of buyers and sellers with respect to these levels. Testing and evaluation of this approach performed to date by Pisharodi has produced promising results (Pisharodi and Langley, 1990b).

Supply Chain Management

Although its evolution has spanned a number of years, the concept of supply chain management focuses attention on the interactions of channel members to produce a product/service that will provide best net value for the end customer.

Perhaps a useful example would be that of the U.S. cotton industry, in which the key channel members include the producers (i.e., farmers), warehousemen, transporters, merchants, and mills. The cotton is grown in the field, warehoused, sold by the merchants, and transported to the mills. In effect, the mill (e.g., Greenwood Mills, Burlington Mills, Milliken & Co.) represents the customer, and the other channel members comprise the additional elements of the supply chain.

Figure 5 is a picture of the supply chain as it pertains to the logistics of cotton flow. As a practical matter, each bale of cotton produced in the United States has its own identity, and logistical value is created for the customer when the specified bales of cotton arrive at the requested location

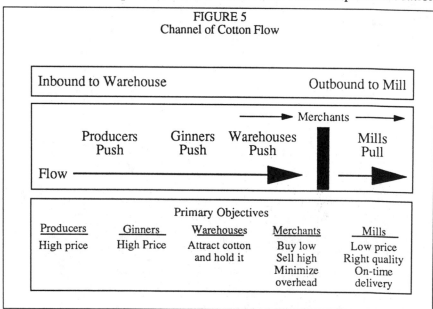

FIGURE 5
Channel of Cotton Flow

Inbound to Warehouse   Outbound to Mill

Merchants

Producers   Ginners   Warehouses   Mills
Push   Push   Push   Pull

Flow

Primary Objectives

Producers	Ginners	Warehouses	Merchants	Mills
High price	High Price	Attract cotton and hold it	Buy low Sell high Minimize overhead	Low price Right quality On-time delivery

in the exact quantity at the time desired. Also shown in Figure 5 are the primary objectives associated with each of the major players in the channel of cotton flow.

Traditionally, there have been a number of impediments to the smooth, effective movement of cotton throughout the supply chain. Some of the principal root causes include the following: (1) conflicting objectives among members of the channel of cotton flow; (2) insufficient incentives for good service throughout the supply chain; (3) inadequate facilities, material handling techniques, and information processing capabilities; (4) general lack of information exchange between key supply chain members; (5) excessive shipping orders at certain peak times; (6) focus on cost minimization rather than service improvement; and (7) emphasis on responding to Just-in-Time and quick response procurement initiatives by customers.

Based on an analysis of causes such as these which tend to produce "bottlenecks" in cotton distribution, the various trade organizations in the U.S. cotton industry have been working for the past few years in a concerted effort to confirm the identify of the suspected causes and to take steps to assure their removal. This type of teamwork effort is indicative of a total supply chain commitment to creating value for the end customer. The results to date confirm the fact that excellent progress is being made.

Another interesting dimension of the concept of supply chain management is the currently popular interest in the topic of Just-in-Time, or quick response approaches to inventory management and product availability. Whereas some feel that the objective of such programs is to reduce or eliminate inventory, the real goal should be the "synchronization of all channel activities in a manner which will create the greatest net value for the customer." When all members of the supply chain achieve this global perspective, the end result is likely to be a degree of coordination and synchronization which assures that the needs of the end customer are met. A byproduct of a well-coordinated system of channel members will place far less reliance on large inventory, which is ostensibly needed to smooth out product flows. Thus, it is likely that the more narrow objective relating to inventory reduction will be achieved as well.

Development of Strategic Alliances

One of the widely discussed logistics initiatives is that of forming strategic alliances with channel partners including suppliers, customers, or intermediaries such as providers of transportation and/or warehousing services. Effectively, this type of relationship leverages a true "win-win" relationship into a strategic alignment of the capabilities of both firms.

Additional benefits to both parties typically include asset productivity, operational effectiveness, and cost efficiencies. Moreover, it is not unusual for one channel member to promote the existence of a meaningful relationship with some prestigious firm with which a strategic alliance has been developed.

A very interesting example of a strategic alliance that centers around logistical capabilities is that of the relationship between Ryder System, Inc., and Xerox Corporation (Langley, Rosen, *et al.*, 1989). Faced with a declining market share owing to increased offshore competition, it was clear that Xerox needed to consider some set of innovative logistical initiatives in order to achieve customer satisfaction. Although Xerox targeted the high end of the market, its offshore competition was targeting the lower end. In order to attack the low end successfully to strengthen its market share, Xerox needed to rethink and rationalize its overall delivery system.

As a result, and with the assistance of Ryder, Xerox trimmed its logistics network from ten to two equipment logistics centers. Third-party logistics providers, including Ryder, performed a number of activities such as supplying warehouse equipment; performing preinstallation assembly tasks; delivering and installing product; training Xerox customers in the use of the equipment; and removing old equipment and preparing for shipping to specific Xerox locations.

A direct consequence of its involvement in third-party relationships is that Xerox has improved its ability to meet its customers' needs. The delivery process has been streamlined, and overall costs have been reduced. Xerox sales personnel, no longer needed to train customers, can concentrate on selling and customer requirements. Logistics is used to gain competitive advantage as it complements, rather than obstructs, Xerox's marketing objectives.

Ryder's role as a third-party provider of logistics services is evidence that a well-managed logistics operation can create value for a customer regardless of whether logistics is performed internally or externally to the firm. The actual degree of value added is dependent on how a company leverages its logistics resources and the ability to recognize the effect a third-party relationship can have.

LOGISTICS AND THE NEW STRATEGIC MANAGEMENT PROCESS

This chapter has dealt with and validated the premise that customer value can be created by logistics and that logistics should be included among the strategic suprasystems responsible for creating value for the customer. As this realization continues to take hold, organizations will rely more and more on the ways in which logistics can help to achieve best net value for the customer.

One of the major propositions advanced early in this chapter is that logistics is in a good position to take advantage of the new strategic management process which is advanced earlier in this book (Carothers and Adams, Chapter 3). This process represents an excellent opportunity for logistics managers to begin viewing their responsibilities on a much different plane than traditionally, one that truly represents a "paradigm-shift" in terms of overall impact and significance.

Even though logistics is regarded as one of the organization's strategic suprasystems, it is also true that each element of the new strategic management process has applicability to logistics. A key task to be accomplished is to complete the transformation and interpretation of the new process specifically to logistics. To this end, Figure 6 identifies the five principal steps in the alternative strategic management process and suggests parallel subprocesses that have applicability to logistics.

Referring to the portion of Figure 6 which deals with strategic suprasystems, we see that recent research has identified interactions, infrastructure, and resource management as likely candidates for inclusion in this category (Rinehart et al., 1990). Interestingly, the interactions management suprasystem has been further subdivided into strategy and structure; the infrastructure management suprasystem into capacity and movement issues; and the resource management suprasystem into facilities, people, and financial.

Also of particular interest is the step relating to the tasks of confirm, correct, and change. In the logistics area, it appears that measurement and control systems such as statistical process control (SPC), quality function deployment (QFD), and/or the use of Taguchi methods represent productive initiatives.

Further research is needed into the applicability of the new process to logistics, but the progress to date is encouraging. In addition to further exploratory research into the conceptual development itself, the issue of implementation is certain to raise meaningful questions to be answered. Efforts in these areas will greatly assist in taking maximum advantage of the leading-edge work that has been done to date on the new strategic management paradigm.

REFERENCES

Bowersox, Donald J., and Robert E. Murray. "Logistics Strategic Planning for the 1990's." *Annual Conference Proceedings*. Oak Brook, Ill.: Council of Logistics Management, 1987, pp. 231-243.

FIGURE 6
New Strategic Management Paradigm Applied to Logistics

- Determination of Responsibility

- Value-Maximization Analysis

  - Creation of product/service attributes

  - Identification of customers' value expectations and perceptions

- Environmental Analysis

- Customer Satisfaction and Competitive Analyses

  - Identification/determination of customer needs and requirements

  - Comparative perceived net value (competitive analysis)

- Strategic Suprasystems Determination

- System and Process Identification and Description

  - Translation of customer value expectations into logistics operational priorities

  - Identification of coordination needed with other strategic suprasystems

- Strategic Suprasystems Management

- Logistics Systems Management

  - Interactions

  - Infrastructure

  - Resource management

- Confirm, Correct, and Change

- Measurement and Control Systems

  - Statistical methods

  - Quality function deployment

  - Taguchi methods

Coyle, John J., Edward J. Bardi, and C. John Langley, Jr. *The Management of Business Logistics.* St. Paul, Minn.: West Publishing Co., 1988.

LaLonde, Bernard J., and Martha C. Cooper. *Partnerships in Providing Customer Service: A Third-Party Perspective.* Oak Brook, Ill.: Council of Logistics Management, 1989.

LaLonde, Bernard J., Martha C. Cooper, and Thomas G. Noordeweier. *Customer Service: A Management Perspective.* Oak Brook, Ill.: Council of Logistics Management, 1988.

LaLonde, Bernard J., and Paul H. Zinszer. *Customer Service: Meaning and Measurement*. Chicago, Ill.: Council of Logistics Management, 1976.

Langley, C. John, Jr. "The Evolution of the Logistics Concept." *Journal of Business Logistics* 7, No. 2 (1986): 1-13.

Langley, C. John, Jr., Mary C. Holcomb, Joel Baudouin, Alexander Donnan, and Paul Caruso. "Approaches to Logistics Quality." *Annual Conference Proceedings*. Oak Brook, Ill.: Council of Logistics Management, 1989, pp. 73-88.

Langley, C. John, Jr., Deborah Rosen, Howard S. Gochberg, Robert A. Dickinson, and Robert J. Quinn. "Logistics and the Concept of Value-Added." *Annual Conference Proceedings*. Oak Brook, Ill.: Council of Logistics Management, 1989, pp. 73-88.

Pisharodi, R. Mohan, and C. John Langley, Jr. "A Perceptual Process Model of Customer Service Based on Cybernetic/Control Theory." *Journal of Business Logistics* 11, No. 1 (1990a): 26-46.

Pisharodi, R. Mohan, and C. John Langley, Jr. "Measures of Customer Service and Market Response: An Exploration of Interset Association." *Proceedings of the 1990 Transportation and Logistics Educators Conference*. Anaheim, Calif., October 1990b.

Rinehart, Lloyd M., Robert A. Novack, David J. Closs, and John J. Coyle. "Rethinking Curriculum Issues in Logistics Management for the Next Century." *Proceedings of the 1990 Transportation and Logistics Educators Conference*. Anaheim, Calif., October, 1990.

CHAPTER 23

MARKETING IN A VALUE-ORIENTED ORGANIZATION

ROBERT B. WOODRUFF
Professor of Marketing, Logistics, and Transportation
University of Tennessee

WILLIAM B. LOCANDER
Distinguished Professor of Marketing
University of Tennessee

DAVID J. BARNABY
Professor of Marketing, Logistics, and Transportation
University of Tennessee

SUMMARY

The realities of extensive competition for world markets demanding ever-increasing quality and value are having a major impact on organizations. More and more of them are thoroughly reassessing and changing management approaches to running the business. Marketing is at the forefront of current attention because of the customer-oriented dimension emerging in these approaches. Marketing has a tremendous opportunity to increase its value contribution to organizations, but only if it reconsiders its role. This chapter presents a framework for understanding marketing's changing role responsibilities in organizations in the decade ahead.

INTRODUCTION

Companies in industry after industry, worldwide, are being threatened by international competition, as they never have been before. The situation has become so serious with American firms that some are calling for a government-backed industrial policy to counter the external threat (Scott, 1989). Many companies are looking for ways to respond. Emerging is a strong sense of urgency to plan and implement strategies for creating advantage in carefully selected markets. Most importantly, providing quality and value to customers is becoming a dominant theme in discussions of strategic direction (Gale and Klavans, 1988; Garvin, 1987).

Ironically, an approach to managing a business called the "marketing concept" has, for decades, urged managers to be customer oriented by balancing the needs of customers with the capabilities of the organization (King, 1965). However, the principles of the marketing concept have proven difficult to implement. Many companies seemed to equate the concept with having the marketing function more involved in all decisions (Hayes, 1988). Yet, just creating a marketing department and a chief marketing executive position will not ensure that the "voice of the customer" is heard in corporate decisions. Rather, all functions of a business must understand customers and their needs, and translate that understanding into well-coordinated strategies that create value and satisfaction for those customers (Shapiro, 1988).

As companies explore new ways to manage, emphasizing a long-run commitment to being customer-driven, marketing will have to reexamine its role. Building on its market opportunity analysis (MOA) expertise for understanding market dynamics, marketing must become a partner with other functions in developing an organizationwide approach to managing value-oriented relationships with customers. This role for marketing is likely to be considerably more comprehensive, integrative, and complex than its traditional role. The purpose of this chapter is to describe a new direction for marketing in the value-oriented organization of the future.

OVERVIEW OF MARKETING'S PARADIGM SHIFT

Tenets of a Value-Oriented Philosophy

With the emergence of global competitive markets has come an emphasis on providing value to customers. Customer value delivery, in its broadest sense, is becoming a part of the vision statement of many organizations. No longer is it adequate for firms to focus on just products or services, but managers must attend to all forms of customer contact as varied as on-time delivery to accurate billing. Obviously, the marketing function must play a key role in helping a firm understand its customers and translate their needs into action-oriented information to all business functions (Stowell, 1989). Figure 1 shows Bower and Garda's (1986)

FIGURE 1
The Value Delivery Sequence

Choose the Value	Provide the Value	Communicate the Value
Customer Segmentation / Value Needs / Market Selection Focus / Value Positioning	Product Development / Service Development / Pricing / Sourcing / Making / Distributing / Servicing	Sales Force / Sales Promotion / Advertising

Source: Bower, Marvin and Robert A. Garda (1986), "The Role of Marketing in Management," in *Handbook of Modern Marketing*. Victor P. Buell, Ed. New York: McGraw-Hill, Inc. Used with permission of the McGraw-Hill, Inc.

conceptualization of a value delivery sequence. Basically, value delivery can be broken down into three stages:

1. *Choose the Value* – Companies must apply MOA technology early to learn about and fully understand what is valued by customers (both end users and trade customers) in different market segments. Customer value requirements can then become the basis for making all decisions within the firm, the first step in being a truly customer-driven organization. Applying MOA knowledge to plan marketing offer strategies for competitive advantage in target markets completes stage one.

2. *Provide the Value* – Companies must develop products and services at price points that are perceived as delivering more value than competitors. To do so, firms must be concerned with the decision of outsourcing or making products in house. Whichever system is chosen, the issues of flexibility and time are paramount. Firms today are becoming concerned with their ability to flexibly build products to customer order across a range of product configurations. Reducing cycle time from order entry to product delivery makes time a competitive tool. A company must meet customer value requirements exactly in as short a time as possible and in a cost-effective way.

3. *Communicate the Value* – A company must create a communications mix that effectively helps customers understand its value offering. To do this, firms must determine the proper role of a sales force, advertising, and sales promotion tools in a larger competitive advantage strategy.

As the three stages show, the nature of value delivery is fundamentally customer driven and reaches across all functions within organizations. In short, bringing the "voice of the customer" into organizational decisions is a companywide responsibility, not just that of marketing.

As firms embrace a value delivery philosophy, the issue of what systems are needed to deliver value becomes important. It is essential that these systems be cross-functional in order to provide a consistent and integrated set of values to trade customers and end users. Furthermore, continuously improving these systems to deliver more value is central to maintaining a long-run competitive advantage. At the heart of the challenge is the notion of carefully managing system variation while enhancing flexibility. Management must set as a goal reducing both common and special causes of variation while improving responsiveness to meet customer value requirements within the parameter of short cycle times. For instance, flexibility is enhanced when a company reduces the lead time needed to bring new products to market or to deliver quickly a customer's special order.

Delivering value and customer satisfaction is inescapably related to the issue of MOA measurement. Today, measuring what various market segments value, creating market offerings to deliver value, and then measuring how satisfied customers are over time are at the core of evaluating a company's rate of improvement in value delivery. Customer satisfaction measurement systems, one aspect of larger MOAs that are rapidly catching on among many businesses as an essential performance evaluation tool, are testimony to the customer-driven orientation required to effectively compete in a global marketplace. A long-run commitment to understanding and meeting or exceeding customer value requirements demands that interfunctional coordination be commonplace within organizations. The leadership within companies must come to realize that giving lip-service to the customer must be replaced by true conviction and that, functionally, "doing your own thing" must give way to a concerted effort across the organization focusing on customer needs.

Paradigm for the Marketing Function

Although many firms are becoming more customer driven, functional specialization still holds an important place within today's organizations. Because of its external focus on the customer, the marketing function must accept responsibility to work closely with its functional constituencies within the firm. Generally, this takes the form of partnering with others across an organization in both planning and implementing marketing strategy. To be truly market driven, a company's marketing strategy has to be developed, enthusiastically accepted, and actively implemented by the entire organization. For instance, the marketing function has the responsibility to supply MOA information to internal customers such as engineering for product design, distribution for product delivery and services, and top management for allocating resources and measuring the effectiveness of the firm versus competition. In this as well as other ways, marketing can become a more effective stakeholder in the firm's delivery of customer and end user value through multifunction processes.

Figure 2 presents a framework for conceiving the marketing function's role in a value-oriented firm. Note that only one of the four functions relates to managing marketing itself. The other three require that marketing be part of cross-functional planning, a supplier of MOA information, and a stakeholder in decisions concerning value delivery. Figure 2 serves as the basic model for this chapter. After discussing the issue of marketing getting its house in order, each of the other three role responsibilities is discussed in turn. The overall purpose of the chapter is to prescribe marketing's new role in any organization, with the vision of competing through customer value delivery.

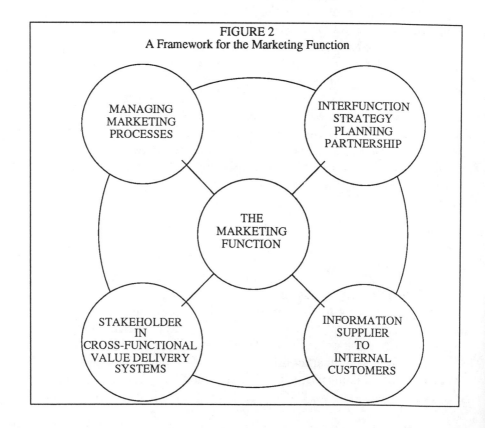

FIGURE 2
A Framework for the Marketing Function

MANAGING MARKETING PROCESSES

INTERFUNCTION STRATEGY PLANNING PARTNERSHIP

THE MARKETING FUNCTION

STAKEHOLDER IN CROSS-FUNCTIONAL VALUE DELIVERY SYSTEMS

INFORMATION SUPPLIER TO INTERNAL CUSTOMERS

MARKETING MUST GET ITS HOUSE IN ORDER

The manufacturing-related operations of many businesses are making impressive progress in improving product and process quality. Results are revealing a consistent theme: it is possible to improve quality and lower costs at the same time (Phillips, Chang, and Buzzell, 1983). A pacesetter in value delivery, Florida Power and Light utilizes quality improvement teams to find quality problems and propose solutions. In 1987 alone these teams submitted nearly one thousand proposals, most of which were implemented. A typical success story from this effort concerned power line switches that were failing. A team implemented a solution that improved the reliability of power transmission and saved $40,000 a year ("Building a Quality Improvement Program at Florida Power & Light," 1988).

At the heart of quality improvement programs is statistical process control (SPC). The principles of SPC are easy enough to grasp. Essentially, this methodology provides a way of analyzing processes to identify problems to resolve. An inescapable reality of processes is that they have variability. Unfortunately, variability leads to unpredictable outputs and the incurring of costs to rectify inevitably poor quality. SPC is a set of tools for understanding processes, identifying the amount of variability, and locating its causes. Corrective action can then be aimed at these causes. Improving quality is a continuous application of these tools and requires a process-oriented way of thinking about work.

Success in applying SPC to operations has increased pressure on other organizational functions to follow the same path. Marketing is not exempt and must respond to this challenge. There is little doubt that similar results are possible. But marketing may have to think about what it does in a very different way.

Marketing managers may not be comfortable conceiving of their work activities as ongoing processes. Yet, that is exactly what they must do. Managers must analyze their work as a series of activities occurring over time so that variability and its causes can be uncovered. Improvement comes from correcting these causes. Figure 3 suggests some marketing kinds of activities that are easily seen as processes.

Initially, marketing managers must think about how work progresses to some output. Flowcharting is an SPC tool that is especially helpful for this purpose. For example, the activities required to fill a customer's order may be diagrammed from the time that an order form is completed by a salesperson to the time that the order is received by shipping. The sequence of work activities revealed will show where error-causing variability in order form completion and handling can happen. Data can be gathered to

FIGURE 3
Marketing Activities Conceived as Processes

Marketing Department   Processes

                Sales   Sales calls
                                   Order form completions
                                   Order filling
                                   Territory planning
                                   Sales forecasting
                                   Discounts implemented

            Advertising   Media placements
                                   Creative design
                                   Ad testing
                                   Budgeting
                                   Couponing delivered
                                   Contest implementation

               Product   Strategy planning
                                   Product modification
                                   Market opportunity analysis
                                   Pricing
                                   Honoring guarantees
                                   Hotline calls
                                   Repair completions

          Market research   Client contacts
                                   Project management
                                   Report preparation
                                   Repeated projects

monitor these critical points in the process to examine variability. Another SPC tool, control charts, is particularly helpful for this monitoring.

Control charts uncover problems but do not identify causes. Managers must launch a search for the special causes of variation in a process. Several SPC tools are especially designed for this purpose, including cause-and-effect diagrams, Pareto charts, and experimentation. For example, suppose that a control chart reveals that order filling errors are unusually high for a particular product. A cause-and-effect diagram can be used to identify all the possible causes of these errors, such as the design of the order form, the number of salespersons using the form, and the place where the forms are filled out. Data may be collected and used to develop a Pareto chart showing which causes are most important. Finally, corrective action can be aimed at resolving these causes.

Applying SPC is a minimum requirement for marketing to contribute its share of value in a value-oriented approach to organizational management. It is a very analytical problem-solving style of decision making, relying on continuous attention to improving processes. Marketing managers must become familiar with this style and the associated tools in order to achieve the same productivity successes evident in the operations side of an organization. Yet, it is just a starting point. Becoming competitive through value delivery will make many more demands of marketing.

MARKETING'S PARTNERSHIP IN STRATEGY DEVELOPMENT

While being customer driven is an organizationwide responsibility, someone must accept a leadership role in cross-functional strategy development and implementation. Thus, an important question for the management of value-oriented organizations is, "Who should play this leadership role?" The answer to this question is not obvious since several organizational groups may lay claim to leadership. However, it is especially important to ensure that a deep understanding of customers, their value requirements, and competitors' strategies for obtaining market position permeates all strategy decisions. That is at the core of being customer driven. Marketing, with its expertise in understanding customer, and competition and market environments, is in a strong position to accept leadership at least in ensuring a customer orientation. In doing so, it would be a mistake to believe that the marketing department should assume the entire responsibility for customer-driven strategy decisions (Hayes, 1988). Rather, marketing must develop partnerships with other functional managers in developing and implementing strategy with a customer-driven focus. Managing such relationships will not be easy.

For marketing to take a leadership role in partnerships, particularly for ensuring customer-driven decisions, several things have to happen. First, marketing must become an organizational advocate for customers. In this way, marketing may be able to help merge top-management organizational strategy decisions with middle management decisions on product-market strategy and tactical planning. Second, marketing must develop greater understanding of the complexities and interrelationships between all value delivery systems of the organization. Such understanding is the basis for managing partnerships with other functional managers in the organization's strategy planning center, however that center is arranged.

Finally, as discussed later, marketing must become considerably more adept at supplying actionable MOA information on competitive market environments to all functional participants in decisions on strategy for value delivery.

MARKETING'S STAKE IN VALUE CREATION

Stakeholders, whether internal or external to the organization, are those entities, people, or groups that affect or are affected by a firm's actions (Mitroff, 1983). The issue of creating value for customers can be seen as a stakeholder problem since external trade customers and end users, among others, have a vested interest in the outcome while internal interests are held by the various functional units within the firm. In the 1960s and early 1970s, U.S. firms were beginning to feel the competitive pinch from global competitors. This shift in market conditions required firms to reorient from an internal stakeholder perspective concerned with negotiations between, say, manufacturing, finance, and marketing to a view that featured both trade customer and end-user value requirements as the guiding influence on an organization's strategy and tactical decisions. The between-function psychology of "they are the enemy" and thus a "winner take all" decision had to change (Yates, 1985). The turf battles that dominated U.S. firms during this period have slowly had to give way to a greater vision of what the firm (and working in the firm) is all about.

With the emergence of modern marketing, the "voice of the customer" was to be brought into the planning and decision-making process within firms. Some firms have been more successful than others in instituting this market-driven perspective. Ideally, marketing's role in the larger organization is to ensure a customer orientation in crucial decision areas: (1) selection of target product/markets as defining where the organization should focus its efforts; (2) definition of product concepts so that product offerings will be perceived by consumers as having the highest value; (3) determining how to instill a notion of "excellence" in the customer service area;[1] and (4) maintaining a customer perspective when resolving inconsistencies and resulting conflicts over functional objectives across the company. If each organizational unit has objectives that clash with each other, then the customer may "enjoy" second position in the minds of various managers. One need only look at the following stereotypes to understand the nature

---

1. Certain companies have developed a customer service culture which translates into a competitive market advantage. If customers are saying things like "dealing with 3-M Corporation is a pleasure and has been for the last ten years," then the value of customer service is being perceived and makes a difference in the mind of customers.

of this cross-functional problem:

Sales	"Ship cases; we are rewarded on volume."
Marketing	"To meet or exceed customer needs, let's have many product configurations."
Manufacturing	"We need long stable production runs without interruption and fewer things to make."
Logistics	"A smooth even flow of product is desirable for a stable and efficient distribution system."
Accounting	"We follow generally accepted accounting principles; we don't have that kind of information."

Each of the above quotes is an example of functional predispositions usually supported by performance appraisal and reward systems. It is incumbent from a customer-driven perspective that all these inconsistencies be resolved in the name of delighting both trade customers and end users – at a profit.

Managing Stakeholder Relationships

Because organizations' need for functional expertise is not likely to disappear in the near future, marketing has a continuing responsibility to

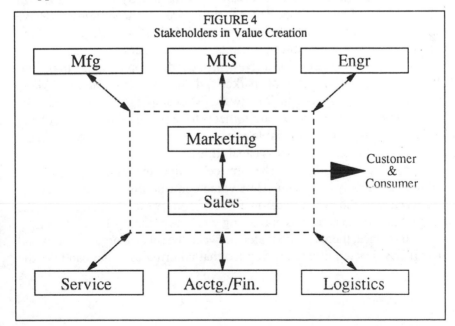

FIGURE 4
Stakeholders in Value Creation

take the leadership in being the chief advocate of customers (both the trade and end users) (Locander, 1989). Figure 4 shows a number of stakeholder relationships that must be managed so that value is delivered to the marketplace. Being market driven means that the arrows depicting inter-functional relationship must be recognized as presenting obstacles and opportunities for improvement. Improvement takes the form of reducing the number and size of variation-producing behaviors. Such behaviors often occur when there is interdependence between the functional units which in the course of their operation can produce variation in performance. Consider the following division of responsibilities from Figure 4:

Marketing – Sales: It is interesting that in many companies these two functions are separate organizational entities. Marketing generally handles the advertising and promotion responsibilities, while sales is concerned primarily with units sold and customer service. It is easy to see that there can be a lack of unified effort toward meeting customer needs.

Manufacturing – Marketing/Sales: While the marketing function is concerned with meeting customer needs, this often leads to unplanned changes that affect the manufacturing planning cycle. These take the form of unannounced promotions, inaccurate sales forecasting in total or by the individual SKU (shelf keeping unit – a term referring to the level of brand specificity, e.g., color, size, model, used for keeping track of inventory), the timing on new product initiates – the list can go on and on!

MIS – Marketing/Sales: Management Information Systems (MIS) will continue to be of critical importance in the future. These systems will have to be much more market based to provide information useful in making decisions concerning products, markets, and customers.

Engineering – Marketing/Sales: New product development has traditionally been plagued by a lack of market and customer information. Many firms fall into the trap of focusing inward in developing new products. The issue of understanding value requirements for a potential new product and then translating them into a viable market offering must be done within the limits of manufacturing process capabilities.

Service – Marketing/Sales: The service component of being customer driven is extremely important. Here value-contributing services that make a difference in the eyes of customers is of concern to marketing. To the extent that service is seen as correcting what the company has done wrong in the first place, there is a mismatch between the service organizations and customer value requirements. Service that contributes value can take the form of avoiding rework and facilitating the installation and use of products so that they perform up to expectations.

Accounting – Finance/Marketing-Sales: The difference between information provided by generally accepted accounting principles and what is needed to be competitive in the marketplace often creates a huge gap between these functions. As an example, the allocation of overhead to new products under development can cause many new products to appear unprofitable. To the extent that the accounting system is outdated and insensitive to the new product development process, companies will have to reconcile the inconsistencies between market needs and traditional accounting practice.

Logistics – Marketing/Sales: Logistics systems are designed to handle smooth, consistent product flows from manufacturer to retailer. Logistical systems are a partner with the marketing function in dealing with the uncertainties of the marketplace (Foggin, 1989). The interface between these two functions must be managed to recognize the tradeoff of building logistics competency to handle variations that can be caused by promotional activities. Similarly, promotions could be dysfunctional in that if the real cost of a given marketing tactic could be understood, the promotion would be abandoned without further thought.

The above relationships are offered to show that the very nature of being customer driven requires an understanding of internal competencies and tradeoffs so that customer expectations can be met and exceeded by a system under control. As companies move to a more customer/consumer-driven culture, the role of marketing will be to continue to improve its own ability to understand what customers need and to translate those needs into internal requirements for the organization.

MARKETING'S ROLE AS A VALUE-ORIENTED SUPPLIER OF MOA INFORMATION

Marketing is accustomed to looking outward toward the external environment when managing its responsibilities. The various departments comprising the marketing function – sales, brand and product management, advertising, market research – have a common purpose of locating customers and planning and implementing strategy toward them. Strategy is multifaceted since an organization must often appeal to both end users and trade customers for the organization to achieve desired performance. Marketing has developed considerable expertise in performing this strategic role with external customers.

Marketing's Internal Customers

Marketing should also ask whether these external customers are the only ones of concern. Under the value-oriented approach to managing an organization, the answer is a resounding "no." Marketing must realize that it has internal customers in various other departments in the organization (AME, 1988: Cole, 1983). After all, a customer is just anyone to whom a product or service is delivered or sold.

In marketing's case, the "product" is information, particularly about various dimensions of market opportunity. Internal customers should include product design, manufacturing, logistics, accounting, financial control, and top management. In fact, any department or group that is in some way involved in contributing value to the organization's offer to external customers needs information on at least some aspects of market opportunity. Marketing must ensure that it has the market opportunity analysis skills to meet these needs.

Consider a case in point. Product design engineers clearly must understand who the end users for a product are, and what needs those end users have. Thus, these design engineers become one of marketing's internal customers. The challenge is to determine exactly what information needs these engineers have, so that appropriate data can be gathered and delivered. For instance, design engineers are faced with many choices among physical characteristics to build into a product. Which characteristics to implement depends, in part, on customers' value requirements. Some value requirements will be sought by end users who have certain use situations in mind. Additional requirements may be those of trade customers, such as desired packaging features needed to facilitate stacking on shelves. Furthermore, competitor strengths and weaknesses in meeting current and future requirements should be considered. Marketing can bring "the voice of the customer" into product design decisions by meeting these information needs.

Internal customers are not likely to need information in quite the same form with which marketing is accustomed to working. For instance, while advertising creative personnel may be comfortable in using data about requirements in the words of the end user, product design engineers will not. Unfortunately, the language of end users may not be very actionable for the design task (Day, Shocker, and Srivastava, 1979). Actionability is best achieved when the engineer can translate each customer requirement into one or more physical product design characteristics. Marketing will have to learn how to assist in this translation process.

Working closely with design engineers, marketing can lead the process of discovering relationships between customers' requirements and product characteristics. A procedure called quality function deployment (QFD) is uniquely intended to assist in this purpose (Hauser and Clausing, 1988; Sullivan, 1986). QFD starts with a listing of customers' value requirements and their relative importance, all coming from MOA studies. Marketing interacts with design specialists and others to explore relationships between these requirements and product characteristics. Competitors' strengths and weaknesses with regard to meeting value requirements are also considered.

Responding to Marketing's Internal Customers

Marketing will have to acquire new skills in order to satisfy internal customers' information needs. Two such skills are particularly noteworthy. First, marketing will have to better understand internal customers' decision-making responsibilities. These responsibilities will largely dictate the uncertainties they face and corresponding information requirements. For instance, accounting may want to provide more managerially useful cost information. Doing so may mean breaking out costs by market and by major customer within markets. Therefore, data are needed on target market selection and customer identification to make this kind of cost system work. Furthermore, marketing must keep accounting informed of changes in target markets and customers so that the cost system can be updated in a timely fashion.

Second, marketing will have to become proficient at constructing MOA information "products" tailored to meet internal customers' needs. In most cases, these "products" will have to address the translation problem mentioned above. Consider the data requirements of corporate level management responsible for allocating resources among business units. They must understand market and profit opportunity for many business units, which themselves are responsible for some mix of different but related products. The translation problem is particularly challenging in this case. A large amount of data on market opportunity and costs for each product and market must be condensed into a summary picture of opportunity across business units. This picture must be sufficiently descriptive for strategic allocation decisions to be made while not overwhelming top managers with detail. Note that MOA information becomes the starting point for top management strategic decision processes.

The Voice of Marketing

For marketing to act as the "voice of the customer" in organizational decisions, it must speak with a unified voice itself. Unfortunately, in departmentalized organizations there is great potential for disunity. As mentioned previously, marketing is typically split into separate departments, each with its own goals, strategies, and tactics. Each is also quite likely to have its own understanding of external market opportunity. One author is familiar with a case where product development designed and tested a new product intended for selected market segments. The product was turned over to the sales department after a forty-minute presentation of its purpose and features. Sales promptly began selling the product to other market segments where they thought sales opportunity was greater. Unfortunately, the product was not designed with these latter segments' customers' requirements in mind.

This lack of cooperation between departments can seriously limit marketing's ability to meet the MOA information needs of internal customers. Ways must be found to break down these departmental barriers to cooperation, so that all marketing units can share a common access to MOA data. Only then will marketing be able to speak as a single "voice of the customer."

Three directions seem particularly important. First, marketing, across all its departments, must have a common framework for analyzing market opportunity. This framework should consider the interactions going on in the external environment that create opportunity (Woodruff and Cadotte,

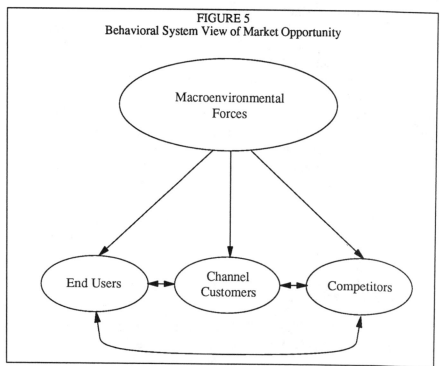

FIGURE 5
Behavioral System View of Market Opportunity

1987). Figure 5 shows the source of market opportunity as exchanges occurring between end users and channel customers, channel customers and competitors (including the firm), and competitors and end users, all influenced by a macroenvironmental context. For instance, the flood of media information about health issues provided by the press is causing people in the United States to become much more knowledgeable about health care. As a result, many are taking a more active role in decisions on the kinds of health care treatments they receive as well as where they go for these treatments. Doctors still play a crucial intermediary role and are an important target for marketing strategy. But hospitals are shifting more of their marketing resources, such as wellness clinics and increased advertising, directly toward consumer and user target markets.

These exchanges form a behavioral system; it is important to recognize that a system can only be understood in its entirety. The MOAs should aim to help managers deeply understand the makeup of the system, how it works, as well as to predict how the system will respond to the organization's marketing strategy and tactics. Yet, many firms seem to lose sight of the systems nature of market opportunity. Organizations commonly parcel out MOA tasks to different departments. For instance, product management and advertising departments may know a lot about end-user markets but little about channel customers. The sales department usually knows a lot about channel customers but not much about end users. Ironically, the department that may understand the most about the entire behavioral system is marketing research. Even here, some companies assign the competitor analysis activity to a separate department that is more responsible to top management than to marketing. Someone must take charge of MOAs to ensure that all marketing departments can share data describing market opportunity. Only then can marketing be the "voice of the customer" by developing, from this behavioral system data, information products for nonmarketing internal customers. One alternative may be to assign MOA responsibility to cross-functional teams that plan strategy for products and markets.

Second, functional managers should develop a common understanding of MOA capabilities. This means that those outside of marketing need to learn more about what an MOA is and what data can be provided. More knowledgeable internal customers can provide significant help in the process of designing information products that will meet their needs.

Finally, the dynamic nature of external environments argues strongly for treating MOAs as ongoing activities, not periodic projects. Yet, this is seldom done. Textbook publishers, for instance, may conduct MOA studies only when a new textbook is planned or at the beginning of a revision cycle every three to five years. In the interim a lot can happen in the market which goes unnoticed. Worse yet, some firms conduct MOAs only when a crisis arises. Organizational values and reward systems must reflect the need for managers in various departments to regularly use MOA data to keep up with changes that are occurring.

Marketing's Value-Oriented Opportunity

Marketing's expertise in learning about the external exchange behavioral system should be invaluable to other functional managers. There is a clear opportunity for marketing to become an effective MOA information supplier to the organization. However, this opportunity will only be tapped when marketing recognizes internal customers and their information needs. In turn, nonmarketing functions must cooperate with marketing for these needs to be met.

CONCLUSIONS AND IMPLICATIONS

Marketing Practice

The practice of marketing is facing a dramatic metamorphosis in the coming years. As we approach the twenty-first century, the practice of marketing will become what, at first, seems to be a paradox. Marketing will become more systematized and yet more tactical. There is no doubt that when systemic tradeoffs are understood, marketing efforts will become more planned, bigger, and less reactionary than they are today. Yet, the need to meet or beat competition in market execution will still be a competitive necessity. The seemingly paradoxical situation can be explained when one understands that firms must build systems that are flexible and adaptable. Flexible adaptive systems will have to be able to react to customer or competitive changes in much shorter time frames. The strategic longer run perspective is in taking the time to build systems which can, if need be, react to tactical requirements immediately.

Thus, marketing of the future will be concerned with providing value to customers by systematically and proactively analyzing market opportunity and executing plans in a short cycle time. This will be done in concert with the other functional strategies like flexible manufacturing, Just-in-Time inventorying, and service quality. As one can see, today firms are wrestling with what it takes to be in the marketplace first with the most value and thereby build a long-run franchise with customers and end users.

Research Opportunities

Marketing's role in the value-oriented organization of the 1990s can also benefit from new knowledge. Research should be encouraged to assist in marketing's transition toward a more organizationwide responsible function. There are research opportunities in at least three areas: (1) understanding marketing activities as processes, (2) understanding customer value and satisfaction, and (3) understanding how marketing organization values and reward systems affect corporate effectiveness.

Marketing Activities as Processes. As mentioned earlier, marketing is not accustomed to viewing its activities as processes with variability. Research is needed to identify typical processes and to learn about their nature. For the most part, this will require studying how marketing managers make decisions. For example, flowcharting of the creative decision by advertising in a sample of firms might yield a picture of an ongoing process with regular activities and decision points. Sources of variability could also be analyzed. Such knowledge might be very helpful in developing guidelines for process improvement.

Customer Value and Satisfaction. Value-oriented organizations all have a common characteristic – managers are market and customer oriented. Yet, these managers may not always know how to learn about customers, including who they are, what needs they want met, and how they will evaluate what the organization offers them. Measurement systems are needed to provide the information that managers need to be market and customer oriented.

Currently, there is extremely wide variation among firms as to how well they measure value and satisfaction perceptions of customers. Furthermore, even the best of organizations will eventually want more sophisticated and practical approaches than presently exist. For instance, current techniques often yield insights only into those product and service attributes most desired by customers at the time purchase decisions are made. Greater understanding of customer value will come from knowing more about the consequences that customers experience from using products in particular situations. Research is needed to discover how to more effectively provide this kind of information. Moreover, research will have to show how customers' desired value is linked to customers' satisfaction evaluations.

Marketing Values and Reward Systems. Finally, marketing departments have typically shared organizational values and well-developed reward systems. There appears to be very little knowledge about how these values and reward systems affect organizational performance. For instance, salespersons are often paid a commission on sales as a significant part, if not all, of their compensation. Commissions are likely to direct how salespersons spend their time across products, markets, and individual customers. Yet, very little is known about the effects of this practice on organizational performance in markets. Research could provide valuable insight into how commission-directed sales behavior affects overall sales, market share, and profit performance by the organization. Similar kinds of research are needed for the many marketing processes.

Marketing Educational Programs

University-based marketing education programs are going to have to change to meet the needs of companies in the 1990s and beyond. The cross-functional nature of delivering value to customers demands that marketing identify and understand the various stakeholders in organizational decision making. The increasing importance of this holistic approach to business will require that educators begin to examine marketing from a process management viewpoint. To do this and to appreciate the "new" practice of marketing, educators are going to have to find legitimacy in studying marketing within the essential context of the organization. This unit of analysis for teaching and research will add emphasis to the theory and practice of marketing in applied settings. The focus on how to configure a worldclass competitor in any industry will be challenging enough, but academic educators and researchers will have to continuously examine how to improve on processes and systems.

The demarcation between university degree programs (undergraduate and MBA) and executive training will begin to blur as industry demands relevance of graduates from business degree programs. Both business and business schools will be moving toward a new "higher" ground in seeking to understand business problems from a richer and more meaningful perspective – one that brings the strengths of academia and business together working on cutting-edge problems.

REFERENCES

AME. "Organizational Renewal – Tearing Down the Functional Silos." *Target* (Summer, 1988): 4-14.

Bower, Marvin, and Robert A. Garda. "The Role of Marketing in Management." In Victor P. Buell (ed.), *Handbook of Modern Marketing*. New York: McGraw-Hill, 1986, Ch. 1, 3-13.

"Building a Quality Improvement Program at Florida Power & Light." *Target* (Fall 1988): 4-12.

Cole, Robert E. "Improving Product Quality Through Continuous Feedback." *Management Review* (October 1983): 8-12.

Day, George S., Allan D. Shocker, and Rajendra K. Srivastava. "Customer-Oriented Approaches to Identifying Product Markets." *Journal of Marketing*, 43 (Fall 1979): 8-19.

Foggin, James H. "The Importance of Quality and Continuous Improvement in Logistics Customer Service." *Survey of Business* (Summer 1989): 40-47.

Gale, Bradely T., and Richard Klavans. "Formulating a Quality Improvement Strategy." *Journal of Business Strategy* (Winter 1988): 21-32.

Garvin, David A. "Competing on the Eight Dimensions of Quality." *Harvard Business Review* 65 (November-December 1987): 101-109.

Hauser, John R., and Don Clausing. "The House of Quality." *Harvard Business Review*, 3 (May-June 1988): 63-73.

Hayes, H. Michael. "Another Chance for the Marketing Concept." *Business* (January-March 1988): 10-18.

King, William R. "The Marketing Concept." In George Schwartz (ed.), *Science in Marketing*. New York: John Wiley and Sons, 1965, pp. 70-97.

Lazer, William, Priscilla LaBonhera, James M. MacLochlan, and Allen E. Smith. *Marketing 2000 and Beyond*. Chicago, Ill.: Dow Jones Irwin-AMA, 1980.

Locander, William B. "Brokering Marketing Into Total Quality." *Survey of Business* (Summer 1989): 31-35.

Mitroff, Ian I. *Stakeholders of the Organizational Mind*. San Francisco: Jossey-Bass, 1983, p. 4.

Phillips, Lynn W., Dae R. Chang, and Robert D. Buzzell. "Product Quality, Cost Position and Business Performance: A Test of Some Key Hypotheses." *Journal of Marketing*, 47 (Spring 1983): 26-43.

Scott, Bruce R. "Competitiveness: Self-Help for a Worsening Problem." *Harvard Business Review*, 67 (July-August 1989): 115-122.

Shapiro, Benson P. "What the Hell is 'Market Oriented'?" *Harvard Business Review* 66 (November-December 1988): 119-126.

Stowell, Daniel M. "Quality in the Marketing Process." *Quality Progress* (October 1989): 57-62.

Sullivan, L.P. "Quality Function Deployment." *Quality Progress* (June 1986): 39-50.

Woodruff, Robert B., and Ernest R. Cadotte. "Analyzing Market Opportunity for New Ventures." *Survey of Business*, 23 (Summer 1987): 10-15.

Yates, Douglas, Jr. *The Politics of Management*. San Francisco: Jossey-Bass, 1985, pp. 134-135.

CHAPTER 24

FINANCE AND THE CREATION OF VALUE

MICHAEL C. EHRHARDT
Associate Professor of Finance
University of Tennessee

JAMES M. REEVE
Associate Professor of Accounting
University of Tennessee

SUMMARY

The objective of any firm should be the continuous creation of value, with the different functional areas of the firm contributing to this goal. This chapter examines one of the functional areas, finance, and the ways it contributes to creating value within corporations and financial institutions.

The traditional functions encompassed by corporate finance include (1) the selection of viable projects, (2) the acquisition of capital from the financial markets, and (3) the management of short-term assets and liabilities. Although the role of finance in an organization committed to linking customer value and strategic systems spans these same activities, the continuous creation of value in today's complex environment may require new approaches and different tools. The first section of this chapter summarizes the new approaches and tools that are currently known and directs attention to areas in which more insights are needed. In particular, attention is devoted to concepts and techniques required for effective capital budgeting.

The second section of this chapter is devoted to issues confronting U.S. financial institutions. These institutions are now being challenged by increased competition from abroad, a situation analogous to that faced by auto manufacturers during the last fifteen years. This section addresses changes that may be required in the management of financial institutions if they are to adapt successfully to a competitive global market.

THE CREATION AND MAINTENANCE OF VALUE

The selection of projects is often called capital budgeting. Although the number of potential projects is unlimited, the implementation of all potential projects is neither feasible nor desirable. Most companies face short-term constraints with respect to skilled labor, engineering expertise, management, and cash. These constraints can be accommodated in the long run, but they are usually binding in the short term; that is, the immediate selection of some projects is simply not feasible. Some projects should also be rejected on the basis of regulatory, environmental, and safety issues.

Even among the set of feasible projects, not all should be selected. Most projects require the sacrifice of cash and other resources before they return cash and/or resources to the firm. Financial analysts generally recognize that only projects which increase the value of the firm should be accepted. In the traditional theory of finance, value is defined as the discounted present value of after-tax cash flows associated with the project. This is still true for an organization committed to quality systems, but in today's complex environment there are previously unemphasized prerequisites for creating and maintaining future cash flows. Two of these prerequisites are: (1) responsiveness to changing conditions in the business environment and (2) cultivation of implicit contracts.

Responsiveness to the Business Environment

It could be argued that these prerequisites are not really new. For example, it is reasonable to believe that corporations should have always striven to respond quickly to changes. With the stable business environment that characterized much of the 1950s and 1960s, however, there was not a critical need for responsiveness. Only during the last two decades has the business environment been subject to rapid changes. Thus, only recently has responsiveness become a prerequisite of global competitiveness.

Rapid change in the marketplace is now a distinguishing characteristic of today's business environment. This is especially true with respect to customer demands, product diversity, and production/process technology. With the advent of increased global competition, consumers now have an enormous array of providers from whom they can purchase goods and services. Faced with choices among providers, customers are no longer a captive audience. If one company does not provide satisfaction, consumers simply choose another company. The long-term well-being of a corporation depends to a large extent on how well it satisfies consumer demand and how quickly it can respond to changes in the desires of customers.

The proliferation of products is another reason why the ability to adapt rapidly is important. Consider products such as the microwave oven, the videocassette recorder, and the compact-disc player. These are major sources of sales revenue today, but they were not even in existence twenty years ago. The ability to design, engineer, and manufacture a new product within a short period of time can often be the difference between success and failure.

Changes in production technologies also have a profound effect on a company's ability to compete. For example, the introduction of computers on the manufacturing floor has allowed many companies to increase output with no increase in costs, thereby increasing throughput. Other applications allow the company to reduce the cost of a product without reducing its value to the customer. With reduced costs comes the creation of value for the firm. This can be in the form of reduced prices and increased market share, stable prices but increased profit margins, or some combination of reduced prices and increased profit margins. Companies that fail to adopt appropriate technologies will be unable to compete on a long-term basis.

In summary, responsiveness to customer desires and flexibility in production technology are now essential to the creation, maintenance, and increase in firm value. Techniques for quantifying the value of flexibility are described later in this section.

Cultivation of Implicit Contracts

A corporation can be defined as a nexus of contracts, some of which are explicit and some of which are implicit. Examples of explicit contracts are easy to identify and relatively easy to value – for example, labor contracts, sales orders, and vendor contracts.

Implicit contracts are no less important, although they are more difficult to quantify. For example, customers may buy a product because they believe the company will continue to support the product with service and additional related products. Travelers may choose to eat at a restaurant from a particular fast-food chain because they believe this company provides a clean facility and a consistent menu. People may choose to work for a company because they believe the company will provide an environment in which they will be able to develop their long-term potential. Suppliers may establish a relationship with a company in the belief that it will lead to continued sales in the future. These are all implicit contracts, and they each have a large influence on the company's ability to create and maintain cash flows in the future. The effect of implicit contracts on firm value can be quite large, since implicit contracts are often a major determinant of future cash flows.

The study of implicit contracting is called stakeholder theory, because all holders of implicit contracts have a "stake" in the company. Traditional theories of finance emphasize stockholder value rather than stakeholder value; that is, the goal of management is asserted to be the maximization of stockholder welfare, which is typically measured by stock price.

It is often asserted that an emphasis on stock value leads to myopic decision making on the part of management; that is, management fails to undertake long-term projects owing to a mistaken focus on short-term profits. This assertion, however, is not supported by empirical evidence. Woolridge (1988) documents the positive response of stock prices to long-term strategic decisions, even though the strategic decisions have a small short-term profit. In other words, strategic actions that create or enhance implicit contracts also increase firm value. As Kaplan (1989) cogently argues, the value of a firm does in fact depend to a great extent on its future cash flows.

Stakeholder theory does not imply that management should no longer try to maximize the welfare of stockholders; it simply states that this welfare can be increased through the careful cultivation of implicit contracts. In other words, firm value (and stock price) can only be maximized when explicit attention is devoted to all stakeholders. For example, increased quality leads to more valuable implicit contracts with customers; a more livable work environment leads to more valuable implicit contracts with employees; long-term relationships lead to more valuable implicit contracts with suppliers. The net result of cultivating implicit contracts is an increase in firm value.

Stakeholder theory is still in its infancy. Although Cornell and Shapiro (1987) provide anecdotal evidence that is consistent with stakeholder theory, there are virtually no empirical tests and certainly none that irrefutably confirm or reject the theory. If stakeholder theory is to become a well-accepted paradigm in finance, then empirical support is required. The valuation of implicit contracts is an area of finance in which more study is needed.

CAPITAL BUDGETING IN TODAY'S ENVIRONMENT

Projects often have side-effects that affect the company's responsiveness to changing business conditions or the cultivation of implicit contracts.

Ignoring these side-effects can lead to the selection of projects that are globally suboptimal. As discussed below, the traditional approach to capital budgeting often fails to adequately address several critical issues confronting today's organizations.

The Traditional Approach to Capital Budgeting

Three areas in which the traditional approach to capital budgeting is often inadequate are: (1) the recognition of project interdependencies; (2) the valuation of flexibility in production/process technology; and (3) the evaluation of projects with long-term strategic objectives. Although most activities and projects span many functional areas, financial analysts often assume that a project exists independently of other systems in the firm. Ignoring possible interdependencies can lead to an incorrect assessment of project value. It is important to determine all the effects on cash flows caused by a project.

As noted earlier, responsiveness to changing conditions is a necessary ingredient for success in today's environment. One way to increase responsiveness is to add projects that increase the firm's flexibility. In particular, some projects can be converted to other uses as business conditions change. This ability to switch makes the correct measurement of risk for such projects more difficult. As shown later in this chapter, it is virtually impossible to value this managerial flexibility with traditional capital budgeting techniques.

Many projects have an impact on managerial strategic objectives. Examples of strategic projects are those that gain market share in a new industry or increase the value of implicit contracts. In either case, traditional capital budgeting is often inadequate to value this feature of a project. Oatman and Buehlmann (1989) argue that when evaluating strategic projects, analysts tend to compare a project with the status quo, rather than to compare it with the environment that will prevail if the project is not undertaken. This can lead to incorrect project selection.

In summary, many currently used techniques in capital budgeting are inadequate for today's environment. An example used in the following section illustrates some of the pitfalls in a narrow application of the traditional capital budgeting approach; techniques for evaluating a more complex project, typical of today's firms, are also illustrated.

The Traditional Capital Budgeting Approach: An Example

In the following example value is determined for a complex project; in particular, the effects of project interdependence and flexibility are valued. To illustrate the difference that these factors make in the evaluation of a project, the value of a simple project is first determined.

The example is based on a firm that is currently producing a single product (Product A) in a multistage manufacturing facility as shown in Figure 1. Each stage is characterized by a group of machines devoted to specific tasks.

As a result of recent technological breakthroughs, the firm can replace the machines in Stage 3 with a single machine that can replicate their tasks. Table 1 contains relevant information about the new machine. Notice that the new machine will require an additional investment today but will cut operating costs in the future

There are three steps in an application of traditional capital budgeting techniques. The first is to estimate the expected after-tax cash flows due to the project. The next step is to find the appropriate cost of capital relevant to this project. Finally, the net present value (NPV) of the project is determined; that is, the estimated cash flows are discounted using the cost of capital. According to traditional finance theory, only projects with positive NPVs increase firm value and should be accepted.

The first step is to estimate the cash flows associated with the project. In this example, replacing the old machines requires an initial outlay of capital; however, the subsequent operating costs are lower. The effects of taxation owing to different depreciation bases must also be considered. A worksheet is presented in Table 2, providing the calculation of after-tax cash flows.

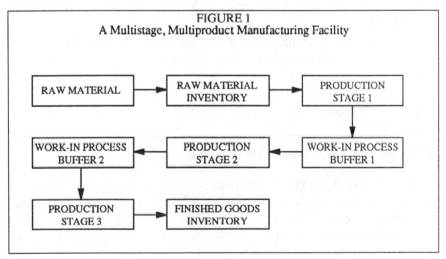

FIGURE 1
A Multistage, Multiproduct Manufacturing Facility

TABLE 1
A Comparison of Costs Between the New and Old Machines

New Machine		Old Machine	
Acquisition cost	$230,000	Remaining book value	$120,000
Market value	$120,000		
Expected life	5 years	Remaining life	5 years
Operating costs/year	$100,000	Operating costs/year	$125,000

The next step is to find the cost of capital for this project. In general, this cost of capital is the weighted average of the costs of the various sources of financing, such as debt, equity, and preferred stock. The cost of equity should be adjusted to reflect the risk of the project. The Capital Asset Pricing Model (CAPM) is often used for this purpose; see Brealey and Myers (1989: Ch. 7-9, 19) for a description of CAPM and its use in estimating the cost of capital. The cost of capital is explained adequately in numerous textbooks and is not the focus of the techniques illustrated in this example. Therefore, detailed discussion is not provided here.

For the remainder of this example, the after-tax cost of capital for this project is assumed to be 14 percent. Given the cash flows from Table 2 and the cost of capital, it is straightforward to calculate the NPV. As shown in Table 3, the NPV is -$27,675. Later in this chapter this is referred to as the base NPV.

Sensitivity analysis would follow in a traditional application of capital budgeting. This additional analysis is undertaken to determine the sensitivity of the NPV to the assumptions underlying the model; that is, how much do the estimates of expected cash flows and the cost of capital influence the NPV?

If the decision were based simply on the NPV, the project should not be accepted. This is a simplistic view, of course; no decision should ever be made on the basis of one number. In a typical firm, however, it is more likely that a project with a positive NPV will be rejected rather than a project with a negative NPV will be accepted.

A Framework for Valuing Complex Projects

Brealey and Myers (1989: 19) suggest a framework that can be applied to valuing complex projects. Suppose the directly measurable cash flows of a project are discounted at the cost of capital in exactly the same manner as in the previous example of a simple project. Let this be defined as the

TABLE 2
Computation of Direct Cash Flows Due to the Project
(All amounts in $)

Panel A
Cash Flows Due to Old Machine

			Year		
	1	2	3	4	5
Depreciation	24,000	24,000	24,000	24,000	24,000
Tax shield of depreciation	8,160	8,160	8,160	8,160	8,160
After-tax operating costs	82,500	82,500	82,500	82,500	82,500
Net cash flow	74,340	74,340	74,340	74,340	74,340

Panel B
Cash Flows Due to New Machine

				Year		
	0	1	2	3	4	5
Initial cost	230,000					
Sale of old machines	120,000					
Depreciation		46,000	46,000	46,000	46,000	46,000
Tax shield of depreciation		15,640	15,640	15,640	15,640	15,640
After-tax operating costs		66,000	66,000	66,000	66,000	66,000
Net cash flow	110,000	50,360	50,360	50,360	50,360	50,360

Panel C
Incremental Cash Flows

			Year		
	0	1	2	3	4	5
	-110,000	23,980	23,980	23,980	23,980	23,980

Explanatory Notes
1. Straight-line depreciation is assumed for ease of exposition.
2. The corporate tax rate is assumed to be 34 percent. The tax shield of depreciation is computed as (0.34)*(Depreciation).
3. The after-tax operating costs are computed as (1-.34)*(Operating Costs).
4. Cash flow is defined as the sum of the tax shield due to depreciation and the after-tax operating costs.
5. Incremental cash flows are defined as the difference between the cash flows of the old machine and those of the new machine.
6. The old machine is sold at book value.

base NPV. The total NPV of the project is the sum of the base NPV and the net present values of all side-effects:

NPV = Base NPV + Present Value of Side Effects

For an extremely simple project, such as the replacement of a motor with a more efficient model, there may be no other side-effects. For more complex projects there may be numerous side-effects, including the interdependency with other systems and the provision of flexibility.

TABLE 3
Computation of Net Present Value for the Incremental Cash Flows
(All amounts in $)

Incremental cash flows

Year

0	1	2	3	4	5
-110,000	23,980	23,980	23,980	23,980	23,980

Present value of cash flows

	1	2	3	4	5
-110,000	21,035	18,452	16,186	14,198	12,454

Net present value = -27,675

Explanatory Notes
1. The cash flows are obtained from Table 2.
2. The cost of capital is assumed to be 14 percent.

Valuing Project Interdependencies: An Example

Suppose the mean processing time for the proposed machine is the same as the mean processing time for the current cluster of machines. A financial analyst might believe that the replacement of the old machines will have no effect on the overall manufacturing process. In other words, the decision to replace the machines can be made independently of any effects on the overall process. Following is an example in which this assumption is incorrect.

An engineering study determines that the mean processing time for the new machine is the same but that the variance of the processing time is less than that for the old machines. Since the machines exist in a sequential system, the project reduces variance in the overall manufacturing process. This reduction in variance is a positive side-effect. One way to measure it is through simulation; for an example of such a simulation, see Reeve (1990).

After simulation, it is determined that the new machine will reduce work-in-process (WIP) inventory by $40,000, a reduction of 20 percent. It is also estimated that as WIP inventory decreases, the overall scrap rate decreases and the manufacturing lead time decreases. Studies at this facility indicate that a 20 percent reduction in WIP inventory results in a 3 percent reduction in the scrap rate. Based on costs of scrap, it is estimated that a 1 percent reduction in scrap saves the firm $1,000 per year in after-tax dollars. Table 4 shows how the direct value of these side-effects can be determined. Notice that this understates the true value, since a decrease in

TABLE 4
Estimating the Value of Systems Interdependencies: Reduced Variance
(All amounts in $)

Cash Flows

	0	1	2	3	4	5
			Year			
Change in WIP	40,000	0	0	0	0	-40,000
Change in scrap		3,000	3,000	3,000	3,000	3,000
Cash flow	40,000	3,000	3,000	3,000	3,000	-37,000
Present value Cash flow	40,000	2,632	2,308	2,025	1,776	-19,217

Net present value = 29,525

Explanatory Notes
1. It is assumed that any reductions in WIP inventory expire with the life of the project.
2. For ease in exposition, reductions in scrap are reported on an after-tax basis.
3. The cash flows are discounted at the cost of capital.

WIP and scrap also leads to increased throughput, reduced time-to-market, and increased effective capacity.

Based on this analysis, the results in Table 4 indicate that the present value of the side-effect due to reduced process time variation is $29,525; this is referred to as the NPV of interdependencies. The mistake of treating the project as though it were independent of other systems leads to an underestimate of project value. In this particular example, the mistake might be sufficient to cause rejection of a valuable project.

The Addition of Managerial Flexibility

Suppose that this proposed machine is capable of producing another product, Product B. For the sake of simplicity, let it be assumed that this machine can produce either Product A or B, but not both simultaneously. Furthermore, the change from one product to another can be made only at the end of the third year; after that, it will be impossible to make the switch. To keep the problem simple, it is assumed that only one switch can be made; if the project is converted to producing B, then it cannot be reconverted to A.

Analysis in Table 5 shows that the expected NPV of using the new machine to produce Product A is $280,276; this is referred to as NPV$_A$. Notice that NPV$_A$ is based on a different concept than that used previously

TABLE 5
Finding the Net Present Values of Alternative Products: A and B
(All amounts in $)

Panel A
Cash Flows for Product A

	1	2	Year 3	4	5
After-tax revenues	132,000	132,000	132,000	132,000	132,000
Other after-tax cash flows	-50,360	-50,360	-50,360	-50,360	-50,360
Net cash flows	81,640	81,640	81,640	81,640	81,640

Net present value (NPV$_A$) = 280,276

Panel B
Cash Flows for Product B

	1	2	Year 3	4	5
After-tax revenues	118,800	118,800	118,800	118,800	118,800
Other after-tax cash flows	-50,360	-50,360	-50,360	-50,360	-50,360
Net cash flows	68,440	68,440	68,440	68,440	68,440

Net present value (NPV$_B$) = 234,960

Explanatory Notes
1. Pretax revenues are assumed to be $200,000 for Product A and $180,000 for Product B. A tax rate of 0.34 is assumed. After-tax revenues are defined as (pretax revenues)*(-1.34).
2. Operating costs are assumed to be identical for each product. Other after-tax cash flows are obtained from Table 2.
3. Each product is discounted at the cost of capital, 14 percent.

to estimate the base NPV. In particular, NPV$_A$ is the NPV for all cash flows associated with Product A; the base NPV is just the NPV of the incremental difference between producing A with either the new machines or the old machines. A similar analysis, also in Table 5, shows that the expected NPV of producing B with the new machine is $234,960; this is referred to as NPV$_B$.

At the time the new machine is to be installed, the expected NPV for producing A is greater than the expected NPV for producing B. If the project is accepted, then the rational decision is to produce Product A and not B. Market conditions might change, however; if customer tastes change sufficiently, it is possible that the price of A will decline with respect to the price of B. In such a situation, it might be profitable for the company to switch products. This capability to switch production has some nonzero value; in other words, flexibility adds value to the project. But how can this flexibility be valued?

Suppose the expected rate of change in the NPV can be estimated for both projects. One approach to valuing the flexibility might be to find the present value of the project, assuming that the switch is made at the end of the third year if it is favorable for the company. Simulation packages are capable of modeling this process, but there is a major problem to this approach: what cost of capital should be used to discount the resulting cash flows?

The previously used cost of capital is inappropriate. This is because the cost of equity is predicated on the notion that the expected future cash flows associated with the project are drawn from a distribution that does not change over time. This assumption, however, is violated by the switching inherent in the project. There exists no method for determining the correct cost of capital in the presence of managerial changes. Therefore, it is impossible to find the NPV using conventional approaches.

Fortunately, the side-effect due to flexibility can be valued with well-accepted techniques from the field of investments. The flexibility of this project is like an option that can be exercised at the end of three years to purchase the NPV of Product B. This option has an exercise price equal to the net present value of Product A (as measured at the end of the third year). Since the flexibility is like an option, it can be valued with techniques from option pricing theory. This particular problem can be valued using the asset exchange option model of Margrabe (1978). Additional inputs required for this model are the variances of the expected rate of change in the net present values for products A and B; the correlation between the two rates of change is also required. A joint study among the marketing, finance, and engineering departments produces estimates for the variances and correlation; they are reported in Table 6. An application of the asset exchange option model for this example is also reported in the table.

As shown in Table 6, the flexibility inherent in the proposed machines has a present value of $42,459; this is referred to as the NPV of flexibility. Ignoring this flexibility could lead to an incorrect decision.

This example is deliberately kept simple for the purpose of exposition. Kensinger (1987), Trigeorgis and Mason (1987), and Kester (1984) provide more detailed discussions on valuing managerial flexibility. More complicated types of flexibility, such as the option to switch at any time, the option to switch to more than one product, and the option to switch back, can also be valued. The procedures to value these options are complicated, but values can be obtained using computers to solve differential equations. See Ballen (1989) for more information on how some corporations are using an options-based approach such as this to value projects. Notice that this option-based approach is particularly relevant for

TABLE 6
Valuing Flexibility: Application of the Asset Exchange Option Pricing Model

The model is defined as:

NPV_F = $NPV_A N\{d_1\} - NPV_B N\{d_2\}$
where NPV_F =   net present value of flexibility

v_A =   variance of NPV_A
v_B =   variance of NPV_B
p =   correlation of NPV_A and NPV_B
v^2 = $v_A^2 - 2 v_A v_B p + v_B^2$
T =   time to maturity
d_1 = $[\ln(NPV_B/NPV_A)+(.5 v^2 T)]/[v T^5]$
d_2 = $d_1 -[v T^5]$
$N\{\cdot\}$ =   the cumulative standard normal density function

Inputs to the model are:

NPV_A =   280,276
NPV_B =   234,960
T =   3
v_A =   .08
v_B =   .08
p =   .2

Model Results

NPV_F =   42,459

Explanatory Notes
1. v_A, v_B, and p are obtained from a joint marketing, engineering, and finance study.

projects that involve flexibility and managerial choices during the life of the project; for simple static projects, the traditional approach works well.

A Comparison with the Traditional Approach

For this entire example, an application of the traditional approach to capital budgeting results in a base NPV of -$27,675 (see Table 3). The values of side-effects are shown in Tables 4 and 6. The comprehensive NPV, referred to as NPV_C, is the sum of the base NPV and the present value of side-effects:

NPV_C = base NPV + NPV of side-effect
NPV_C = base NPV + NPV of interdependencies + NPV of flexibility
NPV_C = -27,675 + 29,525 + 42,459
NPV_C = 44,309

After correctly measuring and valuing the side-effects due to inter-dependencies and flexibility, the comprehensive NPV is found to be $44,309. This example illustrates that cross-systems interdependencies and responsiveness to changing market conditions can be a major portion of a project's value.

CREATING VALUE IN FINANCIAL INSTITUTIONS

The emphasis in this section is on managerial leadership and strategy within financial institutions. Financial institutions are facing increased competition from international firms owing to the globalization of financial markets. They are also facing increased domestic competition as deregulation allows more firms to compete in services that were traditionally limited to financial institutions. In response to this increased competition, financial institutions must develop information systems that allow them to formulate competitive strategies. As shown in this section, an activity-based cost system can be a valuable tool for measuring the profitability of different products, which is a prerequisite to strategy formulation.

Increasing Competition in the Financial Sector

The manufacturing sector in the United States experienced an erosion of competitive strength during the last two decades. Although the service sector was once thought to be immune to similar competitive threats, financial institutions are being subjected to increased global competition at the dawn of the 1990s. In particular, U.S. banking firms are facing extensive competitive pressure from international banks. Of the top fifteen banking institutions in the world in 1990, only one is headquartered in the United States (Citibank). Guenther and Sesit (1989, A1) recently stated that "the message is unmistakable: U.S. banks, once riding high in global finance, are losing their grip on the nation's and the world's credit reins."

In addition to this global competition, deregulation has also increased the number of firms competing in traditional banking activities. Deregulation has also allowed financial institutions to compete in other markets. The net result is a need to formulate strategies that lead to a more competitive posture.

Systems for the Creation of Value

In responding to this competitive challenge, the managerial leaders of financial institutions have the responsibility to identify systems that create value for customers. After the systems have been identified, they must be documented, measured, and continuously improved. (See the chapters in Part B for details of this process.) Just as it is for other firms, the continuous improvement of systems for the provision of customer value is the hallmark of the strategically competitive bank.

For illustrative purposes, an example of a particular system within a financial institution is provided; this includes identification, documentation, measurement, and continuous improvement.

A major regional bank provides corporate customers a cash management service called zero balance accounts. In this service, the corporate client is notified of exact deposit amounts needed to cover checks clearing that day. This is a valued service to clients, since it allows them to invest amounts in excess of those needed to honor checks written on the firm; as a fee-based service, it is also profitable to the bank. This service, the provision of accurate and timely information to the customer, is identified by the upper management of the bank as an important system.

The bank assigned ownership of this critical system to a specific manager. The manager initiated description and measurement of the system. The effectiveness of the service depends on the bank's acquiring Federal Reserve check-clearing data in the early morning for that day's checks. A courier retrieves the Federal Reserve information, and the data are processed at the bank; under ideal circumstances, the information is transmitted to the corporate customer by 11:00 a.m. The manager identified the processing time of these data as the focus of efforts in continuous improvement. Among other activities, the manager implemented courier schemes that allowed the bank to process the data up to 30 minutes faster than the competition. This faster processing time became a competitive advantage and was used for developing new corporate accounts.

As indicated in this example, many banking institutions are beginning to recognize the systems approach as a necessary condition for business success. Successful systems are those that deliver value with minimal waste. To implement successful systems, however, banks need better tools to assist them in measuring and continuously improving the services. Banks also need better tools for matching particular systems to the particular customers that place a premium on the system's output.

New Tools for a Competitive Posture

As discussed earlier, U.S. banking firms are undergoing significant changes as the regulatory reins are altered and the U.S. market is opened to foreign competition. One result is that banks are becoming much more customer oriented. As banking becomes more market driven, banking managers need to understand the relative profitability of both products and customers. A strategy of cross-subsidizing unprofitable product lines with profitable ones is no longer sustainable, given that competitors are able to selectively target the excessively priced products in the profitable line.

There is a much greater need to manage customer relationships toward profitablity than there has been in the past. In the example above, the cost of providing the cash management service must be profitable in the sense that customers are willing to pay a price that provides the bank a return for that service. As a result, financial information systems must reflect the cost of critical systems in providing banking services. An activity-based cost system is one such strategic tool in providing this information; see Chapter 17, "Activity-Based Cost Systems for Functional Integration and Customer Value," for a more general discussion of activity-based systems.

ACTIVITY BASED COSTING IN THE BANKING ENVIRONMENT

Managers of banking institutions must be aware of the cost of banking activities, or they will be unable to develop appropriate product/customer strategy mixes. Meaningful information to be used in formulating strategies can be provided by a cost system that is based on the activities of the firm. Such a system can identify the significant sources of costs, the waste in the process, and the impact of physical activity on the level of costs.

The development of an activity based costing system begins with the sources of cost at the budgetary line-item level. In addition to direct personnel expenses, all other costs are included, such as the costs of facilities, data processing, accounting, advertising, office expenses, loan review, and other indirect budgetary line items.

Although the costs that occur at the budgetary line-item level are primary inputs to the banking production function, many of these costs are not easily traced to particular products or customers. The reason for this lack of direct identification is that the budgetary line items from the general ledger accounts frequently represent costs incurred by a wide variety of products. For example, the salaries of personnel involved in loan review may actually cover many activities that are related to a number of different loan products. In addition, the intensity of activity usage is likely to be highly variable for different types of loans. In such a situation, the portion of loan costs due to loan review personnel is not immediately discernible.

The essence of an activity based costing system is the identification of the important activities necessary to provide the product. Therefore, the budgetary line-item costs must be traced to activities before the profitability analysis can be performed. In the case of loan review personnel, these activities might include interviewing the applicant, obtaining additional credit information, and evaluating the loan. Each of these activities requires time from the loan review officer, which is costly. Given the identification of activities and the determination of activity costs, the portion of loan costs due to personnel expenses can be determined.

A Two-Stage Cost System

The description above is typical of a classic two-stage cost system; a general illustration of such a system is provided in Figure 2. In the first stage, the general ledger expense categories are traced to activity centers.

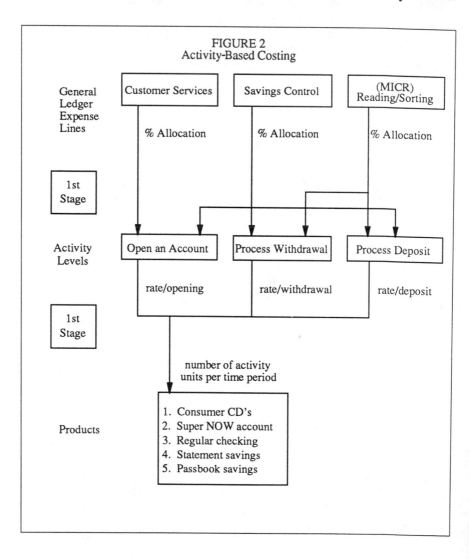

FIGURE 2
Activity-Based Costing

As shown in the figure, the savings control includes all salaries at the branch level that are related to savings. This is not a single activity, but many activities incorporated in one dollar figure. The activities for savings products include opening an account, processing a withdrawal, and processing a deposit. Notice that there are no cost lines in a conventional system for these activities. The cost lines must be broken out from the general ledger line items.

At the second level the activity center costs are traced to products or customers on the basis of a cost driver that relates use of the activity with provision of the product. In this example, the usage of each activity may be different across products, even though all products use the same activity names. The most difficult work of an activity-based system occurs in the translation of general ledger line items into activity centers.

Determination of Activity Center Costs

The activity center definitions and costs can be determined in a number of ways. One approach is to allocate the functional expense lines to activities through information determined from an interview of department heads. This approach takes some time and care if realistic numbers are to be developed. It is not critical that the allocations be perfect; they only need be approximately correct with respect to the amount of effort required to perform the activities.

The interview process essentially takes headcount information and splits the cost of a function into its activity components on the basis of time invested by the department in performing various activities. For example, the loan department can be broken down according to the time individuals spend originating loans, servicing loans, and collecting loans and interest. The total cost for each activity is a function of time resources spent by the department in each of these activities.

One difficulty inherent in the interview process is an inability of interviewees to quantify the percentage of time the department spends on an activity. Department heads are frequently uncomfortable in specifying concrete percentages out of fear that senior management may one day hold them accountable for these percentages. Employees may be less inclined to give truthful information if there is a perceived threat that this information will be used to eliminate jobs and people. Overcoming these considerations can be difficult and requires the commitment of upper level management. In particular, employees must be convinced that this is not a job evaluation. They should be told how their answers will be used and how they will later be able to use the results of the study.

An alternative to the interview approach is the sampling approach. In this approach, the work processes are sampled in order to determine the activity levels. Work sampling involves the sampling and recording of activities performed by individuals over a period of time. Individuals can use a beeper with a repeating countdown function to signal the collection of a sample point. Each recording should include the time, place, activity, and subactivity of work being performed at the time of the beep. Once the observations are collected and summarized, the analyst has a picture of the activity intensities across the organization. These activity centers then form the basis for allocating cost to the product.

Product Costing

Banking products are highly diverse and involve a number of different activities. To keep the exposition simple, only two major products of banks are discussed: demand deposits and loans. Actual product lines are more specific than under this simplifying assumption, but the additional complication adds little to understanding the functions of an activity-based costing system.

The basic building blocks of bank product profitability are the various activities at which cost is incurred over the life cycle of a bank product. Costs for banking products include the costs of activities required to maintain the product during its life as well as the costs of origination and termination. These activities are identified in Table 7.

TABLE 7
Activities Related to Bank Products

Deposit Products	Loan Products
Opening an account (entry)	Originating a loan (entry)
Transacting a deposit	Processing a payment
Transacting a withdrawal	Loan inquiry
Transacting an inquiry	Monthly maintenance
Check processing	Late payment inquiry
Monthly maintenance	Loan losses
Closing an account (exit)	Collection (exit)

The maintenance costs are incurred on a regular basis while the product is active; the origination/termination costs occur twice in the product's life. Therefore, maintenance costs do not amortize over the life of the product but are incurred throughout the life; origination/termination costs do amortize over the product's life. This implies that the maturity or average life of the product is important in the overall profitablity of the product. A product with a short life is unable to support the amortization of the origination/termination costs over sufficient time to achieve profitablity, while longer life products are able to support these costs much better.

The annual maintenance costs and amortized termination/origination costs form the basis of the periodic activity cost due to the product. For each product category, the cost of each activity transaction must be determined from the activity center volumes. For example, suppose general ledger line items are allocated into the activity "processing a deposit." In this example, it is determined that the cost of this activity is $25,000 per month. Suppose also that the number of deposits transacted is 50,000 during a representative time period. Therefore, the cost per deposit is $0.50.

The next step in developing an activity-based costing system is to determine the number of deposits made for the specific product per time period; in this case, it is a demand deposit. If the account has four deposits on average per month, and the cost per deposit activity is $0.50, then the monthly cost from this activity for providing the account is $2.00. Similar analyses should be conducted for the other critical activities of the product.

The total cost of the product for a particular time period is the monthly activity volumes in an account times the rate per activity unit. The amortized origination/termination costs per account are added to this amount. From this analysis the cost per product can be determined.

The activity cost of a product per time period is only a component of profitability analysis. A critical part of the analysis is related to the size of the account. In particular, the periodic activity cost of an account is "scale sensitive"; that is, large accounts produce net interest income that "covers" the annual activity of the account better than do small accounts. This is true because the activity intensity per time period is not directly proportional to the size of the account. Specifically, large accounts likely have similar numbers of deposit and payment transactions as do smaller accounts, albeit in larger amounts. Therefore, the size of the account is the critical volume measure for interest income, but it is less related to the volume of underlying transactions. As a result, small accounts are less able than large accounts to support the transaction costs.

An Application of Activity-Based Costing

The following description illustrates the principles discussed above. The column headings of Table 8 list five activities of another type of deposit account, a savings account. The functional expense line items from the general ledger are shown in the row headings.

TABLE 8
Activity Costs of a Savings Account

Activities

General Ledger Expenses (All Costs Reported in $)	Open an Account	Process Deposit/ With- drawal (Teller)	Process Deposit (ATM)	Process With- drawal	Close Account (ATM)
Customer service	27.50				8.20
Tellers	0.75	1.30			0.80
Bank office processing	0.35				0.25
Read/sort	0.30		0.30		
Savings control	0.50	0.80	0.50	0.40	0.80
Data processing	0.10	0.20	0.10	0.15	0.20
ATM servicing			0.15	0.25	
Total cost per unit of activity	29.50	2.30	1.05	0.80	10.25

The relationship between the expense line items and the activities are obtained through an activity analysis as previously discussed. For example, as shown in Table 8 the customer service department is responsible for opening and closing accounts. The percentage of the customer service department budget related to opening accounts provides the basis for determining the costs of this activity. This percentage is determined from either an interview or work sampling. The number of accounts opened during a period of time can be divided into the activity pool to determine the cost per account opened from this department. In this example, the cost per account opened from the customer service department is $27.50. The activity of opening an account does not stop at customer service, but it also includes a teller transaction for the first deposit and related processing activities. The total cost to open an account is $29.50. A similar analysis provides the remaining major activities for the account.

The total cost per activity can now be related to the actual activity volumes per account; this is illustrated in Table 9. The costs per unit of activity are multiplied by the activity volumes in the account over a period of time. The opening and closing of an account are amortized over the five-year expected life of the account ($1/60 = 0.0167$), while the remaining

	TABLE 9		
	Profitability of a Savings Account		
Activity	Cost per Activity Unit	Activity Volume per Month	Monthly Unit Cost
Open an account	29.50	0.0167	0.4926
Process deposits (Tellers)	2.30	1.50	3.45
Process deposits (ATM)	1.05	0.50	0.525
Process withdrawal (ATM)	0.80	4.00	3.20
Close an account	10.25	0.0167	0.171
Total costs per month			7.84
Annual costs			94.06
Profitability analysis			
Assumptions:	Account balance =	5,000	
	Account interest =	6%	
	T-bill rate =	8%	
Account profitability	Net yield = 5,000 (8%-6%) =		$100.00
	Annual activity costs =		$94.06
	Annual profitability =		$5.94

activities are multiplied by the monthly volumes. Obviously, the shorter the life of the account the greater the period amortization for origination/termination costs. The total cost per month for the account can be determined from these data.

The overall profitability of the account is directly related to the size of the balance. The monthly cost must be covered by the interest earnings of underlying assets supporting the liability balances. In this example, the T-bill risk-free rate is used as a benchmark for liability products. A T-bill rate of 8 percent produces a net yield of 2 percent for the savings account. The annual yield income is reduced by the annual cost to serve the savings account. For a savings account balance of $5,000 the net interest income is barely sufficient to cover the monthly maintenance costs of the account. A lower balance will result in a loss, while a balance of $10,000 would be extremely profitable on an annual basis.

Strategic Analysis

When accurate costs per account are available, the institution has the capability to perform strategic analysis across products and customers. The data recorded in Table 8 represent the activity rates. Because these rates change slowly, they require only infrequent updating. The data in Table 9 can represent either the standard activity usages of savings accounts in general or the actual usages of individual accounts.

If the data in Table 9 represent standard activity usages, then a standard cost per account is determined. The actual cost will be different to the extent the portfolio of savings accounts differs markedly from the standard. For example, if the standard account had a balance of $5,000 and 1.5 deposits on average per month, but the portfolio average was a balance of $3,000 with 3 deposits on average, there would be an unfavorable cost variance. This analysis occurs at the product line level.

The product line is a highly aggregated level of analysis. More preferable is an analysis that occurs at the account level. This is a difficult analysis, best conducted for large customers first and then eventually for all customers. The actual activities incurred by each account can be used to determine cost at the account level. As a result, the bank is able to understand the relationships between size of account, maturity, and transactions costs. This level of analysis allows the bank to segment the market on the basis of profitability characteristics and to prevent cross-subsidization between customers and products.

For example, wealthy clients may incur few transactions and maintain high balances relative to minimum balance clients. The conventional cost system ignores the relative cost advantages of the wealthy client and cross-subsidizes the minimum balance client. The result can be a dangerous situation whereby the bank is vulnerable to competitor pricing and service strategies aimed at the profitable accounts. Accurate cost information can prevent this type of situation. Moreover, fee structures and service structures can more accurately match customer service requirements and profitability objectives.

If profitability can be determined at the account level, then account profitability can be rolled up to the customer level. Specifically, some customers may have multiple liability and asset accounts with the bank; therefore, the profitability of the product portfolio becomes the important level of analysis. A family checking account may be unprofitable, but the mortgage and business accounts related to that customer may be very profitable; the pricing and service structure to the client should reflect the portfolio relationship. In contrast, if the bank offers checking account pricing structures that are unprofitable, then customer profitability analysis should reveal whether customers are selectively picking this service or whether the service is attracting those customers to additional more profitable services.

The customer analysis can support market segmentation and the tailoring of services to customers so as to maintain profitability. For example, one strategy would be to encourage the building of multiple account relationships so as to increase the customer cost of changing to a competing institution.

A sophisticated account management system should eventually be able to determine not only customer profitability, but also profitability at the family unit level. The family level of aggregation is appropriate since decisions will probably affect the complete family account relationship. If a customer perceives a lack of value in a relationship, all accounts related to that family might be moved to a competing institution. The value elements perceived from individual accounts are probably not independent. As a result, the profitability of the complete family relationship may be the most important level of analysis. For example, the bank may be willing to have an unprofitable account for one member of a family if there exist offsetting profitable product relationships for the complete family group.

CONCLUSIONS

In summary, increasing global competition and growing complexity within the business environment require knowledge and commitment if firms are to create value through continuous improvement. The tasks of the finance function within manufacturing firms and financial institutions are undergoing significant scrutiny, with respect to both tools and basic underlying assumptions. Issues surrounding the appropriate objective of the firm, the optimal structure of the public company, the justification of complex capital investments, and the competitiveness of financial institutions are topics in need of theoretical development and practical implementation.

As indicated in this chapter, the capital budgeting problems faced by manufacturing firms are extremely complex. Implicit contracts of the firm play a key role in the creation and maintenance of future cash flows; there is a need for techniques to value these contracts. A prerequisite for optimal selection of projects is for financial analysts to become aware of the interdependencies of projects and how they impact other systems within the company. Recognition of the options inherent in flexible systems is also important, since these options are significant components of firm value.

Financial institutions are also facing a broad array of problems. A financial institution should create and manage systems designed to provide customer value; a prerequisite is to fully understand the services that are required by various customer segments and the cost of providing those services. The customer must perceive that the value of those services exceeds their costs, while the bank must provide the service levels at a profit. An activity-based cost system can provide information to support account, customer, family, and product profitability analysis. The systems that generate service and cost can be evaluated with respect to their contribution of value to customers and the firm. The result is an informed management that is better able to match the needs of customers with appropriate service levels, fee structures, and product attributes.

REFERENCES

Ballen, Kate. "The New Look of Capital Spending." *Fortune* (March 13, 1989): 57-60.

Brealey, Richard A., and Stewart C. Myers. *Principles of Corporate Finance*. New York: McGraw-Hill, 1988.

Cornell, Bradford, and Alan C. Shapiro. "Corporate Stakeholders and Corporate Finance." *Financial Management* (Spring 1987): 5-14.

Guenther, Robert, and Michael R. Sesit. "U.S. Banks Are Losing Business to Japanese at Home and Abroad." *The Wall Street Journal* (October 13, 1989): A1/A12.

Jensen, Michael C. "Eclipse of the Public Corporation." *Harvard Business Review* (September-October 1989): 61-74.

Kaplan, Robert. "Does the Financial Plan Match the Strategic Plan?" *Financial Executive* (July/August 1989): 42-43.

Kensinger, John W. "Adding the Value of Active Management into the Capital Budgeting Equation." *Midland Corporate Finance Journal* (Spring 1987): 31-42.

Kester, W. Carl. "Today's Options for Tomorrow's Growth." *Harvard Business Review* (March-April 1984): 153-160.

Margrabe, William. "The Value of an Option to Exchange One Asset for Another." *Journal of Finance* 33, No. 1 (March 1978): 177-186.

Oatman, Richard, and David Buehlmann. "Supplementing Cost Accounting Courses in Response to the Changing Business Environment." *Issues in Accounting Education*, 4, No. 1 (1989): 161-178.

Reeve, J. M. "The Impact of Variation on Operating System Performance." In P.B.B. Turney (ed.), *Performance Excellence in Manufacturing and Service Organizations* (American Accounting Association), pp. 75-80.

Trigeorgis, Lenos, and Scott P. Mason. "Valuing Managerial Flexibility." *Midland Corporate Finance Journal* (Spring 1987): 14-21.

Woolridge, J. Randall. "Competitive Decline and Corporate Restructuring: Is a Myopic Stock Market to Blame?" *Journal of Applied Corporate Finance*, 1, No. 1 (Spring 1988): 26-36.

CHAPTER 25

MANAGEMENT ACTIVITY FOR COMPETITIVE CAPABILITY*

GREGORY M. BOUNDS
Research Associate, Management Development Center
University of Tennessee

LARRY A. PACE
Professor of Management and Marketing
Louisiana State University at Shreveport

SUMMARY

The range of management activities critical to successfully competing in global markets varies from "radical change" to "no change" or maintaining stability. These activities include creation, innovation, incrementalism, standardization, routinization, maintenance, and execution. The domains of these activities also vary greatly, ranging from strategy to operation, and include value strategy, design strategy, strategic systems, corporate policies, management systems, strategic subsystems, process technology, operating methods, operational tasks, and operational motions.

Jobs and human resources should be designed and developed for these activities. More specifically, individuals should be developed to deal with and participate in different types and domains of activity. At an aggregate level, they must work in concert, as a team, to ensure that the diverse activities of all individuals are integrated to produce a whole and formidably competitive organization in providing customer value. This chapter

*We thank Mel Adams, Tuck Bounds, Earl Conway, Dudley Dewhirst, and Bill Judge for their helpful comments on this chapter.

offers an original framework, the Management Activity Topograph (MAT), which can be used to articulate the roles of all employees regarding these activities, and to diagnose and prescribe human resource needs.

MANAGERIAL JOB DESIGN: THE BASIS FOR HUMAN RESOURCE MANAGEMENT

The growing challenges of global competition magnify the inadequacies of traditional managerial practices, as variously addressed throughout this volume. Although U.S. and Japanese firms still lead the world in terms of market capitalization and financial muscle, trends in the Global 1000 (*Business Week*, July 16, 1990: 111-144) indicate that European firms are developing rapidly. "The hottest market action was in Europe, where the culture of equity investment has taken hold and given companies ever-deeper pools of financing. The European giants will tap those funds to restructure operations, plow money into research and development, and invest staggering sums to improve the infrastructure in the West and bring the East into the 20th century. Economists believe the remaking of the Continent will boost European growth rates by 1% to 2% over the next five years." Managerial leaders should expect global competition to intensify and diversify as even more countries seek economic strength and prosperity. They must prepare their organizations for the globally competitive arena of the future.

This chapter presents a framework to assist in designing managerial jobs to enhance competitive capabilities throughout an organization. To play in the competitive arena, organizations must increasingly and consistently provide customer value. Customers continue to choose an organization's products and services because the net value offered is equal to or is better than that offered by competitors. The challenge to managerial leaders grows with time because competitors improve, customer values change, and expectations rise. Job design and human resource management (HRM) represent critical vehicles for increasing competitive capabilities that meet or lead changing customer expectations. This chapter lays the foundation for HRM with a discussion of job design. This foundation provides the basis for more extensive discussion of human resource issues in the following chapter (see Figure 1).

Productive organizations increasingly rely on automated and advanced technologies to transform and transport information and material. However, people provide the energy, ingenuity, and creativity required for orchestrating the creation of value for customers. To keep ahead of competitors and to consistently meet or exceed customer expectations, human

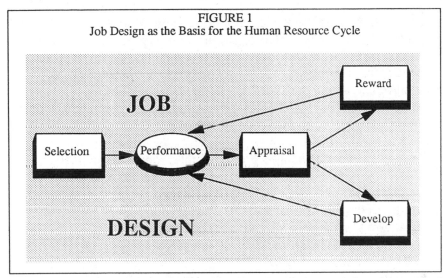

FIGURE 1
Job Design as the Basis for the Human Resource Cycle

resources must be appropriately developed and focused for change and stability.

Over time, organizations must change to competitively provide customer value. Consider the scramble of fast-food chains to offer nutritious food items, low in fat and sodium, for increasingly health-conscious consumers. Once a change is introduced, consistently meeting current customer expectations requires stability in the execution of systems and operations. For example, while fast-food vendors attempt to keep consumers slim, trim, and fit, others attempt to dress them according to their latest needs. With the population bulge of the baby boomers creeping into middle age, a new set of apparel consumers emerges, with expanding waist lines and fatter pocket books. Levi Strauss created the line of casual clothes called Dockers to suit the needs of these boomers, who are buying and wearing fewer tight-fitting blue jeans, as they did in high school and college, but are not quite ready to adorn their Dad's pressed slacks. Levi Strauss changed their value offering to meet changing consumer needs. Their sales rose and profits grew.

Changing consumer demographics, fashions, fads, values, preferences, expectations, and needs dictate that organizations must change their value offerings. While changing and improving the value of product and service offerings, organizations must also improve the systems that provide customer value, and ensure the stable execution of those systems. For example, Levi Strauss improved its service systems by introducing a new information network. Via this network, retailers order and are billed electronically for new inventory. Similar connections with suppliers allow managers to complement Just-in-Time manufacturing by ordering the amounts of various fabric types to match the whimsical moods of the apparel market. With the new information and ordering systems, costs and response times have been reduced. Administrative procedures for ordering materials are cut from three days to a few minutes, shipping cycles are reduced from three weeks to less than six days, and inventories at plants are reduced, yet the hottest selling styles and sizes are made available (*Fortune*, May 7, 1990: 105-107). Such continuous improvements in the means of creating improved value for customers can spell organizational success.

If organizational changes and customer changes are mismatched, misunderstood, or mismanaged, gaps will emerge between what the organization creates as outputs and what constituents outside the organization demand, need, or even tolerate. To ensure long-term prosperity, the organization's strategies, structures, systems, technology, and human capabilities must be integrated to meet or exceed the demands of external constituents. When managers attempt to implement new strategies with outmoded technologies, obsolete and inappropriate structures and systems, or underdeveloped human resources, the result can only be poor performance relative to better equipped competitors.

The way managerial jobs are defined and how managerial resources are managed represent keys to organizational competitiveness. The roles and responsibilities of these managerial resources must require the achievement of two seemingly contradictory objectives: change and stability. Managers must continuously change and improve their organizational capability for producing and delivering customer value, while ensuring stability and consistency in the production of valued goods and services. Competing requires the right mix of activities to encourage both change and stability.

Managers are challenged to accomplish a paradoxical mix of activities to continuously change their organizations for improved performance, while maintaining current performance. This mix will require intermittent periods of change and stability. This chapter presents a framework that describes the range of activities, encompassing change and stable execution, required of managers in competitive organizations. This framework of activities, depicted in the Management Activity Topograph (MAT) described below, provides a conceptual tool for understanding different managerial roles and human resource needs.

The design of managerial jobs and corresponding management of human resources offer a significant customer value advantage for an organization willing to invest in them. Managerial leaders must develop human resources for continuous improvement and for the changes required to become and remain competitive in providing customer value. In an organization that defines the managerial role as continuous improvement of systems for customer value, human resources must be regarded as critical inputs to those systems and must be managed accordingly.

MANAGERIAL RESOURCES ARE KEY

Managerial leaders and middle managers are the key human resources of the organization in the quest for continuous customer value improvement. Operators are important, but managerial resources build the systems that "cnablc" human rcsourccs throughout thc organization. Managcrs arc ultimately responsible for creating, improving, and maintaining the strategy, structures, systems, processes, and capabilities for providing the best net value to customers. Leaders must ensure that managerial resources have the knowledge, abilities, and motivation for these responsibilities.

Managerial job design sets behavioral expectations. Failure to appropriately design managerial jobs and develop managerial human resources effectively jeopardizes long-term organizational competitiveness. The right mix of managerial leader and middle manager behaviors must be in place. Thcsc managcrs sct thc agcnda for thc rcst of thc organization. They do so through their actions on strategy, systems, policies, technology, and operations.

Because of the primacy of managerial resources, this chapter focuses on the design of the jobs for managerial leaders and "middle" managers, in relation to the jobs of operators. Some of the implications for the strategic human resource management (HRM) of managers are also addressed in this chapter. The following chapter by Bounds and Pace more fully addresses HRM's implications for managers and is based on the issues of managerial job design discussed in this chapter.

MANAGERIAL JOB DESIGN FOR COMPETITIVE ORGANIZATIONS

The following pages present the diverse activities that comprise managerial jobs for a competitive organization. These activities are described in terms of the types and domains of activity and are organized into a framework labeled the Management Activity Topograph (MAT).

The Management Activity Topograph

Traditionally, managers have relied on innovation as the primary source of performance improvement, for example, through structural reorganizations. Management also frequently responds to competition with technological innovation of products and services. Once innovation is introduced, managers reestablish control to maintain the gains brought about by new technology investments. While primary reliance on such innovations has been successful in past competitive environments, it will not suffice in future globally competitive markets.

Managers will have to engage in a range of activities to ensure the competitiveness of their organizations. The managerial activities can be described along two dimensions: (1) type of activity, and (2) domain of activity. Do not assume that the words and phrases we use to describe managerial activities bear traditional connotations. Carefully consider their meaning.

In addition to innovation, managers will need to be involved in other types of activities (see Figure 2). These managerial activities range from consistent execution (no change in systems) to creation (unprecedented or radical change in systems). Note that monitoring and measuring activities are not listed as discrete activities in the figure because monitoring and measuring should accompany each of these other activities. Monitoring and measuring will be discussed later in this chapter.

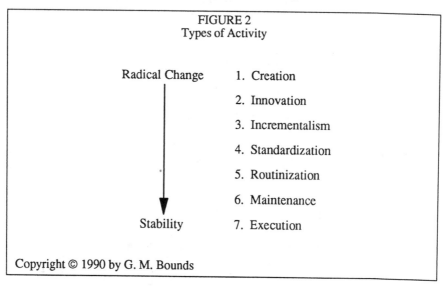

FIGURE 2
Types of Activity

Radical Change

1. Creation

2. Innovation

3. Incrementalism

4. Standardization

5. Routinization

6. Maintenance

Stability

7. Execution

Copyright © 1990 by G. M. Bounds

The domains of change must also be diverse if organizations are to become and remain competitive. As mentioned, managers tend to rely on product and service innovation. Product or service value represents only one area where each of the above types of activities must be applied.

In competitive organizations, the domain may be narrow in scope such as a single technique of work execution or a hand movement within a task. Organizational structure and social mechanisms of organization, which are of somewhat broader scope, may be the domains of change. The scope may be as large as strategic systems or the organization itself.

The following domains of activity are among the most important for competitive organizations: value strategy, design strategy, strategic systems, corporate policies, management systems, strategic subsystems, process technology, operating methods, operational tasks, and operational motions. These domains of activity may be seen as ranging from strategy to operations (see Figure 3).

By combining the typologies in Figures 2 and 3, we can create a two-dimensional layout, such as that shown in Figure 4. One dimension lists the types of managerial activity from Figure 2. The other dimension lists the domains of managerial activity from Figure 3. This two-dimensional layout shows all possible combinations of types and domains of activity. For example, the number "1" on the layout in Figure 4 indicates the combination of "creation" and "value strategy." This position on the layout could be read as "creation of value strategy."

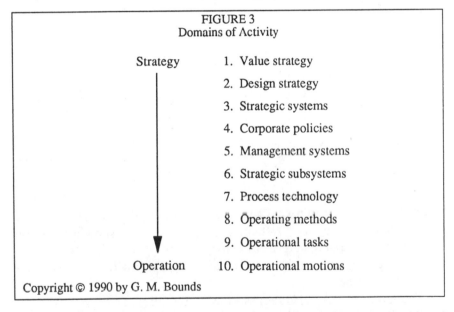

FIGURE 3
Domains of Activity

Strategy

1. Value strategy

2. Design strategy

3. Strategic systems

4. Corporate policies

5. Management systems

6. Strategic subsystems

7. Process technology

8. Operating methods

9. Operational tasks

Operation

10. Operational motions

Copyright © 1990 by G. M. Bounds

The layout presented in Figure 4 graphically depicts the terrain of managerial activity in terms of two dimensions. (1) type of activity and (2) domain of activity. Managerial jobs can be defined in terms of the positions on this two-dimensional layout.

The terminology of Management Activity Topograph and the acronym (MAT) were specifically selected to convey meaning through analogy. The word "topograph" was selected to suggest the science of topography as applied to managerial activity. Topography is defined by Webster as

FIGURE 4
The MAT
(Management Activity Topograph)

Type of Activity										
Creation	1									2
Innovation										
Incrementalism										
Standardization						5				
Routinization										
Maintenance										
Execution	4									3
Domain of Activity	Value strategy	Design strategy	Strategic systems	Corporate policies	Management systems	Strategic subsystems	Process technology	Operating methods	Operational tasks	Operational motions

(1) "the science of drawing on maps and charts or otherwise representing the surface features of a region, including its relief and rivers, lakes, etc., and such manmade features as canals, bridges, roads, etc.," and (2) "a study or description of a region, system, or part of the body showing specific relations of component parts as to shape, size, position, etc." The purpose for drawing an analogy to the science of topography will become clearer later in this chapter.

The acronym MAT also suggests the interconnected nature of management activity throughout an organization. The word "mat" is defined as "anything densely interwoven or felted, or growing in a thick tangle." Thus, the acronym MAT suggests that the competitive strength of an organization with interconnected managerial activity is much greater than one with an aggregation of nonconnected managerial activity. Each of the types and domains of managerial activity is discussed in more detail below.

Types of Activity

For simplicity, systems are generally referred to as the domain of activity. Other domains of activity are suggested in examples and addressed in the following discussion of the types of activities listed in Figure 2.

1. Creation. In creation, old systems, methods, and practices are disregarded or scrapped, and the creator starts with a clean slate. Creators synthesize and develop ideal systems from scratch. Such creative changes are often necessary to overcome old prejudices, limitations, intractable problems, and to explain anomalies. Classical examples include philosophical and theoretical changes, such as moving from the flat-earth view to the round-earth view, from Ptolemy's notion that the sun revolves around the earth to Copernicus' idea that the earth spins and revolves around the sun, and from Newtonian physics to Einstein's relativity and quantum theories.

"Starting from scratch" is a familiar, yet idealistic, concept. We might rightly point out that it is very difficult to totally discard the old and not borrow from existing systems in "creating" a new system, for example, from horse and buggy to "horseless" carriage. Few managerial activities could be considered purely creative. Most are one of, or a combination of, the following types.

2. Innovation. Existing technologies or pieces and parts of existing systems are recombined and reassimilated in novel ways. The innovated whole is fundamentally different from anything that existed before. Consider Henry Ford's advances in mass production systems. Also, consider the product innovation by SONY, which incorporates technology from the world of computers to produce a filmless camera. Images are recorded on a reusable floppy disk that can be played back instantly on any television set. The camera also incorporates a microphone for recording a sound track to accompany each frame. This combination of existing technologies innovates a product unprecedented in its capabilities.

3. Incrementalism. Existing systems are adjusted and modified by slight alterations in existing parts to achieve improvement. Improvement may consist of moving closer to targets, or increasing consistency in outcomes, or cutting cycle times. The importance of incremental improvement should not be overlooked, because the accumulation of a number of incremental improvements can have a tremendous impact. For example, employees at Hughes Aircraft began their effort to build satellites more cost effectively by mapping out every step, from design to delivery. "Working in multidisciplinary teams composed of workers from design, manufacturing, purchasing, and marketing, the Hughes employees iden-

tified 131 steps that were candidates for major improvements, and then they focused on 30 of the most urgent. By making a series of seemingly small changes, such as moving a hole a quarter of an inch so an inspector could more easily insert a testing probe, Hughes cut the time it took to build a satellite control processor – the brains of the machine – from 45 weeks to 22 weeks, saving millions of dollars" (*Fortune*, April 9, 1990: 48).

4. Standardization. Standardization means verifying the operability of systems prior to releasing them for use by others. Standardization requires one to transmit, educate, and demonstrate, so that the resulting system displays statistical capability and predictability for stable, on-target system performance.

Consider an example of the standardization of a work task.[1] On an assembly line, operators assemble parts onto frames that move along the conveyor. After completing each assembly, the worker is supposed to mark the frame to indicate its completion before sending it on the conveyor to the next worker for the next set of parts to be added to the frame. Finding a little free time, periodically, the worker would reach up the conveyor to mark the frame coming from the previous process, prior to assembling the parts. One day the worker marked a frame just a moment before the line was stopped for lunch break. Upon returning to the assembly line after lunch, the worker forgot that the frame had been marked prior to assembly. The worker placed the frame on the conveyor, and it was subsequently included in a final assembly. The defect was ultimately caught at a final inspection, and the unit had to be disassembled and reworked. This defect occurred because of the supervisor's failure to (a) communicate (transmit and educate) the importance of marking the frame after assembly, and (b) initially verify and observe the worker's activities to ensure (demonstrate) that the task was consistently and correctly performed.

5. Routinization. Systems are fine tuned, balanced, and mastered by those responsible for operating the existing system or processes. Routinization represents the subordinate counterpart to standardization by the system owner. The "bugs are worked out" of the system by those who execute the system, so execution becomes more predictable, and performance variations are explained and reduced. The system becomes "second nature" to those involved. The benefits of routinization can be observed in what trainers often refer to as the learning curve that reflects noticeable mastery of a task.

6. Maintenance. The existing system (and mode) of execution is fully maintained and controlled with no changes in order to keep the system

---

1. The example is based on an experience of President Nemoto of Toyoda Gosei but was modified to fit the purposes of this chapter.

stable and consistent in the production and delivery of goods and services. Maintenance may require preventive attention to avoid problems and ensure consistency. In addition, occasional unanticipated events may create crises that must be resolved immediately to maintain system performance.

Consider an example of an unanticipated or special event from the industrial wood products industry. A valve that controls the flow of wax to the wood particles was accidentally adjusted. The decrease in the flow of wax to the wood prior to pressing the wood chips into a board results in pressed boards that fail to bond. The operator observed the decreased wax flow and immediately sought the cause, identified the valve change and made the correction.

7. Execution. Execution means to use, carry out, or engage in something. For example, a system owner executes a strategic system, as a domain of activity, to consistently produce and deliver valued goods and services. While an operator may execute an operational task through physical manipulation of tools, the system owner may execute the system through manipulation of information, for example, directions, requests, schedules, and orders.

Each of the above activities, ranging from creativity to execution, has a place in a competitive organization. Each is necessary. For example, after a new production system is installed, the system must be standardized, maintained, and executed in order to consistently produce valued outputs for customers. After incremental or innovative improvements, the system must again be standardized and maintained, to ensure consistent outputs for customers. The diversity of the domains referred to in the examples above (e.g., product value offerings, tasks, operating methods, systems) suggests that the domains of these activities vary as well. In the following section the potential domains of the above activities are discussed.

Domains of Activity

As suggested in Figure 3, the domains of activity range from strategies to operations. Each of these domains is described and exemplified in the following discussion.

A general competitive strategy to produce and deliver value for customers should exist in every organization. This general strategy should not be considered a ready object for change. Given that managers generally intend to provide value for customers by meeting a specified area of needs or desires, for example, audio sound for musical entertainment, there are many ways they might choose to compete in value creation. Competitive strategy involves two specific domains: (1) value strategy and (2) design strategy. These first two domains of activity, which go hand in hand, are components of competitive strategy.

1. Value Strategy. Value is an outcome for the customer and is a function of the sacrifices required for all that is realized. In the broadest sense, managers typically determine what value will be delivered to customers when they make strategic decisions about whether they will compete on cost, differentiation, or by seeking a market niche. Beyond these broad strategic decisions lie the intricate and varied details about how the organization intends to compete in providing value for the customer, for example, at the business unit level. These details include those about product functionality, ease of use, raw materials, components, configurations of raw materials and components, appearance, reproducibility, consistency, flexibility, image, availability, deliverability, transportability, durability, longevity, costliness, and price.

Managers may choose to compete through other value offerings by emphasizing a particular combination of realized attributes, for example, the low cost, convenience, and transportability of a "Walkman-type" radio, which requires some sacrifice in terms of musical fidelity. The available combinations of relative emphasis on different sacrifices and realizations are seemingly infinite. The combination chosen for the value strategy results from strategic value determination activities, but must also be intertwined with design strategy decisions, for example, regarding current and future organizational capabilities. For example, Coca-Cola decided on an overall European strategy for "closer relationships with retailers, bolder merchandising, cheaper prices, and faster delivery." To accomplish this strategy, Coca-Cola broke out of its traditional role as "image marketer and supplier of secret ingredients to local independent bottlers" by buying local bottlers and managing production themselves (*Fortune*, August 13, 1990: 68).

2. Design Strategy. The second component of competitive strategy involves the organizational means of producing and delivering value, that is, design strategy. "Organization" represents the integrated and cyclical activity of individuals and other assets directed toward a common purpose or objective. Managers may choose to provide customer value by engaging in different combinations of value-providing activity, for example, only the final assembly, distribution, and marketing of a "Walkman-type" radio, rather than the design and manufacture of component parts. Managers may decide to outsource certain components rather than develop the technical expertise and capital required for such activity, like purchasing and managing a production plant.

The available combinations of relative emphasis on different organizational activities are also seemingly infinite. No matter what combination is selected, the design strategy should be intertwined with the value strategy selected. The organization should be capable of competitively producing and delivering the selected components of value for the customer.

Consider as an example of the integration of value and design strategy Conner Peripherals, maker of compact hard disk drives and the fastest growing major manufacturer in America. In the dynamic markets of high technology, where managers "live dog years," one has to do in a few months what others can take years to do; speed and response time can spell the difference between immense prosperity and bankruptcy. In the disk drive market, some competitors choose to invest heavily in R and D to produce the smallest and fastest drives, which they sell at premium prices. These competitors may bring out advanced products, but risk finding no buyers for them. Other competitors choose to be commodity producers by supplying high volumes of a standard disk drive at a lower price. These competitors risk sinking large sums of money into factories that can be outmoded and surpassed by rapidly changing technology or more efficient competitors. Conner pursues a different strategy.

Conner operates according to a principle to "sell first, design, and then build."

> The cornerstone of the Conner company's manufacturing strategy is flexibility. Foregoing the cost advantages of manufacturing its own components, the company buys nearly all its parts from others. It also leases the factory space it needs to assemble and test its drives. Keeping capital investment low is practically a religion with Finis Conner: For every dollar in plant and equipment, his company has $7.17 in sales, compared with $3.59 for Seagate [a leading competitor]. This approach gives Conner Peripherals the flexibility it needs to respond to shifts in demand. In 1988, for example, it was able to pounce on the fastest growing market segment, disk drives for laptop and notebook computers. *(Fortune,* August 13, 1990: 51)

By listening to their customers, developing products rapidly upon demand, and smoothly, smartly, and simply handing off and manufacturing new designs, Conner avoids many of the high costs typically associated with R and D, ownership of factories, and bureaucracy. Conner selected a value strategy for quick response time to customer needs, with frequent and on-demand innovation, and correspondingly implemented a design strategy with the sales, product design, manufacturing capabilities, and systems to match.

3. Strategic Systems. The strategic systems (suprasystems and subsystems) of the organization are derived from the value and organizational strategic decisions of managers. Managers determine what combination of value components to produce and how to produce that value. These decisions implicate the strategic systems of the organization. The strategic systems of the organization represent the "how," the collection of cause factors, for producing valued products and services.

Strategic systems of the organization include integrated collections of personnel, knowledge, abilities, motivations, equipment, machinery, methods, measures, processes, and activities. These systems provide customer value through the design, development, material acquisition, physical transformation, assembly, packaging, image shaping, advertising, configuration, selling, logistical movement, distribution, and retailing of products and services. Not every strategic system will be defined to include all these activities. However, these strategic systems do cut across functional and departmental boundaries and diverse work activities, to form the means of producing and delivering valued goods and services.

For example, consider how President Shoichiro Toyoda of Toyota Motors reorganized product development to improve an already excellent production system. As head of the council that now directs long-range product strategy, he created the position of chief engineer and gave the chief broad responsibilities.

> He has charge of everything associated with the development of a car. First he determines its physical dimensions and suitability for its potential market, then how it will be made and who the suppliers will be. He even helps design marketing strategies and talks frequently with car buyers. . . . Besides getting the cars out, the chief engineer has to stay on top of social, political, and environmental trends. . . . The chief engineer system differs sharply from Detroit's product development practice, where a new-model boss has narrowly defined responsibilities and limited power. The Detroit chief usually works under specific instructions from the product planning and marketing departments. Even if he stays with the project through the manufacturing launch, he almost never has direct contact with dealers and customers. (*Fortune*, November 19, 1990: 72)

4. Corporate Policies. Policies are general statements or principles intended to guide individual thinking during decision making, for example,

"we promote from within." Policies may also define the domain of decision making by designating authority and limitations. Ideally, policies ensure that decisions contribute to organizational objectives. Policies provide guidelines to action and may remove the necessity to reconsider and analyze the same situation each time it occurs. However, individuals should not regard policies as inflexible rules. Rather, policies allow for some discretion.

Policies exist throughout the organization and range in their breadth of coverage. Corporate policies are the broadest and apply to many units and individuals within the organization. Alternatively, the smallest unit, for example, the shipping department, may have policies that pertain only to its own members. Corporate policies form the foundation for these more specific policies. Although all employees may be involved with broad or specific policies, for example, creation of work unit policies, more specific policies are not listed as discrete domains of activity.

Policies are important because of the intended impact on decision making and other behavior of employees throughout the organization. Consistency of policies with the competitive strategy for customer value is critical for competitiveness. For example, the corporate policy to buy only from low-cost bidders may ensure cost containment and favorable budget variances, but may undermine other efforts for customer value. As another example, some companies have policies regarding who can talk to whom and under what conditions, within the company and externally with customers. Such a policy usually discourages the informal communications that foster a customer-oriented culture. Rather than rely on exhaustive lists of policies, some companies have preferred to apply "Occum's Ax" to their policy manuals, reducing them from hundreds of pages, with hundreds of policies, down to ten or twenty general statements.

Policy-makers must carefully consider not only the effect of their formal statements, but also the implicit principles which subordinates infer from decisions and actions, for instance, role modeling.

5. Management Systems. Management systems are organized activities for motivating, directing, and sustaining appropriate behavioral inputs of strategic systems. For human resource (HR) managers, the word "system" tends to conjure up thoughts about the social systems of roles, norms, values, and social mechanisms of control such as evaluations, appraisals, and rewards. The aforementioned strategic systems (suprasystems and subsystems) of the organization are different from the "social" or "management" systems. These management systems include formal mechanisms such as progress reporting requirements, rewards, authority structures, information systems, resource allocation systems, and job design and role requirements, as discussed in an earlier chapter by Bounds

and Dewhirst, Chapter 14. Informal systems also include specific aspects of culture, role expectations, norms, values, and beliefs.

Past failures of the behavioral scientists in helping organizations improve competitiveness have resulted from their tendency to attend to social systems rather than to the strategic systems that provide customer value. HR and other managers must regard social systems as mechanisms to encourage continuous improvement and to ensure consistent execution and operation in the strategic systems.

6. Strategic Subsystems. The strategic subsystems are smaller versions and components of the strategic systems of the organization, that is, a "part" of the "whole." Strategic subsystems may be viewed as components of larger suprasystems, which are the means through which the organization produces customer value. Like suprasystems, subsystems transcend functional and departmental boundaries. For example, the "raw material availability" subsystem of a plant involves activities in production planning, purchasing, accounting, logistical movement, receiving and temporary storage.

7. Process Technology. Process technology is used broadly to mean the elements of applied science needed for doing the work to produce goods and services. In this broad definition of technology, there are two components: knowledge and tools.

Knowledge about how to do things represents a critical part of strategic systems. For example, in relation to goods and services, this knowledge may pertain to the design of new products or product components, such as an optical scanner; the transformation of raw material properties into products, such as plastics and synthetic fibers; the use of energy, such as nuclear and laser technologies; or the extension of human sensation, such as through the use of an electron microscope and ultrasound imaging.

Science remains incomplete without the second component of technology, the tools of the trade. The tools are the implements, instruments, machines, algorithms, programs, or equipment that are used with knowledge to execute the work to produce valued goods and services. These tools may be quite diverse, ranging in complexity from hand tools (such as a hammer), to automated machinery (such as numerically controlled robotics); and ranging in type from computer software (such as CAD/CAM), to production hardware (such as a metal-cutting lathe).

The domain of process technology is vastly important to organizational competitiveness. Consider the potential value to be derived from the marriage of knowledge and tools in the burgeoning field of laser chemistry. "Laser chemists are employing such exotic gambits as 'laser traps' and 'optical tweezers' to grab, slow, and manipulate bits of molecules of living cells. In the process, they are discovering better techniques for such diverse tasks as etching circuits on silicon and unraveling the inner workings of cells" (*Business Week*, July 16, 1990: 160-162).

8. Operating Methods. Operating methods are the ways of using the available technology, that is, knowledge and tools, to do the work to produce and deliver valued goods and services. These operating methods include the standard rules, procedures, processes, and arrangements of tasks used to guide the regular and orderly execution and measurement of work. Operating methods are critical in providing customer value.

Two groups of workers may have the same knowledge and tools at their disposal, yet use them in quite different ways owing to their operating methods. For example, the operating methods of one shift might be guided by a standard procedure to turn off all machines upon shift changeover, and do preventive maintenance prior to producing any parts. Another shift keeps the machines running and monitors the machines, only to stop them for maintenance when something goes wrong or can no longer be ignored. These two shifts have the same technology, knowledge, and skills, yet their operating methods are very different.

The category of operating methods might be broadly conceived to include "soft" methods or interpersonal processes, which are important in addition to the methods directly related to physical transformation of material and labor into goods and services. For example, such "software" is important to ensure that groups function as a team. Milacron employees devised a rule that members of their interdisciplinary product development team should not discuss their deliberations with nonteam members. This rule "broke down barriers between disciplines because a salesman, for instance, might then venture a naive idea about an engineering problem without fear that he would wind up as the laughingstock of Milacron's engineers. And vice versa" (*Fortune*, May 21, 1990: 70).

9. Operational Tasks. An operational task involves the activities of actually doing the work to produce and deliver valued goods and services for customers. These activities include thinking and planning for work, preparing materials and machines, physically transforming or transporting physical materials through manual manipulation of tools or through automated machines, delivering services through physical or mental activity, and monitoring and measuring work outcomes. Operational tasks are the accumulation of specific physical and "mental" events or motions of people and machines, as they act and interface to produce valued outcomes.

10. Operational Motions. Operational motions are the microcomponents of task activities, and include observable physical movements and unobservable mental "movements." Operational motions may be the behavioral movements or mental activities of operators. In addition, the

physical movement or processing activity of other technological tools, for example, of computers and automated machine tools, may be considered operational motions.

As a whole, these operational motions make up the activity of operational tasks. Examples of operational motions include hand movements to control a forklift, hand movements to measure board thickness with a micrometer, signals to communicate to an airline pilot, verbal signals to communicate with co-workers on an oil drill, and manual lifting and placement of subassemblies on an assembly line. Operational motions might be broadly interpreted to include intangible actions, such as visual sensation and mental interpretation to read a micrometer measurement. These operational motions are components of operational tasks that may seem trivial, but cumulatively they can have a big impact on value for the customer.

USING THE MAT

Difficulty Categorizing Activities

Typologies, such as those suggested in Figures 2 and 3, and just described, can be used to reduce or discretely categorize dynamic and real events. Typologies and models represent reality in a form that makes these events easier to talk about and think about. They can provide a valuable prompt to thinking, lead to understanding of relationships, and suggest implications for action. However, by simplifying reality into a model, rarely does one acknowledge all the complexity that exists in real life. The categories in Figures 2 and 3 may certainly overlap in real organizations. Separating out the pieces and parts and labeling them may not be a trivial task.

Consider an example regarding the domains of activity. To compete, managerial leaders must create, improve, standardize, and execute a change process to transform their organization into a competitive organization. Should this domain of activity, referred to above as a "process," be labeled a "strategic system" or a "process technology"? Organization members must address such definitional issues in light of their own particular circumstances, strategies, and management styles. Ultimately, the labeling issue may be moot if managerial leaders implement the change process successfully.

Models can be useful, however. Labeling and pointing out discrete domains of activity can ensure that these important domains of the organization are not taken for granted and overlooked.

Regarding the categorization of types of activity, consider that an event which constitutes change may bear the image of various types of activity, such as creativity, innovation, and incremental improvement. Yet these images may blur together. For example, Heinz discovered that questioning long-held assumptions about cost reduction, innovative thinking, and low-tech incremental improvements can greatly improve value to the customer and returns to the company. Through a process Heinz managers call "paradigm busting," they revisit past approaches with a creative attitude.

Puzzled for years by the frequent breakage of frozen French fries, engineers at the Ore-Ida factory in Plover, Wisconsin, challenged their production paradigm. They examined every step of the production process, from the bays where trucks full of whole potatoes unload, through the plant, where the potatoes are skimmed along conveyors, sliced, and ultimately packaged. The engineers assumed that the uncooked potatoes could withstand routine 3- to 14-foot drops as they tumbled along the production line. However, while the whole spuds weren't breaking or bruising, they were developing microscopic fault lines that subsequently caused the finished fries to fracture. As a solution, they eliminated potato free fall with a few metal slides, to save $300,000 annually (*Fortune*, April 9, 1990: 46-48).

Once again, the issue of labeling activities is moot if the work succeeds. However, labeling and pointing out discrete types of activity can help guide thinking and ensure that important activities are not taken for granted and overlooked.

Who Engages in These Activities?

Traditional organizations have often clearly distinguished between thinkers and doers. However, in competitive organizations, it is not only top management that engages in creative and innovative change. Employees at all levels and in all positions may appropriately engage in various types of activities, although they may do so with very different domains.

Managerial leaders may tend to creatively change value and design strategies that impact organizational strategic competencies. For example, the leader may decide not to outsource optical and imaging systems for an office equipment product, but to develop competencies in optical and imaging systems that might enable entry into other markets. At the other extreme, a line worker may change the methods of executing his or her work, by innovation of activities in accordance with strategic objectives. For example, a worker may derive an innovative pattern for stacking boxes of finished product to reduce breakage in warehousing and shipping, and to increase the efficiency of space utilization. Note that the listing order of these types and domains of change is not intended to convey their worth or value to the organization. Each is necessary, important, and valuable to the organization.

Managers should avoid thinking that only the higher levels of management engage in the conceptual work of innovative thinking or incremental improvement, while the lower level employees only do the "grunt" work to maintain and operate what has been handed over to them without need of thought. By decoupling the type of change from the domain of change, jobs throughout the organization can be described in terms of each type and domain of activity.

The types and domains of activities shown on the Management Activity Topograph (MAT) in Figure 4 potentially represent the jobs of all employees. Thus, the possible combinations of types and domains of activities suggest that even workers assigned to the most specific job activities, for example, stacking boxes of finished product, can engage in innovation and be creative. Thus, "job enrichment" and the challenge of inclusion in managing systems for customer value are a part of every employee's job. However, there are limitations and differences.

Clearly, the job of a forklift driver will differ dramatically from that of the president of the company. These differences can be described in terms of the MAT. For example, the forklift driver may "create," but the domain may be very narrow in scope and concrete, for example, the physical activities of their own jobs or their work group activities. While the forklift driver primarily "creates operational motions," at the position numbered 2 on the MAT, the president primarily "creates value strategy," at the position numbered 1 on the MAT in Figure 4. Although the president or leaders primarily "execute value strategy," at the position numbered 4 on the MAT, operators primarily "execute operational motions," at the position numbered 3 on the MAT.

Prescribing Managerial Roles on the MAT

For an organization pursuing continuous improvement for competitiveness, the MAT can be used to represent the roles of leaders and managers within the organization, for example, prescribe the terrain of various managerial jobs. The MAT also implies the human resource needs of the organization, namely, developmental needs. In this regard, the primary use of the MAT should be as a tool for standardizing a customer value-based strategy throughout the organization. The MAT can be a useful guide to ensure that the management terrain of an organization does not have gaping holes or voids that may jeopardize customer value. Such a tool might also be useful in organizations that are downsizing and flattening their hierarchies. Too often important managerial responsibilities are lost or forgotten during personnel cuts.

The roles of managerial leaders, middle managers, and operators throughout the organization can be characterized and differentiated on the MAT by mapping the terrain of activity for each. For example, the activity of managerial leaders may be characterized in terms of type of managerial activity and domain of managerial activity.

Consider the different roles of various employee groups as depicted on the MAT in Figures 5 through 7. The third vertical dimension indicates the relative focus or intensity of managerial activity through its elevation in each of the positions combining type and domain of activity. These three-dimensional figures suggest that a science of topography be developed for managerial activity.

To assist the reader, the positions numbered in Figure 4 are also numbered on the elevated surface of the three-dimensional MAT layouts in Figures 5 through 7. In Figure 5, managerial leaders have a higher elevation in position 1, that is, creation of value strategy, and a lower elevation in position 2, that is, creation of operational motions. This three-dimensional mapping creates a surface topography that reflects the roles of managerial leaders. Similar topography reflects the roles of middle managers (see Figure 6), and the roles of operators (see Figure 7). Notice that the term *middle managers* may signify those who manage the middle or along the diagonal of the MAT, rather than those who occupy positions in the middle of a hierarchy.

Role Differentiation on the MAT. The MAT offers a means of differentiating the roles of various managers within the organization in terms of the activities required to compete. Note that by describing the jobs of operators in similar terms as that of other managers, the MAT suggests that all employees in an organization may engage in creation, innovation, incremental improvement, standardization, routinization, maintenance, and execution. This view regards operators as "managers" of their own activity or their work group's operational activity. Therefore, the MAT blurs the distinction between "manager" and "worker" on the dimension of type of management activity. Although the distinction blurs, real differences still exist in the domains of their activities and can be described by the MAT in terms of activity intensity. For managerial leaders, middle managers, and operators, the activity intensities will vary, as do their roles.

For example, the topography of managerial leaders indicates that, although their activity covers various ranges of the MAT, their activity intensity concentrates in the region of creation, innovation, incremental

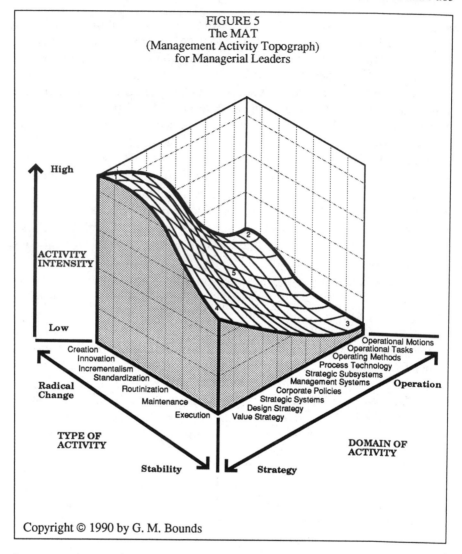

FIGURE 5
The MAT
(Management Activity Topograph)
for Managerial Leaders

improvement, and standardization of competitive strategy, strategic systems, corporate policies, and management systems. By contrast, the topography of operators indicates that their activity intensity concentrates in the regions of routinization, maintenance, and execution of operating methods, operational tasks, and operational motions.

Operators may engage in other activity regions of the MAT; however, their liberty and participation in these activities should be initiated and directed by the owners of strategic systems and subsystems. For example, creation and innovation of operational activity must be consistent with the activities of the owner of the system, of which that operational activity is

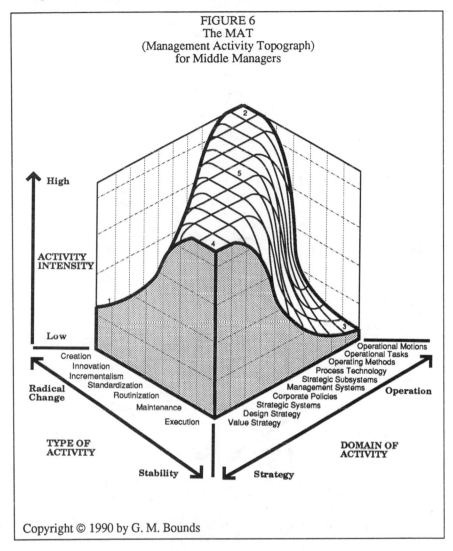

FIGURE 6
The MAT
(Management Activity Topograph)
for Middle Managers

a part. Thus, the diverse activities displayed on the MAT must be integrated for customer value.

The ultimate architects of all domains are the managerial leaders, who hold overall responsibility for strategy and strategic systems. This means that in order to improve systems, managerial leaders will often have to devote some attention to activity domains traditionally considered the exclusive domain of middle managers, for example, process technology.

The role of staff members and specialists can be depicted on the MAT. Staff and specialists may be employed to fill any voids in topography of

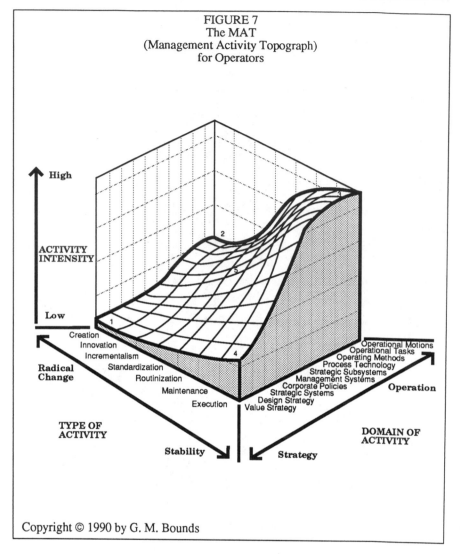

FIGURE 7
The MAT
(Management Activity Topograph)
for Operators

an organization's MAT profiles. For example, the MAT suggests that managerial leaders have a high activity intensity for "innovation of value strategy." In many organizations, managerial leaders make decisions about value offerings based on marketing studies and customer value determination. However, design engineers and other specialists are often employed to do the research and design work to create, innovate, and incrementally improve the configurations of value components for products and services.

Many competitive organizations are reducing the number of staff personnel. Managers and other line employees may increasingly take on the roles that have traditionally been assigned to staff personnel or other experts, to break the traditional division between thinking and doing. However, specialist activities will remain important to competitive organizations. But these activities must be integrated with the activities of others to ensure competitiveness in customer value. The MAT can be used to convey to staff and specialists the context and purpose of their work, and to facilitate the integration of their work with that of other employees.

The MAT indicates that managerial leaders, middle managers, and operators all engage in thinking and improvement activities. All employees are encouraged to use their creative energies and not just to execute routines. Not every individual will necessarily engage regularly and formally in every activity indicated on the MAT profiles. For example, consider the MAT for operators shown in Figure 7. Some operators may devote the majority of their energies to executing motions for tasks, at the position numbered 3 on the MAT. Other operators, in similar jobs, may spend relatively more time thinking about creating improved operations, at the position numbered 2 on the MAT. These more "creative" operators may provide input to system managers through suggestion systems, team meetings, presentations to task forces, or even through temporary membership on task forces. Thus, the MAT of each individual's role may look very different. In aggregate, for all individual operators as a whole, the MAT for operators may look very much like that depicted in Figure 7.

In addition to the three general MATs presented for managerial leaders, middle managers, and operators, other types of positions can be described with the MAT. For example, many organizations have positions labeled first-line supervisor or foreman, whose occupants do more standardization and routinization and less execution of operational tasks and motions. The MAT for the position of supervisor or foreman might be depicted with topographical features somewhere between that for middle managers and operators (see Figure 8). Other organizations prefer not to have one person occupy the position of supervisor or foreman, but choose to develop autonomous work groups or self-managing teams composed of operators who perform their own supervisory activities.

Where to Start. The MAT suggests that the task of creating and improving design strategy belongs to managerial leaders. This task, that is, determining how the organization will provide customer value, involves determining the roles and responsibilities for each employee, that is, MAT surface features. Thus, according to the MAT, managerial leaders must determine the MAT features. This prescription presents a riddle, "which comes first, the MAT or the generation of the MAT." Rather than be distracted by this riddle, someone within the organization must determine individual roles and responsibilities. Just as with the chicken and the egg,

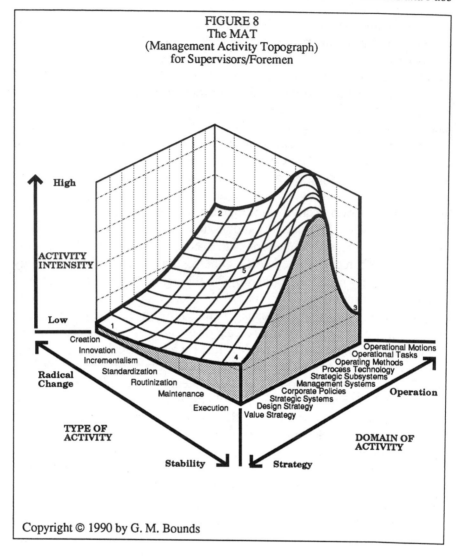

FIGURE 8
The MAT
(Management Activity Topograph)
for Supervisors/Foremen

you have to start somewhere. The ideal models presented in Figures 5 through 8 provide managerial leaders a starting point.

Caveats for Use of the MAT

In applying the MAT to the prescription of managerial roles within an organization, managerial leaders must consider some of the following issues. There are likely to be contingencies not expressed in this discussion, for example, size, technology, organizational complexity, and interactions, which dictate that the content prescribed by the MATs in Figures 5 through 8 should not be considered as absolutely fixed.

The MAT should be used flexibly to assist in prescribing managerial jobs. For example, the domains listed on the MAT should not be treated as an exhaustive list of rigid classifications with no overlap and interdependencies. Furthermore, there are certainly other domains that might usefully be included on a MAT to suit particular organizational circumstances. For example, in addition to process technology, a category labeled "product technology" might be treated as a separate and more specific component of value strategy. Moreover, in characterizing managerial topography for an organization, it might be useful to distinguish between the responsibility for managerial activity and the actual engagement in managerial activity.

THE CONSEQUENCE OF INCONSISTENCY

The Management Activity Topograph may be viewed as an elaboration of the sociotechnical systems theme, which states that the social and technical dimensions of an organization should be congruent to ensure satisfactory individual and business outcomes. Conversely, inconsistency between components of the MAT can have unfortunate outcomes. For example, inconsistency between a management system – such as performance measurements – and value strategy can weaken the fabric of organizational competitiveness.

In the following excerpt from an unpublished summary of assessment conducted by Gregory M. Bounds, the sample organization was engaged in a "change effort" to make its product more valuable to customers by improving design, quality, consistency, delivery, and its ability to meet customer needs. Although the organization had management teams in place to address specific issues, they were making little progress.

The Case of Misguided Management Systems

This industrial products plant has been quite successful in the past. It recently set records for daily production, and continue to make incremental improvements aimed at increasing production volume through capital upgrades and operational adjustments. This plant was once regarded as the industry standard bearer, in terms of quality and productivity. They had the best machinery, equipment, and layout in the industry. Managers standardized their processes and operations well, and workers conscientiously executed their jobs. Managers still run the plant well at current design. Unfortunately, the market has changed and so have competitors.

The routinization which allows this plant to produce record-breaking volumes now works against change.

Proud of past success, managers and employees are quite complacent and satisfied with their current ways of managing and operating. They see little need for change, yet they continue to get "heat" from "corporate" to improve. They respond to pressures to "improve" by reaming even more volume out of the current systems. However, the market for their product has weakened, and they have also lost market share. They are producing much more than they can sell. Recent shutdowns have been necessary to relieve their bulging warehouse. They face continued decline in market share in a sagging market. Competitors have caught up, and customer needs have changed. Yet, most of the managers and workers of this plant see no need for change. The performance measurement system is clearly outdated, and the value strategy of the organization is not diffused throughout the organization.

Customer value and changing customer needs do not drive managerial perceptions of performance. Rather, production volume, efficiency, and unit cost do. The performance measures are inconsistent with the value strategy required to compete. They celebrate record-breaking production volume with a steak dinner for all employees, and the plant shuts down the next week because they can't sell what they produce. Such practices not only send confused messages to the employees, but distract them from the need to continuously improve other dimensions of customer value. Misled by their inappropriate performance measures, they are not in the frame of mind to change their management or operating practices. They blame the economy for market demand's being down and the salespeople for not wooing buyers.

When the market demand was high, production volume correlated nicely with profits. Now the market has slumped, market share has slipped, customer demands and needs have changed, and production volume correlates more nicely with inventory in the warehouse. Production volume, efficiency, and cost measures can be important. However, in this environment these measures are less appropriate as indicators of subsequent profit, and even less useful in driving continuous improvement in customer value.

IMPLICATIONS FOR THE MANAGERIAL JOBS

The managerial activities of value determination and system management should comprise the core of managerial jobs (as specifically discussed in earlier chapters). The MAT depicts job design, in general terms, for several groups of managers within the organization. The implications for designing managerial jobs in accordance with the activity orientation presented on the MAT are discussed below in terms of philosophy, the nature of managerial work, and emphasis on learning to study variation.

Philosophy

To help organizations solve competitive crises, many writers have suggested that managers need to change their philosophy. For example, Peters (1987: 445) has suggested that management through the traditional hierarchy must be changed. He has proposed inverting the hierarchy, so that managers see their role as that of supporting subordinates rather than as commanding subordinates from a position of authority. Peters' suggestion is insightful, but redefining managerial jobs totally in terms of an inverted hierarchy can be incomplete and misleading. Before implementing such a change in philosophy, one must consider the perspective adopted. The perspectives of managers, operators, and strategic systems are discussed below.

Management Perspective. From the managerial perspective, the hierarchy is best seen as led by the top, not inverted. Inversion implies that managers are subservient to the strategies and initiatives of the "subordinates." By contrast, managerial leaders must and will remain the strategic leaders of the organization. They are responsible for determining strategy and driving it through the organization. Subordinate subsystem and operational activity will be unfocused and misguided without strategic direction from managers. Only managerial leaders have both the broad knowledge about the organization and environment and the authority to determine and drive strategy.

Operator Perspective. From the operator perspective, it may be desirable for the hierarchy to be perceived as inverted. When an operator asks whether managers have provided resources, equipment, training, direction, communications, or guidance, then the operators need to perceive that managers have been "supportive." The manager's job is to build systems of the organization which the workers may use to provide customer value.

From the operator's perspective, the managers may be perceived as supporting their activity, responding to their needs, and enabling them to execute work for customer value. Operators may tend to view the organization as an inverted hierarchy focused on helping them apply their specific knowledge to contribute to customer value. However, they must also perceive the role of managers in providing strategic focus and direction for their activities.

Strategic Systems Perspective. The strategic systems perspective encompasses both the managerial and the operator perspective. Thus, "supportiveness" is an operator perception and a byproduct of managers doing their job as system owners (i.e., to create, provide, direct, and improve strategic systems). "Supportiveness" is an operator perception and not a managerial job prescription. The managerial job prescription requires managers to drive a customer strategy throughout the organization and enable operators by building and improving systems. The appropriate philosophical orientation is best described as strategic system management, which is inherently nonhierarchical.

The systems perspective forces managers to recognize that their systems depend on inputs from the organizational environment that must be managed and outputs that must fulfill the needs and expectations of various constituents. Over the long term, in order to fulfill the primary obligation for customer value, the organization must meet the needs of other constituents. Thus, an organization acts as an arena in which the many diverse constituents, internal and external to its boundaries, gain access to one another. These constituents exchange mutually valued assets or resources.

The list of constituents includes employees, investors, suppliers, government regulators, distributors, retailers, purchasers, and end users of the product or service. Each of the constituents competes for access to the assets of the others. These assets include knowledge, skills, money, time, facilities, attention, social environment, and diverse other opportunities. For example, in return for personal development, social affiliation, occupation, money, and fringe benefits, employees offer their knowledge, skills, and abilities for thinking and doing. Organizations compete to attract, engage, and retain the best employees. Exchanges among constituents often involve money. For example, investors provide money for capital assets, and get returns in the form of shareholders' equity and dividends.

Other constituents are less interested in money than in protecting and preserving society and/or nature. For example, food technologists regard the development of the "asceptic" cartons or germ-free food/juice boxes as one of the best technical achievements of the past fifty years. The asceptic container allows safe, fresh, lightweight, transportable nutrition for customers. However, the lawmakers in the state of Maine banned the box to keep containers made of hard-to-separate paper, plastic, and foil from reaching landfills (*Business Week*, September 17, 1990: 36). As another example, consider that companies such as Whirlpool, Digital Equipment, Electrolux, 3M, and General Electric are beginning to design products for disassembly to encourage recycling of components such as the plastic waste that is piling up all over the country. Designers simplify parts and materials to make them easier and less expensive to snap apart, sort, and recycle (*Business Week*, September 17, 1990: 103). In building organizational systems, managerial leaders must consider the many constituents that are not easily reflected in immediate dollar figures.

Within the systems perspective, leaders and managers are the improvers of those systems that provide the means for transactional exchanges among constituents. Figure 9 depicts managers as owners of the systems that enable transaction among five general groups of constituents: employees, suppliers, customers, investors, and societal institutions. The hierarchical view biases the organization toward the investors' financial objectives. In contrast, the system view balances the view of leaders and managers toward creating value for customers, while serving the transactional needs of other constituents. For example, Nordstrom department stores have grabbed market share and developed a loyal customer base by building systems for extraordinary customer service. However, their high standards produce an intense and demanding work environment for employees. To continue "going beyond the call of duty" for customers,

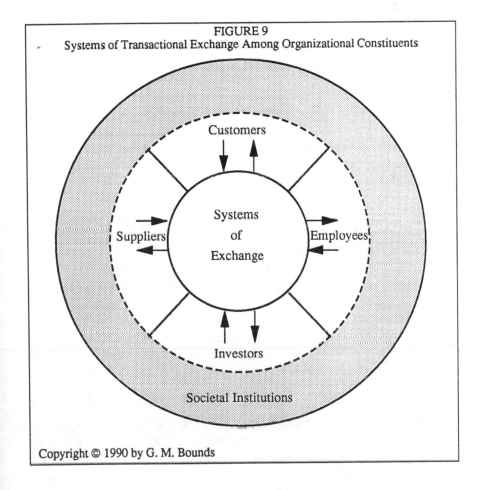

FIGURE 9
Systems of Transactional Exchange Among Organizational Constituents

Customers

Systems
of
Exchange

Suppliers

Employees

Investors

Societal Institutions

Nordstrom must find employees willing to work the systems or make their systems more palatable for employees and its union representation (*Business Week*, September 3, 1990: 83).

In the future, competitive organizations will have systems for efficient and effective exchange of assets among constituents. These systems must be contingent on constituent circumstances, tailored to fit the needs and assets of constituents, and the activities and processes required for exchange. One type of system will not efficiently and effectively serve all organizations. The nature of its customer base and value strategy may predispose the organization to certain types of tasks, systems, and structures.

The Nature of Managerial Work

Some managers are assigned ownership for strategic systems (suprasystems or subsystems) that transcend traditional hierarchical silos and levels. Their work cannot be confined to narrow functional specialties, but broadly encompasses the multiple functions, departments, groups, and individuals that make up strategic systems. Strategic system owners will not simply coordinate functional interfaces through conflict resolution and negotiation, but will architecturally design systems and functional contributions to systems. They will integrate diverse activities for the superordinate performance of systems that transcend local activities.

Those managers assigned ownership for functional activities will work collaboratively under the guidance of strategic system managers to ensure functional contribution to customer value. System owners and functional owners may move freely within a system to engage in various managerial activities. Traditional pigeon holes and positional indicators do not adequately describe these jobs. The content and focus of an individual's work may change frequently as the situation and leaders demand.

The context of the managerial job will be less individualistic and less hierarchical. Managers will not work exclusively with their immediate subordinates and immediate superior, but will do much of their work with managerial work teams led by system owners. These system improvement teams will extend beyond the limited hierarchical work teams implied by Likert's concept of managers as linking pins. Lines of authority, communications, and interaction may seem blurred, but the purpose of customer value remains clear.

Some writers (e.g., Peters, 1987: 661) suggest that organizations should be managed through chaos. Indeed, rapidly changing and vibrant organizations may appear chaotic. However, chaos and confusion are not the means to competitiveness. Managers should not assume that having a hundred cooks in the kitchen, each doing his or her own thing, will yield the best organizational results. Flexibility, adaptability, and breaking traditional barriers are important, but so are purpose, strategic direction, and integration through system ownership and managerial leadership. An organization driven by the managerial agenda prescribed in this book may appear chaotic and disordered, just as the thickly matted tangles of a braided rug or mat. However, a broader view reveals that the tangles are skillfully interrelated to synergistically create a whole that accomplishes an intended purpose greater than that of the individual parts.

Managers Must Learn to Study Variation

Implications for human resource development can be inferred from the MAT, particularly when we consider the importance of variation to managers. To study variation, we must monitor and measure. The managerial activities of monitoring and measuring are not included in the MAT as a discrete type of activity, because monitoring and measuring should accompany each type of activity on the MAT. Monitoring and measuring variation represents the key to confirming the successful execution of each of these managerial activities.

Traditionally, variation has represented uncertainty for managers, and uncertainty in individual behavior usually evokes attempts to control individuals by managers. Variation or deviation from desired standards has signaled to managers that either they failed to adequately communicate goals and standards to subordinates, or subordinates failed to consistently make an effort to meet the goals and standards.

To deal with the variation, managers traditionally increase control in the form of goal clarification, closer supervision, more frequent inspection, and application of contingent rewards and punishments. The implicit assumption underlying this approach to variation is that variation represents some kind of "error" term ascribable to the individual and not to the system or to an individual/system interaction.

Enlightened management realizes that systems produce variation in "individual" performances. Variation should be used to study the performance of systems and individuals within systems. The study of variation can produce knowledge that can be used to improve organizational systems, and not simply to signal a need for increased control over individuals within the system.

The types of managerial activity listed in the MAT suggest the need for the study of variation by managers. To do so, managers must develop knowledge and skills for monitoring and measuring the outcomes of their managerial activities. The needed knowledge and skills include the statistical methods and tools used to study variation. Increased emphasis on these quantitative skills should not be perceived as incompatible with, but complementary to, the need for more vision and inspiration from managerial leaders.

For example, the activities of creation and innovation, prompted by the visionary leaders seeking continuous improvement, involve radical and fundamental change of the domain of focus, such as a new type of production system using numerically controlled diamond etchers to inscribe images on printing cylinders rather than chemical etching. The creation and innovation activities parallel Juran's (1964) notion of breakthrough. A discontinuous change in system performance should result from creation or innovation. The statistical study of variation in outcomes can provide evidence for such change. A favorable discontinuous change may be reflected in a step function increase in performance yields, as depicted in Figure 10. A discontinuous change may also be reflected in the reduction of variation around a target, as depicted in Figure 11.

The activity of incremental improvement may be reflected in gradual increases in yields or gradual reduction in variation, as depicted in Figures 12 and 13. Standardization and routinization to put system changes into place may also be reflected in such gradual improvement. Managers should recognize that whether change is considered discontinuous improvement or continuous improvement is a matter of the rate of change and the time interval considered. Measurement methods and sampling strategies must be carefully considered in studying variation over time. For example, a change that occurred gradually over time may appear discontinuous if samples are separated by a greater time interval.

Maintenance and execution of activity should result in neither gradual trends nor discontinuous steps in performance, as depicted in Figure 14. A maintained system should display stable, predictable random variation around a centerline. Maintenance activity may involve the identification of special causes of nonrandom events, and the elimination or control of such special causes to ensure stable future performance. The managers in charge of maintaining performance should engage in problem solving to fix the special causes under their control to ensure they do not recur. They should also identify causes outside their control that imply needed changes in broader systems. A well-maintained system should display stable performance during execution, even across potentially disruptive events such as shift changes, changeovers, startups, and downtime for preventive maintenance. System stability provides customers consistent value and gives managerial leaders the launching pad for change and continuous improvement.

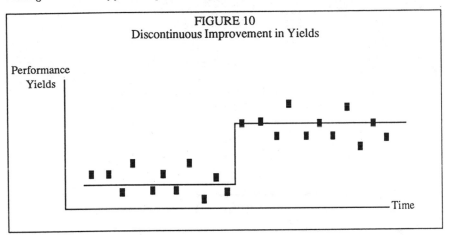

FIGURE 10
Discontinuous Improvement in Yields

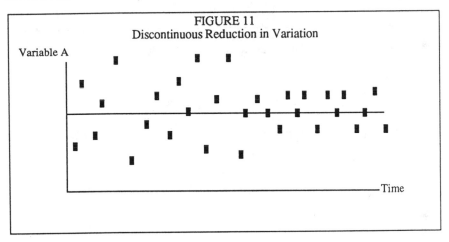

FIGURE 11
Discontinuous Reduction in Variation

Variation should be used to study the results of the managerial activity listed in the MAT, such as monitoring for discontinuous improvement to see if an innovation achieved intended results, as discussed above. Variation should also be used to learn about the domain of focus, for example, systems. Such learning should provide a basis for managerial activity. This means that the study of variation should assist managers in learning about systems, processes, methods, tasks, activities, and the like. Such learning provides knowledge of the means of achieving improved results. It leads managers to understand what they need to change, innovate, improve, and maintain.

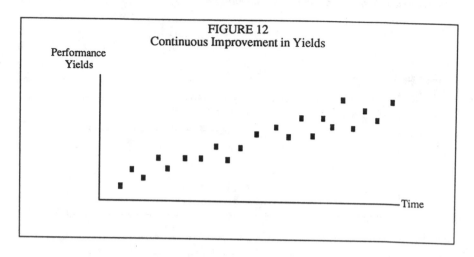

FIGURE 12
Continuous Improvement in Yields

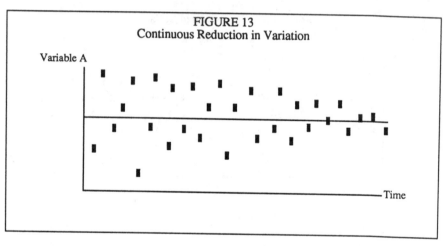

FIGURE 13
Continuous Reduction in Variation

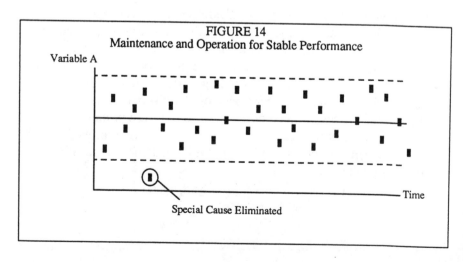

FIGURE 14
Maintenance and Operation for Stable Performance

Special Cause Eliminated

CONCLUSION

The types of activities critical to competing in global markets range in their effects, from radical change to stability. The domains of these activities also vary greatly, ranging from strategy to operation. Job design and role clarification represent the starting points in human resource management for competitive capabilities. The MAT provides a framework for integrating these managerial activities.

Human resources should be developed to engage in these activities. More importantly, as individuals, they should be developed to flow from one type of change to another and from one domain of activity to another. As a collection, they should ensure they work in concerted fashion, as a team, to ensure that the diverse types and domains of activities of all individuals are integrated to produce a whole and formidably competitive organization.

REFERENCES

"America's Fastest-Growing Company." *Fortune*, August 13, 1990, pp. 48-54.
"The Big Brouhaha Over the Little Juice Box." *Business Week*, September 17, 1990, p. 36.
"Built to Last – Until It's Time to Take It Apart." *Business Week*, September 17, 1990, p. 103.
"Coke Gets Off Its Can in Europe." *Fortune*, August 13, 1990, pp. 68-73.
"Cost Cutting: How to Do It Right." *Fortune*, April 9, 1990, pp. 40-49.
"The Global 1000: The Wall Fell Down, and the Continent Took Off." *Business Week*, July 16, 1990, pp. 111-144.
"How Levi Strauss Did an LBO Right." *Fortune*, May 7, 1990, pp. 105-107.
Juran, J. M. *Managerial Breakthrough*. New York: McGraw-Hill, 1964.
"The New World Lasers Are Conquering." *Business Week*, July 16, 1990, pp. 160-162.
Peters, T. *Thriving on Chaos*. New York: Harper and Row, 1987.
"The Soul of an Old Machine." *Fortune*, May 21, 1990, pp. 67-72.
"Why Toyota Keeps Getting Better and Better." *Fortune*, November 19, 1990, pp. 66-69.
"Will 'The Nordstrom Way' Travel Well?" *Business Week*, September 3, 1990, p. 83.

CHAPTER 26

HUMAN RESOURCE MANAGEMENT FOR COMPETITIVE CAPABILITY*

GREGORY M. BOUNDS
Research Associate, Management Development Center
University of Tennessee

LARRY A. PACE
Professor of Management and Marketing
Louisiana State University in Shreveport

SUMMARY

Traditional approaches to human resource management (HRM) have assumed that the individual and the job are the primary units of management. This chapter questions the assumptions underlying this individualist approach. The HRM approach set forth here adds the team and the system as primary units of management. Human resource managers (all managers) must integrate these units, individual/job and team/system, with their strategy to provide customer value. Suggestions are made regarding the development of managerial resources for continuous improvement of customer value and competitive capability. The messages of this chapter apply to all managers and not just human resource professionals.

INTRODUCTION

The challenge of global competition referred to throughout this book makes the effective management of human resources imperative. Dr. Barry Bebb, former Vice President, Reprographics, Xerox Corporation, astutely

---

*We thank Barry Bebb, John Kelsch, and Jean Kinney for their comments on early drafts of this chapter.

characterized the challenge faced by many human resource managers: "The most important change in human resource management in recent decades relates to the rate of change that must be pushed through successful corporations. The world's best corporations are reducing costs by factors of two, reducing product development schedules by factors of two and improving quality by factors of ten every five to ten years. Such rapid rates of improvements require very rapid rates of changes in how businesses operate. The cultural comforts provided by stability in an enterprise environment are not viable in today's rapidly changing global village. Successful corporations learn how to drive enormous amounts of change through an entire infrastructure with frightening speed."

The competitive capabilities that managerial leaders perpetually seek reside as human potential within the walls of their own organizations. The key to competing through customer value lies not simply in process and product technology innovation, but in developing managerial resources. These human resources should be developed for diverse activities aimed at continuous improvement and consistent execution of strategic systems for customer value. If human resources are appropriately developed, all else should fall into place or be strategically put into place by these developed human resources. Thus, human resource management represents the epitome of the popular call for "working on the means to improvement."

Unfortunately, some organizational leaders do not act as if they consider people to be their most valuable asset, despite what their formal policies say. For example, many managers treat human resource development as a necessary evil and seek to minimize the costs of training and education. These managers may see human resource development as justified only to correct glaring deficiencies. They are too concerned about accounting for the costs of knowledge, while ignoring the costs of ignorance. Other organizational leaders seek to control and reduce costs by minimalist compensation schemes, layoffs, and reduced opportunities for advancement. By contrast, other leaders regard human resources as an investment to enhance organizational capabilities for customer value. These leaders recognize that the skills, knowledge, and abilities of their human resources represent competitive weapons.

This chapter addresses the critical implications for the strategic human resource management (HRM) for competitiveness. Based on the managerial job design discussed in earlier chapters, namely, those chapters on the managerial leadership model and the Management Activity Topograph (MAT), implications for general HRM are incidentally addressed. We argue that team and system performance should be incorporated into human resource approaches that have traditionally been focused on individuals and jobs.

For students of continuous improvement, issues of performance appraisal and contingent rewards are those most often on the edge of their forebrains and the tips of their tongues when human resources becomes the topic of discussion. For example, the issue of decoupling performance appraisals and rewards causes many organizations to struggle. An astute thinker might ask: "Since there is natural variation in the skills, talents and experience of people, how does one attract and keep the best? How do we overcome cultural barriers to rewarding teams versus individuals when most of us grew up worshiping heroes? How are leaders and managers of an organization chosen without some type of appraisal system?"

These authors do not proclaim one set of answers to these difficult questions. However, some general principles and suggestions are offered to encourage continuous improvement of strategic systems for customer value. The intent of this chapter is primarily to prompt thinking and inspire managerial leaders to develop their own answers, rather than to offer "proven" recipes for universal implementation. This chapter is not intended to be comprehensive. Painting "the big picture" with a broad brush, we develop and examine only a few of the many implications for the management of managerial human resources. The discussion of these issues is organized around the following general model of the HRM process.

THE TRADITIONAL HUMAN RESOURCE MANAGEMENT CYCLE

The HRM cycle has traditionally been viewed as the process depicted in Figure 1. This model is a skeletal descriptor of what could obviously

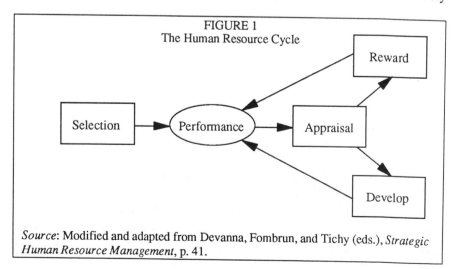

FIGURE 1
The Human Resource Cycle

Source: Modified and adapted from Devanna, Fombrun, and Tichy (eds.), *Strategic Human Resource Management*, p. 41.

be developed at a much higher level of detail. However, for the sake of both simplicity and brevity, we present only the strategically important factors shown in the model.

In the traditional HRM model, job performance is seen as a function of the HR components of selection, individual performance, appraisal, rewards, and development. These elements of HRM suggest generic activities that are performed by HR managers. These elements have been described as:

> *selecting* people who are best able to perform the jobs defined by the structure, *appraising* their *performance* to facilitate the equitable distribution of *rewards,* motivating employees by linking rewards to high levels of performance, and *developing* employees to enhance their current performance at work as well as to prepare them to perform in positions they may hold in the future (Devanna, Fombrun, and Tichy, 1984: 41) [emphasis added].[1]

Implicit elements of HRM underlying this model include (1) job design, which involves the development and arrangement of tasks and duties, the content and methods of work for a position or group of positions aimed at specific purposes or objectives, and (2) organization design, which involves the articulation of tasks, activities, basic departmentalization, authority structures, and integrating mechanisms, production systems, and managerial systems of the organization. Job design and organization design implications were discussed in earlier chapters. The model discussed in this chapter provides a useful beginning framework for the discussion of the essentials of HRM for a globally competitive organization.

Individual Focus

Traditionally, HRM systems have focused on the individual. An individual job is designed, as a part of broader organizational design, with specific tasks and duties prescribed. Individuals typically specialize in training and education to master a narrow domain of work. Focused criteria define the basis for evaluating performance on the tasks and duties. Superiors appraise individual performance in accord with the specified criteria and render judgment as to the adequacy or inadequacy of the

---

1. The terms *people* and *employees* and *human resources* refer not only to the operators and foremen on the line, but also to the leaders and managers of the organization.

performance. Contingent rewards are then administered for the individual, in accord with the individual's performance appraisal. Developmental needs are identified in relationship to the appraisal, and action is taken to correct any deficiencies in current performance or to avoid any anticipated deficiencies in future performance.

Questionable Assumptions

There are many implicit and explicit assumptions on which this individualistic HRM approach rests. Key among these assumptions are the following:

1. The individual is completely (or largely) in control of his or her own performance variation.
2. Supervisors can accurately judge individual performance.
3. Individual contributions to system performance are reflected by the criteria selected.
4. The administration of contingent rewards and punishments at the individual level is motivational and ensures future performance will be satisfactory.
5. Differentiating among individuals with regard to level of performance, level of compensation, and level of status serves important organizational purposes.
6. HR systems that select, appraise, reward, and develop individuals are adequate vehicles for managing organizational change and creating customer value.

The remainder of this chapter calls into question many of these assumptions and offers alternatives for managers of human resources based on systems and management team performance, rather than jobs and individual performance.

Traditional Human Resource Managers

The HR systems of most organizations are relegated to staff specialists or professionals. These specialists do not typically come from the ranks of line management and would not usually be considered as leading contenders for general management positions. They are often narrowly trained in the art and science of their trade, with degrees in organization behavior, industrial relations, HRM, general management, or the social sciences. They frequently do not understand the needs of line managers, the business, or the external customers. Although human resource professionals bear some of the blame for their own shortcomings, most of the blame can rightly be cast on the managerial leaders who fail to strategically manage the human resources of their organizations.

Functional Myopia

Human resource professionals frequently exhibit technical arrogance (as do other functional specialists within the organization) and often feel unappreciated. They complain that "if those insensitive line managers were only intelligent enough or understood our field of expertise, they would appreciate us more." HR professionals epitomize functional specialization, and functional isolation. The result is that they often fail to help develop the organization's strategic capabilities. Sometimes their efforts are even seen as barriers to organizational effectiveness and flexibility. They see most problems in the organization as human resource problems that would best be solved by the addition of staff and budget to the HR function.

In many of the organizations we have observed, the HR professionals are not in touch with competitive challenges and have little idea what changes system managers require. How can they serve without knowing their customers? HRM professionals have often been relegated to administrative activities, such as executing the paperwork of hiring, firing, and other personnel decisions, or handling grievances and mediating disciplinary actions. These personnel activities are necessary, but HRM professionals could play a much more active role in developing the strategic capabilities of their organizations.

Disconnected from Strategy

Traditionally, HR professionals have been narrowly focused specialists with little impact on the strategic thrust of the organization. Their activities frequently lack strategic focus for long-range organizational needs. But even though HR professionals have been much maligned, they should not be fully blamed. The primary responsibility for managing human resources rests squarely with strategic system managers in the line of providing valued goods and services for customers. Human resources should be regarded as assets and system inputs in much the same way as are physical equipment and technologies. Unfortunately, the professionals who could help ensure these assets for strategic purposes are not even aware of the organization's strategy.

Consider an example of the degree to which HR professionals are typically excluded from strategic planning. Recently, an HR manager in a Fortune 500 company stated to one of us that the HR department was now being permitted to examine the strategic plan before it was published. The manager saw this change as a significant breakthrough in his organization's regard for HR. With this kind of disconnection from strategy, it is little wonder that HR managers become maintainers of the status quo in most organizations.

While human resources represent only a part of organizational systems, as an input, they are simultaneously the key to system viability, renewal, and organizational regeneration. Human resources are the vital resource. They give and sustain life in an organization. Managers must invest in these human assets. Organizational and managerial systems must be created to manage these assets. The top managers of the organization are the ultimate HR managers.

Human resources must be managed just as any other asset or system input within the organization. Desired outcomes must be identified and defined, causal variables and leverage points must be identified, and the system must be proactively managed to provide the organization with appropriately equipped managers. Top managers must lead staff specialists and the management of human resources in the improvement of HRM systems and processes. Just like other subordinate managers and staff specialists, HRM professionals are performers within larger strategic systems (suprasystems and subsystems) which are created by top managers. The primary responsibility for performance variation within these systems belongs to top managers who own the critical systems of the organization.

Human resource professionals have largely failed to have strategic and systemic focus in their specialized activities because top managers have failed to articulate strategy, to manage strategic systems, and to consider the HR impacts of strategic decisions. Top managers have failed to lead their organizations to the appropriate human resource agenda. Top managers are ultimately responsible for developing strategic resources. HRM professionals have been misguided and ill equipped for the task of providing the strategic human capabilities for the organization because of the failures of top managers. HRM professionals are not to be fully excused, however. They should also assume personal responsibility and initiate action to ensure that their specialized activities contribute directly to the development of strategic capabilities.

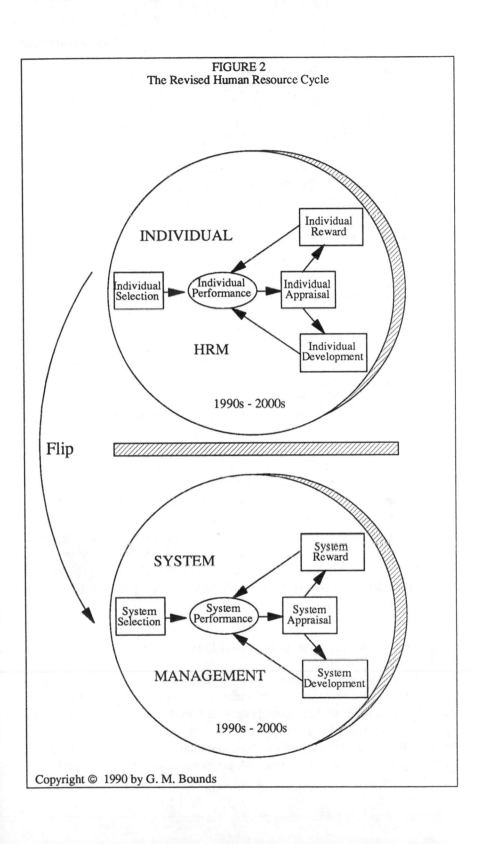

FIGURE 2
The Revised Human Resource Cycle

INDIVIDUAL

Individual
Reward

Individual
Selection

Individual
Performance

Individual
Appraisal

HRM

Individual
Development

1990s - 2000s

Flip

SYSTEM

System
Reward

System
Selection

System
Performance

System
Appraisal

MANAGEMENT

System
Development

1990s - 2000s

THE OTHER SIDE OF THE HRM COIN

The traditional approach to HRM has assumed that jobs and individuals are the appropriate unit of analysis and object of action for the HRM activities of selection, appraisal, reward, and development. The focus on individual performance not only assumes individual control over job performance variation, but it also ignores the impact of systems on individual performance. This focus also reflects a reductionist management approach that assumes that aggregated individual performances ensure overall system performance.

The other side of the performance coin bears the image of organizational systems (see Figure 2).

Different Assumptions

The role activity and role performance of individuals within an organization are intimately intertwined with the broader systems of the organization. An individual's performance is impacted by the methods, rules, materials, technologies, equipment, and other constraints or facilitators provided by the larger system of which an individual is only a part. Individual performance also depends on the timing and consistency of the work execution of other individuals within the system. Thus, individual performance reflects the system performance of a larger team. Conversely, system performance reflects individual contributions and the synergistic and interactive effects of team contributions.

To extend the analogy initiated above, on one side of the coin lies the individual model and on the other lies the system model (as shown in Figure 2). Individuals are selected, their performance is observed and appraised, and they are rewarded and developed. Similarly, strategic systems are created or identified, their performance is observed and appraised, the systems are developed, and the teams of system owners and individual team members are rewarded.

The Blurred Image: System or Individual?

It seems possible conceptually to separate the job/individual performance from the team/system performance, and to consider and examine each, one at a time. In an ongoing organization, however, these two faces of the same coin are hard to separate and examine individually. It is as if the coin has been flipped, and the images on each side of the coin blur and blend together. In a dynamic operating organization, like the flipped coin, we may look closely to discern one image, but the other image remains apparent and cannot be ignored.

The blurring of the images of individuals and systems means that human resource management will be ineffectual without strategic systems management. Just as the coin provides its owner no expendable currency unless it has two sides, a viable and competitive organization must manage individual human resources in conjunction with the management of systems. This statement applies not only to the strategic systems of producing goods and services, but also to the managerial and social systems that encourage the appropriate individual behaviors and contributions to systems.

The Importance of Aligned Roles

Individual learning and development should go hand in hand with organizational learning and development. The "role" of individuals represents the axis around which these two domains of the "flipped HRM coin" spin. "Role" is defined as the summation of the requirements, the set of activities or expected behaviors, associated with a position in an organization. The "role" of individuals represents the conceptual and practical pivot to integrate these two domains. The prescribed "role" of leaders and managers defines the learning and developmental needs of these human resources. For example, managing for incremental improvement of organizational systems through the study and understanding of variation in systems means that managers must develop skills for, and learn about, studying variation through statistical methods.

The prescribed "role" of managers must also be consistent with the social mechanisms and management systems of the organization, which demand and support the execution of that prescribed role. For example, the leaders of organizations formally and informally send messages to subordinate managers. Ideally, the leaders should convey that their role is to continuously improve the systems of the organization for customer value. They do so by role modeling, coaching, the questions they ask in progress reporting meetings, and the appreciation and reward systems they create.

Both sides of the organizational coin must be managed. Systems for production of goods and services cannot increasingly provide customer value without the human resources to create, innovate, improve, maintain, and execute them. Individuals will not likely fulfill these roles for determining and providing customer value unless they have the appropriate human resources for doing so, for example, appropriate skills, knowledge, abilities, aptitudes, and attitudes. Attempts to make an organization more

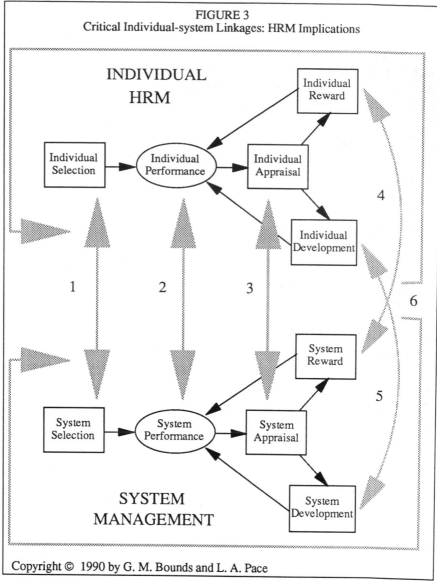

FIGURE 3
Critical Individual-system Linkages: HRM Implications

competitive will fail if managers choose to operate on only one side of the coin, either on the organizational side, for example, through structural modifications, which amount to shuffling the chairs on the *Titanic*, or on the individual side, for example, through massive dosages of individual training that amount to feeding and conditioning a mare for a race with Richard Petty in his race car.

The critical linkages between the individual and system sides of the HRM coin must be managed to ensure competitive capability (see Figure 3). HR managers and the HRM subsystem of the organization must ensure these linkages. These linkages suggest that (1) individual selection criteria must match system improvement criteria, (2) individual performance must be integrated with system performance, (3) individual performance appraisal must be tied to system performance appraisal, (4) individual reward must be linked to system performance, (5) individuals must be developed to practice system improvement, and (6) results of executing these cycles should be linked to renewing of these cycles for continuous improvement.

Failure to recognize these linkages can cause strategic deficiencies and diminish organizational competitiveness. For example, consider the incongruity inherent in the reward practices of a subsidiary of a major corporation. This organization continued paying executives handsome dividends while the organization suffered general decline on several measures, for example, market share, customer satisfaction, quality measures, costs, and delivery schedules.

The basic HRM elements shown in the models in Figures 1, 2, and 3 are used to organize the presentation of these issues. These basic elements include selection, performance, appraisal, development, and reward.

HRM ELEMENTS FOR COMPETITIVE CAPABILITY

Selection

Selection must be a part of human resource management for any organization that envisions a prosperous long-term future. The strategic systems of an organization are improved, standardized, maintained, and operated by the human resources that are vital inputs to these systems. Managerial leaders cannot rely solely on the training and education of existing employees to fill the future managerial ranks. By natural attrition, the ranks of current managers will shrink. People retire, quit, transfer, and leave the organization in other ways. Leaders must ensure an adequate supply of qualified and capable managers. One means is through selection. There are individual differences in capabilities and aptitudes, and these differences are important to individual and system performance. To take advantage of these differences, selection should not be done randomly. Managerial leaders should seek to identify and acquire the best available incoming human resources.

Define the Criteria: What Does "Best" Mean? The greatest challenge to human resource managers is to define "best" and to "measure" the available human resources on these measurable criteria. In the past, it has been important, and probably will continue to be important, for managers to have general education and experience, with some specialty focus. Specialization usually ensures that an individual gets experience in mastering a body of thought at a very deep level. The specialist's knowledge and thinking processes should be pushed toward the cutting edge of the discipline. In receiving education as a specialist in a given field of study, ideally the person practices thinking abstractly and concretely in this domain of specialty. The skills of learning and thinking should transfer to other domains of knowledge.

Too much specialization, however, can breed narrowmindedness and inflexibility, and can interfere with knowledge growth and performance as a manager of system improvement. Managers from various functional disciplines tend to define a situation in terms of their own specialized language and to see the problems narrowly from their limited perspective.

Consider a simple example. Diesel fumes were drifting into a warehouse from trucks being warmed up nearby. Warehouse employees were becoming nauseated, and the work area had to be evacuated several times. Engineering proposed the installation of exhaust fans to remove the fumes. Maintenance proposed the construction of a wall to block off the loading bays. While either solution would have worked, both were expensive. A group of hourly employees met and recommended that the truck drivers come in a half-hour early and move the trucks before work started in the warehouse. Their unspecialized solution was not elegant, but it was inexpensive, and it worked too!

Specialization is useful, but, specialists must be able to broaden their knowledge, with their specialization serving as a base for acquiring new knowledge and skills. In some managerial jobs broad and basic education in engineering, chemistry, physics, mathematics, biology, and other sciences will be important assets. Simply educating and training functional specialists or technicians in management, managerial skills, and activities may not be adequate for some managerial jobs. Successful managers will be those who have learned how to learn and adapt to changing demands. They will continue to acquire knowledge in various technical and managerial areas.

The nature of managerial jobs and job design discussed in other chapters suggests some of the criteria on which available human resources might be judged. The personal characteristics and attributes suggested below reflect the opinions, past experiences, and research of these authors and others who have studied the selection of managers. These criteria provide a starting list for HR managers, but they should be confirmed as valid or invalid by each organization. These personal characteristics include:

creativity, perseverance, tolerance for ambiguity, intelligence, flexibility, a nondogmatic personality open to change, self-efficacy, self-confidence, respect for humanity, interpersonal and social skill for leading, following, and collaborating in teams, quantitative ability, ability to think abstractly, symbolic thinking (representation and interpretation), listening skills, and a balance of individualism and team orientation.

Managers will be increasingly required to think abstractly and to deal with multiple levels of analysis. They will be required to think in terms of intangibles, through abstract and symbolic means, and yet to translate those thoughts into tangible and practical solutions. They will have to think in unprogrammed ways. Use of simple heuristics and formulas will not be sufficient. Specific technical knowledge has rapidly become obsolete. Thus, the most suitable candidates for system manager positions will be those who have learned how to learn and adapt rather than those who have only become technically proficient in a limited area.

How to Assess. Human resource managers are challenged to find reliable and valid ways of measuring these attributes and other attributes that are related to performance as a manager. Traditional paper and pencil tests are not adequate, and neither is any other single method. HRM specialists must discover and create diverse means of measuring these attributes.

Multiple methods help to get a picture of the individuals as complete and unbiased as possible. These methods might include application forms, reference checks, biographical data, interviews, cognitive ability tests, skills tests, personality assessment, peer assessment, subordinate assessment, and behavioral assessment through work sampling, simulation, business games, and group exercises. An example of an innovative selection process is a peer screening for auditor and investigator positions in the Inspector General's Office of the Tennessee Valley Authority. Internal candidates and external applicants for these positions were interviewed by their potential co-workers, who then made recommendations to management. Interestingly, the job incumbents assisted their managers in developing both the criteria and the screening process itself.

Screening and selection of human resources, though important HR activities, only provide raw inputs to the organization. These resources must be further developed and improved to sustain and ensure competitive capabilities over time.

Performance

Performance must be more broadly conceived than in the traditional model. The traditional model focuses on the individual performance in a job. By contrast, more focus should be on team performance in the processes or systems of which the individual is only a part. HRM models must consider individuals/jobs and teams/systems. Some companies are starting to make changes in the way they think about individual performance. For example, in a new plant startup, with which the authors are familiar, an automotive radiator manufacturing organization weighted 80 percent of the individual's performance appraisal toward team contribution and only 20 percent to individual contribution.

Individual performance within a team may be seen as consisting of at least three dimensions: (1) independent contribution directly to the system outcomes, (2) contribution to team efforts by demanding, helping, and supporting other team members to contribute directly, and (3) synergistic and interactive effects of individual members working as a team. Although these three dimensions of performance can be conceptually identified, separating and measuring these dimensions and their effects in actual practice promises to be a formidable task.

Appraisal

Traditional performance appraisal systems tend to rely on an appraisal system, with unilateral flow of information from a single source, wherein the immediate superior passes judgment and informs the subordinate. By contrast, in organizations driven by continuous improvement of systems, managers emphasize appraisal as a means of system improvement to address both sides of the performance coin. Such appraisal will emphasize individual and team performance. In this section, we discuss the weaknesses of traditional appraisal systems and suggest alternatives.

The Split Roles of the Appraiser. Traditionally, performance appraisals have had an evaluative flavor because of the direct connection to individual merit rewards and bonuses and promotion decisions. This evaluative emphasis gets in the way of the important component of human resource development. Figure 1 implies that the appraiser plays dual roles in executing HRM activities (Meyer, Kay, and French, 1964). The first role is that of judge, in determining those worthy of reward and providing a written justification for salary actions. The second role is that of counselor, in determining who needs what type of development in order to improve performance.

Although there may be some exceptions, the split roles of counselor and judge appear to be incompatible. For example, salary discussion may so dominate the annual performance appraisal that neither the boss nor the subordinate is in the frame of mind to make constructive suggestions or to determine developmental needs. Both parties may become defensive, and the discussion may result in argument focused on salary discussion. Most of the boss's attention and thoughts are centered on justifying the action taken. Concerned about excusing or defending his or her performance, the subordinate may fail to hear any constructive comments that might come forth. The result is that both parties are made uncomfortable, or angry, and the discussion has little effect on future performance.

When performance is considered superior, perhaps there will be no problem with split roles for the appraiser. However, given the natural variability of performance over time, most people will be considered either subpar, average, or less than superior at some time in their working career. At any point in time, within an organization that forces distributions of appraisals or otherwise appraises only a fraction of their employees as superior, the appraiser plays the dual role of counselor and judge for that segment of the employees judged less than superior. Within many organizations, this means that appraisers are not fulfilling their role as developers for the vast majority of employees, because of the incompatibility with their role as judge. Failure to develop human resources means waste in valuable human potential and possible deficiency in strategic capabilities.

Systems Ignored. We question the reductionist assumption that traditional performance appraisal for evaluative purposes and individual merit decisions represents a necessary component of HRM. Simple reliance on this approach does not fit a systems approach to management for continuous improvement. In any approach to management, it remains unknown whether bosses have the ability to (1) accurately appraise each individual's performance, (2) separate individual effects from system effects on performance, and (3) reward fairly based on the prior two judgments.

Rather than being a necessary component of HRM, perhaps the traditional performance appraisal of individuals is largely destructive and a hindrance to continuous improvement. Evaluative and judgmental appraisals tend to reduce constructive participation by the individual being assessed. Nonparticipation hinders continuous improvement, because individuals offer a unique perspective not only on their own developmental needs but also on the need for system development and improvement. Such suggestions for system improvement, and the identification of constraints and recurrent nuisances, are regarded as excuse making in traditional performance appraisals. Appraisals should provide a basis for system improvement as well as individual improvement. If the boss plays primarily the role of judge, then he or she may squander the opportunity for system improvement.

Individual Well-Being Jeopardized. An individual tends to have a more positive view of himself or herself than do others of the individual. Negative appraisals from others disconfirm this positive individual self-perception. In cases where individuals are obviously self-deceived and deluded in their self-appraisal, feedback from other perspectives can be helpful and motivational. However, when performance variation results primarily from the vagaries or regular instabilities of larger systems, then negative individual appraisal unnecessarily attacks the individual's self-concept.

Punishing and rewarding individuals on the basis of outcomes over which individuals have no control damages their psychological and physiological health (Davison and Neale, 1982). For example, issuing punishment contingent on outcomes that are not related to the effort or intention of the individual can lead the individual to learn to be helpless. The individual learns that his or her actions are ineffectual and that he or she has no control over the consequences. An individual in such an uncontrollable situation can experience high stress and may eventually lose the ability and motivation to learn new ways of responding or behaving. Once resigned to the "fact" that they have no control, such people may become listless or develop what superiors might call "an attitude problem."

Unfortunately, the traditional individualist, reductionist approach to HRM can worsen this condition by assigning responsibility for failure to the individual who works within the system. Research on learned helplessness and depression indicates that attributing failure to one's self and internalizing the blame can contribute to lowered self-esteem. The people who suffer the most from lowered self-esteem are those who internalize failure and attribute failure to their own personal and stable characteristics, rather than to external factors, such as organizational systems. Traditional HRM activities formally assist the individual in making these internal attributions and distract individual and managerial attention from conditions outside the individual, that is, organizational systems.

Not only can this lack of control cause individuals to be neurotic, depressed, withdrawn, indifferent, or apathetic victims of a larger systemic force; it can also make them physically sick. Recent studies dispel the myth that executives tend to have more cases of heart disease, ulcers, and other stress-related disorders. Rather, blue-collar and middle to lower level managers tend to suffer more stress on the job and, correspondingly, to develop more stress-related disorders. We might infer that some executives create stress for others through inattention and mismanagement of the organizational systems which subordinates must tolerate and attempt to operate.

The effects of punishing people based on largely uncontrollable outcomes and random variation clearly can have undesirable consequences. The destruction of individual self-esteem and self-confidence is particularly disturbing when leaders are pressed by competition to further develop strategic capabilities. Self-esteem and self-confidence form the basis for continuous learning, personal improvement, and effective interpersonal relations.

Attitudes Are Damaged. People should be allowed to think of themselves as conscientious, competent, and committed, if they are indeed so. Unfortunately, individual attitudes can inadvertently be soured because of managerial inability to differentiate system and individual contribution to performance.

Individual attitudes can also be damaged because of stupid or unnecessarily rigid management control systems. Consider the ill effects of making rewards contingent on outcomes, the variation of which is largely determined by systems and not individuals. Rewarding an individual for a chance variation, special cause, or unusual event in performance may send confused messages to peers. The individual may be perceived as undeserving. Resentment may build. Teamwork for system objectives may suffer. Maladaptive, competitive, and destructive behavior may result within the organization.

Consider an example of the destructive linkage between appraisal and reward drawn from a Fortune 500 insurance company. An individual performed her particular job duties skillfully and reliably, made innovative improvements in work processes, and contributed to team performance by assisting others and flexibly assuming other duties as needed. Her supervisor regularly complimented her on her superior work output and team spirit. Unfortunately, she received only an average rating on her six-month performance appraisal, which disqualified her for a merit raise. The mixed signals frustrated and confused the employee. The performance review discussion was predictably heated and not very constructive. Not surprisingly, the subsequent attitude and behavior of the subordinate indicated that the appraisal had not "motivated" her to perform better. In confidence, the supervisor later explained to her that she was unable to give her higher than an average rating because that would require a merit raise, which was not provided for in the budget.

Such muddled approaches to management of human resources result in employee frustration and apathy. Readers might use the degree of frustration or the degree of apathy toward the appraisal process as an indicator of whether their organization has a vibrant and meaningful appraisal process.

The individual performance appraisal process often causes more damage to company performance through destruction of self-perception, self-esteem, attitudes, and interpersonal relationships than it does good through motivation in linking individual rewards to individual performance. Management is often caught in a no-win situation in this regard. In one organization, the recipients of bonuses were kept secret. When employees complained that they didn't know who was being rewarded and thus who their role models should be, management relented and published the names of the individuals who had been given bonuses. This led to bitterness, accusations of favoritism, and more complaining because of the perceived inequities of the rewards. Peers are often more aware than superiors of actual individual contributions to system outcomes and team efforts.

The organization that is pursuing continuous improvement and flexible change requires trusting interpersonal relationships, open communications, cooperation, and collaboration in managing and improving organizational systems. The performance of individuals is largely dependent on other individuals, other processes, suppliers, subsequent operations, and larger systems in general. System performance requires interactive contributions from teams and individuals. Performance appraisal should encourage the development of systems and individual and team capabilities for contributing to systems.

Constructive Appraisal. Appraisals should involve constructive participation by assessors and assessees, and not be overloaded with criticisms, defensiveness, self-justifications, and excuses by the involved parties. The word "constructive" does not mean that tough issues, personal deficiencies, and problems are not addressed. Appraisals should involve candid and honest consideration of any issue relevant to performance. Sometimes egos and self-images will have to be confronted to inspire the changes that are needed. The initiation of new modes of management and managerial job definitions advocated in this book will require such reconsideration and self-examination.

Appraisals should involve two-way communication, with feedback on performance of individuals and performance of systems. Feedback should not be limited to annual or semiannual formal appraisals. Coaching and two-way communication should be frequent activities and should focus on the development of individuals, teams, and organizational systems. Managers should overcome the tendency to avoid confronting poor performance, because it can be a valuable source of information for identifying and improving both individual and system deficiencies. Removing the appraisal from a primarily evaluative context should help managers confront poor performance. When managers perceive their job to be system improvement, then appraisal can be viewed as a constructive activity for purposes of development.

The suggestion to remove appraisal from the purely evaluative context can be misinterpreted. We do not suggest that "judgment," that is, rendering a decision, about personal behaviors and contributions should never take place. Judgment is necessary, but a different kind of judgment. The difference is semantically subtle, yet profound in nature. The difference is like that between (1) a magistrate who hears the facts, pronounces guilt or innocence (judges), and renders sentencing, and (2) a counselor who assesses the psychological state, diagnoses (judges) the causes of the problem, and prescribes therapeutic intervention. One deals only with the results and relies on contingent rewards or punishments to deter or encourage future behavior. The other also deals with the underlying causes of the socially unacceptable behavior.

The difference between an evaluative and an improvement approach to appraisal is also analogous to the difference between the traditional approach to quality control through inspection and quality improvement through the statistical study of variation. (See Figure 4 for a list of some differences.) The orientations and attitudes that accompany these two approaches to quality are very different. Although judgment is required in both approaches, the intentions and the effects are very different. Performance appraisal should be more like the statistical approach to continuous improvement rather than the inspection-oriented approach to quality con-

---

FIGURE 4
Different Approaches to Quality

Traditional Quality Control	Statistical Quality Improvement
Inspection oriented	Management oriented
Results oriented	Means oriented
Screens out defects	Builds in quality
Police	Coach
Minimally acceptable	On target
Just within specifications	Reduced variation
Maintains current standards	Continuous improvement

Copyright © 1990 by G. M. Bounds

trol. The inspection-oriented approach spends too much time trying to screen out defects, or subpar performers, that is, individuals not pulling their weight. With this orientation, inspectors miss the opportunities to continuously improve and develop all employees and the systems within which they contribute to customer value.

Multiple Sources of Feedback. Managers know that individuals do make independent contributions to system outcomes and to their team. However, it is difficult to differentiate the independent effects of individual contributions from system outcome measures. Individual contributions are multidimensional and thus difficult for one person, that is, the boss, to judge. Multiple sources are more appropriate for a developmentally focused appraisal.

For behavioral feedback and development, appraisals should be gathered from peers, subordinates, internal and external customers, and superiors (plural). Each of these sources possesses strengths and weaknesses, but the biases in one will be balanced by the others. Multiple perspectives give a more accurate and comprehensive appraisal. In addition, self-feedback and self-appraisal should be used. Individual self-feedback is somewhat automatic in an organization wherein the managers are using statistical methods to monitor and improve their processes and systems.

Observation, monitoring, and data analysis in the application of statistical methods are specifically intended for process improvement and system development. Since the individual manager is responsible for system improvement, the charting of statistical data indirectly reflects the manager's performance in leading the system improvement. Not only do such data reveal individual developmental needs, but more importantly they help identify constraints and problem areas that need repair in broader systems.

Linking the Roles: Counselor and Judge? In some cases, linking the roles of the appraiser as counselor and judge may be beneficial (Prince and Lawler, 1986). For example, in a job where systems have little impact on performance variation and the individual is a consistently poor and seemingly incorrigible performer, linking developmental counseling and evaluative judgment may be a viable solution. In most organizations, these circumstances are infrequent. In addition, the reader should be aware that certain legal constraints require that formal performance appraisal may be necessary, for example, in identifying and weeding out incorrigible employees.

Some individuals, owing to their personal or job history, may only respond to the "heavy-handed" approach. However, these circumstances are the exception rather than the rule. When managers live up to their responsibility to provide their subordinates with systems, methods, equipment, training, development, and direction, the vast majority of subordinates want to perform.

Statistical Appraisal. Managers who deem it necessary to reward individuals for individual performance must consider issues of statistical variation in making reward or punishment decisions. The manager might question (1) whether the individual actually represents a special cause, that is, an outlier in the distribution of individual performers, (2) whether the individual performance represents a significant trend or run, and (3) whether the individual performance represents a consistent pattern over time that is significantly different from that of other individuals, that is, operating at a different average level of performance than others.

Once managers consider the "statistical" performance of the individual, managers must make a secondary and critical decision: To what does the manager attribute the performance? If one individual performs consistently better than the others, does he or she do so because of individual effort, ability, or skill or because of some extraneous factors, such as equipment, supplier and customer cooperation, task difficulty, material availability, or team assistance?

There may be jobs for which only individual appraisal is appropriate for reward and developmental decisions. In general, however, appraisal should have both a job/individual and system/team emphasis, especially for the HR activities of development and reward.

Development

As mentioned above, the development of organizational systems should be part of the human resource management cycle of activities. Systems both constrain and enhance the performance of individuals, and are thus an important part of human performance. Human resource managers must attend to various aspects of system development, such as structure, policies, methods, procedures, and culture.

Resources for Future Leadership. Human resource managers of some companies have decided to select "future leaders" according to a list of criteria that presumably relate to leadership. These HR managers look for the so-called born leaders. Those selected according to these criteria will be put on the "fast track" to leading management positions. These companies put so much emphasis on selection that they may forget their responsibility for developing all human resources. Furthermore, emergent leaders should be sought from among those who are not labeled "fast-trackers." Some people are late developers, and others are simply different in their approach to leadership. These other potential leaders should not be excluded from consideration by an inflexible selection and fast-tracking system.   Once these "diamonds in the rough" are educated, trained, coached, and equipped, they can emerge as valuable assets for the organization.

Selection of "leaders" should not be viewed as a panacea and "quick fix" for organizational problems. Selecting and hiring "leaders" as a means of improving competitive capabilities should not be used as an excuse not to expend the resources needed for developing all human resources. Certainly good input of human resources is needed, and these must be assessed and selected.   But, more importantly, HR managers should develop the human resources once they are acquired.

Management Education. The individual behavioral capabilities of individual managers must be developed. Managerial resources should develop the knowledge, skills, capabilities, understanding, attitudes, and motivation for the jobs outlined in earlier chapters on the managerial leadership model and MAT activities. The classical functions, such as planning, organizing, controlling, commanding, and coordinating, are not adequate descriptors of the skills and abilities that managers must develop to ensure organizational competitiveness.   The classical functions are adequate only within organizations that are administrative in nature.

Administrative organizations are those that require virtually no system change. The task of "managers" is to oversee and administer the existing structures and systems.   Managers are not required to meet changing internal or external customer needs and values. Performance on financially oriented standards of functional and departmental units may adequately represent system performance. The stable environment of an administrative type of organization does not demand flexibility, adaptability, and responsiveness. In terms of the types of managerial activities listed on the MAT, an administrative organization is characterized primarily by routinization, maintenance, and operation.

An organization driven by managerial leadership, with managers appropriately developed, will be fundamentally different from an administrative organization in terms of managerial behaviors. A traditional thinker may be able to observe the behavior of managers in this type of organization and see planning or organizing activities or see any other classical function taking place. But the managerial behavior of these managers will be much more robust than the classical framework describes. The MAT implies the range of managerial activity required of managers in a competitive organization.

The traditional thinker may object and suggest that his or her classical framework is adequate to describe the behavior of managers in this new type of organization.   The traditional thinker may wring and twist the observed behaviors to impose an old and inadequate framework. However, that which gives power to the managerial leadership model would be cast off and disregarded in the wringing and twisting, just like driving a square peg in a round hole results in a disfigured peg.

Many management and HRM texts (see, for example, Koontz and Weihrich, 1988) insist that Henri Fayol's administrative functions and a systems view are compatible. These thinkers then go on to operationalize the managerial functions but leave the systems view as an abstraction. They prescribe the managerial job with their traditional assumptions of hierarchy, managerial privilege, and a fundamental split between thinking work and doing work. In contrast, the current authors (indeed, all the authors in this volume) call the traditional managerial functions into question and operationalize the systems view! This is the unique contribution of this volume, whether one is examining HRM in particular or management in general.

Interpersonal and Social Development. Leaders of management education and development must not only ensure that managers master the prescribed managerial activities for system improvement; they must also develop the interpersonal and social skills needed to execute the tasks. Team capabilities for leadership, interpersonal interaction, collaboration, followership, and synergy must be developed.

Although the nature of the work will be interpersonally and socially demanding, team building, interpersonal skills training, and cultural change are not to be the primary agenda of managerial development. These skills are auxiliary and help execute the managerial job, but they should not be the driving force of management development. The danger is that managers become distracted from their primary task with their focus on the interpersonal dynamics, social facilitation, and cultural confrontation. In one organization people call such managers "process freaks." Focusing on these social issues can keep managers from attending to their primary tasks of improving strategic systems for customer value. The prescribed tasks of improving strategic systems should motivate management development and behavior, and social and interpersonal skills training should be drafted and pulled in as needed.

We have witnessed the change of managerial behavior brought about by strategically focusing managers and engaging them in the prescribed activities of customer value determination and improvement of strategic systems. The inherently multifunctional nature of this work required collaboration by managers from diverse functions and departments. The managerial attention was focused externally on customers and on systems improvement, and not primarily on interpersonal processes and team dynamics. Nevertheless, communications became more open, levels of trust improved dramatically, interpersonal relations improved, and a team-oriented culture emerged as a result. These social improvements were outcomes of the right managerial activities, role execution, and superordinate, strategic thrust for customer value.

No doubt these social improvements will "facilitate" the continued and improved execution of these managerial activities. However, these social improvements were not explicitly the initial thrust of change. If they had been the initial thrust, the interpersonal challenges might have been too threatening for these managers to handle.

Identification and Nurturance of Potential. Development is a critical component of human resource management. As mentioned earlier, organizations will not be able to rely on development over the long term owing to natural attrition and shrinkage of the managerial ranks. They must select and acquire fresh human resources to replenish those lost and to fill voids where resident members are hopelessly deficient in specific skills and abilities. However, neither can organizations rely on selection to make the much needed and rapid transitions in management required to remain competitive in the next few years or the next decade. To a great extent, organizations must be replenished by developing the employees who are currently on board.

Many people are remarkably talented, and unfortunately this talent often goes undeveloped and unnoticed. People have incredible potential, which if developed represents valuable assets for the organization. We have seen the so-called average people on the job, or even the "dregs" of the organization, exhibit wonderful creativity and ingenuity off the job. In their hobbies they may be creative, talented, innovative builders, artisans, and engineers, yet bored, detached, unmotivated "warm bodies" on the job. Those branded as mediocre often represent the untapped potential of the organization. Perhaps these individuals are not formally educated or they did not attend the "right school." They may rise through some ranks and stagnate at some level because of the organization's failure to continue to develop them. This is a waste of human potential and human assets for the organization.

People Must Learn to Learn. The MAT framework, discussed in the previous chapter, suggests the HR needs for the managers of a competitive organization. Change, innovation, and incremental improvement require managers to question the status quo. Existing systems, methods, and practices are not sacred and unchangeable. An essential goal for management development in an organization pursuing continuous improvement is that managers be equipped and inclined to reexamine their basic values and assumptions, capable of self-evaluation and self-improvement. Argyris (1976) has described this capacity as double-loop learning. He states:

A thermostat may be said to be capable of learning when the room temperature goes above or below the point at which it is set and of taking corrective action. We may call this *single-loop learning*. The thermostat, however, is not able to ask itself the question of whether it should be set at 68 degrees, or if it should be measuring the temperature, or if there are better ways to measure the temperature. To do so would be to question its design and its purpose and would indicate the capacity for *double-loop learning*. (p. 638)

To design and implement new structures and forms and methods not constrained by the status quo, managers must be able to reexamine and reconfigure their values and assumptions about organization and management. Organizational cultural change, discussed in Chapter 15 by Yorks and Bounds, requires that managers question their basic assumptions about management.

Such cultural change through reconsideration and change of basic assumptions, values, and behaviors may be more difficult than one might at first anticipate. People may not only be incapable of double-loop learning, but they may be unaware of this inability. Becoming aware of this unawareness is a primary step to initiate the learning and change process. However, such learned awareness can be threatening and may actually inhibit further learning. Furthermore, the theories that people use to design and execute their actions impede the change process. The theories that people espouse, which may sound something like, "If you want to motivate so and so under such and such conditions with such and such consequences, then behave in the following way," are typically different from the theories according to which they actually behave. People are blind to the fact that they do not behave according to their espoused theories because most of us are not programmed to reflect on our behavior and its impact. People are also programmed not to tell others when they behave inconsistently with their espoused theories.

The consequences of the typical behavioral strategies used by people are that their world tends to be more defensive and less open; they can, at best, engage in single-loop learning. Their problem solving tends to be ineffective for the difficult and threatening issues central to their behavioral strategies, and they are unable to engage in experimentation and learning about the continuous learning process. These people tend not to engage in learning that questions the status quo of ideas, approaches, policies, methods, systems, and relationships, and they tend to attempt to control others unilaterally, and to fear confrontation. Such "defensive routines" serve to maintain the status quo; they must be brought into awareness and challenged, then changed where necessary (Argyris, 1976).

The implications for managerial education are that simply educating at the level of espoused theories will not be adequate for organizations attempting continuous improvement. Most managerial education tends to be the one-way dissemination of knowledge or skills during a training program. Educators may falsely assume that the knowledge will automatically be translated into managerial action on the job without followup activities to demand and support behavior change. Typically, no attempt is made to address the continuous learning process and to establish a means of continued learning in the behavioral setting, that is, the organization, after formal instruction is completed. This lack of continuity results in the "vanishing training phenomenon."

Managers must question and be questioned about the consistency of espoused theories with the theories they actually use. Managers must reconsider basic assumptions about management and their business. Furthermore, given the continuous changing nature of organizations and the flexibility required of them, managers should be equipped for continued learning. Educational programs should provide managers a learning process for continuous development of knowledge and self-teaching. Managers must learn how to learn.

Clearly, continuous learning requires more than simply imparting knowledge or skills to an individual. Individual managers should have the opportunity to practice acquired skills in a job setting that provides feedback and coaching to improve the skills. Role modeling and mentoring will be a necessary component for on-the-job learning and continued development of managers. Feedback, from multiple sources such as the mentor, peers, subordinates, and objective organizational outcomes, provides knowledge of the results of one's actions. This knowledge facilitates the learning process, especially when accompanied by an experienced and knowledgeable coach who assists with advice for improvement.

The implications for leaders are clear. Leaders must be masters and role models of that which they expect from others. Leadership by example teaches subordinates both what to do and how to do it. Managerial leaders should be very careful what they teach subordinates to do by their own actions. This challenge to managerial leaders can be quite threatening. Many leaders are not willing to endure the initial floundering and uncertainty involved in learning new knowledge and skills or questioning old assumptions and practices. It is quite natural to fear being perceived as incompetent, unassured, and imperfect. Successful leaders are more inclined to stick with what has brought them success, to do what they know rather than to learn something new. Leaders must take these risks ultimately to improve themselves and others around them.

Meta-Improvement. Human resource managers should extend the previously mentioned notion of "learning to learn" to their own jobs as HR managers. This means that human resource managers, including leaders, line managers, specialists, and professionals, must improve the means of improvement. The "means of improvement" referred to here include the behavioral activities and processes used to do continuous improvement. This "meta-improvement" job of human resource managers may be summed up as that of continuously learning, improving, standardizing, maintaining, and executing the tasks for competitive improvement prescribed elsewhere in this book.

These prescriptions include the value determination cycle of the managerial leadership model, the systems improvement cycle for system and subsystem managers, and the operator activity management cycle. These cycles of activity, without the detailed activities listed, can be seen in the circles located in the lower portion of Figure 5. These various cycles of activities have been prescribed elsewhere in this volume for the respective types of employees. Thus, the developmental needs of each of these employee groups can be differentiated in terms of these prescribed behavioral activities. HR managers should pursue the implementation and improvement of these models as a part of their managerial agenda.

This meta-improvement task can be graphically depicted in terms of the MAT. The two-dimensional MAT for meta-improvement is shown in Figure 5. This MAT suggests that: (1) these models and cycles of activity must be continuously improved, through creation, innovation, and incremental improvement, (2) these behaviors must also be standardized and routinized as part of regular managerial activity, and (3) these cycles of activities should also be maintained and executed regularly and consistently for continuous improvement and stable performance in the creation of value for customers. Three-dimensional MATs could be drawn, similar to those in the previous chapter, for managerial leaders, middle managers, and operators, to depict their relative activity intensity for each of these meta-improvement activities.

Rewards

Rewards are often spoken of as if magical powers are associated with them. Some people opposed to the use of rewards regard them as the root of all evil, whereas some of those who favor their use regard them as a panacea. The truth lies somewhere in between these two extremes. The danger of rewards derives from their power to influence behavior. The wrong behavior might be encouraged, while the right behavior gets ignored. Reward systems must be appropriately designed, consistent with

FIGURE 5
The MAT for Meta-Improvement[*]

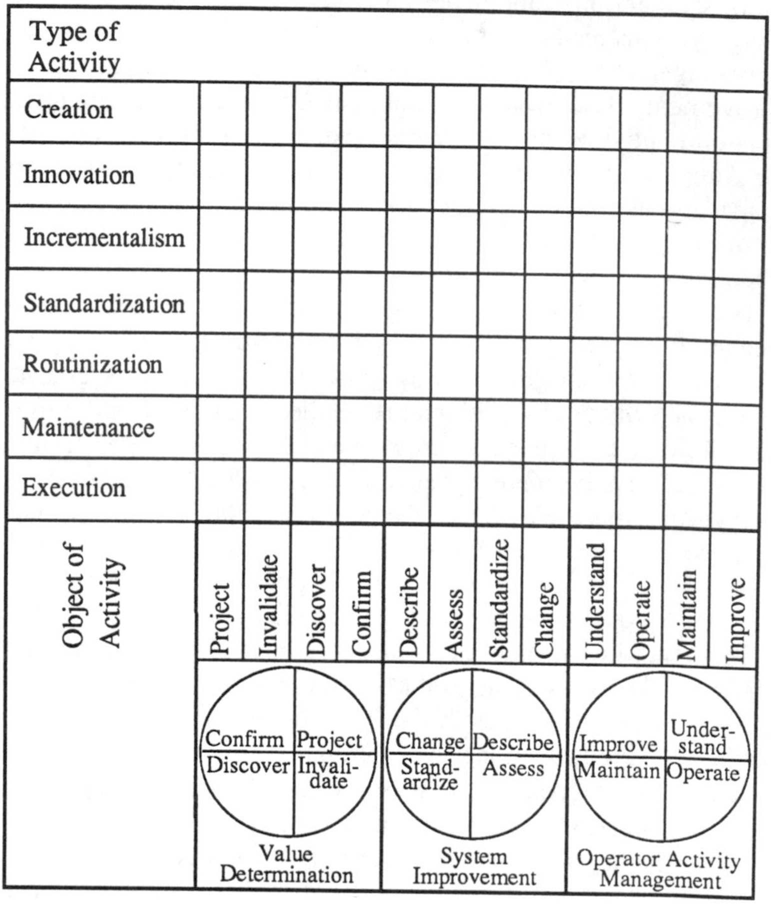

Type of Activity												
Creation												
Innovation												
Incrementalism												
Standardization												
Routinization												
Maintenance												
Execution												
Object of Activity	Project	Invalidate	Discover	Confirm	Describe	Assess	Standardize	Change	Understand	Operate	Maintain	Improve

Value Determination: Confirm, Project, Discover, Invalidate

System Improvement: Change, Describe, Standardize, Assess

Operator Activity Management: Improve, Understand, Maintain, Operate

*We thank Harlan Carothers for his contribution to this particular application of the MAT.

managerial strategy and tactics for customer value and systems improvement.

Individually Contingent. Rewards have traditionally been distributed in a supposedly individually contingent manner. This means rewards are given out to individuals on the basis of individual merit or judged individual performance. One might question whether rewards should be contingent at all. Contingent rewards have their problems; for example, a rewarded outcome tends to be maximized. Maximizing an outcome, such as the production of assembled units when no assembled units are demanded by customers, can result in all kinds of problems, such as excess inventory costs and misallocation of resources. The danger in using contingent rewards is that it is difficult to define and structure a reward system on individual/job specific bases which is consistent with overall system performance.

The positive aspect of contingent rewards is their consistency with our societal norm that the individuals who contribute to the organization deserve a share in the benefits. Ideas about motivation, equity, and fairness suggest that "more effort" should be rewarded more than "less effort," and "greater contribution" should be rewarded more than "less contribution." Unfortunately, when rewards are administered to individuals, competition between individuals for the limited rewards may result, rather than the collaboration crucial for system performance.

Team Rewards. The challenge to HR managers is to design a reward system that takes advantage of the potentially motivational effects of rewards, satisfies norms for equity, and encourages collaboration for system and organizational objectives. HR managers must remember both sides of the performance coin.

We maintain that if rewards are to be contingent, then the application of team rewards for system performance would be most preferable. Furthermore, system performance should be defined in terms of customer value contributions. Team rewards promote collaboration to make the pie bigger for everyone, rather than competition to see who gets the biggest slice. As an illustration of the potential problems with individually oriented reward systems, consider the following example. A middle manager in an accounts payable unit within a larger industrial organization created a self-managing work group of accounting clerks. These clerks worked without direct supervision, negotiating with their "system" manager for support, performance objectives related to customer value, and organizational resources. Quality, schedule performance, and volume of production increased dramatically, while costs plummeted. Customer satisfaction reached new high levels, and morale improved substantially among the group members.

Attempting to reward and recognize the group, the system manager approached his HR representative and asked that the group be promoted as a group. The HR system had no mechanism to do this, and HR concluded that, although each individual could theoretically receive a one-grade promotion, such a practice would violate prescribed promotional quotas. The manager's request was outside of the "arc of the possible" as defined by the current system. Sadly, the team was disbanded because their activities did not fit within the organization's current job design, performance appraisal, and reward systems, and the manager was reassigned.

The results of team efforts in system performance are what customers see in system outputs of products and services. Since the system members interdependently and synergistically produce system outcomes, all members should share in the rewards for system performance. The rewards should be distributed in an equitable manner, without singling out superstars for disproportionate shares of the rewards, unless the team perceives such distribution to be equitable. Reward of superstars may not reflect all the support and collaboration which the apparent superstar received from other system participants. Resentment may mount, and support and collaboration may not be there in the next quarter.

Note that the word "equitable" does not mean equal. It means "perceived as fair" or "justified." Thus, members of a team may be rewarded unequally, yet equitably. Consider the following examples. Executives typically receive higher proportions of rewards from organizational profits; sometimes such a distribution is seen by lower ranks as equitable, but sometimes not. System managers may be regarded as more deserving because of their extraordinary responsibility and contribution to team performance leveraged through system improvement. Often the disproportionate reward of a consistent superstar is seen as fair by team members. Reward of sporadic performers, for example, this month's shining light, is often considered unfair, perhaps because their light shines at the expense of the team, sometimes even through clandestine and unscrupulous individual action.

Consider an example. A plant manager in a fabrication facility was rewarded with a raise and a promotion because he improved the plant's bottom-line performance with regard to its expense budget. However, closer inspection revealed that his success was based on the cancellation of preventive maintenance on the plant's machinery. By the time the neglected machines began to break down, the first manager was a vice-president in another company, leaving his successor literally to pick up the pieces.

Failure to adopt a system view in rewards can have serious long-term consequences. A purchasing agent was given special recognition because he saved the company thousands of dollars by purchasing a less expensive pneumatic torque wrench for use in the assembly plant. Approximately eighteen months later, the medical department noted an increased incidence in tendonitis among the assembly workers. This condition was ultimately traced back to the cheaper, but unfortunately less well-designed, hand gun. In addition to the unmeasured human suffering and ill will, the increased medical claims more than outweighed the dollar savings from buying a cheaper tool.

In most cases, individuals should be rewarded on the basis of the performance of the system or organization of which the individual is a part. The traditional cultural assumption that individual performance simply adds up to team performance (in aggregate) underlies the practice of rewarding individuals for individual performance. In this individualist approach, individuals pursue individual objectives, and team or system outcomes are merely incidental. By contrast, rewarding individuals based on team performance requires different cultural assumptions.

The critical assumptions for teamwork are (1) the individual performance means little without team performance, and (2) individuals should merit reward only through team performance. This cultural value of individual reward through team accomplishment encourages mutual assistance and development among team members. The interactive and synergistic effects of collaboration among managers from different functional areas should result in higher system performance than the simple individualistic and myopic pursuit of local objectives.

The top managers in charge of strategic systems should work as a team. The infighting and competitions typical among functional managers in a hierarchy or project managers in a matrix structure must not occur among system managers. The unit of analysis that serves as the basis for reward must be raised to the level necessary to obtain collaboration for superordinate objectives. This principle should apply at all levels of the organization. If collaboration is required among shifts, then shift managers should not be rewarded simply on shift performance.

If collaboration is required between marketing, design engineering, and manufacturing in new product introduction, then these functional managers should not be rewarded simply on functional performance. Timely release of "technically correct" designs may be the functional criteria for engineers. Such criteria may encourage engineers to hand off blueprints to production, while the designs may turn out to be faulty from the perspective of the production people, that is, too difficult or expensive to implement. A better system might require concurrent engineering, simultaneously designing both the product and the process, with multidisciplinary team participation, and early and frequent contact with suppliers. Within this system engineers would gauge their performance on indicators expanded to include more of the product's life cycle.

Consider another example. Managers of a concrete block manufacturing plant decided to introduce some "healthy competition" between shifts by establishing a contest to see which shift could outproduce the other. Neither shift foreman would shut the equipment down for preventive maintenance. Ultimately, the entire plant had to be closed for costly repairs. Yet management had gotten exactly what it paid for!

Encourage Effort. During initial efforts to change managerial behavior, effort and behavioral progress should be rewarded, even when system outputs have not yet changed. Some companies are rewarding individuals for development of multiple skills and continuous learning. Output change will lag behind such learning and behavioral change. Behavior change must precede system performance change. Leaders should not wait too long to reward behavior change, lest the manager become impatient or feel that change is not appreciated.

Reward Consistent with Strategy. When people think of rewards, the notions of contingencies, merit pay, and bonuses quickly come to mind. However, you should also think of the standard package of salary and fringe benefits as rewards. Furthermore, an organization's salary structures should encourage the acquisition, development, and use of human resources in a way consistent with the strategy to compete.

For example, many organizations are ceasing to treat manufacturing as a second-class activity, since managerial leaders are seeing manufacturing as a weapon for competing. In past decades, factory and operations jobs have commanded neither the glamor, status, upward mobility, nor the money of jobs in other areas, such as finance, marketing, and design. Furthermore, dollars have flowed more freely for research in product design and improvement than for process design and improvement. In order for manufacturing to attract and retain the best and brightest minds, the inducements must be in place for individuals to make that career decision. Only then can operations compete for the best human assets, which are needed to continuously improve the process of how things are made. People who prefer to do so should not have to make personal sacrifices to pursue a career in an area as strategically important as operations and manufacturing processes.

Rewards Mean More Than Just Money. Rewards should be broader than simple financial rewards that come in the form of salary, bonuses, benefits, and stock options. Intrinsic rewards, personal satisfaction derived individually from the activities of collaboration and team accomplishment, are also important, but these should not be relied on exclusively to sustain desired behavior. Intrinsic rewards may seem like a cheap way to sustain behavior but should not be used as an excuse for not developing an appropriate appreciation system.

Human needs and desires for equity, recognition, appreciation, and social esteem require explicit and tangible managerial attention. Other rewards and appreciations for individuals and teams include promotions, lateral transfers into desirable positions, career opportunities for development, opportunity to learn and develop new skills, positive feedback, enriched jobs, challenging assignments, respect, job security, time off, and acknowledgments from customers. These diverse rewards and appreciations should also be designed for strategic purposes.

CONCLUSION

The responsibility for human resource management to ensure the development of the organization's human assets should not be held exclusively by one or a few people. The responsibility for HRM should fall on the shoulders of several people.

Self: Responsibility for self-development, continuous growth, learning, and self-improvement.

Peers: Peers should develop one another for the mutual benefits that team members can derive through overall system improvement.

Subordinates: An overlooked source of ideas for development may be the subordinates, who have a unique perspective on the developmental needs of their bosses and organizational systems.

Superiors: Top managers, leaders, and line managers should assume the primary responsibility for ensuring that their strategic systems have the best available human resources. Human resources should be regarded as system inputs and should be managed for quality and consistency, just like any other set of inputs or subsystem.

Human resource professionals: HR professionals should be consultants, coproducers, and collaborators with system owners and should not bear the primary responsibility for human resource management. They should learn the needs of the system managers and their subordinates and should create supportive subsystems and provide expert advice and consultation to assist in the development of human resources. HR professionals must view strategic system owners as their internal customers and learn to understand and satisfy their customers' requirements.

HR executives must also assume the important role of managing value-contributing HRM subsystems of selection, appraisal, reward, and development. These value-contributing HRM systems must be strategically linked to the creation of value for external customers and to the management of organizational improvement. Rather than focusing on simply developing and motivating individuals, such value-contributing HRM systems will undoubtedly be focused on developing individuals, teams, and systems for strategic capability.

Human resource management represents a strategic activity that must be purposefully engaged to ensure the human assets and capabilities needed for global competitiveness. Managers and leaders must not be distracted from this critical task by the pressures of daily crises and current operations. Given the continuous change required of organizations, ensuring the development of human resources means a continuous retooling effort by managers. While executing the business of today, managers must prepare for the business of tomorrow. Just like the commuter on the beltline around

Washington, D.C., managers must realize that "the road has to remain open while undergoing repairs and expansion." The transitions may often seem endless, messy, and unbearable, but continuous improvement in human resources must be pursued.

REFERENCES

Argyris, C. "Theories of Action That Inhibit Individual Learning." *American Psychologist*, 31, (1976): 638-654.

Davison, G. C., and J. M. Neale. *Abnormal Psychology*. 3rd ed. New York: John Wiley and Sons, 1982.

Devanna, M. A., C. J. Fombrun, and N. M. Tichy. "A Framework for Strategic Human Resource Management." In C. Fombrum, N. M. Tichy, and M. A. Devanna (eds.), *Strategic Human Resource Management*. New York: John Wiley and Sons, 1984, pp. 33-51.

Koontz, H., and H. Weihrich. *Management*. 9th ed., New York: McGraw-Hill, 1988.

Meyer, H. H., E. Kay, and J. R. P. French, Jr. "Split Roles in Performance Appraisal." *Harvard Business Review*, 43 (1964): 123-129.

Prince, J. B., and E. E. Lawler, III. "Does Salary Discussion Hurt the Developmental Performance Appraisal?" *Organizational Behavior and Human Performance*, 37 (1986): 357-375.

E. APPLICATIONS

CONTINUOUS IMPROVEMENT IN A PROFESSIONAL SERVICES COMPANY, BECHTEL GROUP INC. – ARCHITECT/ENGINEER/CONSTRUCTOR*

WALTER D. LEACH, III
Bechtel Corporation
Gaithersburg Regional Office

SUMMARY

Adapting the *customer value* and *continuous improvement* concepts to a professional services firm, in a formal way, has proven to be a challenging task. While Bechtel Group, Inc., has been engaged in the process of implementing "continuous improvement" for three years, with its share of false starts and blind alley tracing, the Commitment to Continuous Improvement (CCI) initiative has demonstrated measurable results in systems improvement and is now poised to move ahead with greater direction, purpose, and leadership. All the early lessons learned are outlined in many texts on the subject of implementing this new approach to organizational life. As is the case with most human endeavors, we learn best by doing, experiencing both the successes and the mistakes.

*The author wishes to acknowledge the following Bechtel individuals who gave freely of their time and expertise to make this chapter come to life, both from a content and an editorial point of view: S. Close, L. Coyle, W. Kerans, N. Knueppel, M. Neuhauser, M. J. Ozcan, H. Pomrehn, and K. Schultz.

INTRODUCTION

The Bechtel Group of Companies (BGI) is in the business of Architect/Engineer/Constructor (A/E) for industrial and government projects that cover a wide spectrum of capital investment ventures. Customers of BGI range from some of the largest corporations and government/public sector bodies in the world, such as Eurotunnel, Kingdom of Saudi Arabia, Southern California Edison, IBM, Nabisco, NASA, Procter and Gamble, Shell Oil Company, Chevron, Union Carbide, Alyeska Pipeline Company, and Mobil Oil, to such small entrepreneurial companies as are engaged in the development and ownership of independent electric power production facilities.

Warren A. Bechtel founded the company in 1898, working on the development of the railroads in the West. The company grew over the years to participate in such major ventures as the Hoover Dam, the San Francisco-Oakland Bay Bridge, mining ventures all over the world, the building of many of the world's nuclear power plants, the planning and building of Jubail City in Saudi Arabia, the Bay Area Rapid Transit (BART) system, and numerous other major infrastructure projects. This effort is best summed up in Bechtel's mission statement:

> Bechtel provides premier technical and management services to develop, manage, engineer, build, and operate installations and perform other related services to improve the standard of living and quality of life worldwide.

As can be seen from the organization chart for the Bechtel Group of Companies shown in Figure 1, the companies are divided along market/business segment lines for marketing purposes and into regional offices for work performance. This structure allows an optimum flexibility in allocating new projects to the location that offers the best synthesis of resources with customer preference. It also means that one of the critical systems that must function well is the relationship system between regional offices and business lines.

COMMITMENT TO CONTINUOUS IMPROVEMENT

As is the experience with many companies, Bechtel's interest in "the new philosophy" was advanced by

- Pressure from prime customers looking for suppliers with "quality management" initiatives.

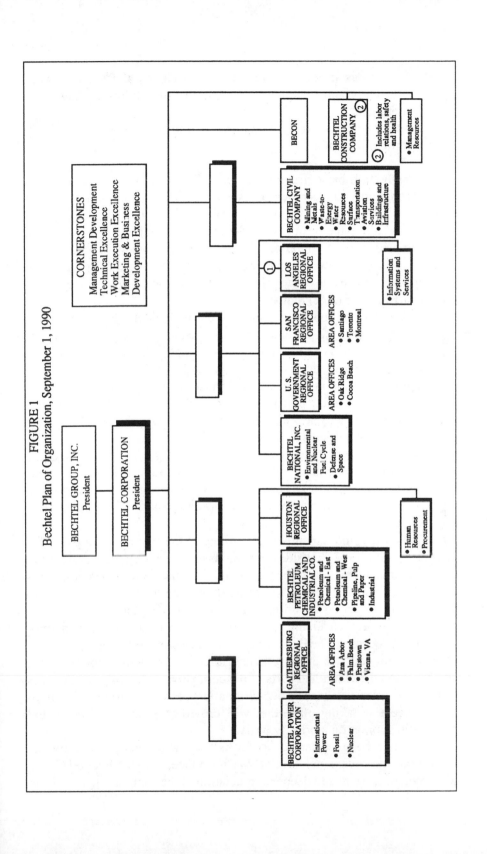

FIGURE 1
Bechtel Plan of Organization, September 1, 1990

- Champions in the company who saw clearly the need to work differently and recognized the logic in the quality management approach.
- An historically strong ethic in Bechtel to be the leader in a highly competitive industry.

Throughout its existence, the owners of Bechtel have taken great pride in their sensitivity to customer needs and their determination to improve continuously the means of producing service deliverables, as a day-to-day way of conducting the business. In the late 1970s and mid-1980s, a more formal or programmatic approach was taken to improve work processes in order to offer customers a more price-competitive service. At that time, price appeared to be one of the primary drivers for selecting services in the Architect/Engineer (A/E) industry.

In late 1987, the top management team of Bechtel's Houston office, representing mainly the petroleum-related business lines, attended one of Dr. Deming's four-day seminars in San Diego. During the seminar, evenings were spent devising strategy and plans to implement the philosophy of continuous improvement in Houston. A formal recognition evolved that, by spending upfront to improve the processes and systems of work delivery, a means now existed to avoid spending the inevitable time and money late in projects to fix errors.

At about the same time, several other large organizations in Bechtel, specifically Controller and Bechtel Power Corporation, were experimenting with the principles of Dr. Deming and other recognized authorities in the field. This effort ultimately led to the initiation of quality management efforts in these particular organizations.

In July 1989, the Executive Committee of the Bechtel Group met for three days with several outside consultants to gain a deeper understanding of quality management and the potential for application to the company's operations. Followup sessions were held over the next several months to identify and concur on the critical processes for BGI senior management to address in their leadership role. Figure 2 presents a graphic display of the chosen processes. The Executive Committee conceived these processes to provide direction for improvement efforts of all systems throughout the company. As the individual parts of the company, such as regional offices or business lines, select their own critical processes or systems, an alignment process is taking place that will provide top-down direction and bottom-up support on a priority basis.

What has been presented so far is the broad picture of how the continuous improvement initiative was introduced into the Bechtel Group of Companies. To have a deeper appreciation of the challenge to transform

FIGURE 2
Satisfied Customers

SATISFIED CUSTOMERS

MISSION AND VISION
* Philosophy of   * Goals
  Management   * Values

1. Satisfying Customer Needs

2. Finding and   3. Developing   4. Performing
   defining   opportunity   work
   opportunity   and customers

5. Developing and applying technology

6. Planning and allocating material resources

7. TEAM BUILDING

* Leadership   * Innovation/creativity
* Teamwork   * Communication
        * Employee development

LONG-TERM REWARDS
SATISFIED EMPLOYEES

a company's thinking and culture to that required for long-term customer value satisfaction and continuous improvement of system performance, it will be helpful to examine the development of the Continuous Improvement initiative in Bechtel Power Corporation (BPC).

A SPECIFIC ORGANIZATIONAL APPLICATION

Starting with the same Deming seminar in late 1987, a BPC employee was given the opportunity to test the Deming approach on a large "operating services" project. Operating services is the engineering, construction, and/or other services work for an operating facility that needs periodic maintenance or upgrade to keep it functional. The question in everybody's mind was:

> Can we apply continuous improvement techniques to what we do in the professional services industry? After all, our business is not an assembly line turning out widgets. Every deliverable is different!

The answer, after five months of testing a model of Dr. Deming's methods, was that evidence showed that a continuous improvement effort would provide positive measurable results and should be initiated throughout Bechtel Power Corporation. Some fragmented basic understanding of Dr. Deming's teachings existed throughout the management and employee population, due to an earlier program called Productivity Management Process. However, senior management had made no overt broad strategic commitment to the new philosophy.

As Dr. Deming has suggested so often, Step 1 was to find a knowledgeable consultant to assist the transformation by exposing management to a new way of thinking about its responsibilities and role – that of continuously improving the systems and processes by which work is accomplished, contrasted with the standard approach of setting goals that the organization might not be capable of reaching. The "paradigm" shift needed is the classic one of starting to examine the means and to stop focusing on the ends. This initial task proved to be enlightening as well as fruitful.

The criteria for the consultant choice were the following:

- Find someone who had implemented a continuous improvement effort successfully in industry as a manager.
- Choose an organization with broad insight into many aspects of applying continuous improvement to many different functional areas of the business with the resources to work with those areas.
- Select a consultant with broad knowledge of continuous improvement who was not an ideologue, tied to one "guru." Draw the best from the best.
- Find someone who understood the behavioral and cultural transformation aspects of management as well as process improvement and statistics.

The search effort interviewed five different groups or individuals who met the criteria to varying degrees. The eventual choice possessed an additional essential skill:

- The ability to present the crucial concepts of customer focus and process improvement along with the compelling logic of the competitive situation in such a way that a tough and demanding management team could relate to it, digest it, and develop an action plan.

Skeptics abound in the management arena when organizational change is required, and the successful introduction of this new way of viewing the world was critical to stimulating the process.

Initial acceptance of the new ideas by twenty-six of the top management team of BPC was achieved through a two and a half day seminar conducted by the University of Tennessee in December 1988. There were two major results: (1) basic understanding of the roots of the continuous improvement philosophy and of what is involved in adopting it, and (2) identification of three cross-functional systems considered critical to the success of Bechtel Power Corporation.

The next step was to develop an initial implementation plan for 1989. The basic elements were to train eighty senior managers of BPC and to carry the cross-functional system identification process a step further. The plan was: (1) to educate twelve of the top management team through a one-week executive level training course; (2) to have two forty-person, four-day Bechtel-tailored training sessions to introduce the theory of continuous improvement to Bechtel Power managers and also give them some of the needed tools to begin work on the identified cross-functional systems; and (3) to train eight company-knowledgeable middle managers to be system team facilitators through an intensive three-week course.

The final piece of the early stage of implementation came in May 1989 at a followup session to the December 1988 top management workshop. Besides reviewing progress, the main agenda item was to begin examining the cultural aspects of transforming the organization. These cultural paradigms were already impacting the change effort and were expected to affect future development. Such items as micro-management, short-term results focus, and fear in the organization were introduced and discussed.

It is important to understand BPC's general implementation strategy. The management team agreed on basic principles, such as establishing management ownership of systems, examining critical cross-functional systems, and making continuous improvement a formalized way to do business. Top-down implementation was considered essential if continuous improvement was not to become "the program of the week." Having the critical systems serve as the drivers of front-line process improvements focused attention on the best use of limited resources. Managers constantly demonstrating their use of continuous improvement philosophy and tools provided a real-time model to convince employees of their commitment.

The top-down element of implementation is related to the concept of *management ownership of systems* and *its responsibility to improve continuously those systems under its purview.* Top-down also relates to a "flow-down" view of cross-functional systems that have nested subsystems supporting higher level objectives.

As discovery work has progressed, the deep involvement of senior management in the continuous improvement process, assuming ownership of systems, has shown itself as one of the benefits of the process. It is not effective initially to delegate participation to lower levels, since direct operational knowledge is essential to successful implementation.

One example of a top-level cross-functional system examination that led to a subsystem is the Management of Projects system. Initially seen as a large and complex system, the Management of Projects team used a nominal-group technique to find the most effective starting point for analysis. The system team first selected cost management as a primary subsystem for intense examination and then chose a major project with good historical data to study. Initial task performance results relating final cost to estimated cost, broken down by a Pareto chart, led to the formation of subteams to look at the estimating, scope control, project staffing, and engineering performance aspects of projects under the project manager's control and responsibility. The initial work on this cost management subsystem is continuing into deeper understanding of the processes.

RESULTS

As BGI has progressed in its quest to implement the continuous improvement philosophy, it has achieved a number of successes and has also experienced difficulties that may be of value to other organizations treading similar paths.

SUCCESSES

A Controller's Application

A successful business partnership is often built on letting each partner do what he or she knows best. Add a strong commitment to continuous improvement and the basis is formed for a partnership between Bechtel and a major national bank in Chicago, which now makes supplier and employee expense payments for Bechtel in all of Bechtel's major domestic offices.

Bechtel's aging accounts payable system was in need of replacement. The company had redone its other financial systems in the early 1980s, but an AP renovation was delayed until late 1988 when the time was right for a radically new system.

The logic was simple. The value-added for an accounts payable department is decided by whether to make a payment. Bechtel and the bank jointly created a new system that streamlined and automated the payables from point of initiation through final reconciliation. Bechtel built an on-line payable system and transmits payments daily to the bank in an industry standard (ANSI 820) format. The bank makes the payments as the payee requests – check, direct deposit (ACH), or electronic (EDI). The system design began in October 1988, and the first payment was transmitted the following May.

A major design principle embodied in the new system was the automatic capture of customer-focused data. Each transaction is time-stamped as it moves through the system from receipt, to approval, to payment. This allows disbursement representatives to maintain control charts for length of time to make payments and to pinpoint out-of-control conditions.

The bank is known for its tireless pursuit of quality. During the summer of 1990, a continuous improvement (CI) team was formed between the bank and Bechtel to improve the payment process even more. The initial sessions led the team to decide on the quality characteristics and the relevant data from their systems to use in monitoring progress. Since then, the team "meets" monthly via videoconference between San Francisco and Chicago to review current charts and supplier requests, and to discuss improvement opportunities. The time between data transmission and acknowledgment (the official "OK to pay") continues to be reduced. The operational data prove to team members and management of both entities that the payment process keeps improving, and the "face to face" contact of videoconferencing enhances teamwork.

An Engineering Application

Calcbusters. The Calcbusters Team was formed to improve the engineering calculation work process. It used the collection and analysis of data along with the knowledge and experience of the team members who normally work within the calculation work process.

The desire to improve the calculations was prompted by the customer's concern with "inattention to detail." Calculation errors identified in prior internal and external audits, technical reviews, and surveillance over the past ten years were collected in order to confirm that this was really a valid concern. Of the total 364 calculations reviewed, 35 percent had some type of error. Based on the Pareto technique shown in Figure 3, it was discovered that 79 percent of all errors fell into four of the sixteen specific error categories or types. These four categories were technical bases, administrative omissions, technically incomplete, and grammatical. Grammatical concerns were not pursued since they did not have an adverse impact on the calculation product. However, it was surprising to find the percentage of calculations that had errors and specifically the presence of technical error types. A target was set to improve the rate of errors per calculation by 50 percent.

The analysis of the problem began by flowcharting the calculation work process for each engineering discipline and constructing a cause and effect diagram to discover the root cause or causes of the errors. The flowcharting demonstrated that the work was being performed according to the engineering procedures and that the work process was not redundant or overly complex. This finding was expected. In addition, the root cause analysis seemed to indicate that much of the problem was the result of higher personnel stress from specific root causes such as late turn on of work, expedited or unrealistic schedules, and overcommitment of personnel.

In order to confirm that these root causes were valid, additional facts were gathered. A regression analysis was performed in order to estimate the correlation between calculation error rates and these root causes. Several scatter diagrams were made. For example, one diagram plotted error rate vs. overtime and another diagram plotted error rate vs. workload as measured by plant outages. Again, what was anticipated and what was actually discovered using facts was inconsistent. No correlation between periods of higher personnel stress, such as overtime, and calculation error rates were evident as shown in Figure 4.

Corrective measures were selected based on the remaining valid root causes such as inconsistent reviews and inattention to detail. A calculation guide for the preparer, a checklist to be used primarily by the calculation checker, and a traveler to track error rate performance for several steps of the work process were implemented. The calculation error rate was then measured over several months. The results were excellent. The technical error rate was reduced by 50 percent and the administrative error rate was reduced by 87 percent.

Much was learned about the importance of using facts and focusing on improving value to the customer. Applying the commitment to continuous improvement to all critical work processes will be of great benefit to our customers and our success.

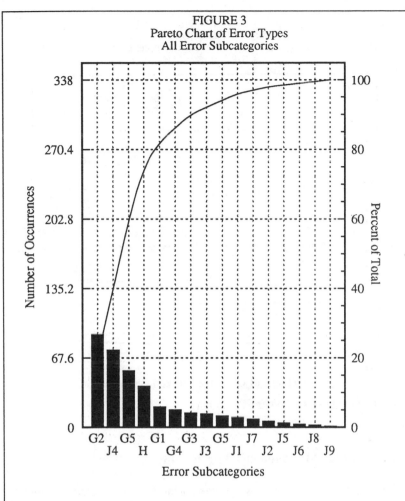

FIGURE 3
Pareto Chart of Error Types
All Error Subcategories

KEY

G - Technical Errors	J - Administrative Errors
G1 - Methodology/Formula	J1 - Pagination
G2 - Bases (Including References)	J2 - Microfilmability
G3 - Numerical Transposition	J3 - Calculation Status
G4 - Arithmetic	J4 - Omissions
G5 - Incomplete	J5 - Incorrect Rev. #/Bars
G6 - Erroneous Conclusion	J6 - Incorrect Date
H - Grammatical Errors	J7 - Incorrect Attachments/Appdx.
	J8 - Incorrect Calc. No.
	J9 - Calc. Missing

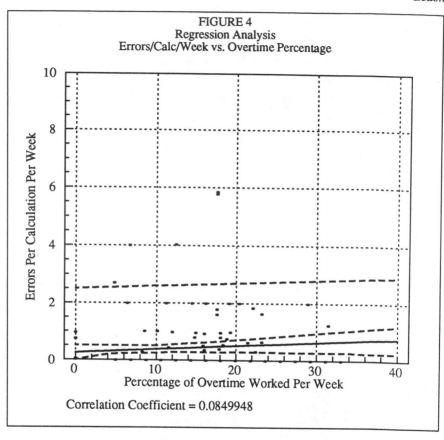

FIGURE 4
Regression Analysis
Errors/Calc/Week vs. Overtime Percentage

Correlation Coefficient = 0.0849948

A Microcomputer Management Application

In February 1990, a partnership was formed between Bechtel and the national accounts division of a large microcomputer supplier. Their mission was to improve the efficiency of obtaining microcomputer products. A steering committee and six process groups formed the teams for improvement. The boundaries of the system are from initial requestor until equipment and/or software is installed, and include all regional offices, departments, projects, business lines, and services (except controller) in San Francisco.

Products from the supplier are purchased at cost plus an add-on percentage. As a result of an improved payment schedule, the supplier has reduced the add-on percentage by 1/2 of 1 percent, with another reduction due in January if payment remains at thirty days or less.

As depicted in the accompanying control charts (Figure 5), the average acquisition time and variation have been reduced in each of the four measured categories. An automated system was developed that contains

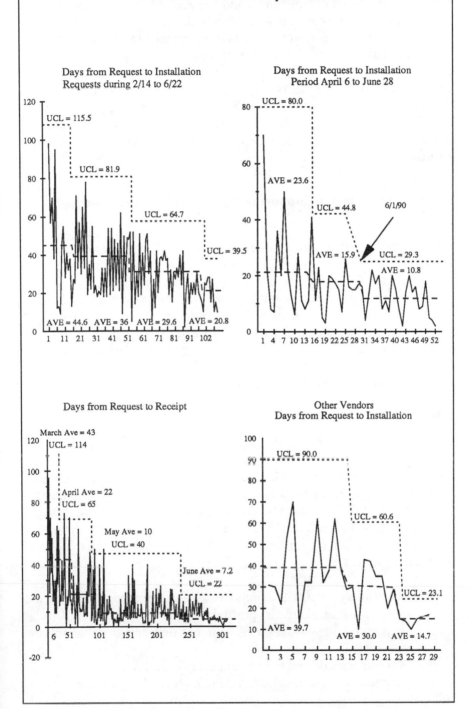

FIGURE 5
Control Charts – Time to Acquire Products

on-line databases of supplier-provided part numbers and prices. This has resulted in improved completeness and accuracy of orders, reduced order preparation time, and easier invoice approval.

Two separate process steps have been eliminated from the twelve-step microacquisition process. Preprinted multipart forms have been eliminated for all orders from the suppliers. Numerous logs, copies, and files have been eliminated. Most notably, copies of requisitions are no longer sent to Central Receiving. Electronic notification of order receipt, ETA, and shipping information has reduced time to status orders. A number of objectives have already been established for continued improvement of this system.

Engineering Design in Support of Operating Services – Nuclear Plant

Eliminating disruptions or delays in completing maintenance or modifications to large nuclear units of electric utilities can save nearly $1 million a day. Quality problems in engineering, in the form of slipped schedules, or lack of fitness for use, can lead to unacceptable levels of rework on the unit. The tracking of field problems back to root causes in putting together the design change packages (DCPs) has been undertaken with a major Bechtel customer, with a measurably improved process as a result. Not only are designs now more accurate and timely, but also the turnaround time has improved. This last item alone can reduce "outage" time for the unit.

PARTNERING with Several Large Chemicals Companies

PARTNERING agreements that rely heavily on strong commitments to continuous improvement principles have been successfully concluded with a number of BGI customers. Working arrangements that feature many of the attributes of PARTNERING have also been in place with other BGI customers. The essential attributes of PARTNERING required to achieve optimum benefits are:

- The primary purpose is to improve quality, lower cost, and increase owner's market share and profitability.
- Continuous improvement of systems that create value for the customer.
- Win/win attitude and trust relationship at all levels.
- Compatible culture, in outlook, initiative, and commitment.

- Integrated management team; shared decisions.
- Commitment to common goals; risk sharing.
- Long-term focus and commitment; permanent core team.
- Meaningful workload; sole source awards.
- Team building and teamwork.

As can be seen by the list, the attributes of PARTNERING relationships fit closely with what is desired by the *customer value* and *continuous improvement* strategy that Bechtel is implementing. Dr. Deming's idea of limiting the number of suppliers and building long-term trust relationships is at the core of PARTNERING. Intimate knowledge of customer values can be gained through effective PARTNERING arrangements.

The benefits to customers are:

- Better focus of their resources on business.
- Lower cost through stabilization of system variables and optimized integration of resources.
- Improved schedules through elimination of bidding.
- Improved fitness for use through better knowledge of customer needs and improved communication.
- Relating project outcome closely to customer market share.

The benefits to Bechtel are:

- Long-term base of work to stabilize resources.
- Reduced overhead through no bidding and shared decisions.
- Improved morale, stability and teamwork.
- Management focus on improvement of work processes.
- Enhancement of technical skills through joint development.

Other Applications in Bechtel

The list of applications is too long to recount fully here; the current list stands at 250. Listed below are names of representative system teams that cover a cross section of organization functions and units and should provide some feel for the depth and the breadth of the CCI initiative in Bechtel.

Drawing turnaround time; microcomputer service request; understanding customer needs, from intelligence gathering to strategy development; project performance to cost; estimating; scope control; project planning and scheduling; project personnel forecasting; project personnel assignment system; performance review system; engineering calculations; engineering drawings; chiefs technical review; lessons learned systems in engineering and start-up; training and development system; vendor drawing control; proposal process; conceptual design process; document change control; expediting of vendor's system; contract administration; accounts receivable; on-line time card process; vendor bid and approval cycle; work packaging process; material takeoff and quantity tracking; and cash management.

ISSUES FOR IMPROVEMENT

- Applying statistical process control (SPC) to a professional service business, such as an A/E. The matters of definitions, collecting operational data, looking at production of one-of-a-kind deliverables as a process, and standardizing processes across projects that are essentially small companies working for unique customers are all part of the differences to be resolved.
- Making time and resources available in a business that makes money only when its people are producing deliverables for specific customers.
- Convincing project managers to sell customers on the concept of continuous improvement when many contracts are short-term, and process improvement efforts may not benefit the immediate customer. This is partly a reward system problem.
- Expecting project managers to make long-term decisions when they are still rewarded on a short-term results basis, as above.
- Continued lack of in-house coaches (facilitators), since many who were initially selected and trained have been assigned to other high-priority work. This is a constancy-of-purpose issue.
- Length of time to see specific results come from complex cross-functional systems has frustrated management, which now wants to study functional processes to show earlier and more tangible results. This has ramifications related to how the organization sees progress and how management stays committed.
- In a professional service business, the complexity of learning about what the external customer values causes frustration, since customers exist at varying levels of their organization and they all appear to have input to buying decisions often made on a team basis. The issue is how to reach a valid conclusion of what the customer values when there are many customer voices.

- Continuing to work in a reactive crisis mode, solving problems rather than finding root causes to improve the base systems. This is more often than not dictated by the external customer.

WHERE DO WE GO NEXT?

While Bechtel continues to pursue its cross-functional systems, management is also exploring the most promising of the strictly functional processes, even though many are closely related to other functional areas. For example, Technical Services has planning and scheduling responsibility but cannot improve that system significantly without input from Engineering and Construction. Alignment of the functional systems with the cross-functional systems is a planning effort that must be completed to eliminate duplications and account for all systems of a major consequence to organizational goals and strategy.

The separate Bechtel organizations are in various stages of developing implementation plans to help with the issues of commitment of resources, with special attention to coaches for teams, and verification of choice of priorities. More time is being spent on communication to the total organization so that all employees will understand CCI better and their role in its implementation. Means to measure progress continue to be pursued, to know if both the right direction and speed of progress are being maintained. A vision of what Bechtel should look like in five years is essential if shared direction for the CCI effort is to be attained.

LESSONS LEARNED

Bechtel has confirmed what has been written in many texts on implementing continuous improvement. We continue to learn as we make progress on our journey. The following list of lessons is offered in the hope that those who read this chapter and have yet to tread the complexities of implementing continuous improvement may find a smooth path to unmistakable benefits.

- Gain commitment and participation of senior management before you start.
- Develop an implementation plan that deals with the issues of commitment of resources, time, and dollars, rewards, and the like, and then share that with the whole organization.
- Find capable and respected champions and allow them to lead the effort.

- Pick processes/systems from which you can produce results in a reasonable time frame (six months) as evidence to the rest of the organization that this approach works.
- Have an adequate number of coaches (facilitators) – internal resources – to help teams.
- Reward risk takers, especially early champions.
- Develop a plan for spreading the approach, once proven.
- Communicate to the whole organization what is going on but be careful that there are proven results to demonstrate that this is not just talk and hype.
- Be prepared to spend blocks of time (three hours) early in process analysis in order to make progress. One-hour meetings will not do it.

CHAPTER 28

LONG-TERM QUALITY IMPROVEMENT AND COST REDUCTION AT CAPSUGEL/WARNER-LAMBERT

WILLIAM JUDGE
Assistant Professor of Management
University of Tennessee

MICHAEL J. STAHL
Associate Dean, College of Business Administration
University of Tennessee

ROBERT SCOTT
Capsugel/Warner-Lambert

RONNIE MILLENDER
Capsugel/Warner-Lambert

SUMMARY

This case documents a long-term quality improvement program with resultant cost reduction in a multinational business unit. Customer demands for functionally perfect capsules necessitated such a program. Salient features of the quality improvement program include long-term top management commitment, Statistical Process Control, cross-functional qualitivity teams, inclusion of influential change masters from plants in five countries, extensive training, and cost reduction due to increased quality.

Capsugel, a division of Warner-Lambert, manufactures and distributes two-piece, hard gelatin capsules to pharmaceutical companies. Capsules are manufactured by a dipping process on high-capacity automatic machines. The gelatin is melted and mixed with necessary dyes and pigments. The finished gelatin solution is transferred to temperature-controlled tanks on the machines, where it is fed continuously to the dipping dishes. Current equipment averages over one thousand capsules per minute, and its productivity is constantly being upgraded.

Capsugel is the worldwide leader in the gelatin capsule market. It offers the highest quality product, the broadest product line, and the widest distribution system in the world. Its four largest plants are located in southeastern United States, Belgium, France, and Japan. In addition, smaller manufacturing operations are located in Britain, Mexico, Italy, Thailand, Brazil, and China.

CUSTOMER VALUE: RISING STANDARDS

Capsugel's customers often fill the capsules with high-speed filling machines that sometimes operate at the rate of 150,000 capsules per hour or forty-two capsules per second. If just one capsule is defective (e.g., too thick, broken, or misaligned), the entire filling machine jams. This is expensive as it means a loss of raw material and production time. In addition, the product undergoes rigorous screenings owing to its obvious impacts on the user's health. In sum, "functional" product quality is very important to Capsugel's customers.

In addition, "cosmetic" product quality is also critical to Capsugel's customers. The color and print quality on the capsules is a major source of information to the end users. As a result, the appearance of the product is an essential aspect of the product's effectiveness.

The third element of quality for this product is the service after the sale. It is through this "service" quality that Capsugel has distinguished itself from its competitors. Capsugel is committed to long-term relationships with its customers, and the service offered after the sale is an integral part of its high-value image.

Although customer demand for quality has always been high, the level of quality expected by customers rose at an accelerating rate in the 1980s. This was because the machines that fill the capsules have gradually become increasingly automated and the cost of downtime is growing. This trend is particularly evident in nations where the cost of labor is high and working conditions are constrained. For instance, in much of Europe, few of Capsugel's customers have a labor pool that is willing to operate the filling machines during the night shift. As a result, they are rapidly replacing labor with high-speed automated filling machines. In order to reduce the labor intensity of the filling process, Capsugel's customers are demanding higher and higher levels of capsule quality so that they can run the filling machines with the least amount of labor. The president of Capsugel summarized this trend as follows: "Nearly fifteen years ago, most of our customers used semi-automatic filling machines. These were relatively labor intensive so defects were caught fairly quickly. Today, most of those machines are fully automated with hardly any operator oversight. In the future, we expect our customers to move to operator-less machines. That represents a whole new ballgame for us – zero defects!"

The practical implications of these rising customer standards are that Capsugel has had to improve quality substantially in order to survive. One plant manager stated: "If we offered the same quality now as we did just five years ago, we would be out of business." As Figure 1 demonstrates, the relative defect level produced by Capsugel has dropped dramatically in response to the customer's rising quality expectations. The market continues to drive inexorably onward toward zero defect levels.

SPC INTEREST: TOP MANAGEMENT LEARNING AND COMMITMENT

Capsugel has always been committed to continuous cost reduction and quality improvement, but at the end of the 1970s most improvements were incremental. One manager described Capsugel's situation as follows: "We are in a mature business. All of the easy gold nuggets have already been grabbed. Now all significant improvements will come from changing the system because all of the variables are interrelated. It was becoming increasingly clear that the old way of doing things was only providing incremental benefits and the increments were getting smaller and smaller. It was like approaching an asymptote."

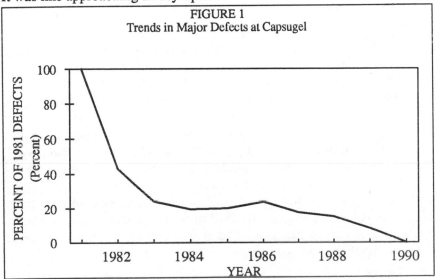

FIGURE 1
Trends in Major Defects at Capsugel

Frustrated with the status quo, the general manager at its largest plant, Charles Hoover, began searching for breakthrough ideas. Hoover considered a wide variety of options, and eventually "it became clear that there is only one way to go: quality improvement. Quality is the only thing that I can see that unites the system of variables. It has become our greatest hope for breakthrough approaches to this business."

Hoover listed a number of reasons why this became apparent. First, some local manufacturers based in the United States reported major breakthroughs of their own through quality improvement programs. "Seeing is believing," he said. Second, a very successful manufacturing consultant insisted that focusing on quality was the key to success. The consultant was very adamant and persuasive that quality improvement "is the wave of the future." Third, Hoover discovered that it was "implementable." He observed, "When you wave the flag of increased productivity, some folks feel like they have to give something up so there is often resistance. Almost no one, however, can argue about improving quality." So in 1982, Hoover began to learn about and experiment with quality improvement projects.

In that same year, many small, niche producers began producing gelatin capsules for their local markets. This provided further impetus to improve its product quality because these "ankle biters" competed only on price. In Hoover's words, "my job is to make sure that this product doesn't become a commodity item . . . we must constantly differentiate ourselves from the competition." Increasingly impressed with the power of improved quality, Hoover required that the rest of his management team become knowledgeable about various quality improvement techniques including statistical process control (SPC).

IMPLEMENTATION: BUILDING A CRITICAL MASS

From 1982 to 1989, the various plants experimented with quality improvement projects and dramatic improvements resulted. Because the management at the South Carolina plant was most committed and knowledgeable about quality improvement and SPC techniques, it became the major innovator. The primary vehicle for progress was "qualitivity" teams. These teams of four to eight individuals were comprised of a wide variety of specializations. Their mandate was to study a major quality problem which they were required to solve over a prescribed period of time. These teams were very successful and they also provided for cross-functional integration, as the teams had representatives from a number of different functions and often examined horizontal systems.

In mid-1989, Hoover was promoted to president of Capsugel. He immediately attempted to spread the SPC approach to the rest of the plants. First, he revised a program that had originated in 1980. This was a program aimed at instilling cooperation between plants that were normally competitive. When one plant successfully implemented an innovation in the production process, it was rewarded in various ways and then required to share that innovation with the other plants. By applying SPC to this program, innovations spread more quickly.

Second, Hoover required that all the plants lower their cost of quality by one-half every five years. The cost of quality was computed as the cost of scrap, inspection, customer complaints, lab testing, and quality appraisal as a percentage of cost of goods sold. The immediate result of this mandate was that each of the plants needed to reduce/eliminate all its inspection operations as quickly as possible. This had dramatic implications for the rest of the process because no longer could the machine operators assume that their defects would be identified and removed by the 100 to 200 percent manual inspections that occurred after the capsules were produced. In essence, this ambitious goal required that the machine operators be responsible for both productivity and capsule quality. This placed greater demands on the production floor to "get their process under control" and "do it right the first time."

Third, Hoover committed much time and capital to training the top thirty-four production managers in an intensive two-week course in SPC techniques and philosophy. Rather than rely on staff personnel, Hoover recognized that the line managers must lead the change effort. As one attendee stated, "We knew management was serious about this program when they flew so many folks from five different countries to Belgium and then South Carolina . . . it must have cost a bundle."

Although the managers came from five different nations, all could speak English as a first or second language. This significant investment of time and money signalled to the rest of the organization that Hoover was serious about quality improvement. Perhaps most significant, the attendees were required to immediately apply their new knowledge to a significant quality problem and present their project to Hoover at the conclusion of the training.

Finally, Hoover made perhaps the strongest institutional change of all: he required all future capital requests to be justified by SPC. Since capital expenditures are the lifeblood of these organizations, this policy required that even the skeptics learn the SPC language in order to do their jobs.

Of course, the program implementation was not completely smooth. Many of the workers saw this program as the "fad of the month club." Many workers had experienced similar "bandwagons" in the past, and they concluded that this would be another one. One middle manager stated, "At first, I thought this would just come and go in six to twelve months like all previous programs that were handed down from on high." As time goes on, however, Hoover's steady commitment is challenging the skeptics.

In addition, many managers recognized that any significant innovation takes time and patience. Being "an American company with short-term American values," many long-time employees were reluctant to change owing to the unrealistic expectations placed on them in the past. While everyone agreed that the program goals were challenging, many middle managers expected to have enough time to show results–again, as a result of Hoover's steady commitment.

BENEFITS REALIZED: TRANSFORMATION OF A MATURE GLOBAL BUSINESS

These efforts showed dramatic benefits, and some short-term successes helped to guarantee future benefits. First, this quality improvement program served to reduce/eliminate the emotional appeals and unsystematic analysis behind capital budgeting that existed in the past. As one plant manager stated, "In the past, folks came with subjective opinions. This led to battles and guys with the loudest voices won. Today, we make capital expenditure decisions with a lot more facts and less emotion. SPC has reduced the turf battles and politics."

Second, it helped to transcend the language barrier. Being spread all over the world, SPC had the unintended benefit of providing a means of communication between parties that spoke different languages. This not only improved communication between the far-flung plants, but it also provided an important communication tool between the plants and their suppliers and buyers. This improved communication reduced friction and raised the amount of information transferred between parties.

Third, quality levels began to improve dramatically and productivity began to rise. The "quality gap" between Capsugel and its competitors has widened, and Capsugel is now proactively seeking out quality problems before the customer demands it. In this way, Capsugel expects to build cost-effectively for the future and to strengthen its already solid competitive position.

THE FUTURE: NEW HORIZONS

All the change masters are now "on board"; it remains to be seen if the rest of the organization follows. The thirty-four change masters are responsible for training and promoting SPC to the other managers and production personnel. Do the change masters have the commitment, knowledge, and skill in relaying this knowledge? As one European manager stated: "I understand these concepts pretty well myself, but frankly, I'm not sure if I have the skill to teach and motivate others to learn." The president of Capsugel predicted, "I'll know that we have arrived when our line managers successfully teach their subordinates SPC techniques and philosophy. Staff assistance is helpful, but real changes come when the line management leads the charge."

In the meantime, these change masters must deal with day-to-day challenges while overseeing the innovation process. Furthermore, there are intense pressures to reduce costs while improving quality. The organization has to learn how to anticipate customer expectations rather than react to customer complaints about quality. These are challenges for the future, but Capsugel appears to be aiming at "breakthrough" innovations at the present.

Quality improvement is increasingly becoming a part of the corporate culture at Capsugel. For instance, the South Carolina plant recently developed its own "quality policy," and it was framed and hung in every manager's office (see Figure 2). These and other changes are convincing managers that "quality improvement is no fad, it's a way of life at Capsugel."

FIGURE 2
Capsugel-Greenwood
Quality Policy

Capsugel is the leader in the production of high-quality, two-piece, hard gelatin capsules and related services to our customers. To continue our position, we must:

Work with and assist our suppliers to provide us with products that meet or exceed our needs. Our product's quality is only as good as our own quality systems and those of our suppliers.

Continually strive to understand, control, and improve our processes and procedures through participation in problem-solving teams.

Do it right the first time. Never forget that you, no matter what job you perform, are responsible for the quality of your work.

Focus on the needs of the customer by providing more and better products and services than our competitors. Routine assessment of our capability and our customers' needs will help maintain Capsugel as the market leader.

Never compromise our values regardless of time pressures or workload.

The Greenwood operation will embrace a restless discontent for the status quo, and thereby strive for improvement in the ways we operate for the benefit of our customers, suppliers, and our employees.

SOURCE: Quality Steering Committee in Greenwood, S.C., December 1989.

CHAPTER 29

GEORGIA-PACIFIC CORPORATION INDUSTRIAL WOOD PRODUCTS – PARTICLEBOARD DIVISION

CHARLES TASMA
Plant Manager
Industrial Wood Products - Particleboard Division
Georgia-Pacific Corporation

STEVEN R. MARTIN
Associate Director
Management Development Center
University of Tennessee

SUMMARY

This chapter examines the work between the University of Tennessee and the Georgia-Pacific Corporation over the course of the last two years. The nature and scope of the joint effort to learn how to improve the quality of the products and processes in nine plants in the industrial wood products particleboard division are discussed. The work at one specific plant is used to illustrate the framework for the systems improvement work. Results and implications for the future are discussed.

ORGANIZATIONAL CONTEXT

With net sales rising 7 percent in 1989 to $10.2 billion and net income rising 41.5 percent to $6.61 billion, the Georgia-Pacific Corporation continues to be one of the largest and most successful producers of pulp, paper and building products in the world. Georgia-Pacific is the single largest exporter of pulp in America. Its product portfolio includes, in the pulp and paper operations, linerboard (used in corrugated shipping containers), printing and writing papers, other paperboard, tissue and sanitary napkins, coarse kraft paper, and raw pulp. In the building products operations, its products include wood panels, lumber, flitches (used for joinery in windows, doors, and mouldings), particleboard, plywood, gypsum, roofing, chemicals, and timber.

Historically, Georgia-Pacific has been a lean, well-managed, conservative growth company. It has long had a reputation for quality products in the marketplace, and, while it continues to enjoy the fruits of that reputation, there are signs that business as usual will no longer guarantee a solid future in Georgia-Pacific operations.

One such signal is a trend in declining profitability that has appeared in its building products operations. In 1988, building products accounted for 63 percent of net sales and 41 percent of operating profits. The same year, pulp and paper accounted for 36 percent of net sales but 58 percent of operating profits. This was the first year in Georgia-Pacific's history in which building products accounted for a smaller percent of total operating profits than pulp and paper. This trend continued in 1989, with operating profits from pulp and paper climbing to $917 million, a 49 percent increase, while building products climbed to $533 million, a 24 percent increase.

As noted in recent annual reports, Georgia-Pacific attributes the decline in profitability in the building products sector to a decreased level of housing starts and increased competition in this segment of the business. This trend is not unlike that being seen in many other industries where rapid market changes and increased competition are requiring greater flexibility and quality at lower cost in order to remain profitable.

The University of Tennessee and Georgia-Pacific began working together when, in 1988, members of Georgia-Pacific's building products operation attended the University of Tennessee's Institute for Productivity Through Quality. After this initial involvement, Georgia-Pacific's interest in the potential application of statistical management methods to plant operations led to the development of a one-week custom course for Georgia-Pacific. The design of this first course was led by Professor Richard Sanders and proved to be the beginning of a long-term relationship between Georgia-Pacific and the University of Tennessee. The intent of this effort on the part of Georgia-Pacific was to improve the process and products in the particleboard plants through the application of systems management concepts.

THE PLAN

The goal for 1989 was to expose each plant management group to the philosophy and methods of systems management and to support their use in improving the operations of the plant and the division. The 1989 plan had four major parts:

1. To provide a one-week seminar on systems management for the management group at each selected site.
2. To help this management group identify and begin to apply these concepts to actual systems within their operation.
3. To offer ongoing support in the form of consultation and management reviews to the managers as they struggled with changing their management approach.
4. To meet, as needed, with senior management to support their efforts to identify and address the management issues at the division and corporate levels.

By the end of 1989, nine plants had been through a custom course at their respective site, had identified systems linked to customer value, and had begun the work to study and improve these systems. An example from one plant may better illustrate the nature of the work within a plant.

In one of the particleboard plants, the management began the improvement work by visualizing the overall plant operations as consisting of distinct systems, each generating a product for an internal customer. Although the internal customers were the main source of information regarding what was important in the product as it was received and used in their operation, the quality characteristics of the final product were concurrently developed and strengthened in much the same way. Emphasis was placed on understanding the "in use" needs and how the product was measured by the external customers. Studying and learning about the internal and external customer needs informed the decisions about where to focus the improvement work. The basic premise of this approach was that, as improvements were made to internal products through the various stages of manufacture, the final products to the external customers would likewise be improved.

Initially, the focus was on the manufacturing system where six internal products with twelve quality characteristics were identified. Operational definitions for each quality characteristic were painstakingly developed so that it was possible to know when the quality characteristic was conforming. The next area worked, the measurement system, required a surprisingly large amount of time and effort. It was critically important that the data generated be both accurate and repeatable. Achieving this desired goal proved to be no small task. Once the operational definitions and the measurement systems were in place, control charts were developed and implemented which revealed the extent of the variation in the system. While the operational definitions describe the expectations from the system with regard to a specific quality characteristic, the control charts show what the system is actually giving in terms of variation.

Sampling methods and techniques were developed and published and required extensive teaching and training to insure the accuracy of the data. A central issue that arose was the difficulty of finding time to collect data and maintain the control charts. To address this issue and to help insure accuracy, an automatic sampling and reporting system was developed.

As expected, the initial data from the control charts indicated many out-of-control situations and, in most cases, confirmed what was suspected about the systems. This confirmation was important in providing incentive to continue the work and direction regarding where to focus. As improvements to the system were made, initially by working on the out-of-control situations, additional improvements could be seen in specific quality characteristics both in the immediate area and, more importantly, in other areas further downstream that had been impacted by the out-of-control situations.

Work continued, with more emphasis being placed on computer control strategies. In a continuous process system such as a particleboard, numerical control systems drive much of the manufacturing equipment. They are a source of variation in the different products being produced on the same manufacturing line. With the use of control charts, excessive variation common to some products and not to others was addressed, and improvements were made to the system. These improvements were reflected by reduced variation in specific quality characteristics.

A separate but equally important issue crucial to the success of the work is the need to strengthen the focus on continual improvement throughout the manufacturing system. Eventually, the nature of the daily work shifts from simply maintaining the system to continually seeking ways to reduce the variation and inconsistencies of the internal and external products. As variation is reduced, the need to react to emergencies also decreases and more time is available for improvement work. In the early stages, the time spent on continual improvement is small relative to the time spent on maintaining the system. However, as priorities slowly change and successes become evident, the shift in work patterns changes and more time is spent on reducing variation. The atmosphere in the manufacturing facility can be changed by all levels of management being involved in continual improvement work. This sends an important and much watched signal throughout the organization.

The goal for 1990 was to begin to see actual bottom-line evidence of systems improvement in the operations at each plant. This was to be accomplished by:

1. Strengthening the support of the plants by assigning a University of Tennessee faculty member to each plant to assist with the systems improvement.
2. Meeting regularly with the division-level managers to help align the division and plant strategy.
3. Encouraging cross-plant learning by holding semiannual meetings with managers from all plants.
4. Assisting with targeted research to better understand the sources of variation in system and process performance.
5. Conducting additional training as needed to help support the learning at the plants.

RESULTS

The involvement between the University of Tennessee and Georgia-Pacific has seen an increasing number of managers willing to grapple with the complexities of trying to change a successful organization while continuing to "run the business."

We have observed a high degree of variation in the level of systems management adopted at the nine different Georgia-Pacific plants. Considering why there is considerable variation across the plants offers the possibility for learning.

When we examine organizations across the country which seem to have had the most success making systems management a way of doing business, several points stand out:

1. There is a perceived urgency to continually learn and get better at their business. This urgency is usually a result of competitive pressures from the market, but it is sometimes created by senior management's awareness of what is needed to survive in the future.
2. Whether or not upper management makes the link between this urgency, systems management, and the success of the business is another critical factor. In successful organizations, continuous improvement is not seen as an end in itself. Neither is change understood as something to be done for its own sake. Rather, management makes sense of such changes in light of the present and anticipated future needs of the business. The emphasis of the firm gets redirected, often by questions asked on a regular basis about variability as it relates to product and process improvement linked to customer needs.

3. The signals in the organization are changed to reflect a new set of priorities. Some of the signal changes are as follows:

a. What behavior actually gets rewarded (and what does not). This is one of the most watched signals in the organization. The rewards may take the form of extrinsic or intrinsic rewards, questions on performance reviews, questions asked at management meetings, and issues that upper managers address during their site visits.

b. What the senior managers spend their time doing. What the management talks about is important, but what it does is more important. Personal commitment evidenced through action is a key indicator of priorities.

c. What the influential people in the organization do about the proposed changes. If they adopt "new" behavior, then the signal is that the new behavior is more than just a fad and others are more likely to adopt it.

These are some of the key differences between organizations that are more successful with adopting a systems management strategy.

If we turn to the nine Georgia Pacific plants, those that seem to be more successful show many of the characteristics described above. For example, at the more successful plants:

1. There is a sense of urgency to get better.
2. The division and plant managers are actively involved in making the link between the study of variation and the success of the business.
3. The signals are changing as managers are getting directly involved in the study of variation, are asking different questions, and are looking at different measures of improvement and as results are being rewarded.

On the other hand, at several of the other plants, there is little evidence of:

1. A need to do anything different from the past.
2. A need for managers to actively study the links between variation and customer needs.
3. Signals changing to reflect a genuine change in management.

What can we learn from this experience?

1. There needs to be more emphasis on the link between customer needs in the marketplace and plant focus. Internally focused improvement work has little value if it is not linked to the customer's changing needs. An example of the type of work that might support this would be work between marketing, manufacturing, and procurement to tie together the understanding of what the customer needs with how to deliver that (from raw material through to finished product). The rate of changing needs of some of Georgia-Pacific's major customers requires that the company stay very close to those responsible for making the changes and selecting the suppliers.

2. There must be a close link between the division strategy and the individual plant strategies in order for the plants to be able to focus the systems improvement work. Every day the plant managers are consumed with problems, projects, and production. Often, there is good intention to do the improvement work, but it gets shifted to a lower priority. Consistent attention and assistance from the division level on how to sort these priorities are critical to the successful change in management attention. A sense of lack of focus on where to do the systems improvement work coupled with a weak sense of urgency about why the work is needed creates disincentives. The urgency for this work must be reinforced from the senior-most level; it must also be linked to customer value and be translated into business measures.

3. The effect of the plants "out front" seems to create a pull effect on the other plants. Some of these learnings can be replicated at the other sites to give them a "jump start." Focused work with one or more of the successful plants to accelerate their rate of improvement seems to make sense as a way to accelerate the effort.

4. Having external people push the effort from the outside via calls and visits is not the optimal way to move the effort forward. Instead, an internal pull effect created by careful selection of key indicators of improvement is a preferred way to support the plant improvement. Having external people who are knowledgeable about the plant's management and operations and available on short notice is important once this internal pull is put in place.

5. Regular meetings to support the cross-plant learning, to reinforce progress, and to stimulate ideas about what works at other sites is a critical part of the reinforcement of the middle management effort.

CONCLUSION

The rate of progress is not what either the senior Georgia-Pacific managers or the University of Tennessee people had hoped for. Nonetheless, progress is evident. It is clear that changes of the magnitude involved in this type of work do not come quickly or easily. As one Georgia-Pacific manager put it, "It's like trying to change the electrical system on a 747 while in flight." There is no formula or blueprint for success, and in the end, the effort will be judged to be successful or not only if Georgia-Pacific's future viability is strengthened.

CHAPTER 30

A SYSTEMS VIEW OF STRATEGIC PLANNING AT PROCTER AND GAMBLE

JOHN SAXTON
Vice President, Noxell Division
Procter & Gamble Company

WILLIAM B. LOCANDER
Distinguished Professor of Marketing
University of Tennessee

SUMMARY

The Procter and Gamble (P&G) Company has been experiencing a major cultural evolution stimulated by a holistic and yet loosely defined concept called Total Quality. Over the past seven years, P&G has examined many facets of doing business in a Total Quality way. This chapter reports on P&G's current thinking about the role of strategic planning in a Total Quality company.

TOTAL QUALITY AT P&G

Procter and Gamble began its Total Quality journey in 1983. This journey has been a bottom-up, not top-down approach. In 1983, a few individuals within the engineering organization became exposed to the teachings of Dr. W. Edwards Deming and statistical process control (SPC) as a tool to reduce variation and product defects within manufacturing. At the same time, P&G was facing serious business problems with disposable diapers. Through the application of SPC, P&G was able to start up new diaper-making lines around the world in one-half the normal time with a

50 percent reduction in the level of defects, a feat that caught the attention and admiration of senior management. By 1985, the interest in quality improvement had evolved beyond SPC to a focus on aligning supplier capabilities with customer needs. While this effort initially emphasized improving raw material quality from our suppliers, by 1987 it had further evolved into a proactive and thorough understanding of the needs of the ultimate consumers of P&G products, as well as trade customers. More recently, a standardized measurement system has been implemented around the world to monitor the level of consumer and customer satisfaction with P&G products.

During the past seven years, P&G has developed a holistic understanding of Total Quality as well as broadened its application throughout the entire company. While still in its infancy, Total Quality has already had a profound effect on the way Procter and Gamble operates. Figure 1 is a P&G training tool used by the Soap Sector in P&G to illustrate four dimensions of Total Quality, which are used to put Total Quality into an overall context. The four dimensions are key elements, concepts, systems, and tools. These distinctions have proven helpful in gaining organizational understanding of this complex and all-encompassing topic.

The six *key elements* of our Soap Sector's quality efforts are constancy of purpose, leadership, empowerment of people, cross-functional teamwork, continual system improvement, and customer/supplier relationships.

Concepts are the fundamental ideas that together establish the mindset for approaching work with a Total Quality perspective. Numerous concepts are used over and over again in a Total Quality organization. The tree diagram (Figure 1) lists a few of them. The first concept is quality first – in other words, quality must never be intentionally compromised. The second is customer driven, which is often referred to as market in – as opposed to product out. In fact, this is the fundamental concept of Total Quality at P&G. Other concepts include doing right things right, viewing all work as a process that can be both understood and improved, viewing the next process in the value chain as your customer, applying a plan-do-check-act mentality to everything, and finally being data based.

The *systems* that have played a key role in our Total Quality efforts to date include strategy development and deployment, the system for launching new products, standardization, information systems, and so on. There are others, but these are the main ones utilized at P&G to date.

The fourth dimension of Total Quality is *tools*, which include not only the seven basic tools and seven new tools used prevalently in Japan, but also tools that P&G has added to the tool box because of their broad applicability across a wide range of situations – tools such as force field analysis, flag charts, and analytical trouble shooting. This cataloging of the

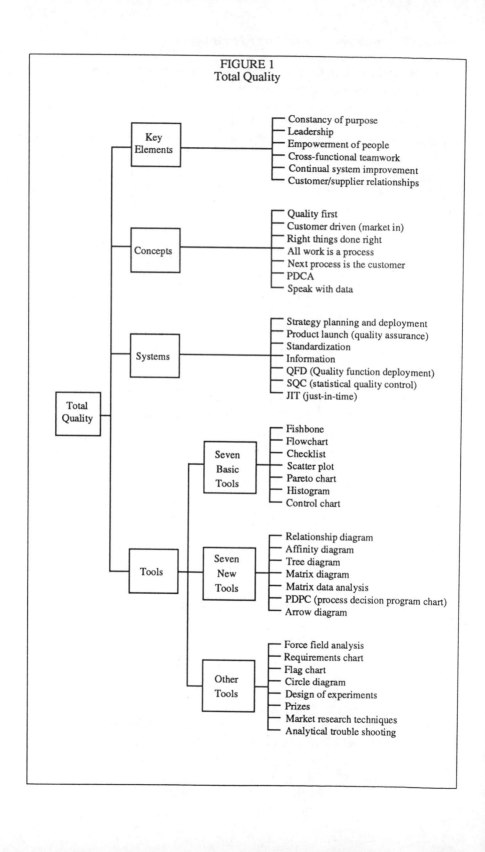

FIGURE 1
Total Quality

Key Elements
- Constancy of purpose
- Leadership
- Empowerment of people
- Cross-functional teamwork
- Continual system improvement
- Customer/supplier relationships

Concepts
- Quality first
- Customer driven (market in)
- Right things done right
- All work is a process
- Next process is the customer
- PDCA
- Speak with data

Systems
- Strategy planning and deployment
- Product launch (quality assurance)
- Standardization
- Information
- QFD (Quality function deployment)
- SQC (statistical quality control)
- JIT (just-in-time)

Tools

Seven Basic Tools
- Fishbone
- Flowchart
- Checklist
- Scatter plot
- Pareto chart
- Histogram
- Control chart

Seven New Tools
- Relationship diagram
- Affinity diagram
- Tree diagram
- Matrix diagram
- Matrix data analysis
- PDPC (process decision program chart)
- Arrow diagram

Other Tools
- Force field analysis
- Requirements chart
- Flag chart
- Circle diagram
- Design of experiments
- Prizes
- Market research techniques
- Analytical trouble shooting

various aspects of Total Quality into the four different dimensions of key elements, concepts, systems, and tools has enhanced understanding by putting everything into a context that makes Total Quality less overwhelming, fully integrated, and yet comprehensive.

At Procter and Gamble, Total Quality is a holistic management approach. It is not a program to be implemented or something that applies only to certain parts of the organization. It requires, in most cases, a fundamental change in the organization's culture since it usually represents a very different way of operating than has existed in the past. As such, it must apply to everything if it is to be sustained and ultimately institutionalized.

TOTAL QUALITY THROUGH STRATEGIC PLANNING

In order to make such a dramatic change in the way an organization operates, P&G has found that Total Quality must be built into the process which is used for developing and deploying the organization's strategy. Figure 2 illustrates the process used for strategy development and deployment within the Soap Sector of Procter and Gamble. The strategy development and deployment process consists of three major phases: the long-term vision, the strategy development itself, and finally, deploying the strategy. In essence, long-term vision and strategy development have been added to the more traditional Management by Objectives (MBO) approach of objectives and actions.

This process begins by getting a very clear idea of the purpose of the organization – in other words, why we are in business. This is often referred to as the mission statement, although purpose is preferable because it conveys permanence. While on the surface this may seem to be an academic question with an obvious answer, it usually prompts a critically important debate within the organization's leadership. Within P&G's Soap Sector, the debate centered on whether we are in business to make money or to provide superior satisfaction to our consumers and customers. As with most Total Quality companies, the conclusion was that we are fundamentally in business to provide brands that achieve superior consumer and customer satisfaction. This does not mean that financial returns are not important. As Figure 3 from the Yokogawa Division of Hewlett-Packard illustrates, this focus on quality, both internally and externally, will result in profit through increased market share and lower cost. While this may seem like semantics, there is a profound and fundamental difference between a company that views its purpose as simply making money as opposed to a company that views its purpose as satisfying consumers. It can be argued that a Total Quality company must have satisfying con-

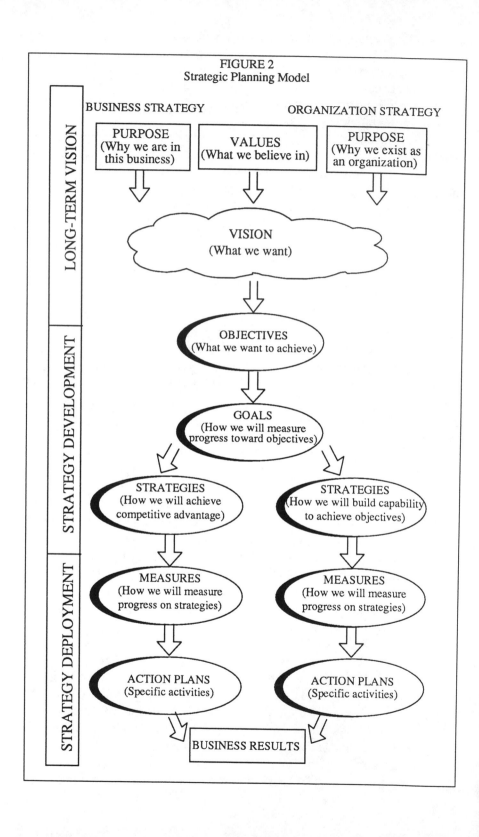

FIGURE 2
Strategic Planning Model

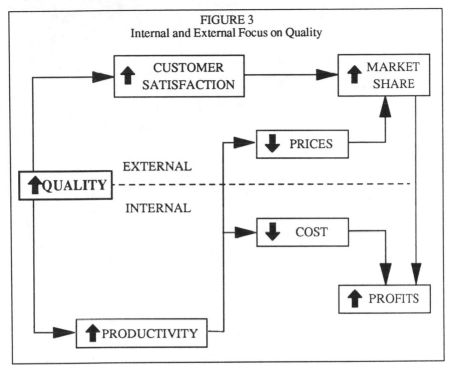

FIGURE 3
Internal and External Focus on Quality

sumers as its first purpose. Certainly, any company needs financial returns
in order to continue to survive and fairly serve its shareholders, but a
single-minded focus on the financial returns, particularly in the short term,
is often the first step toward jeopardizing a company's long-term survival.
As an analogy, consider that everyone needs to eat in order to live, but
hopefully, very few of us would say that we live to eat.

VALUES

Another important step is to clarify the values of the organization –
what we believe in. Values represent the fundamental beliefs of the
organization that never change and should never be compromised. An
organization needs to have a set of common values that are broadly shared
throughout the organization. Over time, these values shape the culture
since they tend to be heavily influenced by the leader(s). In the P&G Soap
Sector, there are six core values (Figure 4) that guide actions on a day-to-
day basis. These values are (1) to have constancy of purpose, (2) to treat
people as our most important asset, (3) to have high integrity, (4) to behave
as an owner, (5) to be a team player, and (6) to have a high degree of
functional excellence.

FIGURE 4
The Procter and Gamble Soap Products Company

OUR VALUES

<u>Have Constancy of Purpose</u>

- Focus on satisfying consumer/customer needs
- Set clear direction and stay on course
- Set priorities
- Stay on strategy

<u>Treat People as our Most Important Asset</u>

- Attract, train, and retain superior people
- Build functional and leadership skills
- Leverage diversity of people and thought
- Recognize and reward contribution
- Involve people in decision making
- Drive out fear
- Communicate openly and frequently

<u>Have High Integrity</u>

- Operate from principles
- Tell people what they need to hear, not what they want to hear
- Meet commitments
- Make decisions based on data
- Establish and adhere to success criteria

<u>Behave as an Owner</u>

- Be proactive and at cause
- Have a high sense of urgency
- Focus on business results
- Tie individual success to business success
- Be innovative
- Aggressively reapply good ideas
- Enjoy your work
- Take appropriate risks

<u>Be a Team Player</u>

- Lead as appropriate/support as appropriate
- Seek first to understand
- Encourage diverse viewpoints
- Think win/win
- Build superior customer/supplier relationships

<u>Have a High Degree of Functional Excellence</u>

- Develop a high skill level
- Be thorough
- Be professional
- Learn continuously
- Provide continuity of assignments
- Focus where we each uniquely add value
- Understand work processes
- Improve processes/systems

For P&G, three of these values that have been part of the culture for a long time are: (1) treat people as our most important asset, (2) have high integrity, and (3) have a high degree of functional excellence. The other three values are areas that the P&G Soap Sector is presently working to improve, notably (1) have constancy of purpose, (2) behave as an owner, and (3) be a team player. These represent values which the Soap Sector is not consistently operating against today but must in the future. Constancy of purpose is needed to overcome a history of new programs each year. Setting a direction and standing by it over time are key to achieving sustained competitive advantage. Constancy of purpose reduces ambiguity and provides the basis for the next value – behave as an owner. Developing ownerlike behaviors in all P&G employees will bring out desired characteristics such as proactiveness, innovation, and individual responsibility which will ultimately lead to business success. Being a team player is a dramatic departure from the company's culture, which traditionally rewarded individual accomplishment. Refocusing achievement-oriented individuals to working harmoniously in a group setting, appreciating diverse viewpoints, and attempting to bring about "win/win" solutions requires a shift in thinking for many people.

Since these are three new values, people must be taught about them. They must be reinforced by management's behaviors and decisions. Behavior consistent with these values must be rewarded.

VISION

Once the purpose is clear and the values are established, the next step is to develop the vision statement – in other words, what we want to create over the long term – both in terms of business success and organizational capability. A vision statement is nothing more than a verbal picture of the future, ideally five to ten years out. It is best to write these statements in the present tense to help bring them to life and to add sufficient detail so that most people in the organization get the full flavor of the desired future state. Once developed, this vision must be broadly communicated and periodically renewed. The P&G Soap Sector vision is to become the best soap company in the world. This goal has been further delineated in a nine-paragraph statement which is posted prominently in all conference rooms and on all bulletin boards throughout the organization.

The most important aspect of a vision statement is that it must be a living vision, used extensively throughout the organization. It cannot be senior management's vision posted on the wall, never to be used again. Decisions must be consistent with the values and vision. Not until the vision statement is used to make decisions will it come to life for the organization.

Once this begins to happen, people will align with it because it makes sense. For example, the decision to shut down a plant has a negative connotation. If management does not use its values and vision statement in implementing the shutdown, its actions will affect the culture of the company for many years to come. The values and vision must continue to be the driving principle that guides management's actions in both good and bad times.

Developing a vision statement should not consume an exorbitant amount of the organization's time; rather, it can be done in a fairly efficient, straightforward way. It must be broadly communicated, then used as the basis for making decisions. In 1980, Procter and Gamble faced a difficult situation when its Rely brand was associated with Toxic Shock Syndrome. The company made a quick, landmark decision to get out of the tampon business. The chairman of the Board later said that the decision, though painful, was an easy one given the corporate value of assuring consumer safety.

Vision statements differ from mission statements. A mission statement provides a definition of the business an organization is in, whereas a vision statement is an expression of hope – hope of what the organization would like to be.

The statement should provide the following for any organization:

1. *Direction.* It should provide direction and definition for the organization. It should establish what the organization wants to succeed in, what it does, and what it does not do.
2. *Focus.* It should focus on the activities that distinguish it from others. It should tell people how and where to channel their efforts.
3. *Value.* The statement should include the values of the organization, how the organization wants to be seen internally and externally, and how it wants to attain its goals.
4. *Meaning.* The statement should be meaningful to individuals both within and outside the organization.
5. *Challenge.* The statement should have a measure of challenge in it. Challenge gives the direction for putting energy to tasks.
6. *Passion.* The statement should be such that those in the organization feel enthusiasm, commitment, and pride.

BUSINESS AND ORGANIZATION STRATEGY

After many years of doing strategic planning, P&G has found that it is imperative that the strategic plan focus not only on the business strategy, but also on the strategy for building the organization's capability to implement the business strategy. The questions that are asked are similar, and many of the elements of the strategic plan are identical. In the case of the purpose statement, for example, functional departments in the organization would ask the question, "why do we exist as an organization?" The answer to this question should identify what competitive advantage will come from that function.

Every functional department in the organization should exist to provide competitive advantage. Over time, management must decide which parts of the organization – be it manufacturing, logistics, marketing, or sales – are going to be part of the company's value-added competitive advantage. In any business, effort should be devoted to those things that will make a difference in the eyes of customers and consumers.

ALIGNING WITH CUSTOMER AND CONSUMER NEEDS

In order to create value, a company must align its organizational units with the needs of its customers (trade) and the ultimate consumers (households). Understanding purchase criteria is a critical first step. It is generally recognized that the following purchase criteria are important for P&G's products:

1. *Performance*. What the product is designed to do; the benefits it provides.
2. *Dependability*. How well the product performs versus expectations time after time.
3. *Price*. What the consumer must pay for the benefits received.
4. *Availability*. The ease of obtaining the product and its in-stock status at the time of purchase.
5. *Awareness*. Awareness that the product exists and offers certain benefits to the consumer. Consumers can be disappointed that no product meets certain needs when, in fact, the product is simply not known to the potential consumer.
6. *Image*. The intangible benefits of a product that fill the emotional needs of consumers. Knowing that the product is "the best" for doing a particular function.
7. *Service*. In some industries, the after sale is extremely important in the purchase decision.

Figure 5 illustrates a "market in" approach to organizational alignment. The consumer and customer are shown at the center of the diagram. Within the dotted circle are the consumer and customer needs which are influenced primarily by each of four functional organizations: sales, advertising, product supply, and product development.

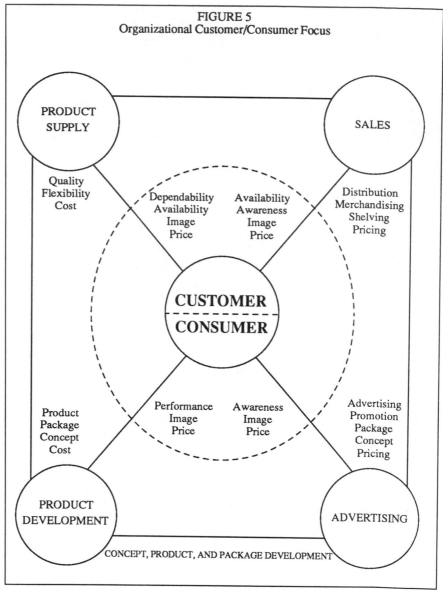

FIGURE 5
Organizational Customer/Consumer Focus

Outside the dotted circle are those internal functional elements that have a direct effect on meeting or exceeding the consumer needs shown inside the circle. For example, the product development function primarily influences the consumer's need for performance, image, and price. In order to satisfy these needs, the product development organization works on the product design, package design, product concept, and product cost. On the other hand, the product development organization typically does not affect things like product availability or awareness. This model provides a clear framework for understanding what each function of the organization should do to maximize P&G's competitive advantage. The role of each functional organization is to provide competitive advantage in one or more of their areas of primary influence.

OBJECTIVES, GOALS, STRATEGIES, AND MEASURES

Once the long-term vision is developed for the entire organization, individual business units and functional departments begin developing their strategy for realizing that vision. P&G's Soap Sector uses a convention that is referred to as OGSMs, which is shorthand for Objectives, Goals, Strategies, and Measures. The objective clarifies what we want to achieve in broadly defined, qualitative terms. The goals are the specific, tangible, quantitative measures that are used to track progress toward the objective. Objectives and goals should be the same for both the business and organization strategies. Next come the strategies – the how – specifically, how we will achieve competitive advantage in order to meet the objectives and ultimately realize the vision. Strategies represent choices that must be made in order to focus everyone's efforts. Once again, progress on these strategies must be measured in specific, tangible terms and reported frequently, often graphically. These measures must also connect directly with the reward system for teams and individuals.

Strategies are a series of interrelated decisions on *how* the company is going to achieve competitive advantage. Strategic choices commit resources. For example, saying that a company is going to be the low-cost producer means allocating resources against building a distinctive competency around total costs. Once a company commits itself to a strategic path, it is not readily reversible. If a company views its direction as easily changed, then management is probably not operating at the strategic level. Strategic direction requires a strong commitment by the organization, and it is intended to have the long-term effect of creating sustainable competitive advantage(s). The characteristics of a good strategy include:

1. *Tough Choices.* It causes managers to choose between significantly different ways of doing business.
2. *Internally Consistent.* If the strategy does not focus a company's actions or polarizes activities, then it is not internally consistent.
3. *Complete and Minimal.* There should be as few strategies as necessary to give the company a complete direction.
4. *Robust.* It is better than the competitor's strategy.
5. *Realistic.* It must be attainable for the organization; it should call for realistic actions and outcomes.

6. *Timely*. Strategy is highly dependent on timing from both an organizational and a market perspective.

Each business unit develops specific strategies and measures for its business. In essence, what we end up with is an OGSM model where the objective represents *what* we want to achieve, and the strategies represent *how* we are going to achieve it, with goals and measures designed to track progress.

This deployment of the strategic plan is typically done only through two or three levels of the organization, at which point it becomes more helpful to develop specific action plans that list the activities that individuals and teams are going to undertake in order to implement the strategy. These action plans then become the basis for individual responsibility and accountability and provide an ongoing tracking mechanism to insure that the appropriate actions are being taken in order to deliver the overall strategic plan. When put all together, these elements make up a relatively simple, yet holistic strategy planning and deployment process that aligns the organization and thereby focuses the effort against the long-term vision.

MEASURES

Several different types of measurement are used in the strategic plan because measurement is critical for any organization. There is a saying at Procter and Gamble that "you get what you measure." In other words, the organization pays attention to those things that are measured, reported, and tracked over time. It is extremely important, however, that measures are quantitative and objective in order to provide a real understanding of what's happening.

In his book *In Search of Excellence*, Tom Peters reported results from a random sample of male adults who were asked to rank themselves in several areas. In terms of their ability to get along with others, 100 percent put themselves in the top 50 percent of the population and 60 percent put themselves in the top 10 percent of the population – not a very objective measure. In terms of leadership ability, 70 percent felt they were in the top 25 percent of the population and only 2 percent knew they were below average. In terms of athletic ability, 60 percent felt they were in the top 25 percent, whereas 6 percent acknowledged they were below average.

Participants in a Procter and Gamble training class were asked to evaluate how well customer needs were being met (Figure 6). On average, these participants rated themselves about a 9 out of 10 in terms of how well their organization was meeting the requirements of their customers. Inter-

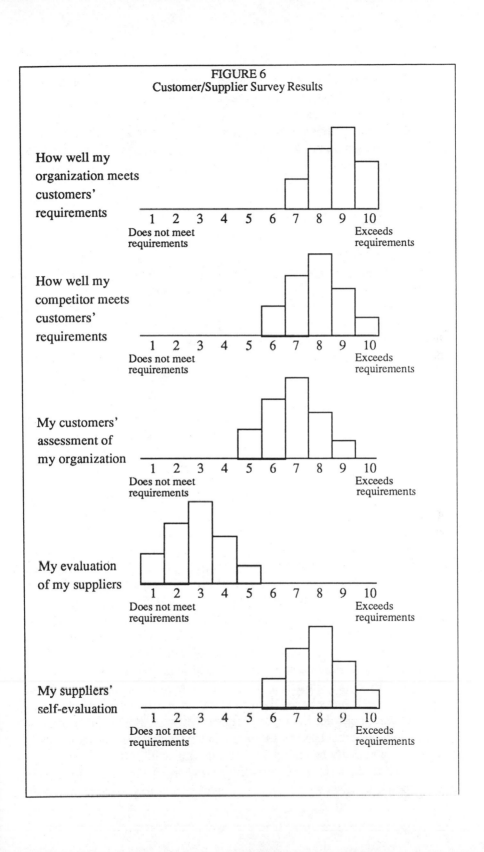

FIGURE 6
Customer/Supplier Survey Results

estingly, they rated their competitors about an 8 on this same scale, but they acknowledged that their customers would only rate them at about a 7 on this scale. When it came to evaluating their suppliers, they rated them only a 3 in meeting their needs. Ironically, they also felt that the suppliers' self-evaluation would be closer to an 8. These examples reinforce the point that, although measurement is important, the choice of the measure is equally important.

ROLE OF THE LEADER

Once the strategic plan is complete and the measures are established, quality visits by the leadership are used to monitor progress and to stimulate corrective actions where necessary. These quality visits are very critical and can have a positive or negative effect on the organization, depending upon how they are conducted. A good quality visit is helpful, and not punishing. This is achieved by focusing on the process which is used to get results as opposed to focusing on the people who are getting the results. Ideally, the quality visit should be a learning experience for all involved as opposed to learning for the subordinate alone. Furthermore, the discussion should focus forward to what will be done in the future as opposed to focusing primarily on the past.

A successful quality visit depends in large measure on the specific questions which are asked. First of all, they must be designed to ensure that the organization being visited is focusing on their most important objectives and the right processes for their achievement. And secondly, they should be positioned such that the organization views the executive visitors as there to help, as a resource to improvement and realization of their objectives.

The role of the leader in this whole process is pivotal. While this is true whether or not an organization is working to become a Total Quality organization, it is even more acute in a Total Quality organization. The leader is depended on to provide clear direction. Without clear direction, no organization has a chance of operating in a Total Quality way. Furthermore, the leader must insure constancy of purpose and avoid annual programs and shifting priorities. Such abrupt changes are debilitating to any organization. The leader must model the type of behavior that is expected of everyone else in the organization and to that end plays an extensive teaching role. Finally, the leader must be able to put things in context for the organization so that what may be seen as competing priorities can actually be understood as synergistic efforts.

In essence, in a Total Quality organization, the leader must move beyond being an inspector of the actions of others to proactively adding value to the organization by doing those things that no one else in the organization is capable of doing.

During a visit to Japan, I was struck by the differences in the leadership behaviors at the best Japanese companies relative to the United States. Figure 7 summarizes some of these observations to show this contrast. The differences are striking, indicating that there is a very different paradigm of what leadership is all about in many Japanese companies compared to what has historically been the case in the United States. The following are just a sampling: patience versus impatience; teams versus individuals; your subordinates are your customers versus your boss is your customer; problems are treasures versus problems are a sign of weakness; the focus is clear to everyone versus everything is important; management's span of support versus management's span of control; continuity versus frequent assignment changes; and finally, probably the most fundamental, management by systems versus management by objectives.

PEOPLE AND REWARDS

People make strategy happen. The relationship between strategy and people must be managed very carefully. Without reinforcing rewards, it does not take long for the people in an organization to become confused about their work, to become disillusioned with the vision, and disconnected from the plan. To insure that the strategic plan is implemented throughout the organization, many factors and their relationships must be understood and managed. Figure 8 shows some important factors to consider. Starting at the top, leadership vision, along with business and cultural strategies, creates both business and organizational expectations. This first relationship is critical to the entire process. From clarity of purpose, values, and vision come the expectations for the entire organization. Senior management must ensure that the vision and strategies are the product of realistic analysis. If organization and business expectations are set with an inadequate understanding of the company's situation, the organization will be charged with a plan doomed to fail, no matter how hard people in the organization try.

If senior management has done the planning correctly, then clarity of vision can empower the organization. Individual roles will be much clearer. People will be able to avoid, to some extent, the paralyzing effects of role conflict and ambiguity. Role clarity leads to individual empowerment and organizational alignment. Role clarity and organizational alignment help produce the expected performance on the part of individuals and teams leading to anticipated results. When results are directly related to rewards, as perceived by individuals, they reinforce role clarity within the

FIGURE 7
Comparison of Management Techniques

Best Japanese Companies	Typical U.S. Companies
• Focus on customer satisfaction	• Focus on profit
• Market in (supply demand)	• Product out (create demand)
• Manage by means/systems	• Manage by objectives
• Holistic approach	• Linear/segmented approach
• Patience	• Impatience
• Incremental improvement	• Breakthrough improvements
• Teams	• Individuals
• Leaders teach	• Staff/consultants teach
• Continuous education (investment)	• Sporadic training (expense)
• Top management has technical background	• Top management has marketing or financial background
• Top management contact with plant/ customers	• Top management distant from plant/customers
• Your subordinates are your customers	• Your boss is your customer
• Homogeneity (conformity)	• Diversity (individuality)
• Problems are treasures	• Problems are a sign of weakness
• Visual communication techniques	• Verbal communication techniques
• Sequential phases of corporate direction	• Independent corporate programs not sustained
• Standardization is essential	• Standardization is constraining
• Focus is clear to everyone	• Everything is important
• Top-down direction is followed	• Top-down direction is resisted
• Everyone is responsible for improvement	• "They" are responsible for improve- ment
• Top people working on TQ	• Staff working on TQ
• Methodical/relentless	• Hit and run
• Make commitments	• Make promises
• Engineers/development in plants	• Engineers/development away from plants
• Management span of support	• Management span of control
• Continuity	• Frequent assignment changes
• Crisis mentality	• Complacency

organization. This reinforcing effect of perceived rewards leads to a new and stronger cycle of empowered behavior on the part of the individual which will lead to enhanced performance and results. In other words, vision, performance, and rewards are as closely related to one another as the mind, the hand, and the eyes are for a human being. Too often, the

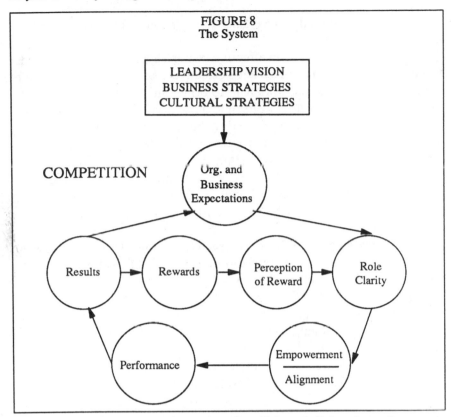

FIGURE 8
The System

strategic planning process is managed as if the mind, hands, and eyes are separate functions unrelated in producing results.

TEAM EFFECTIVENESS

At P&G we have a culture that has historically emphasized individual accomplishment and individual creativity. As we move more and more into a culture that values teamwork and places a premium on being a team player, some teams and individuals have had real difficulty being effective. Three aspects of a team's operation have proven helpful in making a team-based organization effective. The first is role clarity – that is, being absolutely clear on what the team is expected to do and what it is not expected to do. The key principles regarding a team's role are that they should focus only on value-added work – that work which they are uniquely suited to do better than any other team or individual in the organization. Furthermore, the team's role should focus on a few things for maximum impact. Part of the team's role should be to provide a learning environment for each individual on the team and the team collectively.

Finally, the team should make extensive use of subteams and individuals to do the actual work.

The second aspect of team effectiveness is leadership. The team leader is the critical determinant of a team's effectiveness. To that end, the leader must facilitate discussion, work hard to bring out diverse viewpoints, and insure that the team is restricting itself to those areas identified as the team's unique role. The team leader should make frequent use of Total Quality tools both to manage the team process and to model the behavior that is expected of the individuals on the team. The leader must also be the driver to reach resolution on issues since one of the most debilitating outcomes for a team is continued debate without resolution. Finally, the team leader must be a role model which the team can individually and collectively learn from over time.

Numerous techniques have emerged as being effective in a team setting. A few of these are brainstorming, the use of fishbone diagrams, force field analysis, and tree diagrams. These tools enable the team leader to display the thinking of the group graphically in order to avoid endless debate. Another technique that has proven extremely effective in a team setting is why questioning, or as the Japanese call it, asking why five times or until you get to the bottom of an issue. Inevitably, a Total Quality organization will need to master team effectiveness. There is nothing magical about it; it just takes hard work, and once a team is developed and knows how to be effective, it will begin to generate individuals who are equipped to be team leaders in the future.

IMPLEMENTING TOTAL QUALITY

People often ask, if we had it to do over again, would we approach Total Quality in the same way at P&G. The answer to this question is obviously no. As mentioned earlier, our approach has been bottom up, not top down. Consultants and practitioners alike consistently teach that the best approach is to begin with the leader and then deploy Total Quality down throughout the organization. Clearly, if we were starting over today and knew everything we know now, we would follow that advice. This approach is outlined in Figure 9, based on learning from Fuji-Xerox.

Ideally, the implementation of Total Quality should begin with consensus among the leadership which leads to a commitment to take action to implement Total Quality in everything. This is shown as the initial step to reinforce the idea that you should not begin until you have it. With this consensus in place, the first step is education, specifically, on the key elements of Total Quality, the concepts, the systems, and the tools – not all at once, but as the organization evolves in its understanding and then

FIGURE 9
Total Quality Implementation

Obtain consensus among leadership	Spread TQ education	Improve TQ capability within departments	Improve cooperation between departments	Establish a Total Quality system
	• Concepts	• Functional excellence	• Strategic planning	• Link quality control and profit control
	• Systems	• Problem-solving ability	• Strategy deployment	
	• Tools	• Standardize daily activities	• Product launch	
		• Improvement teams	• People development	

needs additional education in order to continue to grow. Once equipped with a basic understanding and tools, the initial efforts are best focused against functional quality, or daily work – in other words, focusing on improving what we do either individually or within a particular department on a day-to-day basis. This generally involves working on problem-solving skills, standardizing daily activities to the current best approach, and establishing improvement teams to begin working on those areas of major opportunity. As functional excellence begins to become established, the organization can move into cross-functional quality, looking at those systems that apply broadly across the board and typically are the highest leverage systems for overall organization results. These systems are typically things like strategy development and deployment, product launch, standardization, information systems, and people systems. The last phase of implementation is merely called Total Quality. This is where the organization brings together profit management with Total Quality, such that there is one holistic approach to operating the business as opposed to separate approaches to doing the work versus managing the profits. Few, if any, companies have evolved to this final step, either in Japan or elsewhere in the world.

At P&G, most efforts are currently in functional quality and cross-functional quality. We are still near the beginning of the Total Quality journey – a journey we expect to continue for decades to come.

CHAPTER 31

CONTINUOUS IMPROVEMENT AT U. S. PAPER MILLS CORPORATION*

THOMAS L. OLSON
President and Chief Executive Officer
U.S. Paper Mills Corporation

JAMES G. SCHMIDT
Technical Director
U.S. Paper Mills Corporation

GREGORY M. BOUNDS
Research Associate
Management Development Center
University of Tennessee

KENNETH E. KIRBY
Associate Professor of Industrial Engineering
University of Tennessee

SUMMARY

For many years U. S. Paper Mills Corporation was run by an entrepreneur who successfully provided value to his customers. His success can largely be attributed to his business philosophies and his depth of experience in all phases of the business. The small size of the company and the fairly small number of regular customers were well within the entrepreneur's ability to keep on top of his customers' needs.

------

*We thank Nancy Gustafson for her diligence and assistance in preparing this chapter.

But what happens when the entrepreneur is no longer active in the daily operations of the business? What happens when the company doubles in size and when many of the new employees have been operating under different business philosophies? What happens when customers make new demands for such things as statistical data and other formal evidence of quality?

It is in such a context that U. S. Paper embarked on its quest for continuous improvement. In this chapter we discuss this quest.

COMPANY BACKGROUND

U. S. Paper Mills Corporation is a small, privately owned business with its headquarters located in De Pere, Wisconsin. It is a producer of corestock used for manufacturing spirally wound tubes and cores. All of its products are made from recycled fibers, and all its products are recyclable. Its customers are located from coast to coast and as far south as Mexico, and include such tissue and toweling industry leaders as James River Corporation, Fort Howard Corporation, Kimberly-Clark Corporation, Scott Worldwide, Pope & Talbot Inc., Wisconsin Tissue Mills, Inc., and Georgia-Pacific Corporation.

The company has two paper mills located in Wisconsin. The De Pere mill produces 100 tons per day of primarily lightweight tissue and toweling corestock. The Menasha mill currently produces 100 tons per day of lightweight corestock and another 165 tons per day of heavier weight corestock. The company also operates two converting plants that make paper tubes and cores. One plant is located in De Pere and the other in North St. Paul, Minnesota.

The principal stockholder of the corporation is Walter R. Cloud, Jr., who, together with his family, owns approximately 60 percent of the company's stock. Walter has over fifty years of experience in the paper industry, all of it with U. S. Paper. He is the founder of the company and the entrepreneur largely responsible for the company's success. For health reasons, he stepped down as chairman of the board and chief executive officer in 1988.

BUSINESS PHILOSOPHY

Although Walter is no longer active in the day-to-day affairs of the company, his philosophies toward business continue to provide much of the basis for how the company operates. Four of his philosophies have been instrumental in the company's success over the years: (1) a firm belief in strong business relationships; (2) an obsession about customer service; (3) a flexibility toward changing conditions based on unchanging values; and (4) a knack for "doing the right thing." Each of these philosophies is discussed below.

Relationships. Walter appreciates the value of strong relationships with customers. U. S. Paper has little interest in simply "making a sale," and has great interest in establishing friendships and developing business partnerships. It has been the company's practice to get to know not just a customer's buyer, but also the other key people throughout its organization. In vendor/customer situations, too often one of the parties is treated as just another name on a rolodex or as a nuisance who is soon trapped in bureaucratic red tape. By contrast, if a friendly partnership exists, the parties treat each other as friends. They jointly find a solution that is mutually beneficial, and the partnership grows.

In addition to developing strong relationships with customers, the company has built up strong, positive relationships with its employees. The company has never had a work stoppage owing to a labor dispute. The union contract negotiations typically last only one or two days. By maintaining a realistic and fair attitude, issues are discussed and mutually resolved before they turn into problems. As a reflection of the company's confidence in its employees' ability to run the day-to-day business, there is no management supervision on second, third, or weekend shifts.

Lastly, the company recognizes the importance of strong relationships with suppliers and others who provide service or value to the business. If a machine goes down in the middle of the night, or if cash flow requires short-term borrowing, it is a lot easier getting help from a friend than it is from someone who is a stranger to the business.

Service to Customers. Walter has an obsession about service to customers. The slogan on the top of the company's letterhead reads "The House of Service for 50 years." Serving customers may mean breaking into a manufacturing schedule, securing special shipping arrangements, or managing customer inventories. U. S. Paper finds a way to serve its customers. This commitment to service has sealed positive relationships with many long-term customers.

Flexibility and Values. Walter believes a successful organization must be flexible. Manufacturing processes, technology, personnel, customers, and their needs are constantly changing. Therefore, U. S. Paper has sought to embrace change and to take advantage of the opportunities that change creates. What has not changed, however, are the company's values. Trust, fairness, openness, compassion, commitment, loyalty, and professionalism have laid the strong foundation for a flexible organizational structure and attitude adaptable to changing conditions. No doubt the small size of the company made it easier both for these values to take root and for employees to recognize the need to be flexible.

Doing the Right Thing. In his relationships and in making business decisions, Walter has had a knack for doing the right thing, strategically and operationally. Finding the company's niche in the stable tissue and toweling corestock market, targeting logical customers, extending special kindnesses or favors to business friends, upgrading manufacturing processes, building employee morale – whatever was right to do at the time, he did it.

NEED FOR QUALITY PROGRAM

When Walter's health required him to withdraw from the day-to-day business in late 1986, the company had changed. With the purchase of the Menasha mill in November 1983, it was no longer a one-mill operation. Sales had grown from $10 million in 1982 to approximately $25 million in 1986. The number of employees and customers had more than doubled.

Not only had the company grown and the man who had kept his finger on every aspect of the business withdrawn from daily operations, but customer demands were also changing. More and more, customers were requesting statistical data and other evidence of quality.

In early 1987, the company's executive vice president, Bob Cloud, and its new president, Tom Olson, were struggling with how to develop and implement a formal quality program. Both men knew that any quality program at U. S. Paper should be consistent with Walter's philosophies of strong business relationships, service to customers, flexibility with respect to change, uncompromised values, and doing the right thing.

In June 1987, Bob and Tom attended a one-week senior executive session at the University of Tennessee Management Development Center. The course consisted of continuous improvement philosophy and training in statistical process control. Both men returned tremendously enthused, but they found it difficult to convey and transfer their enthusiasm to the other managers who had not shared the experience. Both Bob and Tom felt their experience at the University of Tennessee gave them a different insight to continuous improvement than the company's other managers who had not shared the experience.

Around the same time, Bob and Tom had lunch with two managers from a large local paper company who were scheduled to participate in one of the programs at the University of Tennessee. When asked what their company was doing with its continuous improvement program, they indicated some of their people were going to the University of Tennessee; others had been to hear Dr. Deming or to Crosby's college or to some other mecca for continuous improvement training. What became apparent was that not only is it difficult to convey the enthusiasm one gets after participating in a quality training program, but also the matter becomes even more complicated when managers within an organization are trained at different times in somewhat different approaches to continuous improvement.

Another issue resurfaced. What would be the role of managers if, as some companies' continuous improvement programs had done, all decision making were pushed onto the manufacturing floor? U. S. Paper has always believed that a close relationship between management and the workforce is essential and that management must rely on the workforce to identify problems, to assist in finding solutions, and ultimately to run the daily operations. However, from their training at the University of Tennessee, Bob and Tom firmly believed that the great majority of systems improvements must come from the managers. Thus, under U. S. Paper's continuous improvement program, the role of managers must change from problem solving to system improvement and the role of the workforce must change from following instructions to making the decisions necessary to maintain systems.

As Bob and Tom contemplated how to get going, several things became clear: (1) The program must be led by top management, and it was agreed Tom would lead the program with Walter and Bob's full support. (2) The program must be focused on the managers. (3) All managers should hear the same message and preferably at the same time. (4) Managers' new roles should be clearly understood.

DEVELOPMENT OF A CONTINUOUS IMPROVEMENT PROGRAM

In order to generate widespread enthusiasm for its continuous improvement program and to insure a common understanding of the continuous improvement philosophy, U. S. Paper established a partnership with the University of Tennessee Management Development Center and its Institute for Productivity through Quality and together designed an in-house custom course for all managers. Prior to the formal training sessions, two instructors from the University of Tennessee came to Wisconsin, visited the company's work sites, examined the manufacturing processes, and began establishing relationships with the company's managers. The instructors were selected because of their significant experience as engineers and managers in private industry, and their knowledge of continuous improvement philosophy and statistical methods. Perhaps, most important, the company was confident that their personalities would allow them to relate across the breadth of the company's varied managerial backgrounds.

Concurrently, the company sent its technical director to the University of Tennessee's three-week program in statistical process control so that he might be a resource for other managers. The intent was that he could work with the Management Development Center to develop case studies, examples, and problems using papermaking terms to which the company's managers could more easily relate.

During the initial four-day training session held in February 1988, all of the company's managers were exposed to the same continuous improvement philosophy and the same basic training in statistical process control. At the conclusion of the session, each manager selected a system to study. Their task was to define the system, analyze it, and begin using some of the statistical methods they learned to better understand the system, bring it under control, and improve it.

Many of the systems analyzed involved segments of the manufacturing process, such as a comparison of raw material formulas versus actual usage, stock consistency and freeness (drainage) at various points of the process, converting waste, process downtime, and process limp time. Other systems included a wide range of topics, including accuracy of sales forecasts, accuracy of shipping documents, the payroll process, information gathering and dissemination, customer ordering, customer complaints, transportation availability, and production rate measurement.

Most managers followed a procedure similar to the following: (1) define the scope of the system; (2) establish a goal for the project; (3) flowchart the current system; (4) develop a fishbone analysis to identify sources of variability; (5) identify data analysis techniques appropriate to measure sources of variation; (6) gather data and use appropriate statistical tools; (7) analyze data; and (8) begin work on improving the system (bring it under control, reduce variation, and redesign the system).

At a "show and tell" session two months later, managers described what they had learned about their systems. In the lively discussions following each presentation, three significant events occurred. First, it became apparent that many of the "systems" were actually processes or subprocesses of much larger systems. Second, managers began to realize the extent to which the various departments and divisions were interdependent. Third, the organization began to really "open up." No topics were sacred, and virtually all the hot issues, either recent, current, or those that were beginning to simmer, were discussed. How the various departments and divisions interface, how the company relates to and deals with customers, how prices are established for products, how the workforce should be involved in the continuous improvement process, how people should be rewarded – these and many more topics were discussed, often with participation by managers who previously had kept their comments, for the most part, to themselves.

Two months later, the company held another two-day session. Projects were again presented. This time, however, they included some group projects, that primarily involved manufacturing processes. The managers also discussed four company traits from the perspective of how they existed at that time and how managers would like them to be in five years. The four traits were (1) culture; (2) organizational structure; (3) individual manager's backgrounds, skills, and training; and (4) individual manager's role perceptions. Again, the lively discussions during this session bolstered the openness of the organization both to change and to the views of individual managers.

The partnership between U. S. Paper and the University of Tennessee continues to grow. In addition to the regular sessions involving all managers, the company has sent several of its managers to Knoxville to participate in various Institutes for Productivity through Quality. Managers have attended the Three Week SPC Institute, the Senior Executive Program, the Design of Experiments Course, the Cost Management Program, and Alumni Conferences. U. S. Paper believes the University of Tennessee is on the leading edge of continuous improvement theory. Testament to that fact is the number of major corporations that regularly participate in its programs. Even though U. S. Paper is relatively small, through its partnership with the University of Tennessee and its participation in programs attended by major industry leaders, the company is exposed to virtually everything new that is going on in American industry. This exposure, together with valuable input from the University, allows the company to select and adopt those continuous improvement practices and techniques that make sense for U. S. Paper.

MEASURES OF SUCCESS

Continuous improvement is working at U. S. Paper. Confirmation of this fact came five times during one two-week period a little over a year after the program began. Here is what happened during those two weeks: (1) the De Pere mill received notice that it had been selected as the sole supplier of corestock for a greenfield mill being built to produce a premium quality line of bathroom tissue; (2) a West Coast customer notified the De Pere mill that it would no longer be necessary to send a duplicate sample of stock with each carload of corestock because the customer was satisfied with U. S. Paper's efforts both in reducing variation and in lowering the average of a minute substance common to recycled paper but harmful to the customer's process; (3) the Menasha mill was notified it would receive the first ever Certified Supplier Award from a customer who three years earlier considered U. S. Paper one of its worst suppliers in terms of quality; (4) in a formal vendor review, a customer of the Menasha mill rated U. S. Paper its top corestock supplier from among three (one of which was a mill owned by the customer's parent), and furthermore, under the customer's rating procedure, U. S. Paper rated as the top supplier of any product the customer used in its manufacturing process; and (5) after an extensive evaluation process lasting well over a year, the De Pere core plant was selected from a field of three to be the sole supplier of mill cores to a local, major producer of toilet tissue and toweling. Obviously, not every two-week period shows as many significant results. Nonetheless, U. S. Paper regularly sees similar examples confirming the success of its continuous improvement program.

CHALLENGE: WORKING CROSS-FUNCTIONALLY

The more managers investigated systems and measured results, it became obvious the systems of the business are not independent. In fact, the discussions following project presentations demonstrated that the business is a conglomeration of processes and systems often intertwined and confounded by each other and involving several conventional, functional departments. As an example, the ability to deliver a product on time was found to cross sales, scheduling, technical, manufacturing, shipping, and administrative boundaries. Processes within one department are linked to processes in other departments which originally appeared to be independent. The more these links were investigated, it was found that they were not only important but critical. The organization came to the realization that it could best create value for its customers by managing critical, linked, cross-functional systems.

Ironically, to a large extent this realization is simply a return to the company's roots. Walter's knack for "doing the right thing" was actually an ability to make quality decisions by thinking cross-functionally. Until recent years when he stepped back from daily operations and the company grew, he was personally, actively linked to all functional departments of the company.

What Walter did intuitively for many years, the company is now trying to accomplish on a broader scale. The company is attempting to institutionalize the managerial practices of an entrepreneur into the practices of a team of professional managers. As an organization, U. S. Paper must make quality decisions by developing critical, cross-functional management systems focused on creating customer value.

The task is not a simple one. In 1989, the company embarked on its largest expansion to date, a $15 million project for installing a new paper machine at the Menasha mill. The new machine came on line in early 1990. The company anticipates sales from the new machine and other normal growth will raise the company's 1991 revenues to approximately $45 million. The new machine project has monopolized several managers' schedules and has involved large blocks of time from most of the company's other managers. The attention of managers to the continuous improvement program no doubt suffered during the new machine construction and start-up. Moreover, the company has several relatively new managers who came to U. S. Paper with many years of experience in larger, more traditional companies. The company has found that thinking cross-functionally is not always easy for these managers who are accustomed to operating through traditional, strict functional management systems.

NECESSARY CONDITIONS FOR WORKING CROSS-FUNCTIONALLY

U. S. Paper recognizes that certain conditions must exist in order for the organization to make quality decisions and to effectively work cross-functionally. Many of these conditions remain based on the business philosophies of Walter Cloud – namely, strong relationships, obsession with customer service, flexibility toward change, and adherence to the company's value system. Among these necessary conditions are the following:

Strategy. By having strong customer relationships, the company will recognize and understand what customers value and will do whatever is right to provide that value. Critical cross-functional systems must be developed and managed focused on customer value and driven by continuous improvement.

Environment. An atmosphere of trust and openness must exist. Employees and all those who deal with the company should expect to be treated with fairness and professionalism. While individual creativity and initiative will be encouraged, harmony within the organization and with customers must be paramount. A cooperative spirit must permeate throughout the organization.

Structure. Traditional, functional departmental and divisional barriers must be broken down. The structure will be flatter, less formal, and more flexible. Managers will have responsibilities both within and outside traditional reporting lines.

People. The company must retain and attract people capable of thinking and acting cross-functionally. These individuals must be flexible toward change and be more concerned about the organization as a whole than any personal agendas. Before making decisions, individuals must be willing to ask themselves – who else in the organization will be affected by this decision and should they be consulted? And, what other resources, particularly within the organization, can help make this a better decision and promote harmony within the organization?

Training. Rather than mass training the entire workforce on all aspects of statistical process control, workers will be selectively trained in those skills necessary to identify problems, to work effectively as team members, and to maintain the systems with which they work. Managers must understand and be able to use statistical methods to reduce variation. They must understand the sources of variation most important to the customer and prioritize the use of resources in reducing that variation. In short, they must be trained to improve systems. Through formal and informal training, managers must understand the business of U. S. Paper and how their performance impacts the entire organization.

Opportunities. Upper management must create opportunities for individuals to utilize their individual talents and acquire new skills. Cross-functional systems can provide opportunities for managers beyond their regular duties either as leaders of such systems or as valuable resources and team members. Such opportunities offer individuals challenges and a better understanding of how the entire organization operates. The company will benefit from greater flexibility and enthusiasm throughout the organization.

Learning from Examples. The organization should be receptive to constructive discussions of both good and bad decisions and their impact on the company's business. The difference between a quality decision and one that is not is difficult for everyone to understand, and open discussions can lead to both a better understanding and more quality decisions.

Reward Systems. Reward systems, formal and otherwise, should promote the welfare of the entire organization and the willingness to think and act cross-functionally.

U. S. PAPER'S COMMITMENT

U. S. Paper appreciates the desirability *and* the difficulty of thinking and working cross-functionally. Because the company believes that effectively working that way can give it a distinct competitive advantage, U. S. Paper intends both to create and maintain the conditions that foster cross-functional work and to develop those critical cross-functional management systems that will provide increasing value to its customers.

CHAPTER 32

APPLICATION TO GOVERNMENT: U.S. ARMY, WATERVLIET ARSENAL

GREGORY J. CONWAY
Chief, Statistical Methods Office
Watervliet Arsenal

G. HARLAN CAROTHERS, JR.
Senior Lecturer, Institutes for Productivity
University of Tennessee

SUMMARY

This chapter discusses the practical realities associated with implementing systems management using Watervliet Arsenal as an example; as such, it gives us an opportunity to examine the issues unique to government application. There is no pretense suggesting that these changes are complete. Conversely, there has been and continues to be a significant effort at the executive level to improve internal systems for the direct creation of customer value. The primary message learned at Watervliet is that any significant improvement of the value delivered to customers requires a systems management approach, which in turn requires a change in the current definition of management.

BACKGROUND

Watervliet Arsenal, a separate installation under command of the U.S. Army Armament, Munitions and Chemical Command, is located in Watervliet, New York, just north of Albany. Its mission is to perform procurement, fabrication, and product assurance of cannon components for self-propelled and towed artillery, tanks, mortars, and recoilless rifles. It employs approximately 1,800 people executing an annual $140 million program. Its principal customer is the United States Army; other Department of Defense services, the Department of Energy, defense weapons systems contractors, and friendly foreign countries are also served by the Arsenal. Established in 1813, Watervliet is the oldest continuously operating arsenal in the United States and currently operates as a government-owned, government-operated facility.

EARLY DEVELOPMENT OF THE WATERVLIET ARSENAL QUALITY IMPROVEMENT EFFORT

Throughout the years of producing cannon, Watervliet has worked hard to establish and maintain its international reputation as the source of the world's premium quality cannon. In international defense circles, Watervliet Arsenal cannon is synonymous with quality, as well as intensive customer service and support. However, in the late 1970s, and early 1980s, Watervliet management undertook a substantial challenge to further improve production capability and therefore the product and mobilization service provided to the American taxpayer. As a result of a comprehensive modernization program called Project REARM, the most technologically advanced production equipment available worldwide was installed over a ten-year period. Flexible manufacturing, distributed numerical control, CAD/CAM, and factory networking systems were introduced and are now part of the extensive effort.

Although technological development was undertaken with the intent of improving quality, cost, and schedule performance, it soon became clear that technology by itself was not sufficient to achieve the desired results. Emphasis has shifted from technology to improvement of organizational systems and the managerial skills required to make the systemic improvements. This is typically seen as a demotion of technology; it is *not*. Rather, it is a reemphasis and elevation of the vital job of managerial leaders. It is a reemphasis of their responsibility to create, by intent, organizational systems. The purpose of these systems is, ultimately, to create customer value. Technology simply accelerates these systems.

This chapter presents in chronological order the transitions from technology, to statistical process control, to total quality management, to managerial leadership. Concurrent with this chronological report are the following recurring themes:

• The role of external management development resources in the Watervliet program (as offered by the University of Tennessee)

- Government uniqueness
- Application lessons (behavioral and procedural)
- Hyperfunctional development[1]

INITIAL APPLICATIONS, CHROME PLATE, AND SPC

In the mid-1980s, production began on the high-performance 120 mm tank cannon (see Figure 1), the main gun on the M1A1 Abrams Main Battle Tank. A vital design feature of the smooth (as opposed to "rifled") bore of this gun is the chrome plate which is designed to extend the "service life" of the barrel by a factor of ten. During weapon firing, high temperatures, extremely high pressures, and abrasion are the key forces that stress the chrome, causing small (less than 1 percent) but unacceptable amounts to flake off. A significant problem arose in August 1985 when the first production lot was delivered to the Aberdeen Proving Ground and because of chrome chipping off failed the proof-firing test. Although the chrome loss had no effect on either safety or accuracy, the long-term influence on durability was unknown. Thus, an intensive three-year effort was undertaken to improve the expensive manufacturing process and therefore the durability of the chrome plate. A detailed discussion of the analysis and resulting process improvements is beyond the scope of this chapter. Suffice it to say that Secretary of Defense Frank S. Carlucci recognized the product improvements in January 1989 by awarding the Productivity Excellence Award based on the value of a savings of $9 million through improving quality.[2]

Analytical techniques utilized were reviewed and validated with the Management Development Center (MDC) at the University of Tennessee, Knoxville; the techniques learned therein continue to be applied to a variety of applications. A universal lesson learned in the process is that the "problem," that is, chrome loss, was far more complex than initially thought. When multiple failure mechanisms were finally defined, an even more complex matrix of "cause mechanisms" became apparent. The linear and nonlinear interaction of causes had to be sorted out individually and controlled collectively.

---

1. Hyperfunctional describes a functional organization (engineering, procurement, accounting, quality assurance, planning, etc.) that is self-contained and successful by its own functional measure and, at the same time, isolated from other functional organizations and less responsive to the next immediate upper level goals and measures.
2. Improvements resulted in increased acceptance from 70 percent to 99 percent, leading to a substantial reduction in repair and rework and a virtual elimination of scrap. The decrease in chrome loss can be seen graphically in Figure 2.

FIGURE 1

In addition to the technical discoveries found throughout the chrome plating improvement effort, several expected organizational issues were also encountered. The uniqueness of the government/defense environment, with all the associated political and organizational pressures, can have a significant effect on the technical thought process. A problem easily characterized as "chrome flaking" is not so easily characterized in terms of the cause(s) in the process. High-level briefings are good for directing appropriate resources to a problem, but they can also cause the "fix-it-all" syndrome, where an impressive number of costly "fixes" are instituted without regard to statistical validation of their effectiveness. Dr. Deming calls this tampering.

As an analogy, the notion of a brick wall was developed to capture the idea that organizational interaction *among* a wide range of components was essential to the successful implementation of systemic improvement and chrome problem resolution.

The strength of a brick wall depends in large part on the strength of the mortar bonding the bricks, as well as the strength of the individual bricks. Similarly, the effectiveness of the overall organization depends not only on how well the individual components do their functional job, but on how well they work together. The term *hyperfunctional* is meant to suggest a piece of an organization that, in itself, does its job extremely well, like a super strong brick. In larger organizations it becomes easier for an organizational element to become isolated and yet, by its own measures, be perceived to be doing a good job.

In the case of the chrome-plated gun barrel, engineering performance was defined more in terms of the clerical accuracy of the technical data and less in terms of validating the design. Here hyperfunctionality suggests that engineering has engineered in strict terms of engineering measures, and less in terms of the overall organizational goals, that is, to deliver a quality product on time, at the right price, safely.

Figure 2 represents a "put-up or shut-up" chart of chrome plate improvement. Even the staunchest of critics was silenced by the statistically demonstrated fact that over a three-year period the average amount of chrome loss on the 120 mm tank gun had dropped by more than a factor of 10. This improvement has been sustained for more than three years. More than a mathematical game show, the effort represents the cross-functioning of organizations and people implementing changes that were statistically verified. Research and analysis were performed by an ad hoc team, superimposed on the functionally structured organization. In discovering that this was only a *patch,* it was realized that cross-functional systems must be defined and managed as a prime, nondelegated responsibility of executive management.

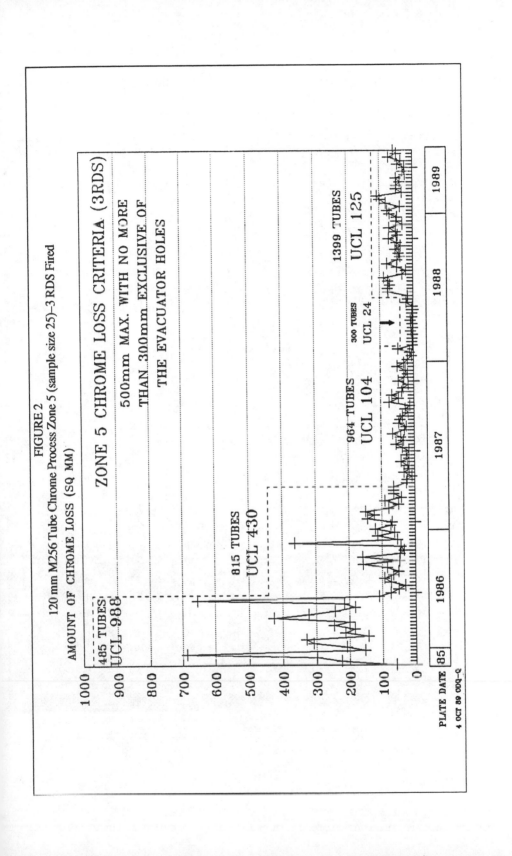

FIGURE 2

120 mm M256 Tube Chrome Process Zone 5 (sample size 25)–3 RDS Fired

AMOUNT OF CHROME LOSS (SQ MM)

ZONE 5 CHROME LOSS CRITERIA (3RDS)

500mm MAX. WITH NO MORE

THAN 300mm EXCLUSIVE OF

THE EVACUATOR HOLES

485 TUBES
UCL 988

815 TUBES
UCL 430

964 TUBES
UCL 104

300 TUBES
UCL 24

1399 TUBES
UCL 125

PLATE DATE

85   1986   1987   1988   1989

4 OCT 89 ODQ—Q

FIGURE 3

Based on the success of the chrome plate analysis, a statistical process control (SPC) effort was initiated with the traditional control charts and yellow stands on the shop floor.[3] Watervliet did not adopt the traditional mistake of wallpapering the shop floor with control charts. In the test operations that were started up, a major problem developed with the use of control charts. The problem was that they *work*. They act as a highly powerful tool that indicates process control and variation. After verifying Deming's pronouncement that 95 percent of variation is due to the systems and 5 percent due to the shop floor operator, it became necessary to rethink the strategy for full implementation of statistical process control.[4]

The Watervliet Arsenal effort revealed and verified that 95 percent of the variation is due to the systems, hence, you have to ask the questions:

What are the systems?
What is the implication to management?
Who owns these systems?
Who's supposed to be working on (*not in*) these systems?

If the purpose of the control chart was to tell the operator about his 5 percent, it seemed to be a waste. He already knew about his 5 percent. If the purpose was to improve the other 95 percent, there was a need to understand what was meant by the system. Why implement a control chart when you have no intention of responding to 95 percent of its relevant signals?

INITIAL APPLICATIONS, MUZZLE SLOTS

In the application of statistical process control, it was found to be unproductive to put a control chart on a job if there is no intention of responding to what it says. The control chart is a powerful instrument. Why start using a microscope to find more problems when it's already difficult to respond to those that are apparent? The key to successful application was to discover what is meant by "the system." For example, in a simple

---

3. Figure 3 shows a typical yellow fiberglass podium-style stand on which a standard statistical process control chart is maintained for the associated manufacturing operation. The chart is used to record measurements in graphical format.
4. Analysis of one year's data on actual shop floor "nonconforming material" reports indicated that the ultimate source of problems (i.e., material, tooling, information, knowledge, training, machine) rests in management-controlled systems in 95 percent of the cases studied. Responsibility for improving these systems was beyond the authority of the shop floor worker.

machining operation performed on gun tubes, a slot about the size of a nonfilter cigarette is cut in the muzzle end of a gun barrel (see Figure 4). A control chart was placed on this machining operation to keep track of the width of the high-precision slot.

The improvements resulted in greater precision of the actual width of the slots and reduced cost. How? By using the same machine, same operator, same raw material, and a cheaper tool (purchased from outside), but with an increased knowledge of *exactly* what tool size, increased knowledge of *exactly* how fast they wear out and increased knowledge of the most effective cutting techniques all made for relatively cheap implementation. What made that possible was a lot of "analytical sweat" that led to the increased knowledge. The *new factor* in the game that used the same old hardware was more precise knowledge of cause and effect. (It's easy to improve quality – just throw away all the bad parts. But this is obviously too expensive a proposition. The need to find out why bad parts are being produced is a precursor of increased knowledge. This is where the statistics played such a big part.)

It was discovered that the existing approach was marginally capable of meeting specifications. This is an example of a typical "tactical," low-level problem. Subsequent analysis showed the following:

1. There was no formal system to check the design for manufacturability.
2. There was no system to verify that the purchased tool performs as expected.
3. There was no system to verify that local measuring capability is sufficient to check design requirements.

Number 2 was especially difficult to understand. Checking the paperwork for the tooling after it arrived at the loading dock is substantially different from verifying that the purchased tool does the job which the original process plan expected it to do. Variation in tool design, variation in tool material (both batch to batch and supplier to supplier), variation in technical data supplied to the contractor, variation in tool setup, variation in availability, variation in geometry, and variation in raw material and geometry are some of the key variables in how an operation is equipped. The equipping system therefore influences the long-term quality level produced at the specific slot-cutting operation. Even more damning is the discovery that a wide variety of organizational functions (procurement, engineering, production planning, and control) are responsible for their own piece of the "puzzle" that finally designs, equips, and acquires an

FIGURE 4

essential tool that is responsible for a simple, but precise, slot-cutting operation.

The implications of 1, 2 and 3 listed above are astounding. If these conditions:

1. design for manufacturability,
2. acquiring tooling, and
3. equipping the operation

influence one simple slot operation, isn't it reasonable to assume that these issues exist in varying degrees for *all other* operations?

Therefore, rather than go the route of "yellow-standism" (i.e., swamping the shop floor with yellow stands and control charts), the Watervliet Arsenal executive board decided[5] to work on the systems that cause the variation discovered in the ten to fifteen yellow stand operations that continue to be maintained. The first problem encountered was in failing to distinguish between function and system. Functions have owners; systems do not (traditionally).[6] Functions have measures; systems do not. Functions work in one building, one floor, one section; systems do not. Functional performance is measured and reviewed at the quarterly management meeting; systems are not. Functions are simple to describe; systems are not. Functions involve a specific number of specific types of jobs reporting to specific managers, systems do not.

The system that "*acquires tooling*" significantly involves procurement, production planning, and manufacturing. Nobody is responsible for the

----

5. The Watervliet Arsenal Executive Board consists of

1. commanding officer
2. civilian executive assistant
3. executive officer
4. deputy director of engineering
5. director of operations
6. director of procurement
7. director of product assurance
8. director of advanced technology
9. director of personnel
10. director of engineering and housing
11. director of resource management

6. A typical organization chart breaks out the functions (engineering, procurement, operations, etc.) as well as the individuals responsible for the function (i.e., the "owner"). Yet the same organizational chart does not show the cross-functional systems (such as "acquiring") or any specific individual therein responsible.

overall performance of "acquiring tooling." Nobody is measured for this system. There is no measure of this system.[7]

The impact of the system that acquires tooling on the job is enormous. It is the single most important source of variation in cutting steel. This powerful entity, called acquiring tooling, is a cross-functional system that was found to be a fundamental aspect of another cross-functional system, equipping the operation.

At this point, another realization was yet to be had. That was the amount of high-level work/dedication and attention required to undertake cross-functional systems management. An interesting discovery in the application of statistical process control to government/defense contracting may be true of most relatively low-volume, high-critical[8] item manufacturers (i.e., a greater use of within-part variation analysis, pseudosampling where every sequential item can and is measured and charted, and finally a greater degree of variation in process setup). Consumer product manufacturing, with high-volume stability and consistent production runs, is in contrast to the defense environment where high changeover, slow-volume production occurs. This is *not* a short-runs application. The statistical techniques that have been found to be appropriate are not extensively different, but they do have some uniqueness in their application compared to those used in the consumer products industry. Currently, there is a lack of a canned SPC training package or program that addresses this issue.[9]

---

7. As an application footnote it was found that 60 pounds of "policy statement" is no match for one sheet of paper specifying management evaluation measures. For example, policy, declaration, posters, etc., all promote management's policy for evenness (steady, constant) of throughput, but monthly quotas drive schedules which drive managers' work efforts, which form the basis of their evaluation. Regardless of how much steady throughput is promoted, only monthly measurements are evaluated and 80 percent of schedule is still met during the last week of the month. The discovery is that managers respond almost *exclusively* to what is measured/inspected as opposed to expected.

8. Large, costly, complex, high-precision components that have high reliability requirements.

9. Another glaring need is the definition and formalization of the "process capability study." Anybody who's ever had his feet in the fires of quality improvement for a specific item or operation knows that a process capability study must define the contributing factors that have or might have affected quality. Simply calculating a Cp or Cpk is only a first step. Design of experiments is great in the laboratory but doesn't tell you what the causes of variation are on the shop floor. An extensive process capability factor analysis may be the missing link between tactical problem solving and systems management.

Early Management Seminars

After consultation with top management, the SPC Office initiated a four-day executive management seminar held in conjunction with the University of Tennessee MDC. During the meeting the top forty executives at Watervliet were introduced or reintroduced to the application of simple statistical techniques. The seminar was effective for surfacing organizational disconnections manifest as individual disagreement. Although, in retrospect, it was too early to introduce the analytical techniques, the begging question was, "If these issues are not getting worked out in this seminar, then when?" The seminar had great value as a communication medium, and it exposed the need for cross-functional management.

As a followup to the four-day seminar, a two-day presentation seminar was held four months later for the top forty managers. Each manager was required to present a project of statistical techniques applied to any aspect of the business chosen by the individual manager. The resulting presentations were evaluated in two categories:

1. Use of statistics (simple to complex).
2. Depth of application (trivial to vital).

Evaluation within the two categories was generally independent in that a strong rating in one category did not guarantee a strong rating in the second. From a managerial perspective, the more important category is the second, that is, the criticality of the application. For example, some managers used only simple, accurate techniques, but they applied them to vital, powerful issues. Others delegated the real guts of the work to their subordinates, had the project prepared for them, and applied the effort to trivial issues. The result was a beautiful looking presentation that meant nothing. The resulting comparison of these two types of presentations acted as a powerful acid test in determining who was genuinely concerned with corporate improvement and who would do only what they were explicitly told to do.

It was interesting to see that some managers, in conducting an analysis of their *own* operation, learned extensive aspects not previously known, fixed problems, and still, without blinking, did not understand the value of what they had done. The implication is that the average manager does not see systemic improvement as part of his job.[10] As a simple graphic

10. The reason for that is simple enough; he's neither rated, evaluated, nor expected to make systemic improvements (as per job description and standard "boss-chat" conducted in the hallway).

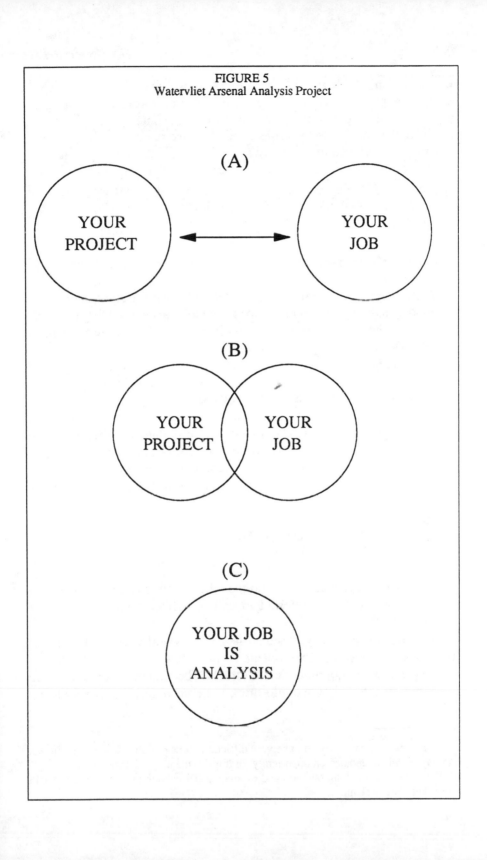

FIGURE 5
Watervliet Arsenal Analysis Project

(A)

YOUR
PROJECT

YOUR
JOB

(B)

YOUR
PROJECT

YOUR
JOB

(C)

YOUR JOB
IS
ANALYSIS

representation of this process, Figure 5A shows two circles, one representing the "project" that was assigned and the other circle representing the day-to-day job responsibilities. As time went on, some managers decided that since they had to do the project and they also ran part of the business, they might as well combine the two. So they applied the analysis to their day-to-day operations (as seen in the merging of the circles in Figure 5B). The goal of this indirect approach is the realization and acceptance of responsibility for analysis and improvement, as seen in the unity circle in Figure 5C.[11]

EMERGENCE OF TQM

After stabilizing the SPC effort at ten to fifteen different operations, the lessons in their uses and limitations were used to develop the scope and priorities of the newly emerging emphasis on Total Quality Management (TQM). The new "buzz phrase" seemed to be "TQM is not a buzz phrase." In the defense arena, managers wrestled to programmatically define TQM according to their functions, rather than as a strategy for changing the roles and responsibilities of management itself. Although the past was scattered with occasional and then sporadic improvement, it became clear that continuous improvement was both a more career-enhancing alternative and a critical path to the long-term survival of the organization. Then the problem became one of defining improvement. Improvement of customer satisfaction seemed to be a powerful answer that suggested *two fundamental* areas of concern:

1. What satisfies our customer?
2. How well are we doing it?

One area is extrospective,[12] and the other is introspective. Watervliet executives would have preferred to call the effort Total Management Quality (TMQ).

The immediate priority, based on the previous works became introspective. The question was, "How well are we providing value to the Watervliet customer?" Two major analytical efforts had been undertaken to analyze thousands of internal "nonconforming material reports" along with the

---

11. As an observation, it proved to be very difficult to do a responsible analysis and *not* find, in one way or another, an opportunity for improvement.
12. Extrospective: Looking outward and evaluating. Discussion of customer value will follow later in this chapter.

yellow stand SPC applications in order to identify systemic causes of quality variation. Two more efforts were undertaken to analyze the corporate quality system and product delivery schedule performance. To simplify the major thrust of these efforts, Figure 6 shows the "basic building blocks" of manufacturing a cannon (or any other item). The basic ingredients – man, machine, tool, raw material, and method – are put together in such a way that quality, cost, and schedule are determined. In the lower right corner of this diagram, a three-dimensional cube has been placed in a three-dimensional coordinate diagram representing the three dimensions of cost, schedule, and quality. Here cost, schedule, and quality are not seen as "good" or "bad," but are simply objective measures of performance.

If an improvement is valid, at least one of these measures (dimensions) should be effected. Thus, to improve the cannon, one or all five "raw ingredients" (on the left) need to improve, and the results should be measurable by at least one of the measures (in the lower right) of cost, schedule or quality. Now the issue becomes, "How do we improve the raw ingredients?" The whole situation gets significantly more complex in Figure 7 where we see Figure 6 has been placed on the right side. In order to improve the raw ingredients in Figure 6, the organizational procedures, methods, rules, and communication shown on the left side of Figure 7 need to be improved. This begins to suggest what is meant by systems improvement. (The danger in this description is that the critical systems are not discovered by examining an individual tactical problem.)

In order to significantly improve the raw ingredients and how they are put together, the systems that supply and manage them must be improved. This is exactly where most quality improvement efforts lose their steam. The conclusion was that the real leverage point for continuous improvement lies in the systems approach.

CROSS-FUNCTIONAL DECISIONS

As a result of the previous analytical studies and in conjunction with the recommendations of the University of Tennessee MDC, the Executive Board determined that three major system efforts would be initiated:

1. Acquiring material
2. Equipping an operation
3. Designing for manufacturability.

Acquiring Material. The system that specifies, chooses and communicates requirements, audits delivery, and actually receives shipment of raw material for cannon production. The focus area was later chosen to be the

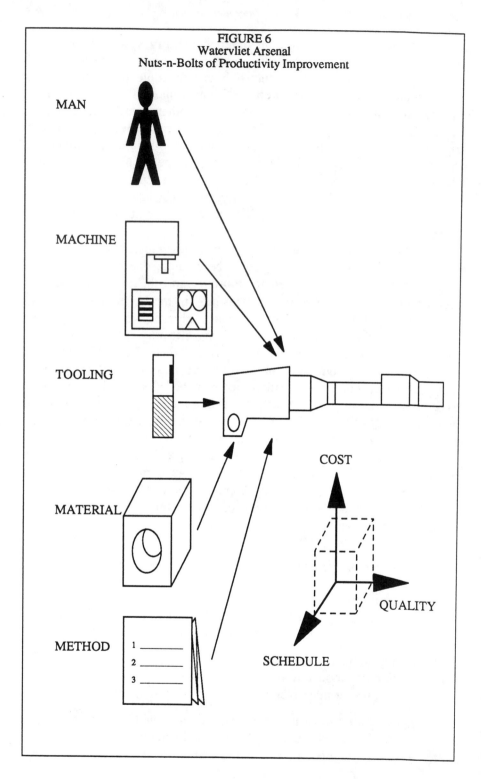

FIGURE 6
Watervliet Arsenal
Nuts-n-Bolts of Productivity Improvement

MAN

MACHINE

TOOLING

MATERIAL

METHOD

COST

QUALITY

SCHEDULE

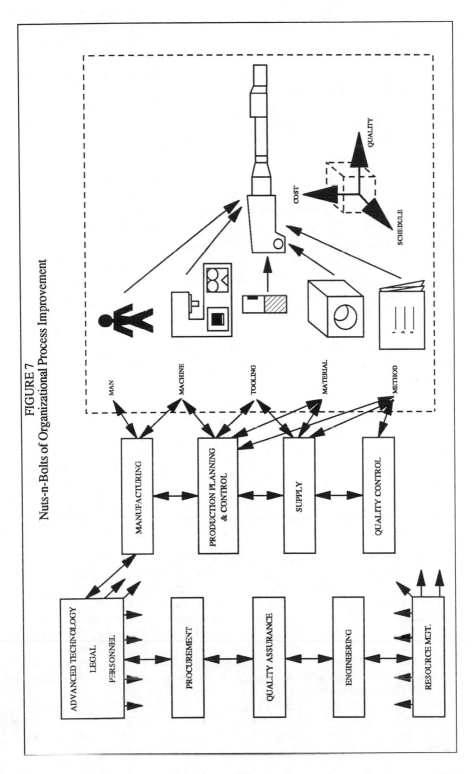

FIGURE 7
Nuts-n-Bolts of Organizational Process Improvement

major components of the 120 mm tank gun, the primary production item of the Watervliet Arsenal.

Equipping the Operation. The system that provides and assures the adequate manufacturing process components of tooling, machine, sufficiently informed and trained operator, N/C computer program, and raw material are positioned at the operation so that each production component can be replicated consistently within engineering specifications.

Designing for Manufacturability. The system that assesses manufacturability in degrees of difficulty, translates that understanding within the design process, and confirms and validates the design in actual replication.

The most fundamental rationale for these particular systems is that they are essential to fulfilling the commitment of management. That commitment is the agreement to deliver a quality product, on time, at the right price, safely. Managing the three systems of equipping, acquiring, and designing is an obligation born in the decision to be a senior executive. The connection is that these systems have a direct impact on the value delivered to the Watervliet Arsenal customer, a value that management has agreed to fulfill. Thus, deciding to be an executive is the same as agreeing to provide value to the Arsenal customer. Agreeing to provide value to the Watervliet customer requires a cross-functional systems approach because functional management techniques do not assure that value is being delivered.

The broad question, "How well do our internal systems perform," can be answered/measured roughly in terms of three independent dimensions: cost, quality, and schedule performance.

The three-dimensional coordinate system (see Figure 8) helps suggest the independent orientation of these three metrics. Common sense tells some and analysis tells others that the three-dimensional measures cost, quality, and schedule are *not* independent measures, but rather highly dependent measures.[13]

13. Reality probably lies somewhere in the middle (i.e., the measures are to some degree dependent and to some degree independent). The irony of the situation is that the "corporate structure" engineers (i.e., executive management) have designed the organizations to conflict. Specifically, the Chief of Quality battles it out with the Chief of Manufacturing. One is rated on quality performance, and the other is rated on schedule performance. Neither is rated on the overall value delivered to the customer. Thus, these two individuals and their associated organizations are pitted against one another. Now bring in the controller, who is rated on cost performance, and there's a glorious three-way battle raging over an illusion. The illusion is that cost, quality, and schedule are separable measures. They are not, and neither should be the measurement and rating of the individual managers. It works, but what works better is when they are all working together toward delivering one measurement of customer value. That common measure could be composed of a combination of cost, quality, schedule, and any other criteria that is important to the customer.

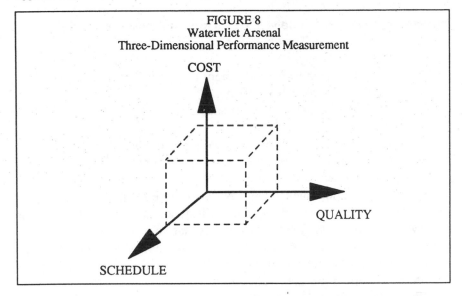

FIGURE 8
Watervliet Arsenal
Three-Dimensional Performance Measurement

The three cross-functional systems were selected on the basis that they all impact the value delivered to the Watervliet customers. Specifically, system 1, "acquiring material," has a substantial impact on overall yearly costs, on shipping and schedule performance, and on internal quality control. The premise behind the thought process is that if different organizational elements work together on a common goal, they will achieve their goal more often than the same number of organizational elements working "somewhat-with" and "somewhat-against" each other. Cross-functional systems work should be considered a higher priority than regular functional work because it more directly impacts delivering customer value.

For example, a critical, early operation in manufacturing gun barrels is the boring operation in which a hole is cut through the middle of the gun tube. A small piece of special carbide steel, roughly the size of a box of wooden match sticks, is used to actually cut steel from inside the gun barrel. This tool, called a carbide insert (because it's made of a carbide and is inserted into the tool holder), is critical to the proper running of the boring operation.

Upon investigating fracturing problems with the carbide inserts (another "tactical" problem), a high-level management team consisting of two directors, five division chiefs and eight branch chiefs, found out that the wrong inserts were arriving at the job site.[14] Further investigation revealed that all functional elements were doing their job properly and all

---

14. Wrong in that marking labels were improper, material grade was improper, and suboptimum geometry was found.

procedures were being followed. Yet it was still possible for the wrong inserts to get to the job. The obvious problems were:

1. Tooling tech data were insufficient ("or equal" was not equal).
2. Tools were improperly marked.
3. Sharpening geometries were inadequate.

Less obvious is that each of these causes was not attributable to any individual component of the organization, but rather to the "seams between" the components. Critical elements had fallen into the cracks between functional components. Who is responsible for making sure these organizational elements work together? Ultimately, the guy at the top. But there are so many cross-functional systems that no one person has enough time in the day to effectively manage them. As the tasking and authority are delegated down into the management system, the "top view," or the integrated systems approach, falls apart.

In the following diagram, the simple icons represent the various organizational elements at Watervliet. Figure 9 shows where the boring operation problem occurred, at the lowest level in the organization (i.e., at the actual machining operation in the lower left corner). Yet to solve this problem, Figure 10 indicates (with a loop) the organizational elements that had to be assembled to understand the various issues. This loop (or amoeba) is the early predecessor of the system called *acquiring tooling* which is a subset of the two major cross-functional systems:

Acquiring material
Equipping an operation.

An underlying assumption that has yet to be tested is that cost, quality, and schedule are sufficient for defining customer value. As of January 1990, Watervliet has focused on the beginning of the organizational improvement cycle called systems improvement; the important work of value determination will begin in the near future.

In the representative case of the carbide insert, an apparently simple, low-level problem had its roots in a complex network of functional procedures involving a wide range of organizational components. Only top-level management had both the requisite "top view" of the cross-functional system and the authority/power to make improvements. Lessons learned in this specific operation can quickly be generalized to include the cross-functional system for acquiring tooling.

In researching the issue of customer value, an aspect of government application of continuous improvement that is significantly unique may

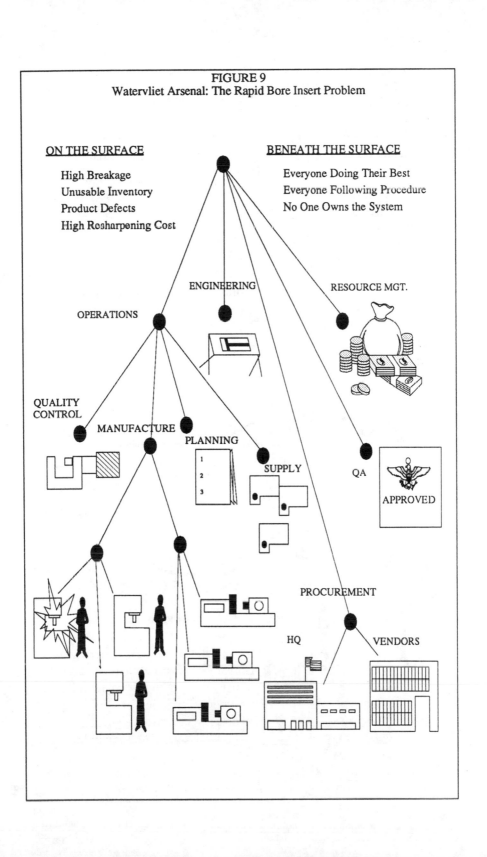

FIGURE 9
Watervliet Arsenal: The Rapid Bore Insert Problem

ON THE SURFACE

High Breakage
Unusable Inventory
Product Defects
High Resharpening Cost

BENEATH THE SURFACE

Everyone Doing Their Best
Everyone Following Procedure
No One Owns the System

ENGINEERING

RESOURCE MGT.

OPERATIONS

QUALITY
CONTROL

MANUFACTURE

PLANNING

SUPPLY

QA

APPROVED

PROCUREMENT

HQ

VENDORS

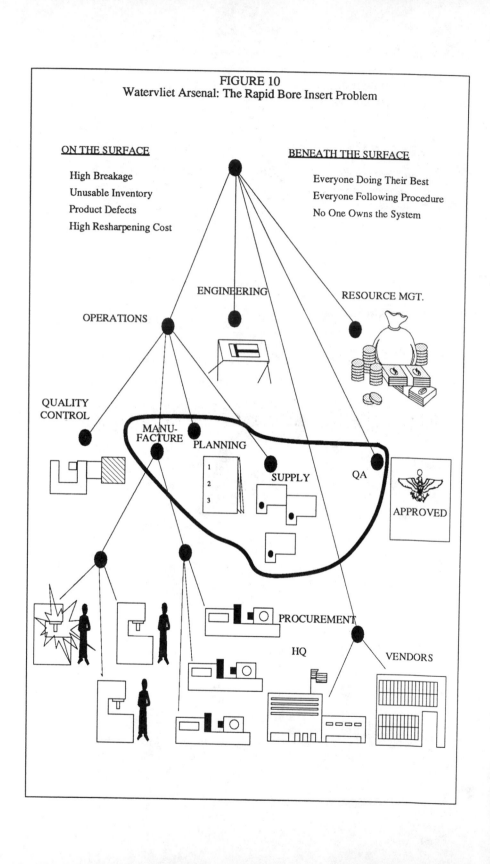

FIGURE 10
Watervliet Arsenal: The Rapid Bore Insert Problem

ON THE SURFACE

High Breakage
Unusable Inventory
Product Defects
High Resharpening Cost

BENEATH THE SURFACE

Everyone Doing Their Best
Everyone Following Procedure
No One Owns the System

ENGINEERING

RESOURCE MGT.

OPERATIONS

QUALITY
CONTROL

MANU-
FACTURE

PLANNING

SUPPLY

QA

APPROVED

PROCUREMENT

HQ

VENDORS

have been discovered. That aspect is the complexity of the customer and his or her associated values.

A QUESTION OF CUSTOMER VALUE

A deceptively simple pair of questions led the executive group head-long into an answer that was difficult to sort out. The questions are:

- Who are our customers?
- What do they value?

What began to emerge was that various organizational elements *legitimately* responded to completely different customers. The customers of the Watervliet Arsenal are:

- The soldier, who uses the guns.
- Logistics headquarters, which supplies the Army.
- Army headquarters.

Also:

- Project managers, who are responsible for specific guns.
- Taxpayers, who are protected by mobilization capabilities.
- Congress, which represents the taxpayers.
- Research-development agencies.
- Department of Defense and other federal agencies.
- Friendly foreign countries.

So who are the customers? Now, to make matters worse, we ask the second question: What do they value? The answers were even broader:

- Weapon accuracy
- Weapon reliability
- Weapon support logistics
- Weapon transportability
- Weapon simplicity
- Weapon cost
- Weapon schedule delivery
- Mobilization requirements.

Obviously, each customer, given his or her individual perspective, is concerned with each of the values to a greater or lesser extent. To simplify this discovery we have created a matrix of customers and values:

VALUE					
Customer	Quality	Performance	Cost	Schedule	Transportability
Soldier	High	High	Low	Low	Moderate
Logistics					
HQ	High	Moderate	High	High	Etc.
Department					
of Army	Etc.	Etc.			
Project					
Managers					
R&D Agencies					
Taxpayers					
Congress					

Obviously each of these customer values isn't just a yes or no answer but rather a continuum of concern. For example, the soldier places much greater value on weapon performance and reliability than on weapon cost. Others may value weapon cost just as much as weapon accuracy.

No doubt, any major private international concern or corporation would have a wide definition as to who is considered "the customer." What is being suggested is that the magnitude of the purpose of government causes a greater magnitude of who the government "customer" is. The resulting complexity of "customer value" of the customer of government is, to the extent of that magnitude, different from private industry.

In conclusion, this point is only relevant in the *application* of cross-functional systems management to government. The process of confirming customer value and managing systems to create that value is identical, government, private, or otherwise. What is different is that in the process of application to government organizations, particularly at the executive level, a substantially more complex customer/value relationship makes cross-functional systems management that much more difficult and that much more important.

CROSS-FUNCTIONAL WORK

"It's a shame those boys couldn't be more copesetic."[15]

---

15. Robert Hunter, American poet.

In order to initiate some tangible work, the Executive Board decided to defer answering the previous questions on customer value and assumed that cost, quality, and schedule performance were close approximations of the primary value(s) of Watervliet customers. Given that cost, quality, and schedule performance are the value(s) that are to be improved in the Watervliet product, the commanding officer and the civilian executive assistant decided that the cross-functional systems approach was going to be undertaken. The ensuing debate within the Executive Board was as spirited as it was complex. The initial problem was in defining the term *cross-functional system*. Any vital system worth considering is one that is rich in organizational issues. An easy, trivial application would minimize debate, but the payoff would be equally insignificant.

In time, a clear distinction was made between a system (acquiring, designing, equipping) and a metric or measurement (cost, quality, and schedule performance). When that distinction became clear, the debate centered on selecting systems that had the following criteria:

1. Significant impact on customer value.
2. Significant cross-functional span.
3. A reasonable degree of local authority to make changes.
4. Identifiable to a specific focus area (e.g., "equipping" would initially focus on a specific machine area).

Clouding the debate was the knowledge held by all that each of these three systems was going to be assigned an . . .

OWNER.

Ominous and foreboding as it was, the implication of being responsible for the undefined, unbounded, and intangible organizational entity was intimidating even for the hardiest of executives. Once the three systems were selected, the question became, do we assign an . . . .

OWNER . . .

first, or do we create a definition and boundary of this entity and then assign it to an owner?

There were two alternatives:

1. Assign ownership, letting the owner develop the scope and definition.

2. Create a definition and then assign ownership.

Since the owner was going to be a director (on the Executive Board) and would be anointed with ownership by the commanding officer (equivalent to the CEO), it became obvious that the owner should be assigned first and that he should develop his own definition, since that's what was going to happen anyway. When the dust settled from this series of debates and the three systems (see Figure 11) (1) acquiring material, (2) equipping the operation, and (3) designing for manufacturability were agreed upon, it was realized that the following factors helped resolve the key questions:

1. Substantial analysis upfront.
2. Lack of awareness as to how much work would be involved.
3. Innocent sounding names ("acquiring").
4. A gut feeling that this "cross-functional" stuff would get us all to work together like we should be – a team.

CROSS-FUNCTIONAL OWNERS

Now the million dollar question was, how do you choose an owner? By what criteria? What are the qualities of a good cross-functional system owner?

At this critical juncture the University of Tennessee MDC recommendation was straight-forward:

#1. Choose an owner such that the success of the effort is made certain.
#2. See number 1.
#3. See number 1.

While certainly not intending to be cryptic, the intention was to reach the understanding as to the more sublime characteristics of success.

Successful executives are successful.
Successful leaders *know* this.
All other criteria are baggage.

Choose an owner that has proven to be successful to such a powerful extent that the success of the cross-functional system is assured.
Some common illusions and trappings are:

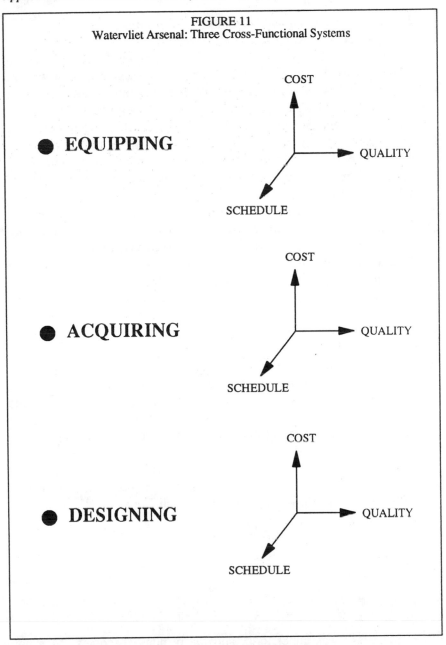

FIGURE 11
Watervliet Arsenal: Three Cross-Functional Systems

Choose an owner who knows a lot about the predominating functional aspects of the system (e.g., choose the director of procurement to be the owner of "acquiring material").

Choose an owner who *doesn't* know a functional lot about the predominating functional aspects of the system.

Choose an owner who wants to do it.
Choose an owner who doesn't want to do it.

The last two suggest a question as to who sets policy, who is a subordinate and who is in charge. With the fundamental changes in behavior that are being called for, volunteers are not necessary. Cross-functional management should not be an "extra-credit" assignment.

If the issue becomes one of undertaking these changes only if everybody likes them, save the waste. The commander and civilian executive counterpart at Watervliet have decided that the cross-functional approach is going to be a vital new responsibility of executives at Watervliet. How systems are defined, how scope is determined, how efforts are manned, and how systems are measured are all legitimate questions requiring substantial consensus building at the Executive Board level.

One question *not* at issue is whether or not we are serious about the effort. The first and most *critical* challenge is "pinning the rose" of cross-functional ownership. Obviously, the response, "I'm sorry, but I don't want cross-functional ownership," is neither explicitly stated nor readily apparent. The commanding officer already owns all the cross-functional systems; the question is how can the executive group be mobilized to assist in the management of this responsibility?

The legitimate objection expressed at the Executive Board level was one of understanding. An executive has a legitimate right to understand and develop the thrust of a task once assigned. The mistake was made one too many times of assuming that the tenets of cross-functionality were understood and accepted.

The chief executive has a balancing act to perform in weeding out and distinguishing lack of understanding from rank insubordination. It was found that behavior is usually a mixture of both, but a very clear progression over time. At first:

- No objections are voiced because the depth and breadth of the task are not understood.

In time:

- The task was understood, and the response becomes, "Are you kidding me? Do you have any idea how much work that will take?"

Which is absolutely correct – so much work in fact, that the role and definition of management itself will need to shift.

Finally, after reasonable wailing and gnashing of teeth, three roses were pinned and three cross-functional system owners began considering this ominous multidimensional organizational entity that lacks definition or scope. Figure 12 graphically suggests the enclosure and assignment of ownership of a cross-functional system while distinguishing this effort from a moderate level tactical problem (i.e., the chrome plate problem seen in the lower left).

CROSS-FUNCTIONAL SEMINAR PLANNING

Enter the Great Value of a Seminar.

"A wise man knows he's going places, so he buys a car and puts gas in the tank. A fool says, I'll wait until I have to go somewhere, then I'll buy a car."[16]

The seminar. Some managers suggested we wait until a sufficient number of organizational issues had been defined, and then plan a seminar. Instead, a seminar date was set, and individuals were scheduled for discussion, presentation, and general attention in public by their peers. The resulting pressure caused the following to occur:

- Systems definitions and scopes had to be developed, and
- Teams needed to be formed.

After deciding on the three cross-functional systems and choosing their owners, the Arsenal's top thirty managers were distributed to the three teams, primarily on the basis of their functional skills and presumed ability to contribute to system definition and assessment. Clearly, the selection criteria are different from those of selecting an owner.

A description of the three cross-functional systems is repeated here for emphasis:

Acquiring Material. The system that specifies, chooses, and communicates requirements, audits delivery, and actually receives shipment of raw material for cannon production. The focus area was later chosen to be the major components of the 120 mm tank gun, the primary production item of the Watervliet Arsenal.

---

16. Ancient Egyptian proverb.

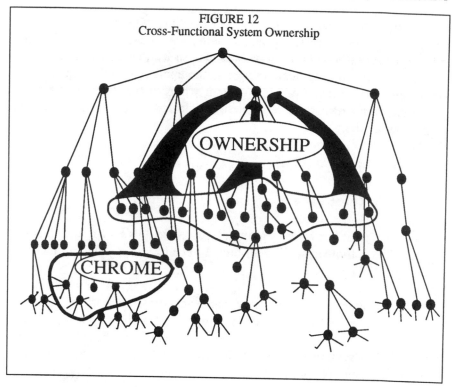

FIGURE 12
Cross-Functional System Ownership

Designing for Manufacturability. The system that assesses manufacturability in degrees of difficulty, translates that understanding within the design process, and confirms and validates the design in actual replication.

Equipping the Operation. The system that provides and assures the adequate manufacturing process components of tooling, machine, sufficiently informed and trained operator, N/C computer program and raw material are positioned at the operation so that each production component can be replicated consistently within engineering specifications.

Given these broad descriptions, each owner further developed and created the scope and definition of his system.

A fundamental problem, particularly with "acquiring," centered on where to draw the boundary lines for the system given that factors such as laws, congressional mandates, and federal and Army acquisition regulations all have a major influence on internal procedures. These factors are external to the direct control of the Watervliet Arsenal. The most common response is, "How can we improve procurement? Our hands are tied!" This issue became known as the "big system versus little system."

The dead end logic says, "Since I can't change the whole system, I'll give up and change nothing." Instead, it was decided to act on the assumption that local improvements could in fact be made and lessons learned could be made available to those who owned the "big system." The next time "big system" improvements are made, we have made a contribution from the perspective of the end user of procurement policy and law.

Application to government organizations is unique in a second area. No doubt *every* major private industry concern has procurement policy and procedure, but only the federal government and major concerns doing business with the government enjoy congressional oversight in the execution of procurement operations. This is not intended to be pejorative, but rather to make a clear distinction between government and most major private concerns particularly in the complexity of procurement systems.

CROSS-FUNCTIONAL SEMINAR EXECUTION

The first full-fledged seminar was a mixture of technical puzzlement over this intangible cross-functional entity and a human behavioral petri dish of unspoken questions such as: What is a cross-functional system? Why am I on this team? What do they expect from me? Why is he in charge? Why is he on this team? What do they mean by acquiring? Who chose these three systems? I wonder what they're really up to. What time is lunch?

Casting thirty plus high-level managers into several rooms to define, scope, and assess a cross-functional system for the first time is like juggling porcupines while riding a square-wheeled unicycle on a hot-picket fence.

The training strategy is really a strategy for changing the cross-functional understanding and techniques throughout the entire organization. Fundamental to the Watervliet Arsenal approach is to start with and *stay* with the executive group until the effort is firmly anchored in an irreversible change process. Figure 13 pictorially demonstrates that, to make sure the wheel is turning and it can't slow down, the torque is applied most efficiently to the axle. Thus, turning the axle is the key to getting the wheel to follow, just as the entire mid- and lower level management will, in time, follow the direction of the key executive cadre.

After three rounds of seminars, spaced three months apart, the following occurred:

- Behavioral issues and interpersonal disconnects began to subside as responsibilities became clear and technical understanding increased.
- Previous works, accomplished by a variety of project teams, contributed to the technical task of systems definition and description.
- Regular weekly meetings began to occur as the size of the task and the pressure of the upcoming seminar were realized.

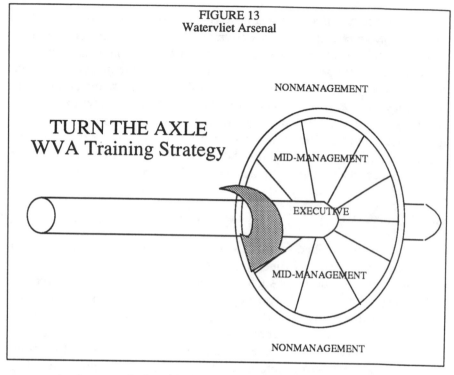

FIGURE 13
Watervliet Arsenal

- An increase in knowledge of how and why other areas need other information to provide a given or requested service helped functional cooperation.
- As in all other efforts, some team members showed themselves as real contributors and again demonstrated their initiative and concern.

As expected, issues concerning the contribution, concern, and responsiveness of team members created tension as the teamwork actually began. The primary issue is: If these senior and midlevel managers have varying degrees of responsiveness within this executive directed effort, isn't it reasonable to assume that there is a concomitant degree of responsiveness in everyday management?

In other words, hard workers showed their stuff *as well* as those who don't work and cooperate too much. The cross-functional systems effort exacerbated any managerial problems that, up to this point, may have been too subtle to detect. Anybody who was highly effective and responsive within this effort proved to be effective and responsive in the daily management of organizational issues. The converse is also true (i.e., those that are less effective and responsive). For this reason, the tendency to "dump" team members was resisted (in order to deal with the situation).

The singular behavioral value that contributed most significantly to bona fide accomplishment was maturity. This is not to be confused with chronological longevity. Maturity was expressed by the professional in that tasks were understood and accomplished without requiring constant overview. Maturity also meant that attitudes became objective and assessments were independent from organization lines. Traditional hierarchical thinking says, "if I work for you, then I'll do the task; If I don't work for you, good luck." In cross-functional systems management, the teams are composed of a wide variety of functional areas that do *not* report to the team owner. Thus, the individual's ability to subordinate the functional concern to the cross-functional effort permitted more efficient use of managerial effort. This is not suggesting that the value of maturity has reached an optimum level; rather, it has been recognized as an essential element.

CURRENT EFFORT

Currently, the teams are in the process of developing and assessing a model of their respective cross-functional systems. Policy statements, standard operating procedures, regulations, and direct experience are all being used to develop the initial diagrams of the system models. On-site walk-through interviews, pulling live documents and actual contracts, drawings, tech data, computer programs and printouts, shop routing sheets, and quality records are all examples of the "nuts-n-bolts" work that takes a completely different meaning when analyzed in the context of validating the actual performance of the cross-functional systems. Future effort will increase the amount of cross-functional systems efforts to evaluate executive performance. Assessment of customer value will begin when the organizational systems evaluation effort has reached the point where it is both self-initiated and self-evaluated.

GOVERNMENT UNIQUENESS AND MANAGERIAL LEADERSHIP

"A chicken in every pot."
In preparing this application chapter, the question arose as to what is truly unique, from a managerial perspective, about government. After much brain- and barnstorming, several themes began to appear:

1. Nothing
2. Complexity of the mission
3. Change mechanism for leaders (time)

Nothing

Management is management. In the traditional definition of management, there's no significant difference. Getting things done through others, planning, administering, approving, and so on – it doesn't matter if it's government or private industry. However, the thrust of this book is to suggest a new definition of management. Within the context of applying that new definition, the following differences may be relevant.

Complexity

Government exists at all times for one purpose: To serve the people. It is by definition subordinate. In providing for life, liberty, and the pursuit of happiness, government should have no purpose within itself. This may or may not be true of private industry, as the name suggests. Private industry serves the stockholders (or the customers?). In government, every stockholder is also a customer of the corporate (government) service. The taxpayer is both the stockholder and a customer. The implications of this duality within the new definition of management is intimidating. The implication is that executive management has a focused responsibility to assess and create organizational systems that provide customer value. Given the staggering complexity of "life, liberty and the pursuit of happiness" as the customer value that is to be provided, it is submitted that the extent to which the complexity of the government mission is greater than the complexity of the corporate mission, government uniqueness is established.[17]

To further simplify, government is different because it's bigger. Legitimately, it has several missions. The purpose of government is so broad in interpretation that entire functions and organizations can easily get lost in "doing their own thing," for their own goals, successful by their own measures, regardless of the value they contribute. This is not an argument for centralization; rather, it is an argument for the need to apply cross-functional management as a primary responsibility of executive management (as opposed to, "Oh yeah, we have some cross-functional teams and I support them greatly. Say, what is it they're working on?").

The breadth of government allows for a pervasive development and growth of the hyper-functional organization.

---

17. In other words, the actual work involved in using the "value determination" cycle discussed in Chapter 5, is much more extensive within the government because the stockholder/customer and the associated values are so complex.

Time-Driven Leadership Change

Another aspect of government that appears to be different is the mechanism for leadership replacement. Oversimplified, yet still accurate, a corporate executive is replaced when he or she voluntarily or involuntarily leaves. In government, the executive is "in" for a set duration of time, i.e. four years, two years, and so on.

Corporate replacement is generally based on performance.
Government replacement is generally based on time.

The issue is behavior. The behavior of the executive and the "just-below-executive" interface may be influenced by the change mechanism, as suggested by the following matrix:

	ADVANTAGE	DISADVANTAGE
GOVERNMENT (Time-based leadership changes)	• Relatively short time to start programs and make changes, etc. • Competence of leader • Short term • Performance is important	• Relatively short time to start programs and make changes, etc. • Competence of leader • Short term • Performance is important
PRIVATE (Performance-based leadership changes)	• Enough time to make substantive changes • Performance is important • Competence of leader	• Enough time to make substantive changes • Performance is important • Competence of leader

The game being played between the executive and "just-below-the-executive" (the civilian "lifer," who is a performance based executive) can be efficient or inefficient. It becomes inefficient when there's a lack of mutual respect that fosters mutual subversion, specifically the existence of the "wait-him-out" syndrome.[18] To the extent that this situation exists, the first victim is the organization that gets crossed signals, and the ultimate victim is the customer/taxpayer who must pay the price of inefficient leadership. The interface between the politically elected/selected, the military and the long-term civilians, is the critical juncture for focus.

---

18. The "wait-him-out" syndrome is the delay and stalling technique used by the subordinate manager when he knows the boss has a limited time left in charge.

Answer the question, "How can organizational systems and managerial leadership create a greater value for the customer?"

To find the proper balance between short-term projects (appreciated by voters and time-based leaders everywhere) and long-term projects (whose benefits won't be felt till I'm gone) is the great skill of a consummate managerial leader. The "eyewash" is necessary for the leaders' survival but clearly not essential in the long-term survival of the organization. In other words, short-term projects that appear to be flashy and tangible are sometimes necessary in the political organization for individual survival and advancement. The danger of these short-term show-projects is threefold:

1. They can be a distraction from the real issues and divert resources that ought to be working on the more difficult strategic issues.
2. They are soothing and give us the impression we've done something substantial.
3. They may provide a misleading sense of organizational progress.

On the other hand, in the course of in-depth cross-functional systems evaluation and assessment, it's almost impossible not to find simple, easily remedied problems that certainly should be fixed and all appropriate hoopla conducted. The term *fixing the flats* has been used to describe such tactical problem fixing. Care needs to be taken to assure that they don't become a distraction.

CROSS-FUNCTIONAL SYSTEMS AND ENTROPY

Entropy is used here as "the tendency of things to move toward disorder and randomness." In other words, if nobody is adding any effort to the situation, it tends to get more disorganized or disorderly as time goes on. Entropy is used in the sense that structure, order, sequence, properness, and clarity *tend* to decay as time goes on unless acted on by an outside force.

A cross-functional system will tend to decay as time goes on unless acted on (managed) by an external force (management).

What's even worse is that fundamental systems existing within organizations tend to be unrecognized, undefined, unassessed, and therefore unmanaged. How can we manage something that's not even defined? A system, such as "acquiring tooling," is composed of both functional blocks (design, procure, test, utilize) and interfaces between the blocks.

As a matter of convenience, it seems easier to manage, measure, and assess the functions as if they are entities in themselves. But cross-functional systems are not traditionally recognized, defined, measured, assessed, or managed.

What a surprise to learn that if a system isn't actively managed, it tends to decay. The laws of entropy apply equally to organizational systems. "But if there's an interorganization problem, bump-it-up." The "bump-it-up" syndrome is symptomatic of a lack of cross-functional management. It says, "If I don't hear about problems, then I assume that there aren't any."

Add in the belief that "bump-it-up," when done, is seen as a fault of the subordinate (are you guys still going at it?). The fate of cross-functional systems is sealed; the rationale seems to be:

1. If there's a problem, bump it up.
2. If you bump the problem up, you might be seen as a trouble maker.
3. If no problems are being bumped up, there must not be any problems.
4. Even when bumps are bumped up, and positively received (thanks for bringing that to my attention), it takes a lot of energy to fight organizational gravity which tends to pull high-level systemic problems down into the delegational trenches where there's usually not enough power to solve them. Granted, there may be the talent and the ability to solve the problem, but there is no organizational "power" to effect change.

Cross-functional management is not something executive management supports. Rather, it is something executive management does. "I support it," suggests an external activity that somebody else is working on and "oh by the way, I think it's very proper and important."

"I support it, so I don't have to actually do it." In fact, "it" will only occur to the extent that the executive does it.[19]

"I support it, and therefore I know that something good is happening." Yet only the drivers of the organization drive the organization. Supporters support; drivers drive. Do we support cross-functional management or do we do cross-functional management? One is an illusion and the other is hard work.

___

19. A quick look at the executive's monthly or weekly calendar immediately shows how high a priority systems management has taken. If systems management meetings are found on the calendar, a secondary question is, "Who initiated these meetings, the executive or a subordinate?"

FIGURE 14
Cross-Functional System Ownership

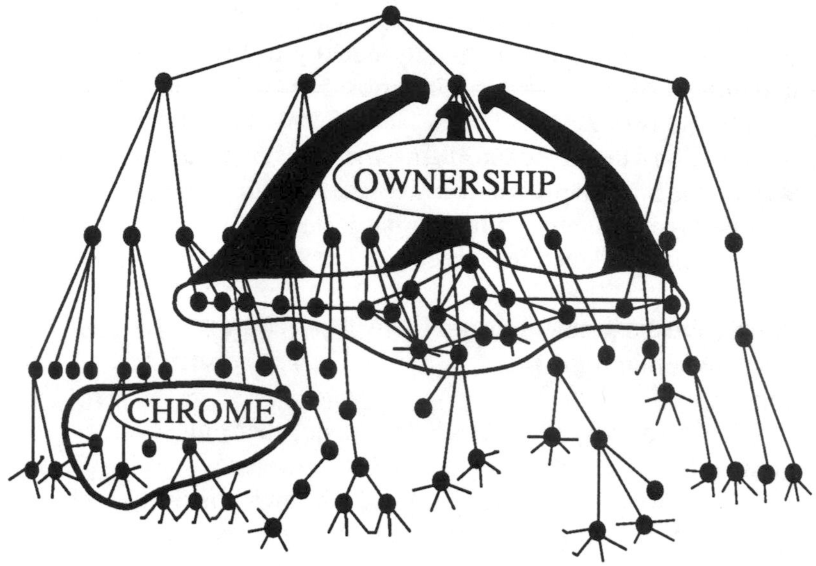

IMPLICATIONS OF DUALITY

As cross-functional systems become defined, the need for their management arises. As the breadth of the task is assessed, the role of management must change. The understanding of the strategic importance of cross-functional systems effort will re-prioritize the executive's time so that tactical problem solving will occur at the tactical level.

When cross-functional responsibility becomes institutionalized, it will become clear that a duality will exist in the reporting of the subordinate. "I know Charlie works for procurement, but he's also part of this cross-functional team. Which one is he really working for?"

"Team" should grow into "system" as institutionalization occurs.

DISTINGUISH:

1. Administration lines
2. Reporting/tasking lines

Administration lines exist for the convenience of administering payroll, vacation time, clerical requirements, and the like.

Reporting/tasking lines are the communication avenues through which tasks are assigned and reports are given. They are the critical element of the "doing" of the business.

The reason why this distinction is made is that in cross-functional systems the reporting/tasking lines begin to resemble a network (spider web) structure as opposed to an hierarchical (tree branch) structure. Figure 14 shows a traditional hierarchical structure that grows into a network structure as the cross-functional responsibility is superimposed on the organization.

The traditional American manager has tremendous difficulty breaking through this barrier from singularity of employee-boss to any multiple form of employee-bosses reporting. "But when it comes right down to it, who does he really work for?"

The answer is, it never comes right down to it. Coming right down to it is a form of organizational conflict. If we are working for one corporation, one entity, then the local goals and objectives are always subordinate to the corporate goals. Traditional managers have a tremendous need to own their people, "they work for me." In cross-functional systems, "they work for us." The issue becomes one of scheduling time after mutually establishing priorities.

In the traditional organization, people need to be controlled, which reinforces the worker reporting to one boss. Cross-functional management requires a mature environment where people are tasked and supported, not baby-sat. In an environment where managers are baby-sitters and a full day's work means that you were physically at or near your desk all day, changes need to be considered.

The growth from hierarchical structures to network structures has precedent in other areas of application; animal nervous systems, complex data management systems, and communication systems are all forms of networks that have to do a job that would be difficult or inefficient in an hierarchical system. Cross-functional systems are the early development of network corporate/government/ organizational systems whose progress is currently being limited by the inherent inefficiencies of hierarchicalism. Personal stature and individual self-importance are values that sustain the perceived need for maintaining the hierarchical organization system. Cross-functional roles and responsibilities will be accepted more readily when managers understand the paradox that the greatest way to acquire/maintain power is to share it.

Yet to share it, it must first exist. In order to exist, it must be created. Thus, one of the manager's most vital abilities is the ability to create. It's not an accident that the notion of a creator is associated with managing.

CHAPTER 33

COMPETITIVE BENCHMARKING AT XEROX

ROBERT OSTERHOFF
Xerox Corporation

WILLIAM B. LOCANDER
Distinguished Professor of Marketing
University of Tennessee

GREGORY M. BOUNDS
Research Associate
Management Development Center
University of Tennessee

SUMMARY

Competitive benchmarking is a technique of gathering information about competitive practice. The primary objective of applying benchmarking techniques is to supply management with the practices that deliver customer value. This chapter outlines the competitive benchmarking process and gives a number of managerial guidelines for implementing the process.

INTRODUCTION

The increased competitive pressures created by global markets have led to a number of new analytic techniques. Since 1979, the Xerox Corporation has been using a competitive benchmarking technique to compare various aspects of its products, services, and processes against various referents. In 1983, benchmarking was integrated into Xerox's Leadership Through Quality Strategy. From 1984 to 1989, benchmarking became internalized as an analytic technique used at all levels of the organization. Xerox's working definition of benchmarking views it as "the continuous process of measuring our products, services, and practices against our toughest competitors or those organizations recognized as leaders."

In essence, Xerox attempts to compare itself on a number of dimensions not only with its direct competitors but also with the best of the best.

The practice of competitive benchmarking fits with the primary themes of this book: (1) creating value for customers and (2) continuously improving the systems that create and deliver value to customers. With an emphasis on satisfying customer requirements, competitive benchmarking orients all employees toward reducing sacrifice and increasing realized benefits that customers derive from the products and services. The nature and focus of the benchmarking process ensures that the means of creating and delivering value to the customer are improved. Thus, the first theme, customer value, is integrated with the second theme, continuous improvement of systems, which are the means of satisfying customer requirements.

BENCHMARKING: WHAT AND WHY?

Benchmarking against competition differs from market research, satisfaction surveys, and competitive analysis. Figure 1 shows how benchmarking differs from the other research techniques. One major point of difference in the figure is that benchmarking focuses on "practices" that satisfy customer needs. While market research focuses on identification and competitive analysis is usually employed at the strategic level, benchmarking's unique contribution is in examining "how" things are done to satisfy needs. A second point of note from Figure 1 is that the sources of information include leading companies and customers of Xerox and competitors. As such, benchmarking provides a better awareness of *what* Xerox is doing, *how* the company is doing it, and *how well* Xerox is doing it. Similarly, this technique provides an awareness of what, how, and how well competition and/or the best are doing.

By benchmarking the methods, rather than simply financial outcomes or other end result measures, managers learn more about how to achieve competitiveness in satisfying customer requirements through benchmarking. Benchmarking the methods directly translates into action implications for improving systems, and lends guidance to how to improve, what to change, and what new systems or alternative practices might be put in place. The diversity of areas being benchmarked also fits with the theme of this book which states that all aspects of systems should be improved. Multifunctional benchmarking and improvement aspects ensure diverse

FIGURE 1
Comparison of Approaches

Type of Analysis	Market Research/ Satisfaction Surveys	Competitive Analysis	Competitive Benchmarking
Generic purpose	Analyze company markets or product acceptance	Analyze competitive strategies	Analyze what, why, and how well competition or leading companies are doing
Usual focus	Customer needs	Competitive strategies	The business practices that satisfy customer needs
Application	Product and services	Marketplace and products The business practices that satisfy customer needs	Business practices as well as products
Usually limited to	How customer needs are met	Marketplace activities	Not limited: competitive, functional, and internal benchmarking are used
Information sources	Customers	Industry analysts/ consultants	Industry leaders as well as yours and competitors' customers

functional contributions to system objectives, from marketing, administration, logistics, to product engineering, accounting, and so on. Customer value is created through systems that cut across all these functions; therefore, functional improvement in all these areas is important.

Why benchmarking? Because it offers a rational way to set performance goals – goals that help firms gain market leadership. Benchmarking also provides a logical and equitable target-setting approach. Target setting can then be used to provide a broader organizational perspective of what is required to gain market leadership.

What to benchmark depends on the desired system improvements that will enhance customer value. Figure 2 shows examples of system improvements which Xerox has identified within companies excelling in various particular aspects of operations.

THE BENCHMARKING PROCESS

Benchmarking can be viewed as either a reactive tool (i.e., problem fixing) or a proactive process for system improvement. The proactive use of benchmarking should be tied to corporate strategies for creating superior customer value. Benchmarking is valuable in that the process forces managers to look externally at what customers value and how other practices meet those needs. Then, an internal examination of processes

FIGURE 2
What to Benchmark

Benchmark	Organization	Features
Insurance	USAA	Customer satisfaction, customer retention
Brokerage	A. G. Edwards & Sons	Financial stability and growth
Quality	Florida Power and Light	Statistical process control
Mail order sales	L. L. Bean	Guarantee policy, telephonics
Customer care	Walt Disney Productions	Training, motivation
Billing	American Express	Billing accuracy and resolution
Transportation	Japanese Railways	Timeliness, efficiency
Customer survey use	Marriott Corporation	Rapid response and resolution

becomes much more valuable to management in that some comparative data exist.

Figure 3 provides an overview of the process that includes the general phases of planning, analysis, integration, action, and maturity. The first four phases include ten steps required to complete a more formulated benchmarking study. During the maturity phase, the process is fully integrated into Xerox's practices. Each step is designed to provide information required to complete the benchmarking process. The steps outlined below are given more in-depth treatment in Robert C. Camp's (1989) book, *Benchmarking*.

Step 1.　What is to be benchmarked? The following must be considered.
- System improvements.
- Product versus process.
- Importance to organization's goals.
- Validation of customer requirements.
- Areas causing the most problems.
- Competitive pressures experienced.
- Is the work process clearly understood?
- Are measurements defined?

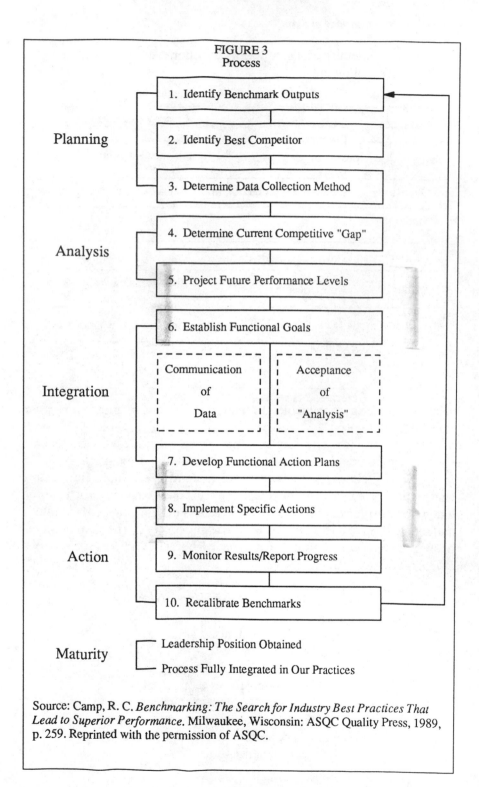

FIGURE 3
Process

Planning
1. Identify Benchmark Outputs
2. Identify Best Competitor
3. Determine Data Collection Method

Analysis
4. Determine Current Competitive "Gap"
5. Project Future Performance Levels

Integration
6. Establish Functional Goals

Communication of Data

Acceptance of "Analysis"

7. Develop Functional Action Plans

Action
8. Implement Specific Actions
9. Monitor Results/Report Progress
10. Recalibrate Benchmarks

Maturity
Leadership Position Obtained
Process Fully Integrated in Our Practices

Source: Camp, R. C. *Benchmarking: The Search for Industry Best Practices That Lead to Superior Performance.* Milwaukee, Wisconsin: ASQC Quality Press, 1989, p. 259. Reprinted with the permission of ASQC.

Step 2.   Identify comparative organizations. Consider the
           following.
    • Similar primary business performance drivers.
    • Comparable product and commodity characteristics.
    • Define "competition" and "industry" broadly.
    • Focus on innovative products and practices.

Step 3.   Determine data collection method. Consider the following.
    • Weigh cost, time, and availability of data.
    • Determine if internal and/or consultant data gathering
      is required.
    • Seek out internal and external experts on subject.
    • Participate on specialized networks.
    • Consider original research through surveys, question-
      naires.
    • Assess sources of information available.

Figure 4 shows the types of information needed for Step 3. Sources of
information with examples are provided for internal, original research, and
external data types.

Step 4.   Determine current competitive "gap." Consider
           these points.
    • Ensure adequate data have been collected.
    • Use qualitative or subjective judgment.
    • Is the gap positive, negative, or at parity?
    • Can the "best" be identified from the analysis?
    • Can your organization be compared to the "best"?

Figure 5 shows a hypothetical example of a gap comparison matrix.
Here a company can compare itself to other organizations across a number
of attributes. This allows for identifying both negative gaps, parity positions, and the best companies by attribute (shown in the dark ovals).

Step 5.   Project future performance levels.
    • Based on Step 4 analysis, plot your organization com-
      pared to the "best."
        – Plot historical trends of your organization and
          the "best."
        – Plot the current performance gap.
        – Project future productivity trends.

FIGURE 4
Sources of Information

Type	Source	Examples
Internal	Library databases	Technical or general retrieval Systems
	Internal reviews	Studies by internal experts
	Internal publications	Newsletters, memoranda
	Internal networks	
Original research	Customer feedback	Focus groups, survey comments
	Telephone surveys	Specific design
	Inquiry service	Specific contract
	Networks	Electronic, external
	Consulting firms	McKinsey, Arthur Anderson
External	Professional associations	American Marketing Association American Society for Quality Control
	Industry publications	Electronic Business What to Buy for Business MIS Week
	Special industry reports	ADL Information
	Functional trade Publications	Materials Handling Engineering
	General management	Industry Week Fortune
	Functional journals	Journal of Business
	Seminars	Annual Quality Congress
	Industry data firms	J. D. Powers
	Industry experts	By Name
	University sources	By Profession
	Company watchers	Wall Street Analysts
	Advertisements	Production Semi-specific
	Newsletters	Boardroom Reports

Source: Camp, R. C. *Benchmarking: The Search for Industry Best Practices That Lead to Superior Performance.* Milwaukee, Wisconsin: ASQC Quality Press, 1989.

- Develop strategic and tactical actions to achieve improved productivity trends.

Figure 6 shows the "Z" Chart which depicts the benchmark gap graphed over time and projected into the future. The benchmark gap shows the degree of required productivity improvement to bring about competitive parity. Note that the breakthrough is shown to be the result of strategic

FIGURE 5
Gap Comparison Matrix

Attribute	Organization					
	Y	**A**	**B**	**C**	**D**	
Unit Cost	$3.29	(3.02)	(2.88)	(2.10)	3.48	.20
Billing Errors	3.2%	(.4)	3.2P	(1.9)	4.7	.15
Inventory Turns	12.6 Days	16.1	23.3	12.9	20.2	.10
PPM Defects	330	991	1323	(219)	(300)	.25
% Customers Satisfied	22.1%	22.1P	(15.9)	(9.6)	24.0	.25
Health Claims Rejected	1.2%	(.6)	(.9)	1.2P	1.3	.05
Weighting	NA	65%	65%	90%	25%	100%

P = Parity   ( ) = Negative Gap

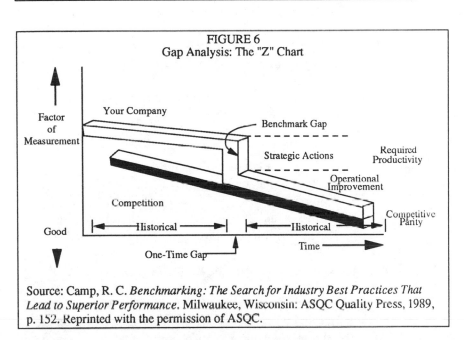

FIGURE 6
Gap Analysis: The "Z" Chart

Source: Camp, R. C. *Benchmarking: The Search for Industry Best Practices That Lead to Superior Performance.* Milwaukee, Wisconsin: ASQC Quality Press, 1989, p. 152. Reprinted with the permission of ASQC.

actions that are followed by operational improvements to maintain parity.

Step 6.   Establish functional goals. Consider:
- Goals based on benchmark findings (factual data of industry best).

- Goals should include how performance gap will be closed.

Step 7. Develop functional action plans. Consider:
- Transactions applied to the new benchmark process.
- Avoid process exceptions.
- Determine efficiency of benchmark practices.
- Plans should address:
  - Implementation responsibility.
  - Step-by-step approach.
  - Expected results.
  - Resource requirements.
  - Task definition with timeline.
  - Measurements identified.

Step 8. Implement specific course of action. Consider:
- Functional action plan drivers and cross-functional effects.
- Line management responsibility for implementation.
- Reinforcement through own internal benchmark network.

Step 9. Monitor results/report progress. Consider:
- Compare progress against Step 7 measurements and timeline.
- Include benchmark measurements in existing performance measurement processes.
- Communicate progress to plans, using identified measurements.

Step 10. Recalibrate benchmarks. Consider:
- Ensure formalized benchmark studies are documented.
- Identify plan for reassessing identified benchmarks.
- Determine if leadership position has been attained.

EXAMPLE: How can these ten benchmarking steps evolve into quality improvement?

One attribute that Xerox customers identified as a critical enabler of satisfaction is accurate and timely invoices. Xerox defined that attribute as Billing Quality, or the relationship between credit adjustments to total invoices produced. The initial step was first to identify internal causal factors for billing adjustments, such as those that are sales and service driven, administrative error, or related to systems. Since only about 5 percent of the errors were determined to take place between the system generating the invoice and customer receipt, the focus clearly had to be on internal processes.

This internal awareness drove the need to look at external billing processes at companies such as Citicorp, AT&T, and American Express. Understanding these and other companies' approaches to billing also allowed Xerox to make necessary conversions to common measurements to ensure a consistency of comparisons. Questions had to be asked to establish a common basis for understanding, such as: "What is the estimator for errors?" and "What is included in the invoice adjustments count?" Only after this common measurement was established could a benchmark be determined. This "benchmark" is a quantitative measurement against which Xerox strives to be the best. Establishing the benchmark is not the final step. For instance, if a 0.4 percent billing quality measurement is identified at American Express, and Xerox is performing at an error rate of 3.2 percent, the annual plan that is developed must reflect this negative gap, with specific actions identified to close the gap by a negotiated timeframe. Progress in closing the gap is measured by an annual recalibration, the final step in the benchmarking process model.

Does the process work? Xerox Customer Administration has experienced substantial reductions in billing errors for the past five years since benchmarking was aggressively introduced into the planning cycle. Continuous quality improvement dictates that there will always be opportunities to deliver more accurate invoices to its customers, but benchmarking has served as an important enabler in ensuring this improvement.

MANAGERIAL CONSIDERATIONS

Benchmarking is successful when management actively demands the activity to the point that continuous benchmarking activities go on within the organization. Thus, the process is institutionalized as part of the company's culture – a culture that supports product or process changes based on benchmark findings.

A checklist of managerial behaviors can help those executives establish a positive posture toward the benchmarking effort.

- Provide leadership in planning and organizing the benchmarking effort.
- Gain consensus on
  - Benefits to be achieved.
  - Partnership companies.
  - Approach to the investigations.
  - Benchmarking team membership roles.

- Support belief that benchmarking is the way more effective work is accomplished; it is not extra work.
- Ensure that benchmark findings are adequately understood and accepted.
- Ensure that performance levels needed and strategies pursued are based on benchmark practices.
- Ensure performance is projected and periodically recalibrated based on benchmark findings.
- Recognize the cross-functional system's implications of benchmarking what customers value.
- Ensure communications process is developed that informs the organization of progress toward benchmark targets and goals.
- Integrate benchmarking findings with the organization's objectives, goals and business plan processes.
- Seek out and publicize examples of successful benchmarking deployment.
- Have patience . . . Effective benchmarking does take time.

A tremendous opportunity for improved benchmarking is to benchmark the integration of diverse functions into cross-functional systems, for example, the collaboration of marketing, product engineering, process design, and manufacturing in the creation and start-up of a new product line. This benchmarking of the process of integration or the process of collaboration may be very different from simply benchmarking functional activities in isolation, or in functional contribution to systems performance. Continuous improvement in this domain offers companies the opportunity for unmatched competitive capability.

CONCLUSIONS

Although Benchmarking has been presented in this chapter as a technique, it is in reality much more. The successful implementation of benchmarking reflects management's belief in the process of monitoring the best of the best and using the findings as part of a continuous improvement philosophy to maximize customer value. Both knowing and doing are part of a formalized benchmark process.

REFERENCE

Camp, Robert C. *Benchmarking: The Search for Industry Best Practices That Lead to Superior Performance*, Milwaukee, Wis.: ASQC Quality Press, 1989.

F. CONCLUSIONS

CHAPTER 34

SUMMARY AND IMPLICATIONS

MICHAEL J. STAHL
Associate Dean, College of BusinessAdministration
University of Tennessee

GREGORY M. BOUNDS
Research Associate, Management Development Center
University of Tennessee

SUMMARY

After a decade of unbridled growth in global competition, such competition promised to be white hot in the 1990s. As more countries experience growing political freedom and gravitate toward market-based economies, as Europe becomes further integrated, as Asian competitors target new industries, worldwide competition should become even stronger. As global competition intensifies, business must develop new ways of managing and competing. Those firms that do not may not survive the intense global economic competition of the 1990s.

In developing a new paradigm of management and organization, the contributing authors of this book develop two themes. The first and *the* central focus of management should be the determination, creation, enhancement, and delivery of best net value to the customer. By net value is meant the difference between what the customer receives and what the customer sacrifices. "Best" refers to the customer's perception of net value from the various competitors in an industry. Three critical dimensions of customer value are quality, cost, and response/delivery time of products and services.

Customers generally do not care about the firm's profitability, quarterly earnings per share, the firm's stock price, or how much the firm shipped last month. Customers vote with their orders and dollars in accordance with best net customer value. Therefore, the mission and philosophy of the enterprise, as well as the goals and objectives of the organization, should focus on the delivery of best net customer value. Delivery of best net customer value will yield higher market share and profitability as residuals.

The primary focus of managerial leaders is not on the competition. Managerial leaders compete by providing best net customer value. The focus is on the customer, *not* on the competitor. Instead of focusing on the Competitor-As-Enemy, managerial leaders focus on the Customer-As-Business Partner.

The second major theme of this book is that management must design and continuously improve strategic suprasystems that focus on discovering, creating, improving, and delivering value to the customer. Such strategic suprasystems cut horizontally across vertical organizational structures and integrate functional silos. A strategic suprasystem is the collection of resources and activities that are crucial to producing and delivering customer value. Indeed, an organization should ask itself why it is involved in an activity, or why it allocates resources to an activity, if the activity is not associated with discovering, creating, improving, or delivering best net value to the customer. The focus of such managerial activity is upon improvement of the suprasystem in order to produce consistent net value to the customer. The managerial focus is not on solving problems without working on the common causes of the variation.

Such new roles for managerial leaders, in terms of focusing on best net customer value and on continuous improvement of strategic suprasystems, are the essence of a new managerial paradigm. It is associated with a revolution in the way managerial leaders and organizations conceive of themselves, as well as the structures, systems, processes, and cultures found in organizations. Several cases are found in the book concerning some organizations' attempts to compete through customer value and to manage some of the associated strategic suprasystems.

The cases near the end of the book describe how some organizations have implemented some of the concepts described in the book. The concept of discovering and delivering customer value has been applied in organizations as diverse as an Army arsenal, which produces cannons, to P&G, which produces consumer goods, and to Bechtel, which designs and builds huge construction projects for worldwide customers. Capsugel defines customer value as traditional product quality since their customers demand consistently perfect capsules to feed automatic, high speed, unattended pharmaceutical filling machines. Xerox benchmarks itself versus the performance of industry leaders to see how others provide best net customer value and operate their strategic suprasystems.

Examples of strategic suprasystems abound. They range from suprasystems at the Watervliet Army Arsenal concerning designing for manufacturability to suprasystems at P&G concerning strategic planning for customer value. Bechtel describes its strategic suprasystems in an engineering design/construction service industry. Georgia-Pacific describes its strategic suprasystems ranging from log purchasing, through wood cutting, and processing to produce consistent wood products valued by the customer.

Pursuing these dramatic organizational changes over the long term is a message of several of the cases. Such organizational upheavals as deemphasizing traditional functional myopia and managing transfunctional suprasystems in order to deliver best net customer value are not quick fixes. Xerox, P&G, and Capsugel have been working at this strategic and cultural transformation over a multiyear time frame.

Top management commitment is another hallmark. Although some efforts may start within the organization, Bechtel, Capsugel, Xerox, U.S. Paper, and P&G all demonstrate that the top management team must be committed to the managerial paradigm shift as described in this book if the shift is to stick.

IMPLICATIONS FOR CHANGE

For industrial organizations to change and move toward this new managerial paradigm, they will need complementary changes in other societal institutions. For example, educational institutions, such as colleges and universities, help develop the human resources that are vital inputs for the organization. Unfortunately, many educational institutions suffer the same problems of functional specialization, myopia, and isolation as the organizations they serve, and indeed help propagate such divisions.

Professors, as consultants and researchers, and students, as employees, bring their functional allegiances and biases to industrial organizations. These human resources reflect and maintain the fragmented and unintegrated organizations they serve. In contrast, the new managerial paradigm requires adaptable human resources capable of more holistic endeavors, continuous learning, and continuous improvement to challenge the status quo rather than reinforce it. Functional specialization will still be important, but only in disciplined contribution to the whole organization rather than self aggrandizement. The management of suprasystems that transcend multiple functions requires more broadly educated and skilled human resources.

The professors, researchers, and students that are the product of their educational institutions, and the managerial leaders, middle managers, and operators that are employed by industrial organizations, must all be prepared to meet these changing cultural imperatives. Otherwise, they risk being deemed irrelevant and unsuitably specialized in today's globally competitive markets. Thus, the changes in educational institutions must complement the changes in the managerial paradigm required of industrial organizations. The managerial leaders of progressive industrial organizations will demand such changes.

Managerial leaders determine which managerial paradigm to follow and build the organizational systems to implement that paradigm. They set the managerial agenda and lead the cultural assumptions, values, beliefs, and practices. Their decisions and actions set the strategic course for the organization and provide the means for following that course. Managerial leaders bear the ultimate responsibility for ensuring the vital resources that sustain and improve strategic systems, that is, the human resources.

Implementing the managerial paradigm described in this volume requires vision, long-term commitment, discipline, adaptability, and diligence from managerial leaders, system owners, middle managers, and operators. For the people at the top of the organization to genuinely lead their organization in implementing this paradigm, they must embody the change, learn it, and live it. Otherwise, they are simply figures of authority and not true managerial leaders.

INDEX

ABOUT THE CONTRIBUTORS

MEL ADAMS is Assistant Professor of Management at the University of Alabama in Huntsville. He earned his Ph.D. in Strategic Management at the University of Tennessee. He has consulted with several companies and the Management Development Center at the University of Tennessee. He has published in several journals and presented papers at national meetings on the role of value-based strategies in inter-firm competition and entrepreneurship.

DAVID J. BARNABY is Professor and Chairman of the Department of Marketing, Logistics and Transportation at the University of Tennessee, Knoxville. He holds a Ph.D. in marketing from Purdue University and an M.B.A. in marketing from Northwestern University. His publications have appeared in *Current Issues and Research in Advertising, Advances in Consumer Research, Ecological Marketing, American Economic Review*, and *Transportation Research Board*. He has been a marketing consultant for General Motors, Union Carbide, TVA, United Virginia Bankshare, Colgate-Palmolive, Midland-Ross, and U.S. Gypsum.

GREGORY M. BOUNDS is a Research Associate at the University of Tennessee, Management Development Center. He earned a B.A. in Psychology at Davidson College, Davidson, NC, and a Ph.D. in Industrial and Organizational Psychology at the University of Tennessee, Knoxville. Dr. Bounds has managerial and non-managerial work experience in federal government agencies and in communications, manufacturing, and agricultural industries. Through consulting and applied research with a variety of organizations, Dr. Bounds gained experience in culture assessment; program development; group dynamics; teambuilding; assessment centers; job analysis; wage and salary administration; implementation of statistical process control; and organizational change toward the management of systems for customer value.

G. HARLAN CAROTHERS, JR. is a management consultant specializing in the implementation of corporate-wide systems for quality and productivity improvement. He has provided consulting expertise to a wide variety of industries including paper, automotive, electronic and printing, as well as governmental agencies. He has had more than twenty-five years of line management with Harris Corporation, Melbourne, Florida. His educational background includes a B.S. degree in physics and mathematics from the University of Southwestern Louisiana, an M.A. degree in human relations from the University of Oklahoma, and his Ph.D. degree in strategic management at the University of Tennessee.

WILLIAM E. COLE is Professor of Economics in the College of Business Administration at the University of Tennessee. He has worked, consulted and conducted research throughout Central and South America, primarily in Mexico and Brazil. His consulting work has included the United Nations Industrial Development Organization, the International Bank for Reconstruction and Development, and the International Labour Office. He holds a B.A. and Ph.D from the University of Texas.

GREGORY J. CONWAY is the Director of Strategic Management at the U.S. Army's Watervliet Arsenal, Watervliet, New York. He has been responsible for directing the newly created offices of Data Management and Statistical Process Control, and has presented extensively within the area of continuous improvement. He received his B.S. in mechanical engineering from the Rensselaer Polytechnic Institute, is a patent holder, a graduate of the University of Tennessee's Institute for Quality through Productivity and has been awarded the Productivity Excellence Award by the Secretary of Defense of the United States.

H. DUDLEY DEWHIRST is Professor of Management, Department of Management, the University of Tennessee, Knoxville. He has ten years' experience with Exxon USA, including staff or management assignments in process development research, operations analysis, and management evaluation. He conducts seminars for business executives in various areas of management and specializes in the management of technical employees. He holds a B.S. from Virginia Polytechnic Institute, an M.B.A. from Harvard University and a Ph.D. from the University of Texas.

GREGORY H. DOBBINS is Associate Professor in the Department of Management at the University of Tennessee. He holds a B.S. from the University of North Carolina, and an M.S. and Ph.D. from Virginia Polytechnic Institute and State University. He has published widely in the area of personnel/human resource management, and organizational psychology. He is currently consulting with a number of organizations and assessing managerial potential.

MICHAEL C. EHRHARDT is an Associate Professor of Finance at the University of Tennessee. He teaches in the Cost Management Institute, the MBA Program, and the doctoral program in Finance. He has published articles in numerous journals and is currently working on topics in the areas of Activity Based Costing, pricing interest rate contingent claims, and valuing flexible manufacturing systems. He received a B.S. in Engineering and a B.A. in economics from Swarthmore College, an M.S. in Industrial Management, an M.S. in Operations Research, and a Ph.D. in Finance from the Georgia Institute of Technology.

JAMES H. FOGGIN is Associate Professor of Transportation and Business Logistics, College of Business Administration, the University of Tennessee. He is a faculty coordinator for the Executive Development Program for Distribution Managers (EDPDM) and the International Logistics Program. He received his doctorate from Indiana University.

KENNETH C. GILBERT is Chairman of the Management Science and Operations Management Program at the University of Tennessee. He is Associate Editor of Naval Research Logistics and has published in *Management Science, IIE Transactions, Decision Science* and other journals. He holds a B.A. from Berea College and M.S. and Ph.D. degrees from the University of Tennessee.

MARY C. HOLCOMB is a Research Associate with the Marketing and Logistics Department at the University of Tennessee. She received her B.S. and M.B.A. degrees from the University of Tennessee and is currently completing her Ph.D. in the area of Logistics and Transportation. Her professional career involved eighteen years at the Oak Ridge National Laboratory in transportation research for the U.S. Department of Energy and U.S. Department of Transportation.

WILLIAM JUDGE is an Assistant Professor of Strategic Management at the University of Tennessee. His research interests focus on three related areas of the strategic management process: (1) board of director and top management involvement in the strategic formation process, (2) the time horizons and speed of strategic decision-making, and (3) the values of the top management team as it relates to strategy formation. Prior to joining Tennessee, he worked for five years in the strategic planning department at Armstrong World Industries, a Fortune 250 firm.

DAVID T. KEARNS is Chairman of Xerox Corporation. He graduated from the University of Rochester in 1952 with a degree in Business Administration. Prior to joining Xerox in 1971, Kearns was a vice president in the data processing division of International Business Machines Corporation. Kearns is a member of the President's Education Policy Advisory Committee, The Business Roundtable, The Business Council, the Council on Foreign Relations, the board of directors of Chase Manhattan Corporation, Time Warner Incorporated, Ryder System, Inc., the Dayton Hudson Corporation, and is a trustee of the Committee for Economic Development.

MICHAEL E. KENNEDY is an M.S. and Ph.D. student in Mechanical Engineering at the University of Tennessee, where he holds an IBM Graduate Fellowship. His M.S. thesis concerns the development and manufacture of a low-cost, industrial robot. His Ph.D. effort is focused in the area of Product Development Methodologies. Prior to returning for graduate degrees, Mr. Kennedy worked as a controls engineer for Pratt and Whitney, West Palm Beach, Florida.

KENNETH E. KIRBY is an Associate Professor in the Department of Industrial Engineering at the University of Tennessee. He came to the University after fifteen years with the Aluminum Company of America (ALCOA), where his last position was that of manager of industrial engineering for Tennessee operations. He is currently a director of the Institute of Industrial Engineers and is active in the American Production and Inventory Control Society and the Society of Manufacturing Engineers. He received his B.S., M.S., and Ph.D. degrees in industrial engineering from the University of Tennessee.

C. JOHN LANGLEY, JR. is Professor of Marketing and Logistics at the University of Tennessee. Degrees include the B.S. (Mathematics), M.B.A. (Finance), and Ph.D. (Business Logistics), all completed at Penn State University. He is 1991 President of the Council of Logistics Management and a co-author of two texts on logistics management. He has published widely in the professional journals such as the *Journal of Business Logistics* and the *International Journal of Physical Distribution and Logistics Management*.

WALTER D. LEACH, III is actively working in the organization effectiveness field since the mid-70s and is currently the coordinator of all Bechtel continuous improvement activities in the Gaithersburg Regional Office in Gaithersburg, Maryland. With a graduate degree in Industrial

Administration from Carnegie-Mellon, Walter has experience working in both the manufacturing and service sectors, as well as external and internal consulting. This disparate background provides him with a unique capability to translate the application of continuous improvement concepts and methodologies from many sources into use in Bechtel. Walter also combines the behavioral and cultural change skills with his experience in computers and the quantitative planning side of his extensive business experience.

MARY LEITNAKER is Associate Professor of Statistics at the University of Tennessee. She consults with industrial organizations in the automotive, pulp and paper, and pharmaceutical industries. She has served as the director of the Biostatistics Laboratory at The University of Tennessee Medical Center in Knoxville and is currently the statistical consultant to the Thompson Cancer Survival Center. Dr. Leitnaker received her B.A. degree in mathematics from Baker University in Baldwin City, Kansas and her M.S. and Ph.D. degrees in statistics from the University of Kentucky.

WILLIAM B. LOCANDER is Distinguished Professor of Marketing at the University of Tennessee. He has held a number of teaching and administrative positions at the University of Illinois, the University of Houston, and the University of Tennessee, and has been honored for excellence in teaching many times. Dr. Locander holds B.S., M.S., and Ph.D. degrees from the University of Illinois. He has worked as a consultant and trainer with various corporations such as IBM, Federal Express, and General Refractories. He is a past president of the American Marketing Association.

STEVEN R. MARTIN is an Associate Director in the University of Tennessee's Management Development Center where he has been involved in the Institutes for Productivity Through Quality for the past four years. He has an M.B.A. and over 15 years managerial experience.

RONNIE MILLENDER is the Director of Manufacturing for Capsugel, Division of Warner-Lambert Company. Capsugel is the industry leader in the manufacture of two-piece, hard gelatin capsules. Mr. Millender possesses a B.S. degree in Mechanical Engineering from Clemson University. He is a registered Professional Engineer in the state of South Carolina and also completed the A.S.Q.C. requirements as a Certified Quality Engineer.

CHARLES F. MOORE is a Distinguished Service Professor in the Department of Chemical Engineering and co-director of the Measurement and Control Center. He has written and presented numerous research papers, contributed to five books in the area of process modeling and automation, consulted with many companies, and taught over one hundred industrial short courses and seminars. He has received numerous prestigious teaching awards. He received his B.S., M.S., and Ph.D. degrees in chemical engineering from Louisiana State University.

C. WARREN NEEL is Dean of the College of Business Administration at the University of Tennessee in Knoxville. The College of Business is the largest professional unit on campus with over four thousand students. The executive education programs of the College extend worldwide with revenues exceeding six million dollars annually. Dr. Neel also recently served in the governor's cabinet having been appointed by Governor Lamar Alexander in November 1985. Dr. Neel is a graduate of Mississippi State University and earned his M.B.A. and Ph.D. degrees from the University of Alabama.

THOMAS L. OLSON is President and Chief Executive Officer of U.S. Paper Mills Corporation. Prior to joining the company in 1987, he practiced law for eleven years, concentrating on business and estate planning. He received his B.A. from St. Olaf College and his J.D. from the University of Wisconsin-Madison.

ROBERT OSTERHOFF is National Quality Manager for Xerox Corporation, United States marketing group. His experience includes over twenty years with Xerox Corporation in operations and staff assignments, including region controller and region quality manager. Mr. Osterhoff has served three terms as a member of the Board of Examiners of the Malcolm Baldrige National Quality Award. Mr. Osterhoff earned a B.A. degree in accounting from Loras College and an M.B.A. from Rochester Institute of Technology.

LARRY A. PACE is Associate Professor of Management at Louisiana State University in Shreveport, where he teaches undergraduate and graduate courses in management. He was a Visiting Associate Professor of Management at the University of Tennessee from 1988 to 1990. Prior to resuming his academic career, Dr. Pace was employed for nine years by Xerox Corporation. Dr. Pace earned the Ph.D. in industrial psychology from the University of Georgia (1977).

WILLIAM C. PARR is Professor of Statistics at the University of Tennessee. He has had practical experience working as a consultant to industry and previously served as senior scientist in charge of statistical development at the Harris Corporation, Semiconductor Sector where he managed an organization of statisticians and support staff providing consulting and training to approximately 4,000 employees. He has published over twenty-five papers on technical topics in statistics and currently performs research in the areas of designed experimentation, statistical process control, and robust methods. He received his Ph.D. in statistics from Southern Methodist University.

JOHN PEPPER is President of the Procter & Gamble Company, a position he has held since 1986. As president of P&G, with sales in excess of $24 billion annually, Mr. Pepper oversees a company that has on the ground operations in 47 countries and whose products are sold in more than 140 countries. Mr. Pepper graduated from Yale University in 1960 and joined Procter & Gamble in 1963. He is a member of the Board of Directors of the Xerox Corporation and is actively involved with a number of professional and charitable organizations including the American Society of Corporate Executives, the Cincinnati Area Chapter of the American Red Cross, and the Cincinnati Youth Collaborative educational effort.

GIPSIE RANNEY is a consultant in quality improvement and statistical theory and methods. She consults with several clients, including manufacturing firms and health care providers. She is an Adjunct Associate Professor of Statistics at the University of Tennessee and a founder of The Institute for Productivity through Quality. Dr. Ranney received her Ph.D. degree in Statistics from North Carolina State University.

JAMES M. REEVE is an Associate Professor of Accounting at the University of Tennessee. He received his Ph.D. from Oklahoma State University. He is a member of the AICPA, American Accounting Association, Association for Manufacturing Excellence, and National Association of Accountants. He is founder of the Cost Management Institute at the University of Tennessee. He has published over 20 articles in both academic and professional journals including *The Accounting Review, Accounting Horizons, Journal of Cost Management,* and *Management Accounting.*

RICHARD D. SANDERS is Associate Professor of Statistics at the University of Tennessee. He is one of the founders of The Institutes for Productivity Through Quality. Over the past sixteen years, he has taught graduate and undergraduate courses in a wide variety of statistical areas, including time series, statistical quality control, and regression analysis. He has served as a statistical consultant to transportation and legal firms and recently has assisted in developing forecasting models for durable good manufacturers. Dr. Sanders earned his B.S. and Ph.D. degrees in business administration at the University of Texas.

JOHN SAXTON is Vice President, Noxell Division of Procter & Gamble Company. His experience includes over twenty years in management positions with Procter & Gamble in manufacturing, product development, and marketing. He earned a B.S. degree in Chemical Engineering from Bucknell University. Currently, he serves on the Board of Directors of the Bucknell Engineering Alumni Association, the National Hispanic Scholarship Fund and Junior Achievement of Central Maryland.

JAMES G. SCHMIDT is the Technical Director of U.S. Paper Mills Corporation. He has a B.S. from the University of Wisconsin-Stevens Point in paper science and engineering and he will complete his M.B.A. from the University of Wisconsin-Oshkosh in 1991. He has completed the three week institute at the University of Tennessee, Knoxville in Statistical Process Control and in Design of Experiments.

ROBERT SCOTT is currently Director, Quality Systems Development for Capsugel Division, Warner-Lambert. He received his B.S. (with honors) degree in Chemistry from the University of Hull, England. Prior to joining Capsugel, his professional career included research and technical management in the synthetic polymer and fibre industry.

WILLIAM T. SNYDER received his B.S. in Mechanical Engineering from the University of Tennessee in 1954, the M.S. and Ph.D. from Northwestern University in 1956 and 1958 respectively. He has been Dean of the College of Engineering from 1983 to the present. Previous positions included Professor and Head of Engineering Science and Mechanics at the University of Tennessee from 1970 to 1983, Faculty Member at the University of Tennessee Space Institute from 1964 to 1970, at the State University of New York at Stony Brook from 1961 to 1964, and at North Carolina State University from 1958 to 1961. He has authored over 50 Technical Papers, and his recent technical activity has been in Industrial Energy Conservation.

MICHAEL J. STAHL is Associate Dean for Research and External Affairs in the College of Business Administration at the University of Tennessee in Knoxville. Dr. Stahl received his B.S. in Electrical Engineering from the State University of New York at Buffalo, his M.S. in Systems Management from the Air Force Institute of Technology, and his Ph.D. in Management from Rensselaer Polytechnic Institute. In the early 1970s, he was the program manager on the design and development of a communications satellite. From 1982 to 1989, he was Head of the Management Department at Clemson University. He has published over 40 journal articles in a variety of areas including strategic management and managerial motivation, and five books including *Strategic Executive Decisions* and *Strategic Management and Decision Making*.

CHARLES TASMA is the Plant Manager of the Taylorsville, Mississippi particleboard plant, Industrial Wood Products Division of Georgia-Pacific Corporation. He is a graduate of Louisiana Tech University, Ruston, Louisiana, with a B.S. degree in Forestry. Areas of work with Georgia-Pacific Taylorsville particleboard plant have included production supervisor, quality control director, continual improvement director and plant manager.

J. TOOMEY is currently a Management Consultant focusing on the identification and implementation of Integrated Management Effectiveness Systems for Government agencies and industrial corporations. His line management experience includes over 30 years with Harris Corporation, Melbourne, Florida and Sperry Corporation, New York, NY. He has extensive experience in Government and Commercial Business areas including responsibilities in General Management, Manufacturing Operations, Program Management and Quality/Productivity Improvement Systems. He has a B.S. degree in Management Science from Nova University, is a member of the Institute of Industrial Engineers and the University of Tennessee's Senior Executive Institute for Productivity Through Quality.

CLEMENT C. WILSON is Professor of Mechanical Engineering at the University of Tennessee. He has also taught at the University of Colorado, University of Kentucky and Purdue University. His industrial experience includes twenty-three years with IBM Development Labs where he received the following awards: IBM Outstanding Innovation Award, IBM Division President's Award, IBM Invention Achievement Award, IBM Quarter Century Club. Dr. Wilson earned his B.S. and M.S. degrees in mechanical engineering from the University of Tennessee and his Ph.D. in mechanical engineering from Purdue University.

ROBERT B. WOODRUFF is Professor of Marketing at the University of Tennessee. For more than twenty years, he has helped students learn about marketing management, market opportunity analysis, and buyer behavior. He also has published numerous papers on market opportunity analyses, consumer satisfaction, and other related topics, as well as coauthored and edited four books on marketing management. Dr. Woodruff has consulted with both consumer and industrial product/service companies concerning marketing strategy, market opportunity analysis, and consumer satisfaction.

LYLE YORKS is Professor of Management Science at Eastern Connecticut State University and a member of the faculties of the Management Development and Executive Development Programs at the University of Tennessee. He serves as a consultant to several organizations in the area of organizational change and has published widely in this field. His most recent books are *Scenarios of Change* (Praeger, 1989), co-written with David Whitsett, and *Dismissal*, (Harcourt Brace Jovanovich, 1989), co-written with William Morin. Articles by him have been published in *The Academy of Management Review, The California Management Review, Personnel*, and other professional journals.